THE BURMAN

HIS LIFE AND NOTIONS

Sɪʀ Jᴀᴍᴇs Gᴇᴏʀɢᴇ Sᴄᴏᴛᴛ (Shway Yoe) was born in 1851 and died, in his 83rd year, in 1935. He devoted his life to the British Civil Service and was involved with Burma on and off for thirty-five years. Just when he first went to Burma is not wholly clear; he went to Malaya (not then British) in 1875, and he may have gone on to Burma in that same year. While in Burma he taught school and wrote articles for both local and English newspapers and magazines.

In 1881 he returned to England to spend several years in study for admission to the bar. (He was unsuccessful in this attempt, but was later called to the bar in 1895 or 1896.) Consequently, he was in England when his first and best-known book, *The Burman,* appeared in 1882.

In 1886, Scott joined the Burma Commission, returned to Burma and became involved in administration there—for the most part in the Shan states—until his retirement in 1910. He was made C.I.E. in 1892 and K.C.I.E. in 1901.

the LORD CHANCELLOR (Sir ...) ... in the King ... and on his ... with Bryce, and especially those ... Britain, and on the ...
... to Bishop ... in 1822, and it ... they ... is different that ... While a ...
school and ... much local and English news ...
... business.

In 1841 he resigned the ... for several years he ...
as draughtsman to the ... VII, was much respected ... about but ... and later editor ... in 1854 ... Presumably ... in England when he ... and lost his only ... Germany ... arrived in 1837.

In 1830 his friend ... Germany ... and became involved in a ... and the ... Kind at the ... in 1831 ...
... his 1832, and K.I.L. in 1834.

THE BURMAN

HIS LIFE AND NOTIONS

BY

SHWAY YOE

SUBJECT OF THE GREAT QUEEN

The Norton Library

W · W · NORTON & COMPANY · INC ·

NEW YORK

First published in the Norton Library 1963

Published simultaneously in the Dominion of
Canada by George J. McLeod Limited, Toronto

Books That Live
The Norton imprint on a book means that in the publisher's
estimation it is a book not for a single season but for the years.
W. W. Norton & Company, Inc.

PRINTED IN THE UNITED STATES OF AMERICA

When anything surprises or pleases a Burman he never fails to cry out, Amè—mother. Following the national example, to whom can I better dedicate this book than to you, my dear Mother? Who else will be so eager to praise; so tender to chide; so soft to soothe and console; so prompt to shield and defend? To you, therefore, I dedicate it; and if this tribute of reverence and gratitude gives you a day's pleasure, it will have been a kaung-hmu—a work of merit.

INTRODUCTION

"THE best thing a Burman can wish for a good Englishman," the witty Shway Yoe wrote in 1882, "is that in some future existence, as a reward of good works, he may be born a Buddhist and if possible a Burman."

"It is a common belief," he also recorded, "that no one can speak Burmese well till he chews betel."

Shway Yoe—"Golden Honest" in Burmese—wrote of his beloved Burma with wit, compassion and a genial openness, matched only by his extraordinary grasp of the significant detail, whether he is commenting on the more suitable kinds of foundation-posts (male, female, neuter) on which a happy house may rest; on the extraordinary legal and religious freedom of the Burmese woman and the reasons for her preeminence in many a business situation; or on the tortures of those who, after an impious existence, instead of progressing along the Buddhist road to Nirvana are consigned to the States of Punishment.

The insouciance of the Burman, even in the face of such potential torments, his gracefulness and spirit, his life and indeed his notions themselves were put down by Shway Yoe with a sunniness and a sharpness of vision which have remained unmatched in the literature on Burma.

Herbert Hoover once called the Burmans the "only genuinely happy people in all of Asia." It is only in a felicitous work like Shway Yoe's that one finds a full and detailed documentation for President Hoover's equally felicitous characterization.

There are, to be sure, occasional statements expressing satisfaction at the superiority of the British flag and rule over the manner of governance which characterized the displaced Burmese kings. It is only in the face of this sort of opinion that one comes back to the reality that Shway Yoe was not, after all, a delightful and erudite young Burman, but rather a delightful and erudite young Scotsman, one named, in fact, James—later Sir James—George Scott.

Adroitness and charm do not make up the whole story of Shway Yoe's reporting.   More important is the vast, authentic and pleasurable detail with which this young public servant drew his picture, in what remains a unique description of the way in which the Burman lives his life and the values and patterns and motives that are the stuff of it.

Burma has, as everyone knows, undergone change since Scott, as a young man of thirty, published his record of how the Burman lives and thinks.   The life in some significant respects has changed, and the notions, in violent collision with those of an alien and occupying British society, have been altered somewhat too.   Yet the basic substance of the tough and resilient Burmese character has survived intact, and with it most of the notions and most of the life Shway Yoe described, only excepting those which he saw as already foredoomed—such things as the education monopoly of the monastery-schools, the childbirth rituals, or the wearing of the men's top-knot.   The tattooing of the male body and the ear-boring ceremonies for girls, then universal customs, are described minutely.   But Shway Yoe, unlike many a modern anthropologist, had the cogency to point out that such customs were not destined to remain very long—were, in fact, dying out.   There was nothing static in the life around Shway Yoe, and there is nothing static in his descriptions of it.   Above all, however, there still remains in this work the essential winsomeness of a handsome, sturdy, relaxed and graceful race, and in this respect, Shway Yoe saw true in 1882.   His vision holds today.

Some may question the republication of a work by a "colonial" writer, but there is much justification for making it available anew. Part of this lies in the fact that James George Scott was not the ordinary colonial Britisher.   In a sense, he was a forerunner of dedicated English friends of Burma like Maurice Collis and the late, great J. S. Furnivall.   He was also an heir to the great British scholar-administrators—Yule, Phayre, Raffles, Crawfurd— who had preceded him in Burma and elsewhere in Southeast Asia.

Like these forebears and successors, Scott went beneath the surface of a Burman's refusal or acquiescence, attractiveness or cussedness, activity and idleness.   He explored deep into the motives which tradition and culture had created, the values from which action or inaction spring.   "It needs something more," Shway Yoe observed, "than passing examinations and being a smart report-writer to govern the people well."

And what wealth of custom, order, piety, superstition, belief, ceremony, celebration, and ritual he found.   Why will a servant not wake his master at the appointed hour?   Because the Englishman's spirit may be away on a visit, and rousing the master while his body is vacant of soul could, at the very least, induce sickness and perhaps something worse.   Little matter that the master will rage at not being awakened on time and accuse the *servant* of oversleeping.

Will a Sunday-born gentleman marry well with a lady born on Wednesday?   Most assuredly not, and nothing but misfortune can come from the union of such an ill-assorted pair.   The planets plainly portend evil for such a marriage, just as they can be relied upon to be benign for a Sunday-Tuesday match.

Every Burman has his *sadā,* his palm-leaf horoscope cast in his infancy at the same time the astrologer confers upon him a name. On the occasion of every important decision—even, in modern days, decisions of state—the horoscope is cast anew, the planets studied and decisions made or postponed, action undertaken or put off.   And no power on earth can make a Burman act in defiance of his stars.   Shway Yoe finds in this some of the explanation for the "laziness" often observed in the Burman's make-up—which is only, in fact, a refusal to act until the stars are more propitious.

The Burman can not, after all, be demanded to act like an Englishman, an American, a Chinese or a Russian, for that matter; and many a foreign diplomat, missionary, businessman and administrator has come a cropper for overlooking the fact.   More than one embassy in Rangoon has writhed in embarrassment after an intercultural *faux pas* based on innocent but unjustified assumptions of common and clear understanding in negotiations.   More than one businessman has lost a contract because he stepped on a hidden but nonetheless sensitive corn.   Many a missionary is remembered, generations later, with a slightly too jocular affection for an unforgettable, if hardly intended, homiletic gaffe.   Too often, in seeking a Burman's cooperation, ignorance of what will and will not bring it about ends in total frustration of the best-intentioned foreigner's effort, with the result that sometimes nasty myths are born and perpetuated about the Burman's character which are hardly justified.

Scott overcame this ignorance and at least made it possible for others, later on, to come to understand that they were not dealing with incomprehensible, and therefore inferior, people. If some of what he observes has ceased to be, much of it remains a vital bundle of factors in the Burman's life today, and today's visitor to Burma, to a sensitive and nationalistic Burma, overlooks these factors only at his own risk.

For too many years, Scott's insights have been available only to persistent seekers of British books out of print. In the United States, Scott is hardly known at all, even to those increasing many who should have memorized every chapter of *The Burman* before departing on assignment to Burma. There has been missing to these Americans, consequently, not only the invaluable information patiently found and most humanely set forth by Scott, but his example also.

James George Scott was born on Christmas day in 1851 in Dairie, a small town in Fifeshire not far west of Saint Andrews, the second son of a minister. His father died when Scott was about ten years old; three years later his mother took her sons to Stuttgart for three years, and there the boys went to school. Returning to Britain, Scott studied briefly at Edinburgh University, but his subsequent stay at Lincoln College, Oxford, was cut short by money difficulties arising from unwise management by an uncle. As a correspondent for *The Standard,* Scott went in 1875 to Perak, Malaya, and shortly thereafter to Burma where he obtained a post as a teacher in St. John's College under the well-known Anglican missionary and schoolmaster, Dr. John E. Marks. During the next few years he wrote articles in *The Rangoon Gazette* under the name of Shway Yoe. He was a correspondent for *The Daily News* for a while in 1879–1880 during a visit to Mandalay, still the capital of the independent Burmese monarchy, and he wrote sketches for the *St. James Gazette,* which were later to appear in *The Burman.* *The Burman* was published while Scott was back in London from 1881 to 1883 studying law for a time. Scott again turned eastward and early in 1884 he arrived as a correspondent in Tongking, the northern part of present-day Vietnam. Here the French had resumed a more aggressive policy toward the court of Annam at Huê and their forces were engaged in campaigns against both Vietnamese and Chinese troops. His book *France and Tongking,* an account of the fighting which he had witnessed in 1884, of his impressions of the Vietnamese, and of his speculations regarding French intentions in Southeast Asia west of Vietnam, was published in London in 1885, seen through the press by his brother. He then returned to London where he succeeded in passing his examinations for the Bar. During his stay in London, a very brief British military campaign resulted in the annexation of independent Burma to the possessions of British-India on New Year's day 1886. Scott returned to Burma in April of that year to join the Burma Commission, an administrative cadre hastily formed to govern the suddenly expanded Province.

Scott remained in the service of the Commission until his retirement in 1910. The sphere of Scott's activities during his last twenty-five years in Burma was almost continuously the Shan States, where he was appointed Superintendent for the Northern Shan States in 1891 and Political Agent and Superintendent for the Southern Shan States in 1902, the post he occupied until his retirement. He was a member of the first and second Siam Boundary Commissions of 1889–1890 and 1890–1891, and served as chargé d'affaires in Bangkok in 1893 and 1894. For his contribution to the establishment of British rule in the Shan States he was made Companion of the Order of the Indian Empire in 1892 and in 1901 he was created Knight of the same Order.

Before his retirement Scott wrote two more books about Burma. *Burma as It Was, as It Is, and as It Will Be* was issued in 1886 shortly after the annexation and was intended to take advantage of the interest aroused by that event. He brought out, in 1906, *Burma, a Handbook of Practical Information,* which included contributions by others and was published twice again. In 1901 the government of Burma put out the five volume *Gazetteer of Upper Burma and the Shan States* as an official publication, and although he had to share credit on the title-page with another, it appears to have been almost entirely the work of Scott. Though it is, next to *The Burman,* Scott's most substantial book, it is now of interest chiefly as an historical source and as a reference work, the stolid pages of which the author was only occasionally able to enliven with his genial writing.

Scott continued writing articles and books in the last quarter century of his life, some of them in collaboration with his third - wife, Grace E. Mitton. *Burma and Beyond,* 1932, was intended to do for the other peoples of Burma what *The Burman* did for the major ethnic group, the Burmans, but it is a poor reflection of the earlier book. Only once during these years did Scott return to Burma. He undertook, some time in 1919, to survey for a private company the possibilities of large-scale cotton growing in Burma. Sir James George Scott died at his home at Graffham, in Sussex, in April 1935, in his eighty-fourth year.

Scott's accounts of Burmese practices and ceremonies are based on his direct observation and experience. *The Burman, His Life and Notions* is the record of Scott's acquaintance with Burma at a time when he was still relatively new to Asia, and when he was in a favored position to learn about the country and its people. Few other writers about Burma have been able to occupy such a vantage point, and he himself was not able to regain it during the rest of his lengthy career. The schoolmaster's post which he first occupied obviously provided great opportunities to one who, like Scott, was endowed with the energy and curiosity to improve them. Scott taught in a missionary school, but it is difficult to think of him as a missionary. There is no evidence in his own writings, or in his biography, which indicates he had any attachment to a Christian communion in thought or membership.

If it seems doubtful that Scott can be classed with the evangelists in Burma, there is no question of his being equally independent of the governing and trading communities of Rangoon. What his feelings about his fellows were is unclear, but he was too intimately associated with the indigenous population to suit most of his European compatriots. The book makes virtually no comment upon officials, but Scott does permit himself some critical remarks about sharp practices of European firms in the rice trade. Despite all this, the younger generation of Britishers in Rangoon, according to the contemporary English-language press, did seem to have accepted him without great qualms.

As a teacher and as a player of football, which he is said to have done a good deal to popularize, Scott must have become friends with a number of young Burmans and with their parents. Scott certainly never lacked for opportunities to meet Burmans and to come to know them. These occasions would be all the more deeply appreciated for Scott's knowing the Burmese language.

Scott's account of a boat race is set at Myanaung, on the Irrawaddy north of the Delta, and he refers to other towns in Lower Burma, but the impression arises that Scott's acquaintance with Burma was most intensely concentrated in Rangoon and its environs.   For some months, a couple of years before *The Burman* appeared, he visited Mandalay, but in view of the feelings of the reigning monarch there toward the British at the time, it seems unlikely that Scott could have achieved an intimacy with up-country Burmans comparable to that which he apparently enjoyed with the folk in Rangoon.   His observations in that still independent kingdom (which the British were soon to annex), aside from those of court institutions, added little but quantity to what he had already accumulated in the south.

In addition to what he could learn from life, Scott was also in those early years reading what observers and recorders preceding him had written, men like Adolf Bastian, Bishop Paul Bigandet, C. J. F. S. Forbes, Albert Fytche, Father Vincenzo Sangermano, and others.   It is interesting that Scott should mention Bastian, the German pioneer anthropologist and traveler in Southeast Asia in the early 1860's, who for some curious reason is almost never cited by writers on Burma.   Perhaps the answer for this neglect is simply the language barrier, no obstacle to Scott with his early German schooling.   Scott also shows an acquaintance with certain books known even now to traditionally-educated Burmans, the religious *Mingala Thok* and *Payeitkyi,* the secular *Lawkaniti* and *Deikton,* and others.

In the end, however, what counts is Scott's distillation of his own experience and observations, perhaps the most important element in the enduring quality of *The Burman.*   Never again, despite a quarter century more in the country, did Scott have the same opportunity to study another culture in Burma.   His service in the Shan States was as an official, aloof and busy, dealing with many different peoples.

Fortunately Scott was able to take a relatively detached attitude toward his experiences.   His status outside the three major European communities in Rangoon of officials, businessmen, and missionaries, and his confining his subject to the Burmans alone gave him freedom to view them directly, and not through colored alien spectacles.   The result is a book which more than any other by a foreigner succeeds in presenting the Burmese way of life without patronizing, without criticism, without romanticising, without attempted justification.   Scott had little interest in the quaint as such.   He does not pine for the good old days, nor did he urge the Burman to reform his ways.   Scott is content to transmit the sense of being a Burman day by day, the pleasures of work, play, and sociability in village Burma.

The Burman still has a relevance for understanding contemporary Burma.   Many details in the picture of the people and society are almost as fresh and clear as when Scott painted them. Where they are fading, it behooves later scholars to describe the reasons and the trends.

Scott's references to ingrained religious practices, whether derived from sacred Buddhist writings or from the folk religion of spirits which persists all over the world as a subsoil beneath the great religions, are perennially valid.   In almost no society has religion been displaced by other ways of viewing the world and man's place in it.   This has been particularly true in Burma.

Mi Mi Khaing has pointed out, in the preface to the recent American edition of her book, *Burmese Family,* that Burmese culture has been less vulnerable to the acids of modernization than that of many other Asian peoples.   This immunity arises out of the identity of the prevailing religion with emerging national awareness and in the absence in Burma of well-defined and firmly maintained distinctions of social rank based upon income, occupation, or sex.

The most striking changes in Burma since Scott's day are nevertheless those consequent upon the process of modernization or westernization.   Such influences spread out, like water on a blotter, from a few points, usually from the ports and certain inland trading and business centers, such as Rangoon, Moulmein, and Mandalay.   Gradually the foreign goods, the foreign education and the foreign ideas imparted therein seep to the villages. Little by little village boys go to the cities for the education, the jobs, the money, and the foreign wares.   The process was slow under the foreign colonial government committed to the principles of laissez-faire, as J. S. Furnivall complained; and it has remained gradual even under national governments explicitly committed to the process of change at a faster rate.   The Burma of which Scott wrote was preponderantly a rural society, and today most of the population are still either farmers or first-generation immigrants to town.

The Burman is important as a document, a record of a way of life prevailing over eighty years ago, yet the book should be appreciated as more than that. Scott described a society upon which the modern world has since made few demands for extreme change, and his description emphasizes the central aspects of the culture, such as religion, family, upbringing, which have long resisted significant change.

Scott employs many Burmese words and phrases in his writing. Fortunately, most of them are defined when used, though not always at first occurrence. A very few remain not wholly obvious when one has come to the end of the book. Scott provides a copious index as an aid. He generally prefers the Burmese pronunciation of names of Indian origin, which are so much a part of the Buddhist heritage. Thus, for example, *Athawka* is for *Asoka,* *Wini* is for *Vinaya,* and so on. Here Shway Yoe is in keeping with modern Burmese folk iconography.

In his preface to the first edition of *The Burman* in 1882, Scott says that eighteen of the sixty-four chapters first appeared in the *St. James Gazette,* an evening paper which made its debut on May 31, 1880. Some unsigned notes in the *St. James Gazette* in the autumn of 1880 have the ring of Scott's style. The first of the forerunners of *The Burman,* signed, like the book, Shway Yoe, appears to be the later Chapter LIII, "Ministers of State," which appeared on June 6, 1881. About half of the *Gazette* essays were taken over into the book virtually unchanged; the others were either reworked or considerably added to. In the preface to the second edition of 1895 only such minor changes were made in the original text as were necessary to take notice of the overturn of the old kingdom. The revision made in 1909 concerned changes relating to British rule of all Burma and to a few references, somewhat irrelevant, to Shan practices. None of these revisions added much either in sense or number of words. Thus *The Burman* is now substantially as Shway Yoe wrote it eighty years ago.

Burma is often recalled by those who have lived there as foreigners as a most hospitable and warmly receptive country. All the Burmese who live in it, whether they be Shans, Karens, Kachins, or the predominant ethnic group which gave its name to the country, the Burmans, receive the stranger according to age-old laws of hospitality. The sensitive stranger, like Shway Yoe, senses and observes these laws and is forever welcome. For those with slightly more calloused sensibilities, Shway Yoe is an excellent guide, companion and mentor to the foreigner who would truly know, understand and enjoy the incomparable Burmans and their land.

John K. Musgrave
Hamden, Connecticut
February 1, 1963

THE BURMAN
HIS LIFE AND NOTIONS

PREFACE

PHONETICISM is said to be "the murderer of history," and there has been a craze of late years to prevent this felony by the adoption of "scientific methods" of rendering Burmese in English characters. I have no doubt that whatever other faults I may be accused of, I shall be greatly blamed for endeavouring to reproduce the pronunciation rather than the orthography of Burmese words. But I may be allowed to contend that the catch phrase ascribing bloodguiltiness to phoneticism, however just it may be in a country where *fonetic nuz* puzzle a long-suffering generation, is most misleading and calumnious where it is applied to a foreign language, and especially to such a language as Burmese. No one who is concerned about the etymology of a language is likely to study it except in the national character ; if he trusts to transliterations, scientific or otherwise, he will most assuredly be little worth listening to. When an author writes in English about a little-known people he presumably writes for a majority of readers who know nothing whatever of the language, and cannot be reasonably expected to have any very great concern in its etymology as long as they get a more or less correct notion of how the words should be pronounced. This is most especially the case in Burmese, where, in very many cases, the orthography of a word supplies but the remotest possible hint of its pronunciation.

The scientific men write bhoora (lord), the Burman pronounces the word păyah ; tsit-tshay (ghost) is a formidable way of reproducing the spoken tăsay ; pa-nya (learning) but inadequately represents the sound of pyinya ; khwon (taxes) is a startling, not to say puzzling, way of suggesting the sound kohn. The matter is made none the easier by the difficulty of finding an English equivalent at all for some Burmese sounds. In the words nyaung, pyouk, gyi, and the like, the *y* belongs to the preceding letter, and has always the consonantal and never the vowel sound. Such words are therefore invariably monosyllables. Again, the nou'pyit sound, which I have written *è* on the analogy of the French *mère*, has as a final vocable no equivalent in English. *Errant* gives the force as an initial letter. The scientific form of *eh* is certainly misleading. The initial *ky* is a great crux to beginners in Burmese. It requires a fine ear to catch the precise sound. An English officer will call for his clerk, Maung Poh Chè, and the punkah-boy will pass on the word for Maung Poh Kyè—tyè it might almost be written. But it is little use multiplying instances. Suffice it to add that a final consonant is always silent—strangled is almost a literal translation of the Burmese word.

Of published works on Burma I have found those of Colonel Yule, Captain Forbes, and Dr. Bastian most valuable in supplying hints as to those of the national customs most likely to be interesting to foreigners. Had Captain Forbes's life been prolonged this book would probably have had no *raison d'être*.

In conclusion, I have only to record my indebtedness to the Rev. Dr. Marks, the head of the S.P.G. in Burma. For over twenty years he has laboured in Burma both as a teacher and a missionary, and there is no Burman in the country to whom his name is not known, and with whom it is not held in reverence. Had it not been for him this work would never have appeared.

The chapters xviii. to xx., and xxiii. to xxvii. in the first volume, and chapters v., viii., x. to xiv., xvii., xxiii., and xxiv. in the second, have already appeared, mostly in a shorter form, in the columns of the *St. James's Gazette.*

June 1882.

With the exception of a few verbal alterations, rendered necessary by the annexation of Upper Burma, this second edition in no way differs from that which preceded it.

November 1895.

This third edition has been more thoroughly revised, in view of the changes during the twenty-seven years since it was written. The system of transliteration adopted by the Royal Geographical Society has been substituted for phoneticism.

Camp Wankan,
    Southern Shan States,
      April 26, 1909.

CONTENTS

CHAPTER I

FIRST YEARS

IT is fortunate for the young Burman that on his first appearance in the world all attention is directed to the mother, and the "little stranger" is left very much to himself till he has attained a stronger vitality. Were it not so, the rival parties of the Dietists and Druggists might quarrel over the relative quantities of the four elements, fire, air, earth, and water, composing the new arrival, and diet and dose him out of existence immediately, in a heroic attempt to attain an equilibrium of forces. The mother indeed is the major point of interest in all countries, but childbirth nowhere entails such penalties as in Burma. Directly the child is born, the mother is rubbed all over with na-nwin (turmeric), and a big fire is lighted as near as the construction of the wooden or bamboo house permits, while rugs and blankets are heaped over her to the extent of the possessions of the family. As speedily as possible the midwife prepares a draught called se sein (green medicine), the composition of which is a tradition with the Wun-swès, and is kept a secret from inquisitive males. This the victim in bed has to drink perpetually during seven days, and for the same period, irrespective of the blankets and the time of year, is heated up with ôk pu. These are big circular or lozenge-shaped bricks. They are heated blazing hot in the wood fire, dropped for a few seconds into a pot full of water, and then wrapped up in cloths and applied to the body of the mother. In addition to this, doses of turmeric are regularly administered, and every now and then she is made to smell samôn-net, a plant (the *Nigella sativa*), which is put in an earthen pot, strongly heated, and then triturated into the shape of a ball.   The odour is not exactly such as one would recognise as calculated to exhilarate any one, but probably after the hot bricks and the se sein every- thing else comes as a matter of detail.   All this is done to drive out the noxious humours which are supposed to be generated by the birth of a child.   On the seventh day the woman takes an elementary kind of Turkish bath.   She sits over a large jar of boiling water, medicated with tamarind twigs and a few other kinds of leaves and grasses, with a blanket over her.   After about an hour of this she has a cold bath, and is then free to do as she pleases.   She usually goes to bed.

It might be supposed that under this treatment death in child-bearing would be very frequent, but as far as imperfect statistics can show the percentage is not much higher than in other countries.   The result, however, appears in another way.   A woman ages up ten or fifteen years for every child she has.   It is satisfactory to notice that in all the larger towns in Lower Burma the more unpleasant features are fading away before the example and influence of women of other nationalities.   In the jungle and in Upper Burma, however, ancient use and wont still prevail, and the young mother of fourteen or fifteen is shrivelled into thirty with her first baby.

If a woman gives birth to a still-born child, a piece of iron is placed in the cloth in which the body is wrapped, or in the coffin if there is one, and at the burial some member of the family says some such formula as " Never more return into thy mother's womb till this metal becomes soft as down."

If a married woman dies before bearing a child (alôn hnin the-thi), a Cæsarean operation is performed, and the alôn is buried in some secret place.   The reason alleged for this is, that were it not done, the husband in future exist- ences would marry this woman again, and she would die in the same way.   Were the embryo not secretly buried it would be disinterred by hmaw-sayās, necromancers, and wizards, who would make evil uses of it.   Children's cauls are as highly thought of by Burmans as they are by English sailors; only where the tar thinks he will be saved from drowning, the Turanian expects to gain the patronage of any great person he may address.

The infant having survived and the mother recovered from her roasting, the next thing to be done is to name the child. This usually happens about a fortnight after the birth. A fortunate day and hour is sought out by some Brahmin astrologer, or a sayā of lesser note, if there is no such dignitary in the neighbourhood. A great feast, as elaborate as the wealth or the ambition and borrowing capacities of the parents admit, is prepared, and all the friends of the family and the neighbours are invited to come. The child's head is usually washed for the first time on this day. The ceremony is therefore called kin-bôn tat thi. A decoction of the pods and bark of the soap acacia (*Acacia rugata*) or kin-bôn is prepared, and with this the midwife washes the infant's head and the guests wash their hands. Most of them bring friendly contributions towards the feast, or perhaps a little money. The mother sits down in the centre of the circle with the infant in her arms, and near her is the father. The company sit gravely smoking and chewing betel for a time, and then some elder, or a near relation of the parents, seems struck with a name, and suggests it aloud. Everybody accepts it on the spot, and falls to discussing the aptness of the name and the accomplishments and virtues of people they have known with that appellation. This is, however, all a pre-arranged thing. The father and mother have settled beforehand what the child is to be called, and have apprised the lu-gyi selected what is to be the result of his cogitations. The midwife then gets a present according to the means of the family, having previously, after the seven days' roasting, received the regulation fee of one pyi, the sixteenth of a basket of husked rice, one mat, and a four anna bit. Then everybody adjourns to the feast, which, with the dessert of le'-pet, salted ginger cut into small strips, ground nuts, fried garlic, the invariable betel apparatus, cheroots, and what not, pass the time till nightfall, when, except in the case of poor people, there is always a pwè which carries on proceedings till the next morning.

The name given thus appears to be entirely a matter of choice ; but this is not so. The consonants of the language are divided into groups which are assigned to the days of the week, Sunday having all the vowels to itself. With all respectable families it is an invariable rule that the child's name must begin with one of the letters belonging to the day on which it was born, but within these limits any name may be chosen. As an immediate consequence it follows that a Burman has a birthday every week, a frequency of recurrence which renders the event monotonous, and precludes the friendly amenities of western nations on such occasions.

The letters of the alphabet are apportioned to the days of the week in the following rough rhyme, which every Burman child can repeat with as much certainty as the English one will display in the recitation of Little Jack Horner :—

> Ka, kha, ga, gha, nga, Taninla.
> Sa, hsa, za, zha, nya, Ainga.
> Ta, hta, da, dha, na, Sane.
> Pa, hpa, ba, bha, ma, Kya-thabade.
> La, wa, Boddahu.
> Ya, ya (the Pali and Arakanese ra), Yahu.
> Tha, ha, Thauk-kya.
> A, Taninganwe.

That is to say, children born on Monday have for the initial letter of their names, K, Kh, G, Gh, or Ng ; for example—Maung, Ngwe Khaing, Mr. Silver Sprig ; Maung Gauk, Mr. Crooked ; Ma Kwe Yo, Miss or Mrs. Dog's Bone ; Ma Khin, Miss or Mrs. Lovable. It will be noticed that in Miss Dog's Bone's names the initial letters of the two words do not agree as to the day. This often occurs, and the first name (Maung and Ma being merely honorary additions) always denotes the birthday. The better class families avoid such a mixing, however, as far as possible.

Tuesday's children have the choice of S or S aspirated (practically the same), Z, Zh, and Ny. For example :— Maung San Nyun, Mr. Beyond Comparison ; Maung Po Sin, Mr. Grandfather Elephant ; Ma So, Miss or Mrs. Naughty.

Those born on Saturday have T, Ht, D, Dh, and N. The aspirated and unaspirated letters have to most Englishmen precisely the same sound, though a practised ear detects the difference immediately. Examples are :——Maung Ba Tu, Mr. Like His Father ; Ma Ne Htun, Miss or Mrs. Sunshine ; Maung Du Wun, Mr. Pole Star ; Mi Nu, Miss Tender.

Those born on Thursday select from P, Hp, B, Hb, and M. For example :——U Po Mya, Old Grandfather Emerald ; Maung Bo Gale, Mr. Little Officer ; Ma Hmwe, Miss or Mrs. Fragrant ; Mi Meit, Miss Affection.

Wednesday has L and W. Examples :——Maung Ho, Mr. Yonder ; Ma Waing Hla, Miss or Mrs. All-Round Pretty ; Ma Hein, Miss or Mrs. Growler.

From noon till midnight on Wednesday is represented as a special day, or, at any rate, under a special constellation called Yahu, and those born between those hours have the alternative of the two Y's, one of which is sounded R in Pali and by the Arakanese. Examples are :——Maung Yo, Mr. Honesty ; Ma Yôn, Miss or Mrs. Rabbit, U Yauk, Old Individual.

Friday has Th and H. Examples :——Maung Than, Mr. Million ; Maung Thet She, Mr. Long Life ; Ma Thin, Miss or Mrs. Learned ; Mè Thaw, (old) Mrs. Noisy.

A is the only letter assigned to Sunday, but the combination with it of the symbol of any other vowel changes it to the sound of that vowel. For example :——Maung Ôn, Mr. Cocoa-nut ; Maung At Ni, Mr. Red Needle ; Ma E, Miss Cold ; Ma Eing Saung, Mrs. Housekeeper ; U O, Old Pot.

A common popular belief is, that, according to the day of the week (or rather the constellation representing that day) on which a man is born, so will his character be. Thus a man's name discloses his probable characteristics to the superstitious.

A man born on Monday will be jealous ; on Tuesday, honest ; on Wednesday, short-tempered, but soon calm again, the characteristic being intensified under Yahu ; on Thursday, mild ; on Friday, talkative ; on Saturday, hot-tempered and quarrelsome ; on Sunday, parsimonious.

Not only has every day its special character and its fixed

letters, but there is also a particular animal assigned to symbolise it, and red or yellow wax candles are made in the forms of these animals to be offered at the Pagoda by the pious. Each worshipper offers the creature-candle representing his birthday, or that of any particular friend or relation whom he wishes well. In this way Monday is represented by a tiger ; Tuesday, by a lion ; Wednesday, by an elephant with tusks ; Yahu, by an elephant without tusks ; Thursday, by a rat ; Friday, by a guinea-pig ; Saturday, by a nagā or dragon ; Sunday, by a kalôn, the fabulous half-beast, half-bird, which guards one of the terraces of Mount Myinmo (Meru), the centre of the universe.

Little candles of this kind are to be had at any of the stalls which cluster about the steps and the base of every pagoda in the country, and they are as freely offered as flowers, and fruits, and gold-leaf.

It will be seen that there is no such thing as a surname among the Burmese. A man may have a dozen sons not one of whom has the same name as his father. Maung, literally " brother," has come to stand practically for " Mister." Po and Shwe and Ba may be applied to any one without regard to his birthday, Shwe implying usually politeness or affection. Nga, used in the English law-courts and by pompous native officials generally, implies superiority claimed by the speaker or writer. Ko denotes friendship, or superior age and dignity in the person addressed. Maung Shwe Than might call himself indifferently—Maung Than, Po Than, Ba Than, Ko Than, Nga Than, or Shwe Than, and might add Maung to any one of these. As a matter of fact most Burmans chop about their name a good deal during their lives. He may begin by being called Lugale Ngè, " Little Wee Man." When he grows up a little the family probably get to call him Lugale Gyi, " Big Little Man." Later, when he begins to think of his appearance and look after the girls—and they begin that sort of thing very early in Burma — he probably calls himself Maung Lugale or Shwe Lugale, " Mr. Littleman," or " Mr. Boy," or " Golden Boy." There are a variety of other changes possible and likely. Finally, when he reaches the age of thirty-five or forty he either readopts the original Ngè and calls himself

U Ngè, "Old Small" or "Old Wee"; or takes U Lugale instead, "Old Boy." To this additions may be made according to fancy. Indeed the possible forms of any given Burmese name would supply a very fair sum in permutations and combinations.

There is a similar freedom with the women's names. Every woman married or unmarried may be called Ma. When she becomes elderly Mè is very often used. Mi implies youth in the person addressed, or affection on the part of the speaker. A young husband or lover usually calls his lady love Mi Mi. She addresses him as Maung, "brother," or familiarly as Taw, or Shin. Ba in Lower Burma is a polite form. In Upper Burma, especially in the Palace, Maung Maung, or Tin Tin, or Teit Tin (prostrating the forehead, Kowtowing) are used in a courteous way. It is considered hardly civil in any case to use the bare name; the office held, or some particular alms given by the person addressed, supplies the easiest equivalent; otherwise some friendly form is employed in speaking. Kin-le is used similarly in familiar fashion or in a friendly way to those of lesser rank. Thus a prince would use it in addressing an A-pyo-daw, a maid of honour.

Sometimes when a boy grows up he does not like the name his parents gave him. He can then change it by a very simple process. He makes up a number of packets of le'-pet and sends round a friend to deliver them to all his acquaintances and relations. The messenger goes to the head of the house and says: "I have come from Maung Shwe Pyin (Mr. Golden Stupid). He is not to be called by that name any more. When you invite him call him Maung Hkyaw Hpe (Mr. Celebrated Father). Be good enough to eat this pickled tea," and then he goes on to the next house. It is not imperative that the letters of the birthday should be adhered to, but it is usually done. Women very seldom change names. It looks too much like a broad hint that they are growing up and have some notion of themselves, or that they have a mind of their own, which might prove irksome to possible husbands.

A careful note is made of the exact hour of birth with the object of drawing up the sadā or certificate of birth

which every Burman has, and carefully consults, with the
help of an astrologer, for the fixing of fortunate days and
hours throughout his life. Sometimes the sadā is drawn
up very shortly after birth, but ordinarily not till the child is
five or six years old. Then an old Pônna, a Brahmin, or
any ordinary astrologer is called in. He records on a doubled
up strip of palm leaf the year, the month, the day and hour
at which the child was born ; the name given to it ; the
planet in the ascendant at the moment of birth and the
house in which it was at the time. This is scratched neatly
on the palm leaf in the usual way with a metal style. On
the other side are a number of cabalistic squares and numbers
from which the future calculations may be made. There are
said to be eight gyo, or planets, and from these the days of
the week are named, Wednesday having a second, Yahu,
which rules from mid-day to midnight. Each of the planets
has its own point of the compass as follows :—

N.

Yahu. 12 Symbol—Tuskless Elephant. Wednesday, 12 P.M. to 12 A.M. Unnamed.	Thauk-kya. 21 Symbol—Guinea- Pig. Friday. Venus.	Taninganwe. 6 Symbol—Kalohn. Sunday. The Sun.
Kyathabade. 19 Symbol—Rat. Thursday. Jupiter.		Taninla. 15 Symbol—Tiger. Monday. The Moon.
Sane. 10 Symbol—Nagah. Saturday. Saturn.	Boddahu. 17 Symbol—Tusked Elephant. Wednesday, 12 A.M. to 12 P.M. Mercury.	Ainga. Symbol—Lion. Tuesday. Mars.

W. (left of table)   E. (right of table)

S.

The stations, numbers, and symbols of the planets are
recorded in a jingling rhyme, which is one of the first things
boys learn in the monastic schools, *e.g.*—

Taninla kya
Ta-sè nga
Ne nya
She yat ga.

Monday's number, I ween,
Is always fifteen ;
The tiger's the beast,
And its place is the East.

There are various ways of calculating the horoscope,
most of them not to be understanded of the people, but the
most popular, because the preliminaries are evident to everybody, is from the numbers given above.   A person born on
Monday remains under the influence of the moon for fifteen
years.   Then he passes into the house of Mars and sojourns
there for eight years.   At the age of twenty-three, Mercury
presides over him and continues to do so for the next seventeen years, and so on to the end, which mounts up to 108
years.   Should he outlive that he would begin the circle over
again.   Another way is to divide the inquirer's age by eight.
If there is no remainder, the horoscope is made up from
the gyo under which he was born.   If there is a remainder,
the Bedin Sayā counts it out round the figure, in the
direction of the hands of a watch, commencing with the
birth planet.   Thus a man born on Thursday, now twenty-
nine years of age, would be under the influence of the moon.
The gyo at the four cardinal points, east, south, west, and
north are happy in their influences, those on the diagonal
rhumbs not so good.   Yahu, and especially Saturday, have
a particularly sinister influence.   A man does most of the
stupid and vicious things in his life while he is in Saturn's
house.   A young man born on Wednesday will need a lot
of ballast to tide him through the ten years of Saturn, seeing
that he enters on the danger at the age of seventeen.

Little gilded and red painted signboards are put up at
all the pagodas, displaying the nan, the symbol, and the
relative position of all the planets.   Sometimes people
worshipping at the pagoda go to the point of the gyo, in
whose house they were born, and offer up their lauds and
candles there.   But this is a mere matter of individual fancy,
and is hardly open to those born in the diagonally situated

houses, for the niche shrines, if there are more than one at the pagoda, are always at the four cardinal points, and if there is only one, as is usual at small pagodas, it is to the East.

The sadā is carefully kept by the parents until the child is old enough to take care of it himself, and thenceforward it is guarded as the most valuable possession the person has. No matter how often the name is changed the new one is never put in the sadā, so that this certificate cannot be trusted to implicitly for a man's name. Some of them are very beautifully engraved and ornamented, but they are naturally not often to be seen. I only know of two in England at the present time (1881), one of which is my own and the other belonging to a travelling Burman. When a man dies, the sadā is either destroyed or preserved as a memento by the family. A great many sadās were found and carried off as curiosities during the Third Burmese War. There is one at Abbotsford.

A curious instance of the firm belief of the nation in the reasonableness of the conviction that the planet under which one is born influences the fates and actions of one's life, is the fact that royalty ordained that the coins and measures used by traders should bear the emblem of the monarch's birthday. Thus for example all the gold coins used in Upper Burma bazaars during the penultimate reign had the figure of a lion on them, Mindôn Min having been born on a Tuesday. The few remaining from previous reigns bearing other symbols were rigidly kept out of the sight of Burmese officials. The Convenor of the Fifth Great Synod, though probably the mildest and best sovereign Burma ever had, would certainly have stood no trifling in matters of this kind, which, if not amounting actually to a part of the religion, were at any rate very intimately connected with it. His son Thibaw Min, however, notoriously indifferent to religion, if a stronger word might not even be admissible, let the old weights remain in use, and probably called it the march of civilisation.

The naming and the construction of the sadā being finished, the principal events in the youthful Burman's life are over, and the children run about in as happy a state of nudity as the respectability of the family permits ; and boys and girls steal grandmamma's cheroot, and potter about making mud pies according to cosmopolitan infantile habit, and not seldom getting up decorous and serious representations of the choral dances and dramatic performances they have seen. The spectacle of a little girl vigorously puffing a big green cheroot while she moulds a heap of mud into shapely form is only a little more startling to the white-faced foreigner than the declamatory passion of a five-year-old princeling. So it goes on till the eighth year is reached; then it is time to go to the monastic school.

On the following page is a copy of the sadā of Shin Thuza. The young lady, I regret to say, is dead. The publication of her horoscope cannot therefore enable malicious persons to work her any harm by means of spells. The side represented is the obverse. I have submitted the figures to two very distinguished wranglers, but they have been unable to detect any system in them.

On the reverse, surrounded by an ornamental border of numbers written in accordance with a rhyme, are recorded in mystic language the details. The young lady was born in the year 1220 B.E. (twenty-three years ago), in the astrological cycle 422, in the month of Ta-bodwè, on the ninth of the waxing moon, and the seventh day (Friday) of the week, in the evening, at thôn chetti gyaw, a little past the third hour, or more exactly, three nayi, two pads, and ten bizana. Then the precise position of the constellation in the heavens is noted. It is thirteen băwa (feet), five finger breadths, three mayaw (grains' length), one sessamum seed (nan), and eight hairs' breadths from the planet. Then it winds up to the effect that this is the horoscope of the maiden, whom, that she may be known by a pleasant name, her parents have called Shin Thuza. " May she live to be a hundred and twenty!" Alas! she did not.

At either side of these details are two identical magic squares, formed in accordance with the well-known Hindoo Law. Over one is written " The Buddha"; over the other " The Law"; beneath the former " Rangoon," and the latter " 650." The two palm-leaves are tightly sewn together, and the writings and figures, done

2	9	4
7	5	3
6	1	8

with a metal style on the dry leaf, are very neatly executed.

The general construction of all sadās is the same, but there are very considerable divergences in the number of figures. In another—I do not say whose it is—there are two circles only in the left portion, and only eight divisions in the right half, while several of the headings to the columns are different. The ti-padi-taing, the "highest post," between the two, also varies. I may mention that, beginning with the second stage on the left, descending and going up the other side, the numbers increase by three : *e.g.* 2, 5, 8, 11, etc. This is the case in all sadās, but they do not necessarily begin with the same number.

CHAPTER II

SCHOOL DAYS

I SUPPOSE Englishmen will never get rid of the notion that monastic schools must needs be dull and dismal, that hours of study only alternate with seasons of austerity and rough punishments. The uninhabited, almost deserted, appearance of the Burmese kyoung ; its isolated position ; the solemn, restful front which it always preserves, no matter how lightened up by profuse gilding and the carved magnificence of its panels and eaves' boards, or how embowered in rich and waving foliage ; the austere aspect and slow-paced gait of the mendicants in their sad yellow robes—all these things inevitably encourage the foreigner in the belief that the monotony and the discipline must crush all life and light-heartedness out of the young scholars.

Nothing, however, can be farther from the actual fact. No Etonian, no old Rugbeian, can look back with greater delight on triumphs on the river or in the football field, than the grown-up Burman does on his early days at the Pôngyi Kyaung. There are no rough games to remember, it is true, no strivings of any kind with members of another institution. Those things do well enough for a cold-country people. The Burman's reminiscences are of a quieter kind. There was the emulation with the chin lôn, the wicker football, to see who could keep it longest in the air by dexterous use of knee, foot, shoulder, thigh, and cheek. How it relieved the body and freshened the mind after hours of poring over little hand-blackboards, covered with cramped words and letters, in the quiet rooms inside. Then there were the games at gônnyinhto, an elementary combination of skittles

and ninepins, played with the big flat seeds of a jungle
creeper. Pleasant they were under the shade of the great
mango and pipul trees and the lofty cocoa-nut and palmyra
palms, and exciting were the games, so that the customary
stillness of the place was rudely broken upon by disputing
voices, till a monk would come out and bring all back to
work again as a penance. Then during the work there was
the fun of the writing hour, when everybody had to write
out maxims and prayers on his little parabaik with a clumsy
pointed steatite pencil. There were always some stiff-
fingered big pupils who could not manage to write their
copy neatly or correctly, and as punishment had to take
the good writers on their backs and march ruefully up and
down the long schoolroom during pleasure. Sometimes
they were thrashed, but the other punishment was the more
dreaded. Then there was the schoolmaster monk, who
would tell fairy stories of the other three great islands which
lie in the sea round about Myinmo mountain ; of the half-
moon-faced western islanders, and the wondrous tree that
bore everything eatable one could wish for and delivered it
ready cooked ; the joys of the six heavens of the Nats and
the grisly horrors of Nga-yè, with its fearful ages of fantastic punishments. Every now and again travelling necromancers and hmaw sayās would spend a night or two at
the monastery, and in recompense for the little delicacies
and odds and ends of food which good-natured neophytes
would get for them, used to tell stories of witchery and
marvel. Sometimes there would be a sā-haw sayā, a kind
of cyclic poet, who knew half the zats in the language by
heart, and would recite a little just for practice. Or a
tattooing sayā would come round and mark some particularly favoured youth with a quaint figure. Discussion as to
its meaning and probable virtues would be carried on in the
shadowy evenings for months afterwards. Varieties of this
kind recur to the old Burman as he thinks of the school
days long ago, and he sighs with as much conviction as
any European that there are no days so happy as the
school days.

English rule has disturbed old customs a good deal in
the province, but even now we may say that, as an invari-

able rule, when a boy has reached the age of eight or nine years he goes as a matter of course to the Pôngyi Kyaung. It is open to all alike—to the poor fisherman's son as well as to the scion of princely blood—for no one pays anything, and it is not carefully considered who it is that fills the monkish begging pots in the daily round.   Thus every Buddhist boy in the country is taught to read and write, and in this respect at least there are but very few illiterate Burmans.   This primary education must by no means be confounded with entry into the monastery as a koyin-gale, or novice.   Strictly speaking, this ceremony ought not to take place before the age of fifteen, and the earlier sojourn is only a preparation for it.   The younger pupils may become boarders in the monastic building if they choose, but they do not assume the yellow robe, which marks them, for however short a time it may be worn, as members of the Assembly of the Perfect.   They wear their ordinary clothes and retain their secular name.

As soon as the boy enters the monastery he is set down in the big schoolroom beside all the other boys, and receives a roughly-made black wooden slate.   On this are written a few of the letters, perhaps the whole of the alphabet.   A little explanation starts him off, and for the next few days he is engaged in shouting out their sounds at the top of his voice.   Nobody minds him, for all the other scholars are similarly engaged in hallooing, and the monks derive a sense of comfort and a virtuous consciousness of doing good from the noise.   It is as soothing as the sound of his mill-wheels to the miller, or the roar of traffic to the cockney.   If a boy stops shouting, it is a sign that he has stopped working— and if he is not meditating mischief, it is probable that he is about to go to sleep, and he is corrected accordingly.   The method is an admirable one for keeping the boys occupied —much more so than civilised Western methods—though I fear a council of English head-masters would scout the idea. The casual foreign observer who goes about taking notes, like Grose or the " Rampant M.P.," passes the ecclesiastical school, and in amazement at the seeming uproar within, declares that monastery schools are hopelessly badly conducted, and without the semblance of discipline.   As a matter of fact, the more noise there is going on, the more work there is being got through.

Doubtless it is a primitive method—doubtless there are thick-headed boys with tough lungs who shout out the ka gyi, ka gwe (the A, B, C) with but the slightest portion of it remaining in their brains. There must be, because sometimes a boy takes a year to get through the alphabet (called the thin-bon-gyi, the "great basket of learning"), the combination of vowel symbols, and the alterations of sound effected by the union of consonants, all of which are mere materials, and only a very small portion of the complicated system of the language. Nevertheless everybody learns in the end, and then they are set to read in the same way, and gradually advance in the immemorial regulation subjects. The first books—all the books, in fact, put in the boys' hands—are religious. They learn the five universal commandments, the five subsidiary rules, the Pali formulæ to be employed at the pagoda—pattering them over till they pour out of the lips with the fluency and precision of water out of a pump. When there are a number at the same stage in their studies, they repeat their lesson word for word after the teacher, sitting in wide rows before him, and all chanting with the same emphasis and apparently in the same key. The effect is very singular when a string of sonorous Pali versicles is being mouthed over in the striking intoned recitative peculiar to these formulæ. The twenty or thirty boys crouching down on their knees, their little heads every now and then bowing down to the ground over their hands joined in supplication, the yellow-robed monk sitting cross-legged on the dais before them, repeating in abrupt, jerky fashion the clauses of the form of worship, which the childish voices instantly catch up, forms a scene which never loses its novelty and attractiveness.

The little schoolboy slowly learns all these formulæ. Even near to and in the larger towns of Lower Burma the amount of secular learning, arithmetic, and so on that is learnt, is of the most meagre possible description. All relates to the tenets of religion—to the existences and teachings of the Lord Buddha. The things thus impressed on the youthful mind sink deep into the memory, and leave their mark on the whole future life of the young scholars. As long as these monastic schools are attended, all attacks on the Buddhist faith must be fruitless.

Besides the commandments, the paya-shekho, and the pareit-yôp-thi, the lauds of the Lord Buddha, and the aspirations to be repeated at the holy shrines, the formulæ to be told over on the beads ; besides these first principles, the young Burman is taught the thin-ki-ya, the rules which are to prepare him for assuming the yellow robe, and to guide him during his longer or shorter withdrawal from the sinful world to the calm tranquillity of the monastery. He must learn that the young novice carefully imitates the decorous pace of the yahan ; does not walk fast ; avoids swinging his hands ; does not smile or laugh in passing through a village, and keeps far away from all secular amusements. The yellow robe, distinctive of the order, is to be regarded not as a garment to cherish and comfort the wearer, not as a robe to adorn the outward man and make it look stately or pious, but merely as a concession to modesty, born of the weaknesses of poor human flesh—and further, as a means of enabling the worthless frame to endure the extremes of heat and cold. In the same way food is to be eaten only to support life. The member of the sacred order must not think of meal times as an occasion for gratifying his senses ; he must avoid dwelling on the tastiness of the food and the gratification to his palate which the pious zeal of a supporter may afford in presenting an unusually dainty meal. Especially must he refrain from eating food to make himself strong and lusty. He must always remember the transitoriness, the misery and unreality of the world, and find relief in the Triple Consolation, the trust in the Lord, the Law, and the Assembly.

All these things are impressed on the young pupil as soon as he is able to read at all, every one of them assuming the fact that as soon as he is old enough, or as soon as he has gone through the necessary preparation, he will assume the yellow robe of the devout, to wear it perhaps for life, perhaps only for a day or two, but certainly to put it on, for without this he cannot attain to the full privileges of a man. His kan (luck) will be altogether one-sided. All the ill deeds he does will swell the sum of his demerits, but not a single good action, no uttermost act of charity or devotion, will be recorded to his advantage for another existence. Without admission to the order, without " Buddhist baptism," no man can count his present existence as other than an animal's. The great gift of having appeared in the likeness of a human being ; the happy balancing of merits and demerits which has resulted in so glorious an opportunity of advancing towards Ne'-ban ; the still greater fortune of existence in a country where the tenets of Buddhism offer supreme chances to the weary seeker after rest from the moil of a work-a-day world ; all will have been recklessly thrown away. It is written that more hardly will a needle cast from the summit of Mount Myinmo across the wide Thamoddaya Sea, more hardly will it touch with its point as it falls another needle standing point upwards in the great Southern Island, than will any given creature become a human being. How are the Western foreigners, black and white, to be pitied, who have indeed by earnest strivings attained the seat of man, but, arrived there, find it all naught because they do not hear the teachings of the Buddha ! How much worse the Burman, to whom all his life long the monastery door stands open, to whom a week's, a day's, an hour's sojourn would offer boundless possibilities, and yet who enters not in. If this be so, what then can be the prospect for the boy who having put his hand to the plough turns back, who entering the monastery as a child, imbibes the religious thoughts and becomes acquainted with the religious creed, and yet fails to seek the " humanity " so easily to be gained ? Better have been born an animal or an Englishman, and scoffed at what he did not understand.

Consequently it may be invariably assumed that the little scholar, as soon as age and acquirements admit, puts on the yellow garb as a finish to his education. This used to include every one. Till the English came and took the country, everybody went to the Pon-gyi-Kyaung. But now there are English government schools ; there are Burmese laymen's schools, which neglect religious education alto-gether, and look to competitive examinations as the end and aim of juvenile existence, as the ne'-ban of school life.

There is a percentage of thirty-five in the " middle standard "
(Government Education Department).   What matters if the
successful halt and stumble in the pareit-gyi ?   There are
two boys who have a chance in the Calcutta University
Matriculation Examinations.   It is a matter of indifference
that the thingyo is as unknown to them as it is to any poor
foreigner.   Nevertheless, notwithstanding their shortcomings
in this respect, there are but few even of these young Burmans who have not become members of the society, if only
for long enough to get their heads shaved and be invested
with the yellow dress.   Still in these latter years there are a
few who have never gone through even this slight ceremony,
and the number may be expected annually to increase as
Western habits spread more widely over the country.   Not
till the monastic schools begin to be deserted will the
Christian missionary find that his labours have had any
effect on the vital energies of the ancient faith of the Buddha.
That day is still far off.   As yet the government and vernacular lay schools have had very little effect in reducing the
number of scholars who go daily to study in the dim-lighted
schoolrooms of the monastery.   Not even in Rangoon have
the monks to call for scholars ; they flock there abundantly
of their own accord.

CHAPTER III

BUDDHIST BAPTISM

THE term baptism as applied to a youth who enters a monastery in the state of probation (called shin) is not, as many people think, a mere idle analogy borrowed from the Christian faith. The novice actually and formally receives a new name to mark his accession to the full dignity of humanity. The great majority of shins, or ko-yins, are little boys of twelve or a little older, but occasionally a man secludes himself from the world at an advanced age. Till a Buddhist has entered the fraternity he cannot claim to be more than a mere animal. He has a lu nāmé, it is true, a worldly name, but so might any ox, or horse, or elephant. It is not till he has subjected himself to the discipline of the kyaung that he can reap the fruits of a holy past and look forward to a more glorious future.

> The devils in the underworlds wear out
> Deeds that were wicked in an age gone by.

Man has less innocence than the animals, and cannot, like them, progress by merely omitting to sin. He may make golden stairways of his weaknesses indeed, but before he can do so he must abandon the world, if it is only for twenty-four hours. Then he becomes an upathaka, a believer, and towards another life will hold the gain as well as answer for the loss in the present one, death casting up the debit or credit.

> Higher than Indra's ye may lift your lot,
> And sink it lower than the worm or gnat.

In recognition of this new-gained power the novice drops

his secular name and receives a bwè, an honorific title, to mark that it is now open to him to escape from suffering. The name lapses when he returns to the world again, but it is sufficient that he has once borne it. He may now add to his kan, merit, and gain for himself a glorious new life by good works.

This is what is meant by calling the ceremony a baptism. The bwè are almost invariably Pali, or Burmanised Pali names, and follow the same rules with regard to initial letters as the lu nāmé. Thus a Maung Po Myat, born on Thursday, might take the name of Pyinya-Zawta, while the bwè of a Sunday child, Maung An, would be Adesa. This religious or Buddhist (on the analogy of Christian) name is, of course, retained by the regular members of the monastery, and a monk is never addressed by any other when a name is used at all. When he becomes old a U is added, as U Adesa, but it must not be forgotten that the use of a person's name in addressing him is considered very far from being polite in Burma, especially to one of rank and dignity such as a mendicant. On the other hand, one who has returned to the world never uses the bwè, not even when he accomplishes some great religious work such as the foundation of a pagoda, which according to a comforting belief ensures passage to Ne'ban after death.

The entry into the monastic order is therefore certainly the most important event in the life of a Burman, since only under the robe of the recluse and in the abandonment of the world can he completely fulfil the law and hope to find the way to eventual deliverance from the misery of ever-recurring existences. The popular time for the ceremony is just at the beginning of Wā, the Buddhist Lent, which lasts from July to October, roughly speaking. Strict Buddhists make their sons stay throughout the whole Wā. During that season feasts, though they do occur, are very much discountenanced, and dramatic performances are energetically denounced by the religious.

According to the letter of the law the intending probationers should have reached the age of fifteen, but this regulation has almost entirely lapsed in Lower Burma, among other reasons chiefly because that is just the most

important age for the boy to be learning English and arithmetic, with a view to getting situations under Government or
in English merchants' offices.   Therefore in the vast majority
of cases shin-pyu thi takes place at the age of twelve, or
perhaps even a year earlier.

If the boy has been a scholar in the monastery beforehand, he is sure to be already prepared in all that is required
of him.   If not, he gets a few hasty lessons in the duties
that will be incumbent on him.   He must address a full
member of the order in such and such language ; he
must walk decorously through the streets, keeping his
eyes fixed on the ground six feet before him, and on no
account gaze round him, no matter what exciting events may
be going on ; he must wear his thingan and du-gut in the
prescribed fashion ; he must eat with dignity and circumspection, and so on.   All these details are set forth in most
minute fashion in a code.   When he has mastered the most
essential portions, and has also given proof of an acquaintance with the ordinary forms of worship, all is ready.   His
horoscope now comes into requisition, and a bedinsayā
or Ponna is called in to determine a lucky day and hour
from the sadā.   When this has been settled, three or four
girls, the intending koyin-gale's sisters, or friends of the
family, dress themselves up in their finest silks and jewels—
often borrowing a large quantity of the latter—and go round
the town, announcing to all relatives, friends, and neighbours
when the induction will take place, and inviting them to the
feast, presenting the little packet of le'-pet usual on such
occasions.   Almost all of these send some little present,
either of money or victuals, to aid in the feast and make it
as grand as possible.   Not unseldom, if somebody else's son
is also going to enter the kyaung and the town is not very
large, the two join forces, while occasionally as many as half
a dozen unite, especially if the families are not well off.

On the appointed day the young neophyte dresses in
his finest clothes, and loads himself with all the family gold
chains and jewellery, and as much more as he can borrow for
the occasion.   He then mounts a pony or gets into a richly
decorated car.   Shaded by gold umbrellas, allowed formerly
on this occasion only in Upper Burma, except to those who

had got a special patent for them from the sovereign, he
passes at a foot-pace through the village.   A band of
music goes before ; all his friends and relatives crowd round
him decked in their gayest ; the young men dancing and
singing vigorously ; the girls laughing and smiling, with
powdered faces and brilliant dresses.   Thus he goes in
succession to the houses of his relations and of all the local
officials, to do them the obeisance due from a younger
member of the family, and to bid them farewell.   They in
turn contribute money towards the expense of the band,
and the solace of the supernumeraries.   This triumphant
march is meant to symbolise the maung-shin's abandonment
of the follies of this world, and to recall Prince Theidat's
last splendid appearance in Kapilawut, amidst a crowd of
rejoicing clansmen and subjects, just previous to his abandonment of family and kingdom to become a homeless mendicant ascetic, and to obtain the Buddhaship under the bawdi
tree.   When the round of visits has been duly carried out,
the procession turns back to the parents' house, where in the
meantime the final preparations for the induction and subsequent feast have been concluded.   The head of the kyaung
to which the young postulants are to be admitted, together
with several of his brother monks, are seated at the back of
the room on a raised dais, in front of which are ranged the
presents intended for the mendicants—heaps of fruit, cooked
food, mats, yellow cloth, and so on.   The " Talapoins "
seated in a row carefully hold up the large lotus-leaf-shaped
fans before their faces to shut out from view the female
portion of the assemblage.   Never is the command to the
holy community not to look on woman more necessary and
more arduous to observe than at a shin-pyu pwè.   Burma's
fairest daughters are assembled, bright in rainbow skirts
and neckerchiefs, drowsy-scented flowers in the jetty tresses,
jewellery flashing on the bosom, the fingers, and ears, the
fragrance of thana'ka lingering over the smiling faces.
Terrible trial it is for the young monk, if any such there
be in the gaing ôk's following, and more imperative the
concentration of the mind on the Payeit Gyi and other
portions of the sacred writ which are loudly chanted as the
postulants return, and the assembly shikhoes to the pon-

gyis, and settles down to observe the proceedings. The boy throws off all his fine clothes and jewellery, and binds a piece of white cloth round his loins. Then his long hair is cut off close to the head. Often the locks are as much as three or four feet long, and are carefully preserved by the mother or sister, the latter often making them up into ta-su, the tails of hair twisted in with her own to increase the size of her sa-dôn—the knot of hair she wears at the back of her head. When the hair has been cut, the head is carefully shaved, the boy holding it over a cloth held by some of his relations. After this the head is washed in the usual way with a decoction of the seeds and bark of the kin-bôn thi, and rubbed well with saffron. A bath is then taken, and once more he puts on the bright paso, and repairs to the presence of the monks. Near at hand the parents have set ready the thingan, belt, ko-wut, and other yellow robes, the begging-pot and other requisites of the shin. The boy comes forward, prostrates himself three times, raises his hands joined in reverence, and begs, in a Pali formula got up by heart, to be admitted to the Holy Assembly as a neophyte, that he may walk steadily in the path of perfection, enjoy the advantages which result therefrom, and finally attain to the blessed state of Ne'ban. The kyaung po-go with his own hands gives him the garments; he is duly robed; the thabeit is hung round his neck by the strap, and then it is announced formally that he is a member of the monastery. He falls in among the other novices who have come with the mendicants. The abbot perhaps exhorts the assemblage for a short time, and then rising while all the people do obeisance, walks off slowly to the monastery, whither the newly-appointed ko-yins follow him, not unlikely helping to carry the presents which have been given at their induction.

The feast at the parents' house begins immediately, and of course ends in a pwè, which lasts till dawn. Sometimes, though this is very seldom the case even in Rangoon, the young probationer comes back again the same night and assumes the lay dress. This *pro forma* observance of the ceremony of baptism is, however, vehemently opposed by all the monks who are worth anything. A few boys remain only twenty-four hours in the yellow dress, long enough to enable them to go once at least round the village begging from door to door in the train of the yahans.   This, naturally, is very little better than leaving the kyaung immediately.   It is considered hardly decent for the shin to leave under seven days of professed membership of the community.   Some stay longer—a fortnight, a month, or two months ; but all the more earnest believers insist that their sons shall remain at least one Wā, throughout the four months of Lent, in the rainy season.   The best course for a fervent Buddhist, who nevertheless does not feel himself, adapted for a monkish life, is to stay over three Wās, one Lent for his father, one for his mother, and one for himself.   It is on account of the importance of the Wā to the shin-pyu that most inductions take place at the beginning of that season.   Yahans count their seniority by the number of Lents they have spent in the kyaung.   A mendicant of twenty Wās must shekho to one of twenty-five, and so on.   An individual who has left the holy community to re-enter the world is called a lu-twet, a runaway.   On the other hand, a man who has been married, and has afterwards entered the monastery, goes by the name of taw-twet, one who has fled from the jungle of the world.   The most revered yahans are those who have held steadfastly by the blameless, austere life of the fraternity since the time when they were first admitted as koyin-gale.   Such are called ngè-byu, white, or stainless from youth, and if they attain to advanced age are always sure of a most splendid ceremonial funeral, whether they have been celebrated for piety and learning or not.

If the shin-pyu stays on in the kyaung, he continues the same course of studies as he began as a scholar.   If he has not already learnt the Payeit Gyi and the Paya Shikho, Pali sermons and forms of worship, or the Mingala Thut, the " Buddhist Beatitudes," he applies himself to them now. The most advanced pore over the metaphysical mysteries of the Abidhamma Konit-gyan, the seven books of the most difficult part of the Bitaghat.   These, with the Thingyo and Thadda, afford ample room for consideration to the longest life.   The modern system of shortened sojourn in the kyaungs has led to very imperfect and limited knowledge of these treasuries of sacred knowledge. Formerly it used to be said that the man who did not know the Thadda, the Pali "grammar," knew nothing. If this position were insisted on now, the number of ignorant people in Lower Burma would be somewhat startling.

But there are many difficulties before you get to the Abidhamma and its cognate subjects. Even in the Payeit Gyi there is a section called Ta-zet, or Ta-zet-thut, which has the credit of sending many a probationer back to the noisy, sinful world. According to the couplet—

> Shin pyet ta-zet,
> Loo pyet a-yet.

> Brandy sends a man to hell;
> Ta-zet spoils the saint as well.

It is a sort of religious *Pons Asinorum.*

Besides prosecuting his religious studies, the shin is required also to attend on the pon-gyis and minister to their wants. He must lay before them at fixed times their daily food, the proper supply of water, the well-used betel-box, and whatever else the monk may require. He must of course go round every morning with the other members of the monastery, the begging-bowl strapped round his neck, accepting meekly, without word of thanks, or glance thrown to the right or left, even when he passes his father's house, the food poured in by the pious. When a pon-gyi goes abroad the neophyte may be required to follow, carrying his fan or umbrella, or perhaps an arm-load of palm-leaf books, if a function is to be performed anywhere. According to the strict letter of the law the ko-yin ought to eat only of the food presented in the morning, but a very great laxity has crept in in this respect, not only with the neophytes, but even among the professed members of the order. It is no uncommon thing for the parents of the youth to send in daily a special meal for him, or even, in the case of wealthy families, actually to keep a cook on the monastic premises to prepare his food. Such sybaritism is not by any means uncommon in Lower Burma, though even there hardly approved of. In any good monastery in Upper Burma, or indeed in any monastery at all, even in Mandalay, it would be promptly put a stop to. But where the monks themselves show the example of carnal weakness, the probationers cannot be expected to maintain the old austerity.

The shin is subject in every way to the discipline of the monastery, but there are very few additional rules really incumbent on him. He has to observe always the Sè-ba Thila, the ten commandments. Five of these are obligatory on all Buddhists at all times : the other five are supposed to be incumbent upon laymen only on sacred days and during Lent. The five universal commandments are :—

1. Thou shalt not take any life at all.
2. Thou shalt not steal.
3. Thou shalt not commit adultery.
4. Thou shalt not lie.
5. Thou shalt not drink intoxicating liquor.

The additional five are :

6. Thou shalt not eat after mid-day.
7. Thou shalt not sing, dance, or play on any musical instrument.
8. Thou shalt not use cosmetics, or colour the face.
9. Thou shalt not sit, stand, or sleep on platforms or elevated places not proper for thee.
10. Thou shalt not touch gold or silver.

These latter five are, it has been said, imposed upon laymen on sacred days, but the burden is very light, the people observing them or not, accordingly as they are observing the "duty-day." If they are not "keeping the feast," they conduct themselves precisely as they would on any other day, and buy and sell and attend pwès in their ordinary fashion.

This laxity is, of course, not open to the shins, but it cannot be said that the regulations, except perhaps as to eating, are very irksome. The seventh and eighth commandments seem by themselves peculiar, but they refer to filthy habits more explicitly set forth in the Patimauk, or book of the enfranchisement, containing the 227 sins which a monk is liable to commit. The ninth refers to the common Oriental dislike to any person of insufficient dignity occupying an elevated place physically above worthier people.

So far, then, the shin is not very grievously burdened in the monastery. But the discipline maintained is very strict. None of the ko-yins or of the boarder-pupils must be out of the monastic limits after the bell has rung. A lay scholar may get permission from the kyaung po-go to sleep at home now and again, but this indulgence is naturally impossible to the neophyte; he must always stay in the monastery. Again, the boarders may run home in the afternoon to get some dinner at their parents' houses, but this the shin cannot do. Breaches of the rules are very severely punished. The culprit's hands are tied high above his head to a post, and the castigator lays on vigorously on the naked back with a stout bamboo. Cases of deliberate cruelty of course occasionally happen, for human nature is the same everywhere, and a Dotheboys Hall is not an entire figment; but they are rare, and on the whole the shin is happy in the monastery, and occasionally in later life looks back with regret to the old, quiet, unruffled, careless life of the pon-gyi kyaung.

In Upper Burma it has actually been his school, for but very few adopt the system of having private teachers to instruct their children; and in Lower Burma it probably contrasts favourably with the uncomfortable hard benches and desks of the English institution, and the still more irksome quietness demanded, and steady, prolonged application exacted by the English teacher. Those who have been to both remember most fondly the long dusky monastery school-room, where they sat on the floor and shouted out their lessons, and now and again slipped out into the air to take the stiffness out of their limbs with a quarter of an hour at chin lôn, Burmese football. In the English school you learned to make money; in the Burmese school you learned to be happy and contented.

CHAPTER IV

LIFE IN THE MONASTERY

A LITTLE before daylight, "when there is light enough to see the veins in the hand," that is to say, in Burma, at half-past five in the morning, in accordance with the dina chariya, the whole monastic community rises, awakened by the sound of the kaladet. This is a big, oblong, trough-shaped bell, made of a piece of wood hollowed out, with little chiselled holes on the side. It is beaten with a wooden mallet, and makes noise enough to rouse the heaviest sleeper. The yahan then rinses out his mouth, washes his hands and face, arranges his dress, the same in which he has slept all night, and recites a few pious precepts, chief among which is the morning prayer: "How great a favour has the Lord Buddha bestowed upon me in manifesting to me his law, through the observance of which I may escape hell and secure my salvation."

There are always a few sleepy boarders, or shins, who have been indulging in the dissipation of whispered conversations till far into the night, whom nothing but a personal attack will awaken, but they are soon shaken up, and then the entire community arranges itself before the image of the Buddha, the abbot at the head, the rest of the brotherhood, pyin-sins, novices, and scholars, according to their order, and all together intone the morning service. This done, they each in their ranks present themselves before the kyaung po-go, and pledge themselves to observe during the day the vows and precepts incumbent upon them. They then separate for a short time, the pupils and shins to sweep the floor of the kyaung, and bring a supply of drinking water for the day, filter it, and place it ready for use; the more advanced novices and others of full rank to sweep round the sacred trees and water them; the elders to meditate in solitude on the regulations of the order. Meditation is beyond all other actions meritorious. The first meditation of the day should be on the miseries of life and the conviction that we cannot free ourselves from them; such thoughts are honourable beyond the founding of a pagoda, or praying for the salvation of all living creatures. Some gather flowers and offer them before the pagoda, to impress upon the mind the virtues of the great teacher and the weaknesses and shortcomings of human nature.

Then comes the first meal of the day, a light refection usually preceded by a homily or grace, to the effect that the rice is eaten not to please the appetite, but to satisfy the wants of the body; that the yellow habit is worn not for vanity, but to cover nakedness; that they dwell in this house not for vainglory, but to be protected from the inclemency of the weather; that medicine is taken merely to recover health, and that health is desirable only that they may attend with greater diligence to prayer and meditation. After the meal all proceed to study for an hour. The ko-yins repeat what lessons they have learnt and apply themselves to new tasks. The early morning is considered especially favourable for committing to memory.

It is now close on eight o'clock, and, arranging themselves in Indian file, they set forth in orderly procession, with the abbot at their head, to beg their food. Slowly they wend their way through the chief street of the town or village, halting when any one comes out to pour his contribution of rice, or fruit, or vegetables, into the alms-bowl, but never saying a word, or even raising the eyes from the ground. It is they who confer the favour, not the givers. Were it not for the passing of the mendicants, the charitable would not have the opportunity of gaining for themselves merit. Not even a glance rewards the most bounteous donation. With eyes fixed unwaveringly on the ground six feet before them, and hands clasped beneath the begging-bowl, they pass on, solemnly meditating on their own unworthiness and the vileness of all human things. There are naturally certain places where they receive a daily dole ; but should the open-handed good wife have been delayed at the bazaar, chatting with her gossips, or the pious old head of the house be away on a journey, the recluses would rather go without breakfast than halt for a second, as if implying that they remembered the house as an ordinary place of call. It is a furlong on the noble path lost to the absentees, and the double ration of the following day is noted without a phantom of acknowledgment.   So they pass round, circling back to the monastery after a perambulation lasting perhaps an hour or an hour and a half. Some mendicants, especially the more austere, return as soon as their thabeits are well filled ; others apparently walk for a certain fixed time, and if the bowl is filled before this time is over, they empty it carefully on the side of the road.   This is not wastry ; the food is eaten by the dogs and birds of the air, and the merit to the givers is the same.

On their arrival at the monastery, a portion of all the alms they have received on the tour is solemnly offered to the Buddha, and then all proceed to breakfast.   In former times, and according to the strict letter of the law, this ought to consist solely of what has been received during the morning ; but a very great number of monasteries have, sad to say, fallen away from the strictness of the old rule.   Only the more austere abbots enforce the observance of the earlier asceticism.   Certainly in the great majority of the kyaungs of Lower Burma there is a man, not a monk, called kappi-yadayaka, or supporter, who provides for them a much more delicate and better dressed meal than they would have if they ate of the miscellaneous conglomerate turned out of the alms-bowl.   That indiscriminate mixture of rice, cooked and raw ; peas, boiled and parched ; fish, flesh, and fowl, curried and plain, usually wrapped separately in plantain leaves ; cocoa-nut cakes and cucumbers ; mangoes and meat ; is very seldom consumed, in the larger towns at any rate, by any but the most rigidly austere.   It is handed over to the little boys, the scholars of the community, or to any wanderers who may be sojourning in the kyaung, who eat as much of it as they can, and give the rest to the crows and pariah dogs.   The abbot and the pyin-sin find a smoking hot breakfast ready prepared for them when they return from their morning's walk, and are ready to set to with healthy appetites.   This question of Sybaritism is a chief source of dispute between the rival sects of Mahā and Sula-gandi.

Breakfast done, they wash out the begging-bowls, and chant a few lauds before the image of the Buddha, meditating for a short time on kindness and affection.   During the succeeding hour the scholars are allowed to play about, but must not make a noise, or indulge in quarrelsome games ; the religious pass the time in leisurely conversation, or in any other way they please ; the kyaung po-go usually has visits from old people, who come to pay their respects, or perhaps the kyaung-tagā, the founder of the monastery, the patron of his benefice, comes to consult with him on various matters, or to converse about religion and good works.   The etiquette observed on these occasions is always very stately and ceremonious.   Whoever approaches, whether it be the poorest villager, the founder of the monastery, or the governor of the district, all alike must prostrate themselves three times before the yahan, and, with uplifted hands, say, " In order that all the sins I have committed, in thought, in word, or in deed, may be pardoned to me, I prostrate myself three times, once in honour of the Buddha, again in honour of the Law, and thirdly in honour of the Assembly, the three precious things.   By so doing, I hope to be preserved from the three calamities, from the four states of punishment; and from the five enemies, fire, water, thieves, governors (literally translated burdens), and malevolent people."   The sayā replies : " As a reward for his merit and his obeisances, may the supporter (tagā) be freed from the three calamities, the four states of punishment, the five enemies, and from harm of what kind soever.   May all his aims be good and end well ; may he advance firmly in the noble path, perfect himself in wisdom, and finally obtain rest in ne'ban."   Whenever the visitor addresses the yahan he joins his hands together, and sitting as he does on a mat, slightly bends the body forward, applying the title of payā, or lord, and making use of the honorific forms of speech specially reserved for the religious. The mendicant on his part calls the layman, of whatever rank, tagā, supporter, or, if the visitor be a woman, tăgama. Somehow or other these conversations, like the addresses of the religious to the people in the rest-houses, always seem to come round to the subject of the merit of almsgiving. The recluse will say that whatever is presented, silk robe, mattress, pillow, betel-box, is purified by the merit of the alms deed. The poor could fill the Lord Buddha's begging-bowl with a handful of flowers; the rich could not do so with a hundred, a thousand, ten thousand measures of grain. The path in the noontide heat is hard to one who has no sandals, and no water-gourd. What, then, will be the path after death to one who has not charity and regard for the ten precepts! Alms deeds can defend a man and protect him against the influence and the sources of demerits which are man's true enemies. Liberality is chief among the ten great virtues; it is the second of the three works of perfection; it is the absolute soul of the five renouncements. With all these a man becomes a Buddha, without them he sinks to be an animal, or worse still, to the fiery chambers of hell.

When the conversation is over the layman bows down three times again, saying, "My Lord's disciple does obeisance"; or U tin ba thi "places his forehead on the ground," rises, backs five or ten paces, and then turning on the right, as he would at the pagoda, departs. There may be quite a long succession of these visitors, and their respects are paid all through the afternoon, if the weather be not too hot.

At half-past eleven, however, there is another meal, usually a light refection of fruits, and this is the last of the day. The pyin-sin are expressly forbidden to eat after noon. Solid food taken after the shadows slope to the east endangers purity. The blood becomes heated, and, moreover, when the stomach is loaded the mind becomes over-clouded and unfitted for meditation. It is worthy of remark that the religious must eat, as they walk, slowly and with gravity, only putting moderate-sized morsels into the mouth, and constantly bearing in mind that food is not intended for the gratification of the flesh, but for the nourishment of the body. The ceremony called a-kat must also be carefully observed, in accordance with the precise instructions laid down in the Wini. When a monk wants anything he must not go and get it for himself, nor direct any one in as many words to bring it to him. He must say to an attendant shin, or scholar, " Do what is lawful," whereupon the food is brought him, and the shin kneels down at a distance of a couple of feet, and, making the customary salutation, says, " This is lawful." The yahan then either takes it from his hand or directs him to place it within reach. The same ceremony is observed in everything, whether the religious wants water to wash his face or hands or to rinse out his mouth, or his sandals and fan when he goes out, or when offerings are made to him by the pious. The desire is of course to impart dignity to all the monk does, and to repress covetousness and inordinate carnal desires, and the custom dates from the very foundation of the order.

After the noontide meal all return to work again. A certain number undertake the teaching of the boys, who are at all stages of learning, from the children at the Thin-bôn-gyi, the spelling-book, up to the Ko-yins, who, in accordance with the law, are learning the Wini, the Whole Duty of the Monk, by heart, with a view to abandoning the world and adopting the religious life. Others set to work to read old texts and the commentaries on them, or go to superintend the professional writers who are copying out manuscripts, carefully scratching on the palm - leaves with sharp steel style. The pyin-sin themselves never do anything of the kind. The writers are all professionals, laymen, and almost without exception from Upper Burma. The sādaik, the carved and gilded box containing the palm - leaf books, stands in the central room near the images, and often shaded by a sacred umbrella. When a learned sadaw makes notes, or writes a commentary of his own, he dictates it all to these copyists, who afterwards engross it. Most of the older members of the kyaung do, however, what an Englishman would call nothing, all the afternoon. They talk with whatever idlers——and there are always an abundance of them——come about the place, and then sink into meditation and many of the weaker of them into sleep. Meditation is the only path to the higher seats whereby a man becomes a yahanda, fit for Ne'ban, possessed of the six kinds of wisdom :—

1. The faculty of seeing like a nat or dewa.
2. The faculty of hearing like a nat.
3. Creative power.
4. Knowledge of the thoughts of others.
5. Freedom from passion.
6. Knowledge of one's own past existences.

They sit therefore for long hours fingering their rosaries, the beads made of the seeds of the *Canna indica*, "Indian shot," which sprang from Shin Gautama's blood, and repeating many times the prescribed formulæ, most often the Thama-tawi Patthana—All is changeful, all is sad, all is unreal ; followed by the Tharana Gôn, the invocation of the Three Precious Gems, the Lord, the Law, and the Assembly. So by abstraction of the mind they hope to acquire the four laws of Edepat :—

1. Absolute power over the will.
2. Absolute power over the mind.
3. Absolute power of execution.
4. Absolute power over the means to the object.

The discipline is terrible to all but a slow-minded man, and we can well imagine one who thus presents himself to the people as a living memento of all that is sacred and perfect in the religion, longing for the extinction of Ne'ban, where he may escape from the misery of recurring lives.

> Ask of the sick, the mourners, ask of him
>   Who tottereth on his staff, lone and forlorn,
> Liketh thee life?   These say, The babe is wise
>   That weepeth being born.

So each one in the brotherhood passes the time each after-noon : some asleep, some racking the brain with mystical musings, some learning, some teaching, while throughout all sounds the din of the schoolroom, where the pupils are shouting out their tasks at the top of their voices.

Between three and four the lessons are finished, and the shins and scholars perform any domestic duties that may be required about the monastery. This done, the day-scholars go home and have their dinner, a few of the boarders perhaps gaining permission to do the same. The ko - yins, being under monastic discipline, are obliged to fast like their superiors. Most of them, and some few of the pon-gyis, go out for a staid and solemn walk round the village and out to the pagoda. Then, at sunset, the unmelodious, far-reaching notes of the kaladet summon all back to the kyaung. The strollers return immediately. None wearing the yellow robe may be without the monastery limits after the sun goes down, which occurs throughout the whole year close upon six o'clock. A short time afterwards the scholars are summoned before the abbot or some of the pon-gyis and recite steadily all that they have learned, from the Thin-bôn-gyi up to the book they have last committed to memory. If the kyaung is large and there are a number of students, this thorough process is, however, modified, and only the work at the moment being learned is required of the pupils. The Pali rituals are chanted with spasmodic energy, abundance of sound in most cases doing duty for a just comprehension of the matter. Very few of the religious could string a sentence together in Pali, far less speak the language, yet most of them can pour forth homilies and dogmata for hours on end, so that the poor ko-yins are not to be scoffed at for their parrot-like volubility. When this examination is over, if the sayā is an enthusiast, or if there is time, that dignitary himself delivers a sermon, or gives an exposition of some knotty passage, or perhaps there is a general conversation on some question of doctrine, or other subject of ecclesiastical interest at the moment.

Thus the time passes away till half-past eight or nine, when the evening is closed with devotions in the presence of the image of the Buddha. All assemble according to their rank as in the morning, and together intone the vesper lauds. When the last sounds of the mournful chant have died away in the dimly-lighted chamber, one of the novices, or a clever scholar, stands up, and with a loud voice proclaims the hour, the day of the week, the day of the month, and the number of the year. Then all shikho before the Buddha thrice, and thrice before the abbot, and retire to rest. None who

have experienced the impressiveness of this ceremonial, called
the Thā-thanā-hlyauk, will readily forget the powerful effect
it has on the feelings.   It is the fit ending of a day full of
great possibilities for all.   If the same routine gone through
day after day becomes monotonous and loses some of its
power for good, yet the effect of such a school, presided
over by an abbot of intelligence and earnestness, must
infallibly work for the good of all connected with it, and
especially so in the case of an impulsive, impressionable
people like the Burmese.   As long as all the men of the
country pass through the kyaungs, the teachings of Western
missionaries can have but little power to shake the power of
Buddhism over the people.   The moral truths of both
religions, Christianity and Buddhism, are practically the same,
and who can give proof of aught else without calling in the
aid of faith ?   The Burman is convinced that no other creed
will suit him so well, and the number of monasteries in all
parts of the country renders it easy for every one to obtain
entrance for his children.   The king sent his sons to the
kyaung, and the poorest and most sinful wretch need not fear
that his child will be turned away from the gates.   Teaching
is really all the pyin-sin do for the people ; but it is precisely
this moderate amount of teaching, revealing as it does to all
the stern simplicity of the monastic life, that keeps the faith
active in the country.   Many monks are supremely lazy, but
so are many of their fellow-countrymen, and if you are
bidden by the Law to meditate deeply on the nature of
mind and matter, of Nām and Rupa, of Seit and Sedathit,
of Thissa and Zan, it is certain that you cannot be actively
employed on other less important matters.

Of late years the rudiments of Western knowledge, arithmetic, elementary geography, and history are more and more
taught in the monasteries all over the country, and Government gives grants to the monasteries for the pupils who pass
the prescribed examinations.

CHAPTER V

TATTOOING

WHATEVER his parents may think, the Burman youth considers the tattooing of his thighs quite as important a matter as his entry into a monastery. If he attains to the full dignity of humanity by becoming a shin, it is no less settled in his own mind that till he is tattooed in proper fashion there may be doubts as to his thorough manhood. Accordingly, very often at a tender age, varying with the spiritedness of his character, he begins to get figures tattooed on various parts of his thighs. When the operation is finished, the whole body from the waist, in a line with the navel, downwards to just beyond the knee-cap, is completely covered, the effect to the eye being not so much of a marking of the cuticle as of a skin-tight pair of *caleçons*, fitting better than the best glove ever made. The origin of the custom may or may not be the shameful reason assigned by foreign writers. No true Burman believes it. But in any case the tattooing looks very well on the olive skin, and I have heard English ladies admire it. The custom will probably never die out. There are, it is true, not a few puny Rangoonites, spiritless sons of the town, who do not get tattooed, but they are ashamed of it and take every opportunity of concealing their weakness. But there is not a single up-country man, not a solitary taw-tha, the sturdy inhabitants of the small towns and villages, who is not decorated with the dark blue tracery. They would as soon think of wearing a woman's skirt as of omitting to be tattooed, and they are strengthened in the feeling by the opinion of the girls themselves.

The operation is not by any means pleasant. In fact in

places such as the tender inside parts of the thigh and at the joints of the knee, it needs more stoicism than most youths can command, to endure it without relieving the mind in speech.   Therefore it is common to put the boy under the influence of opium while it is being done, though some parents will not allow this, for cases have occurred where the youth has died of an over-dose.   For the same reason it is very seldom that more than three or four figures are done at a time.   The part swells up a good deal, and there is danger of fever ; besides that a few days afterwards the itchiness which supervenes is almost as intolerable as the first tattooing, while if the skin is broken by scratching there is not only a nasty sore, but the figure is spoilt.   You not uncommonly hear of cases where the whole surface was finished at one sitting, but you only hear of them because it is unusual, and because the youth is proud of it.

The instrument used is a pricker about two feet long, weighted at the top with a brass figure, sometimes plain, but in the case of good sayās, always carved more or less elaborately in the figure of a bird, a nat, or a bilu.   The yat, or style part, is solid, with a round, sharp point, split up into four by long slits at right angles to each other, which serve to hold the colouring matter.   This style is about four inches long and fits into a hollow pipe, which again joins it to the weighted end.   Thus the length required for free work is gained without too great weight, except where it is wanted.   The tattooer catches the pricker with his right hand, and guides the point with a rest formed by the forefinger and thumb of his left, the hand resting firmly on the person's body.   The dye used is lampblack, the best being that obtained by the burning of sessamum oil, and this is mixed with water as it is wanted.   Good sayās always sketch the outline of the figure roughly on the skin with an ordinary camel's-hair brush, and then the pattern is executed with a series of punctures close together, forming what afterwards fades into a rough line.   Skilful men are very quick at it.   I have had fifteen figures done in little over half an hour.   But then Sayā Chein is a celebrated man.

The figures tattooed are those of all kinds of animals, tigers, cats, monkeys, and elephants being the commonest,

while nats, bilus, and compound animals called tiger-bilus
are also frequent. Each representation is surrounded by a
roughly oval tracery of a variety of letters of the alphabet,
which form a curious and remarkably effective frame. Thus
each animal has a setting of its own. Vacant spaces are
filled up in a similar way, and the top and bottom are
finished off with a scolloped line. Sometimes these letters
are asserted to have a cabalistic meaning, but ordinarily no
greater virtue is claimed for them than that of beauty.
Mystic squares and ladder-step triangles of serious import
are often added in vacant spaces, but all the more important
and valid charms are reserved for other parts of the body
and for special execution, usually too in vermilion. The old
style, and that which prevails still in jungle districts, was to
cover every available piece of skin with tracery, so that the
figures became blurred and indistinct, and on a dark skin
grown old were practically not visible without careful
examination, which, considering the portion of the body,
was embarrassing to both parties. The newer style, and
that specially affected by those with a white skin, is to
sacrifice mass of colour to distinctness of outline. The best
sayās carry about sample-books with them containing clever
drawings, from which the aspirant may select the patterns
he likes best, and mark their relative positions before he
takes the opium. But tigers, cats, monkeys, and bilus
always predominate. To fill up space, and for greater
certainty, the name of the animal is often added in the
figure, after the style of juvenile art on slates, or with a
piece of chalk on blank hoardings.

The Shans tattoo even more extensively than the Burmans. The figures are carried down well over the calf of
the leg and above the navel, while from the upper line
tattooed rays run up to the chest and at the back, after the
fashion of a rising sun, almost to the nape of the neck.
Sometimes the retainers of the Sawbwas, or Shan chiefs,
had every part of the body except the palms of the hands
and the soles of the feet tattooed. Even the face was
covered with the dark-blue markings. Mostly all the men
who tattoo charms and cabalistic figures are Shans. They
claim and are allowed a special skill in such matters, and as

they mutter spells and incomprehensible incantations over the " medicine," are looked up to with profound belief and a very considerable deal of awe.

The tattooing on the loins and legs is universal with all Burmans, and nothing more is ordinarily required ; but there are very few who have not charms of some kind tattooed on the arms, back, chest, or even on the top of the head, which is shaved for the purpose. These figures are of all kinds— lizards, birds, mystic words and squares, rings, images of the Buddha, and sometimes merely a few scattered dots, the latter especially on the face, between the eyes, over the ears, or on the chin. The colouring matter is almost always ver- milion, with drugs and solutions, according to requirement, mingled with it. The blue dye from the lampblack never disappears, but the red colour of the vermilion gradually fades away and vanishes. Nevertheless figures of this kind, more or less distinct, are to be found on Burmans of all ages, so great is the national superstition. Even the town youths, whose limbs are smooth and " unbreeched " as a girl's, are never without some charms of this kind, if it is only the a-nu se, which enables a man to gain the woman he loves. This " drug of tenderness " is composed of vermilion mixed with a variety of herbs and curious things, prominent among which is the bruised, dry skin of the tauktè, the trout-spotted gekko, whose sonorous cry and fidelity to the house where he establishes himself and brings luck, are well known to all who have visited Burma or Siam. It is very sparingly used, a few round spots arranged in the shape of a triangle being of sufficient virtue to ensure the object aimed at. The commonest place for them is between the eyes, but occasionally the se sayā recommends the lips, or even the tongue, and his advice is always followed. This is the only tattooing which women ever have executed on them, and there are not many of them who have it done. The patient is usually a love-sick maiden who is afraid the object of her affection will escape from her, or a girl whom rolling years warn that she must be quick if she would not be condemned to remain an a-pyo heing, an old maid. Except in very desperate cases, however, they always manage to persuade the operator to place the charm on some part of the

body where it will not be visible.   If it is not effectual, there
is always open to them the signal afforded by kindly national
custom to maidens longing for a mate.   They cut off the
lappets of hair, the bya-bazan, hanging over the ears, and the
significance is the same as the white heather of the language
of flowers, " heart for sale."   In Rangoon the tattooing of a
woman has a special signification, not recognised elsewhere.
It means that she wants an Englishman for a husband.
Poor thing !

Another very universal kind of tattooing is that with
a-hpi se.   Almost every schoolboy in the country has a
specimen of this on him, for does it not prevent him from
feeling the pain when he is caned ?   No amount of falsified
hopes in the experience of friends will persuade him that
it may not be effectual in his case, and a flogging is often
courted as an immediate test of its efficacy.   Pride repels
the inquiries of chums as to the results, but the experimenter
is usually very well behaved for some time.   In the case
of older men the a-hpi se acts as a talisman against bullets,
sword cuts, and ills of that kind.   Allied to this are the
thenat hpi, which soldiers and dacoits carry about with them.
These are the horns of buffaloes and other animals, which
may be plain, but are usually elaborately carved with figures
according to fancy.   They must be quite solid down to the
root.   A hollow or flaw of any kind deprives them of their
virtue.   While the man has such a talisman in his hands
he cannot be killed.   A monkey is a very favourite image
to have carved in this way on a sword or dagger hilt, the
reference being to the tale of the Ramayana.   Of a similar
nature are talismans which are especially used by soldiers
and dacoits.   These hkaung-beit-set are charmed or consecrated objects let into the flesh under the skin.   They are of
various kinds.   Some are gold, silver, or lead ; others curious
pebbles, pieces of tortoise-shell, or bits of horn, all of them
with incantations of mystic character written on them.
Many famed dacoits have long rows and curves of them over
the chest, showing in little knobs through the skin.   When
they get into English prisons, an energetic jailer has been
known to cut them out, lest they should be pieces of gold or
silver, or perhaps precious stones, with which the turnkeys

might be bribed. The usual result is to break the robber's spirit. Once the continuity is interrupted the consecration is gone. More peaceable people wear necklaces or bracelets of such talismans in the belief that they are thus proof against malignant witches and necromancers. Most Englishmen in Burma, who are on friendly terms with the people, have been asked to test the virtue of such a charm, by firing at it tied up in a handkerchief. If the incantation is valid the handkerchief will be unharmed, though the muzzle of the pistol be held up to it. In such a case the pistol will burst.

Another kind of tattooing is the mwe se, which guards against danger from snake bite. Similarly the a-kwè a-ka, the shielding, or defending drug, renders harmless the spells of wizards and geomancers, and keeps far away evil spirits of every kind. But the most hideous and weird of the superstitions about tattooing is that connected with the a-kyan se. There are but very few sayās who are acquainted with the necessary drugs and incantations, and fewer people still who have the courage to submit to the operation, for many men are pointed out whose minds have given way under the gruesome process, and who wander about graveyards, gnashing their teeth and fumbling about for human bones to gnaw and mouth. And no wonder, for some tattooers make them chew the raw flesh of a man who has been hanged, while the figure is being tattooed on the breast. Those who go through the operation are called Baw-di-tha-da. Some become Baw-di-tha-da without knowing it, and without the sickening necessity of mumbling human flesh like a ghoul. I knew an instance in a monastery. The patient was a boarder about fourteen years of age. A Shan tattooer wandering about the country spent a couple of nights in the kyaung, and the boy, attracted by the fellow's eerie tales, managed to save up a good many titbits for him from the food going in the monastery. Out of gratitude, and having nothing better to give him, for he was very poor and homeless, the sayā tattooed on the lad a figure with singular drugs, muttering queer phrases the while. Then he went away saying no more than that it would make the boy very strong. In about a month's time the boarder displayed unmistakable signs of being a Baw-di-tha-da. He leapt enormous heights in the air, jumped about and ran at random, carried with the utmost ease things which no one else could move. The abbot locked him up in a sadaik, the box in which the palm-leaf manuscripts were kept; he got out without injuring the lock in any way, sprang on to the roof of the monastery, forty feet high, and turned a somersault to the ground without hurting himself in the least. He had been a boy of very soft, easy temper, and now he became fiery and uncertain, and with his vast strength, very dangerous. He only calmed down when a monk preached the law to him. He was constantly doing marvellous things; one day he walked across the river in front of the monastery, holding a monk's ôk, or food vessel, in his hands. The depth of the water was over six fathoms, but it did not reach higher than his waist. On another occasion a tree which was being cut down fell on him. He sank into the ground and came forth quite uninjured. After some years his parents took him to Magwe in Upper Burma. There he fell into bad courses and became a dacoit. This was terrible for his family in a special way, because in native territory if they cannot catch the dacoit they seize all his friends and relations and put them in jail till they can get hold of the real culprit, and no one can lay hands on a Baw-di-tha-da. At last, however, he was restored to his right mind. A holy ascetic came across him, soothed him with the payeit gyi, and then with a rusty nail and sacred medicines, tattooed out the figure put on with such lamentable results by the Shan sayā. The quondam Baw-di-tha-da is now a staid and respected broker in the employ of one of the best-known English rice firms in Rangoon. He was fortunate; most Baw-di-tha-das have to be killed in their sleep.

But though Baw-di-tha-das are very rare, charmed tattooing is not, and there are some fast young men who seem almost to make picture galleries of themselves with emblems and patterns all over their chests, arms, backs, and the calves of their legs. The colour gradually dies away until at last nothing remains but the blue breeches. These really look well, and they last a man to his dying day.

The following recipes and formulæ to be repeated

during tattooing are taken from a Mandalay tattooer's book :—

For an a-nu se : " I was Kutha Min, I.   At the time when Papawadi was my queen, when I routed the kings of all the seven countries who came suing for her hand. Right beautiful was she, fair as the malla flower when it perfumes the forest with its odours.   I the great Kutha Yaza."

This is to be repeated seven times at various stages in the operation.   Kutha Yaza is the hero of one of the 510 Zats, detailing the previous births of the Lord Buddha.

For an a-hpi se : " Steal gold from the pagodas, fine, bright gold.   Refine it in the fire and repeat the magic words in the house, on the lonely path, before the lucky star, at the pagoda ; repeat them a thousand times save one. Consecrate the water, draw the circle of the flying galôn. Put it under the left arm, under the right arm.   No harm will befall thee, safe and invulnerable."

" A parrot tattooed on the arm will give great favour with princes."

" Take a length of bamboo or of rattan the size of a joint of the merchant's finger, and repeat, pressing your foot against the tha-bye tree, Nat-tha wa-pa, wa-pa nat-tha na. Repeat this seven times and put the joint in your mouth when you are in danger.   There is no better the-nat hpi."

The merchant's finger (let thugywè) is the third—that on which rings are worn.   The forefinger is called let-hno. Hno means to hate, but whether this is the meaning or not —as it were " the finger of scorn "—I do not know.

" Repeat sa ba pa wa wa ba pa wa with the tooth of the wild boar in your palm, with the wild boar's ear as you know.   Draw the circle with pure red gold.   Draw in it a nagā ; then draw sideways the figure of a flying lion.   Write round it ôm gyu-lu gyu-lu thwa ha ya.   Then carry rice, fresh water, betel, tobacco, and le'pet to the pagoda and heap them together.   When you have repeated a thousand times the words of the encircling gāta (spell) put it below the skin. But be careful not to give it to the first man who asks for it.   It is very powerful."   This is another a-hpi se.

Certain stones called amadé, said to be found in the

heads of birds, in trees, and in animals, are highly prized as amulets. They will guard from musket shots, or sword thrusts, from painful blows, or evil spirits. Hmaw sayās always have them. When they are placed on a child's face, or introduced into any one's blood, nat thwin thi, they introduce a spirit. The person so possessed falls into a trance, and may be questioned as to the doings of any other evil spirits in the neighbourhood.

Letters, placed in the magic squares and triangular " in " are la-gyi, na-gyi, ka-gyi, ga-gyi (great *l*, great *n*, great *k*, and great *g*). Other very powerful s'ma, as these tattooed letters are called, are " round " sa, wa, la, and " bottom-indented " da. The arm is a favourite place for them.

The belief of every Burman in the efficacy of these tattooed charms is practically ineradicable. In 1881, in Rangoon, a young man had the figure of the great Peguan byaing, the " paddy-bird," a species of egret, tattooed upon him. This was to be as efficacious in preserving him from drowning as a child's caul used to be considered by British sailors. When it was finished, he suggested that an immediate experiment should be made. Accordingly his hands and feet were tied, and he was tossed over the side of a boat into the river. The under-currents in the Rangoon river are very dangerous, and the poor fellow was never seen again. The tattooers, master and assistant, were brought up on a charge of murder, and convicted of manslaughter, but the great mass of the Burman population thought they were very hardly treated, and that the fact of an unlucky side-wind, some mischance in the calculation from the horoscope, the machinations of an evil-disposed person against the deceased, or something of that kind, which had caused the lamentable issue, ought never to have led to the conviction of the skilled sayās. That they were charlatans was never once hinted.

CHAPTER IV

EAR-BORING

THE first great event in a Burmese girl's life is the nā-twin mingala, the boring of her ears. She is not out of the doll stage till that happens. She may have toddled after her mother to the market with a basket of fruit on her head, long before the ear-boring, but that ceremony is as much an epoch to her as putting on the yellow robe, or getting his legs tattooed, is to her brother. Ever afterwards she will look upon every male as a possible lover. No more taking alternate whiffs at a big green cheroot with little Maung Po ; no more teasing Po Shan to let her have a taste of those fine nettè mangoes his father has got down from Mandalay ; no more dawdling about the streets by herself, watching the small boys playing with the round gôn nyin seeds, or having a hurried glimpse of the puppet play, while she is supposed to be at home looking after the house with her little brother. When she walks out now it will be with her mother, or an aunt, or married sister, as a chaperone ; and if she goes to the play it will be in formal procession, and with all her finest clothes on. Nothing like getting the ears bored to set a girl thinking about the wave of the hair that falls down in lappets by her ears, or the best recipe for the fragrant straw-coloured thanaka, with which she tints her face and charms half the senses of the gallants. It even alters her walk. She sets about practising the coquettish sway of the body in walking, which is considered so attractive, and which a philosophical matter-of-fact Darwinian would probably declare was first of all due to an involuntary throwing out of the heel with each step to keep the folds of the dress modestly closed in front, and to prevent the dainty slipper, just covering her toes and no more, from slipping off the foot. However that may be, it is an accomplishment indispensable to a Burmese belle. She takes as much pains over it as she does with her jetty tresses. In a word, the nā-twin mingala transforms the girl into a woman, just as much as admission to a monastery makes the boy a man. It is her baptism, and is the distinctive mark of her race. Most of the men get their ears bored too, but the ceremony is not so solemn with them, and latterly is not so universal, at any rate not in the towns on the coast.

The ceremony takes place at the age of twelve or thirteen, just when the girl has attained puberty in fact. Her sadā is submitted to a soothsayer, that a fortunate day and hour may be chosen, and that being fixed, a great feast is prepared, and all the friends of the family and the relations are invited. An invitation to an ear-boring feast is a very urgent matter. No one can refuse without a very good excuse, and serious business is often postponed to the demands of such a ceremony. Everybody comes early, and sits down in any place he can find round about the front part and sides of the room, the girl, with all her female relatives about her, reclining on a mat at the back. The bedin sayā stalks about gazing at a mysterious strip of palm-leaf, or apparently wrapped in deep thought. Beside him is the professional ear-borer. He carries the needles, which are almost always pure gold, and even in the case of the poorest, never of any baser metal than silver. Rich people very often have them set at the ends with precious stones. At last the soothsayer gives the sign that the favourable moment has arrived. The ear-borer moves up immediately and passes the needles through the lobe of the ear, sometimes using a cork as they do in England, but more often letting them pass between two of his fingers. The girl, who has been worked up into a high state of excitement and terror by all the preparations, usually struggles and shrieks as hard as she can, but the women round about hold her down, and the band of music in the street outside strikes up a rapid movement and drowns her lamentations, while all the visitors burst into a flood of talk and reminiscences of other ceremonies of the kind that they have witnessed. Usually the gold needle is bent round and left in the wound, but poor people sometimes pass a piece of string through and tie it. This is turned round and passed backwards and forwards daily till the sides heal, and then begins the process of enlarging the hole to receive the na-daung, a big tube an inch long and from half an inch to three-quarters in diameter. This takes a very long time, and is less pleasant even than the first boring. Some do it with a gold or thickly gilt metal plate, which is rolled up and passed through the hole. The elasticity of the metal makes it constantly tend to expand, and so the hole is gradually enlarged. A commoner method, however, is by introducing stems of the kaing, or elephant grass. As many of the little stems of the inner blade as will go through are passed in, and daily their number is added to until a considerable width is attained. When kaing grass is not available, little splints of the thekkè kyaung are made use of. This is the ordinary thatch of the poorer sort of houses, and almost universal in the country districts, but forbidden in the large towns on account of its inflammable character. Then, after a time, the nā-kat is brought into use. This is a curious ear-plug, big at both ends, and smaller in the middle, where the two parts screw into one another. The screw is passed through the lobe of the ear, and the other portion is then twisted on. These nā-kat are gradually increased in size, until at last the orifices are large enough to receive the na-daung, the regular ear-cylinders. These are of various make and material, the latter being formerly regulated by the sumptuary laws in independent territory. The royal family, both males and females, had them of gold, richly set with jewels, often a single large brilliant in front, or a diamond surrounded by a ring of emeralds, while the back was a cluster of rubies. The right to wear these was also extended to the higher ministers and their families. Others wear gold, plain hollow tubes, or with the ends filled up with delicate *repoussé* work. Those who cannot afford this content themselves with solid amber plugs, which, when they are without a flaw, are worth three or four pounds sterling apiece. Finally, the poor content themselves with hollow pipes of glass, coloured in a variety of tints. The shape is somewhat peculiar, a slight irregular concave, if I may be allowed the expression, the front being a little larger in diameter than the back. Some of the princesses wore very costly na-daung, the diamonds, and especially the rubies, for which Burma is celebrated, being exceedingly fine. The men, except those of high rank, very seldom wear them, unless on exceptional feast days. Women ordinarily put them on whenever they go out. Poor people keep the holes open with a roll of paper or cloth. A *chic* damsel very often courts attention by carrying spare cheroots dangling from her lobes. Elder women who subordinate personal appearance to bodily comforts usually do the same thing on a journey. It secures them a smoke whenever they may want it, and the huge green cheroots are not easily carried in the penetralia of the Burmese female dress, while if they were in the travelling box, they might be abstracted by unscrupulous youngsters.

It is curious to notice how much the custom is falling into disuse in the larger towns with the men. Even among the wealthier classes you seldom see a man wearing a na-daung of the largest size. Those of the thickness of a pencil or a little less are still common, but they too probably will pass out of use shortly. Yet this used to be looked upon as the distinctive mark of Burmese nationality. Probably, nowadays, the tattooing is considered sufficient; while the ear-plugs were certainly inconvenient things, and afforded obvious attractions to robbers. But with the women ear-boring is still universal, and probably will continue so as long as the men go on tattooing, notwithstanding the pain of the process. The na-daung are as characteristic of the Burmese women as the flapping tamein.

CHAPTER VII

MARRIAGE

In the Lawkanidi, the book of proverbs relating to ordinary life, it is said that monks and hermits are beautiful when they are lean ; four-footed animals when they are fat ; men when they are learned ; and women when they are married. This recommendation to the married state is no more needed by Burmese maidens than it is by their sisters in other parts of the world, and they have the further inducement that they enjoy a much freer and happier position than in any other Eastern country, and in some respects are better off even than women in England. All the money and possessions which a girl brings with her on marriage are kept carefully separate for the benefit of her children or heirs, and she carries her property away with her if she is divorced, besides anything she may have added to it in the interim by her own trading or by inheritance. Thus a married Burmese woman is much more independent than any European even in the most advanced states. In the eyes of the Dammathat the old idea of the *patria potestas* prevails indeed, and woman is regarded as a simple chattel, belonging entirely to her parents, and to be disposed of by them without any reference to her personal inclinations ; but, as a matter of fact, she may do pretty well as she pleases, may marry the youth on whom she has fixed her affections, and may separate herself from the husband who has offended her, by going before the village elders and stating her case ; and if the complaint is just, her request is never refused.

As yet they have not begun to demand an equal share

of education with the boys, and the only accomplishments most Burmese girls know are how to dress neatly, do up their hair, and powder their faces. This is the single open implication of their inferiority——except in worship at the pagoda, when every woman will pray that in another existence she may be a man——and it is not likely that female education will make much progress for another generation, the popular idea in Burma being that learning is no use to a girl when she has it, and she may, consequently, as well devote all her spare time to making herself look as pretty as possible. Here and there are a few who are deeply learned in Burmese literature. The young wife of one of the most prominent living Burman pleaders in Rangoon has as good a knowledge of the sacred books and as great a fluency in repeating Pali rituals as any pôngyi in the country. But the great majority of girls only know what they pick up from the conversation of their brothers and the men who come about the house. It is therefore greatly to their credit that they manage not only house affairs, but their husband's business into the bargain. A farmer's wife will carry out the sale of the whole rice crop to the agent of an English rice firm in her husband's absence, and generally strikes a better bargain than he would have made himself. If the village head constable is away, the wife will get together the policemen, stop a fight, arrest the offenders, and send them off to the lock-up all on her own responsibility. The wife sits by, no matter what public business is being transacted, and very often puts in her own opinion quite as a matter of course ; in fact, she is virtual master of the house, and henpecked husbands are not by any means uncommon. The last king of Burma, Thibaw Min, was a notable instance. There never was a king of Burma before who remained for three years the husband of one wife. It was not inclination in his case. He had quite a number of *amourettes* ; but the sturdy Supayā Lat and her formidable mother soon got the offending damsels out of the way. There is also little doubt that it was Supayā Lat and her mother who suggested the massacre of the Princes and prompted the defiance of the British Government, which brought about the ending of the Burmese monarchy.

According to the laws of Menu there are three ways in which a marriage can be brought about :—

1. When the parents of the couple give them to one another.

2. When they come together through the good offices of a go-between, called an aungthwè.

3. When they arrange the matter between themselves.

It is understood, of course, that the two latter forms require at least the passive consent of the father, or, if he is dead, of the guardian, mother, brother, sister, uncle, or whoever it may be ; every woman—every young woman at any rate—being necessarily under the protection of somebody. The Dammathat says : " Let the man to whom she is given by her nearest relation be her husband. If the parents or the relations of the girl do not give her away, and she is carried off against their will, even if she has had ten children, they have power to cause her to separate from the man and give her to another ; the man has no right to say that she is his wife. Why is this ? Because a daughter belongs to her parents ? " But, on the other hand, " If a young woman runs off with a young man not approved by her parents, and, having concealed herself for some time, shall return to the village or neighbourhood in which her parents live, and have two or three children, or live there five or ten years with the man after her parents have seen and known of her being there, they shall not have power to cause her to separate from her husband."

According to the old system, the young man was not considered of age to marry till he was twenty-four or twenty-five. The age of the girl was always a matter of no consequence as long as she had attained to puberty. When a youth wanted to marry he told his parents, and they went to the father and mother of the young woman of his choice. If these had no objections, then the young man kept company with the girl, had the run of the house for two or three years, so that they might get to know one another well, and then, if they were still of one mind, the question of dowry was settled, a fortunate day and hour fixed upon, and the marriage carried out. Nowadays such formalities are almost entirely dispensed with. If the parents of both houses are agreeable, the contracting parties get married with most ardent lover-like rapidity. The age, too, has become very much younger. Most lads get married when they are eighteen or nineteen ; thirteen or fourteen is a common age for the girls. Runaway marriages are common enough, and though the parents may be angry, they are usually too easygoing and indolent to take any energetic action in the matter, and let the couple find out their mistake and come and ask for pardon and a house to live in, which is seldom refused. Occasionally in Lower Burma a stern father demands that they shall be separated until the lad has got a situation for himself, but this is ordinarily little more than a mere form of speech. In Upper Burma, where food is scarce and working hands more valuable, the husband is brought to the girl's parents' house and made to do his share towards supporting the household.

The preliminary courting is naturally conducted in the old fashion, best known to those who have had experience of their own in such matters. The parties meet at pwès, the girl perhaps selling cheroots, fried garlic, le'pet, and what not, and therefore being readily accessible to any swain. It must not be supposed that keeping a stall is regarded as anything derogatory. Numbers of perfectly well-to-do women set them up regularly ; some even have daily work in the bazaars, and very often a girl commences occupations of the kind with the view of attracting the young men and securing a husband. Then there are meetings at pagoda feasts, in the zayats and at friends' houses, so that there are plenty of chances of introduction to eligible swains, even without calling in the assistance of the aungthwè. This functionary makes it a regular occupation to know all the attractions, physical and sordid, of all the young women in the place, and for a small consideration, or sometimes merely for love of his trade, brings young couples together and arranges places of meeting for them. He is, of course, most useful where an impecunious youth aspires to the hand of a rich merchant's or high official's daughter. He manages an introduction in a roundabout way to avoid rousing suspicions, praises his client's appearance and abilities, contrives a series of unexpected meetings, and does everything, in fact, to further the project.   There are regular practitioners in the business, and others who dabble in it for want of something to do and from sheer love of scheming.

Courting, whether authorised by the parents or not, is very seldom carried on in daylight.   So much is this the case that the phrase Lu-byo hlè thi achein, " Courting time," is commonly used in ordinary conversation to designate nine o'clock at night, or a little before or after.   The time may be due to the fact that occupation, or the heat, prevent it during the day, but there is an old saw which may account for it, to the effect that in the morning women are cross and peevish ; in the middle of the day they are testy and quarrelsome ; but at night they are sweet and amiable. Authorised courtship, if the term is not too unromantic, is always carried on at this time, and preparations for it are duly made by the girls.   A couple of hours after nightfall the lover, with a friend or two, makes his appearance near the house and dawdles up and down till he finds the old people have gone to bed, or retired from the scene.   Then he goes up the steps along with his supporters and finds the girl alone, or with a companion or two, dressed in her best, with flowers in her hair, powder on her cheeks and neck, and generally prepared for conquest.   The old people are never present, though they can hear everything, and the mother, as I am credibly informed, pauk-kyi thi, has a convenient chink in the bamboo walls through which she can survey operations and prevent too ardent love-making.   Interviews vary in length, and the nature of the conversation may be best left to the imagination.   If one of the accompanying young men has also an appointment that evening he naturally endeavours to curtail his friend's philandering as much as possible, in order that he himself may have the more time in another place to press his suit.   Even in clandestine flirtations the courting is always effected in a formal way like this.   Meetings in lover's loans, or *à quatre yeux*, would ruin a girl's character immediately.   Her own mother would be the first to put the worst construction on such doings.

Little presents are exchanged. The *soupirant* brings a gay kerchief with some love-verses written on it, perhaps his own composition, more probably the erotic sighings of the prince in the last play he heard, or cribbed bodily from a song-book for Kālathas (Corinthians, lads of mettle). The girl gives him some green cheroots, rolled by her fair hands, or a brilliant woollen muffler which she has knitted ; but there is never any of the kissing and caressing indulged in by more urgent foreign lovers. The girl would look upon any attempts of such a nature as highly indecorous, and no doubt it is quite unsuited to her clothing.

When at last everything has been settled — parents' consent obtained, dowry fixed, and a fortunate day and hour pitched upon — the marriage ceremony comes off in the house of the bride's parents. The ritual is very simple and has nothing whatever of a religious character about it ; in fact the celibate pôngyis would be grossly scandalised if they were asked to take any part in it. A great feast is prepared at the expense of the bridegroom or his parents. All the relations, friends, and neighbours are invited, and it is the publicity of the thing that is really the main feature of the ceremony. The old custom that the bride and bridegroom should join their right hands together, palm to palm, in the presence of all the assembled guests, and then should eat rice out of the same dish and feed each other with one or two morsels in turtle-dove fashion, has in many cases died out, and the eating and drinking, the talk of the men in the main room of the house and of the women in the inner apartment, is quite enough to solemnise the union. When the newly-married couple retire into the bridal chamber it is sometimes in the larger towns the custom to shower saffron-coloured rice on them, but this, like the entire seclusion in which the happy pair are supposed to pass the next seven days, is very seldom actually carried out.

In the country villages, however, two ancient customs are still very generally prevalent. The one is to tie a string across the road along which the bridegroom must pass to the house of his intended. He comes in procession with all his friends, carrying the greater portion of the belongings with which he intends to set up house : a bundle of mats, a long arm - chair, a teak box, mattresses, pillows, besides materials for the feast and presents for the bride. ' The people who have put up the string — called the gold or silver cord—usually young men intent on a jollification of their own, stop the happy man, and threaten to break the string with a curse on the married couple unless some money is given them. It is simple extortion, and English district officers sometimes forbid it. Nevertheless the speculation is usually successful. I suppose no one feels very niggardly on his marriage day.

The other custom is much more singular, more ancient, and infinitely more disagreeable. On the night of the marriage a band of the young bachelors of the place come and shower stones and sticks on the roof of the house where the happy couple are, keeping up sometimes such a sustained battery that the thatch or wooden shingles suffer materially, while the furniture and even the newly-wedded couple occasionally do not escape injury. In Lower Burma the lads are usually bought off with a sum of money, and where the officials do not interfere to prevent it, the custom has degenerated into a system of extortion. Not a few lawsuits have sprung out of such sieges. The money paid in toll to this horseplay goes by the name of ké-bo, and is supposed to be devoted by the receivers to making offerings at the pagoda, but the young men nowadays use it shamelessly for their own entertainment. In Upper Burma the blackmail is never demanded, and consequently Father San Germano was puzzled to conceive any reason for the extraordinary practice. Captain Forbes seeing the payment to procure relief, believed that extortion was the sole origin as well as object of the performance. But the learned in Burmese folk-lore assign it a much higher and more estimable beginning. When, after the world was formed, it was first peopled from the superior heavens of the Byammās, of the nine that remained behind, weighed down by the gross earthly food they had eaten, five gradually became men and four women. When these Byammā-gyi ko-yauk, these nine great ancestors of the Burmese and of all mankind, had gradually degenerated, through the substitution of Padalata for the original flavoured earth, and of Thale rice for the leguminous creeper, desire arose among them, and four of the men took the four women to wife. The fifth man naturally resented being left compulsorily single, and pelted the happy couples with stones on their marriage night. Sympathy with the feelings of this archetypal bachelor has perpetuated the stone-throwing by the lu-byos down to the present day, and if there is no dearth of eligible spinsters in our times, the lonely bachelor may be allowed to express his envy of his friend's bliss without being accused of anything but gross cupidity.

After marriage the couple almost always live for two or three years in the house of the bride's parents, the son-in-law becoming one of the family and contributing to its support. Setting up a separate establishment, even in Rangoon, where the young husband is a clerk in an English office, is looked upon with disfavour as a piece of pride and ostentation. If the girl is an only daughter, she and her husband stay on till the old people die.

Polygamy is recognised and permitted, but practically does not exist now in British territory. A man with more than one wife becomes a subject of common talk, and a native official now living is well known all through the delta as the myo-ok with twenty wives. In native territory the right to have several wives was equally little used in practice. Many of the high officials who travelled about over large districts had wives in almost all the towns they visited —a custom in great measure induced by the rule which provided that the mayā-gyi, the chief wife, had to be left in Mandalay as a hostage for the fidelity of the official. But the great bulk of the people are, and always have been, monogamous. King Mindôn had fifty-three recognised *wives*, of whom thirty-seven survived him. His children numbered one hundred and ten, of whom upwards of fifty survived him. Besides the wives, like Solomon, he had numerous concubines. So, indeed, have many lesser people.

The forbidden degrees are few. Marriages with mother, daughter, sister, and half-sister, aunt, grandmother, and granddaughter, are forbidden, but none else. A son may marry his stepmother ; it is expressly mentioned in the

Dammathat. The sovereign always married at least one half-sister to ensure the purity of the royal blood, but, rather illogically, the issue of this union was not by any means necessarily heir to the throne. The son whom the king, or his ministers after his death, named, succeeded, or more commonly still, the son who could best maintain his position by force.

The liberty of divorce is practically unrestricted, except by the elaborate laws respecting the division of property. According to the Laws of Menu a woman may obtain a divorce among other reasons for the following : When her husband is poor and unable to support her ; when he is always ailing ; when he does not work and leads an idle life ; when he is incapacitated by reason of old age ; when he becomes a cripple after marriage.

And a man may obtain a divorce if his wife has no male children, if she has no love for her husband, or if she persists in going to a house where he tells her she must not visit, and so on.

The lawgiver seems in fact to have laid down that marriage is a civil contract which either party can dissolve ; but, unless with good reason, the one that wishes to separate must suffer in property, more or less severely, according as the plea is good or bad.

Property, for this purpose, is said to be of three kinds. Pa-yin, property acquired by, or in possession of, persons before marriage. Let-htet-pwa, property acquired by husband or wife after marriage. Tin-thi, property inherited or obtained by gift. Pa-yin after marriage becomes hnit-pa-sôn, that is, the joint property of husband and wife, but only when it is agreed between them either before or after marriage that the property shall be put together for the mutual benefit.

In the event of a divorce both parties take away whatever pa-yin they may have had on marriage, and the let-htet-pwa is divided either by mutual agreement, or by the decision of the village elders who sanction the separation.

But divorces are far from being so common as most writers would have us believe. The warmth of family affection is one of the strongest traits of the race, and the

Burman is always very kind to his wife, while every girl is taught from her earliest years to look with the highest respect upon man as man, and to defer in all things to his judgment, though she is far more free than the Indian wife. The Burman consults with his partner in all his affairs, public and private, and often is entirely guided by her. She keeps the shop that is to be found in almost every house in the country towns, and usually makes far more money than the goodman himself. It is a simple matter to blame the Burmese for easy marriage customs, but the system speedily puts an end to unhappy and ill-assorted unions, and illegitimate children are exceedingly rare. Finally, unless there is good known cause for a separation the divorced parties are not by any means looked upon with a favourable eye. The man who enters a monastery to get rid of a wife goes by the contemptuous name of taw-twet "jungle runaway," for the rest of his life, while the ta-ku-lat, the *divorcée*, is a perennial subject of joke to the jester in the play :—

> She that's neither maid, married, nor widow,
> Fits all men as a pot does it's lid, O.

That is to say, a divorced woman needs small wooing. Such a woman will not hesitate to cut off the bya-bazan, the lappets of hair that fall down over the ears, the last resource of the despairing and unwilling celibate.

The literature of marriage is not inconsiderable. The tattooing ceremonies, a-nu se, love-philtres, charms, and what not, are referred to elsewhere. There remain a number of singular matters to be taken note of by those who would be happy in married life. Thus the girls are told how they may ascertain a man's character by the colour of his heart's blood—though how they are to ascertain this colour without injury to the subject of inquiry is not mentioned. A lustful man's blood is dark red ; a cross, quarrelsome man's is so dark as almost to be black ; a lazy man's like elephant's water ; a rough-speaking man's like boiled peas : a charitable man's like the flower of the mahā hlega, a species of bauhinia ; while a learned man's heart's blood is beautiful as the ruby.

Similarly useless knowledge is the statement that an

ignorant man's heart is all in one mass, while that of the well-instructed divides itself into three small parts.

As models of married women are held up the Taw le-wa, the most faithful and beautiful of wives, the consorts of four of the chief princes in the ten great Jatakas, treating of the last births of the Lord Buddha. To say that a girl is Taw le-wa win lauk, calculated to become like one of these four great queens, Amaya the wife of Mahawthata, the Solomon of Buddhist kings; Madi, the wife of Wethandaya, world-famed for his charity; Keinnayi or Thanbula, the partners of princes hardly less celebrated, is to pay the highest possible compliment to any woman. But these are somewhat vague and intangible matters. There are other recommendations which appeal much more directly to those intending to get married; to the man that seeks a wife, san-shwe, pure as " test gold "; or the girl who would avoid a linkwe, a " cur of a husband."

Prominent among these is the rhyme of " the hostile pairs," the yan-hpet, who, if they marry, will certainly have a short life.

Some violence is done to the niceties of language in the linga, so that I may be allowed the same in the translation of a portion of it.

> Friday's daughter
> Didn't oughter
> Marry with a Monday's son ;
> Should she do it
> Both will rue it,
> Life's last lap will soon be run.

The same lamentable result would follow if the man were born on Friday and the woman on Monday. Again :

> Saturdays and Thursdays,
> The serpent and the rat,
> You cannot find out worse days,
> Life's short enough at that.

The serpent and the rat preside over Saturday and Thursday respectively. Similar curtailment of life would follow if the union was between Sunday and Wednesday, or between Tuesday and the eighth half-day Yahu. One or both contracting parties would soon die if children of these hostile days married.

On the other hand, there is an elaborate figure showing what unions according to birthdays will be lucky.

The numbers represent the days of the week according to the order. 1, Sunday; 2, Monday; 3, Tuesday; 4, Wednesday; 5, Thursday; 6, Friday; 7, Saturday; 8, Yahu (half Wednesday). The inner numbers represent the man's birthday; the outer the woman's. Those who choose their wives in accordance with this figure will be happy and well-to-do.

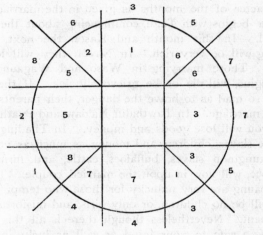

The outer ring the maiden's,
The inner ring the man's.
All ye who would live easeful
On this scheme form your plans.

All these rhymes are learned by the little boys at school, sometimes formally taught them by the preceptor as an excerpt from the Bedin, sometimes, when the yahan refuses to recognise the validity of these books, studied surreptitiously along with the secular plays and song-books. Whatever else a girl may know, you may be sure she can give you the marriage rhymes.

After the marriage has been settled upon, lucky combination of birthdays, parents' consent, settlement of dower and so on, all satisfactorily arranged, the formalities are not yet over. A lucky day has to be sought from the horoscopes of the two chief parties, but beyond this there are a number of obstacles which must on no account be overlooked. In the first place, with the pious the same rule prevails as in England, that no marriages should take place in Lent. This cuts upwards of three months out of the year immediately. Unfortunately a number of persons are so completely in the world of kāma, the seat of the passions, that they care very little whether it is the season of the Wā or not. But almost every one, whether pious or not, considers well the character of the months as given in the marriage linga. The year begins with Tagu, commencing about the middle of April. In this month and Kasôn the next, couples marrying will be very rich. In Nayôn they will love one another. Those marrying in Waso and Wagaung, when Lent begins, will die or be grievously sick. If the young pair are so mad as to brave the danger, their parents should stop the marriage. In Tawthalin, Na'daw, and Pyatho, if you marry, you will lose goods and money. In Thadingyut you will have slaves, children, and money as much as you want. In Tasaungmôn slaves, buffaloes, cattle, and furniture in abundance, will flow in upon the married couple. Tabodwè and Tabaung are very unlucky for those who tempt Hymen. There will be no children, or only girls, and misfortunes will be frequent. Nevertheless though there is all this trouble in getting a wife to your mind, as well as lucky in time of birth, worldly goods, and season of marriage, there are very few Burmans, not in the sacred order, who are not married before they are twenty, and happily married too. As the popular saying puts it—

> Ye hnin nga,
> Lin hnin maya.

> Fish to the water,
> Man to Eve's daughter.

CHAPTER VIII

DOMESTIC LIFE

THE Burman is the most calm and contented of mortals. He does not want to grow rich. When he does make a large sum of money, he spends it all on some pious work, and rejoices in the thought that this will meet with its reward in his next existence. If he never amasses enough to build any great public work, at any rate he subscribes what he can, and is generous in almsgiving. A bountiful soil will not let its children starve ; and so the Burman jogs on through a cheerful existence, troubled by no anxious cares, and free from all the temptations of ambition. His daily round is simple enough. In the morning, after his bath, he loiters about, talking to the neighbours till breakfast time, or perhaps strolls out to the corner of his paddy field, and indulges in a contemplative smoke. After breakfast he probably dozes through the heat of the day, and when the shadows begin to get long, saunters about again. A semblance of regular labour appears when the paddy is being sown or the grain reaped, but even then no one is in the least inclined to disturb himself for the sake of rapid work. It is sufficient that you are always certain in Burma what kind of weather you are going to have. " Another hot day," or " another wet day," is quite as much a matter of course as the rising of the sun itself, and there is therefore no need to hurry operations in case of a change. The evenings are spent ordinarily at a pwè during the fine season, or in amicable converse over a cheroot at a friend's house in the rains. Variety comes occasionally in the shape of a jolting, hilarious journey to a distant pagoda feast, or a trip down the river in the big rice-boat to one of the great milling towns.   And so an uneventful life passes away : the greatest ambition to see the village boat successful at the Thadingyut races, and the village champion cock or buffalo triumphant over all others ; the greatest desire to live peaceably with all men and observe the Ten Precepts ; the greatest excitement the occasional visit of the English district officer, or the suspicion of a witch in that lonely house down by the spirit's pool on the creek.   In Upper Burma formerly this quiet was more apt to be disturbed by the summoning of levies to serve in some special raid against audacious dacoits, or to make a demonstration against reiving mountaineers.   If the myo-wun was a pious man, calls for enforced labour at digging tanks, building pagodas and monasteries, rest-houses and tazaungs, were likely to keep the villager a great deal more occupied than he cared for.   There can be no doubt in any patriotic Burman's mind that the state of the people, regularly taxed though they be, under British rule, is infinitely happier than it was under their king, and all but the officials and their hangers-on longed for the day when the English flag was to float over all the land as far as Mogaung.   There could be no hope for the country, where, even under a kindly king like Mindôn, ill-conditioned governors oppressed the populace with absolute impunity. Complaints were made, but his majesty could not venture to leave his palace for any great distance to inquire for himself, and gold easily dulled the senses of the highest minister round the golden throne.   It is little wonder then that the people, kept perpetually in the lowest depths of poverty, were, if not actually dying out, certainly not increasing in numbers.   There was nothing which so much indicated the popular feeling, and at the same time so irritated the Burmese Government, as the unceasing stream of emigrants to Lower Burma.

Nevertheless, even in Independent territory the Burman preserved his light heart and buoyant disposition.   No calamity is so overwhelming as to make him despond.   Some years ago a large fire occurred in Mandalay, and spread with such terrible rapidity that the inhabitants of a whole quarter were unable to save anything but the clothes they wore. Some of them went the next day to the English missionary chaplain, and told him of the misfortune that had befallen them, and how so completely were they rendered destitute that they had been indebted to the charity of the inhabitants of the monastery for a breakfast that morning. The clergyman promised to do what he could for them, and the same evening went along to view the site of the fire. What was his astonishment to find that the burnt-out victims had rigged up a rude stage among the charred stumps of their house-posts, and in default of a house to sleep in, were prepared to spend the night listening to the love-making of the princes and princesses, and laughing at the caustic witticisms of the clown, not a few of the jokes being inspired by the blackened surroundings. Such defiance of all the ills of fate is very characteristic, and would seem to a Burman mind the most natural thing to do under the circumstances, since it afforded both distraction and amusement.

If any one has escaped the curse of Adam it is the Burman. He does not need to earn his bread with the sweat of his brow, and riches having no attraction for him, when his patch of paddy land has been reaped, his only concern is how to pass the time, and that is no very difficult matter, where he has plenty of cheroots and betel-nut. He can stroll along to neighbour Maung Gyi's, whose son has a knack for wood-carving, and watch him as he deftly cuts out a piece of elaborate scroll-work for the roof of a neighbouring monastery, or finishes off the grim features of a bilu for the English Inspector of Police. Next door the sayā is engaged on a painting, the representation of some palace scene, or of some well-known event in the life of the Lord Buddha. Burmese artists do not, as a rule, paint likenesses, though they are by no means unsuccessful when they make the attempt. Any one but a high official would probably consider it a mark of great presumption and conceit to hang up a picture of himself in his house. There is, however, none of the objection to portrait painting which is so common with some other nations. For example, the Mohammedans will not suffer likenesses to be drawn for fear they should demand a soul on the Day of Judgment, and so some actual human being might come to be left out in the cold. Catlin tells us that the American Indian chief was in a state of great alarm lest his soul might be carried off with his picture. A notion of the same kind appears in the Chinese custom of getting a priest to put in the pupil of the eye, a method which often has rather a ghastly effect when the reverend gentleman is not skilful. Similarly, every Chinese-owned craft, from the sampan to the English-built iron screw steamer, has a couple of eyes painted on its bows, in order that it may see the way. Down in the Straits, and in all places where there are many Chinese, the local steamers, whoever their owners may be are all endowed with eyes. Were they not so favoured, no Chinaman would travel with them as a passenger, or send any of his goods aboard of them. The Burman is not troubled with any such fantastic notions, and has no objection whatever to sitting for his portrait, only, as King Mindôn said to Yule, they prefer a flattering likeness to an exact one. It is seldom, however, that a Burman has a picture gallery in his house, and the village artist usually confines himself to vivid-coloured sketches for the funeral of a pôngyi, or to be hung round the mandut, where the great people sit to look on at a play. The drawing and the perspective are naturally a little faulty, but the details are usually worked out with very creditable skill.

Thus wandering about, seeing what his neighbours are doing, with an occasional visit to the monastery to have some edifying talk with the religious, the villager may spend the time very comfortably. Oftenest however, he stays at home, and waits for visitors to drop in and have a little gossip. The goodwife always has a little shop in the lower part of the building. There is hardly a single house in the whole village where something is not offered for sale: a few dried fish, betel-nut, with the fresh green leaves, lime, cardamoms, and cutch, all ready for making up, half a dozen cocoa-nuts, or perhaps some twopenny-ha'penny knives, looking-glasses, coloured tumblers, and paltry Manchester goods, or where there are many girls about the house, a few home-made lungyis and pasos, waist-cloths, woven at odd times in the loom which stands in the yard or in a corner of the verandah of every house. The stock-in-trade is

intended more as an excuse for people to enter the house and
have a talk than with any idea of making a profit.   Whatever money is drawn is regarded as a kind of pin-money for
the mistress of the establishment.   When the ladies of the
household are in earnest about trading, they start a stall in
the bazaar, and very good hands they are at driving a bargain.
A more regrettable trait is the forcible character of their
language when they are annoyed.   But this, unhappily, is a
characteristic of the fair sex all the world over, whether in
trade or out of it.   Certain it is that the *dames de la halle*
and the Billingsgate fishwives would require all their powers
of voice and vituperation to silence a bazaar maiden when
she sets her mind to it.

   There are as a general thing two meals only in the day :
breakfast at about eight in the morning, and dinner at five
in the afternoon.   There is no difference in the *menu* of the
two meals.   The staple article of food is plain boiled rice,
which is piled up in a heap on a huge platter, round about
which the household arrange themselves, sitting, like pit-men,
on their heels.   The curry which is taken with it is placed
in little bowls, and each one of the party has his own plate,
and helps himself.   Knives are unnecessary ; spoons and
forks and celestial chopsticks are unknown, except in the
houses of a few Government officials and traders in Rangoon,
who have had some experience of English society.   Very
few are able to afford curries of meat or fish, besides that
there are not always unscrupulous people ready to disregard
the law against taking life, and the material is therefore not
always available.   Ordinarily the curry consists of a soup,
or thin concoction of vegetables, in which chillies and onions
figure largely.   The other ingredients are very various.
Young shoots of bamboo are very delicate in their flavour,
if not overpowered by too much garlic.   Wild asparagus,
the succulent stems of a number of aquatic plants and fleshy
arums are constantly used, and may be seen exposed for sale
in every bazaar.   Tamarind leaves and those of the mango-
tree are used by the very poor.   The former have a somewhat acrid taste, the latter are curiously aromatic.   Along
with the curry, which has always a large amount of oil and
salt in it, there are a variety of condiments, notably the

strongly-flavoured nga-pi, without which no Burman would consider his meal complete. Sometimes the big, fierce-stinging kā-gyin, a species of red ant, is used along with this fish paste, sometimes it is fried in oil by itself. As may be imagined, they have an acid and decidedly pungent flavour about them. Roasted turtle's and iguana's eggs, dried fish, and fried ginger are gourmand's adjuncts. There is a particular objection to the smell of cookery, and when anything is fried in oil, or prepared so as to produce a strong savour, it is always done to leeward of the house, and where the fumes may not reach any other dwelling. Such smells are believed to be very productive of fever. Nothing is ever drunk at meals, but each one, when he has finished, goes to the earthenware jar full of water which stands in a corner of the verandah, and rinses out his mouth. It is a lamentable fact that many Burmans in the low country now drink beer and spirits, but this is never done at meals nor in the house, where, indeed, the wife would not allow it. It is deplorable, because it is drinking for the sake of drinking, and is never done in moderation. The tippling Burman goes to the " toddy-shop " for his liquor, and he does not know when to stop. Brandy of the fiery description known to the British soldier as " fixed bayonets," or " chain-shot," is often drunk, but the usual tipple is " Old Tom." A particularly heady mixture of this with cheap beer is affected by confirmed topers. It is contrary to the national religion, and it does not suit the national temperament.

After meals every one smokes—men, women, and children. Facetious people have declared that Burman babies blow a cloud while they are still at the breast. This is in-accurate. They never indulge till they are able to walk without needing the assistance of their hands, but their mothers give them whiffs long before that. The ordinary Burman cheroot is very mild and has really very little tobacco in it. The full-flavoured article to be seen occasionally in London shops is manufactured entirely for English residents. The se paw-leip, the cigar for home consumption, commonly known as the green cheroot, is very large, from six to eight inches long and about an inch in diameter at one end, tapering to slightly less at the other.

It rounds a girl's mouth a good deal when she puts it in.
In the manufacture of it chopped tobacco leaves and pieces
of the stem of the tobacco plant and the pith of the oh'nè,
a species of Euphorbia, are the chief ingredients. Very
often these are boiled with palm-sugar and allowed to dry
before making up. The cover is made of the leaf of the
teak-tree, or of a tree called the thanat, the ends being
tucked in at the point. A piece of red raw silk fastens it
at the end put in the mouth, and some broader pieces of
pith are put there to give it stiffness to the lips. The finer
kinds, such as were only used in Upper Burma in the palace,
are rolled up in the thin white inner coating of the bark of
the betel-tree. The cheroot has an ash like a cinder, and
usually burns holes in the clothes of an Englishman the first
time he tries it. Laid down thoughtlessly on an oily mat, it
is a fruitful cause of fires. All Burman ladies are adepts at
rolling cheroots, and a dozen or two of them form a common
present to favoured swains.

Chewing betel is sometimes carried on simultaneously
with smoking, but most people prefer to economise enjoyment, and only chew in the interval between smokes.
Chewing is hardly an exact expression, and the use of it
frequently leads the experimenting Briton into the unpleasant predicament of having all the interstices between
his teeth choked up with little fragments of the nut, which,
with their indescribable aromatic flavour, stimulate the flow
of saliva for hours afterwards. The Burman splits his nut in
half, smears a little slaked lime, usually white, but sometimes
tinted pink or salmon coloured, on the betel vine leaf, puts
in a little morsel of cutch and tobacco, and then rolls it up
and stows away the quid in the side of his mouth, occasionally *squeezing* it a little between his teeth. It is as well to
be very cautious with the lime and cutch (the juice of the
Acacia catechu) the first time you make a trial. The latter
especially is very astringent. One variety of the nut, called
the Taunggu betel, has effects very much resembling intoxi-
cation. Chewing kôn-thi is an unlovely practice. The
Burman has none of the delicacy with regard to a spittoon
which characterises the American, and these articles require
to be of a very considerable size. The monks are perhaps

the most persistent chewers of the good betel. Smoking is prohibited, but nothing is said against betel, and it is considered a great stimulator of the meditative faculties. The lime used very speedily corrodes and destroys the teeth, and then the old pôngyi has to make the scholars crush up the nuts so that they may not hurt his toothless gums. It is a common belief that no one can speak Burmese well till he chews betel. Demosthenes is said to have put pebbles in his mouth when he was practising oratory.

Alternate smoking, chewing, and conversation serve to pass the day, and after dinner, when the sun goes down, our villager has a bath down by the well to freshen him up. The water is drawn up in a bucket and simply poured over the body. Soap is never used, and particular care is taken not to wet the hair. The head washing is a special ceremony, to be gone through only occasionally, and then with circumspection. Dandies, as a rule, put a solution of rice and water on their hair every day to make it grow long, and cocoanut oil is also very generally used. Both sexes are proud of the length of their hair, and it is not uncommon to see it reaching below the knee and down to the ankles. The men wear it in a yaung or knot on the top of the head, while the sadôn of the women is at the back of the head. Both men and women are in the habit of adding to its size by interweaving false tresses, which are easily got, seeing that everybody has black hair, and that some young member of the family is constantly getting his locks cut off on his entry into the monastery. There is no more sense of shame in using false hair than there is in improving the appearance by wearing fine clothes. At his bath it is usual for a pious person to repeat a Pali charm over the first bucket of water, which is then slowly poured over the body. The object of this is to guard against sickness.

After bathing, the Burman, if he is young, usually puts on his fine clothes, for except in the rainy season there is sure to be a dramatic performance, or a yein dance by the village lads and lasses, or an entertainment of some kind going on at some house in the village. The dress is very simple and picturesque. The paso is a long silk cloth, fifteen cubits long and about two and a half wide. It is

wound round the body, kilt fashion, tucked in with a twist
in front, and the portion which remains, gathered up and
allowed to hang in folds from the waist, or thrown jauntily
over the shoulder.   The body is covered with a short white
cotton jacket, over which another of dark or coloured cloth
is often worn.   Elderly people, and the wealthy of all ages,
when they are paying a visit of ceremony or going to worship
at the pagoda, wear a taing-mathein, a long white coat, open
in front except at the throat, where it is tied, and reaching
almost to the knees.   Round the head a flowered silk handkerchief is loosely wound as a turban.   The old wear a
simple narrow fillet of white book-muslin round the temples
and showing the hair.   This is called a pawlôn.

The woman's tamein is a simple piece of cotton or silk,
almost square, four feet and a half long by about five broad,
and woven in two pieces of different patterns.   This is
wound tightly over the bosom, and fastened with a simple
twist of the ends.   The opening being in front, the symmetry of the thigh is displayed in walking, but a peculiar
outward jerk of the heels which the girls acquire prevents
any suggestion of immodesty.   The loose cotton jacket is
unhappily not so well contrived to display their charms.
Over the shoulders is thrown a bright silk handkerchief, the
same as that used by the men for turbans.   Nothing is worn
on the head except flowers twisted into the hair.   Dressed
in their best, the family sally forth in search of amusement.
If it is a pwè, they will not get home till very late, possibly
not till daybreak, when the yellow line of monks issuing
forth on their matutinal tour may meet them at the monastery gate.   A country dance naturally does not last nearly
so long, though it is kept up much longer than most people
would care to dance a hornpipe or even a minuet.   But a
still more favourite form of amusement is the entertainment
of a sā-haw sayā, a kind of reciter or improvisatore.   He
is paid to come to a house, and the company invited are
asked to choose a subject for him, some of the favourite
zāts, or an incident in history, sacred or secular.   Many of
them, like the cyclic poets, repeat from memory, but there
are others who invent their smooth verses as they go on
chanting.   They may perform in a house, or in a mandut

specially run up for the occasion, or even in the open street. When a well-known sā-haw sayā is going to recite the Wethandaya or the Zanekka Zāts, or when he tells how the Lord Buddha left his father's palace to wear the yellow robe, or how he ascended to Tawadeintha, a dramatic performance is often completely deserted, and the actors have no option but to follow the populace and listen to the improvisatore themselves.   One of the best of the Burmese dramatic writers, U Po Mya, was also particularly celebrated as a sā-haw sayā. He could repeat his own drama, the Wizaya Zāt, from end to end, but had also a particular facility in improvising.

His night's amusement over, the Burman goes home to sound sleep on his Danubyu mat or a coarser one if he has not got that, and rises to spend another day of the same kind.   He cares nothing for the assertion that he leads an aimless, lazy life.   He has enough to live upon, and the writings of all the philosophers say that wealth only brings new cares.

CHAPTER IX

THE HOUSE AND ITS BELONGINGS

IT is singular that in a country where the pagodas and temples will compare in stately grandeur and symmetry of form with the sacred edifices of any part of the world, and where the monastic buildings, though only constructed of wood, strike the most casual observer with their shapely beauty and wealth of decoration ; it is singular where there is a taste for such edifices and abundance of the architectural skill necessary to erect them, that the Burman should in the vast majority of cases live in the flimsiest of bamboo huts. The original cause may be found perhaps in the stringent regulations of the Yāzagaing. In native Burma the shape of a man's house was fixed for him by law according to his station in life. All were one-storeyed, save where exceptional royal favour had granted the spire-like roof to a distinguished noble or a feudatory chief. Brick houses were forbidden, from the apprehension that the inhabitants might take it into their heads to turn them into fortifications. Gilding was forbidden to all subjects, and permission to lacquer and paint the pillars of their houses granted to but a very few, and it was expressly laid down that no one should have an arch over his door. This may account for the paltry and even wretched appearance of most villages, but it is undeniable that though nowadays, they are very considerably more substantial, yet a rich man never by any chance thinks of building himself a grand house, and remains firmly by the unpretentious model of his ancestors. This is the more curious, because they will spare no expense to buy gay turbans and bright-coloured pasos for themselves, and costly

silks for their wives. The ordinary explanation is that every
one can see what clothes you wear, while few people care to
come and spy out what kind of a house you live in, and how
you fare. But there can be very little doubt that the real
reason is a survival of the idea of the old Yāzagaing, as
well as the fact that long years of custom have impressed
upon everybody the opinion that there are only two forms
of architecture, the secular and the ecclesiastical, and no one,
no matter how sure he might be that the Government would
take no notice of his ambition, would brave the denunciations of the religious by adding a spire to his house, or even
adorning the gable ends with carved pinnacles and flamboyant finials of the monasteries. Consequently the one
regular form prevails everywhere.

The Burman's dwelling, then, is always shaped more or
less like a marquee tent, and never more than one storey
high, to avoid the humiliating possibility of the feet of some
one being over your head. But the whole house stands on
posts, so that the floor is seven or eight feet from the ground.
It consists often of only one room, usually, however, of two
or more, and to the front of the house there is always a
verandah, three or four feet lower than the general level of
the house, and as often as not quite open to the street, or the
garden, or whatever may be in front and always to the sky.
The posts which form the main or central part of the house
are usually six in number, and all have their names, such as
Uyu, Kya-hngan, Nyaung-yan. The south post, in the
main part of the house, the Thabye-taing, is the best known,
as being always adorned with leaves and particularly marked
as that in the top of which most probably lives the nat-spirit
of the house. A dead body, after being swathed, and while
waiting for the coffin, is always placed by it.

A house ought never to be built till the foundations have
been thoroughly dug up and shown to a soothsayer. He
will determine, from the substances found, whether it is a
lucky place to build a house in or not. It stands to reason
that the building cannot be commenced till a lucky day and
hour have been sought out. There is considerable care to be
observed in the selection of the timber. Posts are masculine,
feminine, and neuter. Male posts are of equal size at both

ends ; females are larger at the base ; those which swell out in the middle are a-thet ma-shi——without life ; taing bilu, ogre's posts are largest at the top.   As a general rule it may be taken for granted that if a house is built with neuter posts, its inmates will always be miserable and un-lucky ; if the posts are ogres, death and disaster will attend ; male posts are easy-going and harmless ; females, on the contrary, are fortunate and leading to honour.   But it may happen that the character of the piece of ground on which the house is built upsets all these generalisations, so that it is necessary to get a wise man's opinion before you get your posts.   The Deittôn gives many instructions on the subject, and among other things mentions how a man's fortune may be calculated from the Hle-ga-tit, the side pieces of the steps which lead up to the verandah.   The presence or absence of knots, and if the former, their position, determines the luck of the householder.

Poor people use bamboo instead of wood, and make their walls of mats, woven of the same substance, split up. Occasionally, however, they rise to the dignity of common jungle timber.   Richer people make use of the invaluable teak, or of pyinkado (*Xylia dolabriformis*), a wood almost as durable, and equally expensive.   White ants will attack neither of these.   The walls of such houses are planked. The roof is sometimes composed of small flat tiles, but more commonly of thatch.   This consists in most places in the Delta of dani, the leaves of the toddy palm, which are first soaked in salt water, a precaution which prevents insects from destroying them.   Up country a species of grass called thekkè is universally used.   This style of roofing is very satisfactory in every respect but one.   It is cheap, easily put on, reasonably water-tight, but very inflammable, and conse-quently is not allowed in any of the larger towns in the Province.   In the smaller stations, however, it is almost uni-versal, and the consequence is that when one house takes fire, the sparks from it kindle all the others, as a matter of course.   Consequently, as an imperative measure of protec-tion, every house is provided with a long hooked bamboo, called a mi-cheit, by means of which to pull off all the thatch as soon as a fire breaks out in the neighbourhood, and in addition to this a mi-kat stands beside it. This is a broad griddle, or flapper kind of thing, and its object is to beat out the flame which may be caused by a spark lighting on the roof. In addition to this, in many parts of the country, pots full of water are always kept in readiness on the tops of the houses, so that when the hour of danger comes, the householder may douse his roof, and so do the best for himself. In Mandalay, under native rule, some of the pa-gwets, and other outcasts, patrolled the streets all night, to watch for and prevent fires as much as possible.

Another kind of roofing is wā-kat, a sort of flat tile-like construction, six feet long by two feet broad, made of coarse bamboo matting. Bamboos split in half down the centre, and with the knots smoothed away, are also used. They are placed close together, with the hollow side upwards, extending all the way down from the ridge to the eaves, and over these again are placed others with the rounded side up, the whole presenting rather a curious appearance, but making a very serviceable roof and not nearly so dangerous as the leaf or grass thatching. The leaves of other trees are also occasionally used, but the simplicity and cheapness of the dani roof make it by far the most prevalent in the delta, as grass is elsewhere, notwithstanding its danger. In Rangoon and Maulmein, shingles, that is, small wooden slabs like slates, are being very generally introduced.

In the better class of houses the floors are made of planking, but poorer people have nothing better than a series of whole or split bamboos laid side by side on the cross-beams and tied down with rattans. This is not very pleasant to walk on, and has the further disadvantage of being anything but cleanly, for the spaces between the bamboos offer an irresistible temptation to drop all litter and garbage on to the ground immediately underneath the house, and were it not for the pariah dogs the sanitary condition of the place would soon be very bad.

The house is thus simple enough in its character, but the furniture is still more so. Intercourse with the English has indeed brought many Burmans to indulge in English luxuries, and in many houses in Rangoon and the larger district towns, chandeliers, bookcases, pictures, and even statuary are to be seen, besides abundance of chairs and tables, and occasionally bedsteads, while clocks, kerosine lamps, looking-glasses, and lounge chairs are universal. But it is very different in the village houses. There is practically no furniture at all there, for a chair is of no use to a jungle Burman, and without chairs tables are equally useless. Consequently all that is to be seen in a village house is the goodman's box, and a few woven mats and hard bamboo pillows to sleep on. Cots are not used, for one of the Ten Precepts, to be kept on duty-days, is that one must not sleep on a high place. The only furnishings visible are the mats rolled up during the day with the rugs or blankets which serve for bedding. The mats themselves are probably home-made, manufactured from fine strips of bamboo, the best being those with the polished silicious surface outside, which stand any amount of work. Softer, finer articles are made from the skin of the theng, a species of rush, which takes a black dye, and is often worked into patterns, but no one has anything more elaborate, and indeed nothing better could be wished for. A cooler bed could not easily be found. In the country, also, the cooking place during the rains is in the house. During the fine weather culinary operations are carried on in the open air, behind the premises. The cooking range is nothing more than a box, two or three feet square, and six inches deep, filled up with earth or ashes, and on the top of this the wood used as fuel is piled. The cooking utensils and the dining service are equally simple. The former consists of nothing further than two or three earthen pots with lids to them, and a wooden spurtle to stir the contents with. Close at hand is a jar full of water, with a ladle—half a cocoa-nut with a handle through it. These are all the kitchen appliances. In place of table there is a huge round dish of lacquered wood, called a byat. These byats are sometimes as much as three feet and more in diameter, and on them is heaped up in a gigantic pile the rice, while the curry is served in little bowls disposed round about. A young couple have, therefore, no ruinous expenses when they set up house. The inventory of effects necessarily is soon made.

Outside the house there is not much more to notice.

The abundance of land allows every one to have a court-yard of his own. In this the farmer keeps his cart and plough, the fisherman his boat. The buffaloes and oxen of the whole village are usually all together on a pasture-ground kept by some speculative individual, who charges a couple of rupees or so for feeding and looking after them. The care exercised is not very great. Heat and rain kill many of them, where, as is too frequently the case, no shelter is available ; foot-and-mouth disease, and other epidemics, carry off great numbers, and finally, they are not at all averse to killing one another. Consequently the vultures are frequently to be seen on the trees round the village pasture-land. Besides his implements the house-owner has always in his yard a hand rice-mill. Husking paddy has become, near the big towns, quite a separate trade, and abundance of cleaned rice may be bought in the bazaars, but in the village every family husks its own rice, the grain being kept stored in a small granary in the yard. The milling is done by the women, and there are two processes in the operation. The mill consists of two wooden cylinders about two feet thick, the inner surfaces of both roughened in a simple way by the cutting of radii from their centres, the lines being about a quarter of an inch deep. The upper cylinder has a funnel-shaped hole cut through it, to let the grain down, and is worked backwards and forwards by a long pole loosely fastened in, the rice coming out between the two cylinders, and falling on mats down below. It is winnowed either in the primitive way of throwing it into the air, so that the light husk may be blown away, or, often nowadays in Lower Burma, by a hand-worked pair of fanners, introduced since the English occupation.

The rice is not yet, however, ready for cooking. The inner pellicle has still to be removed, and this is done in a big wooden mortar. Two varieties are in use, worked either by hand, as an apothecary pounds his drugs, the pestle being very long and heavy ; or by foot, when the wooden mortar is sunk in the ground. The pestle in this latter case consists of a short, stumpy piece of wood, let into a long lever near the end. This lever is supported on two uprights at some distance from the mortar, and the machine is worked by the housewife or her daughter stepping on and off the bar, so as to raise the pestle and let it fall on the rice in the mortar. The rice is very thoroughly cleaned in this way, and Burmans prefer it to that which has passed between the mill-stones of the European factory. The Derbyshire, or composition stones, do their work only too thoroughly, and remove so much of the pellicle as to take away all the flavour, besides that the great heat caused by the steady grinding tends to the same result. Consequently the pleasant refrain of the girls chanting at their work may be heard all over the village after dark, and when a large quantity has to be prepared for some offering to the Sacred Order on a feast-day, the chanted chorus rises and falls round about the homestead often till long past "midnight cock-crow," till the rising of the "red star" warns them to retire to rest, tired, but happy, for such a good work earns great merit. A sesamum oil-press is also frequently found in at least one house in every village. This is equally simple in its construction. It consists of a deep wooden trough, in which the seeds are pressed by a heavy upright timber fixed in a frame. The weight is increased by a long lever, on the end of which a man sits and guides a bullock which goes round in a circle, thus crushing and turning the seed at the same time.

The carts are very strongly built, and are remarkable for the way in which the floor curves upwards towards the back in the same way as the boats do. In Upper Burma formerly the wheels were mostly composed of one solid, roughly-rounded slab of wood, or in some cases of two semicircular slabs joined together, and these are still found, but more and more rarely, in out-of-the-way places in the upper province, though wheels constructed in European fashion with spokes are mostly in use, and Government now prescribes a three-inch tyre on all district roads. Occasionally in the old days to save trouble the carter started with a square wheel, and trusted to time to round it for him. Padauk (*Pterocarpus indicus*) is the wood most valued for this purpose, but it is too expensive for most people. The wheels are never greased, and make hideous shrieking noises as they revolve. This serves to keep away tigers and wild animals generally when a journey is being made for any distance. At night the carts are arranged in a laager with the high backs outwards, and all inside, including even the pariah dogs, are safe from wild animals. The waggoners used to glory in the strident sound of their wheels, which often can be heard miles off in the forest. A wheel with a creak of particular volume and power of penetration is highly prized, and an experienced driver can tell whom he is going to meet or overtake by the groanings of the axles and the key in which they are pitched. Every bullock in addition carries a square metal bell tied under his throat.

In the yard round about the house there is very often a little garden fenced off in a rough kind of way, but no particular care is taken to keep it neat and free from weeds— no easy matter even for an active gardener in Burma. The favourite plant is always the Bôddha Tharanat (*Canna Indica*, or Indian shot), so named from its seeds, which are used for the beads of the rosary. The flowers are red, or sometimes white. The fable relates that it sprang from the Buddha's blood. His impious and evil-minded brother-in-law and cousin Dewadat, enraged that he was not allowed to have a separate assembly of his own, went to the top of a hill and rolled down a huge stone, intending to destroy the most excellent payā. But the boulder burst into a thousand pieces, and only one little bit bruised Shin Gautama's toe, and drew a few drops of blood, whence sprang the sacred flower. The renowned physician Zewaka healed the great teacher's wound in a single day, and almost immediately afterwards the earth opened and swallowed up the sacrilegious Dewadat. The plants and flowers usually stand demurely in a single row, or perhaps in three or four, like a patch of peas. The *Datura tatula* is almost always found, and among the other mingled vegetables and medicinal plants the *Celosia cristata*, in both its yellow and purple varieties, is a special favourite. But the Burman can scarcely vaunt his success as a flower gardener.

There are always a few domestic animals and pets about the premises. Every family has its dog, which trots about the establishment and makes a terrible to-do whenever a white man appears. The pariahs are magnificent watch-

dogs with their uninflectional, agglutinative barking.   They
sleep most of the day, and at night gather together in bands
and do their best to make up for the want of jackals in
Burma.   There is always a huge band of unattached dogs
about the village, for Buddhism does not permit of the
drowning of superfluous puppies, and these manage to lead a
fairly well-fed life between stealing and devouring the offerings at the pagoda, and the superabundant charity received
by the monks in their morning begging rounds.   It is a
mystery how they managed formerly to exist in Mandalay
and Upper Burma generally ; there were such constantly
increasing hordes of them.   Nowadays the Assistant Commissioner periodically issues an edict, and poisoned meat and
the policemen's truncheons thin out their numbers very
thoroughly for a month or two.   The house - dog often
perishes with his Bohemian acquaintances, and there is much
lamentation among the younger members of the household,
but there is no difficulty in getting a successor, grown up or
otherwise.   The ordinary pariah has a greater turn for agility
than pluck, and the young civilian's English bull-dog would
probably kill more of them, when he is on a tour to the outlying villages with his master, than he actually does, if he
was as smart on his legs as he is with his jaws.   The pariah
is almost as noisy and quarrelsome as a Madrasi, but any
fights there are result as harmlessly as a French duel.
Nevertheless some of the Karen trained hunting dogs will
fasten on to a tiger, or a leopard, or the even more dangerous
wild boar, with the greatest determination.   So esteemed
are they that the sporting owner usually receives an official
message to keep his dogs in safety when the half-yearly
poisoners are about.   Still though buffalo fights and mains
of cocks have been common in Burma time out of mind, the
pariah has never been called upon to develop pugnacious
instincts.

The harmless, necessary cat is not so abundant.   There
are, however, few villages without one or two of them.   What
becomes of the kittens is a mystery.   Perhaps they go wild
and take to the woods.   Perhaps the pariah eats them when
their mother is out foraging.   At any rate the fact remains
that they increase but very slowly.   The Burman cat is

more fortunate than his Malay congener in possessing a tail, but asserts relationship with that animal in the possession of a horny hook, with this difference, that the hard excrescence is at the end of a tail of fair dimensions instead of being humbly situated on the rump, as is the case with the Straits tabby.

There are always some tame villatic fowl about the house. If the householder does not aspire to the ownership of a taik-kyet, a regular game cock, bred for the purpose, he has at least a kyet-hpa, an ordinary cock of combative instincts, and backs him against his neighbour's when occasion offers, through the absence of the constable, by chance, or by the influence of pecuniary profit acting on a sporting disposition. A cock that declines to fight under any circumstances is called a kyet nyaung-gan, and stands in great danger of dying suddenly and being converted into curry. Hens are regarded with indifference except in view of similar possibilities, for their eggs are of no use. A fowl may be killed by accident by a stick thrown at random, but the germ of life in an egg cannot die unless it is boiled or goes rotten. In the former case the boiler incurs mortal danger from breaking one of the Five Precepts ; in the latter the egg is undesirable. In small villages almost every one keeps a tè-gyet, a decoy cock, for luring the wild jungle-fowl. The fore-doomed hunter kills the game, and the pious owner of the decoy bird gets a good dinner. Similarly tè-gyo, pigeons, are bred specially as lures, and so are partridges. Ordinary pigeons, occasionally used for the same purpose, go by the name of gyo ta-nyin. Caged birds are not very common as pets, though every here and there one comes across a hill Mina, who has acquired a fair knowledge of the vernacular, and astonishes passers-by with the unceremonious way in which he hails them. But the Buddhist religion condemns keeping animals in confinement. So much is this the case that in Mandalay, and here and there in other places, there are men who make a regular living by catching birds and selling them to the pious, that they may gain merit by setting them free. Crafty birdcatchers are able so far to disable the bird, without doing it any material or visible harm, that they can catch it again immediately after their tender-hearted customer has gone his way. It used to be a common thing in the palace, during the late king's reign, to let loose a number of birds for the delectation of foreign worshippers at the golden feet, and the expansion of the royal merit. Ill-natured people said all the birds were recaptured in the next room, and appeared again for the next display of charity ; but of that I can say nothing.

Each house, with its ground, is surrounded by a rude fence more or less substantial according to the character of the district. Where there are many tigers or ill-doers, and especially north of Mandalay, where formerly the Kachins might swoop down any night, this is made very high and strong, and is further rendered effective by a formidable array of sharpened bamboos. Except where the British have taken the matter in hand, the village roads are simply places where the jungle is kept from growing. There is no attempt at metalling ; in fact there is no material for the purpose. In some pretentious villages indeed there is a raised path formed of bricks set on edge, and about three feet broad. This is regarded as a public work of great value, and a distinction to the inhabitants of the place. It usually leads to the monastery. In many villages, however, it would be impossible to move about during the rains without some such contrivance. The mud would be too deep, and logs are slippery even to bare feet.

Swinging by a couple of ropes from the roof hangs in the centre of the house a rude basket, made snug with a blanket or some old clothes. This is the baby's cradle, and the mother may often be seen sitting by it crooning and gently swaying it backwards and forwards. Some of the lullabies are very clever. I have tried to give a version of one of the most popular, with as near an approach to the metre as practicable. It is sung to the favourite te-dat air.

SEIN-NI LA-YAUNG

Clouds in Heaven,
Bright as levin,
Dyed with rosy diamond's light,
Did the Nine Gems
Stud your white hems,

> Silver moonbeams
> Cast their chill gleams,
> But to make black darkness vanish,
> Sweet sleep from my babe's eyes banish?
> Fairies wiled him,
> Dreams beguiled him,
> In his cradle wrapped so snugly,
> Cradle carved with nayas [1] ugly,
> Carved with Nats and Kings and Princes,
> Every splendour that evinces
> Royal state and princely usance.
> There he slept, when what a nuisance!
> Comes the light
> To affright
> And scare him back to home from elfin land.
>
> Sweet, my babe, your father's coming,
> Rest and hear the songs I'm humming;
> He will come and gently tend you,
> Rock your cot and safe defend you;
> Mother's setting out his dinner——
> Oh, you naughty little sinner!
> What a yell from such a wee thing,
> Couldn't be worse if you were teething.
> My sweet round mass of gold,
> Now please do what you're told.
> Be quiet and good,
> As nice boys should.
> Oh, you plaguy, nasty brat!
> I must call the great big cat,
> He will come and squeeze and bite,
> Scratch and eat you up outright.
> Puss, puss, puss, you great big pussy!
> Here's a boy so nice and juicy,
> Let the mice have one night's pleasure,
> You shall eat him at your leisure.
>
> Nasty, naughty, noisy baby,
> If the cat won't, Nats will maybe
> Come and pinch and punch and rend you.
> If they do I won't defend you.
> Oh, now please,
> Do not tease.
> Do be good,
> As babies should,
> Just one tiny little while;
> Try to sleep, or try to smile.

---

[1] A naya is a dragon with four legs. The word used here, myat è yin-wè, is specially reserved for royal cradles. The plebeian article is called pa-hket. Throughout, the language is of the most honorific character.

My prince, my sweet gold blood, my son,
Ordained a regal race to run,
Listen to your mother's coaxing,
Listen to the song good folks sing.
> When little boys
> Make such a noise,
> Comes the brownie
> On wings downy,
> Comes the wood sprite
> In the dark night,
> Witch and warlock,
> Mere and tor-folk,
> Kelpie, nikker,
> Quick and quicker,
Gobble all bad babies up.

Mercy, what an awful squall !
Don't you love mamma at all ?
Where's your father ?   Fie, for shame !
He could quiet you if he came.
But he won't ; he lolls and smokes,
With the neighbours cracks his jokes.
He's just as bad as you, tā-te,[1]
Plagues poor mamma and stays away.
> Now I tell you
> This to quell you,
> Both shall rue it.
> Thus I'll do it,
Neither shall have any dinner ;
> You no sweet milk,
> He no meat ilk,
You'll be good when you are thinner.

The King alone you dread on earth,
The wise man said it at your birth,
Said that all the stars would love you,
None on earth should be above you ;
But I'm sure that in the palace
Princes never shriek for malice.
Now I'll sing the eighty ditties,[2]
Known in all the royal cities,
Lullabies so soft and drowsy
E'en the Nat-so could not rouse ye.
Hush, my babe, my prince, my treasure,
List the poppy's slumbrous measure.

---

[1] Tā-te, according to the consent of the Burmese nursery literature, is the typical bad boy.
[2] " The eighty ditties," a very old and well-known palace lullaby.

CHAPTER X

THE EARTH AND ITS BEGINNING

THE Lord Buddha cared very little for speculations, or theories as to the construction and extent of the terrestrial globe, or as to the size and motions of the sun, the moon, and the stars. Shin Gautama was entirely a moral philosopher, concerned with the workings of the mind, whose highest aim was to despise matter and free itself from such trammels in the progress towards Ne'ban. The consideration of natural phenomena was therefore entirely outside the province of the true sage. It is probable, therefore, that the transmogrified Hindu system which does duty for Burmese cosmography was elaborated rather by the Buddha's disciples than by himself. It has been altered only to suit Buddhistic religious views, with here and there the fancies of a lively imagination thrown in, but the outline of it existed before Prince Theidat came.

The Burmese are therefore certainly not responsible for it, but as some knowledge of the system is necessary for the comprehension of various superstitions, phrases, and forms of speech, it may be desirable to give a slight sketch of these astronomical and cosmical theories.

The word lawka means a whole revolution of nature. The world is being constantly destroyed and reproduced, but each lawka lasts an incalculable length of years. It is divided into four periods, and it is not till the arrival of the fourth period that man appears upon earth. During that last period, divided into sixty-four Andrakaps, the life of man must, in each Andrakap, wax from ten years to an Athinkaya (a time represented by a unit and a hundred and sixty-four ciphers, one and a half quintillion years), and then gradually wane to ten years again, on account respectively of the merit and demerit in the world.   We are now in the waning term of the eleventh Andrakap.   The Buddhas only appear upon earth during the waning season of man's life, chiefly, of course, to stay the increasing influence of evil by preaching the law, and also because when man's life is slowly lengthening to an Athinkaya he is not so disposed to listen to their teaching.   100,000 years before the destruction of the world the Déwas come down from their six blissful seats and wander about the earth with dishevelled hair and mournful garb, proclaiming the sad tidings of the impending destruction of the world.   Once again a hundred years before the cataclysm they come, and all mankind strives to raise itself beyond the influence of the destroying element.   The world must be destroyed in any case, but there are three great principles of demerit which determine by what means the catastrophe will be effected.   Concupiscence is the most common and the least heinous of these principles, and the world of the lustful will be destroyed by fire.   Next comes anger, a more grievous sin than concupiscence, and the world ruined by the principle of anger will be destroyed by water. Worst of all is the sin of ignorance.   The world of the ignorant will be scattered about the bounds of space by a mighty rushing wind, which beginning so gently as barely to sway the leaves and flowers, ends by breaking up with its irresistible force the vast bulk of Mount Myinmo and the Sekyawala circle of hills.   Of sixty-four worlds, fifty-six are destroyed by fire, seven by water, and one by wind. Fire reaches to the fifth seat of the Rupa, the beings called Perfect.   Water mounts higher by three seats to the eighth of the Byammās, and wind one seat beyond this.   Out of the thirty-one seats of the world there remain therefore only eleven undestroyed.   The Four States of Punishment, the abode of man, the six blissful seats of Nats ; and five, eight or nine of the lofty dwellings of the Rupa, according to the destroying agent, are altogether overwhelmed and dispersed throughout space.   The seven highest seats of the Byammās and the four of Arupa, where dwell the Immaterials, who having broken all ties with the material world, are ripe for Ne'ban, these eleven seats only remain constantly undisturbed.

Then there is chaos for an athinkaya. When that mighty season has passed, rain begins to fall again throughout infinity. Fire, water, or wind may destroy the world, but water alone can reproduce it, though both the sun and the wind have minor parts to play. The drops gradually increase in size till they reach the volume of five, ten, a hundred, even a thousand yuzanas (a yuzana being about twelve miles English). The wind blows the water together in the spot occupied by the last world. A greasy scum gathers on the surface. The action of the sun gradually hardens this into a crust, which eventually assumes the exact appearance and shape of the last world. The Lord Buddha himself, it is written, did not know which was the first world and which would be the last. Many learned writers say that there is neither a beginning nor an end to the production and destruction of worlds. It will go on for ever like a great wheel, even as the great wheel of the Law itself. Since sorrow then is shadow to life, how should all beings strive to escape from the vortex of existences? In the *Abhidhamma* we read that there are two descriptions of worlds, called Thôn-nya Kabā and A-thôn-nya Kabā, that is to say, worlds to which the Buddhas came, and those to which they did not come. Some think that the latter kind of worlds must have been uninhabited. However that may be, it is certain that the law has always existed. It existed Kalpas and Mahakalpas before the first Budh came to this earth. The Buddhas only revive the knowledge of it among creatures upon the painful ladder of existence. Our present world, called Badda, has been particularly favoured. Already four Buddhas have appeared, and when the dispensation of Shin Gautama shall have passed away, two thousand five hundred years hence, there will come another, Arimadéya, whose stature will exceed the highest mountains in all the Southern Island.

The system of the world as explained by the Buddhist Yahandas is somewhat different from that adopted by western men of science. In the centre is the Myinmo Taung, Mount Meru, the highest peak of all the world. Its

shape is somewhat peculiar, like a cask floating end upwards
in water. A height of 84,000 yuzanas above the sea is
counterbalanced by as many of depth below the surface. It
is supported on three feet, each a huge ruby or carbuncle.
In the space between these feet dwell the Athura, the Nats
who were tempted to drink by new arrivals in the seat of
Toktheeta, and when overcome by the liquor were hurled
into the sea by their crafty rivals. At various heights on
the central mountain are ranged the six blissful seats of the
Déwas, but many of them dwell elsewhere. Thus, for
example, the sun, the moon, and most of the stars and
planets are simply gorgeous dwellings of Nats. Away in the
empyrean, rising perpendicularly one above the other, are
the sixteen seats of Rupa, where the Byammās, the Perfect,
dwell. These have got rid of almost all the passions, but
especially of concupiscence. It is not till they have freed
themselves from all affection for matter and material things
that they can pass beyond to the incalculable heights of the
four seats of Arupa, where the Immaterials dwell in a state
of sublimest contemplation waiting only for the moment when
they shall pass beyond into Ne'ban. Down below the earth,
in a mass of hard rock, are the eight great Hells and the
numberless smaller ones. Surrounding the Myinmo Taung
and girdling round the earth are the seven ranges of the
Sekyawala mountains, with seven seas interposed. In the
sea round about Mount Myinmo, the great Thamôddaya
Ocean, are the four great islands—Ottayakuru to the north,
Pyôppawideha to the east, Aparagawyan to the west, and
Zampudipa to the south. In the Southern Island dwells
the race of man. Each of the great islands has five hundred
smaller ones round about it, and in these islands dwell the
English and other nations other than the Buddhists and
the Indian heretics.

The Thamôddaya sea is too stormy to allow of any
one passing from one of the great islands to any other. The
Southern Island is the largest, and is shaped like a trapezium.
The Western Island is like the full moon, the Northern is
square, and Pyôppawideha is shaped like the moon in her
quarters. The shape of the head of the different inhabitants follows the shape of the island, and the different sides

of Mount Meru give their different colours to each island. Thus the Eastern Island is all white from being opposite to the silver face of the mountain; the Western is green, because on that side Myinmo is of glass; the Northern Island glitters like gold, and the Southern is a pale-coloured brown-like carbuncle. Each island is named from the great tree which grows upon it and forms the sacred insignia of the island. Thus the Southern Island is named from the Zampu tree, the great Eugenia.

The Eastern, Western, and Northern Islands are very pleasant to dwell in, but especially the Northern. There the people live to the age of a thousand years, and always appear to be no more than eighteen. In the other islands they only live to be five hundred. In other respects the Northern Island is a regular land of Cockayne. The fabled Padetha Bin, elsewhere only found in the happy countries of the Nats, grows there. From its bounteous branches hang the most gorgeous dresses of every variety of colour, and the happy islanders have only to take them off. Nor are they at any necessity to till the ground to procure themselves food. From this tree they obtain also an abundant supply of a most excellent kind of rice, already husked to their hands. All that they have to do is to place it on a certain large stone, and it is forthwith cooked, and upon the branches of the trees round about appear the most dainty meats. Truly the Northern islanders have a most enviable existence. But in one respect, like the inhabitants of the Eastern and Western isles, they are unhappy. They are always born back to the same island. They cannot raise themselves in the scale of being, like the otherwise sorrowful Southern islanders. Only in Zampudipa do the Buddhas appear to teach the law and free the people from constant deaths and reappearances. From Tahingaya, the first Buddha, to Shin Gautama, under whose dispensation we now live, there have been twenty-eight Buddhas, and all of them have come to the great Southern Island. To Byammās, to Nats, even to animals and the agonised dwellers in the lowest hells, the blessed words have come, but never to those other dwellers in the islands of the great sea Thamôddaya. Thus are men enabled to attain to the state of Nats, to pass through the seats of Rupa and Arupa, until finally, freed from passion and sorrow and the trammels of matter, they sink into the bliss of Ne'ban.   Therefore have pious writers of old called the Southern Island Ne'ban's ferry.

Down below the earth, in the deepest recesses of the Southern Island, are the eight great Hells, surrounded by 40,040 smaller ones.   Four of the great Hells are called Awidzi, and in addition to other tortures, terrible flames leap from wall to wall across the monstrous space, and extend on all sides beyond for a thousand yuzanas.   The other four are called Lawkantyè, and there, instead of flames, we find hideous cold.   A day in any of these places of torment is as long as thousands of mundane years.

The world having been created is as yet uninhabited. Our present earth, Badda, was peopled in the following way, From the seats of Zān, to which the destructive element had not reached, came down certain Byammās, some say three, some as many as nine.   Holy people as they were and freed from all passions, they existed at first, like Adam and Eve, in a state of perfect bliss and innocence.   They were not as the Kāma, the generating beings of the Four States of Punishment and the Seven States of Happiness—that of man and the six seats of Nats.   But, like Adam and Eve, they fell into sin and thence into misery.   First we read that they prayed for light.   We may imagine that already the spiritual light had forsaken them, for in answer to their prayers appeared the sun, the moon, and the stars.   The holy people had hitherto lived on a flavoured earth, which, however, driven away by their growing desire for matter, vanished and gave place to another species of food, a sweet creeping plant called Padalata.   This was perfect in odour and flavour, but still the appetites of the people grew, and the Padalata was taken away and in its place appeared the Thalé san, a peculiarly fine kind of rice, which grew ready husked, and had only to be put in a pot, when it would cook itself.   But by eating the Thalé rice, the Byammās became more and more gross, until, like Adam and Eve after eating the apple, they attained a knowledge of good and evil, and marriage was instituted.   After this the

Thalé san became more and more scarce. At first, no matter how much was eaten, at night the portion which had been cut during the day reappeared ; but when the first people fell into the sin of lust the rice gradually vanished. Where the rice was cut in the morning, there remained a bare patch at night. Since then man has had to labour, and earn his bread with the sweat of his brow.

Owing to the scarcity, crime first appeared in the world. One man, fearing that his stock would not last him, went and stole from his neighbours' barns. Thus theft was the first crime committed in the world. The man whose rice was stolen at first only scolded the thief, and let him go. The robber, however, did not care for this, and came back a second and a third time. The third time he was seized and beaten. Thus out of the original crime of thievery arose abuse, reviling, assault, falsehood, and then punishments. In this way did crime and consequently law and justice take their origin, and have lasted since the very beginning of the world. Hitherto on account of the happy state in which the people had lived, without crime and without punishments, every one had been equal, and there had been no necessity for marking different grades. As, however, crime increased, and with it revenge, more or less sweeping according to temperament, the people took counsel together and resolved to appoint a man to be ruler over them, who should regulate their affairs and punish wrongdoers. Thus a king was first appointed, and his revenue was derived from tithes given by the people. Each man set apart a tenth of his Thalé san for the support of the king. The tithe system was kept up among the Burmese, the most direct in descent from the original people, until a few years ago. The kings extended the system. The rulers and governors of provinces received in place of salary the tithes of the districts which were under their charge. But King Mindôn Min, finding that with un-scrupulous men the method was liable to abuse, abolished the system of tithes, and introduced the English method of paying a regular salary. It did not, however, work well. Many of the myo-sas, finding that they did not receive their money regularly from the State, continued to exact tithes as before, only secretly and with many cunning devices to hide what they were doing.   It is probable, therefore, that the custom of the ancients would have been reintroduced.

The appointment of a ruler to punish crime was therefore the second source of the law, and the first source of the administration of justice.   The first king chosen was a Payālaung, a person destined in future ages to be a Buddha, and therefore of great sanctity and wisdom, and one who strictly conformed to the five natural and religious laws incumbent on all men, namely, not to murder, steal, commit adultery, drink fermented liquors, or speak falsely.   From these immediately sprang the four thingahas or kingly laws, and the first laws laid down by the Payālaung were with regard to the twenty-five descriptions of theft, the ten kinds of assault, and the twenty-seven kinds of abusive language.

Notwithstanding the institution of a source of administrative justice, crime continued to increase, and those who wished to escape from its evil influences retired to the jungles and there built small houses for themselves, or gained a living by begging from village to village.   Thus rose the caste of the Brahmins.   Those who built themselves houses and acquired wealth by agriculture and trade, were called thaté thu-gywè, rich men, while those who were unfortunate and oppressed sank into the state of poverty and were called thu sinyè.   Thus arose the legal classification of the people.

The first king, Mahāthamada as he was called, probably had a written code, but it has been superseded or lost.   The laws which now guide us were drawn up by Menu, originally a cowherd, but afterwards a minister.   To these laws all others owe their existence, for we read that in Greece, the earliest civilised country in Europe, Menu was styled Minos in Crete, and first gave them laws.   In this way polity was established in the Southern Island.   The original people soon greatly increased, and multiplied, and dispersed themselves not only all over the mainland, but some even went to the smaller islands round about, as did the English to the Pyi Gyi.   Just as the children of one father take different names, so the different peoples took to themselves different titles, according to the part of the earth they settled in.   Just also as some children in a family are good and some bad, so a few races preserved the sacred law of the Lord Buddha, and some fell away into lamentable heresies.   Many of them still retain reminiscences of the teachings of the Great Master.   Thus the Bible of the Christian contains moral precepts in a great measure identical with the sentiments conveyed in the thoughts or sermons of the Lord Buddha.   There is even confirmation in the mention of the ages of Methuselah and other men of old, of the doctrine of the waxing and waning term of human life.   Some learned Sadaws have held that the Lord Jesus is Dewadat, the cousin of Shin Gautama, who was always trying to overthrow the good works of the Buddha ; and it is well known that the Siamese speak of the evil Dewadat as the God of Europe, and the causer of all the evil in the world.   This opinion is not, however, generally held, and the best thing a Burman can wish for a good Englishman is that in some future existence, as a reward of good works, he may be born a Buddhist and if possible a Burman.   For that the Burmese are most nearly descended from the original holy people, their name Byammā or Bamā evidently shows, while no other nation preserves the sacred law more carefully and more exactly in its form as it came from the lips of the Lord Buddha himself.   Moreover, the Burmese monarchs retained the titles given to Mahātha-mada, the first king, and his immediate successors, and therefore they ranked above all others.

CHAPTER XI

THE LADDER OF EXISTENCE

NOTWITHSTANDING the change, the pain, and the vanity
of everything upon earth, yet the Lu-pyi, the Manôt-tha-
bông, the state of man, is desirable beyond all others.
Transience, misery, unreality prevail in all the thirty-one
seats of the world, even in the twenty superior heavens,
where those acted on by Kāma, generating beings, find no
entrance. The Déwas come down to our earth from their
six seats of bliss ; the Byammās, even to the fourth state
of Zān, are occasionally found in earthly guise in the
precincts of holy monasteries ; even Yahandas, who have
entered into Thodda, the current of perfection, and after
death attain the dreamful joy of Ne'ban, the cessation from
existence, even these immaterial beings diffuse a saintly
presence over the Southern Island. The great Lord
Gautama appeared in the seat of man and preached the
sacred law, and he preached it there because all the twenty-
seven Buddhas before him had done the same, and when he
preached it on that soft Indian eve,

> I know it writ that they who heard
> Were more—lakhs more—crores more—than could be seen,
> For all the Devas and the Dead thronged there,
> Till Heaven was emptied to the seventh zone,
> And uttermost dark Hells opened their bars ;
> Also the daylight lingered past its time
> In rose-leaf radiance on the watching peaks,
> So that it seemed Night listened in the glens
> And Noon upon the mountains ; yea ! they write,
> The Evening stood between them like some maid,
> Celestial, love-struck, rapt ; the smooth-rolled clouds
> Her braided hair ; the studded stars the pearls

And diamonds of her coronal ; the moon
Her forehead jewel, and the deepening dark
Her woven garments.   'Twas her close-held breath
Which came in scented sighs across the lawns
While our Lord taught, and, while he taught, who heard—
Though he were stranger in the land, or slave,
High caste or low, come of the Aryan blood,
Or Mlech or Jungle-dweller, seemed to hear
What tongue his fellows talked.   Nay, outside those
Who crowded by the river, great and small,
The birds and beasts and creeping things—'tis writ—
Had sense of Buddha's vast embracing love
And took the promise of his piteous speech ;
So that their lives—prisoned in shape of ape,
Tiger, or deer, shagged bear, jackal, or wolf,
Foul-feeding kite, pearled dove, or peacock gemmed,
Squat toad, or speckled serpent, lizard, bat ;
Yea, or of fish fanning the river-waves—
Touched meekly at the skirts of brotherhood
With man who hath less innocence than these ;
And in mute gladness knew their bondage broke
Whilst Buddha spake these things before the King.

The Light of Asia.

And since that time some few have passed from our
earth to Ne'ban, where the silence lives ; "seeking nothing,
they gained all."   But far the most have failed ; some have
sunk to the Four States of Punishment ; some have risen to
the blissful seats of Nats ; fewer have passed beyond to the
meditative realms of Zān.

It is written that the life of man waxes from ten years
to the huge period of an Athinkaya, and then wanes to ten
years again.   How is it, then, that some men live beyond a
hundred years, and others die almost ere they have drawn
breath ?   The reason is that some have taken no life at all
in previous existences, and that others have, unwittingly
perhaps, destroyed many creatures, and their own existence
is correspondingly graduated.   To maintain his dignity of
man it is absolutely necessary that a human being must
observe, as far as his powers admit, the Five great Precepts.
Failure to observe these will infallibly result in a fall in the
next existence into the States of Punishment.

It will be well to begin the ladder of existence at the
lowest rung, at the worst of these four states.   This is
Nga-yè, hell—the most hideous of all.   Even in Nga-yè

there are gradations: the one mighty seat is divided into
eight great holds, arranged one below the other, all with
punishments so terrible that none can be said to exceed
any other in hideousness. The names of all the eight
great chambers, from Theinzo above to Awizi the nether-
most hell, are given, but a detailed catalogue is unnecessary.
Each great hell is surrounded by sixteen inferior places of
torture called Ôtthad-daret. From west to east the flames
stream through all the mighty space and pass through on
the other side to a distance of a thousand yuzanas, and
from east to west the same. From north to south, from
Nadir to Pole, and Pole to Nadir, it is the same, and yet the
torments of this heat are but a tithe of the gruesome tortures
the sinner must suffer. The life of the Déwas in Tawadeintha is reckoned at sixteen million human years. That
period is but as a day and night in Kālathôt, the second
hell. Thirty such days and nights make a month, twelve
months one year; and the wicked in the Kālathôt hell
must pass one thousand such horrible years. The Nats in
Tôt-thita live five hundred and seventy-six million years,
which is but as one revolving sun and moon to the tenants
of Yawruwa. Of such appalling days they must make up
a tale of four thousand agonising years. The miserable
wretches in Awizi work out the evil of their sins only in
the space of an Andrakap, a period so vast that the mind
cannot grasp it. As if these punishments were not sufficient
to scare the weak and ignorant from sin, it has been revealed
what other tortures await the damned. In one of the Ten
Great Sacred Mystery Plays it is related how a pious prince
was shown the horrors of hell. The terrible pictures of the
sixth book of the *Æneid*, the awful imaginings of Dante's poem,
are outdone by the flesh-creeping minuteness of the Nemi
Zāt. The prince saw men devoured by five-headed dogs,
by famished vultures, by loathsome crows, the flesh being
renewed as fast as the foul creatures tore it away; he saw
others crushed beneath the weight of vast white-hot mountains, stretched on fiery bars and cut up with burning knives
and flaming saws, their hearts slowly scratched and pierced
with fiery needles, flame entering at the mouth and licking
up the vitals, fiends all about, hacking, hewing, stabbing,

lacerating the body with all that the human mind has imagined hideous, and all this, and ten times more, which it were only disgusting to write down, continued with never-abated torture to the wretched victims. The lesser hells are no less horrible ; that of ordure, where huge stinging serpents and gnawing worms fasten on the sinners who are there immersed ; those of burning coals, swords and knives, molten lead, fiery hammers which crush the bones at every stroke ; that where the heart, lungs, and liver are torn out with hooks and slowly sliced and ever renewed. Occasionally the damned are transferred to the Lawkantyè hells, situated in the intermediate spaces between the Sekya worlds, where the tortures are those of frightful cold. Enough, however, has been said about the horrors of hell. The crimes which condemn a man, and the hell to which he is sent, are all duly recorded ; but as one hell is as bad as another, it is unnecessary to recount these particulars. Suffice it to say that the man who scoffs at the Buddha and derides the law, will remain, throughout a whole revolution of nature, an entire Lawka, transfixed head downwards on a red-hot spit, in the lowest hell, hacked, gnawed, crushed, and beaten by all that is most awesome in all the flaming realms. There are twenty-one kinds of people who will fall into the lowest hell. Nineteen, however, if they see the error of their ways, and attend the pagodas with goodly offerings, may be redeemed ; but the hunter and the fisher-man cannot be saved. The impious Dewadat, cousin and brother-in-law of the Buddha, who tried to kill him, suffers terrible punishment. His feet are sunk ankle-deep in burn-ing marl. His head is incased in a red-hot pan that caps it down to the lobe of the ears. Two large red-hot bars transfix him from back to front, two horizontally from right to left, and one impales him from head to foot. But since he repented when he sank into the earth to his doom, he will become a Pyitsega Buddha, under the name of Ahisara, in coming ages.

The State of Punishment above that of hell is that of the Thurakè. Their miseries are various. Some are keepers of hell by day or by night, themselves suffering all the horror of the terrible heat, assuming the form of man at other times. Others feed on their own flesh and blood, and tear themselves with great hooks. Some are six miles high, with projecting crab's eyes, short lids, and a mouth the size of an ordinary mortal's, so that they are incessantly tormented by hunger. Above them are the Pyeitta, who in many respects resemble them in their sufferings. They wander on desert sea-shores and mountains, and in dismal forests, far from the abodes of man, naked and continually lamenting. Some have huge bodies with a mouth no larger than the eye of a needle, so that they can never satiate their craving for food. Others have huge, gluttonous mouths, always seeking to devour, but with no stomach in which the food can be received. Maggots, earth-worms, ants, and the like are often called Pyeitta, because they live on excrements and all manner of filth. This state is the one specially assigned to misers and niggardly, uncharitable people.

The highest of the Four States of Punishment is that of Tareiksan, or animals. Those who do not keep a guard over their passions, who are abusive, and who refrain from giving alms, will fall into the Bông of animals. Just as one man by reason of previous merits is born a prince, while another barely scrapes into human existence as an outcast pagoda slave, a grave-digger, a leper, or a heretic, so there are grades in the state of animals. To be an elephant is of course nearly as good as being a man ; to be a white elephant is usually very much better. Any herbivorous animal is in a better state than a creature which eats flesh. Lions, tigers, and all life-destroying creatures are particularly undesirable transincorporations. The vulture is highly honoured because it never takes life, but lives entirely on carrion. Some animals are particularly esteemed as having been incarnations of the Lord Buddha. Such are the white elephant, the hare, the pigeon. Shin Gautama's first existence was in the form of a little bird, and all the stages he passed through in after existences are recorded in the Ten Great Zāts and the five hundred and ten minor tales. He who would cross the ferry to Ne'ban may learn from them how he may do so, and how miserable the toil is. Who would not seek the higher paths when he sees what the alternative is?

Raised from the Four States of Punishment to the Manôt-tha Bông, where as man the law is open to his study, the creature on his upward path should not be lightly stayed. To rise from the seat of man to that of Nats seems simple. Observe but the Five Precepts, give alms, live peaceably with all men, attend regularly at the pagodas on the appointed days that the image and model there presented to you may strengthen your resolution, do but live a respectable life, and the end is gained ; you pass to the dwellings of the Déwas, there to spend long years of bliss. Good works will do much, but it is especially necessary to observe the Five Precepts. You must keep them in your mind every day, as you put your clothes on your body. The Ten Precepts must be kept on holy days, four times in every lunar month and throughout all Lent ; these, and the daily giving of alms to the mendicants, will save you ; your next existence will be in the Heavens of the Nats.

The Nat-pyi Chauk-tap, the six blissful seats, the highest of the Kāma Bông, the worlds of passion, are ranged on and around Mount Myinmo. Like the eight Hells they all have names, beginning with Zatu-ma-harit and ending with Para-neimmita Wot-thawati. The second and the fourth Heavens are the best known ; for to Tawadeintha the Lord Buddha ascended in three steps to preach the law to his mother, the sainted Queen Maya, and countless Byammās and Immaterials from the far realms of Rupa and Arupa came to hear ; and from Tôt-thita the embryo Budh descended to take flesh as Prince Theidat. The length of life in Tawadeintha is a thousand Déwa's years, that is, in earthly reckoning, nine millions. Similarly the four thousand of Tôt-thita are in human calendars five hundred and seventy-six million years.

Take up any book of fairy tales you have ; revive your recollection of the *Arabian Nights* ; recall any dream when you thought you had made your fortune, and you have a picture of the six blissful seats. A vision of song and dancing, beautiful and fragrant flowers, delicious fruits, palm-trees bearing, in place of leaves, rich garments and priceless ornaments and dainty cates, great gorgeous palaces with crystal pavements, golden columns, and jewelled walls ; a tinkling of gold and silver bells, intoxicating music—everything the most fervid imagination can picture, all are found in these happy realms.   Prince Nemi was granted a sight of them as well as of the horrors of hell.

Passion still prevails, but it becomes less and less sensual the higher we rise.   In Tôt-thita a touch of the hand satisfies love ; in the fifth seat, lovers simply gaze on each other ; and in the sixth, existence in the same place is enough. The Nat of the highest Bông is not far from the twenty superior heavens.

Passage to the Déwa seats is obtained by the strict observance of the precepts and the regular performance of good works ; the step beyond can only be accomplished by the aid of the intellect.   Ignorance is always the chief hindrance to rise in the scale of worlds ; it is especially so in the case of the superior heavens.   The twenty higher seats can only be reached by concentrated meditation ; by the performance of good works, not outwardly by the body, but inwardly by the soul.   The three fundamental principles of Aneiksa, Dôkka, Anatta—transience, pain, vanity—must first be intently examined.   Then we must pass on through the five kinds of meditation, the highest of which is Upekka, which brings perfect fixity, whence originates callousness to pleasure or pain, scorn or affection.   Thus we pass through the successive stages of contemplation which lead us through the sixteen seats of Rupa, each of which constitute the first, second, and third Zāns—Thawtapan, Thakadagam, Anagam ; the tenth and eleventh seats form the fourth Zān, and in the five highest, the Yahandas have entered on Thodda, on the current of perfection.

Thus we reach to the verge of the four immaterial superior heavens.   To enter these we must get rid of all affection for matter.   The thirty-two parts of the body are often mentioned in prayer by pious Buddhists, each part with its forty-four subdivisions.   On these we must ponder till we understand and see the worthlessness of them.   Then we must repeat ten thousand times " the firmament, or the æther, is immeasurable," till at length we reach the first Seit or idea of Arupa.

Thence we progress in contempt for matter till at last

we are delivered from the three Thangya, or false persuasions, and reaching the topmost seat of Arupa, Newa-thangya-nathangya-yatana, tremble on the verge of Ne'ban.

What is Ne'ban?

> If any teach Nirvana is to cease,
>   Say unto such they lie ;
> If any teach Nirvana is to live,
>   Say unto such they err.

The common illustration of the schools will not suffice for matter-of-fact Western heretics. You tell them life is like a lamp, with its wick and its little lake of oil. It may be kindled and extinguished many times, fresh oil may be added, other lamps kindled from it, but at length the oil is exhausted, the flame flickers and dies away for ever. That is annihilation, you say. It is not. When a man dies and goes to Ne'ban he ceases to be individualised ; he is no more agitated by existence, wretched in itself, still more wretched from the woes it reveals in others ; he falls into a calm and never-ending cessation of existence ; he knows nothing of others, or of the world, and so is a stranger to all feelings of joy or sorrow ; he contemplates fixedly the abstract truth, which even the highest Immaterials cannot, perpetually ; but he is not annihilated as the heretics assert ; nor does he slip, like the dew-drop, into the shining sea ; he is not absorbed into the supreme Buddha, as the Brahmins loosely say ; he remains perpetually in a sacred calm, unmoved by any feeling whatever, in lifeless, timeless bliss.

The teachers strive to give a detailed explanation, but who can know? who can tell for certain the composition and economy of even the nearest star? They tell us this : Ne'ban is the extinction of Kan, the soul of recurring existences, the influence of merits and demerits, exemption from which means utter cessation from existences ; Ne'ban is the stifling of Seit, the fire of passions, the entire hundred and twenty volitions and desires ; Ne'ban is the cessation of Utu, exemption from revolving years, from the changes of seasons, from the variations of heat and cold, darkness and light ; Ne'ban is the death of Ahāya, taste, typifying all the senses ; Ne'ban is, in fact, the going out of all that we know as making up a living being ; there remains behind what no one can name and few even picture to themselves, and those who attempt it do so according to their individual fancies. When a person recovers from a grievous illness we can only say that to be free from infirmities is to recover one's health. So we say that a man has attained to Ne'ban when he is freed from the sorrows of existences.

In regard to the Lord Buddha himself, we are told that there are in reality three stages in Ne'ban. The first was the Ne'ban of Kiletha, of the earthly passions, when under the Baw-di Bin, the sacred banyan-tree, he renounced all and became a Buddha. The second was the Ne'ban of Khanda, when near Kôkthenayôn, he expired in the grove of sāl-trees, when the five supports of existence gave way and he finally departed from the thirty-one seats of the world. The third and last, the Ne'ban of Dat, will not be for nearly two thousand five hundred years, five thousand from the day of his death. Then the duration of the Great Master's teachings will have ceased, his cycle will have lapsed, and all his relics from all parts of the world will be miraculously gathered together into the place where the original Baw-di Bin stood ; there will be many wondrous signs, and then all but the memory of him will be gone, the complete Ne'ban will have been attained.

The definition may be vague, and the monks of Burma, Siam, Japan, Ceylon, Thibet, and China may each have their own definition, but there is the same difficulty to be found in all religions with regard to the last mystery. Who can find agreement in the variety of Christian descriptions of the future life, where one places happiness in the eternal singing of songs and in feastings, another in gazing on the Deity, a third, with greater modesty, hopes to creep in by the door of which St. Peter holds the keys ? Buddhists have in their six heavens and twenty superior seats a choice of every kind of bliss, suited to every liking. They have the Islamite delights of sense in the heavens of Déwas with the houri nat-daughters. Then for the various kinds of meditation and mysticism they have the contemplative Byammā seats, while the four seats of Arupa afford room for the most transcendental speculation.

Yet all these ideal realms of phantasy——the dreams of

sense, of contemplation and mystic trance—have nothing to do with the state of Ne'ban. It is not a "nothing" A "nothing" that can be imagined is an all, for according to the laws of thought, non-existence can only be understood in a relative sense. The Buddhist system is much too logical to trouble itself with such incomprehensible problems, and in order to create no false impressions, the teachers surround the last state with the utmost possible uncertainty of expression. The Buddhist yearns to return from the endless whirl and turmoil of existences to the calm of the first beginning.

CHAPTER XII

THE NOBLE ORDER OF THE YELLOW ROBE

That noble order of the yellow robe
Which to this day standeth to help the world.

ALL living creatures are plodding on

the noble Eightfold Path which brings to peace ;
By lower or by upper heights it goes,
The firm soul hastes, the feeble tarries. All
Will reach the sun-lit snows.

The monks in Lower Burma are fond of the comparison
which steam lends them now. The holy fraternity are
pushing on by mail train to the emancipation from constant
successions of new births, while the weary layman toils
along the dusty road on foot, or at best in a jolting bullock-
cart ; the mendicant pushes up the stream of life in a huge
throbbing paddle steamer ; the man yet in the world struggles
along painfully against the current, and whirled about by
eddies in a rude canoe. Why, then, cannot all set forth on
the path alike ? Partly because of ignorance and its consequences ; partly because of the kan which forms each man's
life :

The books say well, my Brothers ! each man's life
The outcome of his former living is,
The bygone wrongs bring forth sorrows and woes,
The bygone right breeds bliss.

A man's kan may be sufficient to gain him existence as a
human being, but not enough to sustain him in the noble
life of the monk. He may enter the noble order, he must,
indeed, if he would be other than a brute beast ; but his
kan, the sum of actions that make up his life, the soul of

transmigrations, forces him to leave and enter the forest of the world, some from want of the gift of continence, some from ambition and desire for worldly power, some from a seeking after wealth, all from the predominance of some one of the hundred and twenty seit that incapacitate a man for the calm meditative life of the pyin-sin.

In the Lord Buddha's time, when a man adopted the faith, the requisites were belief in his teaching, a willingness to live in poverty and chastity, and under strict rules. All the applicant had to do was to renounce the ordinary pursuits of life, give up all his goods, take the vows, and he was forthwith a member of the Thengā. From that time forward he lived in poverty, was dependent upon alms for his food, and upon charity for a shelter for his head ; he was a beikku, a mendicant, and only those who were such were Buddhists. But as the believers increased, it was evident that all could not wholly adopt the religious life. Many had faith, but not faith enough to support them in the strict rule of the society, and soon Buddhists became divided into the two classes of laymen who adopted and believed in the religious tenets, and the religious who abandoned the world entirely, and strove only to lead the higher life. Hence also arose the hierarchy of the order, which exists to a certain extent in Burma, though very far from approaching the completeness of the system of Thibet, where there is a pontifical court, an elective sacerdotal chief, and a college of superior Lamas. In this respect, however, Burman Buddhism is as much closer to the primitive order in polity as it is in exact observance of the ordinations of the Wini. Theoretically, in the sacred assembly there are but three classes :

The shin, the novice, who has put on the yellow robe without becoming a professed member of the order, and probably with no other desire than that of obtaining his "humanity." These are called ko-yins, maung-shins, and a variety of other names.

The u-pyin-sin, those who, having lived a certain time in the monastery, have been formally admitted to the assembly with a prescribed ceremony, whereby the title of yahan is solemnly conferred. These are the pyit-shin, or religious.

Finally, there is the pôngyi, the " Great Glory," who by

virtue of prolonged stay—ten years is the minimum—has proved his steadfastness and unflinching self-denial.

This division of the fraternity is not far removed from the classification of Shin Gautama's own time, when all people were regarded and addressed as dāyaka, laymen, who hear the preaching of the law, but are not yet converted to a firm acceptance of it ; or upathaka, not merely hearers of the law, but steadfast believers and practisers of its precepts.   Nowadays the term dāyaka is applicable to all mankind, for it is open to all to seek for refuge in the Law of Good.

Practically, however, there is a slightly extended distinction of rank.

1. The Shin, the postulant.

2. The Pyit-shin, the religious, the full member of the order.

3. The Sayā, always a pôngyi, the head of each kyaung, or religious house, who controls all the inmates.

4. The Gaing-ôk, the provincial, who has a jurisdiction extending over all the monasteries of a cluster of villages or over a whole district, giving advice in all the affairs of these communities, enforcing the rules against malcontents, and correcting any abuses.

5. The Sadaw, a royal teacher, or vicar-general of the order, who manages the entire affairs of the whole country, both Burma and the Shan States, in religious matters. These live in or near Mandalay, and are summoned thither on their appointment.   There are ordinarily eight of them, all honoured with the title of Tha-thana-paing, *i.e.* supreme in matters appertaining to religion.   It is a mistake to speak of *the* Tha-thana-paing as a sort of Burmese Buddhist pope.   There is no such approximation to the heterodox Buddhism of Thibet, unless indeed the other sadaw-gyis have died, and there is but one remaining.   Since the annexation of Upper Burma, the British Government has allowed the election of a single Tha-thana-paing and given letters patent to the monk chosen.

In the time of native rule the teacher of the reigning king was always created a Sadaw, if indeed he had not been one before he was called upon to take a royal pupil.   The respect paid to him by the king was paid, not as to the head of the religion, but as to the personal teacher. The Burman in his prayers, or rather his meditations for the good of others, prays for his teacher before his parents. The five pleasant things in the world are : the shade of trees, the shade of parents, the shade of teachers, the shade of princes, the shade of the Buddha.

It is this republican tendency of Buddhism that gives it such a wonderful hold on the people. Rank does not confer on the mendicant greater honour, or release him from any of his obligations. The most learned and famous Sadaw must go forth every morning to beg his daily food. If he is very aged and decrepit he may be excused to some extent, but every now and again he must totter forth to preserve the letter of the law and show a proper example of humility. His dress is the same as that of the most recently admitted ko-yin, and in the eyes of the world he holds honour, not because he controls the affairs of the assembly, but because he is so close to the verge of Ne'ban. This feeling extends beyond the order into ordinary life. The religion brings all men down to the same level. The poor man may be a king of nats in the next life ; the wealthy sinner may frizzle in the awful pains of hell. There is no difference between man and man but that which is established by superiority in virtue ; and hence it is that the state of women among Buddhists is so very much higher than it is among Oriental peoples, who do not hold by that faith. The Burmese woman enjoys many rights which her European sister is even now clamouring for.

We have seen that the whole male population of Burma enters the monastery, and that the great majority leave after a very short stay. Some, however, grow fond of the monastic ways, and remain to study and qualify themselves to be mendicants. In becoming pyin-sin they do not acquire any new spiritual power, nor do they constitute themselves directly teachers of the people. In a religious system, which acknowledges no supreme Deity, it is impossible for any one to intercede with a Creator whose existence is denied, in behalf of a man who can only attain to a higher state by his own pious life and earnest self-denial. The religious are merely initiated into a higher stage, and become members of an order in which every individual is aiming at a greater degree of sanctity. The doors of the kyaung are always open as well to those who wish to enter as to those who wish to leave it. The longest stayer has the greatest honour. A visitor monk, who has the greater number of wās, who has passed many lenten seasons in his yellow robe, will be shikho'd to, will receive the homage of the head of the monastery, even if he be a gaing-ôk, and the stranger but a simple pôngyi.

In his ordination, therefore, the pyin-sin takes upon himself no burden in the shape of a cure of souls. He is not a priest like the Christian minister, who undertakes to guide others to salvation. He has no trouble for his food ; a pious and kindly population supplies him far beyond his requirements, and expects no service in return for this support. He has no sermons to prepare ; it is not expected that he will preach the law, and when of his own accord he occasionally does give an exposition, it is not any feeble excogitation of his own, but the thoughts and words of the Great Master himself, or of the highest and noblest of the men of old, that he delivers. His natural rest is never broken in upon by calls to administer consolation and comfort to the sick and the dying. Even his leisure is seldom interrupted to be present at the last rites for the dead. He is not a minister of religion, and all he has to do is to seek his own deliverance and salvation. All that is compulsory on him is the observance of continence, poverty, and humility, with tenderness to all living things, abstraction from the world, and a strict observance of a number of moral precepts, all tending to inculcate these things. It is curious perhaps, therefore, that greater numbers do not don the yellow robe. As it is, however, there is no lack of them.

Previous to admission the postulant must have reached the age of twenty years and have obtained his parents' permission. The origin of this stipulation dates from the earliest times. When Gautama attained the Buddhaship his half-brother Nanda was next heir, and was about to be proclaimed Crown Prince when he was persuaded to become yahan. Thereupon Thudaw - dana, the king, obtained a promise from the Buddha that ever after none should put on the celibate robe without his parents' consent. The candidate must also give proof of a sufficient knowledge of the Pareit-gyi, the Padiseit, the three Bitaghats, and the like. When it is understood that he has given satisfaction in these subjects, his friends provide for him the complete equipment of a mendicant, the sacred eight utensils which a pyin-sin cannot do without. These are :—

1. The dugôt, a piece of yellow cloth of rectangular shape, folded many times and worn over the left shoulder, with the ends hanging down behind and before.

2. The kowut, a piece of cloth worn round the loins and reaching to the ankles.

3. The thinbaing, a square-shaped cloth, yellow like the others, thrown cloak-fashion over the chest and shoulders, and coming down as far as the knees.

4. The thabeit, or begging-pot, worn suspended round the neck by a cord. It is shaped like a large circular soup-tureen with a rounded bottom, and has no lid. This must be carried round every morning to receive the alms of the pious.

5. The kaban, a leathern girdle used for binding on the kowut.

6. The pèkot, a short - handled axe used for splitting firewood and the like.

7. An at, or needle.

8. A yesit, a strainer, or water dipper, an apparatus for filtering the water which he drinks, so that he may not, even unwittingly, take animal life.

To these pareik-kaya shit-ba, these sacred eight utensils, is usually added an awana or yap, a lotus-leaf-shaped fan, made from a single palm frond, with an edging of bamboo or light wood, and furnished with a handle fashioned like the letter S. The leaf used is that of the Talapat palm, hence the name of Talapoins given to the members of the brotherhood by the early Portuguese adventurers in Burma. Every mendicant must have this fan with him when he goes to an assemblage where there are likely to be women present, in order that he may be thus able to shut himself off from any temptation to carnal thoughts. The sight of half a

dozen or more solemn-visaged monks sitting on their mats
and coyly hiding their faces behind these big fans is apt to
raise a smile on the face of a foreigner.   But there is no
doubt that the regulation is well advised.   Women are
disturbers of tranquil meditation.

When these necessaries have been provided, the candidate
proceeds to the appointed building.   This is always a thein,
a consecrated hall, built of teak, with open sides and the
sacred three, five, or seven overlapping and diminishing roofs,
not unlike the Albert Memorial in appearance, but much
larger at the base.   Here the examining body is assembled
to the number of ten or twelve, ordinarily, but a minimum
of four will suffice if the ceremony is conducted in the
jungle.   The senior is appointed upyitsi, or president, and
a secretary is nominated, whose duty it is to bring forward
the candidate and to read the Kammawāsā, the ritual of
ordination.   This is the most gorgeously ornamented of all
the Burmese books.   It is written, not in the ordinary round
character, but in square letters painted on with a thick black
resinous gum, and requires a special education to read it.
The leaves are formed either of the ordinary palm-leaf, thickly
covered with red lacquer, and profusely ornamented round
the border and between the lines with gilded figures of nats
and elaborate scroll-work, or in the case of the more sacred
monasteries, of the discarded waistcloths of kings.   None
might wear these pasos after the Great King of Righteousness had tired of them, and many were therefore made use
of for this purpose.   Portions of them are taken, doubled
over, and then covered with numerous coatings of wood-oil
and a paste composed of this same thitsi, with finely sifted
burnt rice-husks, sawdust, and rice-water, until at last they
become firm as a piece of cardboard, but vastly more pliant.
Then the sheets are emblazoned, and the text painted on,
the whole being enclosed between richly ornamented teak
boards.   Few more splendid-looking manuscripts can be
seen anywhere.   Occasionally copies are found engrossed on
thin sheets of ivory or copper, but those on the royal pasos,
called Wut-lè Kammawāsās, are most highly esteemed.   The
text is always read in a peculiar way, in a high-pitched, jerky
recitative, which is not without a certain impressive effect.

The following detailed account of the ceremony of initiation is taken from the second volume of Bishop Bigandet's *Life of Gautama*, the bulk of it being a translation of the Kammawāsā :—

As soon as the pyin-sin have taken their places, the Kammawā-sayā (the secretary) introduces the novitiant duly clothed and bearing the necessary utensils. The candidate kneels down, and, with his hands raised to his forehead and his body bent, repeats three times :

" Venerable president, I acknowledge you to be my upyitsi."

The assistant, addressing himself to the candidate, says :

" Dost thou acknowledge this to be thy father, and these thy sacred vestments ? "

The candidate audibly answers " Yes," and then withdraws to a distance of twelve cubits from the assembled fathers, whom the Kammawā-sayā addresses as follows :

" Venerable upyitsi, and you, brethren, here assembled, listen to my words. The candidate who now stands in a humble posture before you solicits from the upyitsi the favour of being honoured with the dignity of pyin-sin. If it appears to you that everything is properly arranged and disposed for this purpose, I will duly admonish him."

Then turning to the candidate he says :

" O candidate, be attentive to my words, and beware lest on this solemn occasion thou utterest an untruth, or concealest aught from our knowledge. Learn that there are certain incapacities and defects which render a person unfit for admission into our order. Moreover, when before the assembly thou art interrogated respecting such defects, thou art to answer truly and declare what incapacities thou mayest labour under. Now this is not the time to remain silent and decline thy head ; every member of the assembly has a right to interrogate thee at his pleasure, and it is thy bounden duty to return an answer to all his questions.

" Candidate ! Art thou affected with leprosy or any such odious malady ? Hast thou scrofula or any similar complaint ? Dost thou suffer from asthma or cough ? Art thou affected with those complaints which arise from a corrupted blood? Art thou afflicted by madness or other ills caused by giants, witches, or the evil spirits of the forests or mountains?"

To each question the candidate answers—

"From such complaints and bodily disorders I am free."

The examination continues:

"Art thou a man?"

"I am."

"Art thou a true and legitimate son?"

"I am."

"Art thou involved in debts?"

"I am not."

"Art thou the bondman and underling of some great man?"

"I am not."

"Have thy parents given their consent to thy ordination?"

"They have."

"Hast thou reached the age of twenty years?"

"I have."

"Are thy vestments and sacred begging-bowl prepared?"

"They are."

"Candidate, what is thy name?"

"Wago (a vile and unworthy being)."

"What is the name of thy master?"

"His name is upyitsi."

The assistant then turns to the assembled yahans and says:

"Venerable upyitsi, and ye assembled brethren, be pleased to listen to my words. I have duly admonished this candidate who seeks from you admission to our order. Does the present moment appear to you a meet and a fit one for his admission? If so, I will order him to approach."

The fathers remaining silent, the assistant instructs the postulant to go close to the assembly and to ask that he may be received. The candidate approaches the assembly, and sitting before them in a respectful attitude, resting on his heels, raises his joined hands and says three times, "I beg, O fathers of this assembly, to be admitted as yahan. Have pity on me, take me from my present state of a layman, which is one of sin and imperfection, advance me to that of yahan, which is one of virtue and perfection."

The assistant then addresses the council and says :

" O ye fathers here assembled, hear my words. This candidate, humbly prostrated before you, begs of the upyitsi to be admitted among us ; he is free from all defects, corporeal infirmities, and mental incapacities that would otherwise debar him from entering our holy state ; he is provided with the patta and holy vestments, and he has duly asked the assembly in the name of the upyitsi for permission to be admitted. Now, therefore, let the assembled fathers complete his ordination. To whomsoever this seems good let him keep silence ; whosoever thinks otherwise, let him declare that the candidate is unworthy of admission."

This he repeats thrice, and then continues :

" Since then none of the fathers object, but all are silent, which is a sign that all have consented, so therefore let it be done. Let this candidate pass out of the state of sin and imperfection into the perfect state of a yahan, and thus, by the consent of the upyitsi and all the fathers, let him be received."

The fathers must note down under what shade, on what day, at what hour, and in what season the candidate has been received.

The reader of the Kammawā, addressing the candidate, continues :

" Let the candidate attend to the following account of the duties which are incumbent upon him, and to the faults which he must carefully avoid :—

" It is the duty of each member of our brotherhood to beg for his food with labour and with the exertion of the muscles of his feet, and through the whole course of his life he must gain his subsistence by the labour of his feet (he must not work with his hands, nor beg with his tongue). He is allowed to make use of all things that are offered to him in particular, or to the society in general, that are usually presented in banquets, that are sent by letter, and that are given on the new and full moon and at festivals. O candidate, all these things you may use for your food."

Candidate. " Sir, I understand what you tell me."

" It is a part of the duty of a member of our society to wear, through humility, yellow clothes made of rags thrown about in the streets or among the tombs.   If, however, by his talent and virtue, one procures for himself many benefactors, he may receive from them for his habit the following articles, namely, cotton and silk, or cloth of red (of a Thibetan origin) or yellow wool."

Candidate. " As I am instructed so will I perform."

" Every member of the society must dwell in a house built under the shade of lofty trees.   But if, owing to your zeal and virtue, you procure for yourself many benefactors who are willing to build for you a better habitation, you may dwell in it.   The dwelling may be made of bamboo, wood, or bricks, with roofs adorned with spires of pyramidal or triangular form."

Candidate. " I will duly attend to these instructions."

" It is incumbent upon an elect to use as medicine the urine of a cow or of a black bullock, whereon lime and the juice of a lemon or other sour fruit has been poured.   He may also use as medicines articles thrown out of markets, or picked up at the corners of streets.   He may accept for medicinal purposes nutmegs or cloves.   The following articles also may be used medicinally——butter, cream, and honey."

Candidate. " As I am instructed so will I perform."

The newly initiated yahan is now warned against the four sins, the commission of any one of which would entail the loss of the dignity he has just attained.

The Kammawā - sayā goes on : " Elect, being now admitted into our society, it is no longer lawful for you to indulge in carnal pleasures, whether with yourself or with animals.   He who is guilty of such a sin can no longer be numbered among the perfect.   Sooner shall the severed head be joined again to the neck, and life restored to the breathless body, than a pyin-sin who has committed fornication recover his lost sanctity.   Beware therefore lest you pollute yourself with such a crime."

Candidate. " As I am instructed so will I perform."

" Again, it is unlawful and forbidden for an elect to take things that belong to another, or even to covet them, although their value should not exceed a quarter of a tical (about six annas).   Whoever sins even to that small amount is thereby

deprived of his sacred character, and can no more be restored
to his pristine state than the branch cut from the tree can
retain its luxuriant foliage and put forth buds.   Beware of
theft during the whole of your mortal journey."

Candidate. "As I am instructed so will I perform."

"Again, an elect can never knowingly deprive any living
being of life, or wish the death of any one, however troublesome he may prove.   Sooner shall the cleft rock reunite so as
to make a whole, than he who kills any being be readmitted
into the society.   Cautiously avoid so heinous a crime."

Candidate. "As I am instructed so will I perform."

"Again, no member of our brotherhood can ever arrogate
to himself extraordinary gifts or supernatural perfections, or
through vainglory give himself out as a holy man ; such, for
instance, as to withdraw into solitary places, or on pretence
of enjoying ecstasies like the ariya, afterwards presume to
teach others the way to uncommon spiritual attainments.
Sooner the lofty palm-tree that has been cut down can become green again, than an elect guilty of such pride be
restored to his holy station.   Take care that you do not
give way to such an excess."

Candidate. "As I am instructed so will I perform."

(The pyin-sin who commits any one of these last four
sins is *ipso facto* excluded from the society.   Nothing can
palliate them.   Other sins may be atoned for by penance
and repentance, but one who has committed any one of these
crimes may indeed, if undetected, remain a member of the
order, but inwardly he no longer belongs to it.   He has
become a living lie.)

These denunciations end the ceremony.   The newly
made yahan falls in with the rest, and on the rising of the
council proceeds, in company with them, to his own monastery.   It is thus clearly seen that the mendicant receives no
spiritual powers whatever.   He simply becomes a member
of a holy society that he himself may observe the laws of
the Master more perfectly.   He has nothing to do with
guiding his fellow-monks or the laity.   The latter indeed
may gain for themselves easy merit by pressing alms upon
him, but that can hardly be said to be a merit in the pyin-sin.

They may also go and consult him, and he will read portions of the Law, and explain them as far as his learning permits. He occasionally reads the Law aloud in a rest-house near the pagoda on a feast day ; goes to a funeral, that the pious may have an opportunity of giving him presents, and so laying up a good store towards the kan of a future existence. But it is the teaching of the youth of the country that is his chief credit, and it is this that binds the country to the support of the monastic system.

Sometimes after the ritual of the Kammawā has been gone through, the sponsor of the elected pyin-sin stands up and reads a selection from the full rule of the order, which contains 227 precepts. This is called the Patimauk, or Book of the Enfranchisement, and its composition is attri-buted to the Lord Buddha himself ; but it is much more probably, indeed certainly, like the Kammawāsā, the slow growth and production of a long series of observant apostles. Every possible action of the pyin-sin during the day is anticipated, and the precise way in which it should be performed carefully set forth. The sins he may commit are divided under seven main heads, of which the first, called Parazikan, comprises the four cardinal sins mentioned above. The others may be atoned for by confession to the kyaung-pogo or sayā, who appoints a penance or not as he thinks fit. The punishments are not severe in character, and are usually to water the sacred trees, to sweep out the rooms, to walk for a stated time in the heat of the sun, to carry a number of baskets of earth from one place to another, to sleep without a pillow, or to keep a vigil by night in a churchyard. But a series of infractions of the law would meet with very severe treatment, if not from the heads of the monastery, then from the mass of the people outside. If a pyin-sin committed any one of the four cardinal sins, he would most assuredly be unfrocked and turned out of the monastery doors to the mercy of the people, and they would certainly stone him, and perhaps even put him to death. Such lapses, and even the commission of more venial offences, are very rare, for the weak-minded yahan is always free to turn layman whenever he chooses, without consulting any one but himself and his frailties.

The ceremony of excommunication, thabeit hmauk (literally, inverting the alms-bowl), is sufficiently solemn. The monks gather in a circle round the culprit, and the latter part of the Kammawā, that which is read to drive sickness and evil spirits out of a town, is gravely recited by the abbot, the surrounding brethren responding at the end of each sentence. When it is finished, his yellow robes are taken off him, his alms-bowl is turned mouth downwards, and he is hurried out of the monastery limits. His condition is pitiable. No one may speak to him ; no monk will take alms from him ; he can neither buy nor sell ; he is not allowed even to draw water from a well, or drink from the jars at a wayside zayat. He is as much an outcast as any pagoda slave, and grievous is the penance he must go through before he is once more received into the society even of laymen. It occasionally happens when there is much evil living in a district, or if the people are lax in their religious observances, that the brethren of the kyaung put the neighbourhood under a ban by inverting their alms-bowls, and refusing to go out begging. There is no greater proof of the power of the assembly than the rapidity with which this effects its purpose. The most careless are brought to a sense of their sinfulness in a few days. Such excommunication is, however, more and more rare.

Before the death of the Lord Buddha, the yahans all addressed one another as awutthaw ; but after he had attained the ne'ban of khan-das under the eng-gyin-bin (*Shorea robusta*), a recognition of relative rank was instituted. The inferiors, we are told, called the more advanced in the order, bante, while the juniors were addressed in their turn, by their proper name, or that of their family. In Burma, however, this regulation prevails only to a very slight extent. With the mendicants, as with the royalty, and indeed with the populace at large, it is considered uncivil to mention a person's name in conversation, and his rank, or the kyaung he belongs to, is used instead, or perhaps only the designation of his sacred profession. The laity indiscriminately address all wearers of the yellow robe as payā (lord).

Similarly the " punishment of Brahma," recommended by the great master to be employed against weaker brethren, is

little used.   This punishment was calculated to isolate the
offending brother.   The other yahans were to avoid speaking to him, to the extent of not even uttering a rebuke, if he
indulged in indiscreet talk.   Nowadays, when one pyin-sin
is irritated with another, he does not indeed talk to him, or
go and abuse him, but he advises the people to have nothing
to do with him, and give him no alms.

Indeed many laxities have crept in.   Some casuists
evade the rule against touching gold and silver.   It is becoming lamentably common for monks, otherwise eminently
pious and worthy of respect, not only not to refuse money,
but actually to receive it with their own hands—covered
with a handkerchief.   Such unprincipled playing with the
letter of the law is vehemently denounced by the Sulagandi,
and disliked by the more earnest laymen, even when the
pyin-sin does not personally shave so close to the wind, but
bids one of his schoolboys take the coin and put it in the
box.   Of a piece with this is the roundabout way of getting
anything the monk may especially desire.   He may not
directly ask for anything, if it were even food to save him
from starvation, far less must he bargain for the object he
wishes.   Therefore an elaborate method of exchange has
been invented by a yahan in whom the passion of covetousness was far from being extinguished.   He says, such and
such a thing " is useless to me ; but what is the value of
that ?   I have begging-bowls, iron, clay, and lacquer in
abundance, but my robe is sadly worn and discoloured.
That thengan is seemly and suitable for a holy man.   Thrice
blessed is he that giveth alms, his merit will wax great."
Very often he thus gets the thing he wants without having
to part with previous alms-gifts.   Others, perhaps, a little
more scrupulous, mention to the kappiyadāyaka, the manciple
of the kyaung, that they would be glad to have such and
such a thing, and he provides it out of the monastic funds.
All this trifling with the spirit of the patimauk is, however,
strenuously denounced by the Sulagandi, who in Lower
Burma have gathered a large proportion of the more right-
thinking of the laity to their side.

Some of the regulations of the Book of the Enfranchisement are very singular, but all may be traced to some one

of the fundamental precepts, and are not so ludicrous as some unbelievers would make out, except for the fact that they are set down so precisely when they might have been left to the imagination.

A monk must not build a monastery for himself without the aid of a benefactor. If his piety and talents are not such as to induce a layman to build a kyaung for him, let him patiently remain in the house into which he was ordained. He must see that the foundations of a monastery are not laid in a place where there are many insects or worms, which would thus be killed.

For a similar reason he must not dig himself, except in a sandy place, where there can be no animal life. Neither must he spit, nor do anything of that kind on green grass, nor in fresh water, nor is he allowed to climb trees. There was a discussion in the Lord Buddha's time as to whether vegetation could be regarded as anywhere in the ladder of existence. Shin Gautama, on being asked, said it could not. Still trees and grass must not be destroyed, for they support life in other creatures. A yahan may not drive in a carriage or ride a pony. He must not travel in the same boat or remain under the same roof with a woman, or even with a female animal. When he walks abroad he must neither walk fast nor dawdle and lounge about the streets. He must allow no woman to wash or clean his robes, nor eat food cooked by female hands, if he can get any other ; if a woman offers rice in her hand, he may take but not eat it. He must not look into a brother's thabeit, as suggesting that he does not receive much alms. He must not eat his food to the last mouthful, and must avoid highly-seasoned dishes as tending to heat the blood.

In return for their self-denial the pyin-sin are bountifully honoured by the people, from the sovereign on the throne, who vacates his seat for the thā-thanā-baing, to the beggar in the street who prostrates himself in the dust when the yahan passes by. In the country villages all make obeisance when the mendicant passes, and the women kneel down on each side of the road. Such outward marks of respect are not usual in the larger towns; but there is no lack of venera-tion, and all make way for the monk when he walks abroad.

The oldest layman assumes the title of disciple to the last inducted pyin-sin, and, with clasped hands, addresses him as payā, the highest title the language affords.   The monk's commonest actions, walking, eating, sleeping, are referred to in honorific language, different from that which would be used of a layman, or even of the king, performing the same thing.   The highest officials bow down before them, and impose upon themselves the greatest sacrifices, both of time and money, to build splendid kyaungs for them, and minister to their wants.   Finally, the monk's person is sacred and inviolable.   Nothing he does can subject him to the civil law.   He bears the title of Thagiwin Mintha, Thagiwin Prince, as the heir of the scion of Kapilawut, and receiver of his inheritance.

CHAPTER XIII

THE MONASTERIES

OUTSIDE every village in Burma, no matter how small, there stands a pôngyi kyaung. There may have been no one wealthy enough, or zealous enough, to build a pagoda, or the proximity of some ancient and eminently famous shrine may have rendered unnecessary a general subscription for such a purpose, but there is always a building for the mendicants. Away from the noise of the people—for the monastery must not have secular houses near it—surrounded by great, well-foliaged trees, tamarinds, mangoes, jacks, cocoa-nut, and areca, and palmyra palms, sâl trees, and the tha-bye-bin, to shield them from the heat and supply them with fruit, the monks' position is well calculated to attract those who are tired of the tumult and bickerings and sorrows of the world. There the pyin-sin pass their time without a care to ruffle the tranquil current of their lives ; without trouble as to their food, for a pious and kindly population supplies them far beyond their wants ; with no irksome duties, for nothing is required of them in return ; with no care but how to get through the day with as little trouble and ennui as possible ; seeking nothing but the fulfilment of the Law, and the path to eventual deliverance from the misery of ever-recurring existences ; no wonder many novices come to like the ways of the religious house and yearly swell the ranks of the order, so that there are no signs, two thousand five hundred years after the founding of the religion, of any weakening of its strength.

The first beikkus dwelt under the shade of the forest trees, or perhaps in small huts erected there to shelter them from the pitiless sun and the raging of the storms.   This is the explanation of the circumstance that every Budh is specially connected with some tree, as Shin Gautama with the bawdi-bin, the banyan, under which he attained his full dignity, and the eng-gyin-bin, the *Shorea robusta*, under which he was born and died, and, as we are told, the last Budh of this world cycle, Arimadeya, will receive his Buddhaship under the *Mesua ferrea*.   Hence the regard for trees which the Burmans share with so many other nations, ancient and modern, and the fact that a clump of palmyras and tamarinds seen in the distance infallibly suggests a monastery.   It is not to be supposed, however, that it was the intention of the Lord Buddha that the sacred order should remain far away from mankind in lonesome huts in the depths of the forest.   Very early in his teaching, kings, nobles, and wealthy men vied with one another in erecting spacious and magnificent dwellings for the Budh himself and his disciples.   Most noted among these were the Zetawun Monastery, built by the rich man Anatabein, within which the celebrated Mingala Thôt sermon was preached by the Buddha to a pious-minded déwa ; the Pôppayôn Kyaung and that of Weluwun built by the wealthy dame Withaka and King Bimbathara of Razagyo, to both of which Shin Gautama frequently retired to spend the rainy season of Lent.   These were all magnificently adorned ; and it is expressly mentioned that the pious need spare themselves no expense in constructing and adorning such religious buildings, though the inhabitant of the most gorgeous of them dresses in no way differently from the humblest anchorite, and has no more costly utensils.

Ordinarily the monastery is built of teak, though in many places, both in Mandalay and Lower Burma, brick buildings are being erected, notwithstanding the prejudice that exists against them from their greater liability to damage in the case of earthquakes.   The shape is always oblong, and the inhabited portion is raised on posts or pillars, some eight or ten feet above the ground.   They are, like all the other houses in the country, never more than one story high ; for if it is an indignity to a layman to have any one over his head, it is much more so to a member of the

brotherhood. The space between the ground and the floor
of the kyaung is always kept open and is never used except
by the school-boys, who have not arrived at notions of
personal dignity, and find the locality retired and convenient
for games at gôn-nyin-to, and the discussion of forbidden
eatables, or subjects of conversation. There are always a
few pariah dogs there too, dozing off the surfeit of food they
have had from the morning begging-pots, or the offerings at
the pagoda. A flight of steps of stone or wood leads up to
the verandah, which extends all along the north and south
sides, and frequently all round the building. If the steps
are of stone, or rather brickwork covered with plaster, they
are usually adorned at the foot by propylæa in the shape of
two bilus, or a couple of manôt-thiha—curious creatures,
half man half lion—usually bold enough in conception, if
somewhat rough in execution. Tiers of trefoil heads usually
characterise the parapets when they are of mason - work.
When the ladder is of wood it is covered with spirited carving
in deep relief, representing nats and ogres, dancing figures
and grim warriors, with abundant scroll-work as everywhere
else throughout the building.

From the raised floor thus reached, rises the building,
with tier upon tier of dark massive roofs, giving the appearance of many stories when there is actually but one, for the
reason already mentioned. This style of roofing was allowed
only for religious buildings, for the royal palaces, and for the
houses of a few high officials who acquired the honour by
special patent, and with whom the form and number of roofs
was a matter of regulation settled by the sumptuary laws.
Under British rule it is practically confined to monastic
buildings and the houses of feudatory chiefs. This spire-
like style of roof is called pyathat, and properly there are
but three kinds : with three super-imposed roofs called
yāma, with five roofs called thuba, and with seven, as the
royal palace and the most sacred kyaungs, called thuyāma.
The ends of the gables are adorned with pinnacles or finials,
each with a curious wooden flag at the top and crowned
with a hti, gilt and furnished with bells, copper, silver, or
gold, the whole being elaborately carved. The triple, quin-
tuple, and septuple roofs of the monastic houses, with their

elaborate adornments, there is little doubt found their origin in the opportunity which wood gave for the development of ornament in the way of carving.   If the wooden monasteries are compared with the strikingly similar wooden churches in Norway—at Hitterdal, for example, or Borgund—we have a proof that nature, under like circumstances, always produces like results from human ingenuity.   It may be added that the simple tumulus, which was the original idea of the bell-pagoda, is also found in the Scandinavian *haug*.

The kyaung accommodation is very simple.   It consists in the main of a great central hall divided into two portions, one level with the verandah where the scholars are taught, and most of the duties of the monastery carried on, and the other a raised dais, two feet or so above the level of the rest of the building.   Seated upon this the yahans are accustomed to receive visitors, and at the back, against the wall, are arranged the images of Buddha, a large one usually standing in the centre on a kind of altar with candles, flowers, praying flags, and other offerings placed before it, and on shelves alongside a number of smaller figures of gold, silver, alabaster, clay or wood, according to the popularity of the kyaung and the faith of the neighbourhood.   Close by are placed also the manuscript chests, sadaiks, small shrines, models in wood of monasteries and pagodas, the fans and other religious implements of the pyin-sin and the gifts of the pious, heaped together ordinarily in very careless fashion. The central image is almost invariably placed on the eastern side of the building.   There are occasionally dormitories for the monks, but as a rule they sleep in the central hall, where the mats which form their beds may be seen rolled up round the pillow against the wall.   In many monasteries there is a special room for the palm-leaf scribes, often detached from the main building, as are the cook-room and the bathing-houses.

The whole area of the extensive compound in which the monastery stands is enclosed by a heavy teak fence with massive squared posts and rails, seven or eight feet high. All within this parawun is sacred ground, and the laity, when they enter, take off their shoes and carry them in their hands. This rule applies to the highest in the land, and when a

Shan prince or a high official arrives on his elephant, he must dismount at the monastery gate, and come in reverently barefooted.   Within the one encircling fence there may be, and usually are, quite a number of separate buildings like that described, with their ecclesiastical roofs towering up, dark, or glittering with gold-leaf among the bright green foliage of the pipul and tamarind trees.   Each house has a prior or superior, with his two or three brethren, and a certain number of probationers and scholars, and in the central building dwells the gaing-ôk, or sadaw.   In a corner of the compound, or just outside, there is almost always a thein, a building for the performance of various rites and ceremonies, more particularly for the examination and ordination of yahans.   The ground on which these stand is not only holy now, but has always been so since the Lord Buddha first preached the Law.   When a new thein is to be built it is usually found possible to exhume the remains of an old building of the same kind, thus proving the immemorial sanctity of the site.   Otherwise the ground is dedicated to religion in perpetuity.   The consecration of the ground is, however, rare in these latter times, though several times the British Government has been asked to make a formal grant of land, to be used for religious purposes.   Not far from Rangoon, in the neighbourhood of the Kyaik-ka-san pagoda, there is a thein-gyi, regarded as particularly holy, from the tradition that it is built over the remains of one of the yahanda, who brought the remains of Shin Gautama to Rangoon.

Within the monastery precincts are usually, also, one or two tasaungs, highly ornamented tectums, erected over an image of the Buddha.   Very many zealous priors put up marble stones, or finger-posts, at certain points beyond the Parawun, with inscriptions on them to the effect that U Adeisa's or Pyinyazawta's monastery is to the westward, or southward, and you must not kill animals or conduct yourself in an unseemly manner near it.   It is the ignoring or the ignorance of this injunction which has brought many sporting Englishmen into trouble, and led them to believe that the yahans condemn shooting altogether, and lay themselves out to thwart it ; whereas the intention is only to avoid witnessing, if possible, what they regard as a flagrant sin, and especially to protect the pigeons, which usually flock about the monastic trees.   Not many people in England would think of going to shoot in a churchyard.

The majority of kyaungs in the jungle and in the smaller towns are plain teak wood, or brick and lime structures, with more or less ornate carving and moulding, and interior decorations ; but to see the really gorgeous ecclesiastical buildings one must journey to Mandalay.   There the Kyaung-daw-gyi, the Royal Monastery, is the most striking collection of edifices of their kind to be seen in the world. At the foot of Mandalay Hill, just outside the eastern gate of the city, it extends over an area of a good many acres. Every building in it is magnificent ; every inch carved with the ingenuity of a Chinese toy ; the whole ablaze with gold-leaf and a mosaic of fragments of looking-glass, embedded in a resinous gum, while the zinc roofs glisten like silver in the sun, and the golden bells on the gable spires tinkle melodiously with every breeze.   The huge posts are gilt all over, or covered with a red lacquer ; the eaves and gables represent all kinds of fantastic and grotesque figures.   The interior is no less elaborate, the panels of wall and ceiling are some carved, some diapered with the mosaic mirror work, glistening like polished metal with a rough gold mesh net thrown over it.   The wood-carving is particularly fine ; the effect in some places, where the birds, pecking, taking wing, alighting, and in every other variety of attitude, are so cut as to appear to underlie the profuse flower tracery, being especially clever.   The amount of gilding, spread thickly over every part of the kyaung, alone represents many hundred pounds.   Singular from its plain unadorned appearance is the high, brown teak-wood tower in one corner, to which the Sadaw-gyi and his monks occasionally withdraw, to devote themselves to contemplation and the task of learning to know themselves and the khandas, as well as the Seit and the Seikdathit.   For this withdrawal from their gorgeous surroundings, to indulge in abstract thought, they have the example and precept of the Lord Buddha himself, who, even when he reposed as a babe on the bosom of his aunt Gautami, gave himself over to contemplation.

The whole of the flat land between Mandalay Hill and

the city walls was formerly covered with monasteries, each of them standing separate and enclosed within its own parawun, and almost all presided over by a sadaw, a monk of the highest rank. They were thus entirely independent of each other. One of the most interesting for Englishmen is the Thiho Taik, the "Ceylon Monastery," presided over by Lingayāmā, a sadaw who was in great favour with Mindôn Min, the last king but one. The term taik is always applied to a " bishop's monastery," as implying that his is the chief of a number of kyaungs, all under his care, and in which he makes occasional sojourns. The Thiho Taik is peculiar for its trim appearance. It is very new ; the under part of all the buildings is of brick ; the compound is kept scrupulously clean ; there is not a single large tree in it, and the parawun is a neat sawn-wood fence, instead of being, as is the case almost everywhere else, composed simply of huge stems of trees placed side by side in the ground. The sadaw himself is a very enlightened man. He has been several times to Rangoon to worship at the Great Pagoda, and to decide on questions in dispute. He has, in his library, copies of the English Scriptures in the Burmese version of Judson, and has read them through. Numbers of American Baptists' tracts, and the sacred books of other religions, have also a place in his manuscript chests. These are all deposited in a separate building standing in the middle of the enclosure, and used for no other purpose, except that the scribes sit here making copies of borrowed MSS., or setting down notes of the learned bishop himself. The palm-leaf book is still universal, and the work of making up a volume is therefore very laborious ; for the most practised manipulator cannot, with his agate style and light strip of palmyra-leaf, exceed the speed of an English boy who has just got over the preliminary difficulties of pot-hooks and hangers. The letters scratched on the leaf are made more distinct by the application of crude earth-oil. This serves to darken the writing, as well as to preserve the book. The regular scribes are always laymen, and it is a matter of very considerable unpleasantness to the cenobites, that the cleverest of them are very often uncommonly bad livers, spending all their gains in libations of " Old Tom," or little balls of opium. These vagaries are, however, frequently winked at, for a copyist who can write neatly and with accuracy is far from being common.

The Thiho Taik library is a model in its way. It is nearly the best monastic collection in Mandalay, and is certainly far better arranged than any other. The sadaiks, or manuscript boxes, are arranged in three rows, one over the other; the thôts and zāts—the sermons and birth-stories —of the Lord Buddha below; above them the Cinghalese commentaries and exegeses; and on the top shelf Burmese translations and the explanations of various learned sadaws. Each chest contains a large number of different books, every separate collection of leaves being enclosed between wooden boards, some plain, some carved in high relief, with figures of déwas and demons. Round this is wrapped a kabalwè, a square piece of cloth with inwoven scenes from the sacred books, or portions of the Law, and the formulæ used at the pagoda. Most of these are of silk, very often with narrow slips of bamboo worked in so as to give stiffness to the whole. Instead of this, or sometimes in addition, is used the sā - si - gyo, a riband, about two fingers' breadth, and upwards of a yard in length. This is knitted or crocheted in a peculiarly close fashion, which puzzles English ladies. On it is worked the name of the owner, his titles and distinctions, and whatever other aspirations he chooses to add. They are very neat, and quite easy to read, an advantage which does not always characterise Berlin wool work. The king's grants of forest land, monopolies, and the like, were usually executed in this way.

All the boxes are kept carefully locked, and the door is barred at night, for such a library represents years of labour, and could only with the greatest difficulty be replaced. It is only in Mandalay that libraries of any value are to be found. In Lower Burma the majority of the kyaungs do not even possess a complete copy of the three parts of the Bitaghat, the Buddhist Bible, and some few have nothing beyond a copy of the Kammawāsā, and perhaps a Malla Lingaya Wuttu, a life of the Lord Buddha, or something of the kind. Many others have, no doubt, valuable collections, but the monks are ignorant, they cannot read the books themselves, and they do not care to exhibit them to those who can. Consequently, they moulder away in the bottom of the sadaik, crushed away into the darkest corner of the main room of the monastery. It is, perhaps, not surprising that the most learned monks do not belong to the large towns, but come from remote kyaungs in the depths of the jungle. This is true also of Upper Burma, for though the sadaws in Mandalay are the most learned in the country, they have acquired their reputation in jungle monasteries, and have only been summoned to the royal city when their fame has spread over the land, and the title of royal teacher has been conferred on them.

The main room of Lingayāmā's Monastery contains a great number of curiosities collected by the Burmese Embassies on their travels through Europe. Most of these were presented by the Kin Wun-gyi, the head of the mission, and are in many ways most interesting. Prominent is a large photograph album, emblazoned with the Italian royal arms and containing a fine collection of views. Another album is filled with cartes of members of the Embassy, notably of the lamented Naingan-gyaw Wun-dauk, the portly and good-natured " Pio Nono " of the *Daily News*, who seems never to have missed being photographed wherever he went, and figured in every style, from the penny smudge, apparently taken on a country race-course or outside Battersea Park, to the coloured and gilt grandeur of a Neapolitan cabinet. The author of the *Encyclopædia of Burmese Literature* had no notion of changing the expression of his face, however. He looks stolidly like just having had his dinner in every impression, and the multiplication of photographs serves principally as a means of comparing different styles of art, and exhibiting the great stock of clothing which the worthy Wun-dauk carried about with him.

In addition to the photographs, there is a great collection of engravings, some of them very valuable ; and mixed up with these are to be found some very queer items—old hotel bills, advertisements of gigantic hosiery establishments, with pictures of the same at the top, circus play-bills, shilling view guides, some sheets of the *Graphic*, the front page of the wrapper of *Punch*, and a few railway tickets. These are all carefully preserved, along with many other gifts of the home-keeping pious; rolls of yellow cloth, Dutch clocks, betel-nut boxes, spare spittoons, and begging-pots, rugs, and pots of honey. The images of the kyaung, contrary to the usual custom, are placed in a glass case in the centre of the room, instead of at the east end. This situation is due to their value, most of them being of silver or gold, and one or two studded with precious stones.

The Thiho Taik was certainly one of the neatest and most methodically arranged monasteries to be seen any-where. Unfortunately it was burnt with many others in the year of the Annexation. There were many more gorgeously decorated, and still more that were larger. The biggest in Burma was probably the Maha Yatana Paung-daw, which stood near the great Arakan Pagoda in the suburbs of Mandalay, and was in great part burnt down in 1879. The building, with its encircling platform, measured 440 feet by 200, and was supported by 404 massive teak trees, none less than two feet in diameter, and the central posts, which upheld the topmost tier of roof, must have been quite eighty feet in height. Near Maul-mein, in Lower Burma, there is another kyaung remarkable for the huge girth of its posts.

The brick monasteries are commonest in the neighbour-hood of Mandalay and other old capitals. They are covered with chunam, and in place of having a spire, are themselves built in the form of a pya-that, rising in the shape of rectangular terraces to a considerable height. Round the central hall, which is often divided by a gilt railing across the centre, are a number of cloisters and corridors, which ensure a perpetual cool breeze. Many of these monasteries are adorned with fresco paintings in the hall and in the honeycomb of corridors, representing usually scenes from the Zāts, passages in the life of Shin Gautama, an especially favourite one being the Jataka of Nemi, where the pious prince is represented as a white ghostly figure in a chariot, passing, like the *pius Æneas*, through the dismal abodes of hell and the six heavens of the nats. Some other represen-tations portray the occupations of daily life, such as feasting, hunting, weaving, and the different nationalities to be seen in the country. A very common scene shows the punishment which awaits fishermen in the next existence. The miserable destroyer of animal life is represented as dangling by the tongue on a fish-hook, while demons jerk him into the air, and drop him back into a lake of burning pitch. Many of them have inscriptions below to explain the subject of the picture. Thus in Pagàn :—

"When King Ne-bin Min-gyi reigned in Methila over the ten governors, according to the old books, the Thagya Min came from the nat heavens to help him."

"In the Monastery Yatana Shwe-daing, our Lord preached the Patenôn Tagayo, and remained several days."

"Shin Thumeda (Gautama), in the land of Thudawdana, received the Buddhaship under the banyan tree."

"Payā Alaung Theidat (the embryo Budh, Prince Siddartha), the King's son, married 4000 charming Yathe-mya."

"Our Lord rides on the elephant Nalagiri."

And so on in great variety. One also often finds such a notice as this scrawled on the wall : "In order to be prepared and to gain happiness in the seats of men, of nats, and of ne'ban, the rice-pots are set in order, the images are erected, and the paintings on the walls painted."

The monasteries are built, supported, and furnished by the pious, but there are not a few of them that have considerable sums of money laid away, usually under the control of the kappiya-dāyaka, the layman who lives in the kyaung, and provides for the wants of its inmates. A number of the royal fields round about Aungbinle, where the Burmese army assembled to seek victory before entering on a campaign, were set apart for the use of the Royal monastery at Payā Gyi, and the revenues were kept in a huge money-chest, which was always under the care of a guard of soldiers. Much of the money was devoted to the adornment of the adjacent pagoda. None can be spent on embellishing the monastery itself. That would be as great a sin as if a monk should build one for himself, besides that it would be depriving the populace of much opportunity for gaining merit.

There are a few monasteries of the Pônnas here and there in the large towns throughout the country. These

Brahmin priests were originally brought captives from Manipur, and have been employed as astrologers ever since, their ranks being occasionally recruited by new arrivals. One of the requests preferred to Colonel Symes on his embassy to Ava in 1796 was that he would persuade the Governor-General to send a learned Brahmin and his wife to the capital. The race has been maintained tolerably pure, and the Pônna is readily distinguishable in the streets from the pôngyi. The astrologers muster naturally in greatest force in Mandalay, and their monastery there is situated in a magnificent grove of trees south of the town, and close to the cemeteries. Unlike the native religious, they do not raise their houses on posts above the ground, but follow the Indian custom of having the mat-covered earth for their floor. Foreigners are not admitted into their temples, but there is no objection to the images being brought out by a Pônna for exhibition to his friends. They worship Krishna and twenty-five other deities, but have all but no congregation, few of their faith coming to Mandalay, and those laymen who were carried away at the same time as themselves into captivity having turned to the Buddhist faith.

No yahan is allowed to have a separate monastery built for him until he has spent five full Wā under the discipline of a prior. These Lents must also be consecutive. According to their seniority in this respect the monks obtain names. Thus a pyin-sin who has spent five years—which of course is implied by the Wā—is called Anuti, and is a fit object for the pious to honour by erecting a special kyaung for him. When he has been ten years in the order he is addressed as Myizza-ti, and those who have remained steadfastly for twenty years, attain to the full honour of Mahā-ti. Such a self-denying man is always sure of a magnificent funeral when he dies.

It is a very good point about the life in the monastery that the great austerities and absurd mortifications of the flesh indulged in by the Brahminical houses find no place with the Buddhists, who reject them as unnecessary and unprofitable. The life of the initiated is one of constant self-denial ; all superfluities and luxuries are renounced ; all that is calculated to excite the passions is forbidden ; but there

are no revolting self-inflicted penances such as are regarded
as meritorious in themselves by the followers of the Hindu
creed.   Fasts and penitential deeds are indeed recommended
to those living in the world, but that is because such methods
are the best means for weakening the passions, and increasing
the power of the spirit as against the flesh.   They are not a
part of perfection.   They are not even on the direct way to
the attainment of perfection.   That is only to be achieved
by meditation, by pondering on the various aspects of the
substances and truths in the world.   Therefore the pyin-sin
do not make any difference, except in the case of the very
austere, in the observance of the appointed duty days, during
which it is incumbent on the laity to abstain from food up
till mid-day.   After noontide the yahan never eats.   Considerable scandal is sometimes caused by the tricks of sundry
of the weaker vessels.   They sit all day with their back to
the sun, and if in the afternoon they feel hungry, they ask a
scholar if it is yet noon.   The wily kyaung-tha, thinking to
escape a thrashing on the morrow, promptly answers that it
is a good way off twelve o'clock yet, and brings wherewithal
to solace the hungry religious.   The falsehood, or *suppressio
veri*, on the part of the scholar is a venial offence at his age,
and the yahan escapes sin, for if he breaks the law it is
because he was deceived.   Again, Englishmen are often
puzzled to know, in a country where, even now, clocks are by
no means common, and where they are found, usually show
the wrong time, how it is that the people know what o'clock
it is.   The matter is simple enough when the sun is to be
seen, for its course is pretty nearly the same all the year
round, and the Burman is tolerably skilled in guessing the
time from its height or from the length of the shadows thrown.
But it is different during the rainy season, when the sun is
often not to be seen for weeks at a time.   Here, however, so
say the yahans, whom it most seriously concerns, a singular
dispensation of nature steps in to their aid.   The cocks and
hens of Buddhist countries are not as the tame villatic fowl
of Western lands.   I do not refer to their powers of flying,
which are sufficiently irritating to hungry life-taking voyagers,
but to the fact that the cocks crow at stated hours, four
times a day—at sunrise, noon, sundown, and midnight.

They thus inform the inmates of the kyaung when they must cease eating for the day, and enable them to obey the provisions of the Patimauk. This useful acquirement of the Buddhist chanticleer was acquired in a singular way. Sundry books of the Bedin were burnt as containing unlawful cabalistic teachings. Among these was the Ā-tappana Bedin. When the fire had died out the barn-door flock came and pecked at the ashes, and so assimilated the astronomic lore contained in the book. I never had the opportunity of watching any particular cock to see if he actually crowed four times a day at the times reported. They fly about so, that for purposes of observation they might just as well be jungle fowl.

Thus even the powers of nature conspire for the well-being of the monks. It has been shown how the laity provide them with food and splendid dwellings. It may be unhesitatingly asserted that the most luscious fruits and the most delicate viands all find their way to the monasteries. A single instance will show to what an extent this is carried. In jungle places, where in the dry season there is often a great dearth of water, one spring is always set apart for the kyaung, because it would be a great sin, as well as being unpleasant for the yahan, to drink water which had been stirred up, and for that reason would be more likely to contain animal life. This reservation often compels the entire village to walk a mile or more for a supply of water, a very serious inconvenience to the easy-going Burman. In order that strangers and passers-by may have no excuse for drinking from the monastic well, a yellow cloth is hung over it from a bush or a post erected for the purpose. Here again a stumbling-block and stone of offence is set up in the way of the ignorant or unreflecting foreigner.

Everything near the monastery is rendered sacred, not merely when it is enclosed in the parawun, but as far as the prior may choose to proclaim it. This is especially common in the case of the large tanks or bricked reservoirs which the pious dig in many parts of the country. These are frequently well stocked with fish and turtle, and when the monks declare them sacred, the fish often become wonderfully tame from the abundant food that is brought them by yahans

solicitous as to their welfare. A regular thing after worship
in the Arakan Pagoda at Mandalay is to go and feed the
great turtle in the tank at the back of the cloisters. There
are rows of women selling balls of cooked rice, cakes, and
other delicacies which the pious buy for the consumption of
the sacred reptiles. There was great consternation when, in
March 1879, the tank dried up and many of the huge
creatures died before the people could get water enough
from the river, brought in chatties and household utensils, to
save them from such a sad fate. The circumstance was
supposed to be a sign from the nat guardians of the place
of their abhorrence and anger at the shedding of the royal
blood by King Theebaw in his holocaust of February. But
taking further and totally innocent life seemed a rather
singular fashion of expressing disapprobation.

The dog-fish of the Thihadaw Monastery, situated on a
small island in the middle of the third and lowest defile of
the Irrawaddy, are particularly celebrated, and having been
referred to by every traveller in Burma, the little kyaung
with its stone pagoda (one of the few of that material in the
country) has become a regular show-place for all passengers
to Bhamaw. The great five-feet-long, gape-mouthed
creatures seem to know their bounds, and do not wander
farther than half a mile or so from their sanctuary.

But this is far from being such a remarkable case as
previous writers have seemed to imply. There is a tank
with tame fish at the Maze Monastery near the Shwe Dagên
pagoda in Rangoon. All monastic tanks have fish more
or less tame, according to the good nature and sympathies
of the cenobites, and there is, or was, at least one other
place on the Irrawaddy where the fish were as domestic as
the dog-fish of Thihadaw. This was near the Kyaik-lat
pagoda and monastery, on one of the numerous mouths of
the great river. I knew the place well years ago, and then
there used to be great conflicts between the ill-conditioned,
impious fishermen and the monks. The fish were of the
species called nga-dan, well known on English breakfast-
tables under the name of " butter-fish," and to provide for
the unscrupulous appetites of the foreigner, people used
to come at night to catch the unsuspecting nga-dan. The

yahans had taught the fish to come and be fed when they beat on the bank and cried Tit, tit, tit ; and it was easy to bring them up at any time by following this method. The fishermen came about midnight, and stamped on the bank, and when the nga-dan came, promptly whisked them out with a landing net. The scholars and novitiants had to take turn at watching for these marauders, and if any were discovered, the abbot with his entire *posse comitatus* sallied out to the rescue of his domesticated fish. If the impious life-taker was alone, or if the abbot's was the stronger party, the offenders were incontinently thrashed, and the young ko-yins wielded their cudgels with an energy and knowledge of tender spots which ordinarily made the victim give up his vile practices for the future. If, however, the law-breakers were in force, then the abbot adopted less violent tactics— though it would have gone hard with any hardened sinner who might have ventured to strike a pyin-sin. He simply sat down and preached the Law to them, recited the Ten Precepts, enumerated the horrors of hell, and thus soon choked them off for that occasion at any rate. But the presence and example of the English, and more especially their money, has a very bad effect on weak-minded, un-principled men. In Upper Burma such a contest between wrong-doers and the upholders of the first of the Five Precepts could never have been prolonged—Thihadaw, where such scandals never occur, is indeed an instance of it ; and since the country-side would not rise to the aid of the pyin-sin, they had to adopt other measures to save their friends and enjoy peaceful nights. They persuaded a pious supporter to dig a large tank near the river-bank and to connect it by a narrow ditch with the river. Then they devoted the results of a whole morning's begging to enticing the nga-dan into the tank, beating first at the mouth of their canal and then all along the banks of it, till they had got all safe in the tank, which abutted on the enclosure of the kyaung. But alas ! this was done in the rainy season, and when the hot weather came round the water got shallow and warm, and the fish sickened and died ; and in order to pre-serve at least some of them, the survivors had to be taken back to the river again. When I last was at Kyaik-lat, there were still a good number of the tame fish, tame enough to allow you to stroke them and put gold-leaf on their heads, but there were far from being as many as there should have been had the villagers duly observed the teachings of the Buddha.   The primeval simplicity of the people is fast fading away throughout the province.   The travelling Englishman finds no difficulty in either getting people to sell fowls, or others still less hampered by doubts, to wring their necks and cook them.

The monastery sometimes has a name of its own ; more frequently it is called by the Pali name of the town or pagoda near which it lies, or by that of its prior.   The Thayet-daw Kyaung in Rangoon is so called from the magnificent mango-trees that grow within it.   Well known in Upper Burma is the monastery of U Sandimā, or the Mingala-san Taik, where King Mindôn received his instruction in the religious texts which he knew so well.   The name is usually given by the founder after consultation with the proposed head of the community, and it cannot be said that the consultation results in much originality.

Here and there throughout the country there are a few yatheit, hermits who withdraw into solitude in forests and desert places, and, like the old rathi (from which word of course the Burman term is derived), they live on wild fruits and roots and the chance alms of passers-by.   But as the rathi were closely connected with the Brahmins, and as the custom is not recommended by the Buddha, nor looked upon with favour by the people, it is not of frequent occurrence. Occasionally a very austere monk buries himself in the solitude of the jungle during the season of Lent, in order the better to devote himself to meditation, but even this is not common.   Nevertheless in the rocks above Nyaung-u, near Pagān, there are a few cells dug out high up in the cliffs which are always occupied, as any one who has gone out to shoot the rock pigeons which abound there will very speedily find.   The yatheit comes down, confiscates the bag, and drives away the sportsman with terrible threats of future punishment.   Such caves and holes in the rocks are not un-common on other parts of the Irrawaddy, wherever the ascetic is able to climb up and finds the stratum soft enough to hack

out with his axe and hollow with his finger-nails. There were
a few such cells cut in the rocks at the back of Mandalay
Hill, and visitors to the sacred spot occasionally came across
one of the hermits striding along, wrapped in thought, grasping an iron staff hung with rings, the rattle of which warns
the people to get out of the way and not disturb the holy
man's meditations. A few go away from human society
altogether, just as St. Simeon Stylites isolated himself on a
pillar, and the old Culdee monks from the north of England
and Scotland wandered off to the snowy wastes of Iceland,
there to seek repose and relief from the turmoil of the world.
It is said that the Thadda, the grammar, was added to the
Bitaghat, that the hermits who had withdrawn to the jungle
might not destroy the power of the sermons and lauds by
mispronunciation.

Mandalay Hill is always occupied, for the spot is particularly sacred. King Mindôn used to send thither daily
a hundred fowls which had been bought and saved from
death, and the pious gave them plenty to eat. Similar
proceedings caused the sneer of Purchas, " For men they
hadde not an hospitall that were thus hospitall to fowles " ;
but this is hardly deserved, at any rate in Burma. There
in every monastery the Kappiya-dayaka has a stock of
money, raised by selling the presents given to the monks,
which he devotes in charity to the well-deserving sick and
to poor travellers, while any one is welcome at all times to
shelter and food in the kyaung as long as he conducts himself properly. The yatheit may be looked upon with pious
awe for his austerities and mortifications of the flesh, but the
ordinary pyin-sin is more favourably regarded. The building of monasteries and the giving of presents to their
inmates is a constant strain on the generosity of the people.
It is far more difficult to keep the balance of merit on the
right side in Burma than in other countries. Almsgiving is
a constant and imperative expense, in addition to regular
and personal worship at the pagoda. In Thibet wind or
water drives the prayer-machines for extinguishing sin, and
the goodman acquires merit while he is snoring at night
with his wife at his back. In some parts practical householders are able to calculate exactly what is set down to

their credit, by the expedient of having the prayer-wheels turned when necessary by oxen. But nothing of this kind is practicable in Burma. You must pay your devotions in person, and unless you supplement these by almsgiving, your prospects towards a next existence are not such as your friends can regard otherwise than with concern. Fortunately the more holy the receiver the greater the merit of the alms. To support one hundred ordinary men is not so much as to feed one yahan, and so on in increasing ratio. The merit of giving one single meal to a Buddha outweighs that of supplying ten million Pyitzega Buddhas with food. Thus the kyaungs are always well furnished, and their advantage in affording education to the children further gives them a hold over the country. It will be long before the number of monasteries decreases in Burma.

CHAPTER XIV

SCHISMATICS

THE Buddhist religion is to its adherents the full and entire truth, and has remained almost entirely free from the schisms and dissensions which have sprung up in most other religions, especially in those of Europe, where the progress of science has caused the rise of multitudes of sects. Fully bound by their religion, in the complete sense of the word, are only the worshipper of the fetish whose object of adoration hangs up in his house, or dangles about his neck, and the Buddhist, whose teachers and models of faith rise and fall in flesh and blood before his eyes, vanishing to Ne'ban, there to be freed from all earthly concern, but leaving behind them as a guide to the same last resting-place the sacred World-Law, and at the same time the Assembly of the Perfect, who appear as an incarnation of that Law for the building up of piety among the laity. The yahans have already beaten down the adversaries within them, and, clothed with the yellow robe of transfiguration, exhibit in their persons the glorious results of adherence to the Law. Thus the reverence paid to the monks is a kind of spiritual hero-worship in the sense in which Carlyle speaks of it.

The man yet a slave in the bondage of his lusts and passions gazes in admiration on these models, to whom the recognition of earthly vanity gives strength enough to reject all the allurements of the world and to live only for the future. The spirits are always present to the fetish-worshipper, for hideous devils scare him away from every natural object. So the great secret of the existence of the world is ever present to the Buddhist, and while in the political and social

life of the European nations the manifold character of the
questions of the day attract and occupy the minds and
influence the religious beliefs of the people, the eyes of the
Burman Buddhist are uninterruptedly fixed on the dark
mysteries which surround his beginning, his end, and every
moment of his existence.   His religion enters into every
action of his life, and its admirable system of morality need
fear comparison with none other on earth ; while everything
else appears but as a matter of detail, or a different method
of viewing the same things.   He is not at all unwilling to
enter into discussion as to what is the true religion : whether
only one is the right, whether all have sprung from the same
root and have only now assumed different forms, or whether,
as the Deity gave to the hand different fingers, so He has
given to mankind different paths.   But the arguments of the
proselytiser have but very little success, while, on the other
hand, there is nowadays practically no attempt to gain con-
verts to their own national faith.   This is no doubt in
great part due to the absence of all ministerial duties in the
brethren of the yellow robe, but also to a belief that true
faith can only grow up gradually, and cannot be forced on
the mind.   At the same time there is not a hint of bigotry.
In Mandalay all forms of religion were allowed to be carried
on without the least semblance of opposition.   The solemn
call of the muezzin ; the tinkling of the convent-bell, under
the cross of Rome ; the noisy rites of devil and fire-wor-
shippers ; even the ceremonies of the former fierce enemies
of Buddhism, the Brahmins—all of these were exercised
without the least hindrance, and the processions of the various
forms of faith passed one another in the street with the
most complete amicability.   Even a convert is left unharmed.
There may be a sense of wonder and contempt for the man
who voluntarily resigns his high hopes as a Buddhist for the
probable fallacies of another cult, but there is never any real
attempt at oppression.

Heresies, therefore, never originate with the people ; any
there are come from the monasteries, but even these relate
more to matters of discipline and internal regulation than to
real points of faith.   The yahans are very clever in dispute,
and are far from being averse to it.   The better educated of

them know their ground perfectly well, and are quite able to take full advantage of the strong points of their position. They rely entirely on the holy books, and these they have at their fingers' ends. It is granted by all that they are, almost without exception, entirely free from intolerance, and are quite unable to comprehend the zeal for conversion. A venerable Sadaw in Bhamo came and listened attentively to a Burmese sermon of Dr. Mason, the celebrated American missionary. When it was over he came and complimented him on its depth and grasp, and then suggested that the reverend doctor should go with him to offer up worship before the image of Buddha! The monks do not think, with cynical mockery, that every one should be allowed to go his own way and be blessed after his own fashion; on the contrary, they seek zealously for new truths and explanations of mysteries; but they hold it presumptuous and unwarrantable, in view of the dark secrets which envelop the life of man from its dawning to its close, to set up each his individual opinion with dogmatic certainty as the only true form and the only one that can save. They take their standpoint on the actual state of things, on the misery and sorrow which is externally bound up with the nature of the human body as it exists. They devote themselves entirely to preparing the spirit for its delivery, when it will finally rest, raised above every fear of new change, in the harmonious equipoise of Ne'ban. For this last and highest aim no hypotheses have to be assumed. They require no personal deity who would demand a special place in the system of the world, and in a possible danger to the cosmic system might incur the same risk of destruction. They remain entirely within the clearly defined horizon of their limit of vision, and are therefore very difficult to attack in argument.

Nevertheless schisms have arisen from time to time, and exist at the present day, but they have sprung more from revolt against excessive austerity, or corresponding laxity, than from any real difference on doctrinal points. The Lord Buddha had hardly died before one of the most aged of the disciples, Subhadra, thus addressed the assembled brethren: "Revered ones, cease to mourn. We are now happily released from the rule of the great Sramana; we shall no more be tormented with 'this is allowable' and 'that is not allowable'; we can now do what we wish, and leave undone what we do not care for." To put an end to this scandal to religion, and to fix definitely the bonds of morality, the great disciple, Kathapa, called together, forty-five years after the Buddha's death, in the year 543 B.C., the first great Council, at Rajagriha, in the country of Magadha. Kathapa himself was president. The Wini was read by Upali, whom Shin Gautama himself had pointed out as the most learned of his followers, and the Dharma by Ananda, the personal attendant and favourite disciple of the Budh. During seven months the various points in dispute were considered from all points, and after rulings had been publicly and authoritatively given, the Council broke up. Thus were the three "baskets of the Law" first settled.

But the backsliders were not corrected, and they gradually increased in number, until, one hundred years later, it was found necessary to call together another synod. There was now a considerable body of schismatics, and they formulated a demand for definite relaxations from the severity of the laws. The Council was again held in the country of Magadha (the modern Oudh), this time in the town of Wethali. The king, Kalathawka, built a splendid hall, and when all was ready, himself placed the ivory fan on the ledge of the pulpit, and sent a message to the members of the Thengā who had assembled for the conference, saying, "Lords, my task is finished." The relaxations demanded were then discussed. The most important were as follows:—
Food might be taken until the shade of the sun was two inches in length; whereas Shin Gautama had directed that for the curbing of the flesh none should be eaten after noontide.

Whey might be drunk after mid-day; forbidden as being a component part of milk, and therefore approaching animal food.

Tari, or palm toddy, might be taken, because it looks like water. This was a particularly bold demand, seeing that all fermented liquors are forbidden, and that in modern days the same plea might be urged on behalf of gin.

Gold and silver might be accepted as alms; the use of them being strictly prohibited.

A junior might lawfully copy a senior even in what is wrong; whereas no example could be any valid excuse for a wrong act.

Subsequent permission might cover an act; whereas the Wini required prior permission.

The restrictions against indulgences were to be in force only in the monasteries; and not for those who might be sojourning in villages.

These points, after lengthy discussion, were all given against the dissenters, and degradation was awarded them as a punishment.

Still matters got worse, and in 241 B.C. the great king Athawka, of Pataliputra, brought about the third and last great Council to cleanse the Church. After nine months' public reading of the Book of Rules and of the most excellent Law, 60,000 heretics were expelled from the Church, and it was resolved to propagate the religion far and wide. This last decision was fraught with the most momentous consequences to Burma, for among the missionaries sent north, south, east, and west from Behar were the two, Thawna and Ôttara, who proceeded to the country of Suvarna Bhumi, the "Golden Land," and landing at Thatôn, now north of Maulmein, but then on the sea-coast, proceeded to disseminate the Buddhist doctrines amongst the tribes in the great river-valleys of the country. It is important to notice that the doctrines they brought with them had just been revised and confirmed by a great Council of the Church. Since then, throughout all Burma, the old geniolatry has been displaced by the teachings of the Buddha. The regulations, introduced then in their first purity, have been retained ever since practically unchanged, so that at the present time Buddhism exists in Burma in a form much nearer to that which Shin Gautama taught than is found in any country where the Three Precious Things are held in reverence.

The only sect which has at any time started any doctrinal heresy is that of the Paramats. They reject the worship before pagodas and images, and pray only to the Nyan-daw, the godlike wisdom, which abides like a mountain of fire in the heavens, invisible to mortal eyes, and taking no interest and exercising no influence over mundane things. These

dissenters pay reverence to the ordinary brethren of the
yellow robe, keep the Ten Precepts, repeat the Bawana
(Payā, Tayā, Thengā, etc.) and the Ittipi-thaw, but they
never go near the shrines, and recite their prayers and
invocations in the jungle or in open fields. It is a kind
of reminiscence of fire-worship, an ancestral adoration of the
heavens in the sun, caused possibly by a shrinking from the
suspicion of idolatry. A cardinal fault in them is that they
give no alms, for most religions are at one on the question
that charity covers a multitude of sins. The sect was founded
at the beginning of this century by a pôngyi, called by
his followers Shin Tabaung. He lived at Sinbyugyun,
"White Elephant Island," a place half-way between Mandalay and the British frontier, and the dissent would probably
never have spread beyond that district, or outlived the
life of its originator, had it not been for the king Bodaw
Payā. When the Thenga refused to recognise his claim to
be the fifth Buddha of this world cycle, he espoused the
cause of the Paramats, imposed penalties on all monks who
would not accept their tenets, and went so far as to force
a Thathanabaing, one of the heads of the Order, to marry,
marriage being permissible under the doctrines of the
dissenters. This gave the schism a prominence which it
could not otherwise have attained, and enabled it to last
down to the present time, though its numbers, never very
great, have steadily dwindled away. There are perhaps more
Paramats in Prome than in any other town of Burma, Lower
or Upper. Their most prominent doctrine is that the Shwe
Nyan-daw existed before the world began, and will exist
for all eternity. Ideas may arise from the influence of
exterior objects, but when they have been freed from their
connection with bodily creations, they have an independent
existence, and when once they have come into being continue to live. This is explained by the assertion that the
quasi-deity of the Buddha is founded only on his supreme
wisdom. Buddha means, etymologically, "the wise," and
Shin Gautama was simply an incarnation of the pure
Wisdom. Men believed they actually saw him when he was
already really a deity—nothing else than the inspiring
Nyan-daw, which made the five Khandas appear to have an

actual earthly existence.   Occasionally an energetic Sadaw
excommunicates all the Paramats under his jurisdiction, and
forbids all the laity to sell to them, or have any communication whatever with them, but as a rule they are let alone.
The movement is too feeble to threaten any real danger to
religion, and has never gained many adherents among the
laity.

It is a different matter with the rival parties of the
Mahagandi and the Sulagandi.   Here there are no heretical
doctrines in dispute ; it is simply a question of greater
adherence to the strict rule of the Order.   Instead of, as in
the early days of the Assembly, one party crying out against
the too great austerity of the majority, it is a sturdy protest
of a minority within the Church against the lamentable
weakness and laxity of the great body of the Order in the
observance of the precepts of the Book of the Enfranchisement.   The quarrel is at present limited to Lower Burma,
where the greater wealth of the country and the introduction
of foreign luxuries among the laity have led to corresponding indulgences in many of the monasteries, against which
the Sulagandis protest and preach with feverish energy.
The austere party is strongest in Maulmein, Henzada, and
Pegu, and faction feeling runs so high that street fights
between the scholars of the two sects are very common, and
often so embittered that the English authorities have to
interfere to restore peace in the town, for the laity take sides
with equally bitter animosity.

The questions in dispute are entirely matters of discipline.   The Puritan party, as the Sulagandi may very well
be called, denounce the habit, which is becoming very
frequent, of wearing silk robes.   The Kammawā sets forth
that the thengan should be stitched together of rags picked
up in the streets or in the graveyards, and such panthagu
thengans the Sulagandis wear and glory in.   The Mahagandis, on the other hand, have been gradually becoming
more and more luxurious.   At first new cloth was torn into
irregular pieces, and then sewn together.   Latterly it has
been considered sufficient to tear a corner and stitch it up
again, or perhaps only to rip a portion of a seam, and from
this to the wearing of silk garments was no very great step.

The Puritan party declare that this is simply a scandalous playing with the letter of the law. Again, the Sulagandis eat out of the alms-bowl as it comes in from the morning round, whereas the Mahagandis empty out the thabeit into plates and make as palatable a meal as possible from their collections, which, on the face of it, is a pandering to fleshly weakness. Others, much more bold in their backsliding, do not hesitate to have a special meal cooked for them every morning by the Kyaung-tha-gyi, and sit down to it smoking hot, after their morning's perambulation, while the begging-bowl is handed over to poor people staying in the monastery, or emptied out for the benefit of the dogs and crows. No sophistry, one would think, could explain away this Sybaritism, but the Mahagandis have the assurance to try to make a merit of it, saying that the money expended by the Kappiya-dayaka on the materials for the breakfast is the proceeds of the sale of previous offerings of the pious—rugs, blankets, lamps, and so on—and by thus making use of it, not only do the people gain merit for their gifts of food, but the monks themselves are enabled to extend their charity to the poor or the birds of the air. That is a severe straining of the command that the Ariya should live by alms.

Similarly when the Mahagandi goes abroad he wears sandals on his feet, and protects his shaven crown from the rays of the sun with an umbrella. The austere brother walks the streets barefooted and bareheaded, even though his head may ache and his feet be blistered with the shimmering heat of high noon. Only when he is on a long journey does the Sulagandi allow himself such superfluities as sandals or umbrella. The Mahagandi will receive coin in his own hands, covered by a handkerchief; the Sulagandi will not take it even through the instrumentality of a pupil, or off a ngwe-pa-detha, a rupee-hung tree, at Tawadeintha feast time. Pwès on feast days, or even in the neighbourhood of the pagodas, are denounced by the reforming party; so are balloons with fireworks in them; the habit many monks have fallen into of going to visit Englishmen, with no other object than curiosity; and above all the noisy saturnalia in the monasteries at the end of Lent which

have become so common in Rangoon. It will thus be seen
that the great point at issue is the maintenance of the
original humble character of the brotherhood. The different
vernacular presses of Rangoon flood the country with con-
troversial tracts written by both parties, and the laity adopt
sides and carry polemical discussions into private life. So
fierce had the quarrel become, that in 1880 one of the most
learned and venerated of the Mandalay heads of the Church,
the Thinkazā Sadaw, came down to settle the question.
He was received everywhere with extraordinary honours.
At Danubyu the whole of the populace lined the path up
to the monastery prepared for him, and kneeling down, threw
their hair across the way, so that from the river-bank to
the steps of the kyaung he walked all the way on a carpet
of human tresses. But he did not settle which party was
in the right. After making abundant inquiries and hearing
the most prominent advocates on either side, he halted at
Henzada and announced that he was about to give his
decision. Unfortunately it came to his ears that in that
town, as well as in several others, the Ariya had been betting
freely as to which way he would give his judgment. Thereupon the Sadaw grew furious, denounced both parties alike,
and refused to say anything which would countenance the
claims of either sect. He remained for a considerable time
in the low country, giving numerous addresses for the building up of religion, but never on any occasion throwing out
a hint as to which way he leaned, further than that both
parties should give way a little and refrain from exhibiting
such scandalous dissensions before the heretics. The warfare was calmed for a space, but the old fierce denunciations
have broken out again. The opposing abbots bid their lay
supporters refrain from giving alms to the rival sect. They
recommend all the penalties of excommunication without
having the power to go through the formal ceremony. But
though the Mahagandis have the greater number of followers,
the self-denying Sulagandis have all the more earnest and
rightly-thinking men on their side and will probably prevail
in the end, though a new great synod may have to be held
before that is effected. The head of the reforming party is
U Ôkgansa, a learned Sadaw, whose monastery is at Ôkpo

in the Tharrawadi district.   He was at one time invited to
go up to Mandalay to assume the control of a Kyaung and
spend the rest of his days there.   The Burmese Government
offered to send down a royal steamer with high dignitaries
to escort him to the capital, but the sturdy old " Bishop "
refused to forsake his party until he should be persuaded
that its principles would gain the victory in the end.   And
so no doubt they will, for not even the most casual observer
can fail to see that they, in their bare ascetic monasteries,
are far nearer to the ideal of the founder than the Mahagandis with all the appliances of their richly-stocked
abiding-places.

CHAPTER XV

PAGODAS

SOME one with a greater regard for alliteration than the truth once said that the principal productions of Burma were pagodas, pôngyis, and pariah dogs. As a superficial impression this is neat, and therefore it will continue to be quoted by forcible feebles to the end of their days, in Bayswater or Ealing. It certainly is marvellous how many pagodas there are in the country, far exceeding the number of those raised in the· sacred island of Ceylon, or by the Thibetans and Chinese, pious Buddhists, though they have fallen into sad doctrinal heresies. A Burman does not notice the multitude of the religious edifices in his country till he leaves it and finds how far more sparing other nations are in their places of worship. The poorest village has its neatly kept shrine, with the remains of others mouldering away round about it. No hill is so steep and rocky, or so covered with jungle, as to prevent the glittering gold or snow-white spire rising up to guard the place from ghouls and sprites, and remind the surrounding people of the Saviour Lord, the teacher of Nirvana and the Law. There is good reason for this multiplication of fanes. No work of merit is so richly paid as the building of a pagoda. The Payā-taga is regarded as a saint on earth, and when he dies he obtains the last release; for him there are no more deaths. The man who sets up a row of water-pots on a dusty road does well; he who raises a ta-gôn-daing, or sacred post, who builds a rest-house, presents an image or a bell, or founds a monastery, gains much kutho and ensures a happy transincorporation when he passes away; but the

Payā-taga is finally freed from the three calamities, his kan
is complete, the merits outweigh the demerits, and he attains
the holy rest.   That, at any rate, is the comforting belief,
cherished by the most reprobate.   Little wonder then that,
with such a glorious reward in store for him, the pious man
hoards his wealth for such an object, and that pagodas are so
plentiful in the land.   It avails little to repair a previous
dedication, unless it be one of the great world shrines at
Rangoon, Pegu, Prome, or Mandalay.   In the case of
ordinary pagodas the merit of the repair goes practically
entirely to the original founder.   Hence that puzzle to
Europeans, the building of a bright new place of worship
close to one which a very little care would save from
crumbling away into a simple tumulus.

The word pagoda is seemingly a kind of verbal *hysteron
proteron*, a metathesis of the Cinghalese dhagoba, derived
from the Sanskrit dhatu garba, a relic shrine, and is properly
applied only to a monument raised over some of the remains
of the Lord Buddha.   Such are dat-daw, pieces of Shin
Gautama's flesh ; an-daw, his teeth ; san-daw, his hair ; thin-
gyat-daw, the frontal bone ; hnyat-yo-daw, the jaw-bone,
besides others.   In addition to these there are the sacred
utensils and other articles used by the teacher of the Law,
such as the thengan, the yellow robe ; the thabeit, or alms-
bowl ; the taung-we-daw, his staff; the padi, or rosary, and
other things of the same kind.   These holy relics, however,
could not go far, even if they had been equitably divided
between the great countries professing Buddhism, which
they certainly were not.   Burma alone claims more personal
remains than could possibly have existed.   The same thing
is, I believe, true of Popish relics in Europe, where pieces of
the true cross are as abundant as portions of the dress of
the founder of Buddhism are in Burma.   It is useless
attempting to prove or disprove the authenticity of particular relics.   To admit of the multiplication of shrines,
models of the sacred things are permitted, and these only,
in metal, precious stones, or clay, are deposited under the
vast majority of pagodas.   But images and sacred books
are also so enshrined, and thus arises the classification of
the four kinds of shrines, the Zedi le-ba.

1. Datu zedi, erected over relics of the Buddha, or models of these.

2. Paribawga zedi, over the sacred eight utensils, or their imitations.

3. Oddeitha zedi, enclosing images.

4. Damma zedi, enclosing the sacred books, such as the *Bitaghat thôn-bôn,* the three baskets of the Law, and other sacred volumes, like the *Bagawa,* appointed to be read during Lent.

It may be well to remark that the word " pagoda " is not known at all in Burmese, either in its English or Cinghalese form, any more than the word Mandarin is known in China. Such a building is called a Zedi, from the Pali chaitya, meaning the offering-place, or place of prayer, but the expression Payā, applicable as well to the image as to the shrine, is most frequently used in reference to the more famous centres of worship.

The greatest of the payās, such as the Shwe Dagôn in Rangoon, the most famous of all ; the Shwe Maw-daw, the lotus-shrine of Pegu ; the Shwe San-daw, the depository of the sacred hair at Prome ; and the Mahā Myat Muni, the temple of the most exalted saint in Mandalay ; all these were founded by single individuals, or brothers to whom the most excellent Master had given hairs from his head to deposit in the specified place. How the exact spot was found, and how successive kings increased the size of the first erection, and donations flowed in from the pious in all parts of the world to beautify and preserve the building, all these particulars are recorded in the palm-leaf records of the various temples. Many later Zedi, however, have been erected by villages, or by public subscription in whole districts, as pious memorials, or to commemorate some particular event, as well as for the obvious purposes of public convenience on the duty days of the month. Very many, and among them some of the most beautiful, are, on the other hand, the outcome of purely individual desire for merit. Some, such as the chaste, white Sibyo shrine at Mengôn, near Mandalay, are built in remembrance of individuals ; the graceful pagoda mentioned being erected by a recent monarch in memory of a favourite queen. Under all, however, to render

them sacred, are buried some of the holy things. Without
these, no hti, or umbrella, could be placed on the summit of
the spire.

These objects are deposited in the tāpana taik, a square
chamber, built in the basement of every payā, and always
the first thing finished. Not only one, but many things are
thus enclosed. Captain Cox, who saw the first beginnings
of the huge Mengôn pagoda, describes the tāpana taik of
that vast amount of brickwork. It measured sixty-one
and a half feet square, and was eleven feet deep. The interior
was plastered white and gaily painted, and was divided into
a number of compartments of various sizes to receive the
offerings of the king and the courtiers, the innermost naturally containing the most sacred. The dedicated treasures
themselves were very numerous, including a great variety of
miniature pagodas and monasteries in silver and gold of
varying degrees of purity ; images of the same materials and
of polished alabaster, some of them four feet high ; a number
of gold caskets, probably containing models of the sacred
teeth and bones ; besides these, there was a miscellaneous
collection of other things—slabs of coloured glass, precious
stones, white jars, such as are used by the royal family, and
finally a soda-water machine, then almost as much a novelty
in England as in Burma. The offerings did not strike Captain
Cox as being very valuable, but the then king, Bodaw Payā,
cared a good deal more for his own special glory than for
the raising of religion. Not long afterwards he claimed to
be a new Buddha, and because the Sacred Order would not
recognise his right to the title, turned heretic, and victimised
the monks with renegade zeal.

The relic chamber at the great Shwe Maw-daw offers a
very decided contrast. The Buddha gave two hairs of his
head to two brothers, with instructions to enshrine them on
the Thu-da-thana hill. An earthquake revealed the exact
spot to them, and a host of byammās and nat-déwas came
down to take part in the depositing of the relics. A chamber,
ten cubits square, was prepared, and at the bottom was laid
a slab of pearly white marble, set with diamonds. A similar
slab, studded with emeralds, formed the lid. The Tha-gyā
king placed a golden cradle in the centre of the bottom

slab, and round this were arranged images of the chief disciples of Shin Gautama, each holding a golden bouquet.   The
jewelled casket containing the hairs was placed on the cradle,
and high festival was held for many days.   Numbers of other
images of the Buddha himself, and of many eminent disciples, were placed round the sides of the tāpana taik, and
countless offerings were made, the Tha-gyā king giving
ten billions of gold, each of his queens forty thousand of
silver ; the father of the two brethren one thousand of gold,
and many others equally great sums.   But this was in the
brave days of old, when imagination was vivid and evidence
cursory.

Still even nowadays very costly offerings are often
deposited in the relic chamber.   An almost invariable gift
is a representation in gold of the Lord Buddha, with the
hooded snake raising itself over him, as in the images of
Vishnu in India, or a great model of the Great Master
as he received the supreme wisdom under the bawdi-bin.
Examples of the last may be seen in the South Kensington
Museum, as also of the Sabupati payā, representing him
with the tower-like royal crown, the wings on legs and arms,
and other emblems recalling the king's son who went out
to dedicate himself as the Buddha and the conqueror of
Mān-nat.   Open-handed piety is twice as frequent as of
yore, only the chroniclers of modern days have not the florid
imaginations of their predecessors.

The dedication of a payā is a high festival, but there
is no prescribed ritual in the sacred books, and each individual pôngyi, after reciting the precepts and the Itti
pithaw, has a form of his own, embracing portions of the
law and the sacred discourses.   A prominent function in the
service, as indeed always in giving alms, is the yeset-cha,
the pouring out of water drop by drop on the ground.   The
great king Bimbathara did it himself from a gold cup when
he presented the Weluwun or Bamboo-grove monastery,
and so likewise it is recorded of the rich man Anātabein.
The idea is to share the merit of the action with all creatures,
and at the same time to call to witness, besides the mathôndaye nats, all gods and men, that the donor may have
due reward for his piety.   The same thing is frequently

done in order to legally hand over a gift. As the water falls drop by drop on the ground, the pôngyis read out the formulæ, the substance of which is as follows : " Firm in my belief in the three precious things, the Lord, the Law, and the Assembly, I make this offering that I may be freed from all present and future miseries. May all creatures suffering torment in the four states of punishment reach the happy seats of nat-déwas. May all my relatives, friends, and all men inhabiting this earth and the ten thousand worlds, share in the benefits of this meritorious work. O earth, and ye spirits, guardians of this place, bear me witness to the piety of this gift."

It is worthy of note that it is explicitly stated that the inward dispositions of the giver have nothing to do with the merit resulting from a good work. The merits are strictly proportioned to the degree of sanctity or perfection of him who receives the alms. Hence the glorious release which awaits an otherwise bad man who erects a pagoda.

Zedis are of many shapes and degrees of elaboration, but one common idea may be traced through them all. If you ask a Burman monk the cause of the variations in the form of the payā, he will tell you that the Buddha left no instructions regarding them in the holy books, but had only said that a small mound should be raised over his bones in the form of a heap of rice. Apart from the relation in which the payā stands to the Buddha himself as the representation of the holy one sunk in meditation, the ostensible object is the preservation of relics, and these are to be laid in a shrine, like the lotus-bud of which the zedi is typical, and later by an extending of the lines this got the form of a bell or spire. In the Malla Lingaya Wuttu we are told that the infant Buddha in the womb of Queen Maia resembled a lotus-bud, or a beautiful pagoda, and the conjunction of this idea with the simple original tumulus has undoubtedly led to the typical form as now seen in Burma. The names for various parts of the building all recall the idea of the flower-bud, with its young leaves folded in adoration. Thus the rounded swelling just below the slender spire is called the hnget-pyaw-bu, the banana palm-bud, and on the extreme summit

at the top of the hti is the seinbu, the diamond-bud,
which in not a few poor districts is represented by a soda-
water bottle, which combines the resemblance to a flower-bud
with the good offices of a lightning conductor. The hnget-
pyaw-bu is usually surrounded with lavish adornment of
the sacred lotus. The payās that rise up into a plain cone
or spire are therefore the nearest to the original tumulus,
the top being simply drawn out into a conical point. On
the other hand, the bell-like pagodas are only a direct
imitation of the lotus-bud, and this has led to the more
rounded dome-like forms, sometimes called thabeit hmauk,
the inverted begging-pot. This term, however, is applied
to the swelling-out round part on every pagoda, and
has thence been borrowed to designate special shrines. It
has nothing to do with phallic worship as some have
imagined, nor is there any idea of the resemblance to a
human skull. Such grim reminders of mortality common
in Thibetan Buddhism do not commend themselves to the
Burman.

The buildings are all made of crumbling, sun-dried
brick, for it is enough to gratify the pious feeling of
the moment, and even the long years that the most
solidly built stone edifices might last would only be as
an evanescent drop in the stream of eternity. Thus the
Burman sees no harm in building pagodas of sand, or
even cloth and pasteboard, and in the national annals
the victory which false shrines won over more substantial
erections is a favourite theme. In Lower Burma, the
payās are mostly of the simplest pattern, derived from the
archetypal rice-heap and the lotus-bud. They are solid
pyramidal cones, rising with a gradually diminishing rounded
outline, and surmounted by a hti, or " umbrella " spire, a
construction resembling the musical instrument called a
chapeau chinois, formed of concentric rings, lessening to a rod
with a small vane called hnget-ma-nā on the top. They are
almost without exception erected on more or less elevated
platforms. Burma is quite different from other Buddhist
countries, where the relics are exhibited on great feast days.
The payā is perfectly solid with the exception of the tāpana
taik, situated directly under the spire and the hti, and

there is no means of entering this to view the sacred relics. The addition of spires and the elaboration of the central pyramid are later thoughts, and give hints of the great architectural efforts to be seen in Upper Burma. The peaks of Mount Myinmo are said to have furnished the first notion. In some cases, as at the Shwe San-daw of Prome, the central spire is surrounded at its base by a circle of small gilded temples or zediyan, forming a continuous wall round the pagoda, each containing an image of the Buddha, and suggesting the idea of the Setyawalà hills round the world-girding Thamôddaya sea. In almost all the larger payās there are arched wings on each face of the lower platform, serving, as it were, as ante-chapels, and each containing a large Gautama. It is obvious how easily the introduction of these niche chapels led to the halls and aisles of the Pagān temples. Still this elaboration remains only a sign of architectural genius, and not of greater sanctity, for in every case the building itself serves only as a meet place for meditation and praise in thought or words. The great temples of Pagān, with their galleries, transepts, and corridors, have more of the character of churches in the ordinary acceptation of the word, and the Ananda above all, with its echoing vaults and dim religious light, reminds one especially of some great cathedral of the Middle Ages. But the outward magnificence of the Pagān temples does not win for them the reverence which is shown to vastly plainer bell pagodas.

Of all the shrines, the Shwe Dagôn Payā, the great pagoda of Rangoon and the most venerable place of worship in all the Indo-Chinese countries, is the finest and the most universally visited. Its peculiar sanctity is due to the fact that it is the only payā, known to Buddhists, which contains actual relics, not only of Shin Gautama, but of the three Budhs who preceded him in this world. In the tāpana taik of the pagoda, along with eight hairs from the head of the Buddha, in the eleventh andrakap of whose cycle we are now living, there exist the ye-thauk-palā, the drinking-cup of Kaukkathan; the thengan or robe of Gawnagông; and the taungwe or staff of Kathapa. Little wonder then that the glittering gold spire on the last spur of the

Pegu hills attracts at the time of the annual festival in March, pilgrims, not only from the farthest parts of Burma, but from Cambodia, Siam, and Corea. The stately pile stands upon a mound partly natural, partly artificial, which has been cut into two rectangular terraces, one above the other, each side, as is the case with all pagodas, facing one of the cardinal points of the compass. The upper terrace, which has been carefully levelled and paved and repaved by the pious, rises 166 feet from the level of the ground, and is 900 feet long by 685 wide according to English measurement. The ascent was by four flights of brick steps, one opposite the centre of each face, but the western approach has been closed by the fortifications built by the English conqueror to dominate the town and secure the pagoda, where there was so much desperate fighting in the Burmese wars. Ordinarily with other pagodas, the eastern flight is the most holy and therefore the most cared for ; but the town of Rangoon lies to the south, and consequently this ascent is the grandest.

At the foot are two gigantic leogryphs, built of brick, covered with plaster and gaudily painted. From them up to the platform, the saung-dan, the long stairs, are covered by a rising series of handsomely-carved teak roofs, supported on huge wood and masonry pillars. The heavy crossbeams and the panelling are in many places embellished with frescoes, representing scenes in the life of the Great Master and his disciples, and with hideously curious representations of the tortures of the wicked in the fiery chambers of hell. The steps themselves are exceedingly primitive and dilapidated. They have been manufactured piece by piece, apparently by ardent seekers after merit. Here and there they are made of broad stone flags from Penang and Bombay, but for great part of the distance they consist of simple sun-dried bricks, worn almost into a slope by the pious feet of myriads of worshippers—bare feet too, for none but Europeans are allowed to mount the steps with boots on. The stairs are wonderfully uncomfortable, not merely because they are so dilapidated, but because they are seemingly constructed with the object of preventing any one from ascending or descending with unseemly haste. They are too broad to mount two at a time, and too low to suit occidental tastes taken singly. This method of enforcing respect is characteristic of the Burmese nation, and reminds one of the nails which projected through the floors in the Royal Palace at Mandalay.

The stairs debouch on a broad, open, flagged space, which runs all round the pagoda, and is left free for worshippers. From the centre of this springs from an octagonal bi-nat-daw, or plinth, the profusely gilt, solid brick payā. It has a perimeter of 1355 feet, and rises to a height of about 370, or a little higher than St. Paul's Cathedral. On the summit is the hti, the gilt iron-work " umbrella," on each of whose many rings hang multitudes of gold and silver jewelled bells, which tinkle melodiously with every breath of air. This hti was made and presented by Mindôn Min, the second last King of Burma, and was placed on the summit at a cost of not much less than £50,000. It was constructed by voluntary labour ; and subscriptions in money and jewels, with which the vane and the uppermost band are richly studded, flowed in from all parts of Burma. The old king, " the convener of the fifth great synod," strove hard to have it placed on the pagoda entirely at his own cost and by his own men ; but the British Government rightly and firmly refused, for had this been done it would have been regarded by British Burmans as an acknowledgment of his suzerainty. After considerable correspondence it was handed over at the frontier to native officials and a body of Buddhist elders, by whom it was conveyed to the holy Theinguttara Mount, and there successfully placed in position. The old hti was lowered intact, and now stands on the platform, filled in and gaily painted like a small pagoda or a florid marriage cake, beside a still earlier decoration which it had supplanted.

At the corners of the basement are somewhat Assyrian-like figures of Manôt-thiha, creatures with two bodies and one head, half lion, half man, with huge ears and ruffled crest, and all round about are stone figures of lions displaying an ample show of teeth between their grinning lips. The tale is that long ages ago a king's son who had been abandoned in the forest was found by a lioness and suckled by her. When the prince grew to man's estate, he left his foster-mother and swam a broad river to escape from her. The tender mother's heart burst when he reached the other side, and she died ; and in remembrance of her love, lions' figures are placed at the foot of all pagoda steps, and round the building itself.

The four chapels at the foot of the pagoda are adorned at the sides by colossal figures of the sitting Buddha, and in the farthest recess, in a niche of its own, is a still more goodly figure, the thick gilding darkened in many places by the fumes of thousands of burning tapers and candles. Hundreds of Gautamas, large and small, sitting, standing, and reclining, white and black, of alabaster, sun-dried clay, or the wood of the Pein-nè, the jack tree (*Artocarpus integrifolia*), gilded or plain, surround and are propped up on the larger images. Even the figures in the niches are elaborate carved woodwork, representing figures dancing or fighting, and others flying through the air, or, with head on hand, sunk in meditation ; monsters of the woods and hills and streams. High stone altars for the offering of rice and flowers stand before the lions, the offering being made to the whole pagoda and not to them. Under the Manôt-thihas at the corners are niche altars for burnt offerings. On the outer edge of the platform are a host of small zedi-yan, each with its hti ; tasaungs, image houses, overflowing with the gifts of generations of pilgrims ; figures of the Budh in single, low stone chapels ; tagôn-daing, tall posts, flaunting from which are long cylindrical streamers, of bamboo framework, pasted over with paper, depicting scenes in sacred history, and often inscribed with pious invocations from the offerer ; others are surrounded by the sacred hentha, the Brahminy Goose (*Phœnicopterus rubra*), the emblem of the Talaings, or the kalawaik, the crane of the Burmese. Interspersed among these on the outer edge of the open platform are multitudes of bells of all sizes. Beside each bell, all of which are hung on stout crossbeams supported by two side posts, lie deer's antlers, and pieces of wood with which the worshipper strikes them as he passes. He strikes the bell and then the ground, to call the sky and the earth as witnesses to his prayers. On the eastern side, covered by a

great wooden shed, hangs one of enormous size, inside
which five or six men can stand with ease.   It was presented by King Tharrawaddy in 1840, on the occasion of a
state visit to Rangoon and the payā.   It measures seven
feet seven and a half inches across the mouth, fifteen inches
in thickness, fourteen feet high, and weighs 94,682 lbs.   With
a proper hammer it ought to give forth a splendid sound,
but the ordinary antlers and posts of wood used fail to do
it justice.   It is second in size in Burma to the great bell at
Mengôn, which, apart from the monster at Moscow, is the
largest in. the world.   There is a long inscription on the
Maha Ganda (the great, sweet voice) at Rangoon, recounting the merits gained by the monarch who presented it and
the praises of him chanted by the Nats, the guardians of the
empire.   The bell has a curious history.   After the second
Burmese war, the English made an attempt to carry it off
to Calcutta as a trophy, but by some mishap the Maha
Ganda toppled over, and sank to the bottom of the Rangoon
river.   English engineers made several attempts, but failed
to raise it.   The Burmans, after some years, begged that
the sacred bell might be restored to them, if they could
recover it.   The petition was granted with a sneer, but they
set to work, got it out, and carried it in triumph to the place
where it now hangs.   This success was ascribed by the
thoughtful to supernatural aid, but the common people
chuckled in a carnal and exultant manner over the victory,
and not without very fair reason, for their appliances were
of the most primitive kind.

Buddhists fix the date of the erection of the Shwe
Dagôn Payā in 588 B.C., but the site must have been
sacred for cycles before, since the relics of the three preceding Buddhas were found interred, when the two Talaing
brothers, Poo (dove) and Tapaw (plenty), came with their
precious eight hairs to the Theinguttara hill.   The original
payā is said in the palm-leaf history to have been only
twenty-seven feet high, and it has attained its present height
by being repeatedly cased with an outer covering of bricks
several feet in thickness.   Every now and again it has been
completely regilt.   Sinbyu Shin, king of Burma, towards
the end of the last century, used his own weight in gold in

the process. He scaled twelve stone three, a remarkably good weight for a Burman, and the gold used cost over £9000. The last occasion when the whole vast bulk was gilt was in 1871, when King Mindôn sent down his hti. On every feast-day and uboné, however, numbers of the pious clamber up wherever they can and fix on little squares of gold-leaf, packets of which can be bought at the stalls below for a few rupees. The consequence is that every now and again the spire breaks out in a rash of bright patches, which give it a mysterious, rough, uneven appearance on clear moonlight nights. Of late years a great part of the lower portion has been covered with thin plates of gold brought by the pious from all parts of the Buddhist world.

It is difficult to say what the real age of the building is, if, as sceptical Englishmen tell us, we are not to place implicit faith in the palm-leaf record. Trustworthy documents reach no further back than the time of the Peguan Queen Shin-saw-bu, who reigned in the early part of the sixteenth century; but there is every reason to believe that a pagoda existed there long before her time. The shrine has remained unaltered in size or shape since 1564, and probably will never be altered again. At all times and at all distances it looks imposing and sublime, like the religion whose followers have built it.

At the base of the pagoda hill are many monasteries embowered in their groves of palmyra palms and shady trees; and to the south is a small convent of nuns, not far from the zayat which the king of Siam had built for pilgrims from his dominions. Similar rest-houses line the Saung-dan all the way up to the pagoda, and they always have occupants; while at the season of the feast in Tabaung they are crowded to overflowing. Lepers, and cripples, and nuns in their white robes, line the steps, and cry out in piteous tones for alms from the passers - by. Nearer the top and round the platform itself are sellers of candles and coloured tapers, Chinese incense - sticks, and prayer-flags, along with abundance of gold-leaf. Numbers of young girls sit about with flowers, especially of the lotus, and meats of different kinds for offerings. Others —these always enfranchised pagoda slaves—sell toys and articles for household use. The platform is never deserted. Even long after midnight the voice of the worshipper may be heard in the night air, chanting in solemn monotone his pious aspirations, while on a duty - day, and especially on a feast - day, the laughing, joyous crowd of men and maidens, in their gay national dress, makes the platform of the Shwe Dagôn one of the finest sights in the world.

The Shwe Dagôn Payā is by far the most widely celebrated of the great Buddhist shrines, but there are others which, if not so venerated in other lands, still enjoy an even greater local reputation for sanctity, and attract pilgrims from all parts of Burma and the dependent hills, with now and again a band of pious worshippers from distant countries. Chief among these is the Shwe Hmaw-daw at Pegu, which commands Talaing worship before even the shrine of "the slanted beam" on the Theinguttara hill. The pond close by it was covered with lotus blossoms immediately on the construction of the shapely spire and the great Tha-gyā Min, and countless Byammās and Nat-déwas assisted at the enshrinement of the relics. As with many other fanes, the king granted to the pagoda, and set apart from secular uses for ever, the whole space round it on which the shadow of the original pile fell between sunset and sunrise. Several hundred families were dedicated to its service, and in 1881 large sums were raised throughout all the low country for the manufacture of a new hti and the gilding of the whole surface, while many wondrous signs in the neighbourhood attested the sacred character of the undertaking. Similarly the Shwe San-daw at Prome, with its multitude of bells on the cramped hill-top, enjoys a special reputation on account of the prophecy there spoken by Shin Gautama himself, and the connection of the payā with the national hero - king, Dwut-tabaung, as recorded in the sacred books. In proof of this there exists to the present day, and may be seen at the foot of the hill, a huge stone with an inscription which none but the pure-minded can read, and few even of them understand. In other places examples of this duganan kye-ganan, a kind of cypher-writing, or cryptograph, as it appears to the unenfranchised, exists, and usually records in mystic phraseology and inverted orthography the alms presented to

the pagoda.   Many of the lists of donations are, however,
graven in a less cramped kyauk-sa, or "stone writing," the
givers having probably had a weak hankering after earthly
fame.   Thus a goodly marble slab with a long list of names
may be seen at the Shwe Hmaw - daw, and a tablet near
the Mya Thalôn, the Temple of the Emerald Bed (of the
Buddha), at Ma-gwe in Upper Burma records how Min Din
and Min La - go had in the year 2399 of religion covered
the whole payā with yellow cloth, repaired it thoroughly,
and had it painted red and gold.   An exact account is
given of the amount of materials used and the money
paid to workmen, and the inscription ends up with a prayer
that the family of the donors might be gratified with the
birth of a son.   Near it is a magic stone with the figure
of a hare, surrounded by stars, deeply graven in it to
represent the moon, and a peacock to represent the sun.

A frequent adjunct of many pagodas is the Shwe Zet-
daw, the imprint of the Lord Buddha's foot.   It is too nearly
square to command a painter's or sculptor's praise, and the
toes are all of the same length, as may be seen in the
example carried off by Captain Marryat, the novelist, in the
first Burmese war, and now preserved in the British Museum.
The sole is divided into a hundred and eight squares (taya
shi' kwet), and on them are many lekkhana, representations
of monasteries, pyathats, tigers, kalawaiks, henthas, parrots,
seipputi fish, and the like, to signify that all things were
under the feet of the Great Master.   The number of beads
on the rosary corresponds with the number of squares on the
Shwe Zet-daw.   The most famous example is at the pagoda
of that name east of Mandalay, the great resort of the
Shans, and another well - known one is opposite Magwe,
inland from Minbu, where the mud volcanoes are, "the boiling vats of the nagās."   But there are many specimens all
over the country, not a few with the figure of a nagā, or
sea monster, reared over them.

Most famous among the small pagodas is the Kyaik-hti-
yo, insignificant in size, but unique from its position.   The
hill on which it stands takes its name from the payā, and
is over three thousand five hundred feet in height.   On its
summit are numbers of granitoid boulders, many of them

balanced in a most extraordinary way, and all the more striking surmounted by little shrines. The Kyaik - hti - yo stands on a huge boulder, which itself rests on a projecting rock, separated from the rest of the hill by a chasm, fathomless to the eye, and reaching, so say the villagers, far below the depth of the hill. The boulder stands on the extreme verge of the bare rock, and hangs over it as if a gust of wind or a few extra pounds added would make it topple over and crash down the dizzy height far away into the green valley below. To this shrine people from all parts of the country, but more especially the Talaings, come in the month of February, and cast jewellery and precious stones into the yawning rift, and, clambering up the rock by the aid of a bamboo ladder, cover the payā with flowers and small lighted candles, making it look like a new nebulous constellation from the far-off plains. Inquirers are told with the utmost confidence that the pagoda is five thousand years old. It certainly has been there time out of mind, and the boulder has solely been kept in its place by the hair buried under the shrine, and given to a hermit by the great Budh himself when he returned from Tawa-deintha, the second heaven of the Nat-déwas, on the occasion of his preaching the Law to his mother. Near it is a spring which always flows freely with crystalline water, unless there is evil talk among the assembled people or if the sexes are not separated. A complete Thin - bông - gyi, the alphabet, is graven on the rock. The view from the pagoda is superb ; bounded on the east by the blue Martaban hills, fading away into the dim peaks of Siam, and extending southwards over tangled jungle and yellow paddy lands to the bright waves of the Gulf of Martaban, while to the west the jewelled speck of the pagoda at Pegu almost leads one to imagine the stately bulk of the sacred Shwe Dagôn beyond.

There are many such shrines on the abrupt limestone hills in the Maulmein district, where the devotee has to clamber up bare rock faces, and scramble through treacherous débris, occasionally swinging over perilous deeps on the precarious footing of a rough bamboo ladder ; his offerings tied to his back, and his heart between his teeth. And yet

women are found to make the ascent, especially at the Zwè-
kabin, the precipitous " Duke of York's nose," some forty
miles up the Sittang river from Maulmein, where the
Englishman is lost in amazement as to how they ever got
the bricks and ironwork up the rocks to construct the
pagoda and the hti. Yet thousands of people scramble up
at the time of the annual feast, and the pagoda is as well
adorned with offerings as any in the flat lands down by the
sea, where a rise of a few feet in the ocean would put
hundreds of square miles under water.

Every district pagoda has its special feast and all are
well attended, for even though the locality may be thinly
populated there are always to be found visitors from other
places round about ; partly as a kind of neighbourly cour-
tesy, partly because there is always some fun in the shape
of a travelling troupe, or a marionette play, at a pagoda
feast, and chiefly, there can be no denying, from a feeling of
genuine piety and a real desire to acquire merit. Pagoda
feasts enable a Burman to see the world, as far as it can be
seen in his native land. Without the periodical festivals he
would only stop chewing betel in the wattled bothy where
he was born to go out and smoke a cheroot round his patch
of paddy land, and speculate on the time when the Rangoon
or Bassein broker would come up to buy his crop from him.
Most of the district Burmans would never see the Englishman
and his doings were it not for the annual pilgrimage to
Rangoon to worship at the Shwe Dagôn. During the rest
of the year, unless he lives in the headquarters of an
assistant commissionership, all he sees of the British occupation is a stray visit from a young official out shooting, or
the chance appearance of an inspector of police in search
of a criminal.

Similarly very few Burmans, except those attracted by
business to the capital, would ever visit Mandalay were it
not for the great " Arakan pagoda." The Mahā Myat Muni
Payā is rendered especially sacred by the sitting image of
Shin Gautama there preserved, and is on this account
regarded by Upper Burmans as not inferior in sanctity to
the Shwe Dagôn itself. The huge brass image, twelve feet
in height, was brought over the hills from Akyab in the year

1784 (1146 B.E.).   According to the inscription, the king
drew this Arakan Gautama to the shrine by the charm of
his piety, but the historical books speak only of rough force
of arms.   However that may be, it is a mystery how the
huge masses of metal—the figure was cast in three sections
—were brought over the steep, pathless mountain sides.
The inscription flatters the king, and the monks ascribe the
feat to supernatural help, as they do the faultless joining
together of the pieces.   The image was set up, so says the
legend, during the lifetime of the Great Master.   The utmost
skill and most persistent energy had failed in fitting the parts
together, and the feelings of the pious were fearfully lacerated
by the cracking of the head in their futile struggles.   But
the Buddha, perceiving from afar what was going on, and
ever full of pity, came himself to the spot, and, embracing
the image seven times, so joined together the fragments that
the most sceptical eye cannot detect the points of junction,
while the head was restored to its pristine smoothness.   So
like was the image, and so sublime the effulgence which
shone around during the manifestation, that the reverently
gazing crowd could not determine which was the model and
which the Master.   The resemblance has no doubt faded
away with the wickedness of later times, for unlike most
Burmese images, the Payā Gyi has most gross and repulsive
features.   Inspired by the divine embrace the figure spoke,
but afterwards received the Teacher's command never again
to open its lips till Arimadéya should come to reveal the new
Law.   The shrine in which it stands is one of the most
splendid in the country.   The image itself is covered by a
great seven-roofed pya-that with goodly pillars, the ceiling
gorgeous with mosaics.   Long colonnades, supported on 252
massive pillars, all richly gilt and carved, with frescoed roofs
and sides, lead up to it, and daily from the royal palace used
to come sumptuous offerings in stately procession, marshalled
by one of the ministers and shaded by the white umbrella,
the emblem of sovereignty and the prerogative of the Arbiter
of Existence.   On its first arrival a hundred and twenty
families of Arakanese were assigned as slaves of the payā,
and the number was frequently afterwards added to.   In a
long gallery there is an enormous number of inscriptions,

gathered from all parts of the country, many on gilt slabs of marble, a still greater number on sandstone. All day long circles of constantly renewed worshippers chant aloud the praises of the Buddha, and the air is heavy with the effluvia of candles and the odours from thousands of smouldering incense-sticks. Within the precincts of the pagoda is a large tank, tenanted by sacred turtle, who wax huge on the rice and cakes thrown them by the multitudes of pilgrims. Probably not even at the Shwe Dagôn Payā is more enthusiastic devotion shown than at the Payā Gyi in Mandalay. It is regarded with special reverence by the Shans.

Near the royal city, about nine miles up the river, on the right bank, is a huge monster of a pagoda, built on a low green bluff, running out from the barren, pagoda-sprinkled Sagaing hills. The groundwork of the great misshapen Mengôn Payä covers a square of 450 feet and its height is 165 feet, about one-third of the elevation intended for it when completed; but Mintaya Gyee, the crack-brained monarch who founded it, ran short of funds, and the building was stopped. Nature was jealous of the miniature mountain —the largest mass of brickwork in the world—and an earthquake in 1838 rent the gigantic cube with fantastic fissures from top to bottom, and cast down great masses of masonry, tons upon tons in weight, and yet not sufficient to destroy the main structure, massive and imperishable as Time itself. There it stands, unharmed alike by rain-floods and blistering suns, and laughing even at earthquakes. According to Burmese custom, Bodaw Payā built a model for the guidance of the workmen. This is called the Pôn-daw Payā, and is fifteen feet high. This consists of a bell-shaped dome surmounted by a *sikkhâra*, a pointed spire, and resting on a square plinth of solid brickwork. It is a hybrid between the Shwezigôn and Ananda pagodas of Pagān, and has all the requirements of a place of worship, circuit walls, staircases, ornamented arches, and leogryphs.

Perhaps it was this proud stability which induced King Mindôn Min to attempt an even greater work. He planned a huge shrine to be raised east of Mandalay, under the shadow of the Shan hills. The Yankin-taung Payā was to be larger than the Mengôn monster, and it was to be built of stone.   A fair-sized hill was hewn into blocks to furnish material.   Canals several miles long were dug to convey the stones, and huge lighters were built upon them.   The whole kingdom was called upon to furnish men to labour a few months at a time on the pious work.   Architects, monks, foreigners, were called upon to offer suggestions and make plans.   A French engineer, who declared that, with 5000 men working every day, it would require eighty-four years to complete the original design, came near being crucified on the spot.   After four years' labour the basement, some four feet high, was completed, and then the Convener of the Fifth Great Synod returned to the village of Nats.   Theebaw Min, who succeeded him, was the last man likely to finish the work, and there lie the mountains of squared stones and the heaps of rubble for the centre.   The canals have silted up and the lighters foundered with their unloaded cargoes, and instead of a monument, King Mindôn has simply left a ghastly chaos.   What kan King Mintaya Gyee must have had to get so far as he did !

The whole neighbourhood of Mandalay, Amarapoora, and Ava is rich with splendid fanes ; but a detailed account of them would only weary the reader, as the visiting of them tires out the non-religious observer.   Nevertheless some must at least be adverted to.   There is the Ku-thu-daw, the " Royal Merit House," the richly-gilt shrine built by King Theebaw's uncle, the " War Prince," one of the most compact and tastefully adorned of pagodas, with beautifully carved gilt gates, the main spire being surrounded by a triple square of shrines, each shrine containing a marble slab engraved with a chapter of the Bitaghat on the back and front.   The text of the three volumes of the Buddhist Scripture was carefully collated by the most learned Sadaws in the royal city, and is considered the best extant.

Especially interesting also is the Atumashi, the incomparable payā, the great, oblong, lofty-terraced chapel monastery of Mindôn Min, outwardly plain white, but within splendid with a gorgeously decorated shrine, purple and scarlet, and gold hangings, and velvet carpets.   Here were preserved the gold spittoon, betel-box, kalawaik, and other paraphernalia of its founder.   Unhappily it was burnt in 1892.

Down the river there are hundreds of others of every
variety and degree of decoration.   There is the Naga Yôn
Payā, the whole building wrought into the form of a dragon ;
the huge round-domed Kaung-hmu-daw, and the "king's
victory pagoda" at Sagaing, the "golden cock-scratching,"
on the other side, commemorating a favourite legend of the
boundless charity of the Budh.   There are glistening white
pinnacles, or flashing gold spires, far up the Sagaing hills,
with thousands of steps wending wearily up over the steep,
rough hill-side, and gazing up to them from the Amarapoora
side are great massy temples, frowning over the river with
all the stern solidity of a knightly hold.   Each has its
legend, some tale of bloodshed or piety, some event in
Burmese history, or birth-story of the Buddha.

Most renowned, however, for its pagodas is Pagān, in
many respects the most remarkable religious city in the
world.   Jerusalem, Rome, Kieff, Benares, none of them can
boast the multitude of temples, and the lavishness of design
and ornament that make marvellous the deserted capital on
the Irrawaddy.   Deserted it practically is, for the few flimsy
huts that stand by the river are inhabited only by pagoda
slaves and men condemned to perpetual beggary.   For eight
miles along the river-bank and extending to a depth of two
miles inland, the whole space is thickly studded with pagodas
of all sizes and shapes, and the very ground is so thickly
covered with crumbling remnants of vanished shrines, that
according to the popular saying you cannot move foot or
hand without touching a sacred thing.   Some of the zedis
are all but perfect.   Restored by the pious, they stand out
glistening snow-white, only to render more striking the
hoary, weather-beaten ruins of their less-cared-for neighbours.
Here the bell-shaped, solid pyramid of Lower Burma is
rarely seen.   The religious structures fully merit the word
temple as understood in ordinary language.   To quote Yule,
who gives a detailed account of the principal shrines in his
Mission to Ava, there are all kinds : "The bell-shaped
pyramid of dead brickwork in all its varieties ; the same
raised over a square or octagonal cell, containing an image
of the Buddha; the bluff, knob-like dome of the Ceylon Dago-
bats, with the square cap which seems to have characterised

the most ancient Buddhist *chaityas*, as represented in the sculptures at Sanchi, and in the ancient model pagodas found near Buddhist remains in India ; the fantastic bu-payā, or pumpkin pagoda, which seemed rather like a fragment of what we might conceive the architecture of the moon than anything terrestrial, and many variations on these types. But the predominant and characteristic form is that of the cruciform vaulted temple."

The Irrawaddy just below Pagān widens out like a gigantic lake to over two miles in breadth, and the view of the sacred city from far down the river is particularly fine. Towering above the others rise the great temples of Ananda, Ta-pyi-nyu, and Gawdapalin, like visions of old-world cathedrals strayed into the desert. Round about them gradually rise into view hoary round towers, like a border "peel"; airy minarets as of an underground mosque; apparitions like the pyramids, chiselled into fairy terraced fretwork; huge bulbous mushrooms with slim lanterns on their backs, like the wide studio of a mad architect. There is a memorial line which, placing letters for numbers, declares the sum total of the pagodas to be 9999.

> Hlè win-yo than ta-nyan nyan
> Pagān payā paung.

> The cartwheel's creaking strains
> Pass Pagahn's storied fanes.

Probably, however, there are not nearly so many in anything like a complete state. Pagān ceased to be capital in 1284 A.D. The Emperor of China had sent a vast army to avenge the murder of an ambassador. The Burmese king pulled down a thousand arched temples, a thousand smaller ones, and four thousand square temples to strengthen the fortifications. But a prophecy found under one of the desecrated shrines robbed him of his courage, and he fled to the south ; and ever since Pagān has remained in its present practically deserted state. The whole ground within the old walls is strewn with bricks and mortar. Some of the zedis are strangled with jungle growth, huge bushes spring from their summits and sides and tear the masonry asunder, and with the vast majority no attempt is made to arrest the ravages

of time, but Mr. Taw Sein Ko says in his report of 1908 :
" Numerous terra-cotta tiles have been found in the basements
and corridors of several of the pagodas.   They illustrate
scenes in the *jâtakas* and in the life of the Buddha Gautama.
They are of two types.   In the Ananda and Shwezigôn the
tiles are enamelled green and show Chinese influence.   In
the Petleik pagoda they are of red baked clay and have
South-Indian resemblances.   All three shrines belong to the
eleventh century A.D.   The stone sculptures in the Ananda
are fine, and the pose, drapery, and contour are distinctly
Indian.   In the Sein nyet pagoda, halfway between Myinpagān
and Thiyipyitsaya, of the eleventh century, the Chinese
influence preponderates.   The twin Petleik pagodas are at
Thiyipyitsaya."

Few, if any, contain actual relics.   The cloistered and
terraced temples are simply receptacles for huge images of
the Buddha and others.   The corridors of the Ananda and
Gawdapalin are filled with sculptured groups representing
events in the life of the Great Master, and figures of eminent
disciples and yahanda.   In the central recesses, where are
the colossal figures of the Buddhas, the light is cunningly
admitted from above so as to fall on the calm gilded face,
producing a most weird and striking effect.   But Pagān
would require a monograph itself, and with it should be
compared Shwegu, between Mandalay and Bhamaw.   That
sacred island is a perfect forest of pagodas, and only fails to
obtain wider fame because of the existence of Pagān.   There
are 999 shrines within its limits, and a much larger proportion of these exist intact than is the case with Pagān, though
none of them can compare with the magnificence of the
Ananda.

The question of the architecture of the Pagān temples,
which is so different in style from that found in other parts
of Burma, has been fully discussed in Yule's admirable
Mission to Ava.   He omits, however, to notice the fact
that Anawrata-saw Min, when he established Buddhism in
Pagān, built all the pagodas and temples after the exact
model of those then existing in Thatôn, in the same order
and of the same size.   The town of Thatôn, above Maulmein, was the first settlement of Thawna and Ôttara, the

missionaries from Central India who introduced the teachings of the Lord Buddha into Burma.   There was certainly an ancient Hindu colony there, and its inhabitants may have brought some notions of their architecture with them.   But whether this be so or not, Burmans find source for pride in the admitted fact that "there is nothing in India to compare with the classical beauty of some of the smaller temples, or the stupendous architectural majesty of the Ananda, or the Ta-pyi-nyu."

The following song is taken from a very favourite play, *Sawpé Sawmé*, written by a Pegu dramatist and published in 1880, and gives an idea of the canticles sung at the dedication of pagodas and similar ceremonies.   It is set to a very popular air, the Yôddaya Nan-thein Than, "the Siamese Palace Tune," but I have not ventured to try to reproduce the original complicated metre.   The sikkè or magistrate in question was U Maung Galé, a younger brother of the late U On, long the only Burmese C.I.E., and once second judge of the Small Cause Court in Rangoon.

THE GILDING OF THE SHWE MAW-DAW

> Far-famed and bright, the Shwe Maw-daw
> Is known where'er the Sacred Law
> To toiling millions brings the peace,
> Bids grief be still and turmoil cease.
> Fair glory of Peguan land
> Revered on earth's most distant strand,
> Not more Dagôn's great golden pile
> Hath honour in the Southern Isle,
> Where'er beneath the zampu tree
> The pious bend the suppliant knee,
> Than thou the glorious lotus shrine
> High temple of the hairs divine.
> As leaps on high the funeral flame
> Of some yahan of sainted name,
> A beacon light to Neh'ban's rest
> And haven sure to men distressed,
> So skywards reared, thy shapely spire
> Upsprings a pyramid of fire.
>
> The hoar seer's words are now proved true,
> Spoke ages since while yet all new

The callow world in earnest youth
Revered the Buddha's law of truth,
Ere yet the wiles of lust and wrath
Beguiled men from the Noble Path,
And ignorance of sins, the worst
With which the race of man is cursed :

> *When white men reign*
> *Thy glories wane,*
> *Yet blaze again*
> *While yet they reign.*

High honour to our Sikkè Min,
Who purged away the stain of sin.
Now radiant as a mass of gold,
The temple glitters as of old ;
Ten thousand districts chant his name,
The Sekya systems vaunt his fame,
High winner of the holy rest.
Thrice is the benefactor blessed.
For him the last of lives is run
The ferry past and Ne'ban won.
Great guerdon gains such gift as this,
A sainted name, eternal bliss,
On earth renown will live for aye,
Beyond ne'er more to breathe a sigh.
Whenas the sacred work was wrought
The Tha-gya Min came down unsought,
Sweet music breathed from angel bands
And Déwas sped the workers' hands,
A nimbus shone around the spire
And gleamed each gem with holy fire,
As though on high in lucent coil
The sacred hair did grace the toil,
And once again in hermit guise
The Buddha Prince blessed the emprise.

Hast seen the lotus-bud in prayer
Fold fervent leaves ; with odours rare
Invoke the Buddha's gracious power
To save mankind in danger's hour ?
Hast seen the pôngyi's garb of peace,
The golden robe, strong to release
The suppliant from endless strife,
Unceasing change, the pains of life ?
So prayerful stands the holy fane,
So new-born gleams in golden grain ;
And calmly sleep the hairs divine,
Meet relic for so fair a shrine ;
And hither on the holy day
From far and near men wend their way

And kneeling pray that they may gain
Release from fitful change and pain.
Ah, Saviour Buddha, hear them call
And grant the long, last life to all.

High striving to the upper air,
Great convent of the Sacred Hair,
Thou'st stood upon the foreland's brow
From misty ages e'en till now.
The Budh himself, with his own mouth,
Stood on this hill, and, looking south,
Foretold that on this spot should stand
A fane far-famed in farthest land;
And hither came the brethren twain
And reared with stone of precious vein
A lordly pile and gilt it o'er
And many a monarch added store,
Till last of all our Sikkè came
And joined to theirs a pious name.
From youngest years till hoarest hours,
Peguans all, great fame is ours;
Two Henthas dwelt here, male and mate,
Ten thousand kings kept regal state,
And ever till the kalpas end
Will pious pilgrims hither wend.
Ah, Sikkè, great reward is thine,
Thy fame doth last while lasts the shrine
And ere the shrine falls, falls the world.

Pegu was the capital of the Talaing kingdom of
Hanthawadi. Shin Gautama foretold that it would be
founded in the 1116th year of his religion, and gave two of
his hairs to two brothers, Mahā Thala and Sula Thala, to
enshrine on the Thudathana Myinthila Hill. A pagoda
fifty cubits high was erected over them, and this was the
original of the Shwe Maw (or Hmaw) -daw Payā.

CHAPTER XVI

THE LEGEND OF THE RANGOON PAGODA

AT the end of the last world-period five lotus-buds sprang up on the Theinguttara Hill, where now the Shwe Dagôn pagoda stands. They opened their leaves and disclosed each of them within its chalice a thengan, the holy yellow robe of the monastic brethren. Then a huge bird settled on the top of the hill and laid an egg, and from this was presently hatched the kalawaik, the carrying bird of Vishnu, which seized the sacred garments and flew up to the heavens. This was an omen foretelling the appearance of five Buddhas in the present world cycle, and accordingly the universe which had existed in the preceding kalpa was shortly afterwards destroyed, with Mount Meru, the enclosing Set-ya-wala hills, the six heavens of the nat-déwas, and many of the lower seats of Byammās. Then followed myriads of years of chaos ; then myriads more while the present world called Badda was being constructed atom by atom, and at last the earth was ready and prepared to receive the first Buddha, Kaukkathan. He left his staff on the Theinguttara Hill ; his successor Gawnagông deposited his water-filter beside it, and the third Buddha, Kathapa, added a portion of his robe.

In the time of the fourth Buddha, Gautama, there lived on the Theinguttara Hill a gigantic scorpion, so huge that it devoured every day an elephant, and the tusks of its many victims were set up in a great ring fence round about its den. One day seven foreign ships passed along the coast. The sailors saw the white glimmer of the ivory from far out at sea, and landed to ascertain what it was. They began loading their ships with the precious treasure ; and were working their hardest, when suddenly they saw the giant scorpion coming straight at them.   They rushed on board, cut their cables, and stood out to sea.   But here a new danger awaited them.   A monster crab reared two gigantic claws out of the waters and threatened to crush anything that passed between. But there was no retreat, and, overwhelmed with terror, they drove before the wind.   The vessels just managed to pass through without touching the claws with their yards or masts ; but the scorpion, following in hot pursuit, rushed up against both pincers with its bulky body, and they closed in an instant, crushing and rending the monstrous prey.   The crab itself died of the poisonous food, and the neighbourhood of the holy hill was thus freed from its terrors.

Not long afterwards another ship sailed in these waters. Near Twanté, a town about twenty miles from Rangoon, lived a pious Talaing merchant, who had two sons named Pu, or dove, and Tapaw, or plenty.   These young men heard that there was a famine in the western lands, and set sail thither with a shipload of rice.   They landed at the mouth of the Ganges, and having procured five hundred waggons, loaded them with their grain and travelled into the Wethali country.   There one day their waggons were suddenly arrested, and as it were chained to the earth. While they were seeking for the cause, a nat, who in a previous existence had been their mother, appeared to them and asked : " Desire ye store of gold and precious things, or rather desire ye heavenly treasure ? "   They answered, " Heavenly treasure."   Thereupon the nat bade them go to where Shin Gautama, the embryo Buddha, was sitting beneath the yaza-yatana tree in the seventh period of seven days' meditation, which immediately preceded his becoming perfect.   They laid a sack of rice reverently at his feet, and in return received four hairs each.   The Buddha renamed them Tapôt-tha and Palika, and enjoined them to deposit the hairs on the Theinguttara Hill, beside the relics of the three preceding Budhs.   The place was to be determined by the " takun," a felled wood-oil tree " lying athwart," so that neither the top nor the roots touched the ground.

The brothers, happy in the possession of such inestimable relics, enclosed them in a golden casket, hastened back

to their ship and set sail.   But they visited many a distant
shore without gaining any tidings of the whereabouts of the
Theinguttara mount.   In vain they besought the nats, the
bilus, and yekkathas, good genii, ogres, and demons, of
whom there were many upon earth in those days.   The
spirits knew no more than the men.   At last the king of the
Tha-gyas took pity upon them, came down from the heavens,
and appearing before the seekers in the guise of a nat, told
them to return to their own native land.   There, not far
from their birthplace, Twanté, was the hill they sought for,
and the only being who could point it out to them was the
guardian spirit of the hill, the aged Sulé nat.   But this
guardian nat had lived so long upon earth that his eyelids
had become weak and heavy and had fallen together, so that
he was stone blind.   Before he could help them at all it
would be necessary to restore to him his eyesight, and this
could only be done by hoisting up his eyelids with two great
wooden props.   The Sulé nat was of gigantic stature, and
the two brothers sought about in the forest for the tallest
oil-palms they could find, cut them down, lopped them into
shape, and then went out in quest of the aged guardian
spirit.   At length they found him so thickly covered with
ancient moss and lichens that it was difficult to recognise a
living creature in him.   When he was asked where the
Theinguttara Hill lay he became suspicious, and brought
forward his blindness as an excuse for not being able to
indicate its situation.   But the two brothers were prepared
with their remedy.   They got their two great beams into
position, and after much trouble managed to hoist up his
heavy lids so far that the light fell in a narrow streak on
his pupils.   Sulé then indicated with a wave of his hand
in what direction they were to go, and Tapôt-tha and Palika
set off again on their search.   But here they encountered a
new difficulty.   Instead of one hill they found three, with a
lake in the middle of them, and there was nothing to show
where the staff, the filter, and the bathing robe of the previous
three Budhs lay buried.   They were in despair, but the king
of the Tha-gyās again came to their aid.   He descended
with his subject déwas during the night and united the
three peaks into one.   The next day the brothers felled the

tree on the summit and it fulfilled the required conditions. "It remained poised on its centre on the peak. Its top touched not the ground, and its root touched not the ground. Therefore the place was called in the Môn language, Takun." A pagoda was built twenty-seven feet high, and all the land round about on which its shadow fell between sunrise and sunset was consecrated to it for ever. The déwa king prepared a golden boat to hold the casket containing the hairs, and this vessel circled about perpetually on the lake, and was protected by water-wheels, whose spokes were prolonged into great swords and knives that struck out in all directions and turned without ceasing, except for a moment at midday, when they halted for the space of time during which a woman might draw out a thread from her spinning-loom.

Long after, the royal elder brother of China, King Udibwa, during his wars with the Burmans, was exceedingly anxious to carry off the sacred relics which are deposited in the Rangoon shrine. He prepared a magic figure in human form and despatched it to steal the Budhs' remains. The creature crawled all the way down the Irrawaddy on its stomach until it arrived at the suburb of Rangoon called Kemindine ("the looking-post"). There it raised its head to look for a moment, and was so overcome by the splendour of the shrine that it delayed too long, and when at length it stretched out its hands to steal the relics, the favourable moment at noon was passed, and the whirling swords cut it in pieces. Since then the whole of the treasures have been walled up in the relic-chamber, whence nothing but the entire destruction of the payā could remove them. The marvellous wealth of the shrine has been a fruitful source of wonder and speculation to many. Nevertheless the statement of Sonnerat that the spire, which has now risen to a height of nearly 370 feet, has a narrow funnel descending from the top down to the basement, and that down this shaft princes, rich men, and the religious of all nations cast gold and silver and precious stones, has a foundation only in the imagination of the Gallic writer. The crown or "umbrella" at the top is known to be crusted thick on the upper ring with precious stones, and from it hang scores of jewelled gold bells, placed there in recent times, but to the

mysterious relic-chamber no one has penetrated for hundreds
of years, nor probably ever will.   Neither the shrine itself,
nor the relics, nor the images, are the objects of the adoration of the pious.   The Burman, it cannot be too much
urged, is not an idolater.   He worships neither relic nor
image.   The pagoda and the figure only supply him with a
seemly place to utter the praises of the great Buddha, and
to form resolutions to imitate, as far as he can, the charity
and the sinless life of the great model.

CHAPTER XVII

IMAGES

THERE are few things which more irritate an educated Burman than to assert, or as most English do, calmly assume, that the Burmese are idolaters. The national idea is that idol-worship is especially the characteristic of the lowest savage tribes, and even fetichism is considered a superior faith. Therefore the accusation of bowing down to stocks and stones is intolerable, and the implication is combated with feverish energy. Where there are no prayers, in the technical sense of the word, there can be no idolatry. No one, not even Shin Gautama himself, can help a man in his strivings to lead a holy life. None but the individual in his own person can work out his special salvation, and he tries to do so by setting a splendid ideal before his mind. The words uttered before the impassive features of the Budh are not a supplication for mercy or aid, but the praises of the great Lord himself, through the contemplation of whose triumphant victory over passions and ignorance the most sinful may be led to a better state.

There is no Supreme Being; the Buddha himself, who even while he was on earth was no more than a perfect, sinless man, no longer exists to make intercession, were there any such power to which one might appeal. The only thing to be done is to praise, and in praising to strive to imitate, and through imitation to attain to the perfect knowledge, and so to the final deliverance, the exemption from the four burdens of heaviness, age, sickness, and death, which is the restful absorption of Ne'ban.

The worshippers of all creeds have always sought for a

special place wherein to pay their devotions. The Burman erects a pagoda over sacred relics, and puts up an image of the great Lord of Truth there, not to worship, but to afford a means to the pious of localising their feelings and concentrating their thoughts on the supreme model. The candles and smoky oil lamps, the fruits and flowers offered on the shrine, are no more signs of idolatry than the offertory bag placed on the altar by the Christian priest. The Yatana Kalapa is perfectly distinct on this point. Under the heading U'bhato Kotito Panha we find it written : " It is bootless to worship the Buddha ; nothing is necessary but to revere him and the memory of him. Statues are only useful in so far as they refresh the memory ; for as the farmer sows the seed and gathers in the grain in due season, so will the man who trusts in the Buddha and holds fast by his sacred Law obtain the deliverance and pass into Ne'ban. The earth and the Buddha are alike in themselves inert."

There is thus no doubt left as to what the great master and his interpreters intended. The worship of thè payā is nothing more than a simulation of the devotion which would be paid to Shin Gautama were he still upon earth. The Buddha is admired, he is lauded, he is tenderly loved ; and this devotion is extended to the figures which are erected in remembrance of him, in recognition of his blameless life, the supreme wisdom which enabled him to teach the Law, and the great compassion and benevolence with which he regarded all living things. The characteristics of a Budh are the exercise of the Three Great Works of Perfection, the constant practising of the Ten Great Virtues, and the Five Renouncings ; and to attain the deliverance, all must diligently strive to observe these. The Three Great Works of Perfection are :—

1. Assistance afforded to parents and relations.

2. Great offerings made in this and previous existences, coupled with strict observance of the enactments of the Law.

3. Benevolent dispositions towards all sentient beings indiscriminately.

The Ten Great Virtues are :—liberality ; observance of the precepts of the Law ; retreat into lonely places ; diligence ;

patience ; fortitude ; wisdom ; benevolence ; truthfulness ; indifference.

The Five Renouncings are the giving up, for holiness' sake, of—children ; wife ; goods ; life ; one's self.

This cannot all be effected in one existence, unless piety has been exhibited in many previous lives.   Much depends on one's kan, the accumulation of merits from past time. Just as the fruits on a tree are some of them good, some bad, but have little or nothing in common with each other, or with those that went before, or may come after, so it is with a man's kan.   But the diligent observance of the holy precepts, and especially the exercise of open-handed charity, will always tend to reduce the number of lives to be endured before the deliverance comes.

Prayer there is none in the technical sense of the word, and the doxologies repeated at the shrines are mostly those learnt in childhood at the monastery school, or special compositions of each individual for himself.   There is nothing laid down in any of the Buddhist religious books concerning the formulæ of prayer.   Whatever there is, is taken from the Apyin Aung-gyin, the record of the triumph of Shin Gautama over the outer foes, Mān-nat, the spirit of evil, and his daughters, and the Atwin Aung-gyin, the triumph over the inward foes, the kiletha, the passions of mankind.   Many, however, repeat little more than the tharana-gōng, the form with which the pôngyis almost invariably commence worship : " I worship the Buddha ; I worship the Law ; I worship the Assembly."   This, with the aneiksa, dôkha, anatta, " change, pain, illusion," forms the sentence to be repeated on the rosary.   A very usual form of doxology commonly taught to the scholars of the kyaungs, and therefore retained through life, is the following :—
" Awgatha, Awgatha, I worship with the body, with the mouth, and with the mind, with these three kans.   The first, the second, the third ; once, twice, until three times.   The Lord, the precious one ; the Law, the precious one ; the Assembly, the precious one ; these three precious things. I, the worshipper, most humbly, with fervid zeal, with clasped hands, pay reverence, give offerings, and with pious gaze bow me down.   Thus by this worshipping I gain merit and

increase in earnestness and purity of heart, and am freed
from the Four States of Punishment; from the Three Evil
Things, starvation, plague, and warfare; from the Eight
Chambers of Hell; and from the Five Enemies. And at
the end, when the last existence has come for me, may I
pass into Ne'ban."

Such "prayers" are addressed not merely to the image,
but to the whole pagoda, and not even on the platform of
the latter. It is common for the pious at any period of the
day to repeat their devotions simply in the direction of the
pagoda, and often from a spot where hardly even the summit
of it can be seen. The pilgrims to the Shwe Dagôn Payā
in Rangoon prostrate themselves at intervals from the
moment they catch sight of its glittering spire; but they
repeat nothing further than the above, or some more fanciful
formula, such as this: "Awgatha, Awgatha, Awgatha, I
worship the footsteps of the great, the brilliant Buddha, to
whom even the savage hunters turn, and the fierce dragons
on the mountain tops and in the abysses of the hills. In
the far land of Thiho (Ceylon) there, where, in the wilderness of woods, far from human dwellings, temples and
pagodas rise up 84,000 in number, in the caves and the
deeps; there I worship, there I bow me in devotion." By
far the greater number, however, repeat simple Pali sentences,
of which they have long forgotten the meaning, if indeed
they ever knew it. Many of the pyin-sin can repeat whole
books and chapters in the sacred tongue, without having
any but a very confused notion of the meaning of what they
utter. Yet even this parrot-like performance has its merit,
for it brings the mind into a fit state to contemplate the
great ideal. A conclusive proof of this is recorded in the
Malla Lingaya Wuttu, the life of Shin Gautama. There
were many bats who lived in a cave in the time of the last
Buddha, Kathapa, and great numbers of yahans were in the
habit of resorting to this cave to meditate and give themselves up to devotion. These bats learned to repeat some
of the phrases which they heard, but could not understand,
and this pious exercise resulted in such benefit to their kan,
that on their death they migrated to the seats of nat-déwas.
Afterwards, when Shin Gautama was preaching upon earth,

they again appeared upon the seat of man as yahans, and, attending diligently to the precepts of the Law, were the first, as disciples of Thariputra, one of the chief followers of the Buddha, to comprehend the sublime law of the Abhidamma. If dumb creatures then can win such rewards for piety, how much more a man who repeats his sentences with at least a consciousness of what their import is.

Similar to this feeling with regard to the Pali jargon, of which every Burman knows more or less, according to the length of his stay in the monastery or the depth of his religious sentiments, and prompted by a like idea, is the offering of little nan-tagôn. These prayer-flags—kyet-sha-taing, as they are sometimes called—are made of paper, cut fancifully into figures of dragons, lizards, and the like, with embroidery-work round their edges. In the centre is written some pious reflection or aspiration, and the offerer places it on the shrine. Most of those sold ready composed for the worshipper are in Pali, those which he writes for himself, in Burmese. Samples of these inscriptions are :—

" By means of this paper the offerer will become very strong."

" By the merit of this paper Wednesday's children will be blessèd by spirits and men."

" May the man born on Friday gain reward for his pious offering."

" This paper is an offering for people born on any day of the week from Sunday to Saturday."

" May the man born on Monday be freed from sickness and from the Three Calamities."

Very often nothing but the names of certain days of the week are written on the nan-tagôn ; but sometimes a friend of humanity, or a man with a particularly large family, covering with their birthdays the whole week, simply writes down the names of the days in any order he pleases. The commonest form at the stalls round about the Shwe Dagôn is this simple, bald list, and indeed Rangoon is particularly badly supplied in this way. There are other small flags or streamers made of coloured cloth, some of them, especially those presented by the Shans, stitched with many

plies until they stand out quite stiff. Others again are
made of varnished strips of zinc. These have nothing
written on them, and stand simply for the advancement in
piety of their offerers, as do the candles representing the
various nan, the animals which stand for the days of the
week. Other offerings are flowers, single or arranged in
bouquets, and almost invariably distinguished by the heavy
sweetness of their odour. Candles and tapers, of all sizes
and styles of manufacture, abound ; some a couple of feet
high, or occasionally much more, made of long, narrow
coloured tapers, plaited together over an ordinary solid one,
some plain white, others coloured all the hues of the rainbow, European manufactured sperm or paraffin articles, and
home-made tapers of the crudest style of dip. Side by side
with these are placed smoky oil-lamps, consisting of a little
flat saucer full of oil, with a wick composed of a bit of cloth
or a few threads of cotton roughly twisted together. The
candles are simply softened with a match at the bottom and
made to stick on the ledges in front of or round about the
figures of the Buddha. Incense sticks and scented wood are
often burnt on stone altars erected specially for such fire
offerings.

The worshippers, if they are men, squat down, neither
kneeling nor sitting down, but resting the body on their
heels as miners who are accustomed to low workings do.
The body is bent a little forward, and the hands are joined
together and raised to the forehead. The women kneel
down altogether, and for this reason take especial care to
cover up their feet, sometimes getting a friend to tuck their
skirts over them. All are of course barefooted. The
sandals are removed always at the foot of the pagoda steps,
though these may begin in some places many hundred yards
away from the shrine. Before commencing the repetition of
the formulæ, three prostrations are made with the forehead
to the ground, and the same is repeated at the close, and on
rising to depart you must turn to the right. It is usual to
hold some offering between the hands during worship—a
prayer-flag, a flower, or something of the kind—and this is
afterwards reverently deposited on the altar. A favourite
offering, instead of real flowers, is pauk-pauk. This is the

variety of rice known as kauk hnyin, fired dry on a pan. It swells up and cracks open, and the grains are then dyed red, green, or yellow, while some are left plain white. The resemblance to flowers or flower-leaves at a distance is sufficiently striking. It is a work of merit to go about lighting tapers and candles which have blown out, or lamps which have got choked up, watering flowers, and so on.

The statues of Shin Gautama, then, are only his visible representatives to keep alive in the hearts of his flock feelings of love and adoration, and gratitude to the Great Master who strove so long to teach the Law, and was ever so pitiful towards earthly suffering. Like the Egyptians, Buddhists have large images, but stand diametrically opposed to them in the way in which they regard them. All the Egyptian's energies were directed to conquering the hostile powers of nature. He sought with anxious care to preserve the mummy in the recesses of huge mountains of stone, in order that the soul returning after the period of 5000 years might enter again its old home. He built for eternity, and hoped to defy decay and outlast the world. The Buddhist laughs at this notion, seeing that for him the stream of time levels and carries off every existence with it. The rising again of spirits has for him nothing but a suggestion of devilish arts. The idea raises in his mind a threatening of evil, as well to the living as to the disembodied spirit. Instead therefore of devising any such uncanny measures for the preservation of the corpse, he strives rather to destroy it as soon as may be on the funeral pyre, or even to blow it into small atoms with fireworks and bombs. Similarly, his images are made of mouldering brick. Where is the use of laboriously carving figures in the hardest stone, when the most indestructible of them could only last for a time, which is but as a ripple in the stream of eternity? Therefore the marble and brass Gautamas are but few compared with those of brick and mortar, or wood, and the crumbling away and rotting of these is viewed with the utmost equanimity. There will always be piety enough to keep the tazaung full until the cycles end.

The popular division of the Gautamas is into the classes of standing, sitting, and lying. This is somewhat crude, but

it is perpetuated by a curious notion that though a man may
present all three kinds of images, he must do so in a special
order : the standing first, then the sitting, and last the lying
down.   As many as one pleases of one style may be presented, but you must not reverse the order : one dare not go
backwards.   The vast majority of images represent the
master in a cross-legged attitude, in which he attained the
Buddhaship, seated under the bawdi tree.   This sitting
figure is called Tinmyinkwé.   The left hand lies palm upwards in the lap ; the right hangs over the knee.   The ears
reach to the shoulder, and the face is calm and passionless.
On the top of the head is a little knob or point.   This is
called the mani-daw, and represents the hair which Prince
Theiddat cut off with his sword when he first put on the
yellow robe.   It was left a quarter of an inch long, and
never grew again.   In attaining to the supreme wisdom, the
Prince attained to the Ne'ban, or annihilation of the passions.

Less common are the Shinbinthalyaung, the recumbent
figures representing the Budh as he died and attained to the
Ne'ban of earthly existence, reclining between the two sāl-
trees.   He lies on his right side, and is often represented
with numbers of his lamenting disciples ranged around the
couch.   To these are not uncommonly added circles of the
kings of the earth and the heavens, bilus, galôns, nats, yekkathas, and a variety of other creatures.   The figures of the
latter often display some artistic skill in the modelling and
the expression of the features, which it is impossible to show
in the placid countenance of the teacher himself.   The Shinbinthalyaung very often have the emblems of the Shwe-zet-
daw carved on the soles of the feet.

Finally there is the Mat-tat-kodaw, or erect image, also
called Mat-yat-daw, where the master is represented in the
attitude of preaching, the right hand elevated, but still with
the same calm, unmoved visage.   These Mat-yat-daw are
usually very large, and are far more common in the temples
of Upper Burma than in the bell-pagodas of the low country.
They are often Sapupati Payā, representing the Budh as a
king with crown on head and the royal wings on arms and
thighs.   They are usually very large, like the recumbent
figure.   The standing figures in the Ananda at Pagān must

be over forty feet in height, and form a very impressive sight. Light sufficient to illuminate the whole figure cannot be admitted at the comparatively low gateways of the shrine. Cunning architects have therefore cut slits far up in the chapel roof, and a narrow stream of light falls full on the gilded face of the Buddha. The effect is most solemn and awe-inspiring. The devotee passes through long dim corridors, where his foot falls soft on the mouldy pavement, and the smell is as of a charnel-house, and there is silence throughout the whole vast temple, broken fitfully by the eerie chant of a fellow-worshipper far away through the passages, and suddenly he comes on the chapel and sees before him the sad tranquil face, with a glory shed over it, and the hand stretched out as if in warning or benediction. One can then understand how it is that many of the ignorant and unin-structed do actually worship the Gautama as if it were an idol, and the Englishman involuntarily takes off his hat as he enters the sanctuary.

The statues in the great lonely fanes at Pagān are cer-tainly far more impressive than those in the smaller but more gaily-decked-out niche-shrines of the solid pyramidal pagodas of Lower Burma. The four great Mat-yat-daw in the Ananda Payā represent the four great Buddhas of this world-cycle. Kauk-kathan, as the first law-giver, is placed in the east; Gawnagông in the southern image chamber; Kathapa to the west, and the Buddha of the present religious period in the northern shrine. Kauk-kathan is made of the sweet-scented dantagu tree; Gawnagông of jasmine wood; Kathapa of brass, and Gautama of fir; but they have all been covered with plaster and gilt, and the material of which they are made is only known by tradition. An especially favourite figure to represent standing is Dibinkāya Payā, the fourth of the twenty-eight Buddhas whose names are recorded as appearing in successively destroyed worlds. It was this Buddha, the "Light-bringer," who first announced to Shin Gautama that he, then a fervent yahan, would here-after, after many worlds, attain the supreme wisdom.

The temples of Pagān and other places in the upper territory are built specially for the reception of great images, and as the public zeal is concentrated on these, there are comparatively few surplus figures, and these mostly scattered along the sides of the dim corridors. In Lower Burma, however, where the sacred buildings are more particularly relic shrines, the images are more of an adjunct to the payā, and there is a most extraordinary multiplication of them. In each of the four image chambers round the base of the pagoda, besides the chief figure there are numbers of other Buddhas of all sizes, and these overflow into dozens of tazaungs, or image houses, all round about the central payā. This reserve stock is due to the unceasing desire for kutho. If a man cannot build a pagoda, or has not money enough to erect a monastery or a rest-house, there is at any rate no one so poor but he can gain merit by dedicating a Gautama ; and so images of brass and marble, plaster and wood, and sun-dried clay, flow in a never-ending stream to the great district shrines. There has long ceased to be any room for them except in the image-houses, and there they remain, seldom visited by any but the very religious, and gradually becoming grimed and mouldy with age, notwithstanding the Yéthonpwè, at the new year, when the women come and wash them down. It is a maxim that devotions may and ought to be repeated before every image, but it is not often that a worshipper is seen in the tazaungs, and the offerings of candles and incense sticks, flowers and pauk-pauk san-pan (pop-corn), are few and far between. Nevertheless the houses are crammed with figures of all sizes, from huge ten feet high Sagaing marbles down to little clay painted and gilt specimens that you can put in your pocket, and that idolatry-detesting Britishers often do so serve and afterwards exhibit as having actually " been worshipped." Big and small, they are crowded together as close as they can be, the small ones reposing in the hand or the lap, or round about the sides of their bigger facsimiles. Sometimes, as is the case in a great long building at the Kyaik-than-lan Payā at Maulmein, the centre is occupied by a gigantic recumbent figure, the tinmyinkwe being placed in orderly array all round the sides facing the central dying Budh. Sometimes the figures stand side by side on steps rising one above the other with a small open space in the middle. The halls are always quite full, the most recently erected being apparently just spacious enough to hold all the images ready to put into it.

Few statues stand unprotected in the open. At Kyauk-taran, on the Irrawaddy a few miles below Prome, there are a number of Gautamas cut out of the rocky face of a bluff overhanging the river. The ridge is about eighty feet high altogether, and the figures are thirty feet above the level of the water. They are all honestly cut out of the rock, and not, as some people think, simply brick and plaster erections —an idea induced by the habit of painting them white, or covering them with gold-leaf, occasionally indulged in by people anxious of bettering their chance towards a new existence. There are about fifty of them altogether, varying very considerably in size, some being very large. A similar work may be seen on the hill-side above Sagaing, opposite Ava. There the Buddhas, each in his separate niche, are carved at regular intervals, and the rock face sweeps round in a segment of a circle, the platform in front being strongly built up with a masonry revetment.

On the opposite side of the river, near the village of Sagyinwa, formerly a suburb of the old capital, Amara-poora, is a gigantic sedent figure built perfectly open and uncovered. It is situated close to a half-mile-long wooden bridge which once crossed the lagoon there, and the Budh gazes across the waters with eternal meditative smile. Round about are ranged double and treble circles of pigmy Zedi-yan, over which it towers to a height of ninety feet or more. The neighbourhood is practically deserted now that Mandalay has become the capital. There are almost no worshippers of the giant Buddha except the small colony of monks from the kyaung hard by. The birds will drop seeds between the crevices of the bricks and plaster, and another decade will probably see the great image torn out of all possibility of recognition.

Such a phenomenon actually does exist near the ancient Pegu town of Zaingganaing, on the opposite side of the river from the capital of the old Peguan kings. One of the singular pyramidal limestone rocks, common in the Tenas-serim Province, has been built with the aid of bricks into the form of an enormous Gautama. On the top of the

head, glinting white through the trees, appears the slender
spire of a small pagoda.   The jungle growth has spread all
over the hill, or image, and the outline and features of the
Budh struggle to be seen through a heavy fog of varied
green.   Such monster images exist here and there all over
the Eastern districts.   They are all exceedingly ancient,
and are regarded more as glorifications of the Great Master
than as recognised places for devotion.   The pious deposit
offerings and chant their sentences before them as they do
everywhere before the features of the Buddha, but otherwise
the people regard them more with the curiosity of the
foreigner than with the adoration of the devotee.

Among the more ignorant and superstitious classes it is
not at all uncommon to find particular images regarded with
especial awe and reverence, on account of the tale of some
prodigy displayed.   The sacred order and all true Buddhists,
however, strenuously discountenance the idea of any miracles
being wrought either by particular images or by holy relics.
It is for this reason that the latter are in Burma all walled
up and not brought out for the inspection of worshippers as
in other Buddhist countries.   The Kammawāsā in its denunciation of the claiming of magic powers is also considered
to forbid the assertion that any particular statue displays
more than usual power——a power which could not fail to
lead directly to idolatry.   The passage runs as follows :
" No brother must arrogate to himself what goes beyond the
power of human nature, and he must not boast of exceptional abilities.   Whoso gives out with evil intentions that
he possesses supernatural powers, saying that he has
attained zān, or ne'ban, or command of religion, or undisturbed repose on the path that leads to the deliverance ;
he is no Sramana ; he is no son of Sakya.   As a broken
palm-tree cannot be again united, as a twig broken from the
stem cannot be joined on again, so is that religious man,
who falsely declares that he has attained the superhuman,
fallen away from the true Sramanas, separated from the sons
of Sakya.   So long as life lasts must this be avoided."

Nevertheless unprincipled yahans, fearing that the piety
of their district is growing slack, or wishing to attract
benevolent pilgrims to their neighbourhood, undoubtedly

do occasionally originate, or at any rate stimulate, the belief in prodigies. A common wonder is that of the Tat-daw pwa, growing images. I am not aware that they are made of meteoric stones or any such substance. The carnal and unregenerate are wont to asssert that these images only grow at night and then in sudden jumps. In any case, they never grow very big.

A more unusual miraculous discovery actually resulted in the growth of a small fishing village into a prosperous town, and, owing to this latter circumstance, into the head of one of the subdivisions under the British Government. This is the station of Myan-aung on the Irawaddy. A Gautama rose out of the ground there. That was, however, not the wonder. It perspired! It perspired a thick, sticky exudation which precluded the necessity of using the milky juice of the thapan thi (*Ficus racemosa*), the gum usually employed in fixing gold-leaf on the images or pagodas. The tidings soon spread far and wide, and people journeyed from distant towns to see the wonder and to plaster on fabulous quantities of gold-leaf. The hamlet rapidly grew into a town. The surrounding country was taken up and cultivated, and Myan-aung is now as pretty a little station as any you will see on the great Irrawaddy, and is one of the principal centres of the great Henzada district.

Another little fishing village, farther down the river, below Maubin, possessed in 1879 a singular image. This Buddha in most unusual fashion suddenly began to develop a moustache. It was not much to speak of, and was certainly not pretty, but there was undoubtedly a growth of some kind on the upper lip. The phenomenon, however, never had more than an exceedingly local interest. A moustache is not an appendage that appeals to a Burman's finer feelings to any great extent, and if Shin Gautama had one in life he would certainly have shaved it off. Therefore the swampy, mosquito-haunted district failed to better its fortunes. A good many people came and gazed on the ugly bristles and made offerings, but they went away again, and the enthusiasm was strangled before it was well born. The military assistant commissioner of the district declared in an off-hand way that it was a fungus of a new kind, or some hitherto undiscovered lichen, and had thoughts of chipping a bit of the lip off and sending it to the British Museum. But he refrained, and the villagers missed even this poor chance of notoriety.

There are a few images specially noteworthy with less questionable reason. One of these stands half-way up Mandalay Hill under a lofty teak tectum. It is a gigantic standing image profusely gilt all over, and pointing with steadfast finger full at the glittering central spire of the palace rising gracefully over the throne of the Ruler of Existence. As a half-way house on the toilsome ascent of the hill it is always frequented, but the superstitious wayfarers gaze through the gilt railings more with the awe due to the guardian spirit of the capital than with the fervency of the worshipper. It has been burnt since the annexation.

In the chapel on the summit of the hill, looking over the wide, fertile plain towards the black, jagged Nat's Peak, haunted by goblins and wraiths, the silver windings of the mighty Irrawaddy and the barren pagoda-sprinkled Sagaing hills beyond, there is a singular statue. A notice begs the religious to put their gold-leaf, not indiscriminately all over the figure, but only on the eyeballs. The zeal of many years causes the pupils to start from their sockets as if the Buddha were horrified by some gruesome deed of sin perpetrated in the golden city below. The last time I was there I heard a matter-of-fact Briton marvelling how it was that the goodly nuggets had not long since been removed by a sacrilegious hand. It seems to be always Englishmen who think of these things first.

A hundred yards from the foot of the sacred hill in a tall brick building is a great marble Buddha, probably the biggest monolith in the world. The sitting figure must be quite twenty-five feet high, and scores of tons weight. It does the Mandalay workmen great credit that with their primitive appliances they should have been able to mount so ponderous a figure on its pedestal. In a wide square round about are arranged little six-foot shrines, each containing a gilt image and all looking towards the central Buddha. It is not the least wonderful of the many wonderful things to be seen round the foot of Mandalay Hill.

The casting of a brass image is a public festival, and the scene of general rejoicing. The people gather from miles round about, and there are plays and feastings for several nights, whether the Buddha is presented by an individual or by public subscription. The whole assemblage takes an interest in the proceedings, and rejoices in proportion to the success of the casting, which is effected in the same way as with bells. When the image is finished and ready to be dedicated, a great procession is formed ; a band of music and dancers go at the head ; the most wealthy men deem it an honour to be allowed to bear a hand in carrying the statue ; men, women, and children from all the surrounding country, dressed in their gayest clothes, follow on foot or in brightly decorated bullock-carts to the bottom of the pagoda steps. Then the Buddha is carried up and solemnly deposited in the allotted place, myatta-thappè, in religious phraseology, a term not to be rendered without many words in English. It includes all the meanings of seemliness, dignity, beauty, splendour, and awe-compelling majesty. The ritual of the monks at the consecration of an image is, as in the case of the dedication of a pagoda, vague, and decided by individual opinion. Such a formal presentation service is called Nekaza, and is declared by the Sulagandi sect to be superfluous. The lineaments of the Budh are worthy of honour wherever seen, at the pagoda or in the workman's shop.

The figures of Shin Gautama are not in themselves by any means handsome as works of art. The national skill in wood-carving is well known, and the little wooden lay figures made at Henzada and other places are remarkably clever in their variety of expression. None of this skill appears in the religious images. The modeller or sculptor is held fast by ancient custom. He must make his image of a particular pattern and with the recognised expression. The object is to portray the death of all human passions and earthly feelings. The calm, eternal sleep-like smile symbolises the attainment of ne'ban, the cessation of being, the end of the cycles of transincorporation of souls. This is all that is intended to be represented, and it is held out as a hope to the struggling sinner among earthly miseries.

The model to be followed would be worthless did the face express the hopes and fears and pleasures of wretched mortality.

The following triumphal song is taken from the same play of Sawpé Sawmé as the chant in celebration of the gilding of the Pegu pagoda, and is set to the same Yoddaya nan-thein than. The Mahā Myat Muni is the "Arakan Pagoda" in Mandalay.

ON THE IMAGE PRESENTED BY THE PEGU INSPECTOR TO THE MAHĀ MYAT-MUNI

Fair springs the sun at dawning
    From out the forest's green,
The nine gems on his nat-front
    Shine gloriously at e'en.

The rainbow weaves nat-raiment,
    Sweet is the lily's breath,
The malla flower is winsome,
    That weeps the Saddan's [1] death.

But fairer is the image
    That Hanthawadi sends,
Amid its gold and silver
    The pearl with ruby blends.

The maiden from her finger
    Drew off her jewelled rings,
The men brought costly diamonds
    And wealth of precious things,

And as 'mid shouts and clangour
    The flames leapt red as gold
All joyous cast their treasures
    Into the hissing mould.

So high hath Buddha honour
    In Hanthawadi's soil,
So gladly seek believers
    Release from earthly toil.

---

[1] The Saddan is the White Elephant, the last incarnation of Shin Gautama before he was conceived in Queen Maia's womb.

First great Sandathuriya [1]
   The Master's features wrought,
He sought the Budh's permisson,
   Nor failed in what he sought.

And I, the poor Inspector,
   Fired by as holy zeal,
Present a copied image
   And trust for equal weal.

That 'tis a precious alms-gift
   Great prodigies attest,
The Buddha's six-fold glory
   Gleams nightly on its crest,

And whenas it was casting
   Byammās and nats untold
Came down and cast rich offerings
   Into the holy mould.

Yea, myriads of all creatures
   From every earthly seat
Rejoicing cast their alms-gifts
   Before the Buddha's feet.

With close-clasped hands men bowed them,
   With fervent minds they prayed,
That Buddha some great token
   Might grant them for their aid.

Then from the lordly image,
   Aglow with brilliant light,
There streamed both fire and water
   Upon their dazzled sight,

And diamond rays and ruby,
   The Six great Glories blaze,
The Buddha's Nine great Splendours
   Blind their adoring gaze.

---

[1] The King Sandathuriya, while the Buddha was yet alive, obtained his permission to make a statue of him. This image is the great twelve-foot high brass Tinmyinkwe, now the chief centre of worship in the Mahā Myat-muni shrine.

> There's many a goodly image
>   In Mahā Myat-muni,
> But Mamyay [1] shall be aged
>   Ere it a fairer see.
>
> And I, the poor Inspector,
>   May lay me down in peace,
> For when this life is ended
>   Existences shall cease.

It is a very usual practice at the casting of bells and images for the onlookers to throw gold and silver articles of jewellery into the ladles of melted ore.

[1] Mamyay is a common poetical contraction for Mandalay. Man is also frequently used.

CHAPTER XVIII

BELLS

" THIS Bell is made by Koo-na-lin-gala, the priest—and weight 600 viss. No one body design to destroy this Bell. Maulmein, March 30th, 1855. He who destroyed to this Bell, they must be in the great Heell, and unable to coming out."

This inscription runs round the rim of the great bell at the Kyaik-than-lan pagoda at Maulmein. It is hardly a fiftieth part of the Maha Ganda at Rangoon, which, in turn, is a great deal smaller than the huge monster at Mengôn, near Mandalay ; but it is noticeable as being the only bell in Burma, as far as I am aware, which has an English inscription on it. The circumstance is scarcely to be considered in the light of a compliment, for the bell has not the character of exceptional sanctity, and there is a lengthy Pali inscription on the upper part giving further particulars, and commending the pious donors to the safe keeping of the 5000 nats who guard the faith, the tutelary nats of the universe, the nats of the earth, the air, the forest, and the city ; but there is nothing whatever in the shape of menaces to such as may have evil designs on the bell. Koo-na-lin-gala, the priest, however, no doubt thought this English addition very necessary and by no means unwarranted ; for only two years before, after the conclusion of the second Burmese war, in 1853, the British troops had tried to carry off the sacred Shwe Dagôn bell, and had gone the length of getting it on board of a ship. Unfortunately the vessel turned over, and Maha Ganda, the " great sweet voice," was capsized into the mud at the bottom of the Rangoon river.

The good mendicant, therefore, who superintended the casting of the bell for the Maulmein payā doubtless thought that none but the utmost terrors would serve to scare off the sacrilegious Briton, and therefore it is with punishment in awidzi, the lowest of the eight chambers of hell, ordinarily reserved for parricides, assaulters of an ascetic, and railers at the Buddha, that all who meditate harm to the Kyaik-than-lan bell are threatened. The fiery monk may rest happy. The bell has hung unmolested from the big crossbar, resting on its two huge teak uprights, and will doubtless long remain safe on the somewhat cramped platform at the end of the Taungnyo range.

The love of bells in Burma is somewhat remarkable. Every large pagoda has some dozens of them, of all sizes, hanging round the skirts of the zedi, the image-houses, and sacred posts. One or two were put up with the central shrine itself; others have been added at various times by the religious. Most of them have long Pali inscriptions on them recording the praises of the Lord and the aspirations of the giver. Here and there are a few with Burmese dedications, presented by poor, simple jungle people, the monks in whose district did not know Pali, or had the grace to say they were not learned enough to write an original composition in that language. Every Burman has learned a certain number of Pali formulæ to enable him to worship at the pagoda, but few even of the most renowned sadaws have anything like a thorough knowledge of the sacred language. Hence, when there is a modest monk in the kyaung, the simple cultivators have to fall back on their own vernacular, and produce plaintive appeals like the following :—

"This bell was moulded with great care and much expense, and is humbly offered by Maung San Ya, of the hamlet of Nga-pe-u, in the township of Maubin, and Mama Gyi, his wife, who seek refuge in the boundless mercy of the pitiful Buddha, in the majesty of the eternal Law, and in the example of the venerable Assembly of the Perfect, the three gems. They visit the precious things faithfully on the appointed days. Applaud, ye pious! They humbly strive to gain for themselves merit. May the good nats who guard the forest and the field look smilingly on them and

protect the poor man's crops.   May the nats who dwell in
the air and the earth defend from evil creatures the two fat
bullocks which plough the fields.   May the guardian nats
of the house and the city keep from harm Chit U, their son,
and little Ma Mi, their darling daughter.   And may the
merit of this offering be shared with their children and with
all living beings.   May the excellent Lord pity them, the
good spirits smile on them, the holy assembly receive them.
So shall Maung San Ya and Mama Gyi gain much merit
and rejoice in presenting this bell.   Weight, seventy-five
viss."

Such dedications are found here and there, but they are
not common, for half the honour of presenting the bell is lost
if the common crowd can read what is written on it ; and
doubtless Maung Chit U, when he has been to an English
school, and has got a place under Government, or in an
English merchant's office, will be rather ashamed of the
quaint humility of his father's offering.

The bells are not intended to summon worshippers to their
devotions.   There is no necessity for such a call where there
is no formal service.   Every man is responsible to himself
only for his religious state ; no one else has anything directly
to do with him, or can give him help.   The monks themselves display but little concern in the spiritual state of the
laity.   If a man is to attain a favourable change in a succeeding existence, it must be by his own exertions.   He
knows the regular duty-days, and on these and on the special
feast-days he goes to gain kutho for himself and better his
chance towards a new transincorporation.   If he is a fond
man, he parcels out the merit acquired by his devotions
among those members of his family or friends who have not
been to the pagoda.   The use of the bells is to direct attention to the fact of the lauds of the Buddha having been
recited.   The worshipper, when he has finished, goes to one
of the bells and strikes it three times, to bring to the notice
of the guardian spirits and the four worlds what he has been
doing.   There are always a number of deer's antlers and
billets of wood lying near the bell for this purpose.   None
of them have clappers, and metal is not used to strike them.
There is no objection whatever to a non-Buddhist striking

the bell ; it is indeed rather a kindly action, for the more
clangour there is the more likely the nats are to observe the
devotions going on.   After the bell itself has been struck it
is proper to strike the ground, so that the spirits of the earth
may know as well as the guardians of the air.   Most of the
bells have a fine tone, and a flick with the finger is sufficient
to cause a vibration through the whole twenty-five tons of
metal in Maha Ganda.   What sound the Mengôn bell,
second only in size to that presented by the Empress
Catherine to Moscow, is capable of producing, will never,
probably, be known, for the supports have given way,
and half of the rim rests on the ground.   But, as
Colonel Yule says, it would have at any time required a
battering-ram to bring out its music.   It has, since the
annexation, been hung by the enterprise of the Irrawaddy
Flotilla Company.

Besides those suspended round the precincts of the payā,
the hti, or umbrella, on the top of the edifice, is always
hung with a multitude of bells.   Those on the more sacred
shrines are very often entirely gold or silver.   Several on
the Shwe Dagôn are of gold, studded with precious stones,
and are worth many hundred pounds sterling apiece.   These,
of course, are furnished with tongues, and the slightest
breeze causes a constant harmonious tinkling, dear to the
worshipper's heart.   The object of these bells is identical
with that of those below on the platform——to attract the
attention of the good spirits in Tawa-deintha, and other
abodes of the nat-déwas on Mount Myinmo.

Though the bells are very well moulded, the mode of
casting them is of the most primitive possible character.   A
mould of clay is formed to represent the inside.   This is
covered with bees'-wax to the proposed thickness of the
metal, and over this again is placed a heavy layer of clay,
mixed with chopped paddy straw.   Through this outer
covering there are a number of funnel holes in parallel rings
at distances of six or nine inches, and through these the
molten metal is poured in, melting and taking the place of
the bees'-wax, which flows out at the bottom.   Straws inserted
through the clay let out the air and steam.   Thus the bell
is formed in a series of rings one above the other.   The

copper and tin are melted together in small open-air furnaces round about, and the crucibles are carried in little wicker baskets. Large bells usually are made in a pit dug in the ground. The metal images of the Buddha for the pagodas are cast in a similar way. When the mass has cooled, the outside is polished, and any flaws there may be are patched up. Then the inscription is chiselled on, and the bell is solemnly dedicated.

The casting is made quite as much a ceremony as it used to be in the Middle Ages in Europe. The whole district gathers to see the operation. Songs are sung, and bands clash and play while the actual casting is going on, and sometimes the vast multitude is wrought up to such a state of enthusiasm that women and children throw in their necklaces, and gold and silver rings and bangles. Traces of these are to be seen in the inside of many bells, in the shape of whitish or yellowish streaks. The workmen sometimes, in the case of large bells, try to strengthen them by twisting iron chains round the inner mould in the midst of the bees'-wax. Such a chain cable is distinctly to be seen in the great ninety-ton Mengôn bell. Since the " Great Monarch " of Moscow became a chapel, this is actually the biggest bell in the world.

The shape of Burmese bells is not handsome. They come straight down to the mouth like a barrel—not expanding at the rim, like those of European make, but their tone is very sweet. In Burma bells are entirely reserved for pagodas. A Burman never has a bell in his house ; and it would, in fact, be no use to him there if he had it. Englishmen do not use them either, so that throughout the whole country the bell is only used for sacred purposes.

The following is a translation of the inscription on the bell numbered 15219 in the Indian section of the South Kensington Museum :—

" The Victor, the All-gracious " [referring to Gautama, the Lord Buddha].

" The gist of the discourse on worship, as it appears in the beginning of the Dhamma-set, is as follows :—One must give goods in alms ; one must preach the Law : these two things are good deeds both for this world and for the next ;

they lead into the four meggas and the four palin-sas, the
paths by which a man may pass to ne'ban. Without
charity you cannot attain to ne'ban; so it is written in the
Pali, in the texts, the Tagata and the Tiga, and the commentaries on these sacred books.

"A seemly place is this, a goodly and far-famed place
[the shrine where the bell was set up], renowned throughout
the four systems of ten thousand worlds, among the Nat-
déwas, the Athuras, the Byammās, the Thagyas, the
Nagas, the Gôn ba Yekkhas [the guardians of the Thagya
realms], and all such beings to whom reverence may be
paid.

"The Pagān Min [who was deposed during the second
Burmese war in 1852, and died of smallpox in 1880], who
has received the divine authority, the king of this country,
gave to me, as to one of his pages to whom he gives commands, the title of Maha Min-gaung Kyaw Din, because I
was an old and true servant of his, listening reverently to all
his commands; this title he gave me with power over three
districts, with mercy abundant, like the earth and all the
precious things.

"I, the giver of the bell, the famous man, the Yewun
Min, was staying in the sweet-smelling town of Ma-u, of
which I collect the revenue for the king, and with me was
my wife, my life's breath, Mèh Shwe Gôn, like to the
pollen of a lily, from whom I will not be separated in all the
existences to come, out of which we hope soon to escape,
and therefore we give praises now in order to advance in the
Meggas and the Po [the four great attainments]; we adore
before the Lord Buddha that we may embark on the golden
raft of the noble path which will conduct us to the final
plunge into ne'ban; we two, brother and sister [commonly
used for husband and wife], have given this bell as an offering to the seven precious things.

"The exact weight of the bell in current reckoning is
2500 kyats weight. In this attempt to merit ne'ban our
method was as follows:——We took our own weight in gold
and in silver and bought copper and other metal [lawha,
the Pali word used, implies *five* metals—gold, silver, copper,
iron, and lead], and mixed them well together.

"In the year 1209 [1847 A.D.], in the hot season, at a fortunate hour, I had it moulded, setting my heart on giving it in alms. As I wrote this inscription I offered up abundant prayer that no enemies or troubles might come nigh me, and that I might obtain ne'ban. Then I dedicated it.

"Now will I record all the alms which I gave and erected within the sacred enclosure of the pagoda, round the slender spire. I gave a tagôn-daing, the price of which, with all incidental expenses in putting up and everything, was five hundred rupees; that was the alms exactly. At the foot of the tagôn-daing I built four small pagodas, making bold to offer them in alms. In addition to these I built, outside the pagoda enclosure, a monastery and a rest-house. I, the Yewun Min, wished earnestly to give the greatest alms of any in fragrant Ma-u-myo, of which I collected the taxes. I, the Yewun Min, and my wife, my sons and my daughters, the four chief parties, together with my servants and slaves [presented these things]. I persuaded them all to give alms that they might attain to ne'ban, the deliverance; that they might prepare for themselves the way, difficult and full of swirling eddies. Let the four congregations — let men, nat-déwas, and all creatures, unite in praise.

"Such are all my offerings; these alms dedicated all together, in order to gain merit, to rise and progress to ne'ban—to the world just before it [the last of corporeal lives]. May I be freed from the four states of punishment; the three great kaps [fighting, famine, and plague]; the eight evil places, from which a man is born biind, dumb, and otherwise crippled; from the five enemies; from unfortunate times and seasons; from bad-intentioned people; may I escape all these when I die. When new glories wake up, I will give praise; in the king's palace, the golden dwelling where the king lives; I will ponder well and chant aloud the praise of faith. Very high, even to the skies, rises the pagoda given in alms by the Ma-u revenue collector, the Yewun Min payā, the pious founder. All men and nat-déwas, when they behold it, will cry out eagerly in praise, they will shout Thādu [well done, thou good and faithful servant], with united, limitless clamour.

"The good that I have done in this world ; all the alms that I have given [may they be for the benefit of] my parents, teachers, cousins, and all my relations ; all who in Zampu-dipa are kings of the earth, all queens, their sons and daughters ; nobles and all men of rank, officers, and all people of the earth in the thirty-one seats of the world. All the merits I have gained, may they be shared with these. I give them and share them freely. The alms are manifest. I have given them. This good work, when I forget it [*i.e.* in my next life], may it be counted to me in the time of the Buddha Arimadeya, when he is revealed. The friendly witnessing nats will bear testimony, as they wring the water from their streaming hair."

The allusion to the witnessing spirits refers to the Mathôndaye nats who testified that Shin Gautama was the true Buddha. Mān Nat, the spirit of evil, came and claimed the throne under the Bawdi-bin as his, and appealed to all his countless retinue as witnesses that he was the true Buddha, and the rightful possessor of the throne. They replied with a great shout. The Lord Buddha had no one to call in evidence but the earth, and to it he addressed himself. The earth replied with a violent quaking and a roar that scared away all Mān Nat's noisy host. The Mathôndaye nats stand as representatives of the earth, and it is to gain their testimony that a cup of water is always poured out whenever an offering is made. Hence their wet hair. At the Shwe Zigôn pagoda between Nyaung-u and Pagān, the Mathôndaye nats are represented under umbrellas and with books. Their images almost always display them wringing the water out of their long tresses. It is to draw the attention of these nats that the worshipper, after striking the pagoda bell, strikes the earth.

The small bell in the South Kensington Museum, in the case close by the larger one, bears the following inscription : —"In the month of Tabodwè [February], on the fifth of the waning moon, in the year 1204 [1842 A.D.], on a Sunday at about four in the afternoon, this bell was cast and moulded of pure copper. Its weight is 594,049 kyats [this is an absurd misstatement, or a gross piece of flattery to the king]. There are four lions on the hanging apparatus. Its height is nine fingers' breadths; the diameter five inches; the circumference fifteen; the thickness twenty-four (lines?). It is called the Mahati Thadda Ganda (the great, sweet sound). The man who had this royal bell moulded was the Burman king Tharrawaddy, Kônbaung Min."

CHAPTER XIX

A PAGODA FEAST

A PAGODA feast in Burma is one of the most frequent, as well as one of the most picturesque sights in the country. Each shrine has its own special sacred day; and the annual celebration of it is made the occasion of a general picnic, the congregation of people, from all parts of the surrounding districts, being bent no less on pleasure than on pious observances. Reverence for the shrines of various saints in different parts of Europe gave rise to the great fairs which were general until the end of last century, and survive even now in out-of-the-way places. Doubtless, if the Burmese were a commercial people, and cared for the putting together of pieces of silver, these gatherings might degenerate into occasions of barter and bickerings of trade—just as, if they were a practical people, their zat-pwè might blossom into something of a more real character, as the old mystery and morality plays gave birth to the modern drama of Europe. But the Burmese do not care for any of these things; and the pagoda festivals retain therefore the character they have always had, of ostensible religious assemblies. Still their most obvious characteristic to the ordinary public mind is very different. Youths and girls look forward to them as seasons of mirth and flirtation: long nights at the open-air theatre, feastings and perpetual amusements, the pleasanter because lasting no more than a couple of days. Elderly people have no less liking for them. They meet their old friends, and receive and recount the gossip of half a dozen districts; and there is always a succession of new acquaintances. It is a joyous holiday; and it is sanctified by the thought that the few hours spent at the payā gather up stores of kutho, not less certainly profitable than the social delights of the "duty day" are pleasurable.

The greatest of all the pagoda feasts is, of course, that of the Shwe Dagôn in Rangoon, with its pilgrims, not only from the farthest parts of Burma and far-away Shan hills, but also from over the seas, from Siam and Cambodia and the Corea. But the vastness of the gathering and the proximity of the great town spoil the national character of the festival, and introduce too many elements of nineteenth-century civilisation in the shape of merry-go-rounds and hack carriages. A "jungle" feast is not only more characteristic, but more appreciated in its way by both town and country folk.

There are three old Talaing pagodas near Rangoon, Kyaik-ka-san, Kyaik-ka-lo, and Kyaik-waing, whose annual duty days are looked forward to with pleasure by all the people round about. The feasts all occur in the month of Tabodwè, corresponding to our February or March. I have a suspicion that, were the proper date adhered to, all three would have the same uboné; but such a lavish squandering of the good a popular religion provides for us would hardly meet with lay approval, even if advocated by the most holy of hermits. Accordingly the three pagoda days occur at intervals of a week, without reference to the crescent or waning moon; and latterly, with singular convenience for Burmans occupied in business in Rangoon, have usually been fixed for Sunday; so that English merchants are not troubled with the sudden ailments of their clerks at this season so much as used formerly to be the case. The Kyaik-ka-san is probably the most sacred of the three; containing as it does a tooth and bone of the forehead of Shin Gautama, brought to Rangoon by a yahanda, a blameless mendicant, over whose remains in Rangoon a huge thein-gyi, or ceremonial building, has been erected. Kyaik-ka-lo is, however, seemingly the more popular. It stands on the summit of a little hill about fourteen miles north of Rangoon, and is built of laterite blocks, now faced with bricks covered with plaster. The shrine was built in the second century before Christ, and,

ninety feet high itself, is surrounded by twenty-four smaller
zediyan of a much later date.

Great crowds of people go out every year from Rangoon,
starting early in the morning, so as to avoid the heat, though
in February the bracing winds of the cold weather have not
altogether gone.   Most of the travelling is done in bullock-
carts.   These conveyances are not nearly so fine as the
Mandalay vehicles, but they are neat enough ; the pole is
elaborately carved at the end, and above all they are roomy,
and allow " Jack Burma " and his family to loll about as
they please.   Bamboos are bent over to form a hood, and
over this is thrown a kullagā, a piece of tapestry-work
formed of pieces of many-coloured cloth sewn on to a red
blanket so as to represent figures ; the scenes being usually
taken from some well-known play or from the court.   They
are eight or ten feet long, and four or five broad, affording
a capital shelter from the sun, and combining the advantage
of being easily moved when there is a breeze, with the still
greater merit of looking very gay and bright.   The party
starts off before daylight, young master Lugalé being left
behind to guard the house till the rest come back, and testi-
fying his disapproval of the responsibility of this duty by
strenuous howls.   The Madrasi sepoy lines are soon passed,
and we get out into the undulating country beyond, and
pass through the gardens and orchards which abound along
the Prome road.   The ground here is not suited for rice,
and there are large areas covered with mango, jack, ma-yan,
a kind of acid plum (which the perverse Englishman persists
in calling Mary-Anne), and other fruit-trees, with pine-apples
in long rows beneath their shade.   The Chinese have great
market-gardens here, miracles of neatness, but far from
savoury in their odours.   They never miss a chance of
making money, and accordingly this morning turn over a
few pice by selling sugar-cane to the girls, and bamboo pipes
of palm-toddy to the men.   The Shans, also born gardeners,
to whom the fruit-trees mostly belong, are very pious, and
join in the pilgrimage with their quaint offering-flags made
of slim frameworks of bamboo, woven across in diverse
patterns with vari-coloured cotton threads.   A little farther
on we get beyond the region of the market-gardens, and

pass between monotonous stretches of secondary jungle with no houses to be seen, though behind the strip of tangled bush there are wide expanses of rice-land with little bamboo huts dotted here and there in clusters. But the sun is getting high, and about half-way on the journey old Maung Gyi declares he is hungry, and draws up the cart under a bank in a shady hollow. The bullocks are turned loose, and preparations made for breakfast. The entire house service has been brought with us. It is not very extensive, certainly. A couple of earthen pots with covers, and a flat wooden spoon to stir up the rice or curry ; a ladle made of half a cocoa-nut, with a handle in it ; a big round flat dish of plain lacquered wood to place the entire feast on when it is ready ; and a few bamboo, lacquered cups, without handles, with perhaps a plate or two, complete the list. The provender is equally simple. A heap of plain boiled rice, dried fish, chillies, onions, nga-pi, some salt and oil—that is the sum total. But it is eaten with zest and good appetite, and the little stream furnishes wherewith to wash it down. Then the ladies produce cheroots for the party from the recesses of their bamboo plaited pahs, and light up for everybody if they are good-natured.

Numbers of other carts have come up and stopped or passed on in the meantime, and, hilarious with his breakfast, Maung Gyi challenges neighbour U Hpe to a race ; and forthwith the bullocks are brought into a shambling trot, and amidst much prodding with sticks and cries of " Hé noa " and " Tun-n-ng," and other sounds understanded of cattle, a fairly level race is kept up for half a mile or so. Then the carts are pulled up, and their inmates burst into loud talk, having been hitherto precluded from expressing their triumph or chagrin from a fear of biting their tongues off in the jolting, or of being choked with the dust. Notes are compared as to who is coming and who has stayed away, and then fresh acquaintances are sighted in the passing throng ; and so with much good humour and pleasant meetings the fourteen-mile journey is safely got over. Arrived at the zayat, the rest-house, which marks the point whence the path to the shrine strikes off from the highway, the cart is turned aside among the low bushes ; the oxen are cast off and tethered up, the mats and bedding spread out below the cart in readiness against bed-time. Then our party breaks up to seek friends in the crowd ; the girls taking off their travelling-dress and putting on their finest tameins, an operation which it would puzzle English women to do in public with equally scanty raiment and equal modesty. But they do it deftly ; and, after touching up their complexion with a little fragrant thana'kha, are off, followed shortly by their brothers, who, in the absence of a looking-glass, have some difficulty in winding on their turbans to their liking. However, that is eventually done, and the remaining hours of daylight are spent in pleasant talk with friends, and wanderings through the shrub-growth and tall grass which cover the spur, at the end of which is the pagoda. The little tank, a brick-built pond, which lies at the foot of the hollow, falling away from the monastery, is a great rendezvous, and many of the older people climb the slope to have some talk with the abbot.

At nightfall there is a general gathering in the cleared space where the stage for the puppet-play is erected. The monks of the kyaung are not Sulagandis, and do not prohibit the acting of a play so near to the sacred precincts. Besides, it is the Wethandaya Wuttu, one of the ten greatest birth-stories ; and there is a troupe of famous manipulators from Rangoon. The marionette play is more esteemed by the people than the legitimate drama, and it is more suited to the neighbourhood of the relic-shrine. Nevertheless, a zat-pwè, got up by the amateur actors and actresses of the village of San-gyi-wa, a mile back on the road, is also well patronised, so that all tastes are consulted.

The people sit round about in a dense crowd, smoking and chewing betel, many of the young men strolling about and flirting in the impromptu bazaar which some business-like girls have started. This goes on till daylight, the audience alternately sleeping and looking on and applauding. At early dawn, the offerings are made to the yahans, and all crowd to the shrine to recite their sentences in praise of the Lord Buddha. After breakfast there is more gossip and conversation with friends. A few of the old people listen to the reading and expounding of the Law by the superior of the monastery, but the young continue the amusements of the day before. The cool of the evening, or the following morning at latest, sees all on their way home again, the fun being kept up with, if anything, increased zest. Every one is in high spirits. There has been much merit gained by the pilgrimage, and the personal enjoyment of the trip has been no less satisfactory. Gay turbans are hung up as flags from the carts, and songs and choruses are frequent and jovial. Many a marriage is settled at these pious picnics. There is such abundant opportunity for love-making at the open-air encampment, where the old people are so engaged in talking with relations and friends whom they have not seen for the last twelve months, that they forget how craftily they utilised similar opportunities when they were young themselves. Besides, at the end of February, Lent is beginning to loom up, and in Lent nobody can be married, and those girls who do not care for the watery courtship of the New Year's Feast in April are often induced to be complaisant at the country pagoda feasts. Many a young couple have special cause to remember the happy ride back. The Buddhist faith may be as dreary, without hope, without belief in the world, as many say it is, but no one would imagine it so who looks on the gaily-dressed laughing crowd of men and maidens who throng to the country pagoda feasts.

CHAPTER XX

DUTY DAYS

THERE are four uboné, or duty days, in every lunar month, on which all good Burmans are expected to go and worship at the pagodas. These are the eighth of the crescent, the full moon, the eighth of the waning, and the change, of which the second and the fourth are the more sacred. As the monks have nothing to do with looking after the spiritual state of the people, it is entirely a matter to be settled by one's self whether any particular worship day is to be observed or not. If you conclude that strict religious observances are only necessary for your spiritual well-being on the day of the full moon, or at any rate that you may leave out the eighth of the crescent and waning moon, then the uboné does not concern you at all, and you may proceed about your ordinary business without being considered a reprobate. The very devout may go to the pagoda on all the four sacred days of the month ; but if you choose to omit one or several, or substitute an ordinary day for that provided by religious custom, there is no one to take you to task for it. Were a Burman never to go to the pagoda at all, or fail to do so for any considerable time, he would indeed soon get a very bad character among his neighbours, and might even be formally excommunicated by the yahans. There is, however, practically no constraint save the force of public opinion. But the duties of worship are so light, and so dependent in their details upon yourself, and there is so much amusement to be got out of a visit to the pagoda on an uboné, that few, even of the most worldly-minded, miss any great number of the appointed days, and a special festival is always carefully observed.

With the really devout, a worship day always commences on the previous evening, that of the apeitné, or day of preparation. In most country villages, and occasionally even in the larger district towns, where there is more dissipation than devoutness, a few old men, as a voluntary work of merit, go round about the place beating the kyizi, the triangular gong, used only for this and similar religious purposes. The instrument is suspended by a string to a stick carried over the shoulder, and as the sounds vibrate, rise and fall, quicken and die away with the winding and unwinding of the cord, those who intend to keep the duty day well make ready for a start to the pagoda. Mats, sleeping-rugs, blankets, and eatables are gathered together ; and the whole family, with the exception of a couple of the children and an old woman or so perhaps, left behind to look after the house, set off in a body, preceded in some cases by a kyizi of their own, struck at intervals by the head of the family, who slings it on a bamboo, to the other end of which, as a kind of equipoise, is fastened a lamp. The purpose of this ceremony of striking the gong is to announce to the four worlds the good work on which the party is engaged. They make their way to one of the numerous zayats, erected round the pagoda for the accommodation of pious people. If the family be a wealthy one they have probably such an open-sided, floored shed of their own, erected for the general use, but virtually reserved for themselves when required. If they have not, or if the shrine is small and the rest-houses few, they put up in one of the general zayats, where they can always find a quiet corner to settle in. There they sleep, or, what is better, tell their beads and meditate.

Some time before daylight the food intended for the yahans is cooked, and when the sun rises a message is sent to the monastery that everything is ready. The alms have been put together in a heap in the middle of the zayat, in front of the permanent platform on which the mendicants take their station after they have arrived in a long procession of Indian file. In the meantime numbers of other more comfort-seeking laymen, who have slept at home, come trooping in from the town, also bringing offerings for the pagoda, and food for themselves and the pyinsin. When a

congregation has been made up, or when the family party
is complete, the senior monk recites the Ten Precepts incumbent on all upathaka on duty days, and adds some
portion of the sermons of Shin Gautama, the other pyinsin,
sitting behind their big fans to hide the women from their
sight, occasionally making the responses. Finally the
Payeit-gyi, or some similar litany of praise, is intoned;
all the congregation joining in the chant, with upraised
hands clasping a flower or some other symbol of offering.
With this the service ends. The yahans rise from behind
their fans and file back to the monastery again, the food
being carried after them by the pupils or the donors. When
this is done the worshippers set about preparing their own
breakfast—unless, indeed, as is probable, it was cooked at
the same time as the food for the yahans. Each family eats
separately, arranged in a circle round the great byat, or
platter of rice. If, however, any one has some particular
delicacy—the celebrated nga-pi gaung fish paste from Payā
Gyi, in the An-gyi township, iguana's eggs from Shwe
Gyin side, or pickled tea fresh from the Shan hills—he
gives of his abundance to those round about; and any
solitary stranger from a distance is always sure of an invitation to join some breakfast party. When all have finished
eating, the fragments that remain are thrown out for the
pariah dogs and the crows. Additional merit is of course
gained by this act of charity. For the rest of the day, with
the exception of the time that may be spent in repeating
doxologies before the image of the Buddha at the pagoda,
nothing is done. Every one is dressed in his best and goes
about meeting his friends, or lolling comfortably with a
cheroot in the zayat waiting for them to come to him. Vast
quantities of betel-nut and pickled tea and local gossip are
discussed. The racing-boat the Bassein men are getting
ready to send for the October contests in Mandalay; the
brass image Maung Waik, the extra assistant commissioner,
is going to dedicate next month; the old witch down at
Ywa Thit Gyi, who has caused the murrain among the
Thu-gyi's buffaloes, and the nuisance it is that the English
ayebaing will not allow her to be tied to a bamboo and
pitched into the river in the good old fashion, to prove that

she really does trade in the black art; the new style in Manchester-flowered turbans that Ah Lôk, the Chinese pedlar, has brought in his boat from Rangoon—all these, and a great variety of kindred topics, are considered under all their aspects.

It must not, however, be supposed that all the people take this easy-going and frivolous view of duty days. Diligent seekers after kutho behave very differently. They do not merely limit themselves to the customary forms of worship and offerings. They sleep little, or not at all, the night before; telling their beads instead, and reading good books, some of the discourses of the Buddha, or portions of the greater zāts. All necessary business is transacted the day previous to the uboné, and neighbours are exhorted to observe the festival properly. After one simple dish in the morning, they eat nothing for the rest of the day; or perhaps on certain occasions do not break their fast till after mid-day, a custom very general on the first day of Lent. Instead of staying in the noisy zayat, where the assembled people are talking of light matters, laughing and diverting themselves, they retire to a tazaung on the pagoda platform, or to some place shaded by trees, where they finger the hundred and eight beads of their rosary, muttering, "All is transient, sorrowful, and vain; the Lord, the Law, the Assembly; the three precious things"; and meditate on the example of the Lord Buddha and the excellence of his Law. To vary the monotony of this performance, they go for an hour or two to one of the monasteries to talk with the prior or some learned brother, or perhaps to hear him read and expound one of the jatakas, or birth-stories.

So the duty day passes. By sunset most of the worshippers are making their way back to their homes; but a few zealous spirits remain all night in the zayat, and only return with daylight on the following morning. This simple round of celebration is repeated four times in every lunar month, with here and there a feast-day of some particular shrine thrown in, when the only difference is that there is greater ceremony and a more or less large influx of strangers, according to the sanctity of the pagoda.

The sole distinction between Lent——lasting from the day after the full moon of July to the full moon of October ——and the rest of the year, is that all laymen are expected to be much more regular in their observance of the weekly religious days. It is not a season of fasting, but simply of stricter execution of religious duties. No marriages, feasts, or public amusements are held, or only by the graceless ; and some of the yahans retire into the depths of the jungle, where they can devote themselves to meditation with greater security from interruption. The custom of regarding these three months as peculiarly sacred undoubtedly rose from the habit of the monks, in the first days after the Buddha's teaching, remaining steadfastly in their monasteries in Magadha during the period of the annual rains, devoting all their time to pondering over the Sacred Law, and expounding it to any laymen dayakas, or upathakas, inquirers, or believers and searchers after the truth, who came to consult with them in their dwellings ; seeking to enter the current of perfection, and, attaining the state of arahan, to float into Ne'ban, the state of joyless, painless calm. Nowadays all are expected to study the Law for themselves ; but in order to prepare themselves worthily for the Wā, the wealthier people often call in the more learned yahans to deliver exhortations in their houses. Numbers of relations and friends are invited, who bring presents for the holy man, in the hope of sharing the merit of the transaction. Portions of the holy books usually are read on these occasions, especially the much-admired Wethandaya Wuttu. The doctrine inculcated by this zāt is charity ; and malicious people do not hesitate to say that the giving of alms is the invariable theme of the pyinsin. But I have at least as often heard the praises of wisdom from the Lawkanidi recited at such Lenten lectures, and a portion may be quoted here : " The ignorant bow down before the wise man. The riches of the wise man are like a bubbling spring, a fountain that never runs dry, and that, however constantly you may draw from it, is ever filled anew. The beauty of women and the sweetness of the sugar-cane bring satiety, but the words of wisdom never pall. The lazy man will never get learning. Any man may be endowed with riches, beauty, rank, youth ; but without

knowledge he is but as a beautiful flower that hath no perfume. The fragrance of flowers is refreshing; more so is the
light of the cool moon's rays ; but the greatest delight comes
from the words of wisdom. The sun may rise in the west ;
the summit of Mount Meru may be bent like a bow ; the
fires of hell may languish and die out ; the lotus may spring
on the tops of the mountains ; but the words of truth and
wisdom are always the same."

Similarly the riches of man are said to consist in his
learning, his family, and his good name ; of a woman in her
beauty ; of a great man in his rank, influence, position, and
the number of his slaves ; of a monk in his austerity ; of a
serpent in its poison ; and of a pônna in his oaths and his
prophecies.

Thirteen kinds of pride are enumerated. To lie in the
cool shade, with the power of the heavens at his command,
and to be victorious over his enemies, is the pride of the
tha-gya king. The galôn delights in flying throughout the
skies above or below. The naga prides himself in his
wondrous works, bright and glorious. The lion's pride is
to overcome his enemies and destroy all opposition. The
merchant's pride is to have obedient slaves and abundance
of gold and silver. The soldier's to enter a town with the
clash of the cymbal and the pomp of military music. The
peasant's to finish his toil honestly and well. The yahanda
finds his pride in the power of wisdom and in books. The
prince in triumphing over routed enemies and enriching
himself with their spoil. A woman's pride is to talk in a
pleasant and amusing way. A man's to be celebrated and
feared for his strength of mind and body. A doctor's to
effect successful cures with his own medicines, and a pônna's
pride is in his wisdom and knowledge of the Bedin.

The significance of all this and a deal more similar
useless information is that during the Wā the sacred books
should be studied, while all youths should receive their
Buddhist baptism by putting on the wā, the yellow robe of
the cloister—a Burmese play upon words which has a further
significance to the young neophytes, in the reflection that
" wā " also means a bamboo, which yahans do not spare,
Lent or no Lent.

CHAPTER XXI

THE END OF LENT

THE end of the Wā, or the full moon of Thadin-gyut, is always the occasion of a regular carnival of enjoyment, which in Rangoon has latterly shown a tendency to degenerate into uproarious saturnalia. The dismal season of the rains and of Lent, when there were no pwès anywhere, no feasts, no courting to be done wherever the parents were at all strict, no amusement of any kind to be had, except the somewhat tame diversion of a gossip with kindred spirits at the pagoda on the duty days—all this has passed away. Plays, ahlu pwè and kyi-gyin pwè, are to be seen in every quarter ; young brothers who have just finished their three months as novitiants in the monastery and have come out into the world again are wild with excitement at their regained freedom, and infect their sisters with enthusiasm for gaiety of all sorts ; the town is illuminated, feasting goes on everywhere, and the street plays are so crowded that you cannot secure a decent place unless you come down early in the afternoon, or at any rate before nightfall.

But all public festivals in Burma are religious in their character, and the rejoicings at wā-gyut are not less so than those at wā-win, when every one was preparing for the austerities of Lent, instead of the relaxations of the coming cold months. Accordingly the merry season is ushered in with a great feasting of the monks. This sôn-daw-gyi pwè is not so extensive, properly speaking, as the legitimate festival of that name a month later at the time of the Tawadeintha feast, and as a matter of fact is much more modest in its character in the small towns and villages.

But in Rangoon it has assumed in recent years a form which gives a great deal of offence to all the more serious people, and is especially condemned by the austere Sulagandis. Instead of having the offerings displayed in their houses and giving them to the yahans when they come round in the grey of the morning, the new fashion with the inhabitants of Rangoon is to carry all the alms to the monastery over-night, set them up in goodly array, there and then hold receptions, sing songs, dance, play musical instruments, and generally turn the quiet monastery into the semblance of an uproarious " penny gaff." This objectionable innovation has gradually arisen out of the practice of a few of the more pious old people who at the end of Lent used to go in the evenings with ahlu for the pyinsin, listen to some pious discourses, or the recitation of some sacred zāt, and then return betimes to bed. But now the frivolous find monks not less carnal-minded than themselves. Subscriptions are raised for weeks beforehand to make a grand display. One of the yahans is asked to grant the zayat near his house for the occasion. Some of the monks of the Thayet-daw kyaung in Godwin Road, which is the chief sinner in this respect, are even so shameless as actually to go touting about for people to take their zayats, or at times even part of the monastery itself.

Then at nightfall, on the full moon, the people begin to troop in. Those who have taken the management of the almsgiving are there before. We enter by one of the little wooden bridges, and come across a pya-that, a presentation spire, immediately, glittering bright in the moonlight and the glaring torches which are gathered thick farther on among the pôngyis' dwelling-places and the mango-trees from which the monastery takes its name. The spire has just been deposited, and the band has barely stopped the music which sounds so strange within the sacred parawun. But there is more coming that will be a far greater shock to up-country notions of religious propriety. The first place we come to is a zayat, and Maung Maung, the dispenser of hospitality, recognises us and calls us up. All his female friends are arranged in a row at the back, dressed in their finest, and before them, just as at the Tasaungmôn alms-feast, are heaped up piles of fruits, savoury curries, cakes, biscuits, and sweetmeats of all kinds, intended for the monks ; while scattered about are great *repoussé* silver bowls full of sherbet, gold and silver cups, lamps, mirrors, and all the familiar adornments, fit enough for a private house, but singularly out of place where a gay piece of tapestry hung up barely conceals the image at the eastern side of the rest-house.   Maung Maung offers us some lemonade, and we light cheroots, exchange a few compliments with the ladies, and pass on, just as a noisy half-dozen of young Englishmen from one of the mercantile houses come scrambling up the ladder-like steps.   It would be well if these gentlemen would re-member that each of the houses is to all intents and purposes a private assembly for the night, and that, though the host always welcomes them, he understands English, and does not by any means relish the mocking comments which are lavished on everything, and still less is inclined to approve of the criticisms passed on the ladies.   But then there are so few Englishmen in Burma who understand the very shortest sentence in the language that they may be pardoned if they mistake for a promiscuous saturnalia what is nominally a religious ceremony.   We leave them joking with Maung Maung and the hostess, as she offers them some beer—beer in a monastery !   But then it is known that Englishmen will be there, and the Burman's notion is that an English-man only leaves off drinking beer when he drinks brandy, so this last indignity is not objected to by the yahans.

Farther on we come to the place we are specially in search of.   The master of ceremonies here is our friend Maung Po Si, a Patama Byan, a certificated theologian and long resident in Mandalay, qualified, therefore, to be a yahan himself, and from his previous experiences, one would think, not at all likely to countenance such open contempt of the provisions of the Wini, which treatise his success in the above-mentioned "theological tripos" implies that he knows by heart.   But "Mr. Grandfather Oil" is very em-phatically in the world of kāma ; he is far from having beaten down the passions, and his place is the most start-lingly secular of them all.   He has got the kyaung of a myizzi mati, a pôngyi who has been ten Lents in the Order, and ought therefore to scorn such desecration for any purpose whatever, and certainly should not be tempted by the offer of a feast for his palate. But the fact remains that not only has he given up the front part of his kyaung, all but the elevated dais on the eastern side, where the images stand and visitors are received, but there is actually a play going on, trumpets braying, drums beating, and the bamboo clappers sounding high over all. It is a zāt, a birth-story certainly, but that does not make it any less a sin for the pôngyi to be so near, and with all those thirty pretty girls looking on too. The monk is behind the curtain which shuts off the undesecrated part of the building, it is true, but he can hardly be asleep with all that music, surely, and it is a crime for a member of the Order to listen to music. Yet who is to condemn him to penance when the prior's house is very little better? In some of the kyaungs, indeed, the younger yahans take very little trouble to conceal the fact that they are looking through the chinks of the slight hangings which cut off their sleeping-places from the noisy throng on the other side. The Englishmen, when they come round, push aside the kalagas to see what is behind, stumble over the peeping postulants, and scare the conscience-stricken "ascetics" almost out of their senses, under the impression that it is a bilu who has been enabled to gain access, and is going to devour them incontinently. Nevertheless there is no check in the revelry. It goes on until far into the night, and increases in noise the later it gets. The liquor which has been brought for expected visiting foreigners cannot be left behind in the kyaungs; they are not low enough for that yet. Consequently, the laymen must drink it. The result is that as time goes on there are quarrels and fights; and in this very Thayet-daw kyaung in the Thadin-gyut of 1879 a man was stabbed and died within the limits of the parawun. Little wonder that the strict Sulagandis are gaining over many of the more respectable inhabitants of Rangoon, for even this horror has not diminished the popularity of the wāgyut alms-feast.

The noise and hubbub go on till far into the morning, and when at last the people go, the monks may be supposed to have a little rest, for they can hardly have slept much

before, however steadily they lay on their mats. The offerings
are eaten next morning, and it is greatly to be feared that
there are many abstentions from the morning's round of
alms-begging. Such dissipation must scatter to the winds
any merit acquired by diligent piety and meditation in the
long weeks of Lent. It is only to be seen in Rangoon and
a few other places where many foreigners congregate. The
description is from the " country mouse " point of view.

In country towns, revels of this kind are never seen, and
even in Mandalay, though there are festivities in abundance,
the monasteries are never invaded in this scandalous way.
The difference is that between the primitive Buddhist and
the highly sophisticated latitudinarian. A more harmless
and decidedly prettier custom is the illumination, called
taungpyi pwè, of the pagodas and the town. In Rangoon
a very fine effect is produced by hanging the Sule Pagoda,
in Fytche Square, all round with Chinese lanterns, from the
base up to the top of the thabeit-hmauk, where the body of
the shrine begins to narrow into the spire. The rings of
coloured light narrowing upwards in a veritable pyramid of
fire, produce one of the finest sights of the kind to be seen
in the country. The street lamps, however, somewhat
handicap the simple means of illumination open to the
inhabitants, and to see the illumination of a town at its best
one must go to a place where there are no street lamps.
There all the pagodas and many of the private houses are
lighted up, and the contrast to the ordinary gloom is startling. Candles are placed on posts at intervals of ten paces
in every street, and the sè-eing gaungs have very plain-worded
instructions as to what will happen to them if any of the
lights in front of the ten houses of which they have charge
go out. Mandalay Hill at such a time was a fine sight and
still is, though it is no more a royal town. The two covered
ways which lead up the steep uneven sides to the pagoda
and the richly gilt Gautama on the top, look like streams of
flame, or fiery serpents from the haunted nat-taung, under
the shade of the Shan hills. But the monasteries which
cluster close in to the foot of the sacred hill are all as dark
and still as on any night in the middle of the Wā. No
unseemly orgies are permitted there. In the town, on the

other hand, all is noise and merriment.   Bands of music
and dances figure at the corners of all the chief streets,
provided by the chief burghers, who take the place formerly
occupied by the king himself, or by the ministers under his
orders.   The capital used to be crowded with umbrella-
bearing chiefs and officials, Shan sawbaws, and chieftains of
the mountain tribes all come down with their bands of wild
followers to do homage to the Lord of the Rising Sun, for
the greatest of the kadaw-né, the beg-pardon days, was
always immediately after Lent.   Having brought their minds
into a sedate and tranquil state by the observances of the
Wā, it was fitting that men should come and make submission
and do obeisance at the golden feet.   Mandalay is a very
different town now from what it was in royal times, but the
old traditions still linger.

At the same season there is an illumination on the river.
As soon as it is dark the villagers row out into the middle
of the stream and set adrift a multitude of little oil-lamps,
each fastened to a little float of bamboo or plantain stems.
The lamps are simply little earthenware cups filled with oil,
and each supplied with a small piece of cotton for a wick.
Thousands of them are sent out by a single village, and the
sight from a steamer suddenly rounding a bend and coming
upon a bank of these little stars of light afloat on the river
is very singular.   In the distance it looks like a regular sea
of flame, and as there is plenty of oil, on the night of the
full moon there is a constant succession of these shoals of
twinkling lights floating down the whole length of the
Irrawaddy from above Bhamaw to China Buckeer, every
village sending its contingent.

This ceremony, called ye-hpaung hmyaw thi, or mi-
hpaung hmyaw thi, launching water or fire rafts, is in remembrance of a universally honoured payā-ngè, a lesser
divinity called Shin Upago, who lives down at the bottom
of the river in a kyi-pya-that, a brazen spire, where he
zealously keeps the sacred days.   In a former existence he
carried off the clothes of a bather, and for this mischievous
pleasantry is condemned to remain in his present quarters
till Arimadeya, the next Buddha, shall come.   Then he
will be set free, and entering the thenga will become a

yahanda, and attain Ne'ban. He is a favourite subject for pictures, which represent him sitting under his brazen roof, or on the stump of a tree, eating out of an alms-bowl, which he carries in his arms. Sometimes he is depicted gazing sideways up to the skies, where he seeks a place that is not polluted by corpses. Such a spot is not to be found on earth, where every stock and stone is but the receptacle of a departed spirit. The notion is like that of the Tibetan monks, who look upon the earth as simply a vast graveyard. They carry human finger-joints strung together for a rosary, eat their food out of a human skull, and instead of horns for trumpets use the bones of a man's forearm. " We are dead," they say, " and dead men have nothing to do with the things of the living."

Of a similar character to this illuminating of the pagodas, the town, and the river, is the letting loose of fire-balloons, from the end of Lent to the Tawadeintha festival in Tasaungmôn. The balloons are sometimes very big, but they are simple enough structures. A bamboo framework is covered over with the thick, coarse, home-made paper manufactured from the bark of the mahlaingbin (*Brousso-netia papyrifera*), which also supplies the material for the black parabaik note-books. At the bottom, across the open mouth of the balloon, is a little platform, on which pitch is heaped, and with torches attached to it. The balloon is then tethered to the ground. The torches and resinous matter are lighted, and when the strain on the stays is considered sufficient, they are cut, and the balloon goes off. They are dangerous in large towns, and are forbidden there, but the Burman considers that the law applies only to the ground round the town, and dozens are let off every year from spots only a hundred yards or so outside of municipal limits. Not unseldom dôn, rockets, and other kinds of fire-works are attached to them, not by any means tending to make them safer for the houses below. This mi-eing byan, as it is called, is in honour of the Sula-mani payā, a pagoda erected in Tawadeintha, over Mount Myinmo, by the Thagya, king of the Nat-déwas. When Prince Theidat left his palace, his wife, and forsook all to become a Buddha, he rode as far as the river Anawma and leaped over it on his famous

steed Kantika. Then he drew his sword, cut off his long
hair and threw it into the air, where it remained suspended,
till the Tha-gya-min carried it off in a basket and had his
Sula-mani shrine built over it. Hence the offering of fire-
balloons.

Thus offerings are made on earth, water, and in the air.
The whole month, from the full moon which ends Lent till
the feast commemorative of the nogāna alms of Thuzata,
is distinguished by specially abundant ahlu to the pagodas
and to the beikku. A peculiarly pretty offering is that
called a pan-taing, a pyramid somewhat like a pya-that,
entirely composed of flowers in wreaths and nosegays, which
is conducted with much dancing and sounds of music, to
be laid before the great image. Fantastic tin shrines and
lanterns made to hold big, two-inch thick candles, often
plaited of long tapers made of different coloured wax, are
presented, and along with these, huge monkish fans, each
adorned round the edge with tags of gold-leaf and little
pictures; big muslin dragons distended on hoops and long
streamers to be hung from the poles surmounted with the
sacred hentha, or the kalawaik, are also frequent. It is also
customary at this season to make the monks large offerings
of honey—pya-ye hlu-thi. This can hardly be called a
separate festival, but as the honey is only given in these
months, it affords sufficient cause for the exhibition of plays
and energetic dancing on the way to the monastery.

All these religious observances, sufficiently mixed up
with secular enjoyment, are accompanied by other occupations which cannot be said to have anything directly to do
with religion. Such is the preparation of the boats, and the
practice for the races, which always take place in Thadingyut. They must wait, however, till Lent is over; and the
racing boats are almost always kept under the abodes of the
yahans, so that even here there is ground for the assertion
that all great public feasts in Burma are connected with
religion. But the Burmans are very far from being sad
worshippers, and any one who has been in the country in the
months of October and November would be inclined to
assert that the whole round of existence in Burma is made
up of junketings and pleasure-parties.

CHAPTER XXII

NATS AND SPIRIT-WORSHIP

NOTWITHSTANDING that Buddhism has been the established religion in Burma since shortly after the third great council at Patalipootra in 241 B.C. (283 of the sacred era), and that the purest form of the faith exists, and is firmly believed in, yet, throughout the whole Ashe Pyi (the Eastern country), both in Upper and Lower Burma, the old geniolatry still retains a firm hold on the minds of the people. Missionaries say that it is a natural revolting of the human mind against the denial of the existence of a Supreme Being, superior to man, and controlling his destiny. Government officers assert that the retention of the prior religion (for it is undoubtedly a kind of second religion) is due to the fact that surrounding, and scattered about amongst the Buddhist Burmans, are numerous tribes—Karens, Kachins, and others—who have no form of belief but nat - worship, the reverencing of the spirits of nature. As a simple matter of fact, it is undeniable that the propitiating of the nats is a question of daily concern to the lower class Burman, while the worship at the pagoda is only thought of once a week. For the nat may prove destructive and hostile at any time, whereas the acquisition of kutho at the pagoda is a thing which may be set about in a business - like way, and at proper and convenient seasons. It is just the difference between avoiding a motor car and avoiding the circular saw in a timber mill.

Before proceeding further, it will be well to discuss the word " nat " itself. General Phayre and Bishop Bigandet did not finally settle whether Nat is derived from the Sanskrit term nath, meaning " master, husband, lord," or not. The question may be philologically interesting, but is not likely to be definitely settled till the languages of " Farther India " are better known.   What concerns us is the fact that " nat " means in Burmese two distinct kinds of individuals.   It may be applied to the inhabitants of the six inferior heavens, properly called déwas, who figure in Hindu mythology, and have thence been transferred to the Buddhist world system. Kings and virtuous people are rewarded with happiness in these six seats after a good life upon earth.   The Tha-gya min, the king of the nats, or déwas, comes down to earth at the beginning of the Burman year, and remains here for three days, and his subjects generally display great solicitude for the pious state and welfare of mankind, but otherwise they are matters of no concern to dwellers in the lupyi unless as objects of envy.   Perfectly distinct from these are the nats of the house, the air, the water, the forest,—the spirits of nature, fairies, elves, gnomes, kelpies, kobolds, pixies, whatever other names they have received in other countries. Burmans never have any confusion in their mind on the subject, such as may occasionally occur to a foreigner.   The genii and peris of Eastern story, though doubtless springing from the Hindu déwas, have no real analogy in Burmese literature, any more than the idea of the *devil*—etymologically connected with the word dév-a or déwa—has anything to do with the joys of Tawadeintha and Tôtthita, the best-known heavens of nats of the superior order.

The worship of nats, of the spirits, then, has nothing to do with Buddhism, and is denounced by all the more earnest of the pyin-sin as being heretical and antagonistic to the teachings of the Lord Buddha.   King Mindôn, who was a true defender of the faith, and possessed of a deeper knowledge of the Pali texts than many of the members of the Assembly of the Perfect, fulminated an edict against the reverence paid to the nats, and ordered its discontinuance under severe penalties, but the worship was never really stopped, and can no more be stopped than refusing to dine thirteen at table, to walk under ladders, to cross knives, or to refrain from throwing spilt salt on other people's carpets.

The term spirit-*worship* hardly conveys a proper notion. Even the Karens and Kachins, who have no other form of belief, do not regard them otherwise than as malevolent beings who must be looked up to with fear, and propitiated by regular offerings.   They do not want to have anything to do with the nats ; all they seek is to be let alone.   The bamboo pipes of spirit, the bones of sacrificial animals, the hatchets, swords, spears, bows and arrows that line the way to a Kachin village, are placed there not with the idea of attracting the spirits, but of preventing them from coming right among the houses in search of their requirements.   If they want to drink, the rice spirit has been poured out, and the bamboo stoup is there in evidence of the libation ; the blood-stained skulls of oxen, pigs, and the feathers of fowls show that there has been no stint of meat-offerings ; should the nats wax quarrelsome, and wish to fight, there are the axes and dahs with which to commence the fray.   Only let them be grateful, and leave their trembling worshippers in peace and quietness.   For the Karen all nature is filled with nats, every tree and stone and pool and breath of air has its spirit.   The dead are only separated from the living by a thin white veil, through which, however, none but the gifted can see and venture to speak to them in words.   So the Caffres leave an open space in their line of battle that there may be room for the spirits of dead heroes to join in the conflict and fight on their behalf.

The Burmans are naturally not so wholesale nor so demonstrative in their recognition of the existence of spirits. The yahans would not endure it, and Buddhism has at any rate a somewhat softening and reassuring power.   Nevertheless evidences of the fact of the belief are universal and not to be mistaken, in all parts of the country, whether among the Government school educated youth, or among the bumpkins, who follow the plough, and crush the clods, and know the jungle better than anything else upon earth.   At the extremity of every village, the Ywasôn, there is a nat-sin, a shrine for the nat or nats of the neighbourhood.   This varies very much in size and character.   Sometimes it is a mere bamboo cage, hung in a pipul or other tree, or slung on a post, a bird-cage kind of construction, with an image inside, and a little hole through which the superstitious can introduce their offerings, tiny water-pots, oil-lamps, and little morsels of food. Often, if the village is larger, the shrine is much more pretentious, assuming almost the size and appearance of a zayat, a large tectum or roof, gabled and supported with red posts, the platform ornamented, and with a dais at one end, on which a representation of the nat is placed at the feast time, which, in imitation of the pagoda festivals, occurs at a regular fixed season. At other times these images are kept stowed away in an adjoining chamber, built for the purpose. It is particularly irritating to an educated Burman to see these absurd figures, which remind one of nothing so much as the fetiches of the prognathous African. Two gaudily dressed puppets, masquerading with spire-like crown, and royal, sharp-pointed swords, represent the much-feared nats, Shwe Pyin-gyi and Shwe Pyin-ngè, the Nyi-daw, Naung-daw, the Royal Younger Brother and the Royal Elder Brother, who command much respect in the neighbourhood of Mandalay and in Upper Burma generally. A still more dreaded spirit is one whose representation figures in a shrine at Tagaung, one of the ancient capitals of the country, half-way between Mandalay and Bhamaw. He appears simply as a head on a post, four feet high or thereabouts. A spire-like crown rests on his head, his eyes protrude and goggle in semi-globular wrath, asinine ears and a Punch-like nose complete the likeness, for he has no mouth, and his body is that of a dragon. Every one avoids his temple as much as possible, but the inhabitants of the village bow in that direction before they venture to do anything, and passing boatmen kindle lamps and offer flowers, of which he is said to be particularly fond, and fruit, for the nat has an incorrigible habit of giving people the stomach-ache when he is offended, and death punishes the recalcitrant. "Tagaung colic" is a recognised ailment with the Burmese faculty. The demon is said to have been one of the ancient kings of the place, who acquired his power from magical arts which he learned in Northern India. Three famous pagodas in the defile take their names from episodes in his life; and his two sons founded the dynasty of Prome. Oftenest of all, however, the nat-shrine contains no figure. It is occupied only by the viewless spirits of the air.

First in the list of personal spirits may be considered the

kosaung nats, a kind of confusion of ideas between the proper
spirit and the butterfly spirit, and representing as it were the
genius of each individual, a kind of materialised conscience.
They are twelve in number, six good and six bad, six male
and six female, and regulate the life and doings of their
protégé accordingly as the benevolent or the malevolent gain
the upper hand.

Next to these comes the eing saung nat, very often
called Min-magayi, the guardian nat of the house. For
his comfort the tops of all the posts in the house are covered
with a hood of white cotton cloth, for it is in this situation
that he usually takes up his abode. In almost every house,
at the end of the verandah in front, you will find a water-
pot full of pareityé, water over which certain gathas, magic
spells, or religious formulæ have been uttered by the astrologer,
or the prior of the district. This water, which is replenished
once a month, or oftener in cases of danger from disease, or
when a member of the family is absent on a journey, is every
now and then sprinkled about the house as a protection
against bilus and spectres, ogres and tasés. When the
water is consecrated in this nyaungye-o, which is of a special
shape, something like an overgrown Indian spittoon, there
are always a few twigs and leaves of the thabyé tree floating on the top. These are mostly taken out and hung round
about the eaves, but occasionally left in the water. The
inordinately superstitious sometimes keep a small thabyé
bin (the sacred eugenia) growing in a pot in the house, so
that its benign influence may keep harm away. Talaing
houses may usually be known by the cocoa-nut hanging up
at the south side of the building. This is covered with strips
and tags of yellow or red cloth, and is offered to Min-magayi,
whom they call the king of the nats. Of these spirits (called
kaluk in their language) they say there are thirty-seven distinct varieties, but Min-magayi rules them all. These are
the " thirty-seven nats of Burma," but whether they were
borrowed by the Burmese from the Talaings or not seems
at any rate doubtful. At the beginning of the wet season
they always wrap up the cocoa-nut afresh, and when the
rains are over make new offerings of money, glutinous rice,
eggs, jaggari, and fruit, in order that the eing saung nat may

keep away fever from the household. It must not be supposed that the nat guardian of the house has necessarily
any affection for those who have built the place where he
has taken up his abode. He probably regards them only
with cold indifference, however generous they may be in
their offerings, and were he not propitiated by these gifts he
would almost certainly display his anger by doing the
inhabitants some grievous injury. But then he dislikes his
haunts being intruded upon, and if a stranger comes at an unwonted time—a burglar at midnight, for example—it is quite
likely that the eing saung nat will attack him violently,
scare him out of his wits, or give him the colic. Thus without any really estimable purpose in his mind, Min-magayi
may be a considerable protection to his worshippers, just as
an "awful example" is useful to teetotallers.

Beyond this guardian, or demon of the house, there is
the guardian nat of the village, the ywa saung nat, of whose
shrine at the end of the town I have already made mention.
None of the lower-class Talaings would ever think of eating
a morsel without first holding up his platter in the air, and
breathing a prayer to the village nat. They are particularly
fond of putting up shrines to the nats under the le'pan tree,
from the wood of which coffins are frequently made. A
feast must be held every three or four years in honour of
this nat, at which the natkadaw, a woman called the nat's
wife, dances. This is done in order that sickness may be
kept away. Should an epidemic actually break out, a very
elaborate ceremony is gone through. Probably first of all
the figure of a spectre, or of a bilu, is painted on an ordinary
earthenware water-pot, and this is solemnly smashed to
pieces about sundown, with a heavy stick or a dah. As
soon as it gets dark, the entire populace break out into
yells, and make as much noise generally as they can compass, with the view of scaring away the evil spirit who has
brought the disease. This is repeated on three several
nights, and if it is not then effective the yahans are called
in to give their assistance. The prior, with his following,
repeat the Ten Precepts, chant the Payeit-gyi, and then one
of the sermons of the Lord Buddha is declaimed, the same
by the preaching of which he drove away the pestilence

which was devastating the country of Wethali. If this last ceremony is not effectual the village is abandoned. The inhabitants leave the sick and the dying to their fate, and go off to the jungle, where each household camps out by itself for a time. Before they return again, the yellow-robed monks, in recognition of much alms, read the Law up and down the street between the houses. When they have gone back to the monastery, the nat's shrine is repaired, and abundant offerings deposited. Having thus made their peace with the representatives of both religions, the people return to their houses, light fires, cook rice for new offerings, and then enter upon their ordinary pursuits as if no interruption whatever had occurred.

This is what would take place in any ordinary Burman village. But among the Talaings, and in the more retired places in the jungle, occupied by ignorant uncultivated Burmans, the function called ywakyathi would be carried out, which is much more purely geniolatric in its character. This is sometimes done when a prominent man in the hamlet is sick, more often when there is danger of a contagious disease. A great feast of cooked rice and meat, roasted fowls and ducks forming a prominent part of it, is heaped up on a platform specially erected for the purpose some distance outside the village. Everybody in the village is required to have some part in the ceremony. A few are sent out beforehand, who dress themselves up in a fantastic way, and pretend to be bilus, evil nats, and witches. With them are others who feign to be dogs, and rush about on all fours, barking and howling ; others represent pigs, and grunt and nuzzle about with their noses in the ground. After this performance has been carried on for some time, the remainder of the villagers come out in a band, and, through one or more spokesmen, demand of the possessed whether those lying sick at home will recover, and whether the bad spirits are satisfied with the offerings. It is specially ordained at these exhibitions that no one shall be called by his real name ; such mention, if made inadvertently, would expose the person addressed to considerable danger, even if he should make no sign betraying himself, for he certainly would not answer. The quasi tasés always reply that the

sick will recover and the plague leave the locality. Thereupon the villagers rush off like madmen into the surrounding forest, and run about hither and thither in a reckless
way with an open cloth, or the end of their waistcloth, in
their hands. Some of them suddenly make a plunge with
their cloth over a bush or a tussock of grass, and then closing
it up carefully, hurry breathless back to the village. The
leip-bya or " butterflies " of the sick man are supposed to
have been captured. The paso, or cloth, is carefully opened
and shaken over the patient's head, and the leip-bya is
supposed to return to its proper habitation. This operation
is repeated several times, in case a wrong " butterfly " might
have been captured, or lest the actual one should have
escaped on the way. Then everybody returns. The function
is not without its danger, for it has happened that the
temporary mimes have become permanently possessed of
evil spirits, and as witches and wizards have proved as great
curses to the neighbourhood as any pestilence could have
been. Which things are an allegory. The whole ceremony
is beginning to get into very bad odour in the more settled
parts of the province, and respectable people avoid having
anything to do with it, while those who have taken a part
are ashamed to own it.

All these nats are directly connected with a particular
locality, and therefore well known to, and regularly propitiated by, the inhabitants of that place. But there are
abundance of nats to be found elsewhere, away from villages
and houses, and all of them equally ready to resent any
injury which the passer-by may unwittingly do them.
When a Burman starts on a journey he hangs a bunch of
plantains, or a twig of the tha-bye tree, on the pole of the
buffalo cart or the stern of the boat, to conciliate any spirit
whose beat he may intrude upon. The fisherman makes
offerings in his nat-sin every time he launches his dug-out;
the lonely hunter in the forest deposits some rice and ties
together a few leaves whenever he comes across some particularly large and imposing tree, lest there might be a thi'pin-
saung nat dwelling there. Should there be none, the
tied-back twigs will at any rate stand in evidence to the
taw-saung nat, the demon who presides over all the forest.

When there is a boat-race, the opposing crews have a preliminary row over the course with offerings placed on the
prow for the nat who guards that stretch of the river.   And
so on through numberless examples.   Some nats achieve
fame, and are known far and wide by special appellations.
Such is Maung In Gyi, a spirit who is feared in all the
district round Rangoon, and away eastward and northward
as far as Pegu. He lives in the water, and causes death.
A special festival is celebrated in his honour, or rather in
deprecation, in the month of Waso, the same in which Lent
begins.   Others more especially known in Upper Burma
are Byindôn, Shwe Pyin-Gyi and his brother, and a drunkard
nat called Maung Min Gyaw, to whom great quantities of
rice spirit are offered.   Uyingyi is a spirit universally known
among the Talaings.   The chief spirit of a district usually
goes by the name of A-shin Gyi, the great lord, or, among
the Talaings, Okkaya.   Then there are generic names ;
there is the Hmin nat who lives in woods, and shakes those
he meets so that they go mad.   There is the Upaka, who
flies about in the clouds to spy out men whom he may snap
up.   There is the Akakaso who lives in the tops of trees,
Shekkaso who lives in the trunk, and Bumaso who is
content with a dwelling in the roots.   The presence of
spirits or witches in trees may always be ascertained by
the quivering and trembling of the leaves when all around
are still.

The Talaings, and many of the Burmans in the Irrawaddy delta, have a regular nat-feast just before harvesting
begins.   The figure of a woman is fashioned out of straw,
and a tamein, kerchief, and other portions of female dress
placed along with it in a bullock cart.   Great quantities of
kauk-hnyin, "sticky rice," are heaped up, and the whole
driven in procession round the ripe paddy fields.   The
figure is then set up in the place where the paddy is to be
stored, and the offerings are usually swept away by the
boys of the place, whose appetites overcome their fear of
the nats, Bumadi, the guardian of the earth, and Nagyi, the
guardian of the grain, to propitiate whom the feast is held.

There is a theory that persons who are executed or meet
a violent death become nats and haunt the place where they

were killed. They are called nat-sein. Advantage is taken of this to guard the capital. When a town is founded, at each of the four corners of the city walls and under the gate-posts people are buried alive. Their spirits thereafter hover about the place and bring disaster on strangers who come there with evil intentions. Monks and nuns who lead bad lives and break their vows are also believed to pass into demons when they die. There is therefore a constant and lamentable recruiting of the forces of the nats and tasés.

In some places certain nats have qualities ascribed to them which are not entirely obstructive and obnoxious. For example, in a nat's house at Nyaung-u, before the figure of a spirit called Apé Shwemyosin, lies a twisted, curious-shaped stone, which has magic powers ascribed to it. The sick come and try to lift it up. If they are successful they will soon recover health; if, on the other hand, its weight is too much for them, the inquirers will die. Similarly, on the ascent to Mandalay Hill there is a little chapel in which, besides three figures of the hentha, the Brahminy goose, each said to contain a sacred tooth brought from Ceylon, there is a flat, oval stone, with mystic characters inscribed on it. Many resort there to ascertain the probable issue of an intended journey or enterprise. If the stone proves heavy, the sign is bad.

The belief in spirits naturally induces a corresponding faith in omens. The Deitton, an astrological book constantly in the hands of Bedin Sayās, but carefully excluded from all monasteries, gives a great variety of them; auguries from the flight and number of birds seen, omens from the barking of dogs, the movements of bees, and the laying of eggs by fowls. Rules are given for choosing the site on which a house is to be built, and omens drawn from the substances found in digging the foundations. Posts are called male, female, or a-thet ma shi, neuter, according as they are of the same girth throughout, larger at the bottom or in the middle. Under ordinary circumstances, houses with female taing are fortunate, with neuter disastrous. Posts which are largest at the top are called taing bilu, "demon beams," and are especially unhappy.

If a hen lays an egg upon a cloth, its owner will lose money. To come across mushrooms at the beginning of a journey is a most fortunate sign. A snake crossing the path always denotes delay, whether in a lawsuit, a journey, or a warlike expedition. If a dog carries an unclean thing up into his master's house, he may get thrashed for it, but the man will become rich ; and so on in infinite variety.

All this belief in supernatural powers tends to produce abundance of experts who profess to be able to explain signs and to control the evil spirits. Every district possesses its nat thungè, or nat meimma, a spirit woman who dances at the nat feasts, and at ordinary times is consulted by the superstitious on all kinds of subjects connected with her trade. She is asked where so-and-so, lately deceased, is, to what seat of the world he has migrated ; where absent persons are, and what they are doing ; what facilities there are for special undertakings, and when they should be begun.

The Bedin Sayās claim similar knowledge, and are equally abundant. Numbers of them may be seen at any time of the day sitting under the trees on the way up to the Shwe Dagôn pagoda, writing and rubbing out figures and letters on their black note-books, and drawing a comfortable income from an unfailing succession of inquirers. Sometimes such a magic-worker, wishing to establish a reputation, or having a spite against somebody, performs the ceremony called pônnaga taikgyin. He carries off some cinders from the funeral pyres of people who have been burnt, and collecting a large assortment of such charred pieces of wood, puts them secretly in the house of the person whose feelings he wishes to work on. At night the spirits come and keep up a battery of stones on the unfortunate man's roof, all attempts to find out where the stones come from being as unavailing as they were in a similar instance in the suburbs of London not very long ago.

It is consolatory, however, to know that piety will protect any one from the attacks of malevolent spirits. Numerous stories told by the yahans prove the virtue of the gâtas to guard against evil. If the victim has only knowledge and strength of mind sufficient to recite these religious formulæ,

the wiles of the nats are harmless.   In case of the utmost
need, even the ordinary tharana-gôn, the payā, tayā, thengā,
is of much avail, if only uttered with faith.   It is with the
idea of keeping away bilus, tasés, and demons that the
members of the yellow robe are often summoned to death-
beds.   There is no thought of the monk administering
spiritual consolation to the dying man.   The good influence
of his pious presence keeps away evil spirits, and nothing
more.   No exhortations of the yahan can alter the balance
of merit and demerit which is already cast up for the dying
man.   On the other hand, in out-of-the-way parts of the
country, and especially in the hills, spirit shrines are not
unseldom found actually inside a monastery compound.

CHAPTER XXIII

RICE CULTIVATION

A GROWING number of millions of acres are under cultivation in Lower Burma, and of this total all but some three hundred thousand acres are devoted to the planting of rice. Tobacco, sugar-cane, cotton, and oil-seeds of different kinds, as well as fruit-trees, form the other crops. Upper Burma has a greater number of crops, and the proportion of rice is far from being so overwhelming, though almost everywhere it is the chief crop. The alluvial lands of the Irrawaddy delta produce by far the greatest quantity of rice. It is certain that the best quality grain comes at present from this part of the country, but this may be due to more practised agricultural skill or long-continued tilling of the land. Hardly any possible number of crops in a season could apparently exhaust the fertility of the soil. Any part of the country, however, may be used for the cultivation of rice. The laziest farm is a swamp-land, where the ordinary rainfall is sufficient to produce the sodden ground requisite for a rice crop. Such low-lying plains and the riparian lands, annually flooded by the overflow of the river, are naturally best suited to Burmese indolence and are earliest taken up. Farther up the country, where the rain runs off the surface quickly and the land is too high for the south-west monsoon floods, it is necessary to resort to irrigation, either by the obvious method of dams or by ingenious water-wheels. Finally, there is the laborious taung-ya cultivation, where whole hillsides are cleared of trees to produce a crop. This hard work is left to mild aboriginal or other tribes, whom the Burman has long ago bullied out of the fat lowlands.

Malicious people have declared that the only things a
Burman does well are steering a boat and driving a bullock-
cart. This is a libel ; he can cultivate rice remarkably well.
Unfortunately, however, as far as a vindication of his
character as a worker is concerned, this does not imply any
severe labour. Here the Burman is a victim of circumstances. So rich is the soil of his native land that it has
only to be scratched to burst with plenty ; the ploughing of
the land cannot be described in any other way. The south-
west monsoon rains, commencing early in June, soon reduce
the ground to a soft sea of mud. When this has come
about, the Burman proceeds to plough it. His plough is a
single-barred harrow, or rake, with three long teeth of tough
acacia-wood ; a high bow or loop of bent wood rises from
the cross-bar, and standing on this, the farmer is dragged
backwards and forwards till the ground is reduced to a
smooth surface—no very difficult matter. Oxen are frequently
used, but more commonly the mud-loving buffalo, partly
because he regards the toil as a pleasure on account of the
mud, and partly because of his greater strength. Lazier
farmers still adopt the primitive method of making the
children drive the buffaloes and plough-oxen up and down
in the mud and water so as to poach it up well ; and then
a log of wood is drawn over it to smooth it down. None of
the farms are large, the average being somewhere between
ten and twenty acres ; so that this work is soon over.
Nurseries are prepared at the same time on somewhat higher
ground, where the seed will not rot with excessive moisture,
and here the grain is sown broadcast.

Agricultural operations are now suspended for a month
or six weeks. By about the beginning of August the
ploughed fields have become somewhat less fluid, and the
plants in the nursery, called pyokyèlè, have grown to a
fair size. These are then pulled up and carried off to the
prepared lands. A kaukseiktan, or knobbed stick, is used
to make holes in the ground at intervals of a few inches,
and into each of these holes a couple of plants are inserted.
This work is left to the women and children, many of whom
prefer their hands to the stick. The farmer squats on one
of the solid ridges, which intersect the ground and serve as

footpaths, and with a huge green cheroot in his mouth, leisurely contemplates the operation. Everything is now in the hands of nature, and the agriculturist may lounge round his farm in peace till November ; unless, indeed, excessive rain floods the ground and rots the crop, when a new planting out has to be gone through. The harvesting near Rangoon is entirely done by men from Upper Burma, or even by Indian coolies. They work for very little, and it saves the farmer a good deal of time and dignity to get all the cutting done for him. Accordingly, from October till December the steamers down the Irrawaddy used to be crowded with King Thibaw's subjects, all of whom had to leave behind them with their Myo-sa, or his delegate the Myo-wun, who vicariously "ate" the township between them, a pledge either of property or of some member of their family, that they would return to their country again. When they got back, very little of their hard-earned gains escaped the voracity of the royal officials. Now they come down by train, and after a trip or two learn enough to keep their money from enterprising fellow-countrymen. These anyathas, as they are called, behave remarkably well in British territory, notwithstanding the assertions of the rural police, who, being unable to detect dacoits, declare that these are all Upper Burmans who have come down for the harvest. They are really, however, mostly simple, quiet people, who are kept very much in awe by the bluster and town-knowledge of the down-country farmers, and work away zealously with their queer sickles, looking like the ordinary English article worn to half its original size by long use. It is worthy of notice that the grain is not mown close to the ground as in Europe. Except where there is a market for straw, very little more than the ears are cut off, and the straw burnt in the hot weather of March and April supplies a scarcely-needed fertilising to the soil. The reapers usually receive their payment from the farmer in grain, but they naturally convert this into money, or more portable goods, before they start off home again.

It does not take long to cut the crop, and then the corn is brought in to the homestead, commonly on rude sledges, more seldom in carts. The threshing-floor does not take much preparing. It is simply a portion of the field swept clean. It is sufficiently hard from the broiling sun, and a stake is driven into the centre of the circle. Two lines of sheaves are arranged round this, head to head, and the grain is trodden out by slow-moving bullocks in good old lazy fashion. The Christian Biblical precept, not to muzzle the ox that treadeth out the corn, does not fail of observance with the Buddhist farmer. Then the paddy, that is, the unhusked grain, is winnowed. In some places hand-winnowing machines of a simple pattern are used ; but ordinarily a far more primitive and easy method, corresponding to the substitution of oxen for threshing-flails, is in use. A man stands on an elevated platform and capsizes baskets of paddy brought from the threshing-floor ; the rice falls on a sloping bamboo mat and so to the ground, the wind blowing away a great part of the bits of broken straw, chaff, and light grain. The system may not be very thorough, but it saves an immense amount of trouble, which is the chief consideration. All that now remains to be done is to carry the grain off to the big rice-boat lying in the creek. There it is stowed in bulk ; and after a day or two, the farmer makes a start, dropping leisurely down through the network of creeks into one of the main streams, and so making his way to Rangoon, or Bassein, whence he will return in a few weeks with fine Chinese neckerchiefs for his daughters and perhaps a gay Manchester paso or two for himself and his sons— unless, indeed, the Madras money-lender has snapped up all his receipts down in town, or some of the robber-boats that infest the creeks at this time of the year have pounced upon him and carried off everything but the boat and the paddles.

Rice-farming would be profitable as well as easy work were it not for the reckless squandering of almost all the cultivators. The average rent per acre is under three shillings ; the average produce of the land per acre is from eighty to a hundred bushels in the more fertile parts, while elsewhere the yield is from forty to fifty. The selling price of rice per maund (80 lbs.) in Rangoon is between 4s. 6d. and 5s. Agriculturists, therefore, ought to grow rich. But they are too fond of gambling and building works of merit to accumulate money, and their carelessness results in the constant death of their plough-beasts, so that matters usually remain exactly at the same level if the farmer does not actually get into permanent debt. The Scottish Highlanders have a pious wish, " May the free hand always be full ! " If it is not always full in Burma it is consoling to think that it is seldom absolutely empty. Still, when the grandson succeeds he ordinarily finds that there is as little actual money hoarded up about the place as there was when the grandfather Po Gyi spent so many borrowed rupees at his uncle's funeral.

If rice cultivation is easy work in the low country, it is very different with the taung-ya, or hill clearings. Here the dense underwood and forest growth has to be cut down ; and the more there is to cut the better the crop, for the soil needs fertilising badly, and all that is cut down is burned. Work is begun about January ; everything is felled, bushes and all ; and after the fallen logs have dried some time in the sun, the brushwood is heaped up round about them and the whole is set on fire. Some of the logs smoulder for weeks —perhaps till the first rains come. Then the ground is rudely dug up with hoes, and the ashes turned in. Cotton-seed is ordinarily mixed with the rice, which is of a quite different variety from that produced in the plains. It is sown broadcast, and the farmer has thereafter only to keep down the weeds, but this is not by any means a light task. The crop is ready by October, and furnishes little more than enough to support the family or community. The scanty manure provided by the wood-ashes is not sufficient to last more than two or three years ; and when the crop is secured the party proceeds on to a new settlement, there to repeat the same laborious process. A very ingenious device for lightening the toil is resorted to where there is much heavy timber. Beginning at the bottom, they slightly cut the lowest trees on the upper side only, gradually increasing the depth of the notch as they advance up the hill, until at the top of the clearing they cut the trees completely through. These fall on the row immediately below them, and by their weight knock it down ; and so the felling process is continued down to the bottom. Occasionally a tangle occurs where some sturdy tree refuses to fall, and the clearing it away becomes a matter of very considerable danger. This taung-ya system is very wasteful as well as laborious, and annually draws down upon itself the denunciations of the English forest officers. But the hill-tribes who adopt it are too few to support themselves in any other way. They were long ago driven out of the plains by the Burmans, and now cling to their old nomadic life with a degree of obstinacy which Government officials, in a variety of ways, have found is not to be tempted by any tale of the present security and plenty of the low country, or even of the valleys among the hills. Rice, therefore, continues to be produced with the minimum and the maximum of labour ; but none of the hill rice ever finds its way out of the country, and seldom even down to the plains.

The rice season, as far as the English merchant is concerned, commences in January and ends about May ; but though this is pre-eminently the " busy season," there are purchases made in greater or less quantities all the year round. The relations between the great English rice firms and the simple jungle cultivators have not always been of a very elevating character, and it can hardly be denied that the fault lies wholly at the door of the foreigner. Missionaries in Burma are wont to mourn that their teachings are often rendered wholly nugatory by the want of scruple, and it might almost be said of honour, displayed by the great Rangoon rice firms. The good padres teach their proselytes that Christians are all honest and truthful. The ingenuous lads enter as clerks in a rice-mill and discover that Englishmen scarcely differ from the " poor heathen," except in being more lordly in the way of doing the thing.

Years ago, when there were not nearly so many mills as there are now, and not a quarter so many ships in the harbour during the rice season, things went on pretty equably. One day one firm would give a rupee or so more per hundred baskets, and the next day it would be another. But soon the mills began to increase in number and more ships came, and it was harder to get paddy. Then rival firms began to bid against each other. There was demurrage before their eyes, and it was terribly expensive work keeping the mill

establishment up to its full strength. And so prices rose
and rose until they became absurdly high, and no one
profited but the hawks that preyed on the simple Burmese
cultivators. Then the English merchants held a meeting,
and all pledged themselves not to give more than the
current market rate for paddy. This seemed a fair enough
agreement ; but after a while it was found that the boats all
gravitated towards one or two firms. A little investigation
showed that this was due to the fact that though they paid
the ordinary rate, according to the compact, they had a
smaller measuring basket than their neighbours. Accordingly every one went on reducing the size of his basket
until the system became as ruinously absurd as ever it had
been before. Then there was another meeting, at which it
was unanimously agreed that this state of affairs would
never do, and that it was absolutely necessary to come to
some definite understanding. A committee was appointed
which, after some deliberation, concluded that, if, in addition
to abiding by the market rate, every one were bound to use
a basket of a certain fixed size, there would be no chance
for unfair speculations. A standard basket was therefore
fixed upon ; and the competitors were supposed to start fair
again. But in no very long time, one firm put a false
bottom in the basket, another wedged in a board ; and so
on, till matters got back to the old way. This state of affairs
is hardly creditable to mercantile honour, and it certainly is
by no means profitable.

Independently of this, paddy has gone up in price at an
alarming rate of late years. The first heavy rise was in
1877, at the time of the Madras famine. That was also
the time of the resolution to have a standard basket.
Rice was wanted in any quantity for the famine districts,
and millers gave an altogether fabulous price for grain.
The game went on merrily, introduced the scandalous
" paddy morality," and lasted long enough to make the
cultivators think the new prices had come in for good.
Far too many Burmese farmers are heavily in debt to
the " chetties," the money-lending caste of the Madras
coast. The agriculturists have borrowed money to build
a pagoda or a monastery ; to give a grand feast on the

occasion of their marriage, or their father's death ; to buy
a new yoke of oxen in the place of those that have been
carried off by disease ; to get seed-grain to sow their
tracts of paddy land, the last season's gains having been
lost in some gambling transaction when they were down
in Rangoon. They have got into the chetty's books in
some way at any rate ; and hapless is the man, Burman or
Englishman, who has dealings with the fat, shaven-headed
Madras money-lender. He will be charged eight, ten,
twelve per cent a month, or even more, before there is an
end of the transaction. The chetties, therefore, took a particular interest in the rise of the price of paddy. High
prices ensured their being paid ; moreover, handling such
unwonted sums of money made the ever-careless Burman
reckless. He gambled, he gave great feasts, he got deeper
and deeper into debt with the money-lenders. Consequently
it was desirable that the prices should not go down ; and as
men of business the chetties understood how that was to be
done ; they made the Burman farmers hold back their grain.
The Rangoon firms were in desperation to meet their contracts, the ships could not be kept waiting ; and so prices
were maintained at nearly famine rates. This more than
anything else brought about the unlucky legerdemain with
standard baskets. The appearance of the chetty element
in the trade upset everything. They are charming men
of business, and know all about bulling and bearing, and
all the other civilised expedients of trade. Poor " Jack
Burma," listless and good-natured as he is, would never
have thought of such things of himself; but he is in the
hands of his master. Not a single village in the jungle,
however remote, is to be found without its bare-backed
money-lender. He hovers round the paddy nursery ; he
watches the men planting out the handfuls of half-grown
rice ; he makes the farmer hold back the threshed-out grain
till he gives the word : then he fixes the rate and all but
takes the money himself.

The English merchants have struggled against the
system, but with small success. They have laid out heavy
sums in advances. The farmer is paid for the next year's
crop before ever it is sown. This is generally only practi-

cable with men who have not yet fallen into the clutches of
the chetties, and the result has been almost invariably to
drive them into the money-lender's arms.   The Burmese, it
it is to be feared, have not sufficient stability of character.
U Myaing or Maung Po never had so much money before in
their lives as the advances figure to.   They do not know the
value of it, and proceed to squander the rupees forthwith ;
and so, long before the paddy is delivered they are heavily
in the usurer's books, and then Maung Po and U Myaing
have to do as they are bidden.   Moreover, the system in
any case could hardly be a safe one.   The cultivator might
die ; there might be a flood or a jungle fire ; many things
might happen, in fact, to prevent the advance boats from
ever reaching the Puzundaung creek.   Consequently many
English firms have given up the practice, and instead send
agents away up the creeks, far into the jungle, to negotiate
with the farmers on the spot and try to secure paddy before
rivalry has had time to raise the price.   But even this expedient does not answer well.   The chetties do their best to
throw obstacles in the way.   It is not without expense, and
it impresses the cultivators with a notion of the great demand
there is for paddy.

The telegraph, they say, ruins business.   The paddy
season opens in February with a price of, say between
seventy and eighty rupees a hundred baskets.   The merchants declare they will not be forced into materially increasing this rate, and the home firms charter a number of ships.
Meanwhile the price of paddy steadily rises, while rice in
England steadily goes down ; and by the time the vessels
discharge their cargo in Liverpool or London, milled rice is
not very much dearer in wholesale shops than the raw paddy
in the Burmese boats.   New mills are constantly being
started—which would seem contradictory, were it not that
all the firms starting them have business of another kind ;
teak sawmills, cotton or piece-goods trade, silks for Burmese
men and maidens, or jute and grey shirtings for Upper
Burma and the hill tribes.   Rice will certainly always be
wanted, and there is any quantity of it to be had in Burma.
A little more of the sterling probity which used to be
associated with the name of the English merchant would

do no harm in Rangoon rice dealings, and would win that respect from the farmer which heavy payments and cunning never will.

Rangoon still continues to be the largest rice port in the world. From January to May the river is crowded with shipping—huge iron and steel sailing craft that have been chartered beforehand, and carry off thousands of bags in their capacious holds ; and a constant succession of " ditchers," as the steamers passing through the Suez Canal are called, which come " seeking," and seldom have to go away without their full complement of " five parts cargo rice," or " Europe milled." The steamers are displacing the sailing ships, and the shorter passage now makes it possible to carry fully husked rice home without the danger of heating, which was supposed to be avoided by the partly husked " five parts cargo rice." Harbour-masters and river-pilots have a busy time, and gather together many pieces of silver against the later months of the year, when they will have abundant leisure to spend them. Coringi coolies swarm in the town, and their monotonous chant, " Eh-ya-mah-la Tah-ma-lay, Madras Ag-boat Tah-ma-lay," may be heard at any hour of the night or the morning, floating over the river. The British sailor overflows into the town and sings noisy old salt sea-songs round about the Sule pagoda, gets mad drunk on arrack, and not unseldom clears Dalhousie Street with a linked-arm rush, heedless of the red-turbaned guardian of the peace, who keeps out of the way in the meantime, but will break poor drunken Jack's head with his truncheon if he finds him helpless and strayed from his fellow-roysterers.

The Puzundaung Creek, where all the mills are, is as busy as an ant-hill all day long, and all night too, when some of the mills are lighted up with Jablochkoffs or later forms of electric light, and the silvery rays shine ghastly on the black and bronzed mill-workers. Here we have the Madrasi coolies again, making noises, according to their nature, as a kind of assertion that they are doing hard work. The lank Chittagonian firemen, with their aquiline noses, are coated with coal-dust, and divide their time between firing up and having a whiff at the hubble-bubble when Sandy,

the Scotch engineer, is not looking. There is a cluster of
Chinese carpenters, chipping away with their queer thick-
headed axes and planes, which, with characteristic perversity,
they pull towards them, instead of pushing away as other
workmen do. Here is M——, the English "assistant" at
the mill, his hat and coat all covered with rice-dust, which
hangs in queer fashion on his eyebrows and moustache. He
is in high spirits. "We've got twenty-four pair of stones
going to-day, more than anybody else in the creek;" and
he goes off to see how the Burmese girls are stitching up the
rice-bags, a duty of which he is particularly fond, and over
which he spends a quite unnecessary amount of time. There
is R——'s voice on the other side of the creek. He is
storming at some men in the cargo-boat, who have done
something wrong—anchored in the wrong place, or not
started for the upper mill at Kemendine last night as they
ought to have done. R—— has a voice which is the terror
of every loitering coolie and dawdling boat-wallah in his
employ; and he will be as hoarse as a North Sea pilot by
nightfall, and will want a "double-barrelled" whisky and
soda to moisten him before dinner. He wants company
down to "the Point," and presently comes skimming across
in his gig, manned by Chittagonian Kalassies, and we drop
down the creek—they call small rivers creeks in the East—
to where it joins with the main Rangoon stream. The
Pegu river, tapping the country north-east and north of
Rangoon, comes in at the same place; and there is a great
crowd of paddy-boats here in the early morning. Each firm
has its brokers, middlemen who make the purchases from
the farmers that come down with their grain. They have
been here since daylight, and fly about in their little dug-
outs from one seller to another. The great point in a broker
seems to be power of lungs and fluency in abuse. The
amount of yelling that goes on at "Monkey Point" would
silence the bookmakers' ring at Epsom on a Derby day.

R—— has not come down to this pandemonium for
nothing. There are a couple of big ships in, which must be
filled, or there will be demurrage to pay, and a "canal-
wallah" is expected this afternoon or to-morrow morning;
so that the wheels must be kept going their hardest.

Accordingly, we paddle about here and there, and whenever we come across the little canoe flying the flag that marks R——'s brokers, sundry signs pass, which result in three great paddy-boats mounting the red flag too. They presently weigh anchor, and drop up to the mill. R—— is a smart man of business, and is very scornful about the representatives of several other firms, who lounge on the bank, smoking cheroots, and throwing sticks into the water for their dogs to fetch out. It is not directly a matter of money that is in question. The cultivators know pretty well what they are about, though you might not think it when you hear a man refuse ninety-two rupees a hundred baskets, and afterwards settle with a broker for eighty-eight. Those passes with the finger on the nose meant a good deal more than appeared. Another brick in the bottom of the basket, a three-inch batten wedged in somewhere, was the significance of that wink which sent the broker off in such a hurry.

At last it is over. There are no more boats to be had ; and we are not sorry to turn back, for the sun throws its beams fiercely back from the water in a way that gets below the broadest solah hat. R—— is in great glee : "Thirteen boats, by George ! Next best to the Imperial Firm ; and then there's the launch to come back." The Imperial Firm is the biggest concern in Rangoon, and has sometimes as much as a lakh out for "advance boats," *i.e.* money paid to cultivators before the rice has been planted out from the nurseries, or perhaps even before it has been sown at all. The launch about which R—— is so solicitous went away last night far up the Pegu River to intercept boats coming down with paddy for sale. There are sometimes great bargains to be made in this way. The boatmen have come a long distance, and are tired with paddling. The tide is making strong when the steam-launch comes up. There is the welcome prospect of an end to their labours, and above all there are no outbidding rivals to interfere. R—— instituted the system, and for a day or two had the game all to himself; but now the other firms have got wind of it, and there are sometimes famous races for a big boat, which must somewhat astonish the simple jungle wallahs, and certainly do not reduce the demands of the hleshin, the owner of the boat. R—— is in luck this morning. We have hardly gone a hundred yards when the "Mah Hlah" comes puffing round the point behind us, with a boat on either side, and three towing astern.

And now we have got back to the mill. The Burmans are discharging their paddy, which is stowed in bulk, into a big cargo boat. The regulation basket is in use, and we do not peer too inquisitively into the bottom of it. The owner of the boat is perched on the lofty carved stern of his craft, and placidly smokes a great cheroot. Presently he will come down and make his way to the office, where he will get a great pile of rupees to carry off, tied in the end of his paso. The greater number of them will probably find their way into the hands of the oily chetty, who is squatting on the bank there. The rest our hleshin will most likely gamble away.

Meanwhile, a long string of coolies is carrying the paddy from the lighter into the godown, a gigantic shed, where there is already a mountain of grain. We skirt round it, and go to the other side. There a few hundred more coolies are running off with more baskets to the mill. The paddy is thrown into huge receptacles on the basement, winnowed, carried up in lifts to the top of the house, three stories high, where it is first of all passed over a long sieve. Here the stalks, leaves, stones, and stumps of cheroots are separated from the grain, which is then passed between two revolving stones, just sufficiently wide apart to grind off the outer husk without breaking the seed. Then it is rewinnowed in fanners, and passed over finer sieves, where the broken grains fall through, while the part-cleaned rice goes on to fresh stones. It is found that perfectly clean rice will not stand the long sea voyage, and the grain as it is sent in the sailing ship has still the inner pellicle, and is mixed with about twenty per cent of unhusked rice. This is what is technically known as "five parts cargo rice," or simply "cargo rice." Since so many steamers have begun to go through the Suez Canal, the amount of "white rice" milled in the province has been steadily increasing. Rice of a specially fine quality, with a glaze on the surface, is manufactured for Italy. Clouds of rice-dust float all over the mill, and settle everywhere, making queer spectacles of the dark-skinned Madrasis. The dust is carefully swept up and sold to Chinamen, who fatten their pigs upon it. The milled grain descends to the ground-floor again, and pours in a stream through shoots into bags standing ready on weighing machines. There is a crowd of Burmese girls ready to sew them up as they are filled, and another band of coolies to carry them off in the cargo boats ready to convey them to the ships away up in the Rangoon harbour. Paddy that came in a Burmese boat in the morning may by night be safe stowed in the shape of milled rice deep down in the hold of a ship bound " to the Channel for orders." Everything is used but the paddy husk. That is passed out from the fanners, and pours in a great stream from wooden shoots into the creek. There it floats backwards and forwards with the tide, and creates miasma and narrows the river ; still no other feasible means of getting rid of it has yet been devised. Several engineers and others in Rangoon have tried special furnaces for consuming the husk, but with no very great measure of success. Mr. Cowie's system is probably the best ; but it requires a special kind of boiler and furnace, and has not as yet been generally adopted. The economy in fuel as well as the advantage to the river would be immense if the scheme were perfected.

And so we have seen the paddy sown out and mown, and passing from the hands of the cultivators, through the mills, into the great ships that carry the rice away to all parts of the world.

CHAPTER XXIV

A GRACIOUS PLOUGHING

LIKE the "royal elder brother" of China, the king of Burma ought to go out once a year to plough the fields. Thibaw Min did not do it during the first two years of his reign, and, as far as I am aware, was equally heedless throughout the later years also. The consequences ought to have been disastrous. According to tradition, the failure of the Lètwin mingala to come off should have caused a drought all over the country. But the Mo hkaung did not ensue ; on the contrary, there was Mo kaung : an aspirate makes all the difference between a water-famine and seasonable showers. King Thibaw went very little indeed out of his palace. The annals of the country supply too many instances of kings, who, having gone abroad, found on their return to the palace gates that a usurper had taken possession of the throne in the meantime, and had no better greeting for his predecessor than a short shrift and a red velvet sack in which to plunge his body into the Irrawaddy. This unlovable custom had great weight with King Thibaw ; but it was unwise of him to entirely abandon so venerable a tradition as the Lètwin mingala. It was at this ceremonial that one of the earliest marvels in the life of the Buddha Gautama happened. The king Thudawdana, with eight hundred noblemen save one, was ploughing the fields at the annual festival. Many country people came to see the great sight, and the city emptied itself. The maids who had charge of the little Prince Theidat laid him down under the shade of a tree and went to look on. The infant Buddha rose up as soon as they were gone, and sitting

cross-legged in the fashion in which he is ordinarily represented in the images, became sunk in meditation. The
careless maids all through the hot afternoon forgot about
their princely charge, until the returning crowds and the
setting sun reminded them of their neglect. Then they
hurried to the tree and found that the Zampu tha-bye had
maintained its shadow in the exact same position all day
as it was in when Prince Theidat was first laid down.
Notwithstanding the arc the sun had described, the shade
had all along hung over the head of the meditating Payā
Alaung.

The festival has therefore special reason to be celebrated
by the descendants of the solar kings. It was also in every
way a most picturesque fête, pleased the people, and offered
a valuable opportunity for squeezing money out of them.
King Mindôn never omitted it, even when he was grown
old and portly, and little able to follow the slow-stepping
bullocks. The ceremony took place in the beginning of
June, about the time when the south-west monsoon usually
breaks in Mandalay. The order went forth that the king
would come out on such and such a day, and the people
were enjoined to get ready. Not to see him—far from it.
The right of a cat to look at a king in Mandalay was not
well established. The Amein-daw was issued in order that
the heads over ten houses, the Sè-eing gaungs, might see
that the road in their district was in proper repair, and that
the yazamat had not got out of order. The yazamat, or
king's fence, was a kind of lattice-paling put up in every
street in the walled town, and in any of those in the suburbs
through which the king was likely at any time to pass.
It was formed of thick diagonal spars made into hurdles,
which were lashed to heavy posts sunk in the ground at
regular intervals. The whole was whitewashed, and often
flower-pots stood on the top of the posts to enliven the
structure a little ; and it certainly wanted enlivening a good
deal. The lattice-fence undoubtedly looked very neat and
tidy, as a long straight road lined with Lombardy poplars
does ; but it became terribly tiresome, when you found all
the streets looking exactly the same, with this six-foot-high
heavy wood fence standing within a couple of feet or so of

the walls of the houses, and shutting out all view of these wooden structures. It had, however, to be kept in constant repair, and the house-reeve has to go round carefully to see that none of the whitewash had been rubbed off, nor any of the transverse bars sprung with the sun. Behind these the entire populace had to stay when the king, or any one of the queens, went out. Woe betide the wretch who was caught outside them when the procession had started. He might consider himself lucky if he escaped with only a belabouring from the fasces of the shrieking lictors. No one was supposed even to look through the little diamond-shaped holes. As a matter of fact they did ; but by way of condoning for the offence, they rendered it more difficult by planting flowering shrubs between the bamboo houses and the lattice-work.

The procession on the route out to the Lèya, the royal acre, to be ploughed, was magnificent. The king was clad in all his robes of state : the paso with the daungyôp, the pea-cock sacred to royalty ; the long silk surcoat, or tunic, so thickly crusted with jewels that its colour could not be seen ; the tharapu, the spire-like crown, also a mass of precious stones ; the twenty-four strings of the Order of the Salwè across his breast ; and over his forehead the gold plate, or frontlet. The great gates in front of the stairs from the Hall of Audience were opened for him. Except the King of the Golden Throne no one might pass through them ; there was the low red postern at the side for meaner beings—a shrewd device to make every one bow his head to the palace, whether he liked it or not. His majesty mounted the white elephant, which none save he might ride—for is not the noble creature a king himself ?

The king mounted the Lord White Elephant at the palace of the latter, to the right of the Hall of Audience ; but the princes and ministers, all of whom came to attend the great function in their robes of state, might not enter their howdahs till the stockade of the nandaw had been passed. Then they fell into line in order of precedence, the wuns and wundauks wearing their official mitres—tall red velvet hats, with the top curled back like a nautilus, and the base surrounded with a row of gilt spear-heads. The long crimson velvet cassocks edged with rich brocade were also worn, and every one paraded all the umbrellas, gold, or vermilion, or green, that he was entitled to.

Thus they pass through the official town into the suburbs. The road taken is that by the east gate, whence, in a line with the steps of the Hall of Audience, a broad way runs straight away to the blue Shan hills ; or at least to where, in Mindôn's reign, the great Yankin-taung pagoda was being built, a few miles from where the hills rise, steep as out of a lake, from the flat rice lands. A death-like stillness prevails after the procession has passed the two timber guard-houses, between the tall columns of the eastern gate, surmounted by fantastic, triple-roofed teak pavilions, looking like Chinese joss-houses with their flamboyant carvings. The people are no doubt all there—we speak as those who know— crouching on their stomachs and peeping as best they can through yazamat and leaves of the bushes and legs of the soldiers that line the royal path all the way, striving their utmost to get a glimpse of the king and the splendour of his retinue ; but they are not to be seen, and no one so much as sneezes. Thus the richly carved and gilt royal monastery is passed on the left ; and immediately afterwards comparatively open ground is reached, stretching out on either side of the high, raised road. A little farther on, half a mile or so from the eastern gate, a halt is made at the selected portion of the lèdawgyi. Ploughs stand ready in a long row, extending away as far as one can see ; for all the princes and ministers must plough as well as the king. The royal plough is thickly covered with gold-leaf ; the part on which his majesty stands—for it must not be forgotten that the Burmese plough is something like a giant rake, and is not really a plough to English ideas at all—is gold, roughened with pearls and emeralds. The milk-white oxen that draw it rival the Lord White Elephant in the splendour of their harness. Crimson and gold bands hook them on ; the reins are stiff with rubies and diamonds ; heavy gold tassels hang from gilded horns. The gold-tipped ox-goad his majesty wields is covered with jewels and flashes like a rod of fire in the sun.

The king ploughs a couple of furrows—or, rather, passes

the big rake once up and down the rain-sodden field—and then stops ; for he is portly, and short of breath now. The ministers, no matter how fat they are, have to go on plough-ing as long as the Arbiter of Existence chooses to look on. At last he declares that enough has been done, and prepara-tions are made to go back again. He doffs his royal robes, for the tharapu, with its spire and jewelled ear-flappets, is burdensome, and the long surcoat, with its thousands of precious stones, is said to weigh about a hundred pounds. The Lord White Elephant is relieved too. He stalks back unencumbered, with his household of thirty retainers fussing about him with fans and swaying umbrellas.

The king gets into an open car, something like what Roman racing chariots are represented to have been. It is of course adorned as richly as everything else, and is drawn not by ponies or bullocks, but by men, eight of them pulling at each of the flexible shafts. The object is to prevent any one, the driver for example, sitting higher than the king. The English carriages presented at various times to different Burmese monarchs met with little approval. At first it was thought that the king was to sit on the box ; but then it was found that with this arrangement there was nothing for it but that the driver should run by the side and therefore maintain a constant erect attitude in the presence of royalty. When it was found that the king was supposed to sit inside, with the driver two or three feet above him, a burst of indignation suggested that it was an insidious plot to put an insult on the majesty of the lord of the umbrella-bearing chiefs. For a time the vehicles were put away as lumber ; but an ingenious handicraftsman adorned them with pya-thats—five-roofed ecclesiastical or royal spires. They were now, when drawn by men, suitable for royal occupation ; but unfortunately the solid teak-wood spires made them top-heavy, and especially unstable on rough Mandalay roads. They therefore degenerated into paraphernalia for exhibition on a kadaw day, or gauds for a procession at Tawadeintha feast time.

The king consequently returns on his low, gilt, native-made carriage, reclining on a mattress placed on the floor. He is now dressed in the ordinary national way, with a light linen jacket and a slender pawlôn (a fillet of book-muslin wound round the head), showing the thin white hair tied up in a little knot on the top of the head. The chief ministers are round about, fanning him assiduously; and he is in extreme good-humour, chaffing the Kin Wungyi, the astute prime minister, on the way he let his bullocks straggle away at random and the difficulties he got into in trying to turn them at the end of the field; while the stout old Naingan-gya Wun-dauk is rallied about the absurd state of heat he was brought into by his exertions. Possibly, if a venture-some and inquisitive subject were to be seen now, the king might pardon him for his rude gaping. But nobody knows in what temper the king is, and the silence is as death-like as when the party moved out. As soon, however, as the great procession has passed and has wound its way into the palace, the hitherto deserted streets are crowded again. Pwès begin with startling suddenness at every corner. Bands strike up; long lines of candles illuminate the streets at nightfall; rockets are let off, fire-balloons ascend, and every-thing is given up to rejoicing; for the lèdawgyi has been graciously ploughed, and the Lètwin mingala is a presage of abundant crops.

It is needless to say that the persons mentioned are now all dead and that the British Government does not maintain the Lètwin mingala. The spectacle of the Lieu-tenant-Governor balancing himself on a harrow with the Commissioner of the Northern Division and the Judicial Commissioner for Upper Burma as acolytes, or rivals, would not be impressive. A striking spectacle has gone and cannot be revived.

CHAPTER XXV

A HARVEST FEAST

ONE of the pleasantest and most social of Burmese country festivals is the ceremony which goes by the name of Tamanè Hto-thi. It occurs in the month of Ta'saungmôn, or of Na'daw, when the harvest is over and the first of the new rice piled up in a heap near the farmer's house, or perhaps stowed away in the capacious bottom of the hnaw, the big rice-boat, with its stern rising ten or fifteen feet above the surface of the water, and ready to start for Rangoon whenever its owner shall have hit upon a lucky day for commencing the voyage. In order to acquire a store of merit as well towards the next existence as towards the journey immediately in view ; to back up the verdict of the astrologer from the horoscope with the good wishes of the holy men of the monastery ; and, above all, to have a feast such as generally comes in somewhere in all Burmese religious proceedings, the cultivator resolves to give away twenty baskets or so of rice in alms and presents to the yellow-robed monks and his neighbours. A special kind of rice is always used on these occasions. Englishmen generally are unaware probably that there are a great number of varieties of rice, and that they differ very much in their flavour. Most people imagine that all rice has the same taste (no taste, they would probably say) ; and distinguish in a rough material way between Patna rice, which is very small, and Rangoon rice, which is considerably larger in the grain, and finally Carolina rice, which is bigger than any of them. A Rangoon merchant would go a little farther, and say that there are two varieties—the nga-sein, which he likes best and gets most of, and the nga-kyauk, which comes in more sparingly. But beyond these—

and they are not the varieties most in favour with the Burmese for their own consumption—there are at least thirty different kinds. There is the byat sabā, the "tray" rice, which is considered the best, but, like most of the other sorts, will not stand the rough treatment of the steam mill-stones, and breaks in pieces. Then there is the myi-she, which has a long awn, and the myi-tôn, which has no awn at all; the taung-pyan, "winged rice," and the nga-chywè, "buffalo grain"; and so on through a long list, ending up with "black rice," which is not by any means bad eating. But of all the kinds, kauk-hnyin, "sticky rice," is the variety always used at the harvest feast. It is mixed with thin sliced cocoa-nut, sesamum seeds, ginger, onions, and pepper, all stirred together and well boiled; and the resulting mess is called tamanè. The rice is well named. It is very emphatically sticky, and even when taken alone is not very easily digested; but when it comes in the form of tamanè, the result is usually a widespread attack of colic throughout the village. This, however, comes after the festival, when the fun is all over, and does not concern us in any way.

When the farmer has made up his mind as to the day on which he is going to have the feast—a date which, of course, cannot be settled without consulting the wise men of the village and much pondering over the palm-leaf horoscope —he sends out a few boys with a number of packets of "pickled tea" to all the young men in the place, requesting them to be good enough to eat it and to come without fail that night to his homestead in order to help him to husk his rice for the tamanè hto-thi. A few girls are also asked to come; and they bring their friends for the sake of company, and the mothers follow for the sake of propriety. Thus there is quite a large assemblage at the farmer's when night falls and the business is to commence. There is a good deal of preliminary tea-drinking and smoking of cheroots and chew-ing of betel and le'hpet, and a great deal of laughing and talking. The girls profess to be astonished to find so many young men there; they had not imagined their host was meditating such extensive preparations, and thought there would be nobody there but his own and his wife's younger brothers. That is exactly what they will say next week

when they attend a similar assemblage at Htun Aung's
house at the other end of the village.

But after an hour or so they settle down to do a little
work. The young men—kālathas, they call themselves—
"Corinthians, lads of mettle"—have brought with them a
number of wooden mortars, with a heavy pestle working on
a lever; and these they set up and commence to husk the
rice. The process is very simple. A few handfuls of the
paddy are thrown into the mortar, the workers step off and
on the lever which raises and lets fall the solid wooden
pestle, and the husk is every now and then blown out and
the grain stirred up a little. The Burmans infinitely prefer
rice husked in the national way to that which is sent out
from the European steam-mills. The big Derbyshire or
composite stones do their work only too effectually; they
take off not only the hard shell, but also the inner cuticle of
the grain, which contains the chief flavour; and, moreover,
the heat which the steady grinding induces, scorches out a
great deal of what taste remains. Therefore at every house
there is to be found the primitive national apparatus in
which the girls of the household every morning or evening
prepare the rice for the day's consumption. But to-night
they are relieved from such hard work. The village youths
for once in a way exert themselves; and all the girls have
to do is to wash out a few dishes and prepare the bamboo-
lacquered platters, the pyramidal ôk, in which the tamanè is
to be carried to the yahans and the pagoda to-morrow, and
get ready the palm-leaves in which less exalted people will
receive their modicum of the stew. The whole actual work
might be finished in little over an hour, but that is the
intention neither of the giver of alms nor of the assembled
young men and maidens. They have come much more for
merriment than for merit. Else why that great pile of
le'hpet? For the condiment is an anti-soporific, and if you
take enough of it, you will be able to see all through a forty-
eight hours' play, and give your friends an outline of the plot
before you lapse into a slumber lasting twice round the clock.

Accordingly, after a quarter of an hour's work, the
"prince" of the local amateur dramatic company jumps off
his perch, and commences the "White Dove" song from the

Zawtagômma melodrama, which the old sayā at Pegu has just brought out, and which is having a tremendous run all through the low country. The song is about the Saddan mere, the lake of the Lord White Elephant, where golden lotuses flower perpetually, where the gorgeous yin-dwin bird sails on the silvery waters, great butterflies flap about with painted wings and sip the nectar of the fabled jasmine, and peacocks stalk proudly on the jewelled margin, while around roam elephants white, red, and black in happy security. The singer has hardly finished when the lu-byet, the village jester, breaks in with a travesty of the whole thing, mocking at the tremolos and the lofty style, and taking off the peculiarities of the singer. He went out to a lake too, and launched a canoe on it, but he was capsized by a huge creature that came up from below; and then he found that he had got into a slimy buffalo wallow, out of which he only escaped after great peril from the horns of its three outraged owners, who butted him under the surface many times; and at last, when he crawled out, he was so brown and dirty that some passers-by took him for a hermit, and gave him some rotten plantains in alms. Before the "prince" has time to show any bad temper, a girl commences a coquettish ditty, somewhat after the fashion of the English "Paddle my own canoe," about a poor wife whose husband comes home and storms and growls and abuses because there is no rice ready cooked, softens down when he has crammed himself with curry and rice, but breaks out into grumbling again at night because his wife cries and will not go to sleep. Such tyranny the young lady declares she will never expose herself to, or at any rate "she'll be no submissive wife." Then there are a few love-songs, wherein the girls are compared with the maids of the palace in Mandalay, and the Mandalay girls generally (who are *ex officio* pretty) with the daughters of nats, with Madi, the model wife of Wethandaya (the prince who in his next existence became the Lord Buddha), with flowers and stars and gems, and whatever similes lovers all the world over are in the habit of making. The swaying of the body as they walk, the turning in of the elbows, the fragrant powder on their cheeks and necks, and a few other items which would not commend themselves to a Western admirer, are recorded with enthusiasm and delighted precision of detail; and when an hour or so has been passed in this way, a little more rice-husking is done, and the girls set to work getting ready the onions and sesamum seed, and slicing up the cocoa-nut kernels. This sort of thing goes on all the night through. There is half an hour's work, and then an hour of singing and story-telling and gossip; about the great Shinbinthalyaung, the gigantic recumbent image of Shin Gautama dug up lately near Pegu; of the two min-laungs, the embryo kings, who have been revealed there, and the third one, who is foretold by the old theit-sa, the prophecy which declares that he will restore the ancient Talaing kings and revive religion; of the new hti which is being set up on the pagoda of the lotus tank, and its exceed-ing splendour, each single one of the concentric rings having been assigned as a particular favour to one out of many competing districts. Then there is a discussion as to the new fashion of turbans, the one plain colour with worked flowers on it, which has supplemented the old thinner style with more braid-like patterns; and the present rage for waist-cloths with many-coloured stripes in place of the old wavy and dog's-tooth fashion. Then the girls are rallied about the method in which they dress their hair—all of them in the style just declared treasonable in the upper country. Queen Supayalat has hit upon some particular set, or plaiting of her tresses, which she thinks becomes her very well, and a royal order has come out making it penal for any meaner damsels to adopt the same method. Conse-quently all the maidens from Taungoo to Kyauk-Hpyu and the A-eng Pass to Malawun have made up after the queenly model and flatter themselves that it is *chic*. There are always ghost stories at these gatherings, tales about the three farmer brothers that were killed just after harvest time three years ago, and now haunt the dense patch of swampy jungle down by the creek as nat seins, and sometimes scare the fishermen out of a night's work by the violent agitation of the tree-tops on a still night; and then there is that old hag in the lone house at the far end of the village, who is certainly a witch; it must have been she who gave the old sikkè the tet, poor old man, and he a payā-tagā too, founder

of the pagoda on the slope of the "Brother and Sister Hill";
and there is little Ma Mi; the old beldam looked at her over
the fence on the fifth of last waning, and the poor thing lost
her sweetheart before the change of the moon, and had all
her fine false hair stolen only three days ago: proof enough
that of the *jettatura*.

It is long past midnight, when all the cocks of the
village crow together, deriving their knowledge of the exact
time from the diet of burnt astrological books, pecked at by
their ancestors long ago, when the objection to cabalistic
works was much more violent than it is nowadays; and
sometimes daylight is coming in, and the sound of the
morning chant steals over from the monastery, when the
party breaks up and all go home.   The kauk hnyin has
been all husked, and, mixed up with the other ingredients,
is simmering away over the fire.   Every one has a virtuous
consciousness of having gained considerable kutho in
addition to having spent a very agreeable time.   Few go
to sleep.   They have eaten too much le'hpet for that, and
in an hour or two some of them will be wanted again to
take the tamanè round.   That is done about eight o'clock
in the case of the monks.   The farmer himself and his
family carry it to the monastery in the spire-shaped lacquer-
box, and having paid the usual reverence, deposit it before
the superior, who looks on calmly without a word of thanks,
or even the semblance of a recognition, but says before they
go, that if they keep the Ten Precepts and live virtuously,
they will escape the Four States of Punishment and be
delivered from the Five Enemies.   Then the "supporters"
wheel on the right, and depart home to make up the portions
for all their friends and neighbours.   These are usually taken
round by the girls, who go in bevies of three or four, dressed
in their finest clothes and with flowers in their hair, and
deliver the dainty with compliments, and injunctions to eat
it immediately.   By six o'clock in the evening, when the
sonorous wooden bell of the monastery is summoning in all
the scholars, the entire village is asleep; and they do not get
up very early next morning.   Nobody in the whole place has
been drunk; and if there is an opium-eater in the village, he
was not asked to the feast and had none of the tamanè.

CHAPTER XXVI

SILK-GROWING

REARING silkworms, though a very profitable occupation, is not looked upon with any favour in Burma. To get the silk the pupa must be killed ; and the taking of life in any form is an impiety always looked upon with great horror by all good Buddhists. Silk-growers are classed together with professional hunters and fishermen. The Four States of Punishment yawn for them, and their portion will be in the lowest abyss of the lowest hell. Still there are colonies of silk-growers in various parts of the country ; but they live apart from the rest of the inhabitants as a rule, and often have entire villages to themselves. Colonel Horace Browne who, more than any other Englishman took an interest in the ways and occupations of the districts under his charge, states that the cultivators near Prome, where more silk is produced than in any part of Burma, are nearly all Yabeins —a race of the same stock as the Burmese, but despised by them independently of their crime in the way of habitually taking animal life. So much has the cultivation of silk become identified with them, that to Burman ears the term Yabein is virtually synonymous with that of silk-grower. They usually live on the hillsides, occupying themselves like the poorer Burmans and Karens, with taung-ya cultivation ; burning the forests on the slopes and sowing the ground thus enriched with the wood ashes, with rice, cotton, or oil-seed. The system is viewed with very little approval by the government officials, for the taung-ya soil, hardly exhausted by the single crop raised off it, immediately produces a dense shrub-growth of no use to anybody, certainly not to the foresters.

Silk-raising is therefore encouraged as a means of stopping the ruination of the timber. It is a very simple matter, involving the least possible amount of toil, and at the same time being on the whole very profitable. Moreover, the Burmese mulberry-bush, which is quite distinct from the ordinary *Morus Indica*, does not grow well on the alluvial soil of the low lands, while it flourishes on the hillsides, where the Yabeins mostly live. The silk obtained from the caterpillars fed on the leaves of the hill-shrubs is very much better than that obtained from the mulberry-bushes of the plains. Thus it happens that all parties are likely to be pleased. The English Government foresters will gradually find means of putting an end to the timber-burning, which they detest ; the richer Burmans down in the lowlands will neither have the temptation to increase their income at the expense of their piety, nor will they have that piety shocked by an organised system of taking life ; while the Yabeins in their own hill-villages will be allowed to do as they please, and will accumulate tidy sums of money into the bargain.

It is certain that neither the silkworm nor the mulberry-bush is indigenous in Burma. It is said that the first cocoons were brought from China in the reign of King Anawrata Saw. Others again maintain that the Chinese taught the Shans, the Shans the Karens, and these the Burmese. In some places among the more superstitious hill-tribes the mulberry-tree receives a kind of worship. In any case it is more probable that both the silkworm and the tree were introduced from Western China, down the valley of the Irrawaddy or the Salween, than that they came over the hills, through turbulent mountaineers, from India. The shrub does not grow much more than ten feet high, and seldom produces good succulent leaves for a longer period than three years. After that the plants are apt to get coarse and stringy, and the cultivators ordinarily abandon the plantation, or root out the bushes and plant new ones. As the shrub will not flower it is propagated by cuttings, and new shoots are constantly being planted so that there may be an unfailing supply of young and fresh leaves. The Burmans call it the posabin, "the tree the silkworms eat." There is another tree—that from the bark of which the coarse paper used for the para-baik, or note-books, is got—the leaves of which the caterpillars will eat ; but the silk thus obtained is much coarser, and recourse is had therefore to the mahlaing-bin only when the mulberry-bushes give out.   In any case, however, it is undeniable that, as yet, the silk produced in Burma is of a very inferior kind.   It is rough and coarse ; but it is all the better suited for the strong lungyis and pasos in use for ordinary every-day wear among the people, the finer fabrics all coming from China or Manchester.

The whole process of growing the silk is of the simplest possible character, and is exactly suited to indolent people who have no conscientious objections to the killing of the pupæ. Silk can, indeed, be spun from the cocoons, out of which the moths have escaped ; but it is very much coarser even than the ordinary silk, and commands somewhat less than half the price.   Except the occasional trouble of strolling out for a few leaves, there is almost nothing to be done ; and the whole operations are carried on in the rickety bamboo hut of the cultivator, within a yard or two of the place where his food is cooked.   The caterpillars do not seem to care a bit for the smoke or the dirt ; and the pupæ are equally callous to the fumes of tobacco which circle about them con-stantly during the few days that remain to them before they are stewed.   The female moths are placed upon pieces of coarse cloth, with palm-leaf lids put over them.   The eggs stick to the cloth, and form a compact little circle.   A day or two over a week suffices to produce the larvæ, and these are then thrown upon flat trays, made of strips of bamboo plaited closely together, and guarded by a slightly raised edge.   For four or five days the little caterpillars are fed on finely-chopped mulberry-leaves, the tenderest that can be found.   After that they change their skins, and, beyond getting plenty of leaves, do not receive much attention. They are sturdy creatures, and they would need to be, for they are often very roughly treated.   The trays are scarcely ever cleaned, and if the larvæ are to be shifted from one tray to another, they are scraped up in handfuls and thrown down as if they were so many chips of wood.   Gauze or mosquito netting is usually thrown over the trays to keep away the ichneumon flies, which otherwise would deposit

their eggs in the silkworm's back and kill him.   In about a
month's time the caterpillar is full grown.   He is then
bundled into a fresh tray, in which there lies, wound about
in the form of a spiral, a narrow-plaited bamboo strip.   The
ripe larvæ are thrown into this with as little ceremony as if
they were pebbles.   In about a day's time they have spun
their cocoons, fastening them to the strips of bamboo.   These
are torn off and kept in baskets for a day or two, when a
pot with water in it is filled with the pupæ, and then set to
simmer over a slow wood fire.

From a triangle over the pot is suspended a small bamboo
reel, and down below, near the pot, is a wooden cylinder.
The reeler is usually a girl.   She fishes about for a time in
the simmering vessel, and, catching a few threads of silk,
passes them over the reel and down to the cylinder, to which
they are fastened.   She then turns the handle of the cylinder,
winding on the silk, and at the same time constantly fishing
up and fastening on new filaments, which she does by means
of a light bamboo double-pronged fork.   Not the least
trouble is taken to keep the silk clean.   Any rubbish that
may be floating on the surface of the water is wound on to
the cylinder without an attempt being made to disengage it.
When all the silk has been got off the cocoons, and wound
on to the cylinder, the pupæ are taken out of the water and
fried in oil to furnish a dish for the family dinner.   They
are not by any means unpleasant, tasting, barring the oil,
very much like roasted chestnuts ;   and indeed the dish is
considered a great dainty.

The silk-growers mostly sell their silk.   A loom is to be
found in almost every Burman's house in the country ; and
in Prome and Shwe-daung, as being close to the place where
the silk is produced, great quantities of articles of dress are
made for sale.   The native-grown silk is only used for every-
day clothes of simple patterns, the more elaborate being all
worked from imported Chinese silk.   The silk is bought
raw, the separate filaments twisted into a thread by means
of a wheel, and then made up into hanks ; these are boiled
in soap and water, and are then ready for the dye.   The
commonest colours are green, yellow, orange, different shades
of red and light blue ;   black and dark blue are only in

favour with the Shans. The dyes are obtained from various jungle seeds, roots, flowers, leaves, and barks; the yellow dye obtained from the wood of the Jack-tree (*Artocarpus integrifolia*) being reserved for the monkish robes. After being dyed, the thread is unwound again. The weaving machine is very much like the old hand-loom still occasionally seen in out-of-the-way parts of England. The operators are almost always young women, and they are very clever at working the treadle and shooting through the shuttle, while talking all the time to village gossips or admiring swains. Some of the tameins, made for the richer women, are extremely intricate in pattern and require between twenty and thirty shuttles. The treadle raises and lowers the alternate threads of the warp. Except the rough dresses and the most complicated in pattern, however, not many native-made clothes are worn now. The townspeople prefer the showy and cheaper imported articles, and, though the Manchester goods are too frequently "doctored" and do not last long, yet this does not trouble the Burman much, for he is fond of a change of dress, and, unless he is very poor, will never wear a paso, except about the house, after it has been washed. All the more elaborate designs are, however, native made. The "dog's tooth" pattern is almost confined to Amarapura or Sagaing court looms, and since the fall of the monarchy is hardly seen at all. The acheit paso or tamein, of a complicated, wavy, sprigged design, which middle-aged Burmans remember as being the cherished object of desire of their young days, is now considered rustic. Young Rangoon will tell you that you may always know a taw-tha (a jungle wallah) at the pagoda feast by his wearing an acheit paso and nothing else except his turban; and although the waist-cloth may cost from 150 to 400 rupees, that does not redeem it in the town-bred youth's eyes.

CHAPTER XXVII

LACQUER WARE

FOR a long time it was assumed that Japanese and Chinese lacquered goods were simply papier-mâché. A popular fancy for the ware has brought to the knowledge of all who care for the information that it is really wood of different kinds painted over with the juice of the urushi tree. Should fashion ever inspire a similar enthusiasm for Burmese productions of the same kind, it is probable that it may be supposed that these also are composed of solid wood, and people will wonder at the extreme thinness and flexibility of the finer specimens. But it is only the coarsest ware which is thus produced. All the better boxes and cups are made of a woven basket-work of strips of bamboo ; the varnish used on them is, like the Japanese lacquer, the sap obtained from the stem of a tree, and has nothing whatever to do with the insect-produced lac, such as English varnishers employ in solution with alcohol. I am not botanist enough to know whether the urushi (*Rhus vernicifera*), the Japanese tree, is identical with the Burman thi'si (*Melanorrhœa usitatissima*), or even whether it is of the same genus or order. Thi'si (literally wood-oil) is dark in colour from the moment it is gathered, whereas the urushi sap is described as being light yellow when first extracted, and only turning black after considerable exposure to the air. The urushi has been cultivated by royal order for hundreds of years in Japan ; but in Burma, though the Forest Department declares the thi'si a reserved tree, there is no attempt at organised cultivation, and the thi'si-bin grows wild in the jungle. Not even near Nyaung-u, where nearly every household in the town is occupied in the trade, is there any attempt at regular planting of nurseries. Nevertheless it is plentiful enough, and affords a magnificent spectacle when it is in flower—a huge forest tree covered so thickly with creamy-white blossoms that the leaves cannot be seen. The flowers have a fragrant scent not unlike that of apples, and the needy and practical Burman often makes a very acceptable curry of the buds. In full-grown trees the average height to the first branch is thirty feet, and the ordinary girth six feet from the ground is nine feet. Charcoal-burners have a predilection for the wood, which would not meet with approval in Japan; and it is much used for anchors and tool-helves, being very close and fine-grained. It is too heavy to float when green, but dried it is not particularly weighty. The sap may be collected at all times, except when the fruit is on the trees, from Pyatho to Tabaung—the first three months of the English year. Then it is thin and does not produce such a brilliant polish. The mode of collection is simple enough. Incisions are made in the stem, and the sap trickles into bamboos placed to catch it. When it is to be kept any time there must be a depth of two or three inches of water on the top, otherwise it would dry up and become solid. The water, however, does not improve it. The best varnish, called thi'si ayaungtin, is that which has been just drawn from the tree; the second quality contains twenty-five per cent of water, the inferior as much as fifty.

The articles lacquered are chiefly drinking-cups and betel-boxes, the latter consisting of a cylindrical inner case, in which are fitted two or three trays for holding the lime, betel-vine leaves, cutch, nuts, and other ingredients for betel-chewing, the whole covered by an outer lid reaching to the bottom of the inner case. Ordinary kôn-it, betel-boxes, are three or four inches high and two and a half to three in diameter. Articles of the same shape are made of all sizes up to a couple of feet or more in height, these last being used for holding clothes and women's working materials. The bi-it, ladies' toilet-boxes, are often the most delicate and carefully worked. The actresses always carry splendid specimens about with them to contain their combs, oil, scent, the white lead and thana'kha for the complexion, and a few tresses of false hair. Other articles are the pyramidal tamin-sa-ôk, used for carrying food to the monasteries and the pagodas, fashioned somewhat in the style of the sacred spires, of five or seven roofs, and of all sizes from eighteen inches to the huge things, the height of a man, which the king sent under the royal umbrellas to the Arakan pagoda in Mandalay. Byat, platters of all sizes, up to the gigantic circular tray as big as a small table, used for dishing up the family dinner, are always made of wood, like the Japan ware. The people do not think much of them, and they are therefore almost always quite plain, either black or red. There is no inferiority to the Japanese in capacity for sketching fantastic designs. The future may see great developments in this branch of the art, but at present it is practically untouched. It is unfortunate that enterprise so far has taken the form of making "peg" tumblers and cigar-cases instead of developing national forms.

The process of manufacture is as follows : Little basket-like boxes of the required shape and size are woven of fine bamboo wicker-work, upon round chucks of wood prepared and firmly fixed for the purpose. The bamboos used, which are usually split and cleaned by the women and children, are of different kinds, that called myinwa being the most highly esteemed. Similarly, the yet, or woven basket-work, is of different degrees of excellence, the kyaungleinyet being the finest. Some of the Shans and better workmen at Nyaung-u are celebrated for the delicacy of their work. On this is then evenly applied with the hand (so that the slightest particle of sand or dirt may be at once detected) a coat of the pure wood-oil. This is then put away to dry—not in the sun, which is apt to pucker and blister it, but in a cool airy place. Some careful workmen have often an underground room prepared specially for the purpose. After three days it is quite dry and hard, and is then liberally and evenly covered over with a paste called thayo. This is made in a variety of ways, the commonest being a mixture of finely-sifted teak sawdust, thi'si, and rice-water. But instead of the sawdust, or often mixed with it, finely-ground bone-ash, or paddy-husk burnt and strained through a cloth, is kneaded in. In the coarse, common articles for every-day use, tempered clay and some other materials are often used; but this being thicker and less putty-like, is apt to scale and come off in flakes, especially if at all roughly used. This thayo is allowed to dry quite hard, and the box is then fastened to a rude lathe, which is turned with one hand, while the other is employed in polishing the box. This smoothing-down is effected with sifted ashes, or some-times with a piece of silicious bamboo, which is as good as fine sand-paper. When this is done the box is ready for a fresh coat, which almost invariably consists of a mixture of finely-powdered bone-ashes and thi'si. This, after drying, is polished in the same way as before. We have now a box of a brilliant glossy black, in itself very pretty and fit for use anywhere. But this is only the end of the first stage; none but the byat and common wooden platters are left in this state.

The ground colour of the great majority of the boxes and cups is red; but some of the black wood-oil is required to rise through it and define the pattern. This is effected in a most ingenious way. The black box is put on the lathe again and turned round, while the lines and spots, and the form of the black pattern generally, is sketched on with a sut, or split stile, charged with thi'si. The drawer has no guide but his eye. There is no preliminary mapping out, yet a practised hand will never make a mistake and spoil a box. The fresh thi'si thus put on stands up above the general level of the surface. The whole box is now covered with red paint; and when this is dry the box is put on the lathe again, and the operator turns it round and rubs it steadily with ashes. By this means the red paint is removed where the lines of thi'si rise above the general surface, and the black pattern stands out clearly on the red ground. A quaint chequer-work is also always produced, where the slightly projecting edges of the bamboo wicker-work raise the black wood-oil through the vermilion layer. Still, however, it is not finished. No box is complete with-out three colours; and this last shade is applied in an equally simple and effective way. The desired pattern is incised with a graving-tool called a kauk—often nothing more elaborate than a pin firmly tied to a piece of stick. Then the whole box is coated over with the new colour, and this is in its turn polished off on the lathe till nothing remains but the lines of the engraved pattern. If another colour is required, a similar process is gone through.

When the design is complete, a clear varnish of another vegetable oil, called shansi, with a dash of thi'si in it, is applied all over as a last touch, unless indeed a very high polish is required. This is effected by rubbing gently with the powdered petrified wood found so useful in imparting a gloss to the alabaster images. The patterns are none of them very intricate, and are handed down as heirlooms from father to son, so that the same family will have all its ware made on a few clearly-defined models, and there is no fear of "spoiling a set." The invention does not as yet soar beyond scroll-work and line-figures of infinite variety; but should a foreign demand spring up there would be no lack of skill to meet it; just as the Rangoon tattooers have taken to copying pictures out of the *Graphic* on English sailors' breasts.

The supreme test of excellence in the manufacture is when the sides will bend in till they touch without cracking the varnish or breaking the wicker-work. Connoisseurs can discriminate between Shan, Nyaung-u, and the ware of other places, by the shadow thrown on the inside (which is varnished plain red or black), when the cup or circular box is held at an angle of forty-five. Three colours only are used besides the black groundwork; but variety is produced by graduating their intensity of shade. They are red, green, and yellow. Red is prepared from finely-ground vermilion mixed with shansi. The Nyaung-u people prefer a vermilion called hinthapadi ywè, prepared by themselves, to that procured from China and used elsewhere. The home-made stuff seems to be much brighter in tint. Myeni, red ochre, is used only with the coarsest work. For yellow, yellow orpiment is ground down and washed several times until a pure, impalpable powder remains. This is mixed with a pellucid gum, and when required for use, worked up with shansi. Green is obtained by adding finely-ground indigo to the yellow orpiment until the required tint is obtained. Red and yellow are, however, always the pre-dominating colours.

The thi'si is turned to a variety of other uses besides the manufacture of lacquer-work ; applied to wood, or to marble and clay images, it enables them readily to take on gilding. It is used as a waterproof varnish to all the umbrellas in the country, and makes them as impervious to rain as if they were made of wood, while it protects the palm-leaf against the rays of the sun, which otherwise would burn it as brittle as an egg-shell. All the racing and war-boats in Burma are painted with it, and the best caulking in the world could not make them more water-tight. Finally, boiled down thick it furnishes the material for delineating the square heavy characters of the sacred kammawa-sa, the ritual for the admission of brethren to the sacred order.

The oil is usually put in the sun for a short time before being used, and it is at first of a light brown colour, soon darkening into a brilliant black. It seems to be of a par-ticularly mordant character, and raises huge blisters on the hands of some people, leaving marks of the ashy-white colour suggestive of leprosy. Hence strangers suspected of being afflicted with the terrible malady always declare they are thi'si workers ; and many people avoid these latter, in case they might find they had been holding communication with an outcast. A lotion composed of fine teak-wood saw-dust, mixed with a little water, is used as a cure for blains. Many of the workmen periodically swallow small doses of the wood-oil, under the impression that it acts as a preven-tive. The capriciousness with which the varnish acts, leaving some men quite unharmed and punishing others severely, has given rise to a proverb in Nyaung-u :—

> Thi'si is a witness
> To a burgher's fitness ;
> If bad, he's marked an outcast ;
> If good, not long can doubt last.

CHAPTER XXVIII

NGAPI

THERE are few articles of food which meet with more energetic denunciation than the favourite Burman condiment, ngapi, which means literally pressed fish. The frogs of France, the rats and puppy dogs of China, the diseased liver of the Strasburg *pâtés*, the "ripe" cheeses of most European countries, and the peculiar character of game in England, with its occasional garniture of "rice," all meet with condemnation from those who dislike such dainties. The smell of ngapi is certainly not charming to an uneducated nose, but the Backsteiner or Limburger cheese of Southern Germany is equally ill-calculated to evoke approbation on a first experience. An old herring barrel smells strong, but there is nothing in nature that more than ngapi hath an ancient and a fish-like smell. Travellers on the steamers of the Irrawaddy Flotilla Company are wont to rail in no measured terms at the fish-paste which forms an invariable and obtrusively evident part of the cargo, yet no Burman would think a dinner complete without his modicum of ngapi, and it is a noteworthy fact that one form of the condiment is of frequent appearance on English dinner-tables in the East, under the name of balachong, a term borrowed from the Straits Settlements, but which designates nothing more nor less than a specially prepared variety of ngapi. In the same way there are equally various opinions with regard to the celebrated Durian, a fruit found as abundantly in the Tenasserim province as in the islands of the East Indian Archipelago, and equally highly prized by Burmans. Some Englishmen will tell you that the flavour

and the odour of the fruit may be realised by eating a
" garlic custard " over a London sewer ; others will be no
less positive in their perception of blendings of sherry, noyau,
delicious custards, and the nectar of the gods, while a somewhat objectionable smell is regarded as doing no more than
suggest, or recall, a delightful sensation.   I am not aware
that any Englishman has been equally enthusiastic with
regard to balachong, but there is no doubt that ngapi seinsa
[" raw-eaten fish-paste," so called because it is fit for consumption without being cooked] is identical with this much-
used substitute for anchovy sauce, and is often brought
direct from the Burman bazaar by Madrasi butlers, who
declare it has come all the way from Penang, and charge
correspondingly.

Of ngapi there are three main kinds — ngapi gaung,
taung - tha ngapi, and ngapi seinsa.   Each of these has
its special varieties, getting their names from the township
where they are prepared, or from the species of fish used
in their manufacture.

Ngapi gaung, or whole ngapi, is the most prized and
the highest in price.   That made at the village of Payāgyi,
in the Angyi circle, not far from Rangoon, is celebrated
from the rocky promontory of Modain, with its golden
pagoda, to the barren solitudes of Mogaung, the Burmese
Siberia.   It may be made from any kind of fish, but the
varieties preferred are the nga-ku, an amphibious, slimy fish,
found in ponds and ditches wherever there is plenty of mud,
and something under a foot and a half in length ; and the
nga-gyi, a fish very similar in general appearance and size,
but called by the English the scorpion-fish, and very much
dreaded for the wounds it causes with the pectoral spines.
The great object in the preparation is to keep the fish quite
whole, not so easy a matter as would at first appear.   The
process is as follows : A great mass of the fish, some of them
only half dead, are thrown together into a big wooden
mortar, and a man stands over them and works about with
a curious cleaner made of a bamboo, the end of which has
been slit and frayed into a kind of stiff brush.   By this
means it is surprising how soon the fish are scaled, and how
effectively it is done.   The larger specimens are, however,

almost always cleaned by hand, the shoulder fins and the tail being also removed. They are then thoroughly rubbed with salt and tightly packed in bamboo baskets, each of which is well weighted down. They are thus left for from twelve to twenty-four hours, the superfluous juices of the fish straining out at the bottom. Then they are cautiously taken out one by one, well rubbed with salt again, and laid out on a mat in the sun to dry. On the second day they are equally carefully packed away in huge earthenware jars with abundance of salt between the layers of fish. These jars are then put away—no easy matter with some of them, which might have served to conceal the forty thieves of the *Arabian Nights*—in as shady and cool a place as can be found. Gradually the liquid rises to the surface and evaporates by degrees, leaving a layer of solid salt on the top. Sometimes this fish-brine becomes alive with maggots, when the fish have not been sufficiently pressed, or have not had enough sun. When this occurs the liquid is drawn off the top and more salt is added, but in no case are any of the fish rejected. Usually the fish are ready for the market in a month's time, and will keep as long as may be wanted. They are eaten roasted, or fried somewhat in the same way as the "Bombay ducks," well known to the Anglo-Indian gourmand; sometimes also they are made into curries, the cook taking as great care as the manufacturer to keep them quite whole. The salt used is in many places, such, for example, as the Angyi township, made on the spot. The soil there is strongly impregnated with salt. Water is run through it after the ground has been ploughed. The water is then collected in a tank, whence it is taken to pots, placed over furnaces, and evaporated to dryness, and the salt obtained is piled on sloping boards so that the bittern may run off.

A specially esteemed variety of the ngapi gaung is that called the nga-tha-lauk, after the fish of the same name, the hilsa, or "Indian salmon," which would be perfect, were it not supplied with bones all through its body, seemingly utterly irresponsible and unconnected with the spine. This handsome fish, silvery, shot with purple and gold, is not scaled, nor âre the head, tail, or any of the fins removed.

Each fish is cleaned and rubbed with salt in the usual way and exposed to the sun. Then they are spread out on the floor of a shed on mats, and mats are also put over them, and on these are placed weights of some size. This is all that is required. In four days at the outside they are ready for sale, and are then handled with most reverential care by both buyer and seller, for the hilsa is a fish that the foreigner loves, and therefore always commands a good price.

The second kind is that called taungtha ngapi, that is, pounded fish, or fish-paste. It also frequently goes by the name of damin ngapi, from the bamboo trap in which the fish are usually caught. This is the form of ngapi which has earned the bad name for the whole preparation. It is made almost exclusively from shrimps and the smaller kinds of fish. These are spread out as they are caught, without the addition of salt or any cleaning whatever, on mats in the sun. There they remain for two, or perhaps three, days —by which time their condition is better imagined than closely investigated. They are then thrown into a huge wooden mortar and pounded together, with a liberal addition of salt. It does not take any very heavy work or length of time to reduce them to a state of mash, in which one fish is not to be distinguished from another. The whole is then heaped up in a great mound under a shed near the house, and several hollow bamboos, with little holes here and there in their sides, are thrust into it. Out of these a liquor, called nganpya ye, runs, and is carefully collected in jars set there for the purpose. This as well as some other fishy oils are greatly esteemed for culinary purposes, and fetch a good price. When these juices cease to run freely, the fish-paste is ready for sale, and is dug and shovelled out in an unceremonious way, contrasting very markedly with the loving care taken of the " whole fish ngapi." In the country boats it is usually carried in bulk, piled up as corn, or salt, or commodities of a like nature might be loaded ; and therefore a boat which has once been used for this purpose is easily known again. In English steamers it is, of course, packed in jars, but the odours are none the less fragrant on that account. This is the true and only mode of preparation, and the marvellous tales related by some foreigners of the burial of the fish in the earth for periods varying from a week to a year (!) are due either to a guileless nature or a too powerful imagination. The soil of Burma needs no manure.

The fish most sought after for damin ngapi are those belonging to the family of cat- and dog-fish, from the circumstance that they have no scales, and therefore make a smoother compound. Some of these attain a huge size, the tame dog-fish at Thihadaw, above Mandalay, being quite five feet long, and blessed with mouths that would take in a leg of mutton. Many of them also have the peculiarity of breathing air, rising to the surface of the water and opening their mouths for the purpose ; while, when the inland pools dry up after the rains are past, they are capable of making long journeys overland.

Seinsa ngapi is made entirely from prawns, and comes chiefly from the Tenasserim coast, Beit (the English Mergui) and Tavoy being the centres of its manufacture. The prawns are spread out on mats in the sun as soon as caught and left there till they are fairly well dried. Then they are mashed up by hand, abundance of salt being added, and are stirred up several times a day regularly for three days, lying out in the sun all the time. After that, the paste is ready for use, and is packed in small jars. Properly, seinsa is that made from the prawns exposed immediately after being caught. When some hours elapse before they are spread out to dry, the resulting ngapi is called yetpyan ; and if a whole day elapses before the exposure, yet-ôk. The greater the delay, the more powerful the smell and the more piquant the flavour—a fact for Englishmen to remember when they take balachong. Ket ngapi is simply a variety made of large prawns, which are heavily pressed in baskets called ket, before they are put out in the sun to dry. They are then pounded with salt and pressed again, after which they are ready for consumption, either as they are or after frying.

Notwithstanding the open disfavour with which the English regard ngapi, the Burmese hold by it as the most savoury and necessary portion of their dinner, and vast quantities are exported to Upper Burma, where the manufacture, owing to the smaller fisheries, is not equal to the demand.   The indignation which a crusade against the condiment by a young civil officer with more zeal than discretion caused in 1880, will not soon be forgotten. Cholera was rather bad in Yandun, one of the great places for ngapi, and the Assistant Commissioner, convinced that the heavy smells must be the cause of it, issued an order forbidding the manufacture of the fish-paste, or its sale in the public markets, as well as that other cherished but strong-smelling dainty, prawn-head oil.   The result was an avalanche of petitions to the Chief Commissioner, and something very like open riot in the town.   Equanimity was not restored till the too energetic official was removed to another station, and the lugyis pointed exultantly to the fact that as soon as they began to make up arrears in the way of ngapi consumption, cholera left the place.   Nevertheless, Yandun is not a charming place of residence to a man with a sensitive nose.

Fishermen are promised terrible punishments in a future life for the number of lives they take, but popular sympathy finds a loophole of escape for them.   They do not actually kill the fish.   These are merely put out on the bank to dry, after their long soaking in the river, and if they are foolish and ill-judged enough to die while undergoing the process, it is their own fault.   Nevertheless, some strict people hold by the doctrine of the Manichæans, who asserted that the soul of the farmer migrated into herbs so that it might be cut down and thrashed out.   The baker becomes bread and is eaten.   The killer of a deer becomes a deer ; of a fish, a fish ; and so on.   But nevertheless, if all the fishermen became monks one day, the next would see some of the pious trying their hands with the cast-net.

CHAPTER XXIX

PLAYS

THERE is no nation on the face of the earth so fond of theatrical representations as the Burmese. Probably there is not a man, otherwise than a cripple, in the country who has not at some period of his life been himself an actor, either in the drama or in a marionette show ; if not in either of these, certainly in a chorus dance. It would be wrong to say that there is no other amusement in the country, but it is indisputable that every other amusement ends up with a dramatic performance. When a Burman is born there is a pwè ; when he is named there is a pwè ; when a girl's ears are bored ; when the youth enters the monastery ; when he comes out again ; when he marries ; when he divorces ; when he makes a lucky speculation ; when he sets up a water-pot ; builds a bridge ; digs a tank ; establishes a monastery ; dedicates a pagoda, or accomplishes any other work of merit ; when there is a boat or horse race ; a buffalo or cock fight ; a boxing match, or the letting loose of a fire-balloon ; a great haul of fish, or the building of a new house ; when the nurseries are sown down, or the rice garnered in ; whenever in fact anything at all is done, there is a theatrical representation. Finally, there is a pwè, as grand as his friends can make it, when the Burman dies.

The plays are always given in the open air, and any one that pleases may come and look at them, and stay as long as he likes without paying, or being expected to pay, a single pice towards the expense of the performance. A large shed has indeed been erected in Rangoon, nightly performances take place, regular troupes are engaged for a definite period, and money is charged for admission ; but the idea is an English one, and opposed as it is to ancient custom and the old free attractions elsewhere, meets with barely enough support to keep it going. The giver of the pwè simply constructs a small roofed enclosure for himself, if the pwè is held on open ground, and fits it up with a bedstead covered with mats as a kind of private box, with a few chairs and plentiful mats round about it. To this reserved space he invites a few of his most intimate friends, sending them the ordinary little palm-leaf packet of pickled tea by the hands of his daughters or sisters. All other places in the circle are open to the first comer, and when a pwè is announced, women may be seen early in the after-noon strolling down, with rolls of mats on their heads, to secure good places. Abundance of refreshments and materials for smoking are taken, for it will be sunrise before the play is over. The commonest place for a pwè, however, is in the street opposite to the giver's house. All traffic is unceremoniously stopped. There is nothing to be done but to hoist up the hinged front wall of your house, or throw open the windows and go out on the verandah, if the con-struction of the building is more solid, and there you are with the theatre come to your doors. There is no trouble with the stage. A circular space is covered with mats and it is all ready. This is called the pwè-waing. In the centre is a branch of a tree, or the stem of a plantain palm stuck in the ground, which goes by the name of the pan-bin. Yule and others have endeavoured to discover some for-gotten meaning for this centre of action, comparing it with the altar of the old Greek stage, but probably it never had any greater significance than to mark the centre of the arena and prevent the audience from crowding in too much so as to curtail the space. The actors when questioned about it always say that it is there to represent a forest, such as forms part of the scene of action in every play. This of course is merely an answer, and not an explanation. Europeans of an inquiring turn are apt to complain of this Burmese (and Scotch) method of supplying information. Why such a phantom attempt at representing a forest should be made, when no effort aims at portraying the palace which is of equally regular appearance in all zāts, is not by any means evident. The property box of the company indeed serves as a throne, but this is an accident, and if there is no property box, there is no throne. The people take up positions long before the performance commences, and no doubt the pan-bin serves no deeper purpose than to indicate to intending spectators where the action will take place, and where therefore they may deposit their mats without being turned out later for being in the way. Further than the central tree and the mats nothing is required till the play begins. Then round about the pan-bin are arranged, as footlights, a number of small earthen-pots filled with petroleum, usually the thick black crude oil brought from the wells at Yenangyaung. Bits of rag or cotton seed are used for wicks, and the cups are replenished by the actors as occasion may require during the progress of the play. They are freely used throughout by both performers and audience as a means of obtaining lights for their cheroots. It is somewhat trying to the dramatic sense when the princess of the piece after a prolonged ngo-gyin, a dolorous wailing for her sad fortunes, driven from her love and strayed far in the jungle through devious paths to the immediate neighbourhood of bilus, ogres, ghouls, and horrid creeping things, when thus forsaken and finishing off with the sense of an impending danger, she proceeds to light a great green cheroot and placidly blow great clouds till her turn comes again. No less startling is it, when in the middle of a sonorous declamation from the king a half-naked youngster scuttles across the stage to get a light and scrambles back again. Englishmen, not understanding the progress of the play, notice these things more than anything else, and get an impression that the whole thing is ludicrous and unreal. This is very far from being the case. When the Yindaw Ma Le, the Mandalay *prima donna*, sang, or when the famous puppet player, Maung Tha Byaw, is performing, there is not a sound, the whole great crowd—and it must not be forgotten that the performance is in the open air—is hushed to its farthest limits, and not till the passage is finished does the usual buzz and chatter begin again. Those who have heard it will acknowledge that this spontaneous tribute must be as gratifying as the loudest stamping of feet and whistling on fingers of a London theatre. In fact a Burman might perhaps be justified in doubting the enthusiasm and admiration which finds vent in whistling.

The acting as a whole cannot be said to be satisfactory. The circumstances are against it. Who could "lose himself in his part" in the centre of a crowd of people all smoking and often talking? Moreover the subjects treated are so romantic and remote from ordinary worldly events that no one can be expected to realise them. Finally, who could keep it up for ten hours at a stretch? Nevertheless, individual passages are occasionally wonderfully well done. The piteous wailings and desolation of the princess; the majesty of the king; the grim savagery of the demon, are often very effectively delineated, while the clowns are almost invariably exceedingly clever. They are chosen for their ready wit, many of the jokes being extempore, as well as for their power of facial contortion. Caricatures of the performances of the other actors and comic songs form their chief stock-in-trade, and the text of the play is very far from being adhered to. It is an undoubted fact, if scarcely complimentary, that the clown has much more to do in the play and is very much broader in his jokes when Englishmen are present than when there is a purely national audience. The prolongation of the comic parts is due to a courteous desire to please the visitors, buffooneries being much more readily understood than high dramatic art, while the coarseness is unfortunately due to the same impression which makes a Burman always produce brandy and beer for the refreshment of a white man, the idea namely that that is what he likes best. None of the higher class troupes, more especially those from Upper Burma, will, however, condescend to this sort of thing.

The company formerly was always made up in Mandalay, or said it was. There are other troupes, but it is usually taken for granted that they cannot be better than second-rate. The delta Burman is firmly persuaded that "far birds have fair feathers." In their humble phraseology they say, "In the Low Country we are not up in the humanities." This is not exactly complimentary to longer

English rule and civilisation, but in one sense it is true.   In
Upper Burma every one is taught in the monasteries, and
having no other relief from Pali doxologies, becomes saturated with the phraseology and ideas of the zāts.   Thus,
from the theatrical point of view, the Mandalay youth starts
with a distinct advantage over the Lower Burman who
potters away in lay and elementary Government schools
over addition and multiplication and the sterilities of the
First Reader.   To qualify for the first ranks, therefore, the
ambitious Peguer starts for the Royal City of Gems, practises
as much as he can there, and watches the most celebrated
players.   Then, after a time, he obtains an engagement, and
turns up in Rangoon as a quasi anya tha.   The stage
managers, usually old actors who have made some money
and are inclined to take their ease, go up to Mandalay
during the rains, when comparatively little is doing, the wet,
combined with the four months of Lent, making pwès few
and far between.   There they cast about and get together
a company, entering into a written engagement with the
actors, male and female, for the season, which lasts about
seven months, from Ta'saungmôn to Nayôn (roughly,
November to May).   The manager makes all arrangements,
and usually takes up his headquarters in some town or large
village whence he can easily move to the surrounding places
where the company may be wanted.   The salaries paid are
very good.   A first-class prince or princess commands from
800 to 1000 rupees for the season.   A good lubyet, or
jester, will get five or six hundred.   After these come the
actors who take such parts as the king or the maids of
honour.   The dancers, that is to say, those who simply
dance and do no more, get about sixty rupees ; the saingthama,
the musicians, receive forty.   The company have not more
than two or three rehearsals together before they commence
their tour, but this does not matter much, because every one
knows his part well, and the cue is not a matter of supreme
importance.   The zat-ôk (the manager) draws all the money
from the performances.   As much as 450 rupees have been
paid for a two-night performance.   This, however, was exceptional, and it was a marionette play with the great
Maung Tha Byaw in the prince's part.   Very few people

could afford so much as this. The best engagements are those known as ahlu pwè, given by a rich man in celebration of some religious festival, or to commemorate some event in his family, such as the donning by his son of the yellow robes of the monastery. The elders of the village, or the custodians of the pagoda, often collect money for the performance of some of the religious zāts, depicting avatars of the Lord Buddha. Then there are subscription pwès, where some energetic lover of the drama suggests the propriety of a play to the inhabitants of the village, or of a street in the town. He goes round gathering subscriptions, and then negotiates with the zat-ôk for as many nights as the manager is inclined to give for the money. This system has unfortunately led to abuses. Sharp individuals have discovered the possibility of collecting three or four hundred rupees among the people, paying the manager two hundred out of this, and keeping the rest for themselves. The dodge has been too often tried in Rangoon, but in the smaller towns it is still practicable, and is far too often carried out. Besides these performances by accredited companies, there are others called kyigyin pwè, given by professionals anxious to make a name for themselves, and for this purpose giving gratuitous exhibitions. These are naturally very uneven from the difficulty of getting a complete company together. But in all cases the vast majority of the spectators pay nothing at all. The guests invited by packets of le'hpet usually contribute a rupee or two towards the expenses of their host, but otherwise the entire cost is defrayed by him.

The pwè is begun by the arrival of the band, which, with characteristic Burmese disregard of the value of time, ordinarily comes upon the scene several hours before the actual commencement of operations. They occupy one side of the stage, and tune up their saing and play away vigorously while the people gather. The zatthama and zatthamā, the male and female artistes, drop in casually along with the spectators. Each is ordinarily accompanied by a servant to carry their dresses and help them in robing. All of them, women as well as men, make their preparations in full view of everybody. Each lady has a toilette-box with all the necessaries for making up. Many are the hints the village maidens receive in the way of touching up eyebrows, artfully swelling out the sadôn with false locks of hair, intertwining the raven tresses with red and white fragrant flowers, toning the complexion with thana'ka, and so on. The young men look on critically while the princess scans herself in the little hand-mirror and tranquilly completes the touching-up and other feminine mysteries so little dreamed of by ordinary European swains. No one has the slightest appearance of recognising the ludicrousness of the thing, or of deprecating the exposure of little female wiles and vanities. The zat-thamā wears her acting skirt indeed when she arrives, but everything else—the tight-fitting lace jacket, the stiff brocaded wings, the jewellery, the pagoda-like crown—is put on by the side of the stage at the bamboo rack which supports the masks and necessary changes of dress. The audience either looks on with stolid earnestness, or takes no notice whatever.

Finally, having smoked all through the toilette, the princess and the maids of honour quietly seat themselves— squat would be more accurate, but does not sound nice—at the edge of the pwè-waing, and continue to smoke till everything is ready and their call comes. Then they simply stand up and are on the stage immediately. They do not cease smoking then, except during a long song. The men are equally calm. The king chews betel and salivates copiously between observations or speeches, but in so doing he can only be said to be the more realistic. Incidental ballets are introduced to relieve the monotony of the dialogue, and the maids of honour and the clowns perform wonderful feats of winding themselves about as if they had no bones, picking up coins with the mouth bent back to the ground, doubling themselves up so that the toes touch the forehead, and so on.

Sometimes there are great fights at these pwès. A young man has got surly because there is such a crowd that he can see nothing of what is going on, and runs up against another equally inclined to quarrel for the same reason. Or perhaps he is angry because some one has supplanted him in a flirtation with one of the girls who have established a temporary bazaar in the outskirts of the crowd. Or there may be a dispute as to the ownership of a mat. There are a few loud words; a woman's voice joins in. Next minute

the two are smashing away at one another with their long
hair streaming over their faces and down their shoulders.
Friends join in, and almost before you can realise what has
happened, the actors disappear, the women and children run
off home, and the street is filled with an excited crowd of
men swaying backwards and forwards, and fighting promiscu-
ously.   For this reason pwès are now never allowed in towns
without permission from the civil authority, and numbers of
policemen are always at hand to nip any riot in the bud.
With the same object performances are only allowed in
large towns about the time of the full moon, when there is
abundance of light, in case the street lamps should be put
out.   The worst row of the kind I ever saw, however, was
started by two of the Burman policemen themselves.   They
quarrelled about the merits of two apyodaws, talented *danseuses*, and the crowd, relishing the absurdity of the thing,
backed up the quarrel with such energy that broken heads
were plentiful and a ward in the infirmary was filled.

Foreigners very often make the mistake of taking the
performances of children's companies to be actual zāt plays.
Even Captain Forbes, usually so accurate, falls into this
error in speaking of a representation of the Wethandaya zāt.
This must simply have been a yein, an adaptation of the
great drama for performance by the little choral dancers.
For people who do not understand Burmese well—among
whom, of course, the late Captain Forbes was certainly not
to be included—the mistake is very easy.   They are far
prettier to look at, and much preferable in every way to
the actual text of the birth-story, mainly because they are
not so dismally drawn out, and can ordinarily be got
through in an evening.

The dramas are all founded on the tales which Shin
Gautama told of five hundred and ten of his previous
existences, or on events in the lives of kings and heroes
in India.   None of them are original.   The story in every
instance is taken from the Hindoo, the adapter in most
cases not even taking the trouble to nationalise the names
of places and characters.   It is only in the extemporising
of the clown that anything really characteristic comes out.
The Hindoo sense of humour is vastly inferior to the

Burmese. The term zāt or, still more so, wuttu (*i.e.* a real
story) is properly applied only to the religious plays, the
five hundred and ten Jatakas. The work of fiction not
necessarily religious is called a Pyazat, an *acting* play.
Thus you speak of the Utena Wuttu (given in part by Yule),
but of the Zawta Gômma Pyazat.

Ten of the religious dramas stand out prominently from
the others. These are called the Zatgyi Sèbwè, and are
designed to show how the Lord Buddha in turn overcame
all the deadly sins. They are named: (1) *Temi*, (2)
Zanecka, (3) *Thuwunnashan*, (4) *Nemi*, (5) *Mahawthata*,
(6) *Buyidat*, (7) *Sanda Gômma*, (8) *Nayidda*, (9) *Widuya*,
and (10) *Wethandaya*. Several of them are very interesting.
The *Wethandaya* is probably best known on account of the
real pathos of the story and the beauty of the composition. It illustrates the boundless pity of a Budh. The
prince—Gautama's last incarnation on earth previous to his
appearance as Prince Siddartha or Theidat—gives away
everything he possesses, even to his wife and children. The
Nemi and Buyida zāts, or wuttus as they are called indifferently, are also very popular on account of the particulars
they give of the nga-yè, the great hell, and the country of
the nagās, fabulous creatures, like the kraken, that sleep
deep down below, far beyond the ken of mortal man. The
similarities between Norse mythology and Buddhist cosmo-
gonies have often been noticed, and the legend of the kraken
or nagā is not the least singular.

Of the other more secular plays, U Hpo Nya is the most
celebrated recent author. He was killed in King Mindôn's
reign by the Tabè Mintha, one of the most brutal of the
royal princes, and for whose son's head King Thibaw twice
paid a thousand rupees. The young man, however, lived
long after King Thibaw himself had gone. His father's
victim, U Hpo Nya, was particularly celebrated for the
sweetness and melody of the songs introduced in his pieces,
these songs, of course, being practically original. No one
before or since is equal to him in this respect. The *Wizaya
Zat* is probably his masterpiece, and forms one of the stock-
in-trade of every company in the country. Maung Hpe, the
son of a former wungyi, or minister of state in Mandalay, is

another popular and voluminous writer. An ever favourite play is the *Ramazat*, the fight of the monkeys and the men in Ceylon. It was performed by a palace troupe specially sent down to Rangoon by King Mindôn on the occasion of the proclamation of Queen Victoria as Empress in India. Everything was of the best possible kind ; the royal drum and cymbal harmonicons, the trumpets, the flutes, even the bamboo clappers, were of an excellence never before known in Rangoon. The players were famous wherever Burmese was spoken, and the play lasted five nights. The general opinion was that it called forth more admiration of King Mindôn than loyalty for the Empress among the delta people.

All that has been said of the zāt pwès, those in which men and women act, applies with equal force to the yôkthe, or marionette pwès. It is well known that the Burmese esteem these more highly than what Englishmen would call the legitimate drama. The action in the puppet-shows is much more complicated than on the plain mat stage, the dialogue is very much more refined, and there are none of the *lâches* perpetrated by individual zatthama striving for effect. Especially there is never, even with the provocation of a number of Englishmen present, the least semblance of coarseness. Further, supernatural beings, nats and bilus, elephants, dragons, ships, thrones, and properties of all sorts can be introduced which are impracticable on the limited arena of the mat platform. The elocutionary powers of the performers behind the curtain, the verve and passion of the songs, the accuracy and melody of the recitative, to command success must be at least as good, if not better, than the best of what is met with in the pwè-waing. Added to this there is the manual skill implied in moving the strings attached to the heads, limbs, and joints of the puppets, which are often exceedingly cleverly manipulated. The national preference for the marionette play is therefore not entirely without justification.

The action takes place on a raised bamboo platform some thirty feet long, the puppets performing on the stage in front of a curtain which screens the manipulators down the whole length of the erection. One end of the stage is devoted to scenes at court, and is adorned with a throne, golden umbrellas, and other royal insignia. The other extremity represents, with artfully-arranged twigs and tufts of grass, the jungle and forests to which, during some part of every play, the prince and princess are sure to have to fly. The puppets, which are frequently as much as two or three feet high, are always gorgeously and expensively dressed. The larger ones are all cut in wood, and the carver's skill often turns out very clever presentments of rugged-faced old men and exuberantly jovial lubyets. Most of the zāts, which deal greatly with the supernatural and fabulous, are only represented as yôkthe pwès. No amount of technical skill could represent in the public streets an athurein, a creature (destined incalculable ages hence to be a Budh) whose height is a few thousand miles, and who produces eclipses in his play by taking the sun or moon in his fingers or between his toes.

Curious as it may seem, the puppet players often acquire a far more really personal reputation than the legitimate actors. The zatthama mostly get a name for dancing as much as for anything else. The Yindaw Ma Le, who came from a village near Meiktila in Upper Burma, indeed, was equally celebrated for her voice and her graceful movements, but the yokthethama become renowned for dramatic fervour, for tender passion, for dry wit, just as thoroughly and personally as if they actually appeared before the audience. Except the *prima donna* just alluded to (now dead) there are few professionals celebrated on the stage who are not far better known as first-class marionette players. These performers are all men and boys. None of the female parts are ever taken by women. Maung Tha Byaw was unequalled in "prince's" parts. He was recognised as Thabinwun; every stage-manager, every zat-ôk in the country received his word as law. No tenor with a *voce fenomenale*, no bird-voiced Patti, was more sought after nor received with greater honours. His name became a proverb in the mouths of people who never heard him. "Tha Byaw Hé," a Mergui man will say when he makes a marvellous haul of fish or gets a super-excellent cheroot. A journey of his to Rangoon produced a popular saw, corresponding to the English "killing two birds with one stone." Maung Tha Byaw said he was going to worship at the Shwe Dagôn pagoda. He gave a performance or two, and made several (Burmese) fortunes. Hence the saying—

> Payā lè pu yin
> Leip u lè tu yin.
>
> You go and worship and dig turtles' eggs.
>
> Turtles' eggs for prayer
> Reward the pious player.

Maung Tha Byaw was not only a good singer, but himself wrote very good songs, and was particularly clever at coining in phrases the wisdom of many with the wit of one. No other "prince" has ever attained to his fame. Best known among the clowns was Shwe Lôt Gyi, who had the knack of making local jokes wherever he happened to be, and took the fullest advantage of the scope which the language afforded him in the way of punning. Just after the railway from Rangoon to Prome was opened, Shwe Lôt Gyi was performing in a piece where the prince and his servant, the clown, wander away into the forest and fall into a state of great destitution. The prince bewails his sad fate in a dolorous tedat (a tune appropriate to such lamentations), and finishes by asking what they are to do. The lubyet replied, "The English have just opened a railway here. You go and trespass on it, and I'll lay information against you and get the reward." The idea showed considerable acuteness in a man who had never seen a railway before.

Among the "princesses" many youths have been noted for the sweetness of their voice. The two best were Maung Tha Zan and, running him very close, Maung Mu, both of them, like Tha Byaw and the clown, Mandalay men. The accuracy with which they imitated the female voice was wonderful, the more so as every song abounds with trills and turns which would expose the least roughness. Neither in the recitative, the tremulous erotics, nor the doleful wailings of the maiden for her absent lover, would the stranger ever suspect the performer's sex.

The plays are performed during the day only in a few and exceptional cases, such as the arrival of a great man, who cannot stay over the night, or when a local feast, limited in its time, occurs. The great and legitimate season is the night, and frequently a play, especially a puppet play, extends over six or seven successive nights. The majority of the audience stay the whole time, from seven or eight o'clock at night till sunrise. It is not, however, to be supposed that they hear it all through. Abundance of mats and rugs are brought, and not a few, after listening till midnight or thereabouts, calmly curl themselves up to sleep, and slumber away for two or three hours, heedless of the braying of the horns and the crash of the cymbals only a few yards off. Then they wake up and fall in with the progress of the piece with as keen interest as if they had heard every word of it. Most of the young people, however, prime themselves with the anti-soporific le'hpet, " pickled tea," as the English call it, and bid defiance to drowsiness. This condiment is as regular a crown to a Burmese dinner as cheese is to an English one, and with the same idea, possibly erroneous in both cases, that it promotes digestion. It is almost exclusively produced in Taungbaing, in the Shan country, by a hill tribe called Rumai, better known by the Burmese name of Palaungs. The Burmese mix with it salt, garlic, and assafœtida, douse it in oil, and add a few grains of millet seed. The leaves forming the basis are the leaves of an actual tree as distinguished from the bushes of China and Assam. Hooker called it *Elæodendron orientale*, while Anderson asserted that it was really *E. persicum*. Of late years Assam planters have bought Taungbaing seed for their gardens. One of the grievances which Englishmen have when they attend a pwè is that they are always induced by their host to take pickled tea, and perceive in it nothing but the overpowering horrors of the assafœtida. Pwès and assafœtida are therefore associated with one another to the detriment of both.

Few foreigners can detect one tune from another, or the recitative from any one of them. Consequently most declare there is only one tune, or no tune at all, according to the capacity of generosity in them. The same thing has been said by an inappreciative Burman of the "vipers" of the Royal Scots Fusiliers. He admired the conscientiousness and pertinacity with which they defied the mosquitoes under the shade of the trees, and droned away on their pipes all through a tight-tunicked and perspiring Rangoon afternoon garden party, as the observant Burman imagined, at one endless tune. The national music is not written down, and each actor has a variation of his own, but the smallest girl in the audience would detect a kayāthan from a dobatthan with as much readiness as any English boy would distinguish " Drops o' Brandy " from the " Old Hundred "! But there are some people who do not like the Italian opera, and even say so.

The following short outline of the *Zawtagômma pyazat* will give an idea of the style of the more popular drama, as distinguished from the purely religious birth-story. The writer was an old player himself. He lived at Pegu, and the *Zawtagômma* was perhaps his most successful effort. The text has been published at one of the vernacular presses in Rangoon, and the sketch given is a translation of the Zat-lan, the " path of the play," prefixed by the editor. " In the country of Pyinyawwada, of which Yazôtta was the sovereign, the name of the Southern Queen was Thunemadewi, and that of the Northern Queen Thukethidewi. The Queen of the Southern Palace was about to bear a child, and the king issued an order that her majesty of the North should attend on her. This was very irritating to the Northern Queen, and she resolved to ruin Thunemadewi, and for that purpose conspired with Shin Gwe Ni, the midwife. As soon as the child was born it was to be killed, and set afloat on the river in an earthen pot, and the *accoucheuse* was to say the Head Queen had been delivered of a still-born baby. A twin son and daughter were born, and Shin Gwe Ni put each of them in a jar and launched them on the river, and went and told the king that they were still-born. Yazôtta, the king, was very angry, and punished his consort by setting her to dig the ground and carry water for the palace. The Queen of the North was promoted to be Head Queen, and her daughter, Pyinsarupa, was made tabin-daing (*i.e.* she was set apart as wife for the next king, and not allowed to marry).

" With regard to the bodies of the prince and princess.

the prince was carried down the Yamuna river and the Thuwuna nagā swallowed the body, and the spirit of the prince entered into the ruby that hung in the necklace of the dragon. Not long after the nagā became nervous and uncomfortable in his mind, and proceeded to the monastery of the recluse Bedaseinda, in the Thiriwunna forest. There he went to keep the ten holy precepts. As soon as the ya-theit saw the necklace with the ruby in it, he knew by his bedin that the spirit of a young prince was enclosed there. He therefore represented to the dragon that it was unseemly to wear precious things when he was observing the injunctions of the law. The nagā therefore gave him the necklace in alms, and having kept the ten precepts the prescribed number of days, returned to his own place. When the prince was born anew from the ruby, the ya-theit gave him the name of Zawtagômma, and explained to him all that had happened in the prince's last existence.

" The princess's body was carried away into the Southern Ocean, and there the fish kegga-thitha, whose head is shaped like a sceptre, ate her up. The spirit of the princess entered a pearl in the fish's head and dwelt there. A violent hurricane came on, and the fish was carried up into the sky and fell down inside the enclosure of the recluse Bedaseinda. When the ya-theit cast eyes on the pearl, he knew that a princess was in it, and he gave this pearl, called the myissa, to the Zawtagômma prince. From the precious stone was born in seven days the princess, and she got the name of Palèthwè. The ya-theit knew from his mystic books that in the former existence they had been brother and sister, and told them all about it.

" When they grew up he told them they were to go back to the old king and queen's capital in the Pyinyawwada country, and on their way they were to make offerings and give the pearl to the Gyo nat. But the prince forgot all about the Meittu Gyo, and the spirit therefore became very angry with him. While they were travelling on, the nat separated them by means of magnets, which attracted the iron in their bones, and drew them away to the devils on either side, to right and to left, who held the magnets.

" Meanwhile, in the Pyinyawwada country, Zawtagômma's

father and mother, and his stepmother, the former Northern
Queen, had all of them gone to the country of nat-déwas
(*i.e.* died), and there was no king to rule over the land.
The Pyinsarupa princess, therefore (who had been kept
single to marry the new king), according to ancient custom,
sent out the pôtthwin yattā (a chariot which has no driver,
and stops where the horses will), and it hurried away from
the palace and came and stopped beside the sleeping Zawtagômma. When he woke he entered the chariot, and the
horses returned straight to the capital. The prince then
ascended the throne and married Pyinsarupa.

" In the meantime, the princess who was born from the
pearl came to the house of a pônna and his wife, and was
delivered of a child there. One day she covered the baby
with an emerald green neckerchief, and laid it on the bank
of a lake while she went into the water to bathe. But a
bird, called kemayekka, swooped down from the skies and
carried off the green scarf, baby and all. Then it flew to
the palace of Zawtagômma and circled round in the air
above it. The prince shot at it with a bow, and it fell down
and died, and vomited up the green scarf, and the baby,
still alive. As soon as Zawtagômma saw the infant and the
neckerchief, he knew that they were Palèthwè's, and clasping the child in his arms, he set out to find the princess, and
wandered far and wide.

" Palèthwè herself, as soon as she had obtained permission from the pônna, set off in search of the prince and
her child. The Brahmin priest, with the aid of his mantras,
made her assume the appearance of a man, and despatched
her to seek Zawtagômma in the disguise of a harp-player.
He also instructed her that she would meet the prince on
the way, but she was not to reveal herself to him : she was
to explain how it was that the two had been separated by
the Meittu Gyo nat, and say that she had met Palèthwè,
and that the princess had gone to Pyinyawwada ; Zawtagômma himself was to take the counsel of the Bedin wise
men, and return to his own country, where he must offer
sacrifices to the ten gyo nats, whereupon he would meet the
princess Palèthwè, the wife he so tenderly loved. All these
instructions the pônna gave to the princess, and then let

her go. Everything happened as he had foretold. She met the prince and he followed her advice. They returned to the Pyinyawwada country, and all was happy."

The above is the merest outline of the story. The piece is very long, and there is abundance of incident. The prince's servant, and usually also the two holy men, do the comic part of the business, but this is always so purely personal a matter that the printed text can give no real notion of what actually is said. It serves merely to point out the lines which the lubyet must follow in his impersonation. The stage books, written on palm-leaf, contain but very few detailed speeches, and merely indicate the story, and throw out hints to the actors. The following is one of the songs sung by the prince in his wanderings through the forest in quest of Palèthwè. It is written to the tune of the "Chase in the Tawmawyôn Forest," that in which the king goes to hunt in the epic of the Ramayana. The wut or wutdaw referred to is the penalty of suffering the same punishment, or death, which has in a former existence been wrongfully or needlessly inflicted on others. Thus the great minister, Widuya, spoken of, who was an avatar of the Lord Buddha, had in a previous life dragged a frog by the leg so that it died. Hence he is dragged at the tail of the fierce Nat's horse until he dies himself. The prince fears that some such evil destiny is working itself out on him. The jingle of the rhythm is intended. The whole play is of the "raging rocks and shivering shocks" pattern.

FATE

The wind breathes chill
Across the rill
That cuts the forest track ;
The haze to mist
Whitens, I wist,
And I am lost, alack.

The branches spread
Dull green and red
Flat o'er the sullen stream ;
Comes through the gloom
The gibbon's boom,
And shrill the parrot's scream.

Ah, sad the scene ;
But yet, I ween,
A sadder wight am I ;
The thuyaung seed [1]
Gives lovers rede,
But sears my tortured eye.

Ah, cruel spite,
Ah, cursed night,
That tore my Queen away ;
More comfort here,
In jungle drear,
Than in the golden day.

The fog's death-cloud
Hangs like a shroud
Upon the shagg'd hillside ;
The tall trees mope,
The wild beasts grope,
Nor know what may betide.

Yet the great sun
Needs cast but onc
Fierce eye upon the gloom ;
The mists all rise,
Mix with the skies,
And rainbows deck his loom.

Ah, wretched wight,
Such omen bright
Gleams not upon my fate ;
Nor faint, nor bright,
Hope's golden light
Lends me no heart to wait.

The story old
Of Nat so bold
Creeps o'er my harassed thought ;
Haply this hill
He treadeth still,
And here that horror wrought.

In warlike guise,
With wings on thighs,
He scales where eagles flag ;

---

[1] The fruit of the thuyaung bin, a kind of half shrub, half tree, has a curious resemblance to the figure of a woman, and *soupirants* are wont to detect fancied likenesses to the object of their affections, and deduce favourable omens from the discovery.

His magic steed
Hath such great speed
The lightnings seem to lag.

Ah, fateful law,
Ruthless Wutdaw,
Widuya, art thou feared ?
From life long past,
Thy sin at last
Eftsoons must dree its weird.

Nor soon, nor late
With calm, cold gait
The Wut relentless tracks ;
Nor prayer, nor fees
Will bring release,
'Tis blood for blood it lacks.

Thy limbs fast tied
The Nat doth ride
O'er gorge and cliff and plain ;
At his horse heels
Dragged, no faint steals
O'er thee to spare one pain.

Though blood forth gushed
And brain was crushed,
Thy heart was panting still ;
Lingered thy breath,
Nor came glad death
Till ye twain reached this hill.

The fiend sprang down,
And from its crown
He hurled thee many a rod,
With eldritch glee
He hurled e'en thee
The great embryo god.

So the old Wut
With stealthy foot
Nor pity e'er evinces :
So must some crime
From ancient time
Have robbed me of my princess.

Methinks 'twas here,
This place so drear,
That great Widuya died ;

Here or elsewhere,
With praise and prayer
I seek him for my guide.

Ah, still the Wut
Its baleful fruit
Doth bring before mine eyes.
  See, bright and clear,
  The Saddan mere
And round the mountains rise.

Like jangled chime,
Or tangled rhyme,
The piteous tale is told ;
  The Saddan Min [1]
  By death solves sin
Committed once of old.

Thrice wretched she,
By destiny
Marked out the blow to guide ;
  She, then as Queen
  Thubadda seen
Had erewhile been his bride.

But beauty's curse
Hath made her nurse
Greed most akin to hate ;
  The milk-white tusk
  She sought to busk
With glories six her state.

Then her behest
She hath addressed
To Thawnôtto, the hind ;
  Fell hunter that,
  As Dewadat
Hath felon deeds designed.

---

[1] The Saddan Min is the Celestial White Elephant, an avatar of the Buddha Gautama.   Hence it is that white elephants are so revered and regarded as the symbol of universal sovereignty.   Thubadda had been the Saddan's queen in a previous existence.   She repents, dies of sorrow, when she hears of the Lord White Elephant's end, and afterwards, in consequence, becomes a Yahanda in the time of the revealing of the Buddha.   Mèbadda is the actual consort of the Saddan.   She became, in after existence, Yathawdaya, the wife of Prince Theidat, before he left the palace and devoted himself to acquiring the Supreme Wisdom. Thawnôtto, the hunter, became the wicked Dewadat, cousin and brother-in-law of the Lord Buddha, and now languishes in Awidzi, suffering punishment for his attempt on the life of Shin Gautama.

Then he with guile
His purpose vile
With yellow robe conceals ;
The Monkish garb
Hides the sharp barb,
Nor aught of sin reveals.

And when he nears
The silver mere's
Fair jewel-studded edge ;
Then like a snake,
Through baleful brake,
He parts the golden sedge.

His arrows' tip
With poison drip,
He rears his cobra head ;
The bowstring twanged,
The dart deep-fanged
Its course too well had sped.

Thy heart is cleft,
Thy life is reft,
Now, reel'st thou, milk-white King ;
The woodland hushed,
And darkness brushed
O'er earth its sooty wing.

The silent moon
Doth fright the noon,
And Death e'en breath restrains ;
Save one wild scream
Might check the stream
Of blood in murder's veins.

Mèbadda, Queen,
The deed had seen,
She caught him e'er he fell ;
Would staunch the flood
Of red heart's blood
That fiercely forth doth well.

Ah me, 'tis vain,
Wild with heart-pain
Forth flies the frenzied wife
To seek for foes,
Or mayhap those
Might save the Saddan's life.

Ye who doubt truth,
The boundless ruth
Of the all-pitying Budh ;

Now list ye well
What then befell,
And quit your scoffing mood.

Straight to the cave,
Where crouched the knave,
He walks with gentle mien ;
   Himself bestows
   The tusks' white snows
For Thubadda, the Queen.

Ah, cruel Wut,
Why strayed my foot
Unto this hateful spot ?
   See low I bow
   To earth my brow ;
Be mine less awesome lot.

Here erewhile trod
The embryo god,
Now all is dull and blear ;
   O'er land and sea
   I seek for thee,
My Princess, even here.

By lonesome lake,
Through forest brake,
I'll track each rumour's breath ;
   Where roams the bear,
   By fierce beast's lair,
I'll seek thee e'en past death.

But, 'gainst the Wut's
Fierce power what boots
To strive with eager zeal ?
.   .   .   .   .
   Peace, doubting heart,
   No fate can part
True lovers fond and leal.

As an illustration of a purely religious play may be given the *Nemi Zat*, one of the Ten Great Birth Stories. It is occasionally represented as a yôkthe, or marionette play, but it is rather expensive to put it on the stage well. It was " preached " in the monastery of Meggadawun, during the stay of Shin Gautama in Mèthila, of which country he remembered to have been king in a previous existence. The following is the story in brief :—

In old times the King Mingadeva ruled over the country, and for many years was entirely given up to pleasure and worldly passions, till one day his barber showed him a grey hair—"a flag of the king of death," as it is commonly called in Burmese—which he had found on the royal head. The king was struck with this *memento mori*, and immediately saw yawning before his eyes the abyss of mortality. The vision scared him, and he gave up the gay raiment and idle pleasures of earthly glory and wandered into the desert to end his life as a hermit. His self-denying piety gained for him on his death elevation to the seats of the Byammās, and all the 82,000 princes who succeeded him on the throne of Mèthila followed the example of their ancestor and retired into hermits' cells when they felt their end approaching. Mingadeva, from his blissful superior seat, followed with earnest solicitude the fortunes of his dynasty, and when at length he saw that it was drawing near its close, he returned once more to earth. He was conceived in the womb of the then Queen of Mèthila, and was born of her, and received the name of Prince Nemi. From his earliest years, as the pônnas discerned from his horoscope, his mind was firmly and unwaveringly directed to the prescriptions of religion and to pious observances. Once when he felt a doubt in his mind as to whether the outward giving of alms or inward self-contemplation was the more meritorious, the Tha-gyā King himself came down and instructed him that abundant charity would indeed secure him a new birth in the heavens of Nat-déwas, but that only the cultivation of the mind could ensure a rise to the blessed regions of the Byammās. The Déwa King was so attracted by the religious spirit and piety of the young prince that on his return he spoke of it with admiring delight to his subject Nats. Their curiosity was excited by the account of such distinguished qualities in a man, and they begged the Tha-gyā Min to procure for them the acquaintance of so holy a personage. Accordingly the king gave orders to a young Déwa named Matali to descend to the earth and invite the young prince to a visit to the nat-heavens.

It was the day of the full moon, and all the inhabitants of Mèthila were assembled in the streets and on the pagoda

platforms to observe the ceremonies of the holy day, when a
great wonder happened.   While the full moon shone high
and clear in the heavens, there appeared through the clouds
a glowing light in the east, so that all the people cried aloud
in astonishment that two moons had arisen in the sky at the
same time.   But as the light gradually neared and neared,
it became evident that it was a nat-chariot with the young
Déwa inside.   Matali advanced to the prince and invited
him to enter the car and proceed to the realms of the
blessed.   Nemi stepped in without fear, and when he was
told by the charioteer that there were two ways open to
him, of which one led through the horrors of Nga-yè, and
the other through the Elysian fields, he at once desired to
visit both.   First they went down to the eight vast burning
chambers, and saw the pains of the damned in the fiery
gloom of hell, and then they ascended and viewed the pure
delights of bright paradise.   After Nemi had met in audience
the highest king of Nats, he returned to earth to give to his
subjects a true account of what fate would befall them after
death, according as they followed the path of virtue or of
vice.

After many peaceful and honoured years, when Nemi
at last saw his hair begin to grow grey, he, like his predecessors, entered the state of Yahanda and abdicated the
royal power.   The same venerable custom was followed by
his son Thalarazana, the last of the roll of kings, who, when
old age began to snow upon them, devoted themselves to the
holy order in the town of Yathemyo (Kappilavastu).

It is evident that such a play as this, though it offers
plenty of incident, is for this very reason the more difficult
to put on the stage, and can hardly be satisfactorily produced at all except as a marionette play.   No zāt furnishes
more subjects to the Burman artist than that of Nemi, and
pagoda corridors all over the country are decorated with the
scenes in hell, which are much more easily pictured to the
mind and the eye than the pure joys of heaven.

CHAPTER XXX

DANCING

DANCING, though an accomplishment in which every Burmese man or woman is more or less proficient, is, as elsewhere in the East, never carried on simply for personal amusement. That custom, together with the elaboration of the two sexes dancing in couples, is entirely a Western invention. If a great man wants dancing he hires people to do it for him. If indeed he becomes greatly excited at a boat-race, a buffalo fight, or a religious procession on its way through the town to the pagoda, he may tuck up his paso tightly round his thighs and caper away till his bare legs tire, but he does so ordinarily with a ludicrously solemn aspect, as if the performance were a part of his official duties, and to be got through with as much stately dignity as the dispensing of justice from the magisterial bench. It is a concession to the excitability of his nature, and he would be very much offended if next day, when he had calmed down to his ordinary composed demeanour, an Englishman were to compliment him on the agility he displayed, or the complexity of his evolutions on the previous day.

With the young people it is different, but only to a certain extent. Most of them, if they have any aptitude that way, practise dancing for the sake of the applause and admiration it may get for them when they perform in a village procession, at the initiation of a young friend into a monastery, or at one of the great religious feasts, such as Tawadein-tha, or even at a funeral. But as a general rule no lessons are taken other than watching noted performers. The ambitious usually confine themselves to practise in out-of-the-way places by themselves, trusting to natural ability and good ear to help them in the harmonious movement of head, limbs, and body, to the sound of the music.   The women who dance as professionals in the plays have to go through a very rigorous course, not that there are any complicated steps to be learnt, but that they may acquire the pliancy of body necessary for the indiarubber contortions into which they have to writhe their bodies.

There are therefore no distinctions of dances, according to regular varieties of movements.   These are pretty well regulated both by professionals and amateurs according to individual fancy.   If such a thing as an " encore " existed in Burma, it would probably puzzle the dancer to repeat the step exactly as it has been gone through before.   This of course refers to individual dancing, and does not by any means apply to the yein pwès, where a carefully-trained troupe goes through pre-arranged movements with well-drilled precision.   There may be said to be really only two kinds of dancing : individual, or it might almost be called irresponsible dancing, such as is seen in the plays and at various religious or social ceremonies ; and the yein pwès, the figure, or " country " dances, where much practice and working together is imperatively necessary.   A zatôk, or theatre manager, will tell you that there are four or perhaps five kinds ; the dancing of the zat pwè, the regular drama ; that of the yāma zat (the Ramayana), which is of a much wilder and more energetic character ; the dancing of the anyeinthama, the trained companies of ballet-dancers, who perform in the palace before the king and princes to the sound of the pattala, the harp, or the flute.   These are simply glorified yeins, and the *danseuses* are often most gorgeously dressed with gilded pyramidal crowns, and wings on their legs.   Fourthly, there is the bônshe pwè, a performance of much the same kind, except that it is gone through to the music of the instrument of that name, a long kettle-drum-like thing, much the same as the tom-tom of India.   This latter variety is considered old-fashioned, and is not often seen now, notwithstanding that it is called Byaw, after the great Thabinwun, who was particularly fond of it.   The fifth style of dancing, according to the player's idea, is the performance

of the ordinary domestic youth on festive occasions, when he
prances about like an extremely self-conscious turkey-cock
in the style that suits his capabilities best.

There are a great variety of names for special dances,
but in all there is the same waving of hands and weaving of
paces.   The hands, fingers, elbows, and shoulders are twisted
about as if they were circular-jointed ; the legs are doubled
up and extended in the same fantastic and tentacular fashion,
while the body seems to wind and bend in any direction
with equal facility.   Europeans as a rule find nothing to
admire in the dancing except the marvellous sensitiveness to
time, and the extreme tension in which every muscle of the
body is constantly kept.   The solemnity of face is paralleled
by the expression of the waltzer who is convinced that he is
becoming giddy.

Little though the dancing of the men resembles European
saltation, that of the girls is still farther from active motion
and definitive figures.   This is no doubt in great part due
to the Burmese female dress.   The tamein is simply a square
cloth folded round the body and tucked in so that the opening is down the front.   This necessitates some adroitness
even in walking, and renders all active motions incompatible
with modesty.   When they dance the skirt is sewn or pinned
down the front, so that the girl is, as it were, in a narrow
bag, reaching down to her feet and trailing about on the
ground in an eighteen-inch or two-foot train.   Even thus
hampered their dances are much more animated than those
of the Indian nautch girls, but still do not go greatly beyond
posturing.   Nevertheless, the natural and graceful attitudes
into which they throw the body, and the cleverness with
which they manœuvre their hands and arms, so different
from European awkwardness with these members, is not
without a charm.   It is quite a common thing to see a girl
bend over backwards till her lips touch the mat upon which
she stands, and pick up from the ground rupees thrown there
by the spectators.   In Mandalay I have seen a performer
double up all her members, head and all, into a space represented by the length of her trunk, and compact enough to be
put into an ordinary-sized portmanteau.

The zatthamā, the professional actresses, usually dance

to their own singing and often improvise with wonderful
cleverness, when performing before a celebrity, or any one
whom it is especially desired to honour.   Many of them
acquire a reputation that extends all over the country, and
are often sought for in vain by the wealthiest play-goers.
Chief among them was the Yindaw Ma Le, the " Mandalay
Diva," who was known to every English official or man of
importance who visited Mandalay during the twenty years
before the annexation.   Unlike most Eastern women, she
kept remarkably well, and though her voice failed latterly,
she made up as well as she did nearly twenty years before,
when she sang in Amarapoora, the City of the Immortals.
There were few Englishmen who saw her perform before
Lord Mayo in Rangoon—she was sent down specially from
Mandalay by King Mindôn for that purpose—who could
have believed that she was then close on forty.   The want
of a national court no doubt prevents any other dancer from
taking the place which she has left for ever.

An accomplishment greatly affected by the coryphées is
the extraordinary faculty of moving local muscles, the remainder of the body being perfectly quiet.   Many of the
men, especially the clowns of the piece, can do the same
thing, but it is usually brought in by them only as a mockery
of the lady.   She will extend the arms alternately and cause
the muscles to rise and fall and twitch so vigorously that it
may be seen yards off.   Similarly the bosom heaves as if
violently agitated by passion or exertion, while the face
remains perfectly impassive.

These displays are all, however, comparatively uninter-
esting to foreigners.   The posturing and waving of hands,
however graceful and supple, become tiresome, and the more
so the oftener they are seen.   But it is different with the
yein pwè, the choral dances, which are very often executed
by amateurs, and imply considerable skill and long practice
under competent instructors.   The *coup d'œil* is very attractive, and the effect of the different groupings quite as good as
anything to be seen in the incidental ballet of the European
stage, while the brilliance of the dresses and the ebbing and
flowing chorus of the dancers add to the picturesqueness of
the whole.   The yein flourishes most in small villages, where

the most promising of the youth of both sexes are taken in charge by a skilled sayā, who trains them assiduously together until they have attained perfection.   Even in these dances the sexes do not mingle.   There are meimma yein and yaukya yein, the former usually eschewing complex movements, and sitting in rows on the ground, richly decked with bracelets, and dalizan necklaces falling over their silken vests or tight-fitting lace bodices.   The dancing consists of the usual pirouetting, or perhaps it ought to be called winding, on both feet, with much serpentine movements of the arms and the head.   The loosening of the elbow-joint is greatly practised by Burmese girls with a view to these performances, and also under the impression that it is elegant in itself.   From early years the arm is so manipulated that the forearm can be bent back so as to form a curve outwards, and this accomplishment is steadily exhibited on all occasions in public by a belle who has acquired it.   Very often the meimma yein is performed by a body of girls, who succeed one another in successive groups.   All are seated at first.   The chorus is led by a woman, who herself does not dance, and is usually the instructress of the troupe.   She begins in a low recitative gradually swelling until at last the first group rise and go through a stately performance.   They are succeeded by the next row, who are more lively in their movements, and so on to the last, who are usually young girls, and are much more rapid and varied in their figures than their elder predecessors.   Finally, all join in some complicated evolutions, and finish up seated in some pre-arranged figure.   But as a rule the meimma yeins, though pretty enough as a mere spectacle, have not sufficient action to redeem them from the accusation of tiresome sameness brought against individual dancing, and they are always so discreet that they might be performed by Sunday-school teachers.

In the men's dances it is different.   At the commencement all are seated, four or five in the front row, and forming a column of perhaps ten or more rows.   The conductor gives the sign and all bow down with closed hands raised to the forehead in salutation to the great man in whose honour the dance is given.   Then they begin singing in

chorus in the usual way. The song treats in a rambling
way of the past history of the village, its ancient glories and
heroes ; its victories in boat-races, boxing matches, or mains
of cocks. Interpolated are catch phrases for the guidance of
the dancers. At a certain word all spring to their feet ; they
sway to the right, to the left ; white handkerchiefs are drawn
from the belt and waved to the measure of the refrain, peeled
white wands replace them ; they pirouette simultaneously,
they troop round in procession in movements resembling
figures in the Lancers or the Haymakers, the time varying
with the measure of the song, dying away in plaintive sounds
almost to quiescence, and then suddenly rising to excited
movement of every limb as the words tell of a let-pwè, in
which some local hero of the fancy did glorious deeds, or a
fight long years ago when the village spearmen carried the
day. Then the measure changes again, the alterations in
time being always heralded by some such refrain as to yein
daw tha, le maung yo wa, a kind of warning hung out
after the manner of the first word of a military command.
Occasionally, a yein troupe which has acquired particular
skill and renown travels about the country on special invitation. Rangoon is often supplied with its " country dances "
in this way, the townspeople not having the time, or being
too numerous to form a good company for themselves. But
they very rarely become regular professionals in the same
way as the play actors do ; they never perform ostensibly to
gain a living, and the dances always occur on some fête day,
whether in their own place or in the village to which they
have been invited. Their instructor always receives a sum
of money to recompense him for his trouble and to pay for
the expenses of his troupe. Yein pwès are performed ordinarily in private houses or on a public platform, when it is
a religious or special festival. A yein is a favourite way of
greeting a great man, or an English official on his arrival
in a village. It is not so expensive as a zat pwè, is more
quickly arranged, allows the sons and daughters of the chief
people to distinguish themselves, and lasts just as long as the
person it is intended to honour pleases.

CHAPTER XXXI

MUSIC AND SONGS

THERE are no teachers of music or singing in Burma, and there are no written scores. A musician commences his career by diligently listening to the performance of a good band. By and by he enters the village orchestra as a clapper player, and so learns the time and the peculiarities of various tunes, just as actors rise from the posturing and choruses of the children's and country yein pwès to the full dignity of dramatic performers. As a natural consequence there are occasionally variations, and indeed every pulwè, or flute-player, has his own particular mannerisms, but these are never so great as to materially alter the character of the air, and such tunes as the tedat, apudaik, lôngyin, and so forth, which occur in every zāt, are as familiar to everybody as "God save the King" and "Auld Lang Syne" are to an Englishman. Nevertheless it is very difficult for a foreigner to catch the air, and I have not been able to get an English score of any of the really old national tunes. The melody given later on was taken down from the playing of a well-known pwè leader in Maulmein, and has been harmonised for the town brass band by Mr. W. G. St. Clair, formerly of that place, to whom I am indebted for the score. So true is it to the air that many wealthy Burmans have the band to play at domestic festivals, funerals, and the like, and are satisfied to have the one tune played over and over again a score of times. But the kayāthan is of modern origin, and, as Burmans always say, in the English style, though Englishmen will persist in saying that there is nothing English about it. It has somewhat absurdly been adopted by the

British army as "The Burmese National Anthem." It makes not at all a bad quick march, but it is about as appropriate for a national anthem as "Champagne Charlie is my name." In the acknowledged national airs it is very difficult to get a definite rhythm, the music being apparently, at any rate to all but experts, a mere succession of recitative, more or less Wagnerian in its style.

The instruments of a full Burmese band always include the following, whether the occasion is the orchestra for a play, the music for a dance, for a wedding, an ear-boring ceremony, or a funeral. A saing-waing, an elaborately carved, circular, wooden frame, painted in parts, standing between two and three feet high, and five feet or more in diameter. Round the inside of this are hung drums of graduated sizes, which are struck with the hands of the performer, who sits in the middle. The alternate dry and saturated state of the atmosphere renders constant tuning necessary, and this is effected by tightening the drum-heads, and also by smearing on with the fingers a paste made of burnt rice husk. The music produced is rather thin in itself, but by no means unpleasing. Similar to it in construction, but not standing so high, is the kyi-waing, the only difference being that graduated gongs take the place of the drums. The gongs are of course beaten with a knobbed stick, and not with the hand. These ponderous instruments can only be carried about in a cart, and their owner keeps perpetual guard over them, sitting in the centre, cheroot in mouth, for they cost a very considerable sum of money. Fair specimens of both the drum and the gong-harmonicon may be seen in the South Kensington Museum. In addition to these, there are in every band two or three hnè, trumpets or clarionets, with a broad bell-shaped mouth, which is movable and ordinarily but loosely attached. The noise of these is always very prominent, and is not relished by people who do not care for the bagpipes. There is also a similar number of pulwè, or pyue, a rude kind of flute. The best pulwè-player is always the leader of the band. Then there are ya-gwin, big cymbals, and than-lwin, little cymbals, and the patma, a long drum like the tom-tom of India and beaten with the hand in the same way. Finally there are the wa le'kôt, each formed of a length of bamboo, extending to five feet occasionally, and split down the centre. These castanets are always in the hands of the most recently joined, and therefore most zealous, members of the band, and are clapped together with an energy which usually makes them unduly prominent. The above instruments serve to constitute a full band.

Besides these, however, there are several other musical instruments used by themselves, and learners—even those who are members of an orchestral band—usually avail themselves of the aid of a teacher to acquire accuracy and delicacy of touch, especially in the case of the harp. The saung consists of thirteen silken strings stretched on a boat-shaped wooden case, with a long, curved handle. The Burman boat, low at the bows, rises to a very considerable height at the stern, and is so like a harp frame that there is a stock story of a country peasant, for the first time in Mandalay, believing that the gilded royal boats in the moat were gigantic harps being seasoned for use in the palace. The sounding-board is formed of thick buffalo-hide, and the instrument is tuned by pushing the strings up or down the curved handle, and so tightening or loosening them. Only the young men play, and the accomplishment is not very common. The handle rests on the left arm and the right hand touches the strings, while the singer plays his own accompaniment. A similar instrument is the migyaung, the crocodile, a sort of guitar with three strings, stretched over a hollow sounding-board, shaped like that uninviting saurian. It is somewhat too primitive, however, to be popular, except with sentimental people. Finally there is the pattala, or bamboo harmonicon, as some call it. This instrument has always evoked approval from even the most fastidious of foreigners, as a singular instance of sweetness of sound produced from most unpromising materials. It consists of a carved and painted box, long and narrow and with high rising ends. From each of the corners of these sides are suspended strings, which hang down in a parabolic curve over the low centre of the box, and to these strings are attached flat strips of bamboo, placed at close intervals. Their tone is regulated by the more or less complete thinning out of the centre of the under side, and little sticks are used to strike them with. The notes produced are surprisingly clear and melodious.

Fiddles may often be heard played with greater or less skill, especially on the pagoda steps by blind and deformed beggars, but the instrument is not national, and is never, or but rarely, found where Europeans have not penetrated. The same may be said of the young Burmans who play in Rangoon on the concertina and the English fife and piccolo. It is flattering to national pride to notice with what accuracy and rapidity they pick up English airs.

But except at funerals and other solemn occasions instrumental music is looked upon not so much as a means of enjoyment in itself as an accompaniment to the human voice, and mere orchestral concerts would never draw the crowds which a single good singer can always command. The recitative character of the music is always more evident in the singing than in the instruments, and each " prince " or " princess " has individual peculiarities in the way of trills and staccatos introduced into the legitimate air. As the young musician learns by hanging about the band, so a vocalist follows an acknowledged great singer about and imitates his style, or at any rate learns the tunes and the words. The latter are, however, very immaterial, for the language itself is so pliant that it is easy to express the ideas in rhythm as you go on. Maung Tha Byaw, the great singer of his day, always made his songs as he sung them, and this was so well known that whenever he appeared, whether in a regular play or only to sing a few airs, there were always thirty or forty reporters sitting round to take down his words in their parabaik. This peculiarity of the Thabinwun occasionally got him into trouble. A somewhat incomprehensible piece of palace etiquette rendered it treasonable to sing a thanzan, a new song, before the king. Maung Tha Byaw several times, whether through too great laziness to learn the words, or from the force of habit, transgressed this rule, and was several times ordered out to execution. But he sang to the taunghmu and the pagwet, and these grim customers, the gaoler and the executioner, unable to resist the melody of this latter-day Orpheus, hid him away and exhibited some less talented person's body in evidence of having carried out their orders. Then when the next palace concert came on, the king—his late majesty—would grow tired of the ordinary vocalists and regret that the great improvisatore was gone. Whereupon Maung Tha Byaw would promptly come forth and sing his sweetest. He was killed in this way several times, but in the end died a natural death, about the same time as his contemporary Yindaw Ma Le.

The honours he received were quite on a par with European estimation of musical talent. He had a patent to carry a golden umbrella, and, as Thabinwun, had magisterial powers to punish those who offended him or refused to obey his edicts. Two lictors went before him to clear the way, a white cloth being tied round their fasces as a distinctive mark. When he performed in a play a low yaza mat, or royal fence, extended across the front of the stage, and at the ends were planted his golden hti and a banana-tree. The latter distinction was also granted to Maung Tha Zan and Maung Mu, singers only inferior to the Thabinwun himself.

If the tunes are not easily reduced to regular rules, the difficulty with the metres is not less. There exist, indeed, written laws ordaining the number of feet to the verse, but they are as lightly regarded as is consistent with their recognition at all. Much more precision is indeed expected in the old tunes than in those of modern date, but even with them song-writers of the present time allow themselves considerable freedom. The original linga are all very short. Thus the pyo has but four syllables; kabya, four; yatu, six and four; luta, four; yagan, six and four; ègyin, four, five, and six; hmawlôn, four and six; paikzôn, four; legyo, four; sagyin, four, five, and six; and so forth. In the thanzan, or new tunes, however, the compass of the lines often approaches the portentous length of some of Walt Whitman's *Leaves of Grass.* Such modern tunes are the kayāthan (so-called English), dobatthan, nabethan, nanthein yodaya (Siamese), and pyigyithan (Chinese). Such compositions as the lôngyin and ngogyin cannot be designated otherwise than as musical prose, with occasional fits of metre, prompted by their dolorous character. They are the threnodies and the laments of *divorcées*, unhappily all too common (in plays and song-books). Such, too, are the saungbasa, the ardent epistles of separated sweethearts.

The question of rhyme is even more puzzling. Some compositions not intended to be sung, such as notably the sèhnityathi bwè, songs about the twelve months of the year, giving an account of their characteristics, the pwès that take place in them, and so on, are written with regular final rhymes, while the other laws of prosody, shi'-lôn tabaik, kolôn tabaik, and so forth, are fairly strictly observed. But in the songs of the plays and such-like productions, rhyme runs absolute riot, so that it is quite common for every word in a line to rhyme with the corresponding word in the second verse of the couplet.

Thus in the kayāthan, translated below, there are abundance of lines like the following :—

> Thuza lo lo
> Muya po po.

Or—

> Ma yo le hnan kyauk
> A-po le tan lauk.

Or in the Tedat—

> Ta ko dè pa
> Ma so bè hma
> A ngo thè hla.

Such rhymes occur in an abundance that makes them the most prominent characteristic of the verse, but it is impossible to reproduce them except in another monosyllabic language. English, of all others, offers the greatest difficulties to the translator.

I have done what is possible to reproduce the following kayāthan, "The Sound of the Trumpet," as nearly as possible in the varying metre of the original. Those who are best able to judge of the success of the attempt will be the most lenient in their criticism. I may mention that the tune was originally composed to the words of a song in honour of the accession of King Thibaw, but words on all manner of subjects have been written to it since.

RANGOON MAIDENS

O, the girls of Rangoon town,
They are fairies who've come down
From seats of nats, beyond the skies, sure here their likes are none.
And the fragrance on their cheek,
Gad, it makes a man feel weak,
And their hair so black and glossy with jet wavelets in the sun.
Ye maidens fair,
With graces rare,
Your faces and your ways they are a pair:
Nat-maidens are renowned,
But to say this I am bound—
If you were mixed
We should be fixed,
For who could tell the fairy from the fair?
You're so slender
And so tender,
You are like Wethandaya's queen,
And when Barani is seen,
Who goddess is of flowers on the green,
Men say,
'Amè!
Such a likeness, I am sure, ne'er was seen.'
Ah, when we meet by chance,
My heart's all in a dance,
You're so dangerously, murderously fair.
The diamond ear-ring's light
Like a meteor glows at night,
With the lightning of the hair-pin in the midnight gloom of hair.

The Southern Queen,
The right-hand Queen,
She who sits supreme, alone
By the monarch on the throne,
She the greatest of the Four;
List, sweet maids whom I adore,
Dark-skinned or fair,
Slim, *débonnaire*,
She has robes, a kingdom's joy,
That two hundred looms employ;
But the silken flowers you wear,
You may dare with her compare,
Rangoon maids.
With gay kerchief o'er the bosom,
With sweet swaying of the shoulder,
Without art
Ye inflict on one or two some
Wounds that love will hardly solder
In the heart.

O that curve in the round arm !
It has wrought men grievous harm.
Like the sylphs when they're at play,
Like the maids of Mandalay,
>>Without display
>>In everyday
>>Quiet dresses they
>>Are busked and gay
As the daughters of the palace, as the maidens of the skies
In their natural, their usual array.

O ! could I but sing what I think,
My heart would no more on the brink
Of despairing love struggle and sink,
Ye maidens to heavens the link ;
>>Each passer-by
>>Who casts his eye
Upon the buxom Hanthawaddy girls,
>>Though he be sage,
>>His feelings wage
Fierce war within his brain-pan till it whirls.

Dewa daughters, fair, fair,
Rosebud fairies, ware, ware,
Born men's hearts to snare, snare,
>>Can I paint your ways,
>>Better sound your praise,
>>In verse
>>That's terse
Than thus : You're fair as any maid in Mandalay.

Barani is a daughter of nats, corresponding very much
to the classical Flora.

Madi, the spouse of Prince Wethandaya, is always
regarded as the model wife.

Amè ! "mother !" is the invariable exclamation of all
Burmans on all possible occasions of astonishment, anger,
doubt, or delight.

The name Hanthawaddy, properly applied to the whole
province, is, in songs, usually employed to designate Rangoon,
for rhythmical more than any other reason, just as Mamye,
or Mye, or Man stands for Mandalay.

"Rosebud fairies," called bôngyo, are daughters of nats,
who having stayed in the country of the déwas for a thousand
years, are obliged to come down to the seat of man again.

They are born from roses.   Such charming houris apparently particularly affect Rangoon.

The following is the score as written down by Mr. St. Clair, now and for many years, editor of the *Singapore Free Press* :—

KAYA-THAN

Next to the "Sound of the Trumpet" the Dobatthan is probably the most popular air, and is certainly the next most familiar to the English ear. It may be called the refrain-song, and is remarkable for the long dwelling and trilling on the last note of each stanza. The do is the seed with which aim is taken in the game of gônnyinhto, and pat, or bat, is to twist or spin. The metre here is not so complicated :—

SERENADE

Love united,
Troth so fondly plighted,
Love's light with life first lighted.
Sigh, my dear,
In me here,
Long with fear,
Now thou'rt near ;
Long and sigh, my dear.

Flew the storm-cloud,
Rose and shrieked the winds loud
Came I yet and lowly bowed.
Cold as lead
Here I sped,
For love dead
Bent my head,
Lonesome for love dead.

The thein-nats play,
See through wild rain I stray,
Drenched, but sad from thee away :
Sad and lone.
Sweet, my own,
Be not stone,
Hear me moan,
Sweet love, hear my moan.

Love, the cloud-rack,
Flashed blue gleams of hope back,
Broke and furled its fringes black ;
Here I wait
At thy gate ;
Open straight,
Be not late,
Hot with hope I wait.

My pet is fair
With flowers twined in her hair,
Kerchief gold-meshed like a snare,
Like a net
Fairly set
Hearts to get,
Sweet my pet,
Mine lies in that net.

Courtly story
Tells of queenly glory :
My queen's as fair and more, aye.
Eyebrow tint,
Just a glint,
Slightest hint
Of art in 't,
Eyebrow's pencilled tint.

Painted cheeks sweet,
Nosegay where all scents meet,
See, I throw me at thy feet.
There is none
To be won,
No not one
'Neath the sun,
Like my love there's none.

The thein-nats are certain spirits, or superior beings, who
preside over the showers. It rains whenever they come out
of their houses (the stars), to sport about and have mimic
fights in the air. The thunder and the lightning are the
clashing and shining of the celestial arms. When the sun is
in the house of the goat it is very hot, and the thein-nats do
not come out. To arouse them from their lethargy, if the
rains are long of coming, it is a common custom in country
places to have a lônswéthi, a tug-of-war. A chain or a
stout cable is got, and the villagers divide themselves into
two parties, and pull and shout and get up as much excite-

ment as possible, to stimulate the thein-nats to exert themselves also. A lônswèthi sometimes continues for nearly an
hour without definite result.

The "painted cheeks," or "fragrant cheeks," so frequently
mentioned in all these love-songs, refers to the thana'kha, a
sweet-scented, straw-coloured powder made from the bark
and roots of the *Murraya paniculata*, a flowering shrub of
the citron species. Some girls, and especially some actresses,
have particular recipes for making up the cosmetic into a
moist paste. It is applied with the finger, and a good deal
of skill is exhibited in putting on the requisite amount.
Unpractised hands usually smear on far too much, and it is
as unsightly as a badly whitewashed outhouse. On others it
is barely visible. All girls use it, and not a few town dandies.

The following may be regarded as somewhat of an
approach to the European *vers de société*. I have not
attempted to imitate the original metre :—

THE CIGAR-MAIDEN OF MADEYA, NEAR MANDALAY

> Thy cheroots, so deftly fingered,
> Famous are in Burma's land,
> Many a chief has fondly lingered,
> Watched the maiden's nimble hand.
>
> Madeya, I'd spare to sing thee
> For cheroots and dainty maids,
> For their crispness doth but bring thee
> Sorrow from the palace blades.
>
> By the throne's great gilded grandeur
> Sits the prince, cheroot in hand,
> And behind him little Ma Nyo,
> Pearl of all the village band.
>
> Burnt up all my love and sighing,
> Like the ash of his cigar ;
> Hopes dispelled and idly flying,
> Like the smoke he puffs afar.
>
> Thy cheroots so deftly fingered,
> Madeya are silver-white,
> But the prince that came and lingered,
> Stole away the hamlet's light.

CHAPTER XXXII

THE TAWADEINTHA FEAST

NEXT to the uproarious merriment of the New Year's feast in the spring, the festival of Tawadeintha is probably the most joyous and striking of the Burmese religious ceremonies. It is not of universal observance. Some districts keep it up with much more pomp than others, but are not always equally enthusiastic every year in the way in which they celebrate it. In Rangoon and Mandalay, however, it is carried out regularly with greater or less magnificence, and preparations for the procession and the performance of the mystery play often go on for many months beforehand.

The feast commences on the first of the waning moon of Ta'saungmôn, about the beginning of November, and lasts over three days. It is commemorative of the Lord Buddha's ascent from the earth to preach the Sacred Law to his mother, Maya, then a Queen of déwas in Tawadeintha, the second nat-heaven. He was staying at the time in the country of Thawatti (probably the place now called Fyzabad), in the Zetawun monastery, and thence in three steps compassed the distance to the nat-heaven, situated above the Myinmo Taung, the centre of the universe. He had just finished a display of miracles on an immense road, constructed by him from one side of the world to the other, before a crowd covering an area of thirty-six yuzanas. The leader of the heretics who challenged the display of wonders, a man named Purana, was so overcome with chagrin that he tied himself to a weighted jar and was drowned. Arrived in the nat-seat, the Buddha preached a sermon on the duties of filial gratitude, to a vast congregation of byammās, nat-déwas, and arahats, and having expounded the Law which was to lead them into the noble path of deliverance, descended again by a magnificent ladder composed in separate strips of gold, silver, and precious stones, to the ne'ban kyaung, where he received the usual pious offerings of the people on his arrival, on the day of the full moon of Thadingyut.

To recall this event in the Buddha's life is the object of the feast, and the preparation of the stage often takes considerably over a week, notwithstanding the facility with which bamboo buildings are run up in Burma. A platform is prepared, from twenty to fifty or sixty feet in height, according to the subscriptions and the scale on which it is intended to carry out the performance. Over this is raised a gaily-decorated pya-that, the tower-like spire with seven diminishing roofs, characteristic of sacred buildings, and leading up to it is a sloping way, representing the Saungdan, the path by which Shin Gautama ascended. Sometimes there is a similar sloping descent on the other side, figuring the ladder which led down to the monastery in the neighbourhood of Sampa Thanago, but more often the ascent and descent are compassed on the same slope, which comes to an abrupt end six or eight feet from the ground, on a level platform, covered by an ordinary roof, if it represents merely the earth, or the sacred pya-that if it does duty also for the ne'ban kyaung. Half-way up there is sometimes a covered stage, representing the Ugandaw hill, on which the Lord Buddha found purchase for his final step to the nat-déwa country. On the first day of the feast, usually about eight o'clock at night, the whole scene being lighted up by the brilliant moon, occasionally rather spoilt by smoky torches and the evil-smelling fumes of open crude-oil lamps, the procession begins. The image of the Teacher of the Law, always represented sitting cross-legged, is mounted on a little carriage, fitted to run on a tramway reaching right up to the top, and is dragged up by means of a rope and a windlass. This is done slowly and in a rather jerky fashion, partly because the apparatus does not admit of greater expedition, but principally to prolong the function as much as possible, so that all the people may see it and greater merit may be gained. Surrounding the Buddha is a great company of worshippers from all the higher seats of the universe, earthly kings in royal dress, the white umbrella borne over their heads, and ministers and pages at hand with trailing robes and gorgeous peacock fans; nat-déwas and their rulers in rainbow hues, with wings on arm and thigh ; byammās from the thoughtful realms of the upper sky ; a glittering throng, all uniting in praise to the Saviour of the World, the chant rising and falling on the night air as they slowly ascend. As a general thing it takes quite an hour to get up.   There are many doxologies to be sung, and the performers, all laymen from the town, have paid many rupees for their dresses and want as many people to see their grandeur as possible.   Technically, on the first night the image should go no farther than the Ugandaw hill, but, as already said, this half-way house very often does not exist at all, and even when it does there is usually no more than half an hour's halt, and then the procession goes on to Tawadeintha, the spire-covered platform on the summit.   There the gay throng gather round the image in the attitude of adoration, and a man with a powerful voice stands behind it and declaims the sermon written down in the sacred books as having been preached on the occasion.   The subject is filial piety.   " I, the great Sramana, the mightiest of all beings, the teacher of ne'ban and the Law ; I, the all-powerful, who by my preaching can lead my mother into the path of salvation and the final deliverance ; I, who know all things and have beat down the passions under my feet ; even I, with all this can but repay the debt due to one of the breasts that suckled me. What then can man offer in love and gratitude to the mother who nourished him at her breast ? "

The sermon takes very much less time than the ascent. There is a Burmese proverb—

> Sa nahtaung thaw
> Taye pyaw.
>
> When the pôngyi preaches
> No harm the sleeper reaches ;

that is to say, no great evil can befall you when you are assisting, in presence of body, if in no other way, at the exercise of so meritorious a ceremony as the expounding of the Law. Accordingly the great crowd, who have been looking on with much interest at the progress up the taper-lit saungdan, commence generally to prepare for sleep in the zayats which surround the place where the stage is, or failing accommodation there, curl themselves up as comfortably as may be under the bullock-carts which brought them thither. A still greater proportion, however, gather together in circles to have a gossip, and this talk, accompanied by much smoking and chewing of pickled tea and betel, goes on till far into the night. An excuse for the scant reverence paid to the sermon, to which none but a few white-haired men and women listen, is, that what part of it is not in Pali is in such suggagyi, such a lofty and stilted style of Burmese, that no one can follow it. Accordingly the discourse is hurried through and the per-formers come down, and after putting off their fine clothes receive the congratulations of their friends. The image remains all night in " Tawadeintha," and the following even-ing the descent is made with similar ceremonial, and so the dramatic part of the festival is concluded.

But this is very far from being the whole of the proceed-ings. On both days numerous presents are made to the yahans and offerings to the pagodas, and these are carried round about the town and by circuitous routes to the monas-teries, so that the greatest amount of pleasure and publicity may accrue to the donors.

Chief among these offerings are always huge spires, some of them fifty feet high, representing Tawadeintha, and similar to that on the summit of the stage platform. They are made of bamboo covered with pasteboard, glittering with gold and silver paper and painted in many colours, and are carried by ten or twenty men, on long bamboo poles. Round about them dance all the youth of the quarter or village they are presented by, young men and girls, all in their brightest clothes. In Rangoon scores of these offerings wend their way to the monasteries under the shadow of the great Shwe Dagôn.

Mingled up in the procession come white umbrellas, gold umbrellas, lofty bamboo poles with gilt balls quivering and swaying at the top, big pasteboard images of nat-déwas, bilus, princes, and animals, from the crawling turtle to the familiar two-legged (or six-legged, which you please) horse, all of them surrounded by their group of vigorous dancers. Most characteristic of the day are the padetha-bins, a sort of Turanian Christmas-tree, representing the fabled wishing-tree of the Northern Island and the heavens of the nats. In those regions the fairy branches bear whatever is wanted, from a savoury ragout to a complete suit of clothes. Upon earth the quivering bamboo twigs carry, dangling by strings, whatever the bazaar shops will supply, packets of scented soap, matchboxes, razors, clasp-knives, little looking-glasses, coloured-glass tumblers, candles, and dolls ; and piled round the roots are heavier and more useful articles — blankets, mats, bales of yellow cloth, and earthenware or lacquer begging-bowls. These trees, each with its attendant band of dancers, are carried round and finally deposited before the house of the head of the monastery. Occasionally a ngwe padetha is offered, if the inhabitants of the wealthy districts of the town are particularly pious. This silver padetha is a tree similar to the rest, except that from its branches hang exclusively rupees and smaller silver coins, each wrapped up in a piece of tinsel or coloured paper. These silver trees, some of which are worth from 500 to 1000 rupees, are more frequently presented to the pagodas than to the monasteries. In the former case the custodians of the shrine take charge of the money for the purposes of repair and the payment of watchmen ; in the latter, the kyaungthagyi, the kappiya da-yaka, or lay steward of the monastery, receives the money, as indeed he takes the miscellaneous collection from the other wishing-trees, and dispenses all for the benefit of the kyaung and the giving of alms to poor travellers. It is noticeable, however, that the ascetic Sulagandi monks would altogether refuse to accept such a temptation to break their vows as a silver rupee tree.

Spires and umbrellas, padetha-bins and hobby-horses, hover about the streets on the way to the monasteries all day long throughout the duration of the festival, and at night, after the mystery play is over, the bands which have been performing sedulously all day crash out again on the night air, and fragments of plays and songs are to be heard everywhere. Chief among the night amusements too is the presentation of the naga, the huge serpent-like dragon, a great monster often considerably over a hundred feet long, formed of thin paper, distended on bamboo hoops. Each of these has a handle attached to it and a lighted taper fastened inside, and is carried by a man. The body is white, shading off into a blood-red head and jaws, and as the creature writhes its long folds and twists and darts from side to side of the road, the effect from a distance is very fine and startling on a first view. He plunges and coils about till the candles are nearly burnt out, and then is deposited with other offerings on the pagoda. All through the day and night there are generous people about, ready to give meat and drink, cheroots and betel, to any passer-by who chooses to afford them an opportunity of acquiring merit, for any act of charity accumulates kutho, even though the object aided be base.

The offerings to the monks are also not confined to the fruit of the padetha-bins. On the third day of the feast the image of Shin Gautama is carried away from the bamboo erection and dragged through the town in the early morning, the monks following with their begging-pots and receiving the abundant alms prepared for them at the Sôndawgyi feast, which is intimately connected with that of Tawadeintha, and commemorates as much the Lord Buddha's issuing from the ne'ban kyaung at Sampa Thanago to beg for his food on his return from the second heaven, as the pious gift of nogana, made after the long fast, by Thuzata.

CHAPTER XXXIII

A SÔNDAWGYI FEAST

IT is written that in the solitude of Uruwela a woman named Thuzata vowed an offering to the spirit of the place if she should have a male child. The prayer was granted, and the offering prepared. A thousand cows, new-calved, were milked; five hundred more were fed with this milk, and then with theirs two hundred and fifty more, and so on until the six noblest and best of all her herds produced a milk of surprising flavour and richness. This was boiled with sandal and fine spice in silver vessels, and fine ground rice, from chosen seed, set in new-broken ground, was added. Wonderful signs attended the preparation of the offering. A tha-gyā brought fuel to the fire; the great Brahma held an umbrella over the silver lota; four kings of nats sat by and watched; while subject spirits infused rich honey into the nogana. When it was ready Thuzata sent a servant to clear a place under a tree in the grove that she might make her offering to the wood-spirit. Sunama, the servant, found Shin Gautama sitting under the bawdi-tree. It was the day on which he attained the ne'ban of the passions, on which he became the Lord Buddha, and his face shone with a splendour beyond that of nats. Sunama returned and told her mistress that the spirit of the grove had appeared in person to receive the offering. Thuzata poured the nogana into a golden cup, worth a hundred thousand pieces of silver, such a cup as is always presented to the payalaung on the day wherein he becomes Buddha. Then she went to the grove, and prostrating herself humbly, made her offering, turned on the right, and retired. The Lord Buddha bathed

in the river Neritzara, at a place where more than 100,000
Buddhas had bathed, before obtaining the supreme intelligence.   Then he divided the nogana into forty-nine mouth-
fuls, ate it, and mounted the throne, whereon he sat for
forty-nine days tasting no food, and combating Mān Nat,
the spirit of death and sin.   But ere he lapsed into meditation he threw his golden bowl into the river.   It ascended
the stream swiftly, floated steadily for a short time, and then
sank in a whirlpool far down, leagues beyond the earth into
the country of the nagās, where it fell against the golden
bowls of the three previous Budhs with a clang that re-
sounded throughout the four worlds, and all things worshipped the present Lord :

> King and high Conqueror ! thine hour is come.
> This is the night the ages waited for.

This event in the life of Shin Gautama is commemorated
in the Sôndawgyi pwè.   Sōnthi is a sacred word set apart
to denote the eating of members of the Holy Assembly, and,
in remembrance of Thuzata's historic offering, the mendicants are feasted annually by the pious, with a splendour
and profusion far exceeding the ordinary alms poured daily
with unstinting hand into the begging-bowl.   The date of
the feast does not exactly correspond with the original event.
According to the chronicle, the Lord Buddha attained the
first state of ne'ban in the month of Kasôn, about April,
whereas the feast of Tawadeintha, with which the Sôndawgyi is always immediately connected, is celebrated after
Lent, at the full moon of Ta'saung-môn in November.   The
festival is essentially one of the town rather than of the
country.   Except the New Year's Feast, none of the
religious celebrations can be really called universal, and the
Sôndawgyi perhaps least of all.   Villages and small country
towns cannot get together the splendour necessary to distinguish the occasion from the ordinary domestic feasts, or
even from the daily almsgiving to the mendicants.   It is
therefore in a large town like Rangoon, where there is a
certain amount of money, and a facility for acquiring or
borrowing ornaments and frippery, that the festivities are
best seen.   There the *fête*—the word is more appropriate

than any implying more of a religious character—assumes
the appearance of a gigantic reception, or *conversazione*.
Streets and quarters of the town make up a common purse
for general decorations and the erection of stages for hired
troupes of actors, in addition to individual effort.   The dates
are arranged beforehand so that no two streets shall make
their effort on the same night, and so lessen the enjoyment
of the public, or draw away from the expected number of
spectators.   A committee is elected, or appoints itself, and
having got as much money as possible, hires the best available dancers and actors for the zat pwè, if possible a puppet
troupe also, and in addition, as many unattached mummers
and clowns as can be got, whose business it is to dance up
and down the street in the guise of dragons, snakes, nagās,
and demons of all sorts, and amuse such of the visitors as
cannot get near enough to see the set play, or prefer walking
about talking to their acquaintances.   Bands are engaged
in profusion, flower-garlanded arches erected at the ends of
the street and at intervals along its length, and gay Chinese
lanterns hung up everywhere.   Complimentary packets of
le'hpet, pickled tea, serving as invitations, are sent out in
profusion, but the non-receipt of one of these does not
deter anybody, and all comers of whatever nationality are
welcome.

Nowadays the monks are wont to complain that the
presents customarily made them at the Tawadeintha feast
are not nearly so valuable, or even so satisfactory, as they
used to be.   But it is different with the Sôndawgyi *fête*.
There the emblems of the archetypal nogana are all edible
and of the most sumptuous kind.   In every house the offerings for the ascetics are set out for display all night long
and make a goodly show, if the process can hardly be supposed to improve them for consumption.   Mountains of
cooked rice send out spurs of beef and pork, with flat lands
of dried fish and outlying peaks of roasted ducks and fowls,
the legs with their claws and the neck with the head and
beak being extended as if they had been drawn out tight to
exhibit their greatest length.   Ngapi, fish paste, in all its
malodorous varieties of ngapigaung, seinsa, dhamin, nga-tha-
lauk, abounds, and loads the air with suggestions of a fish-

curing village, or an unclean fishmonger's in the dog days. Chinese patties of sugar and fat pork, plates full of fried silkworms, maggots from the top of the cocoa-nut tree, salt-pickled ginger and fried garlic, and a variety of other dishes beyond the ken of occidental cookery, abound all down the long tables.   Alternating with these, and perhaps more pleasant to look at, are heaps of fruit, oranges, citrons, shaddocks, plantains, with here and there a late durian or two, rivalling the ngapi in its odour, and the brick-red or purple rind that conceals the luscious " snows " of the delicious mangosteen.   Plentiful tins of sardines and Reading biscuits, with somewhat muddy-looking Bengali-made lemonade, give evidence of the progress of " civilisation " ; and plates of betel with the fresh green leaves of the betelvine suggest how the morrow's afternoon will be passed in well-filled meditations by the pôngyis of the neighbouring monastery.

The house itself is decked out on a corresponding scale of magnificence.   To the uninitiated foreigner an ordinary Burmese hut presents about as unfavourable raw material for decoration as can well be imagined.   Built of rough teak planking, or of split bamboo mats, and raised a few feet off the ground on posts, it resembles a marquee tent in shape and in size (according to the principle of the old Joe Miller story about the stone which was as big as a lump of chalk). On all ordinary occasions there is not a vestige of furniture in it.   A row of earthenware pots with water, a couple of wooden boxes, and the rolled-up mats and blankets whereon the household sleep, are the only things to be seen.   The sides and ceiling are grimed with the smoke of the fire that cooks the daily meals ; the floor stained with smudges of oil and red blotches of betel.   Yet this unpromising shanty the Burman transforms into a palace chamber, or stage-like fairy bower.   The sides of the house are thrown up towards the street, so that the room assumes the appearance of a verandah.   The floor is covered with thick bamboo matting finely woven, over which bright-flowered rugs are spread. The dingy sides of the house are draped with flags and kullagās, elaborate stitched pieces of tapestry, ten or twelve feet long, and reaching down to the ground.   White, or brilliant-coloured chintz, or paper, forms a roof studded with red, blue, or green stars and rosettes of tinsel paper. Great mirrors, swinging and other lamps, statuettes of wood or stucco, candlesticks with glass shades, clocks, German half-crown engravings, and gay Chinese lanterns hang or stand about. The floor is literally covered with silver and gold cups and betel-boxes, of all sizes, from that of a soup-tureen down to a breakfast cup. Some are plain ; some of that *repoussé* work at which the Burmese silversmiths are so clever. The great majority of these are of course borrowed from friends (of another street or quarter) or hired for the night from the chetty pawnbrokers. A few chairs and tables stand about for any European visitors who may come, and they are sure of a friendly welcome. At the back of the room in a long line, behind the mirrors and statuettes, sit the girls, decked out in their most expensively embroidered skirts and gayest silk neckerchiefs. They are literally loaded with jewellery. Round their necks and over the bosom hangs the broad network of the dalizan, formed of silver or gold fishes and flowers linked together. The nadaung, the huge gold plugs or circlets in their ears, sparkle with rubies and emeralds. So do the bracelets on their arms and the rings on their fingers. Each girl as she sits is worth many hundred rupees. It is probably for this reason that they are made so inaccessible, seated behind the lamps and lights. If admiring swains could get at them, so could other individuals, whose regard for the jewellery might exceed that for the commandments. The young women may therefore be supposed not to care so much for the Sôndawgyi *fête* as their brothers. Most of the girls are of course daughters of the house. If, however, the householder has not womankind enough, he simply goes into the bazaar and hires as many personable-looking damsels as he may find necessary. They are as much a part of the display as the silver cups and the looking-glasses. A band at one end of the room discourses music fitfully. Occasionally a girl, too young to have attained to the dignity of jewellery, gets up and dances and sings for a while. Musical instruments of different kinds, pattala, hnè, and migyaung, harmonicons, trumpets, and alligator guitars, lie scattered about here and there for the amusement of skilled visitors, and there is always somebody thrumming or tootling away on them.

The whole scene is an unceasing round of laughter and gaiety. The host and hostess and a few old women bustle about and receive the visitors, point out the most noteworthy parts of the display, have a few words of conversation, and offer refreshments. The guest drinks a cup of singularly washy and saccharine tea or lemonade, smokes a big green cheroot, or chews a fid of betel, compliments the owner of the house, declares he never saw so much magnificence in his life, and departs to go through the same performance in the next house. Englishmen are always welcome. Seats are brought for them ; the master of the house sits by while they are under his roof, explains everything to the best of his ability, and produces the inevitable bottle of brandy or beer, without which no European is supposed to be able to endure existence. The reception begins at eight, or half-past, and lasts for an hour and a half or so. Then every one who is coming has arrived, and has gone the round of his friends, so that the domestic display is pretty well over. The gorgeously-arrayed females gather up their skirts, and go off home under a guard of their male relatives, and having put off the greater part of their jewellery, come back, each with a huge green cheroot in her mouth, to see the play and join in the fun. A few of the older people remain indoors, steadily chewing betel, comparing notes as to past displays, and speculating as to whether any other street in the town will be able to surpass the display of Eighteenth Street. Not a few placidly go to sleep, notwithstanding the din without, the strident sounds of the band, the shouts at the buffoonery of the clown, and the confused chatter of thousands of voices. Outside there is no slackening in the jollity. From the lofty stage representing the second heaven of the nats, portions of the Law are declaimed ; the celestial beings deliver themselves of suggagyi, lordly sentiments, revellings in exuberant verbosity, all night long, and the constantly-shifting audience never thins away. Farther up the street a huge pasteboard demon is gambolling unwieldily, half-a-dozen dancers twirling and twisting vigorously within a foot or two of its great tusked jaws. At intervals some of the youths of the street, or some of the visitors, worked into a state of excitement by the music, dance enthusiastically in an unattached kind of fashion for a few minutes, and then suddenly break off with a laugh. Some of the young men spend most of the time flitting about the extemporised stalls, tasting at one place fish jelly, at another queer salads, having a violent flavour of garlic ; here smoking a cheroot, there chewing a packet of pickled tea, and flirting in turn with all the girl vendors, who look very coquettish with the red or white flowers in their glossy black hair, and the fragrant, yellow thanaka toning down their complexion. Not in the least shy they are, and quite ready to bandy Oriental compliments with new acquaintances. It is with many of the younger folks the pleasantest part of the feast—and is not the old duenna sitting behind—what matter though she is asleep—to play propriety ? And so the merriment goes on all night, fit occupation provided for all : sleep or high moral declaimings, combined with the clown's comedy, for the elderly ; abundance to eat, and a surfeit of gossip for the lazy and middle-aged ; and indiscriminate love-making and dancing and noise for the young. At length, with dawn of day, which in those low latitudes corresponds with the rising of the sun, the ascetics come round in grave yellow procession, their hands clasped round the thabeit, their eyes downcast. The bowls are filled, the rest of the feast is carried humbly to the monastery by the donors, and the Eighteenth Street Sôndawgyi pwè is over. The celebrators sleep all day ; the state of digestion of the monks is not a matter for discussion ; and those visitors who have got new ideas from what they saw last night, lose no time in making use of them for the better glorification of their own *fête*, which comes off a few days later.

CHAPTER XXXIV

A WORK OF MERIT

" THE wisdom that made Asia mild " laid down no command
which is better observed in Burma than the first of the Five
Rules : Thu a-thet go ma that hnit (Thou shalt not take
any life at all). Hardened convicts will not harm the
vermin that infest their mattresses. A story is told of a
man who allowed the snake that had killed his father to
wriggle away unmolested through the tall elephant grass.
I myself have seen a Burmese mother take up between two
bits of bamboo the scorpion that had stung her little son,
and simply throw the hideous creature out of the house. So
far does the command to beware how they harm any meanest
thing in its upward path lead earnest Buddhists. Mr. Edwin
Arnold tells how, in a distant age, the great Lord Buddha
offered up himself to preserve " this breath of fleeting life "
in an animal :

> Drought withered all the land ; the young rice died
> Ere it could hide a quail.

When between the hot walls of a nullah, our Lord spied, as
he passed, a starving tigress, with two little cubs whining for
the nourishment her shrunken frame could not give them.
Then, heeding nought but the immense compassion of a
Budh, the great yahan bethought himself :

" Lo ! if I feed her, who shall lose but I ? " and, throwing
off his priestly robes, came forth with a " Ho ! mother, here
is meat for thee ! " and died.

" So large the Master's heart was long ago," before he
came upon earth for the last time to teach the Law and give

the millions peace; not only when he came down from the hills, where in austere fastings he had been pondering to win the secret of "that curse which makes sweet love our anguish," and appeared before King Bimbasara to plead for the flocks that the white-robed Brahmin priests destined for sacrifice on the altar. The idea has always been a favourite one with Buddhists. A favourite myth is that of the hare. Kalpas since the Lord of ruth appeared on earth in the form of that animal. All creatures were making offerings to the Buddha who was then engaged in preaching the sacred Law. The hare bethought himself that he too must give some alms. But what had he to give? Man might bring costly gifts; the lion found it easy to offer the tender flesh of the fawn; birds of prey brought dainty morsels; fish could produce no less tasty signs of devotion; even the ant was able to drag along grains of sugar and aromatic leaves; but the hare, what had he? He might gather the most tender succulent shoots from the sunny forest glades, but they were useless even to form a couch for the teacher. There was nothing but his own body, and that he freely offered. The Supreme Lord declined the sacrifice, but in remembrance of the pious intention, placed the figure of the hare in the moon, and there it remains as a symbol of the queen of night to the present day.

Similarly just a little below Mandalay on the river, near the Ava road, there is a huge, castellated pagoda, the Shwe Gyet-yet, raised in commemoration of another performance of the Budh, in an avatar countless ages ago. The tale is that in a season of grievous dearth, when all flesh was dying of famine, the great Master, then in the shape of a jungle-fowl, spied a holy pilgrim in the last extremity of want. There was none to pity him, none to save him from death, and the Budh, conquering, even in that distant time, one of the latest lost of the ten deadly sins—the love of life—surrendered himself to save another. Hence the pagoda standing out boldly on a great rock over the river. To the east is a representation of a fowl in stone, recalling the event; and before this, daily by the pagoda slaves and others, and on feast-days by hundreds of worshippers, plentiful heaps of gilded grains are strewn.

These personal examples furnished by the teacher of neh'ban and the Law himself have only served to emphasise what is seen on the admission of every new member to the holy assembly. One of the articles with which, in addition to his dress and begging-bowl, every postulant must provide himself, is a strainer, without using which he must drink no water. The object is, of course, to prevent him from destroying life in the shape of the small animalcula to be found in water. Some zealous and scientific proselytiser endeavoured, by the use of microscopes, to persuade the people that this was of no avail, seeing that even in the strained water there was abundance of animal life; but a council decided that, provided the water had been filtered, if the ascetic could detect nothing living with his unaided eyes he was at liberty to drink the water without incurring blood-guiltiness. The attacks of science on Buddhism failed as completely as the efforts of most missionaries.

The mingled pity and dislike with which professional hunters and fishermen, whose occupation implies the regular taking of life, are viewed by Buddhists, is well known, and makes itself evident in the fact that the villains in most plays are hunters. Fishermen are perhaps not so much decried—possibly on account of the plea brought forward on their behalf, that the fish die of themselves, being taken out of the water, and not through any direct action of their captors. It is in connection with fish, however, that one of the most curious national works of merit takes place annually —furnishing, like all Burmese festivals, occasion for much fun and frolic.

The violence of the rain during the five or six months of the south-west monsoon floods the country. Not only do the rivers, which in many places rise regularly as much as thirty or forty feet above their hot-weather level—not only do they overflow their banks, and make wide seas of the neighbouring flat lands, but great lakes spring up everywhere. These are gradually stocked with fish of all kinds, most of which, by the sudden fall of the water, are cut off from all chance of retreat to the large rivers, where alone there is safety. Steadily the water goes down, the hot sun sucks up the pools, till at last the end seems to be come. The river is far away, and there will be no rain for months. Another day or two will suffice to bake and split into long fissures the bottom of the puddle, wherein are yet hundreds of animate things, from the whiskered mud-fish to the lordly hilsa, the salmon of India. Then the seekers after merit come out, bearing with them big chatties, huge earthenware jars, the size of some of which makes the story of *Ali Baba and the Forty Thieves* seem very much more credible. Girls and boys, old men and old women, go tramping about in the soft slush, capturing the fish and dropping them into the jars of water. Great laughter there is over the wild plunges and flounderings of the boys, the little screams and " a-mè lele, a-mè le-taw " of the girls as they step upon a fish, which whizzes away with a suddenness that is apt to disturb the equilibrium, or slip with one leg slowly but irremediably into a hole—perhaps a last year's buffalo-wallow—out of which they are only extricated after much teasing and tickling by the boys. Then there is the stalking and driving of a great nga-gyi into a corner, whence with a flop and a muddy dash he escapes into the middle again, amidst a chorus of the inevitable amè ! (" mother ") which springs to a Burman's lips on all possible and unexpected occasions. There is the caution to be observed in seizing the stinging mud-fish, the gingerliness with which, when he is caught, the waving whiskers are avoided ; especially the control over yourself to be maintained if he does sting you, lest you should spoil all your chance of merit in a moment of irritation, by doing him an injury. Sometimes the fish are caught in nets ; but this reckless wastefulness in the matter of combining merit with merriment is not very favourably viewed by the neighbourhood.

At last the fish are all caught and crowded together in the sin-o—the water-jars. There is, perhaps, a considerable pause before they are liberated. The nga-hlut pwè usually occurs a little after the carnival of the water feast, when everybody is doused with water ; and if the fish have been rescued from their danger some time before that, they have to wait in their uncomfortable quarters all the longer. The *fête* seems to be celebrated with more enthusiasm in Maulmein than in any other large town in Lower Burma.

In Rangoon the spruce merchants' clerks are apt to sneer at it as a "jungle feast," and rather laugh at the gatherings on the banks of the "Great Royal Lake." But in Maulmein it is different. There everybody enters into the spirit of the thing with religious fervour. A great procession is formed, and winds its way along the long snake-like up-and-down street that constitutes the great part of the town. At the head comes a band of young men dancing—some with their faces whitened with chalk, others grimed with soot ; some extravagantly dressed as princes and ogres, others scantily arrayed in a tucked-up waist-cloth—capering and prancing along with the waving of hands and fantastic pacings characteristic of the national dancing. Behind them, in a bullock cart, is the band, the huge saing-waing, the circular frame with its octaves of drums, on which the performer, smoking a big green cheroot all the while, thumps away with great vigour and in excellent time, accompanied by some trumpets, a flute or two, and a young fellow with a noisy bamboo clapper. Then there is an indiscriminate crowd of well-dressed, excited people, carrying huge umbrellas, white and gold ; big spires ; young fellows on hobby-horses ; men with long bamboos, gilt from butt to tip, looking like fishing-rods, with which one might bob for whales. Mingled with these are the carts carrying the jars of fish. In the middle is a great long platform on wheels, supporting a pasteboard and bamboo and painted mat model of a steamboat. The captain, in a gold-bordered cap, occupies the greater part of the ship forward, and yells orders to the man at the helm, who ports and starboards with surprising rapidity and impartiality. The chief engineer divides his time between stoking up the smouldering cigar-stump and the cotton which supplies the smoke from the funnel, and whistling violently on his fingers. A man stands at the side, heaving the lead (a joint of bamboo stuffed with cotton). It seems to be "And a half, nine," when some one is hit on the head, and "tin bām milla ne"—three fathoms and no bottom—when the lead fails to touch any-body. A lady in English dress, with her face brought to the proper colour with chalk, represents the passengers. This performer is of course a boy, and usually affords most amusement to both native and English spectators. The fun goes on all the way with jokes at the expense both of the performers and the lookers-on, and shouts and roars of laughter at every new buffoonery. At last they reach the spot on the river-bank selected for freeing the fish, and after a few pious formulæ have been recited, the contents of the jars are capsized into the water. Many of the fish are already dead, and not a few are so sickly that there is little chance of their escaping being eaten by cannibal brethren ; but this does not disturb the equanimity of any one. A great kaunghmu has been done, much merit has been gained, and there has been great fun over it. The motley procession wends its way back again, and everybody goes at nightfall to see the great kyi-gyin pwè given by some public-spirited and drama-loving quarter or street in the town.

CHAPTER XXXV

THE NEW YEAR'S FEAST

ALTHOUGH religious festivals and *fêtes* are so abundant in Burma, it is undoubtedly true that none of them are universally observed in all parts of the country, except the New Year's Feast. In localities where the people are exceptionally pious, the end of Lent may be more carefully observed than elsewhere, some devoting themselves especially to pious observances, others to the more worldly ceremonies of the sôndawgyi feast. The Tawadeintha festival is an annual observance in some districts, in others it practically passes over unnoticed. Similarly with all the minor *fêtes*. But it is not so with the thi'gyan pwè. All over Burma, from the smallest jungle hamlet to the crowded streets of Rangoon and the straggling suburbs of Mandalay, the New Year is ushered in with the old formalities, and with perennial enthusiasm. Not an hour is cut off from the allotted number of days, and every item of the old practice is carried out with the same vigour.

For this reason the "Water Feast," as it is called by Englishmen, has forced itself on the attention of the most careless observer, and every one who has written about Burma devotes a greater or less amount of space to a description of the good-humoured merriment with which the New Year is introduced. I do not propose, therefore, to do more than allude to the lesser known formalities observed on the occasion.

The month Tagoo, the first of the Burman year, occurs in the spring, and New Year's Day is in the earlier half of April. But it does not fall annually on the same day. It

is a movable feast, and the date of the commencement
of the year was regularly fixed by the royal astrologers in
Mandalay, who made a variety of intricate calculations, based
on the position of various constellations.   Since the annexation the duty of fixing the date of the new year has fallen
on the Chief Secretary to the Local Government.   The
object is to determine at what time the king of the tha-
gyās will descend upon earth, for it is his arrival which
will inaugurate the year.   The Déwa king is fairly punctual,
and the descent occurs always between the 9th and 12th
of April.   For some few years he has appeared on the 11th,
and scoffers in Rangoon declare that he will probably continue to do so to save the pônnas trouble.   These gentlemen
annually draw up a thi'gyan sah, a kind of prophetic
almanac for the year, relating what is likely to happen, and
whether it will be prosperous or not.   These vaticinations
depend upon a variety of circumstances.   The tha-gyā
min may come down wielding a spear, when there will be
disturbances in the land ; a water-jar, when the rains will be
abundant and the crops good, a torch or a simple staff.

It is from those objects that he bears with him, all of
which are ascertained by previous inspection of the heavens
and comparison with ancient precedents, that the astrologers
are able to determine the exact time when the descent will
be made.   Other particulars are learned from the animals
on which the nat-king rides.   Sometimes he has a cow or
a buffalo for a mount; at other times he bestrides a nagā,
when there are sure to be very heavy rains ; a galôn, on the
other hand, presages violent squalls and atmospheric disturbances.   When the tha-gyā min goes on foot with a
lantern in his hand and shoes on his feet, it is a sign that
the heat will be very great and prolonged.   Besides this the
king of the superior heavens, the Bumazonat, the spirit
guardian of the earth, exercises also a considerable influence
on the coming year, though he has nothing to do with its
commencement.   The pônnas, therefore, are at great pains
to find out his exact position at the beginning of the month
Tagu—whether in the trees, the flowers, or the paddy
stubble.   Each of these temporary habitations has its special
signification, and the discovery of them is not only valuable

in itself, but serves as a most satisfactory corroboration of
the truth of the events prognosticated by the movements
and surroundings of the tha-gyā king. The conclusions are
all carefully noted down in the thi'gyan sa, and great piles
of these are carefully preserved in the archives of the
monkish library, seldom to be looked at again.

Besides the events which are to happen in the coming
year the astrologers are also able to determine whether the
tha-gyā min will remain three days or four days upon earth.
If he stays three days it is called a matulè year, if four,
tawtulè, and the water-throwing is carried on a corresponding time.

All these points are settled some time beforehand, so
that every one in the remotest part of the country may
have due notice, and then information is sent to the heads
of monasteries, and the chief districts, and all is made ready
to receive his nat-majesty with proper honours. When at
last the day comes round, all are on the watch, and when
the wise men give the signal, tha-gyā min kyabyi, the king
has come down, a cannon is fired off, and forthwith all the
people come out of doors with pots full of water, the mouths
of the jars filled up with fresh green leaves and twigs of the
sacred tha-bye tree. A formal prayer is said, and the water
is poured out on the ground, and all are happy. Many
years ago an event happened which singularly impressed
true believers in the royal city. Just when expectation was
at its highest and all ears were strained in expectation of
the roar of the cannon, there was a terrific thunderclap, which
made all the town quiver, and demonstrated the accuracy of
the pônnas' calculations. There was no more thunder that
night, and the ranks of the pious received great increase
during the ensuing week. In country towns and villages
every one who has a gun rushes out into the street at the
appointed hour and fires it off. Most wonderful blunder-
busses and old flintlocks and ancient rusty horse-pistols
make their appearance, warranted to make a noise, but
capable of little more. After this ceremony is over a few
go to bed,—for the descent is usually made at midnight,—
but the majority sit up and talk.

With the earliest glimmer of light all rise, and taking

pots full of fresh clean water, carry them off to the monastery to present them to the monks—not to throw over them, such liberties are never taken with the brethren. After having made their kadaw, "begged pardon with water," to the sacred order, they set off to the pagoda and there commence the yethôn pwè, the washing of the images. It is not to be supposed that these really require cleansing any more than the recluses do, but it renders them myatta-thappè, an expression not to be rendered by many words in English. It combines all the meanings of cleanliness, beauty, stateliness, proper position, majesty, and repose ; and the laving with water is merely a recognition of this fact. The work is usually done by women, and they reverently clamber up and capsize their silver and earthenware goblets of water over the placid features. There are scores of them at work, and the ceremony is soon finished. Then all set off home again, and the jovial part of the festivities begin. All along the road are urchins with squirts and syringes, made of tin and bamboo, with which they have been furtively practising for the last few days, and their experience develops itself in extreme accuracy in catching you with a stream of water in the ear. Young men and girls salute one another mostly with cups and goblets of water, and stifled screams and shouts of merriment rise everywhere. Before breakfast every one is soaked, but no one changes, for it is fine warm weather, and there is lots more water to come.

During the day there is a regular going round to pay the compliments of the season. It was a great kadaw day in the palace at Mandalay, and all the nobles and officials went to "beg-pardon," and worship at the golden feet—not with water, however. Similarly inferiors pay their respects to their superiors and masters, children to their parents, scholars to their teachers, and juniors generally to seniors There is water everywhere, more especially on those parts of your dress which cling most uncomfortably to you. The girls are the most enthusiastic in the matter, and as they generally go in bands and have a copious reservoir in the shape of big jars along with them, the unprotected male is routed in no time. Some zealous people go down to the river or creek, wade into the water knee-deep, and splash

water at one another till they are tired and the thing begins
to seem monotonous. No one escapes; in fact no one would
care to get through the three days with dry clothes, for the
wetting is considered a compliment. A clerk comes up to
his master, shikhos to him, and gravely pours the contents
of a silver cup down the back of his neck, saying ye-kadaw
mi, " I will do homage to you with water." A polite but
less humble form of speech is ye-laung-thi, to " pour " water
over ; while equals, and the young people generally, yepetthi,
" splash " one another with the utmost vigour. It is to be
observed that dirty water is never used. The barbaric
innovation of squirts is a sign of decadence.

Foreigners do not object to the custom, except perhaps
some of the more pompous and stolid natives of India, whose
minds are incapable of appreciating a joke in any form
whatever. The rollicking Chinaman takes it up with the
utmost zeal, and sets about the thing in the most business-
like way. The last time I was in Maulmein one of the
storekeepers in the main street had rigged up a garden
hydrant in front of his house and connected it with the
well. A coolie was engaged to work it all day, and a
continuous jet of water, sufficient to put out a small conflagration, streamed from the nozzle the entire duration of
the feast. Not only was Boon Tek enabled to drench
everybody, but he advertised his machines and made a good
thing of it.

But the Chinaman was exceeded in zeal by a young
Englishman in Prome, not many years ago. He was a
Government official, and there were two friends dining with
him. A note came round to him from a neighbour in the
next street saying that the yepetthi girls were out and would
be round his way shortly. So he forthwith made preparations. The Madrasi " boys " got a huge bath tub on to the
verandah, and tin pannikins were placed handy, and the
dinner proceeded. But unfortunately there was no one put
to watch for the arrival of the girls, and the first notice of
their appearance was a well-directed stream of water in the
nearest man's shirt-front. To sally forth was the work of an
instant, but it was found that the tub was in the possession
of the enemy, and only served to eke out the abundant

supply they had brought with them in big silver bowls. The three Englishmen were soaked through at the first discharge.   But the Assistant Commissioner was not to be discomfited so easily.   He rushed through a perfect cascade, and seizing the first damsel he came across, incontinently plunged her in the bathing-tub and soused her under.   This filled the rest with dismay, and they forthwith took to their heels and ran, followed as speedily as her clinging garments would permit by the offended beauty who had been so unceremoniously treated.   The occurrence was rather unfortunate, for the girls were all daughters of some of the principal Burmans in the town, and it is a very grave impropriety for a man to lay hands on a woman even in joke ; how much more to duck her in a wash-tub and wet all her hair !   That young official had no more compliments paid him at New Year's time, to his own loudly expressed regret.

The most ludicrous story I have heard on the subject of the water-feast may serve as a warning to Englishmen who arrive in Burma in April.   The victim reached Rangoon on the second day of the water-feast, and having no Indian outfit got himself up in a tall hat, frock-coat, and the rest, to go and present a letter of introduction.   After much trouble and irritation, caused by the meanderings of his ghari-wallah, not by any means alleviated by the heat—for the sun is usually at its hottest in April—he arrived at the desired house, and proceeded upstairs.   On the verandah he found three or four Burmese girls, who forthwith asked permission to throw water on him.   He naturally supposed they were asking whether he wanted to see the master of the house, and nodded violently.   Whereupon they capsized their bowls of water over him, including the hat in the libation.   The astonished man took it to be a custom of the country to cool down over-heated foreigners, but thought the inclusion of his hat an unnecessary detail.   Just then the owner of the house appeared, having retired previously to get some money to buy himself off a ducking, and having been informed of the state of affairs, burst into a fit of such violent laughter at the griff's notion of the ceremony as roused in the latter a wrath so fiery that it almost dried him again.

A special feature of the New Year's Feast was the formal washing of the king's head, called thi'gyan daw gyi. It is not to be supposed that his majesty washed his head only once a year, or that it is at any time an operation to be lightly undertaken, any more than it is by the humblest of his subjects. But at other times the ceremony was called hkaung-se mingala or thi'gyan daw hkaw, and was not attended with so great solemnity as characterised the function at the opening of a new year. Formerly the water for the purpose was annually brought up from Hkaung-se Gyun (Head-washing Island), a little rocky islet situated on the river opposite Maulmein. Hkaung-se Gyun is fabled to hang, with its little cluster of pagodas and monasteries, by an invisible cord from the heavens, and has therefore long enjoyed a special sanctity, not by any means reduced by the springs of clear bubbling water found on its limited surface. Therefore for long it supplied all the water for the royal head-washing. Latterly, however, it was abandoned, and with this there is a curious history connected. After the war of 1826, it was settled in a general way between the commissioners that the river Salween should form the boundary between Burma and the newly-acquired British province of Tenasserim. But later a question arose as to the ownership of the islands, and especially of the rich rice-growing Bilu-gyun, north and south of which the three rivers flow into the sea. After much fruitless palavering it was determined to leave the decision to chance. A couple of cocoa-nuts were tied together and taken some distance up the Salween and thrown into the water in the middle of the river. They went down bobbing gaily till they came to the place where the conflicting currents of the Gyaing and the Attaran come in, and there they twirled and twisted about in an aggravating way until at last an eddy caught them, and, carrying them past the old town of Martaban, decided for the Dayè outlet, through which they were swept away to sea. Thus the "Ogre's Isle" became British territory, and with it the little Hkaung-se Gyun. Nevertheless for many years water was still carried up to Mandalay for the thi'gyan daw gyi, till at last Pegu was annexed to the British crown. Then it seemed undignified to carry the sacred water, not only from the stranger's land, but so many miles through alien waters, and so it was necessary to seek for another place. Where could a better be found than the mighty Irrawaddy itself? Accordingly from then on till there ceased to be a king of Burma, the necessary amount was drawn from the centre of the river by the Ye-kyi-wun, a minister specially appointed for that purpose.

As in so many other cases the amenities of the thi'gyan pwè have led to the extorting of money. In the good old days, and in the country districts still, it was the practice for benevolent people to keep open house, and give food and dainties to all passers-by, with tea and flavoured drinks, cheroots and betel for those that preferred them. To lighten the expense, contributions, called kèbo, were invited from friends and neighbours, and out of this has sprung the system of blackmail prevalent in Rangoon. A bevy of girls go into an Englishman's house and sprinkle him with lavender-water, or the moss-rose bouquet, so much in favour with Burmese belles. After a little badinage, they produce plain water, and threaten further operations unless something is given them. This they usually get, and if Englishmen complain of shameless extortion it is their own fault. The fair speculators are not such as any respectable girl would care to be seen with, and the prettinesses with scents are no more national than the scents are themselves. A provincial beauty would infinitely prefer a good honest ducking with vulgar water to the mawkish sentimentality of *eau de Cologne*. Some of the results of superior civilisation are very undesirable.

On the final day of the feast a gun is fired at noon to signalise the ascent of the thi'gya min to his happy realms again, and then all is over. The squirts are laid by for another year; clothes are hung up to dry, and nothing remains but to wait and see whether the pônnas are more successful than usual in their prognostications for the year.

The origin of the custom is no doubt the rain-making, described by Professor J. G. Frazer in *The Golden Bough*, but the Burmese explain it by a legend. The thi'gya min had a bet with a rival and the loser lost his head. This could not be allowed to be defiled by touching the ground, so it was caught by a daughter of Natdewas. Seven of them take it

in turn to hold the head, and when the head passes from
one goddess to another the New Year begins.   The head is
burning hot, and has to be cooled with pouring on of water.
This is recalled by the splashing of one's neighbour with
water at the New Year time.

CHAPTER XXXVI

A BOAT-RACE

IT is four o'clock in the afternoon, and the sun is still beating down fiercely on the mile and a half broad stretch of water which extends far above and below Myanaung. But the whole population of the town, and excited family parties from a score of villages round about, are gathered on the banks of the Irrawaddy, and bustle about regardless of the heat. Girls with flowers in their hair, and the brightest of dainty silk handkerchiefs floating over their dazzling white jackets; their costly skirts trailing on the half-muddy, half-dusty grass, and the long loops of their dalizan necklaces swinging about on their bosoms, hurry hither and thither with unwonted activity, regardless of the detriment to the fragrant yellow cosmetic on their cheeks and necks, and heedless of the occasional remonstrances of the guardian duennas, hardly less excited than themselves. Young men, ordinarily scrupulous as to the jaunty set of their flowered turbans, and the carefully-arranged folds of their hundred or two-hundred rupee waistcloths, now rush backwards and forwards, apparently aimlessly, their gaung-baungs twisted on anyhow, or hanging loose round their necks, and the cherished paso girded up tightly round their loins, reckless of creases; while they have not a word to say, or even a glance to throw, at the fairest of the country's daughters. Staid old men are gathered together in knots, all talking together at the pitch of their voices, and jingling bags of rupees in one another's faces; every now and then one group rushing off to another and swelling loud talk into shouting, in a fashion of which you would not have believed the phlegmatic old gentlemen capable, if you had seen them three days ago. Everywhere is bustle and excitement and anticipation. Even the township policemen have lost their ordinary official swagger, and are engaged in eager converse with individuals who, in ordinary times, command their attention in quite a different way.

There is very good reason for it. The full moon of Thadingyut is past ; it is well on in October, and it is the time of the boat-races. For weeks past the Myanaung boat has been spurting up and down the long straight reach, or having a heavy training paddle to Akauktaung and back again, and now at last the great day has come. Myanaung has challenged Thônkwa, hitherto the unconquered champions of all the low country, and the race, in best-and-best boats, is to come off this afternoon. The down-river men with their boat, and pretty nearly the entire body of their fellow-villagers, arrived last night, and none except the privileged have seen anything of them yet, to enable them to judge whether they are in as fine form as they were last year when they rowed the Bassein boat to a standstill. No wonder there is excitement, for Myanaung is but a young subdivision, sprung up since the English occupation, with no speciality for paddlers, and Thônkwa cherishes a name for prowess on the river from far back in the old Burmese days.

But suddenly there is a lull in the buzz of talk, and every eye is directed up the river. The boats have started for the preliminary row over the course. It is necessary to propitiate the guardian spirits of the river, and the votive offerings are therefore to be made At the stem of each boat crouches a man holding with outstretched arms a bunch of plantains, some cooked rice, flowers, and betel, for the soothing of the water-kelpie. This precaution must on no account be omitted. Who knows what disaster might not otherwise happen ? The flouted nat might upset the craft with a flip of his finger, or cling to the keelson of the boat and tire to nothing the sinews of the brawniest arms. Therefore goodly alms are given, so that all may rest with the prowess of the rival crews. This breather serves also another purpose. It enables the spectators to have a final view of the antagonists, and to lay their last rupee or not on their champions according as their judgment or loyalty bids them. Not a man of them will back the enemy's boat. If they have not supreme confidence in the superiority of their representatives, they simply refrain from staking all they possess. But in all the vast crowd there is not a man who has not a money interest of some kind in the race. There is U Ôn, the district magistrate, in the " grand stand "—a primitive erection run up in half an hour with some sticks and bamboo matting ; he is a Thônkwa man by birth himself, but nothing will persuade him to back the fishing village against the subdivision over which he now rules. Why, he has practically built and furnished all the money for the Daungsatpyan himself. The water-craft which he learnt in his native place has only prompted him to hang with greater loving care over the lines of the boat when it was building, and Ba Tu, his eldest son, wields the steering paddle in the Peacock, the pride of Myanaung. Now the old gentleman—he pulled a good oar himself twenty years ago for the very town he now longs to beat—moves about uneasily, gets up and sits down, winds and unwinds his white pawlôn, and can hardly refrain from shouting out, for the Peacock is just passing, and Ba Tu gives a yell and flourishes his paddle, and there is a great shout of " Yauk-kya ! " from the Myanaung partisans. Yauk-kya, or yauk-kya ba-tha, means simply " man " or " man, the son of his father," but it is a defiant challenge, or an inspiriting cheer to the Burmese. They are a fine, strong-looking lot, the Myanaung crew, perhaps a little too fleshy, and therefore possibly deficient in staying power, but all young, and worked up to a state of nearly frantic enthusiasm by the presence of their sweethearts and the momentous duty that rests upon them. Their weatherbeaten old trainer paddles alongside of them in a little canoe, and begs them to be calm at the beginning and not rush themselves out at the start. The boat is a beauty, and does credit to the old magistrate in the sweeping curves of its lines. Low and as light as skilled hands can make it, it draws only a few inches of water, and does not rise much more than a foot above the surface. So thin are the sides that the boat is tourniquetted together with twisted wire

and bamboo, and the seats themselves serve more to stiffen
it and prevent a wrench from doing any harm, than as
conveniences for the paddlers. There are twenty-four of a
crew all told, and the boat is fifty feet long. It is painted
all black, save at the bow, where there is a brilliant representation of the peacock, from which it takes its name. At the
end they come with a great spurt, shouting and bending to
each stroke, and another great yell rises from the bank to
assure them of the approval of their townsmen.

A length or two behind them comes the Thônkwa boat,
paddling along composedly to the time of their celebrated
rowing song, a mysterious, gusty air that has suggestions of
the swirl of the river eddies and the rustle of the wind in the
tall kaing-grass that lines their native creeks, in its varying
measure. It comes over the water gently enough now, but
many is the time it has swelled like a hurricane-blast and
left the opposing boat foolishly as if it were at anchor. The
Thônkwa crew are as different as possible in appearance
from their robust young rivals. There is probably not a
man under thirty among them, but there is not a superfluous
ounce in all the wiry twenty-four. Every thew is tough as
whip-cord, with long struggles against the rush of the current
in the flooded creeks ; every face and arm and shoulder is
deep brown with exposure to the wind and the sun, for not
a man among them but is a fisherman, and thinks nothing
of the wild squalls that sweep over the delta and ruffle the
swift current into a dangerous surge. No wonder they have
an unbeaten record ; and U Ôn fidgets about uneasily
when the famous pè-nin of the Thônkwa boat salutes him
obsequiously as the boat sweeps up.

No one knows how old Ko Kya-gyi is. His withered
face and shrunken body suggest that it is time he was giving
up fishing and endeavouring by assiduous piety to get his
balance of kan somewhat more on the right side towards
another existence, but he is tough as buffalo hide still, and
no man in all Burma has a greater name than the ever-
victorious Thônkwa steersman. None like him to keep a
boat straight in the conflicting eddies that have thrown out
many an apparently conquering boat ; none like him to
gauge the strength of his crew and spurt just at the right

moment ! From start to finish he has all his wits about him, and the stem of the boat is full on the winning-post all the time. Four years ago, when the Hlaing men seemed to be carrying all before them, it was Kya-gyi's generalship that won the day. Therefore the Myanaung magistrate is a little disconcerted at the homage paid him by his old rowing mentor, but none the less he puts on another hundred rupees with a Thônkwa lugyi who comes up at the moment. The Thônkwa men come with a bit of pace just at the finish too, and with a he-la, lu-la, yauk-kya, ba-tha, hé, dash past the winning-post.

This winning-post is not such as is used in English boat-racing. A boat is moored right out in the current with its head to the stream. At right angles to its length a long hollow bamboo stretches across the bows, and through this is passed a rattan, the end projecting an inch or two beyond the mouth of the tube at both sides. The contesting boats have each their own side and keep their own water, and the bow-paddler rises and snatches at this pan as the boat whisks past. It thus becomes a sign and proof of victory and is planted in the bows of the winner. Not a little skill is wanted on the part of both the man at the bow and the man at the stern. The former has to be sure in the eye and quick of hand, and the latter must take especial care to bring the boat past at the proper distance. It is not so very simple a matter to pull out the long cane at the terrific pace with which the boats come up, and the pan must be carried off to ensure the verdict. Sometimes both men seize it at once, and then they are almost certainly swept out of the boat, and as a rule both lose the rattan. Then it is a thaye pwè, a dead heat. But if one has the pluck and presence of mind to stick to it, then his boat has won.

Now the offerings have been made and the boats turned round, no very easy matter in the swift current with their great length. But it is effected dexterously enough. The Myanaung boat paddles up to the winning-post and young Aung Zan tries the pan to see that it runs smoothly in the bamboo, and Ko Kya-gyi swings in the stern of the Thônpanhla—the Three Fair Flowers, as the Thônkwa

boat is called—to make sure that his man will have his
proper amount of cane to grasp at.   Then both boats get
under the bank to avoid the force of the current, and paddle
leisurely up to the starting-point, a mile or a mile and a half
up the river.

The din and bustle on the bank now become greater
than ever.   Every one is talking and stating his views as
to the result of the race, and nobody is listening to him.
Betting goes on freely, and the chink of rupees is heard perpetually.   It is announced that the sporting English extra
assistant-commissioner from the divisional town has given as
his opinion that "the fishermen" will win ; they are in better
condition and cooler-headed than their opponents, and will
win at the finish.   There is a minute's dejection at this, and
then it is all effaced by the discovery that the Chinese storekeepers have put their "bottom dollars" on the home boat.
That is good news, for the Tayôk is a good judge of anything that can be betted about, and it is very seldom that he
drops money.   So the talk goes on till the last coin is staked.
Welshers have not yet been introduced into Burma, and
there is now nothing to be done but relieve one's feelings in
talk, and puff furiously at big cheroots, with an occasional
rush into the water to see how far the boats have got up.
Old U Ôn tries to talk to the young Englishman, but it is
no use, he can't keep either his mind or his eyes off the boat,
and the Ayebaing improves the occasion by attempting a
flirtation with the daughter of the house.   But he might
as well talk to the winds.   She is far more excited than her
father, and would be dancing about if it were not for the
restraint of her old nurse, who is too blear-eyed and rheu-
matic to be anything but ill-natured.

But at last there is a hush and every eye is turned up
the river.   The boats are turning, and come drifting down
to the starting-place.   There is a minute or two of backing
and fussing about so as to get the boats straight and the
bows level, and then, with a loud shout, they are off to a
start by mutual consent.   A roar of pent-up excitement
comes from the crowd all the way down the banks to the
grand stand and then swings back again like a wave on the
flat sea-sand.   Served by their magnificent boat and their

younger strength, the Myanaung crew jump off with the
lead and continue to draw away until half-way down the
course, where they are clear and have a bit of daylight to
spare. The backers of the Peacock are wild with triumph,
and already see victory before them, but the Thônkwa
party are perfectly composed and declare that things could
not be going better. Quarter of a mile from home old Ko
Kya-gyi lets out a yell, and though there is no apparent
quickening of the stroke, the gap, which for the last few
hundred yards has remained unaltered, suddenly disappears,
and the Thônpanhla creeps steadily up the Peacock's
thwart, and at last Aung Zan, the Myanaung bow, sees the
enemy's boat for the first time since the start, and a few
seconds later the rival bow is level with him, and the nose
of the Three Fair Flowers shows in front to the length of its
figure-head. The noise on the bank is simply deafening.
Incoherent shouts of despair and encouragement and delight
burst from every throat ; old women tear down their scanty
hair and work with their arms as if they themselves were in
the race ; girls rush to the water's edge heedless of the mud
and splashing that will ruin their silken skirts for ever ;
young men and boys rush up to their necks in the water
and yell with frenzied eagerness, for it is only a boat's length
to the winning-post, and Thônkwa leads by a foot. Old
U Ôn can stand it no longer, for the last minute he has
been shaking all over as if he were in a palsy, and his tongue
and throat are as parched as if they were choked with slack-
lime. He rushes forward with his hands in the air and
shrieks Yauk-kya in a key that cuts through the din like
a steam whistle. Yauk-kya—the cry is taken up ; Yauk-
kya, ba-tha—every mother's son of you—the Daung, the
Flower, swè le le ; row for your lives ; row for your un-
vanquished name ; and the two bows fling their paddles from
them and rise for the struggle. The wink of an eye too
soon and he will miss his grasp, the flick of a finger too late
and there will be nothing to seize. A great hush falls on
the vast crowd as if they were all stricken dead, and then
both men disappear in the water, clutching apparently simultaneously at the rattan. An agonising five seconds, and
then Aung Zan comes to the surface brandishing on high

the pan ; the Thônkwa bow felt the scratch of it on his palm as it disappeared through the tube.

The scene that follows is beyond description. The victorious crew spring up to dance, but the relief is inadequate. They can only escape frenzy by plunging into the river. U Ôn tucks up his waistcloth and dances round in mad delight till his stiff old legs will bear him no longer. Pompous old lugyis caper and plunge and shout ; younger men can only relieve their feelings by flinging themselves in the pools on the bank and rolling about wildly in the mud ; girls, who at ordinary times would hardly dare to raise their eyes to look about them, dance and shout in ecstasy, and their married guardians join in the rout. Bands from a dozen villages round about strike up, but the professional dancers who came to perform in honour of the victors are fain to look on while their intended audience go through unpremeditated figures. It always seems marvellous how the people ever get gravity of demeanour again after a great boat-race.

The contest is technically not over yet. It is a hle-pyaung lu-pyaung, that is to say, the crews have now to change boats. The Thônkwa men take the Daungsatpyan, and the home crew man the Three Fair Flowers. But to all intents and purposes the victory has been won, and the home representatives are the conquerors. The two boats paddle up again, and the fishermen go right away and win with the most consummate ease. This sets money matters on a more comfortable footing, but the Myanaung people are not a whit disconcerted. They won the real race, that in which each crew rowed in its own boat, and they receive the arguments of the Thônkwa contingent with the most self-satisfied composure. The record of the champions has been broken, and the veteran Ko Kya-gyi has at last sat in a losing boat.

A general adjournment is made back to the town. The country people have all come in their bullock waggons, and these are drawn up in comfortable places under the trees. The victorious crew go in procession up and down the main street, preceded by bands and every one in the place who can dance. Feasting is general, and then all move off to the plays, of which there are three or four, while some un-wearied spirits can only find relief for their exultant triumph in yein dances and irresponsible performances of their own. Till dawn of day the revelry goes on, but there is nothing like drunkenness. It is exceedingly seldom that you see a drunken Burman out of Rangoon, where they claim to be Europeanised. For a couple of days the excitement lasts, and then the strangers wend their way homewards, and the township calms down to its usual quiet. But for years the great event will be talked of at the local feasts, and the Yein choruses of three or four generations will tell of the gallant struggle when the Daungsatpyan beat the Thônpanhla and broke the long supremacy of the Thônkwa rowers.

It is a great pity that these old contests are not kept up with the spirit that used to characterise them. In 1877 the then Chief Commissioner of British Burma, Mr. Rivers Thompson, believing that they led to unrestrained and dangerous gambling, issued an order forbidding all govern-ment officials to have anything to do with them, and advising that great races should be discouraged as much as possible. This policy was continued by Mr. Aitchison (late Sir Charles), and there seemed some danger that the art of making fine racing-boats would be lost, while all the fun and jollity of the old ye-pwè, kôn-pwè, land and water sports, were put an end to, without any decrease in the amount of gambling. The habit is as engrained with the Burman as with the Chinaman, and if there are no boat-races to bet on there are lots of other things, from pony matches to gôn-nyin-to, on which sporting votaries might stake their money. There were still local matches between adjacent villages held, but they were but a sorry imitation of the old festivals, and have unfortunately led to the unpleasant speculations of the West being introduced. "Barneyings," in-and-out rowing, and all the unlovely customs of Western professionalism have sprung up as a consequence of the degradation of the old manly sport. Sir Charles Bernard, who was an ardent athlete himself, did a good deal towards reviving boat-racing. Sports have been held on the Great Royal Lake at Rangoon, it may be hoped only as a prelim-inary measure to the encouragement of longer contests on

the great rivers again.   The surest way of putting an end
to " roping " and false rowing with the object of mere money
gain, is to reintroduce the old honest, enthusiastic rivalry.
Where every rower feels that the name of his village depends
upon the prowess of his arm, there will be no " sugaring "
and ignobly waiting, in Sheffield handicap fashion, to " have
their heads loose."

All the races in the low country are rowed in hlaw hle,
or hlaw laung, that is to say, in paddle-boats.   Up country
there are frequently contests in hkap hle, " pull-away boats,"
rowed with oars, but even there the national paddle predominates.   It may be mentioned that the coast men are
by far the better rowers.   In the Mandalay October races
in 1881, a scratch Bassein boat challenged all comers, and
was victorious in every match.

There are a variety of boats, mostly, however, made on
the same model, of which the launggo is the type.   This is
simply a canoe hollowed out of the trunk of a tree, the
sides of which are drawn out by charring and inserting
wedges ; then the boat-builder chips out the centre.   The
laungsat is only a little larger and more commodious, plank
sides being added to the solid keel, if it may be so called.
The huge hnaw, or rice-boats, are made in the same fashion.

Of a different style are the pein-gaw, huge, ungainly,
barge-like things, used principally at Yenangyaung for
carrying oil.   Along the sides, projecting over the beams of
the boat, and reaching aft to the house raised on the quarter-
deck, are tagin, a sort of platform for the polers to walk
backwards and forwards on.   Pihn-gaw keep mostly in
shallow water, so that their ungainly weight may be moved
along by poles, which is much quicker and less laborious
work than rowing.

Barring exceptionally fine racing-boats, the hlawkadaw,
or hlawga, the king's despatch boats, were the finest specimens of boat-building.   They were gilt all over, even to the
kat-tat, or paddles, and the stern rose high up in the air for
the accommodation of the steerer.   The express boats, or
hpaungpaw, had usually a representation of the kalawaik,
the carrying bird of Vishnu and national emblem of the
Burmese, on the bows, and had often as many as sixty

paddlers.   Down stream they went faster than a steamer ; but they are never seen nowadays.

In the Rangoon Boat Club regattas on the Royal Lakes, a British four usually rows a Burmese ten to fourteen paddle-boat.   Honours are fairly easy with perhaps a balance in favour of the paddlers, who always get off at practically top speed.

The Intha leg rowers of the Yawnghwe Lake in the Southern Shan States, when they row in their own boats, seem likely always to beat even the best picked Burman crews.

CHAPTER XXXVII

CHESS

I DO not say that the Burmese invented chess, either for the world or themselves. As latter-day English dramatists "adapt" from the French, so Burmese play-writers steal from the Hindoos, and possibly the game of chess was got in the same way. But there is a considerable diversity in one respect. The plays are rendered into Burmese with a stupid fidelity. The sayās do not even take the trouble of altering the names of men and places, and the only difference in the pieces is that the lubyets, and occasionally even the actors of higher parts, introduce "gag" of a comic and local description to satisfy the national demand for fun and frolic, and to carry down the prosiness of the staid Hindoo. Chess may have been taken over in a similar way, and altered after the same fashion. I remember once, indeed, hearing an enthusiastic player in Rangoon claim the invention of the game for an ancient Talaing queen. She was passionately fond of her lord; he was equally fond of fighting; and to keep him by her, and at the same time out of the dangers of the wars, she invented the game of chess. The story has a certain pathos about it, and it would be pleasant to believe it true; but I never came across any other Burman who had ever heard the story, and am afraid the old sitduyin player was romancing. But if the Burmans did take the first notion from India, they have greatly altered the game, and not less improved than altered it.

It is generally believed that it is to the Hindoos that the world owes this most purely intellectual of games. Sir William Jones was quite positive on the point, and quotes from the Bhawishya Puran. This seems all the more mysterious when he proceeds : " The beautiful simplicity and extreme perfection of the game, as it is commonly played in Europe and Asia, convinces me that it was invented by one effort of some great genius ; not completed by gradual improvements, but formed, to use the phrase of Italian writers, by the first intention." But the European game is as different from the old Hindoo as the Burmese is from either. The Sanskrit name was cha-tur-anga—literally, the four members of an army : elephants, horses, chariots, and foot-soldiers. But the Hindoo game had four armies on the board ; yellow and black against green and red. Each army had a corner of the board to itself, and there were usually four players. One of the allied armies on either side attacked the immediately opposed force in flank, and therefore had an immense advantage at the start. Moreover, the allies were never sure of one another. It was allowed, and even recommended, to indulge in treachery. The black king might, in the heat of battle, attack and depose his yellow friend, uniting the two armies under himself against the green and red foe. However consonant this might be with the national character, it can hardly be claimed as a special beauty in the game. A ship, or boat, also figured somewhat mysteriously in the warfare. Moreover, the rule that the piece to be moved was determined by a throw of the dice, by still further complicating the game, virtually ruined all scientific play, and robbed it of more than half of its interest as an exercise of purely intellectual skill. When a cinque was thrown, the king or a pawn had to be moved ; when a quarte, the elephant ; a trois, the horse ; a deux, the boat. With such a method it was impossible to forecast the game —or, in fact, to work on any leading idea at all. Nevertheless, the Hindoo game is undoubtedly very ancient, and has certainly the oldest history of any known form of chess. It is alluded to in the most ancient law-books. The wife of Ravan, King of Lunka (Ceylon), is said to have invented it to amuse her spouse with the image of field war while his capital was besieged, 5000 years ago, by Rama, with his wild hordes of barbarian mountaineers, derisively called monkeys, or satyrs, in the great Indian epic. The Hindoo game, then, if it really be the first idea, has been no less altered by us than by the Burmans, as well as by the Persians.

The Burmese arrangement of the pieces differs entirely from the Hindoo, though we may, perhaps, imagine a reminiscence of the four armies in the arrangement of the pawns. The pieces are as follows :—

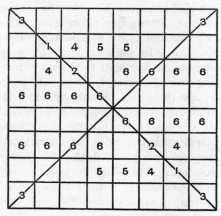

1. Min = one king.
2. Sikkè = one lieutenant-general.
3. Yittā = two war-chariots.
4. Sin = two elephants.
5. Myin = two horsemen.
6. Nè = eight pawns, or foot-soldiers.

The king has the same moves as in the English game, but cannot "castle." Sikkè can move diagonally in advance, or retrograde one square at a time. The yittās have the same power as the English castle or rook. The sins have five moves, one square at a time—one direct forward, two diagonally forward, and two diagonally backwards. An elephant cannot walk straight backwards, nor can he go sideways. The myins have precisely the same power as the English knight. The pawns act in the same way as in the English game, except that in the initial move they can only advance one square. They may become sikkè, in the event of that piece being taken, by advancing to the diagonal line which stretches across the board. When, however, the pawn replaces the dead leader, he is not allowed to remain on the square where he gained the distinction. He must be placed as one of the eight surrounding checks, at the player's option, and therefore often falls a victim to his new-gained eminence.

From the Q.'s pawn to the Q.'s R.'s pawn, the nè are placed on the third square. From the K.'s pawn to the K.'s R.'s pawn, they are placed on the fourth square in direct *échelon*. The first move, therefore, takes a pawn. The pieces may be arranged behind the pawns according to fancy or judgment. The formation represented in the figure is considered the best among Rangoon players.

Either player, however, may adopt another line of battle. He may strengthen either wing, or expose the king, according as he estimates his opponent's abilities, or the peculiarities of his play. In some respects this may be done in such a way as to be tantamount to giving a piece to an inferior player. The pawns, however, never vary in position. The board is a huge thing like an enlarged foot-stool, or a tea-table with rudimentary legs, the players squatting on mats. There is always heavy betting on the games; and when a famous player comes in from the district or over from Maulmein to measure strength with the Rangoon cracks, the excitement is wonderful, and often furnishes occasion for free fights, such as the Burmese, in their sturdy, hot-blooded way, delight in as much as any schoolboy or devotee of town-and-gown rows.

The Burmese game, as well in the names and powers of the pieces as in the liberty of individual arrangement, is thus, it will be allowed, much more like a real battle than any other recognised form. The elephant is particularly well calculated for defending the king where he is most vulnerable.

War-chariots are decidedly more appropriate to active warfare than castles. Indeed the Briton must acknowledge that the English nomenclature is bad. There was a time certainly when bishops used to buckle on their armour, and charge across the field of fight; but their disestablishment in that way came about long before the day of Mr. Miall. Boadiceas and Shan amazon leaders are too rare nowadays to have queens careering about the board as a regular thing, dealing slaughter for their less nimble spouses. The Burmese general has powers sufficient to elevate him above his men, and is yet not so loftily supreme as the mail-clad knights of romance; while if he is laid low, it is not too violent a change for the gallant foot-soldier who may win the marshal's bâton. On the whole, the Burmese game is undeniably a good one; far superior to the Hindoo, or the Persian, though possibly not requiring the skill and calculation of the European form.

It may perhaps be said that the Burmese would be more likely to get their game from their Mongolian relations than from the Hindoos. This is historically improbable, and a comparison of the games bears out the belief. The Chinese, as usual, claim for themselves priority in the discovery of the game. Unfortunately, however, they fix a date when it was invented, and this is long after the time when the Aryan game is first spoken of. Three hundred and seventy years after Confucius (B.C. 174), Hung Ko-chi sent a warlike expedition into the Shensi country, under a mandarin called Hem Sing. After one successful campaign, the troops went into winter quarters. Shensi lies in the north-west, and the weather was very cold; and the soldiers thought of their families, and wanted to go home. Hem Sing, who was a great military genius, invented the game of chess to occupy their minds and foster their military ardour. The soldiers were so delighted with it that they forgot the inclemency of the weather, and their wives and children at home, in the excitement of the new game. So the winter passed away, and in the spring-time Hem Sing took the field again and conquered the entire province, in consequence of which Hung Ko-chi assumed the title of Emperor, and chess was held in the greatest reverence ever after. So says the book of Chinese Annals.

The Chinese game is a very odd one. The pieces are played, not on the squares, but on the lines. I should have mentioned before that in none of the Eastern games are the squares differently coloured. Midway between the opposed forces flows a river. The king on either side is shut up inside a fortress, out of which he cannot move, but can shift about from one side to the other as much as he pleases. On either side of the fortress are two princes, his sons, who are equally bound to stick to the side assigned to them. There are a couple of elephants in either army, which, however, being very heavy, cannot cross the slender plank-bridge thrown over the stream for the passage of the other troops.

They therefore remain on the defensive. There are also pieces called pau—bombardiers or rocket-men—with curious powers. They can move the whole length of the board, in the fashion of the castle. If an adversary's piece intervenes, they can take the pawn or piece immediately behind it, but cannot kill direct. Students of the Persian game will be reminded of the power of their elephant. It will be seen from this cursory description that the Burmans can hardly owe their game to the Chinese. Shin Gautama sent us Buddhism from " the Middle Country " ;[1] it is possible that the game of chess came from India also. But if so, while Burmese Buddhism has hardly changed at all, and remains much more like the original teachings of the Master than the faiths of Ceylon, Nepaul, and Thibet, the game of chess has been greatly altered, and I think I may venture to say vastly improved.

[1] Myizimadetha, not the " Middle Kingdom " of the Chinese.

CHAPTER XXXVIII

GAMES

A VERY favourite game with Burmans of all ages is the gônnyinto pwè. The name is very suggestive. Gôn or hkôn means to jump, and nyin is to deny or bluster, and there is no doubt of the fitness of the implication. A more noisy and contentious game, not even omitting the uproariousness of the English enormities known as grab or pit, it would be difficult to find. Most writers on Burma have passed over gônnyinwaing lightly, as a simple, harmless, children's game. It would be well if it were only that, though the monks at the pôngyi kyaung often sally forth in great wrath (most dangerous for their future state), and armed with a stout bamboo, to put a stop to the clamorous disputes of the schoolboys over their seeds. But the police officers would tell a very different tale. Grown-up men play also, the quarrels sometimes end in assault and murder, and always in reckless gambling. Beinshu, opium-eaters, who with all respectable Burmans stand for types of iniquity, a kind of epitome of vice, often have as much as two or three hundred rupees on a single game, and the results of unrestrained gambling are best known to civilised people who frequent Monte Carlo. Consequently the police keep a sharp eye on grown-up gônnyinto players, and if a party is caught, they are all punished heavily for gambling, the daing, or keeper of the ground, being fined heaviest of all. For there are regular alleys kept for the purpose, the daing, or proprietor, carefully smoothing the ground, moistening it delicately in the hot weather, and keeping it from getting sodden during the monsoon. He charges his customers a small fee for the right to play, usually an anna in the rupee, keeps a supply of seeds ready, and acts as umpire in cases of doubt, or when a tie has to be played off.

The game is played with the seeds of a huge creeper, the *Entada Pursætha*, whose pods are five feet long and six inches broad, and the beans are large flat things, about an inch in diameter, and shaped like a lily or lotus leaf, or the flattened-out gizzard of a fowl. They are made to stand on the stalk side, flat face foremost, a little more than a diameter apart in a long row, and the object of the player is, as in bowls and ninepins, to knock down as many as possible. The players use seeds called do, exactly similar to those they aim at, or occasionally iron rings, and the distance from which they do so is agreed upon beforehand, but is never less than five or six yards. The do is spun away in crossbow fashion from the forefinger of the left hand, drawn back by the thumb and finger of the right. As the seeds aimed at are all in a line, there is plenty of room for skill in the way of putting a heavy bias on, as well as in the by no means easy matter of preventing the bean from jumping up and missing altogether. Some old players have a wonderful knack of getting a strong parabolic curve on, which succeeds in levelling a great part of the line. The difficulty of the thing cannot be realised till one has made an attempt one's self, and the result of a few experiments is usually greatly to raise the estimation of gônnyinto as a game of skill.

There are a great many ways of playing it. First, it may be premised that the ordinary value of a seed is two annas, about threepence—that at any rate is the price usually charged by the daing, who always has a great supply of them. Having got his seeds, the player puts down as many as he pleases in the row, five perhaps or ten. There is usually a preliminary dispute about some one who has not put down so many as the others, yet claims an equal chance of winning in the game. These quarrels, after having been noisily fought for a quarter of an hour or so, are referred to the decision of the ground keeper, who settles the matter off-hand, seldom knocking a man out as long as he is sure that he has no more seeds to stake. Then it has to be settled who is to have first shot, naturally among good players a very considerable advantage. This is settled by a preliminary

tournament for the best of one or three shots, the players
following one another in the order of their success in the
trial.   Then it is settled how the game is to be played.
Sometimes it is the obvious, elementary way of each man
taking the seeds he knocks down, sometimes it resolves itself
into a contest for everything staked, the man who knocks
down most taking all the seeds.   There are of course numerous bets, but they are more frequently disposed in backing
one player against another than in selecting a single individual as the probable eventual winner.

This method, however, of endeavouring to knock down
the greatest number of seeds, which is of course the commonest with children, is not so much affected by grown-up
gamblers as other elaborations of the game.   A favourite
form is that called ngalet ngalôn, where the object is, in
five shots to knock down five seeds, neither more nor less.
This is not so easy as it might seem, for the seeds are not
like marbles, and it is hardly less difficult to make them go
perfectly straight than it is to put on the proper " side."
Most men try to knock down all five at their first attempt,
and then let their remaining seeds go anyhow.   Veterans,
however, declare that the safest way is to knock down the
fifth from the end of the line with your first shot.   It then
lies as a kind of barrier to prevent the other four, when
knocked down, from rolling about and upsetting more than
the proper number.   The seeds when hit hard certainly have
very eccentric methods of spinning and wobbling about.   If
there are ties, the men of course play off, and the winner
takes the whole pool, if the collection of seeds may be so
called.   The best play is almost always seen in these ngalet
ngalôn contests.   The children's form, that of knocking down
the greatest number in one or three shots, is called pwet-tha,
and is certainly the commonest, except with the avowed
gamblers.   There are besides these two main forms many
other variations occasionally introduced, the commonest being
daungpyit and pedan.   In the former the seeds are placed
in the usual line, but all except the centre are lying on their
sides.   The players stand much farther away, and the object
is to hit the seed standing up.   Any one who does so carries
off all.   If one of those lying down is hit, the seeds from it

to the extremity of the line are taken.   In pedan the seeds
are placed in a big circle.   Some one seed, either at one of
the sides or at the back, is fixed upon to be hit.   Any one
who does so takes all, but if any other seed is knocked over
you have to pay forfeit, and add one to the circle.   This is,
perhaps, the most outrageously noisy form of all, and, like
the daungpyit, is very seldom played by any but children.

The daing or ground keeper's services are constantly
being called for.   A long-armed man is accused of delivering too far forward ; some one has got an exceptionally big
do to aim with ; one of the seeds knocked over does not
fall down flat, but leans up against another ; somebody hits
a seed already knocked down by somebody else, and by
means of it manages to level some of those left standing,
though his own seed never touches them ; cases of this kind
are always cropping up and being referred to the umpire
amidst boisterous statements and precedents referred to by
everybody present, for the betting spectators are often more
deeply interested in the matter than the actual players.
Then the police burst in and carry them all off to the
lock-up, and they are duly fined for gambling, and English
residents who look upon gônnyinto as only an elementary
kind of marbles are astonished that people should get
themselves into trouble for such a trifle.   But for all that,
gônnyinto, in its way, requires quite as much skill as either
bowls or curling, and judgment and delicacy of touch are
quite as essential as in billiards.

Curiously enough, taking gônnyinto for mere childishness,
most foreigners look upon " Burmese football " as a game.
This is certainly not the case in so far as a " game " is a
striving between one or more competitors for supremacy.
There are of course different degrees of proficiency, but one
man cannot be pitted directly against another to see who is
the better player, as you do with two lawn tennis or racket
players.   Primarily chinlôn, as it is called, is simply designed
to exercise the body, to restore elasticity to the back and
limbs cramped by sitting, reading, or writing, or even by
playing chess or gônnyinto.   The ball is composed of
wicker-work, strips of rattan interwoven in bands so as
to leave a number of pentagonal holes, and is about four

inches, or a little less, in diameter. It is extremely light, and the object is to keep the ball as long as possible in the air without touching it with the hands. Thus a single individual may play it all by himself, or there may be a circle of players who catch the ball as it comes round their way, keep it up as long as they can, until an ill-judged stroke sends it away from them to somebody else, who proceeds in a similar manner. To play it of course the feet must be without shoes and the waistcloth is tucked up close round the middle, so that the legs may be quite free. It is worth while watching a good player. He starts the ball on his knee, knocking it up, and standing on one leg all the time, or perhaps rapidly changing the knee. Suddenly he sends it up high, catches it with a back stroke with the heel, repeated perhaps several times. Then he receives it on the knee again, gradually and gently reduces the force with which he strikes it, lets it slip down to the instep, and jerks it back and forwards between the top of the foot and the knee for a time. Then from the knee he sends it into the air again, clips it between his cheek and his shoulder ; then lets it run down the side to be caught up with a side stroke of the foot, or behind to be sent up by the heel, or forwards to be caught again by the knee. The last is the most difficult, because if hit too soon with the top of the thigh, the ball simply flies outwards, and cannot be saved from falling to the ground, while even in catching it with the knee, care must be taken to hit it gently. Another very difficult manœuvre is to jump into the air, catch the ball between the feet and jerk it up again before reaching the ground. Nasty tumbles are the usual result of first attempts. A good player will keep the ball up until his strength gives way, and most Burmans, if they are not ambitious to attempt difficult strokes, can keep the chin-lôn up a very fair time. But it is not easy all the same. No part of the arm must be used, and using the toes is also barred, though in any case, with them a stroke would almost inevitably prove a failure. Still though spectators may stand and look on, and the players may try to give one another difficult strokes, the skill displayed in negotiating which is always applauded, yet chinlôn cannot be called a game, any more than dancing the Highland Fling can, for judgment as to superiority in either case must be a mere matter of personal opinion, and cannot be governed by hard and fast rules.

These are practically the only outdoor national games. Boxing is a very common institution, but there is no ordinary practice in the evenings, and when a let-pwè comes off it is a regular ceremony more resembling what would be called in Europe a match, or a tournament, than a game. A good deal of agility and skill is shown, leaps into the air, and kicks with the bare feet, and violent upward knocks with the knee finding a place which would not be allowed by the "fancy." The first drawing of blood decides a contest, however slight the injury may be. But boxing is not common now. Among the Karens near Maulmein it is still regularly kept up, and no young man would be successful in his courting unless he had taken part on some occasion or other at a let-pwè. In Rangoon nowadays contests are of regular occurrence at feast times, but the displays are in sheds and entry money is charged. Elsewhere they are not often seen, and the rule that no women shall be present is always rigorously kept.

What may be called indoor games are numerous and various. There is a game very much like the English one known as Fox and Geese. There are three big tigers, and eleven or sometimes twelve little ones. It is called legwet kya, and the object is for the big tigers to hunt down on a draught board and eat the little ones. If, however, the cubs can corner the big ones, and prevent them from taking a leap, the latter have to succumb—starve to death in fact. Another game called pasit, or chwe pyitthi, or ansa pyitthi is a steeplechase kind of arrangement, and is a favourite with children and simple country people. It is played on a board shaped and divided like that in the figure.

Cowries are used instead of dice, and the object is to complete the tour of the board as fast as possible, and to take as many opponents as you can on the way. Thus if there were two playing, the first thrower would enter at *a*, and having reached *b*, would continue from *a* to *c*, from *c* to *d*, and so on. The second would commence at *a* also, but

proceed first to *c*, thence to *d*, and so on.   A third would
start from *e* towards *f*, and a fourth in the remaining arm.

The method is as follows.   Six cowries (chwe) are taken
in the hand and thrown into a plate or cup ; if one falls
upside down it is called sè, and counts ten ; two, called pa,
scores two ; three, thôn, is the same in value ; four, le, equals
four ; five upside down, called taseit, scores twenty-five.   When

all are on their backs, it is called baya, and counts twelve.
When all six fall on their faces, chauk, and the value six.

You have three throws to start with, and can only enter
with a ten or a twenty-five ; after entering you can have
only one throw at a time.   If you are lucky enough, you
may enter two or even three racers, but if you throw three
tens running, or three twenty-fives consecutively, the hand
is lost to you, you cannot enter even one.   If you overtake
an opponent and come on to the same square with him,
you kill him and he has to go back to the starting-post, but
only if you fall on the same square, and not if he is on one
of the shaded squares, called poh or kyah, which are coloured

red or green on the board.   In this latter case you lose your throw.   The game is won by returning home first.   Thus the first player having rounded *g*, comes down the middle course and finishes at *h*; the second player at *i*; the third at *j*, and so on.   Any number can play, and if there are four, or more, and even numbers, partnerships are formed.   When three or more play, it is called mèthida.

The game is simple and harmless enough, and as there is little chance of gambling over it, pasit is but little in favour with people in the big towns.   Tônbu lein, cheating with the weight of the lime used in betel-nut chewing, is much more to their taste.   This lime, a little of which is smeared on the leaf of the betel-vine that wraps round the nut, is, if of fine quality, often sold by its weight in rupees.   Two confederates arrange a speculation together.   One of them picks out an eligible-looking bumpkin in the street, some rice-farmer, who has come in with his boat-load of paddy; or a raftsman, who has brought down a lot of teak logs; or a pious man come to worship at the pagoda.   He gets into conversation with the intended victim—asks him for a light for his cheroot, perhaps, and brings round the talk to tônbu. Then he says he has got a fine sample of it, and draws a packet out of his pocket.   The unsuspecting taw-tha admires it and is asked how much he thinks there is.   He guesses three rupees weight.   The speculator happens, singularly enough, to have a little pair of scales in the folds of his waistcloth.   The lime is duly weighed, and the countryman proves to be right—Burmans have a natural faculty for estimating by the eye.   The scales and the lime are put away, when up comes the confederate, who has been loitering about at a distance.   He pretends to recognise a friend in our farmer, with his old-fashioned zig-zag paso and red-tanned face.   After explanations he asks who his friend— the man with the tônbu—is.   The latter immediately introduces himself, produces his lime again, and asks the new-comer how much he thinks there is.   He says right off, " Two rupees weight "; our taw-tha breaks in, " No there isn't." " Bet you a-seit (a quarter century, twenty-five rupees) there is."   All Burmans love gambling, and the farmer straightway tables his pieces, thinking he has got rather a " soft " thing.

The scales come into use again, and the lime weighs two rupees—it is another packet. That night the two rascals are drunk together, and the farmer makes an offering to the nats, persuaded that there is something supernatural in the matter.

Pitch and toss is common enough in Rangoon now, as is also the three-card trick, introductions of Western industry. Pitch and toss is called myauk pan—myauk is the lion and unicorn on the old " Jan Kumpani's " coin, while the pan, the " flower," is the laurel wreath on the other side. Two rupees or pice are spun, and the bystanders call. One says two tails, and if they turn up, he wins double his stake ; similarly if he is equally fortunate as to his guess of two heads. If he hedges with a head and tail, he only wins what he laid. The " tossing shilling," and the " lucky penny," of Box and Cox, one of which had no head and the other two, are not by any means novelties in the Pabè-dan and other disreputable streets in Rangoon.

Another sleight-of-hand trick at which the town loafers are very skilful and are constantly deluding the unwary, is a performance called kyotothi, tilting at the string. A narrow strip of hide is doubled across, and the doubled end being in the centre, it is wound round and round in a complicated way. Then one of the bystanders is asked to place either his finger or a stick into the centre. The thong is then un-wound, and if the man has his finger in the doubled-up end he wins, otherwise the manipulator gathers up the money. It is obvious that manual dexterity may do a great deal in a venture of this kind, and the operator usually makes a good thing of it.

Cock-fighting is also a favourite pastime, and though forbidden by the authorities, is still carried on more or less openly in country villages and quiet streets in the towns. Thibaw's uncle, the deposed Pagān Min, who died of small-pox in 1880, was so fond of the practice that he went by the name of the cock-fighting king. In sporting villages pretty nearly every house has its kyet-hpa, or its taik-kyet, the latter, splendid-looking birds, being bred specially for their pluck in fighting.

Buffalo fights, which used to be great festivals in the

Tenasserim province, especially round about Amherst and Tavoy, have, under the influence of the British Government, almost totally died out. Each village used to have its champion, songs were composed in its honour, and special guards appointed to look after it, and the conqueror brought as much honour to the village as a personal victory of the inhabitants would have done. But they were nearly as brutal exhibitions as Spanish bull-fights, and only a little less dangerous.

Field sports are barred to all but professional hunters by the religious objection to taking animal life, though when a Burman does enter upon the pursuit, he is always an enthusiastic and skilful sportsman and generally a clever shot.

CHAPTER XXXIX

LUCKY AND UNLUCKY DAYS

It has come to be considered an axiom that the Burmese are irredeemably lazy. Some authors who have written about the country ascribe a very great number of additional bad qualities to them ; others are more favourable ; but all are unanimous in the declaration that they are lazy. The reverend missioner, Father San Germano, who was almost the first European to write a definite account of Burma, is the most unkind critic of all. He gathered together a great deal of information about the country during his long residence, but the opinion he formed of the people would be crushing were it not so strongly at variance with that expressed by a Christian priest who has been still longer in Burma, and whose knowledge of everything connected with it yields to none, the late Bishop Bigandet. But it is as well to see ourselves as others see us. The good father says : " The Burmese are distinguished for that timidity and servility which is the characteristic of slaves. . . . There is no contempt, oppression, or injustice they will not exercise towards their fellow-men when they can assure themselves of the protection of government. They are thus vile and abject in adversity, but arrogant and presumptuous in prosperity. There is no one amongst them, however mean, who does not aim at the dignity of mandarin (minister)." But the chief characteristic of the Burmese " is an incorrigible idleness. Instead of employing their time in improving their possessions, they prefer to give themselves up to an indolent repose ; to spend the day in talking, smoking, and chewing betel, or else to become the satellites of some powerful mandarin.   The same hatred of labour leads to an excessive love of cunning, and also to thieving, to which they are much addicted. . . . It would seem that it is impossible for this people to tell the truth; nay, a person who ventures to do it is called a fool, a good kind of man, but not fitted for managing his affairs."   Still the padre has a little good to say of them: "Besides giving daily alms to their talapoins, they all lay by something to be applied to some sort of public benefit.   They are very fond of thus signalising their gener-osity, and will often deprive themselves of comforts to have the pleasure of being benefactors to the public."   This is an unlovely picture.   But the good father was apparently very unfortunate in his acquaintances.

It is pleasant after this to turn to a soldier's opinion. Major Grant Allen says: "Unlike the generality of Asiatics, the Burmese are not a fawning race.   They are cheerful, and singularly alive to the ridiculous; buoyant, elastic, soon re-covering from personal or domestic disaster.   Free from the prejudices of caste or creed, they readily fraternise with strangers, and at all times frankly yield to the superiority of the European. . . . Indifferent to the shedding of blood on the part of their rulers, yet not individually cruel; temperate, abstemious, and hardy, but idle, with neither fixedness of purpose nor perseverance.   Discipline, or any continued em-ployment, becomes most irksome to them, yet they are not devoid of a certain degree of enterprise."

This is a much better certificate, but still we are accused of laziness.   Let us now turn to the last and the best authority on the subject (from an English point of view), Colonel Horace Browne, at one time Commissioner of Pegu, and always very popular with the Burmese.   The Burman, he says, "displays much spasmodic energy and general laziness, much love of feasts and shows, much disregard of the sacredness of human life, and much tenderness for the lives of inferior members of the animal kingdom, much arro-gance and inconsiderateness when placed in high position, and last, though not least, much general truthfulness, and, amongst unsophisticated villagers, the very unoriental trait of being unable to tell a specious falsehood."

The hauteur complained of towards strangers is principally due to the fact that the stranger is not a Buddhist, and has not as a boy been admitted into a monastery. To a Burman such a man is no better than a buffalo or a dog. In those of low degree this feeling shows itself in pitying kindness, in those in high positions in arrogance and insulting rudeness.

The unpleasant allegations of Father San Germano may be considered cancelled by the advocacy of the two military gentlemen, but there remains the united charge of unwarrantable laziness. Let us see what can be said for the defence on this point.

It may be taken for granted that the whole human race is more or less hampered by a dislike for work when there is no necessity for doing it. In addition to sharing this weakness, the Burman is fettered by a multiplicity of fortunate and unfortunate days. When he is born, his sadā, or horoscope, is cast, detailing minutely the moment at which he appeared, and the influence the presiding constellation has over him personally ; and this sadā must be carefully examined before anything can be done. But beyond this there are a great variety of unlucky days which more or less concern everybody, and have to be avoided if a man is to hope for success in his enterprise or his journey. To enlist the sympathy of maritime England, I will begin with the superstition about Friday :

> Thaukkya ye gyaung
> Ma thwa kaung.

> On Friday boats sailing
> Cause weeping and wailing.

On the contrary, if you begin the study of a subject on Friday you will become an authority on it. Thursday is also a good day ; but if you commence on Tuesday or Saturday you will soon die. Saturday is a bad day for everything, especially for fires—a fact which the Fire Brigade would probably corroborate. But doubtless it is somewhat irritating for an Englishman when he wants to commence a journey, and has everything ready except the bullocks for the cart, to find that he cannot persuade his servants to buy or engage them till Sunday, because such a proceeding would bring disaster on everybody connected with it. He declares it is dilatoriness, or the desire to stay and see some feast ; whereas it is a matter of conscience, and was taught to the Burman in a rhyme when he was a little boy at school. Similarly there are regulations as to the days proper for washing one's head. This is a regular ceremony, performed only once a month or so, partly because it takes a long time with the Burman's luxuriant hair ; partly because many people, especially in the small Talaing villages in Pegu, believe that too frequent washings would disturb and irritate the genius who dwells in the head and protects the man. Therefore when you collect the bark and saponaceous seeds and other material for the operation, you must remember that it is unlucky to wash your head on Monday, Friday, and Saturday. In the same way, parents sending their boy into the monastery must remember not to cut his hair on a Monday, a Friday, or on his birthday. A Burman's birth-day, it must not be forgotten, occurs once a week, and his name recalls the day.

This circumstance gives rise to a number of barriers to the proceedings of the children of particular days, all of which are taught in the linga, the doggerel rhymes of the monastic and lay schools. Pyatthada ne (unlucky days) are as follows : Thursday and Saturday in the months of Tagu (April), Wagaung (August), and Na'daw (December). The months do not exactly correspond. Tagu, the first month of the Burman year, is really half April and half May ; Na'daw, half December and half January, and so on ; which must be remembered in the months mentioned below. Thursday and Saturday mean that the people born on those days are invari-ably unlucky in the specified three months, and had con-sequently much better remain at home, talking, smoking, and chewing betel, even though it irritate good missionaries, like San Germano, than endeavour to do work of any kind which could only result unfortunately. The monastery rhyme may be rendered as follows :—

> Tagu the hot, Wagaung the wet,
> Na'daw the dull and chilly,
> Scowl on the serpent and the rat,
> So rest ye, willy nilly,—

the serpent being the sign of Saturday, and the rat of
Thursday. Similarly the sons of Wednesday and Friday
are debarred from work in Kasôn (May), Tawthalin (September), and Pyatho (January):

> Kasôn, Pyatho, and Tawthalin,
> These months are right unlucky,
> For Friday and for Wednesday
> At home or in Kentucky.

Sunday and Monday are bad days in the months of Nayôn
(June), Thadingyut (October), and Tabodwè (February):

> The tiger and the gusty roc
> Must shun Nayôn and Thadingyut,
> Eke Tabodwè with dripping lock,
> Whate'er they do 'twill bear no fruit.

The tiger is the symbol for Monday; the Galôn, or roc,
for Sunday. Tabodwè is the foggiest month of the year.

The Waso (July), Ta'saungmôn (November), and Tabaung
(March), those under the sign of the lion (Tuesday), and
the tuskless elephant, Haing—which represents the dark
planet Yahu, and makes an eighth day of Wednesday after
noontide—are shut out from active labour:

> In month Tabaung, 'twixt hot and cold,
> Ta'saungmôn, Waso breezy,
> Yahu and Tuesday's human fold
> Must take it precious easy.

On the other hand there are Yet Yaza, "kingly days,"
during which the Burman will display "much spasmodic
energy." Such are Friday and Monday in April; Saturday
and Thursday in May; Tuesday in June; Sunday and
Wednesday in July; Friday and Wednesday in August;
Thursday and Saturday in September; Tuesday in October;
Tuesday and Yahu (noon to midnight on Wednesday) in
November; Friday and Wednesday in December; Thursday
and Saturday in January; Thursday and Tuesday in February;
Saturday and Wednesday in March.

> Cease to weary,
> Whose lot's dreary,
> On these kings of kingly days.

It must, of course, be borne in mind that these days are only lucky for those who were born on them, and not for everybody.

With all this the Burman is in a very considerable difficulty between lucky and unlucky days. If he declines a piece of work because it is his unlucky season, or undertakes it, but delays commencing till his fortunate time shall come round, the foreigner accuses him of laziness in the one case and dawdling in the other. Yet many Englishmen would not sit down as one of thirteen to dinner.

It would be bad enough if this were all ; but there are other matters calling for the observance of the Burman if he would consult his well-being. It is ordained for him by paternally solicitous astrologers in what directions he must not travel at certain seasons of the year. This is regulated by the nagā hlè. The Nagā is a huge creature, half dragon, half serpent, coiled round the world, and gradually and steadily crawling in a constantly repeated circle ; so that his head is now in one place, now in another ; the circuit being completed in a year, and following the direction of the hands of a watch. You can journey from the tail towards the head with safety, but not from the direction of the head towards the tail, for then you would go straight into the monster's jaws. It is safe to go across in any direction. As long as you know the position of the head, therefore, you are safe ; and this is recorded for you in the usual linga :

> From March to May, all April through,
> The huge Nagā towards Mount Meru
> His belly turns, his back to south ;
> The west he frights with open mouth ;
> His tail curled up holds all the east.
> Mark well how lies the grisly beast.

From June to August, therefore, the head is to the north, and you must not go southwards ; from September to November the west is barred to you, and from then on till March it is dangerous to go north.

The difficulty an Englishman occasionally finds in getting boatmen to go in a particular direction, or porters to carry his baggage across country, is therefore easily accounted for without any necessity for stigmatising the Burmese as hopelessly lazy and averse to steady labour.   The fact that men are always to be got eventually is no argument against the general belief in the theory, for the English persuade people to all manner of iniquity.   Staunch members of the Order of the Yellow Robe will tell you that the brandy-drinkers and the opium-eaters (whom the English Thathana-baing, the Archbishop of Canterbury, and other good people believe to be so very numerous in Burma) are very frequently proselytes, and, at any rate, have been much influenced by the white foreigners.   And probably every officer in the Commission who has at length got together a band of men to journey towards the nagā's jaws will bear out the assertion that they must have been a bad lot, and drank raw spirits and chewed opium enough to gladden the heart of an anti-opium society man in search of a frightful example.

It may be asserted that the unlucky days were invented as an excuse for laziness ; but the prevalence of the system with regard to other matters disproves this.   For example, the blind god is supposed to laugh at barriers of rank and time and space ; but most Burmans have a profound belief in the yan-pet linga—the rhyme of hostile pairs, referred to in the chapter on marriage.   Again, in forming a partnership for purposes of trade, or the like, a due regard must be paid to birthdays.   Lucky combinations are as follows :— Sunday and Friday, Tuesday and Thursday, Saturday and Wednesday, Monday and Yahu.

When you get a Burman on his lucky day, he will display an amount of " spasmodic energy " which has surprised many travellers into calling him hard-working.   The boatmen on the Irrawaddy and the Sittang often row six, eight, and even ten hours at a stretch, on no more solid food than cold boiled rice, with a fragment or two of salt fish or curried vegetables.   But that is when it is their " kingly day."   Try them on a pyatthada day, and they will not even drift with the stream.

CHAPTER XL

THE BUTTERFLY SPIRIT

IT is a matter of common knowledge that Buddhists deny
the existence of a soul or spiritual principle in man. Each
new being, spiritual nature as well as bodily substance, is
the product of what has gone before, and differs entirely
from the previous being. That faculty which performs all
the actions referred by other religions to the soul is by the
Buddhist system placed in a sixth sense called manaw, the
heart, or faculty of knowing. This sense is as material in
its action as any of the others which are denominated seeing,
hearing, tasting, and so on. The manaw is, it is true, the
most important of all the senses. The eyes, the ears, all
the others, are merely channels to communicate impressions
to the purely intellectual faculty of knowing ; but it is not
a separate something, distinct in composition and existence
from the material body. The quality and keenness of perception of the manaw is a matter of serious importance to
its owner ; for it is only by meditation that a man can attain
to the higher heavens, and the act of meditating can only be
conducted by the sixth sense. The observance of the
precepts and the performance of good actions meet with
abundant reward in happy births on earth or in the six
heavens of the nat-dewas ; but the inward good deeds of
the soul are incomparably more meritorious, and therefore
the pondering on the lawki seit, the ideas of creatures yet
under the influence of the passions, and on the lawkotara
seit, which are the ideas of those happy beings who have
entered into the current of perfection and move about in the
regions of pure spiritualism—the consideration of these and

of the seitathit, or results immediately connected with ideas, throughout all the five stages of meditation up to upekka, lead to rewards in the twenty superior heavens, where the contemplative gradually frees himself from the thanya, or false persuasions, and acquires a contempt for matter.

All this action has its place in the manaw, or the seat of knowledge, and is duly explained to the Burman when he is in the monastery school, and afterwards, perhaps, in discourses of the Yahans in the rest-houses on feast-days, or other suitable occasions. Unfortunately, however, the matter is, to say the least, a little obscure, and not by any means easily to be grasped. Accordingly, the superstitious Burman having got a confused lot of big words into his head, after letting them simmer there for a while, evolved from his internal consciousness the notion of the leip-bya, or butterfly spirit.

This personation of the soul in a fairy-like form had natural elements of attractiveness in it; and the consequence is that the error of the unphilosophical Burman long ago has grown into a present national belief, and it is universally accepted that the life of man resides in the leip-bya and dies when it disappears. The man at the point of death opens his mouth and the butterfly escapes from the body, but only to die at the same time. Many strange things are explained by this doctrine. For example, the leip-bya is the cause of dreams. It is not absolutely necessary that the butterfly should remain constantly in the body; death will not necessarily ensue from the separation. When the man is asleep, therefore, it leaves the body and roams about far and wide. But in these wanderings it can only go to such places as a person to whom it belongs has previously been in. A straying from known paths would cause extreme danger to the sleeping body, for it might happen that the butterfly would lose its way and never return, and then both would die—the body because the animating principle was gone, the leip-bya because it had no earthly tenement to live in. The butterfly is enabled to perform these journeys through its existence as thwe seit, or soul of the blood; and it is the state of this blood which makes the leip-bya more or less inclined to roam, and directs its movements. If the blood is feverish or excited in any way, the butterfly necessarily becomes restless, and wanders about more or less rapidly and into more or less strange places, according to the degree of perturbation.   Therefore it happens that the soul thus exist-ing in itself, and straying or flying at random, sees extremely strange and fantastic visions on these voyages.   An elabora-tion of this notion divides dreams into three special varieties : those which occur at the beginning of sleep, those about midnight, and those in the early morning ; or the false, the mixed, and the true.   Bedin-sayās and wise women are for this reason always very particular in their inquiries as to the precise time at which the dream occurred.   If they foretell wrongly it is, of course, because the questionist made a mistake as to the time when his vision appeared to him.

These night wanderings of the butterfly spirit are not without their dangers.   In addition to other hobgoblins and spectres, Burma is especially plagued by evil spirits called bilus—creatures in human guise who devour men.   If they will eat the corporate man, there is small doubt what will happen to the fragile butterfly spirit should it come across such an ogre.   Cases do happen when the leip-bya is gulped down, and then the man has slept his last sleep.   More often, however, it is only a case of leip-bya lan ; the soul is scared, and in its terror sometimes runs into unknown regions, from which it is unable to retrace its steps, when of course it dies and with it the owner ; or it rushes home to its bodily dwell-ing-place with such precipitation that the whole system is disorganised and sickness follows.   This butterfly theory, therefore, offers a grand field for quack doctors, of whom there are unfortunately a very large number in Burma. When a man falls ill they dose him with all the drugs and simples they have in their little bamboo phials.   If he does not get better after taking even the fungus from the roots of the bamboo, culled in the eclipse, or vegetable soot pre-pared at the change of the moon, then there can be only one opinion ; the leip-bya has had its system shaken by some ghoulish sight ; or perhaps it is being kept in durance vile by some tasé, some demon (in the sense of the Greek δαίμων), or by a sôn, a wizard.   In this case no bodily medicine can be of any use, were it even that celebrated nostrum, the green powder, which contains 160 different ingredients. A witch doctor must be called in, and he resorts to the leip-bya hkaw. This ceremony is very much like that made use of in ordinary cases of oppression by evil genii, nat-sos, and witches. Offerings are laid outside the house, or perhaps outside the village, at night—heaps of cooked rice, bananas, salt fish, and other eatables ; and the malevolent being, whether ghostly tasé or material witch, is begged to eat this rice instead of the butterfly spirit, and to let the prisoner free. Few are hardy enough to watch and see what happens ; but the few who have done so agree in the discovery that the demon appears in the shape of a pariah dog, which does not differ from other pariah dogs in spirit, inasmuch as it will run away if you throw stones at it. The offerings are repeated till a change takes place. Perhaps the tasé is greedy, eats offerings, leip-bya, and all, and kills the man. Perhaps it is appeased. Then the butterfly spirit returns safe to its owner again, and convalescence sets in. This is called leip-bya win. Bilus are never successfully negotiated with in this way ; they are too voracious. They occasionally appear in broad daylight upon earth ; but may always be recognised, since they have red eyes and cast no shadow.

A particularly difficult operation is to separate two leip-byas that were intimately united in life. This is especially the case when a mother has died leaving a little infant. If the leip-bya kwè is not resorted to, the butterfly of the little one will follow the mother, and the child will die. A wise woman is therefore called in. She murmurs some mantras, and then places a looking-glass on the floor near the corpse. Still muttering, but with more and more rapid gesticulation, she drops a filmy shred of cotton down on the face of the mirror, and with frenzied words entreats the dead mother not to retain the infant soul, but let it come back to its earthly tenement. The fleecy down slowly slips down the mirror face and falls off into the handkerchief she holds below, and is then gently placed on the breast of the child. A similar ceremony is occasionally gone through when a husband or wife is more than usually overcome by the death of the yoke-fellow.

The whole notion is of course foreign to Buddhism, and

is viewed with great disfavour by the members of the sacred assembly, but they are no more able to put a stop to it than they are to suppress nat-worship in the subsidiary form in which it still exists. It is somewhat discouraging to those who have the welfare of the people at heart ; yet still when one comes to highly civilised countries such as are found in Europe and finds ghosts only a little less demonstratively believed in, a load is removed. The world is very small after all.

The leip-bya idea, like a good many other peculiarities of the Burmese, occasionally gets them into trouble with foreigners. It is the cause of the great unwillingness all Burmans have to wake a sleeping man. It is obvious from the above explanation of the character of the leip-bya, that it would be highly injurious to rouse a man suddenly from his slumbers. His butterfly might be wandering far from the body, and probably would not have time to hurry back to its tenement. Then the man would certainly fall sick, or at any rate would be indisposed for a time. Consequently, it is useless to tell a Burman servant to wake you at a certain hour. He will come in at the appointed time and look wistfully at you, and wish something would fall down and make a noise ; but he himself will tread as softly as a housebreaker, and will not even have the heart to instigate somebody outside to make a disturbance. The Englishman has not got " humanity," it is true ; he has not been in a monastery, and is therefore not really a " man " ; but there is no knowing but what he might have a leip-bya for all that. Consequently the master is not wakened, and gets up an hour and a half after he wanted to, and storms at the poor Burman for a lazy scoundrel who snores away till the sun is as high in the sky as the pagoda spire, let alone a tari palm.

The same thing occurs out in the country villages. An English assistant commissioner rides unexpectedly into a small townlet in his subdivision and calls for the headman. That worthy is having his afternoon siesta, and the good wife announces this with a composure which almost surprises the young sub-janta wallah into swearing. He says, " Well, then, wake him, and tell him to bring his accounts along to the traveller's bungalow." Old Ma Gyi shudders at the very thought, and flatly refuses. The Englishman gallops off in a fury at the d—readful impertinence of the people, and Ma Gyi calls together all her gossips to hear of the brutality of the young wundauk, who actually wanted her to imperil her goodman's life. It needs something more than passing examinations and being a smart report-writer to govern the people well.

CHAPTER XLI

CHOLERA SPECIFICS

OCCASIONALLY a whole Burmese village or a quarter of the town seems to be seized with sudden madness. Without a moment's warning, apparently, and moved by one common impulse, the able-bodied scramble on to the tops of their houses and fall to work to beat the wooden or mat roofs with bamboos and billets of wood. The old and feeble stand down below and thump unmelodious drums, or bray their loudest on raucous trumpets, while the women and children dance round about and open their mouths and yell. No one has any right to talk about pandemonium till he has been scared by the sudden bursting on the night air of this diabolical uproar. New-comers in Rangoon, mindful of the scares which have been frequent of late years, on hearing the outburst for the first time, are apt to believe that the long-prophesied rising of the "budmash" population has at length commenced, and that the ferocious Burman has started on the war-path. They are the more inclined to believe it because the outbreak always takes place at night, and, at a distance, suggests nothing so much as a general free fight. But it is nothing of the kind ; nothing could be farther from it. It is, in point of fact, the regular sequel to a religious ceremony. Cholera has appeared in the district. There have been a number of deaths, and the population is aroused to a sense of the danger. The terrible epidemic is of annual occurrence, notwithstanding all sanitary precautions, at the beginning of the south-west monsoon in May. The first heavy bursts of the rainy season wash all manner of surface impurities, animal and vegetable, into the wells

and tanks, and cases of sporadic cholera are the consequence. So says the civil surgeon; but the Burmans do
not believe him. They are convinced that a nat-so, some
evil spirit, has taken up his abode in the place, and is exact-
ing revenge for some real or fancied insult. They accordingly take this means of forcing him to quit; and if the
malignant nat can be supposed to have any nerves whatever,
it certainly ought to be effective.

The brethren of the monastery discountenance the practice as far as they can—as indeed every one not afflicted
with a dulness of hearing might be expected to do. It is a
remnant of the old geniolatry, and, having nothing to do
with pure Buddhism, confounds the dewas of the six heavens
with the heathenish spirits of the old wild tribes. But cholera
is a pestilence that regards not the yellow robe of the mendicant any more than the gay paso of the frivolous; and so
the pôngyis hold the ceremony which immediately precedes
the wild riot called thayè tôpthi, and display their opposition
no more violently than by getting out of the way as fast as
the dignified walk prescribed to the Assembly of the Perfect
permits.

It is related that long ago, at the time of the beginning
of religion, the terrible pestilence swept over Kapilawut, the
city of Thudawdana, the father of the Lord Buddha. Only
at the intercession and by the merits of the prayers and
good works of the saviour of the world and his assembly,
was the plague stayed, and the city saved from desolation—
hence the function called pareit yôtthi. Cholera has broken
out in the village. Several deaths have occurred in succession with the terrible suddenness which is characteristic of
the disease. The dirges played by the bands for the dead
fade into one another and break out all down the street.
Then one of the chief men of the place makes preparations
and begs the monks to come down from the monastery. A
raised dais is put up at the back of the room for the accommodation of the yahans, and covered with mats. Offerings
to the holy men are arranged in a long row before the platform—rice, fruit, flowers, betel-boxes, pillows, cups and bowls.
Alongside of these are placed the vessels which the monastic
superior is to consecrate—nyaung ye-o, sacred to the use of

the religious, and pareit-o, so called from the ceremony. These are partially filled with water, leaves of the thabye bin, a species of *Eugenia*, are put in, and along with them coarse yellow string wound round a small stick.   When all is ready the monks come down in the grey of the evening, moving, as always, in slow procession of Indian file from the kyaung, followed by their disciples carrying the large monastic fan, or perhaps an arm-load of palm-leaf manuscript books.   Meanwhile, and all through the ceremony, the people from all parts of the village come in, each person bearing his pareit-o, with its supply of thabye bin leaves and modicum of yellow string.   The pôngyis, their eyes fixed humbly on the ground, take their allotted seats without a word to any one, not even to the master of the house.   All the people kneel as they come in, and remain in the half-kneeling, half-prostrate position customary before members of the thenga.

The abbot of the kyaung then begins the service, longer or shorter according to the capability or inclination of the officiator.   Certain formulæ reciting the praises of the Lord Buddha are always chanted ; the Sèba Thila, the Ten Commandments incumbent on all believers on worship days and on the earnest always, are usually declaimed.   Sometimes it ends with this ; sometimes, if the abbot is an enthusiast, the law is preached.   Then he extends his hands over the collected vessels and consecrates them, and the religious ceremony is over.   The yahans rise and file back to their kyaung as solemnly as they came.   The presents made to them are carried off at the same time, some by the boy pupils, some by the donors.   The people then take away their pots to their houses, and shortly afterwards, at a given signal, the wild clattering on the roofs begins.   This lasts till the performers are exhausted.   Fortunately that usually occurs within half an hour.   If the malignant demon can hold out so long, it is much more than most Europeans can, and their futile remonstrances and threats sometimes add to the general din, especially if, as not unfrequently happens, the disturbance is repeated for several nights.

There is this much, however, to be said in favour of the custom, that it often actually does stay the spread of cholera

—no doubt owing to the diversion of mind produced by banging away on the top of your roof, and the confidence and hope which the operation induces. Moreover, so much damage is done to the house itself that repairs take some time, which also serves to keep the mind occupied.

When the thayè tôpthi is over, the people return to their houses, where the pots with their consecrated contents are. The yellow string is unwound from the sticks and divided into lengths. Some people hang it all round the eaves of the house in little bags, others tie pieces of it round the left wrist, more especially those who go about much. At a time when there is cholera about, most of the young men may be seen with these wristlets. A Rangoon clerk detected wearing one colours with annoyance, and says his parents made him put it on. He very probably throws it away, but the same night he will have a fresh piece on. The thread is coloured with dye obtained from the wood of the jack-tree, the same which supplies the colouring matter for the monkish garments. The thabye bin leaves are kept in the pot, or scattered about the house. The tree is particularly highly esteemed by the Burmese. A species of it, the thabu thabye bin (the Malay apple, *Eugenia malaccensis*), is celebrated as the largest tree in the island which lies to the south of Mount Myinmo. Sprigs and leaves of the thabye bin are cut, prayers and supplications for absent friends and relatives offered up before them, and then the twig is thrown into a pot of water. A song has been composed about the tree itself, and is one of the most popular of those that do not belong to the category of love-songs. The jester in a play has always an unfailing draw when, wishing to testify his regard for some one, he declares he has cut down an entire thabye bin and thrown it into the river that his friend may enjoy good health. The joke lies in the contrast between this and the couple of leaves in a small pot used by people ordinarily.

It might have been expected that contact with English civilisation and doctors would have put an end to the riotous absurdity of the thayè tôpthi; but it has not by any means. In fact the house-beating goes on more vigorously in Rangoon and the larger district towns than elsewhere. This is partly because cholera is more frequent there on account of the crowding together of the people, and the greater chances of the water being polluted ; and partly because in small villages the people very often simply abandon the place, if there seems any danger of the malady getting a firm hold. Cholera is almost certainly fatal to any Burman attacked. The usual remedy adopted is a very astringent decoction of the rind of the mangosteen fruit, but it is seldom given soon enough to be of any use ; and the Burman habit of trying to keep air away from the patient as much as possible, pretty nearly renders useless any effect the remedy might have had. * All the windows and doors of the house are covered up, and a cloth is usually thrown over the sick man's head, so that he can hardly draw breath. Under these circumstances the man smitten with cholera invariably justifies the national belief that he is doomed. Any means, therefore, of keeping away the epidemic is eagerly seized upon, if it is only the embarkation of the whole population in unlimited gônnyinto playing, as was recently recommended as a favourable diversion to the public mind in Prome. No amount of reasoning or remonstrance is likely to put an end to the infliction of the thayè tôpthi. The Government officials are helpless against the superstition, and English police-inspectors have simply to stand by foolishly with their hands to their ears till the clatter and clamour dies down.

CHAPTER XLII

MAKING GOLD

THE Burmese have no more escaped from the craze for the discovery of the philosopher's stone than other civilised peoples. Even at the present day there are numbers of goldsmiths and other handicraftsmen in the principal towns of Lower Burma who might be prosperous and happy, did not the craving for the discovery of a means of making gold perpetually disturb their minds, and impel them to waste their earnings in dabblings with mercury and strange-looking mineral and vegetable products. Mercury is what the experimenter always starts with. Every would-be discoverer commences his researches with mercury; and it is on this account a matter for congratulation that it is so expensive; otherwise, we might have far more people doing damage to themselves and others than is even now the case. A very great fire in Rangoon was caused by a searcher after secrets capsizing his crucible while suddenly pouring in mercury. For greater secrecy, and because his horoscope said it was a favourable time, he was working at three in the morning. His house took fire; and when day dawned the whole of Edward Street—one of the wealthiest inhabited by Burmans—was a heap of smouldering ashes. The originator of the fire, instead of being abused for his carelessness, was condoled with, because he was able to assert that the accident happened at the supreme moment, when he was trembling on the verge of the great discovery that would have made his own and all the neighbouring goldsmiths' fortunes. But accidents of this kind are not of frequent occurrence. The damage is usually limited to burnt fingers, and constitutions shattered with the red fumes of the heated mercury.   Sometimes, however, men who have lost their possessions in attempting to make gold, fall upon the notion of repairing their fortunes by making money—coining as it is called in ordinary parlance.   Luckily, few have the skill requisite for this smashing business ; and the counterfeit coin put about is such as should hardly deceive any man who has ever seen a genuine piece of money before.

Naturally with so many people experimenting, there are always rumours of the discovery having been made.   Indeed, methods are known by which the great object can be attained—with proper care and the selection of a favourable hour.   One of these is quite infallible, and is so regarded even by those who have tried it many times without success.   If there has been any failure it is because of some miscalculation in selecting a lucky moment from the sada, the horoscope which every one possesses ; or because some unavoidable hitch in the operations allowed the propitious hour to pass.   That there is any doubt about the feasibility of the process no one dreams of hinting.   Have not skilled sayās exhibited the metal—undoubted gold—which they have made?

This method is as follows.   On the slopes of Kyaikhtiyo, the hill on which, perched on a gigantic boulder, stands the famed pagoda of that name, grows a peculiar kind of tree, the stem of which is flattened out in a singular way, so that it gets the name of se nga-pè, from a flat flounder-like fish called nga-pè.   This tree is cut down, and the trunk is chopped into little pieces, which are then squeezed in as effectual a way as the limited machineries in a Burman's household can do it.   The chips are pressed between two stones ; or the bullock-cart is passed over them ; or the good man of the house puts his teak box on the top of them, and summons the family to sit upon it.   Any way, the chips must be well squeezed ; many failures are due to remissness in this respect.   The chips are next thrown into a long crucible, half filled with mercury, and the mixture is subjected to the heat of a roaring wood fire. By this simple process, the sayās have obtained pure gold —a little mixed with ashes, if there has been too much of

the se nga-pè, but otherwise pure enough to content the
most fastidious assayist.   The only time I ever witnessed
the operation, we were prematurely choked off by the wood
smoke and the red fumes of the mercury ; and when we
went back again towards sunrise, we got nothing but a
quantity of very malodorous charred wood.   There was a
mistake somewhere in conducting the experiment.

There is another method well vouched for, and it is much
less trying to the temper and constitution than the other,
though perhaps a little more difficult of execution ; seeing
that a good deal depends upon extraneous help, which is not
always available, and then only in special localities.   You
get a small piece of paladôtta, copperas, or green vitriol,
and persuade a fish to swallow it.   Any kind of fish will
not do.   You must seek out the nga hkônma, a silvery fish,
which grows to the length of about a foot, and is, I believe,
known to science as *Barbus sarana*.   It is most certain if
you introduce the copperas into the living fish, let the creature
loose, and catch it again.   If you are in a hurry, however,
it is sufficient to put the copperas into the dead creature's
stomach.   When it is taken out again it is quite changed in
appearance.   I have never been fortunate enough to see the
thing done, but sayās say the change is quite remarkable.
This new substance is put into a mass of copper, and either
allowed to remain there till the change comes about, or
heated in a crucible to accelerate the process.   In a successful experiment half the metal should become pure silver,
and the other half remain copper, the two being on separate
sides of the vessel and not mixed up together.   This method,
competent alchemists say, is infallible ; but somehow it does
not seem to enrich them.   Perhaps they spend their gains
in searching after more lucrative processes.   When you
can make silver, the desire to make gold is doubtless only
intensified.

I will mention only one more method, which was more
satisfactory than any while it lasted, but was brought to an
abrupt end by the exhaustion of the raw material.   A ship
was driven on shore near Negrais, the promontory on the
south-west coast of Burma, and was broken up in a violent
storm.   Among the wreckage was discovered a small quantity

of some substance, which those who found it called a-yet hkè (congealed or solidified spirit), on the analogy of yè hkè (ice). How they came to try it I do not know ; but after a while it was found out that this was the grand secret. A small fragment of this stuff proved thoroughly effectual in converting the baser metals into gold. No matter what it was tried on—tin, copper, lead, iron—the result was always satisfactory, and the discoverers travelled about the country for a time turning other people's scraps of metal into gold. Then the supply of the a-yet hkè ran out ; and the great question is now where to get more of it. The invention of compressed beer created hope ; but the acquisition of that article was disillusionising. It had not the magical properties of the a-yet khè, and it was not good to drink. There is here, perhaps, a promising field for sympathetic Western industry. It may be hoped that the wrecking of the ship had nothing to do with communicating its special virtue to the compressed spirit ; otherwise we might have an alarming series of maritime disasters all round the Gulf of Martaban. Burning houses to get roast pig would be a trifle to this.

These are a few of the methods adopted, and they may be taken as samples of them all. None of them are more scientific, and the three I have described enjoy the reputation of being entirely successful in the right hands. But the practice is much discountenanced by the pious. Alchemy is specially denounced by the Lord Buddha. It tends to induce covetousness ; and the striving is in itself the best evidence of a love for the things of this world, which incapacitate a man for the contemplative states of zān and arupa —how much more, then, for ne'ban. The monks, the Assembly of the Perfect, of course denounce it ; for, in addition to the consulting of horoscopes—itself, though universal (the pôngyi himself had one drawn up when he was a week old), a Brahminical practice, and remote from true Buddhism— there are numerous other observances connected with alchemy which are still more heretical. In addition to consulting his sadā for a lucky hour, the alchemist frequently also obtains omens through the augurs from the bones of a sacrificial fowl. It is arranged that the thigh bones of a chicken shall be examined. A condition is imposed that the bones shall exactly correspond, or that there shall be certain defined differences. The hollows of the tendons, for example, shall be like or unlike, the bones shall be even or uneven, and so on. This being accurately settled, the bones are, after the chanting of bedin, and cabalistic spells, held up side by side, and critically examined. An experienced eye is necessary to read the result properly, and interpret the full signification of the omens. Fortunately, or unfortunately, as you like to take it, if there are two augurs present, they almost always differ, and the intending experimenter is left free to follow the opinion that he approves of, or which fits in best with his plans. This superstition, besides being abhorrent in itself, on account of the taking of life, is particularly objectionable to the mendicants, as implying that there are others besides themselves commanding respect and receiving reverence. The openly avowed alchemists are therefore a much abused body. But they have the consolation of knowing that almost every Burman has tried his hand at eggayat htothi and failed. There are very many monasteries where experiments have been made notwithstanding theoretical denunciations.

CHAPTER XLIII

SUMPTUARY LAWS AND ETIQUETTE [1]

UNDER native rule the sumptuary laws in Mandalay were exceedingly strict and most elaborate in their character. Out of the capital the regulations were equally in force, but never, as a matter of fact, came into action, because the country governors took very good care to replenish their coffers out of the money-bags of every one who chanced to be fortunate in his speculations. Speaking generally, officials were the only rich people ; but in no country in the world was the official rank more open to competition, or more subject to the caprice of the king. The last mayor of Mandalay, who was also Governor of the Rafts—that is to say, Lord High Admiral—was not many years before little better than a slave, and owed his first start in life to a lucky accident. Several others of King Thibaw's most prominent advisers were among his personal attendants before he ascended the throne. There is, therefore, nothing of the caste prejudice of the Hindoos to be found in Burma. Burmans will often declare there is caste, but what is called by that name is nothing more than the arbitrary settlement by the sumptuary laws of what a man might wear and what was forbidden ; what language he may use and what must be used to him. Captain Forbes, in his book on Burma, said that these prohibitions extended in native territory to the names which might be given to a man. The term Shwe, meaning gold, was, he said, restricted as a name to people of rank. This is certainly a misappre-

[1] Since the annexation of Upper Burma these sumptuary rules are no longer law, but they are observed by very many good citizens even under British rule.

hension. It may have been an ancient law, but it was not enforced in the last years of the Burmese empire, and it does not seem to have been enforced even in the times of the haughtiest and most unreasonable monarchs, such as Tharrawaddy and Mintaya Gyi. The appellative was perhaps not so common as in British territory ; but as far as the law was concerned, the poor man might call himself and his children Shwe as much as he pleased ; only he had to be very careful how he used any of the gold he might possess in decorating his person or in adorning his house.

If the regulations did not apply to the name a man might have, they certainly did to the language he might make use of. Oriental forms of speech in self-depreciation are familiar enough. They are universal with all the nations of the East, and even turn up in the democratic West in the petitions of " your humble, obedient servant." The magniloquent and supreme nga, as applied to one's self, is not peculiar to Burma ; while hnin, addressed to an inferior, is only a little more contemptuous than the *Er* of the small German courts. The difference between the various ranks is far more distinctly marked than this in the employment of different forms of speech ; an entirely special language as applied to the royal blood, and in a scarcely less adulatory way to the members of the Assembly of the Perfect. A man " dies " ; a monk " goes back " to the blissful seats whence he came, or to ne'ban ; a king " ascends to the village of Nats " ; one of the six heavens of happiness, where the passions still reign, and in the contemplation of which Buddhists find consolation for the otherwise dismal forebodings of their faith. The Buddhist religion is thoroughly democratic. A man only is what he is through his actions in past existences. The accumulation of merits must therefore vastly outweigh the demerits in the kan of a king. However badly he may act in his regal existence, he cannot fall below the lowest seat of the dewas—at least, so official language declares. Similarly, an ordinary man " walks " ; a mendicant " stalks," or " strides," or " paces with dignified gait," or whatever may be the English honorific equivalent of the Burmese chwa ; while a king " makes a royal progress." The latter expression was emphatically correct as far as personages of the Burmese royal blood were concerned. The descendants of Mahā Thamada never went on their own legs in the open air. If they did not mount an elephant, some official was honoured with the weight of majesty on his back. In the same way, while a humble subject " eats," a pôngyi sônpônpethi " assimilates," or " nourishes his body with the alms of the pious " ; and a king demeans himself to nothing less than " ascending to the lordly board." You may " call " or " invite " an ordinary man ; to an ascetic you may " suggest an interview " ; you would be a reckless man indeed if you sought a formula which in the faintest imaginable way would suggest to a king that you wanted him to come to you. When your visitor departs, if he is on familiar terms, he says, Thwa-mi nŏ, " I say, I'm going," and you politely respond, Thwa-ba, " By all means, go away " ; if he stands a little in awe of you, he says, Thwa-daw-mi, " Honoured sir, I take my leave " ; on the other hand, when, after a conference with a holy brother, you take your departure, you say, " My lord's servant does obeisance " (literally, " kowtows with his forehead "). When there was a king he did not give you the chance to say anything ; he flung out of the throne and disappeared behind a blue curtain, while your eyes were fixed on the ground a couple of feet before you.

And so it goes on through a triple language, which makes Burmese of the palace an unknown tongue to the best foreign scholar. Tales are told of the ludicrous mistakes of men, who to ordinary people could speak Burmese, and therefore imagined they might venture on it with the king. Thus it was with a bluff English manager of one of the numerous mills which King Mindôn built and kept going till he got tired of them. This gentleman, in replying in the affirmative to some remark of the Lord of the Golden Palace, horrified the court by saying hôkde instead of the prescribed tin-ba payah, " I think with your majesty." The expression to palace ears was much the same as if some one were to say to His Majesty the King of England, " Right you are, old cockie." The court language is still kept up by all Burmese in their intercourse with superior officials.

If the proprieties of language were carefully observed, the regulations as to wearing apparel and ornaments were far more minute, and guarded with the most jealous care. The almost wretched character of the houses of Upper Burma, as compared with those in the lower territory, was very apparent ; but what struck a stranger even more was the absence of the gay dress which is so pleasant and picturesque in Pegu and the seaboard provinces. There was indeed no law against any one wearing the most brilliant paso he could get ; but the money was wanting to support the character. A man with a fine waistcloth would be considered to have the money at the back of it, and might have to sell his dress to meet the contributions demanded accordingly by the local official. In Lower Burma, every one has a feast-day dress, however poor he may be. He gets the money for it by a week's work, perhaps backed up by a lucky bit of gambling. Then he is at liberty to strut about and do nothing till the clothes get shabby, when he has to bestir himself again. In British territory, too, he might decorate his kilt with any number of representations of the peacock. An Upper Burman would have been promptly put in gaol—he would even have run some risk of being killed outright—if he ventured upon one. Peacocks were for personages of the blood-royal. Most people in independent territory wore no coats at all ; but if they did wear coats, they had to be of the simplest possible " Chinese cut." Long-tailed taingmatheins, surcoats and the like, were reserved for officials, with regulations as to buttons, gold or otherwise, and other minutiæ which must have severely taxed the memory of informers and chamberlains.

As we ascend in the social, or rather the official scale,— for all dignity came from office, or from a special patent from the king—distinctions thickened. Naturally in the land of the umbrella-bearing chiefs, the huge htis afforded a prominent and obvious mode of marking rank. The umbrella is twelve or fifteen high, with an expanse of six feet or more across. A poor man had nothing to do with these big umbrellas whatever, unless he were employed to carry one over his master's head. If he owned an umbrella at all, it had to be short in the handle and otherwise of Western dimensions. Royal officials about the palace had their umbrellas painted black inside ; country people, and those

not directly connected with the royal abode, had the palm-leaf
as near the original colour as the varnishing with wood-oil
permitted. Some had permission to cover the wide surface
with pink or green satin; others, more honoured, might add
a fringe, either plain or embroidered. A golden umbrella
was given by special grace to the highest wuns and the
royal princes. A white umbrella belonged to the king
alone and to religion, and not even the Eingshemin, the
heir-apparent, when such a person existed, was allowed to
use it. Matters were still further complicated by the number
of umbrellas. Nine white ones marked the king; the Eingshemin had eight golden ones; and the rest of the royal
personages numbers corresponding to their achievements, or
the regard the king had for them. If they achieved too
much, however, and became popular, they died. Distinguished statesmen and generals might have several gold
htis, which were duly displayed on all public occasions,
and were put up in the house in prominent places. The
king's "agent" in Rangoon had only one, which very fairly
represented the consideration in which Great Britain was
held, and the official rank thought good enough to communicate with the Chief Commissioner. A favourite trick
of the king, Naungdaw Gyi, was to issue perpetually new
edicts as to the length of umbrella handles and the proper
measurement of the paso. District officials used to make
large sums of money in the way of fines in those days, and
occasionally themselves fell victims. There was nothing of
the kind latterly, unless we may consider the queen Supayalat's announcement as to the way in which her hair was
dressed, being patented as her sole prerogative, an instance
of the same nature. Nevertheless, the general distinctions
were very tenaciously held by. Innocent, unwitting Englishmen got themselves into serious trouble in Mandalay by
going about carrying silk umbrellas with white covers. The
offence was high treason and merited death. None actually
underwent the supreme penalty, but there were a few who
had vivid denunciations for the stocks.

The metal, size, and construction of spittoons, betel-
boxes, cups, and the like household furniture for different
grades were rigidly demarcated, and afforded the most

minute evidences of the owner's rank and his precedence in that rank. Anklets of gold (kyegyin) were forbidden to all children but those of the royal family on pain of death. Silk cloth, brocaded with gold or silver flowers and figures of animals, might be worn by none but the royal blood and such of the wunkadaws, the minister's wives, as received a special grace enabling them to use it. Similarly the usage as to jewels and precious stones was very carefully laid down. Very few besides the king and his kinsfolk might wear diamonds. The display of emeralds and rubies was restricted in like manner, and so on with other precious stones less esteemed by Burmans. All rubies above a certain size found in the country were the property of the king, and the hapless digger as a rule got nothing in return. His head paid the penalty if he listened to the temptings of black merchants from India, and chipped it so as to bring it under the royalty size. Kadipa panat, velvet sandals, were allowed to none but persons of royal blood. The use of hinthapada, a vermilion dye obtained from cinnabar, was very jealously guarded. The kamauk, a great wide-brimmed hat, was an honour eagerly sought after by the lower rank of officials. The institution was not very ancient, and was primarily due to a prophecy that Burma would come to be ruled by a hat-wearing people. To cut out the Englishmen, therefore, the kamauk was invented, and was looked upon as a great distinction. Hundreds more instances might be given of the yazagaing, the sumptuary rules; but the above will probably suffice to exhibit their scope and character.

Our present Burmese subjects delight in nothing so much as in their immunity from these enactments; and perhaps the permission to bury their dead in any way they please is the most popular privilege. In Mandalay, exclusive of the ceremonial at the cremation of a monk, which is identical all over the country, five kinds of funeral were ordained by the yazagaing. First, that of the king; then of any member of the royal family. Even if one of them were executed, he was put in a red velvet bag and committed to the waters of the Irrawaddy. Third in order were the funerals of those who died in the enjoyment of ministerial office—not always a certain thing, if the recipient did not die shortly after his promotion.   Then came the obsequies of thutés, " rich men," people who had royal edicts conferring that title on them ; and finally the rites of poor people, which were practically no rites at all.   They probably would not even have been buried were it not for sanitary reasons.   But now in all Burma the poorest man, if he can borrow the money, may have any honours he pleases for his dead.   He may shade the catafalque with golden umbrellas, or white ones for the matter of that ; he may hire elephants ; he may fire guns, as long as he does not do it in the public thorough-fares ; he may have any number of bands of music ; he may erect a pagoda over the ashes of the deceased ; he may revel in all the honours restricted by the yazagaing to the most privileged dead ; and, in consequence, he may suffer in pocket as much as he dares.   Further, he may heap up honorifics in his conversation and correspondence to the utmost of his desire and capability ; finding infinite gratification in the fact that in former days the use of a single one of them would most assuredly have resulted in his being lodged in gaol, there to be treated according to the way in which he was able to satisfy the rapacity of his guardians.   If yazagaing was unpleasant when it was in operation, the contemplation of it certainly affords an unfailing pleasure to those who are exempt from its provisions.

CHAPTER XLIV

WIZARDS, DOCTORS, AND WISE MEN

WIZARDS and witches are very common in Burma. The thing runs in families, and on the Chindwin river in Upper Burma there is a village called Kale Thaungthut, "the small town at the top of the sandbank," where the entire population is credited with supernatural power of this kind. They have a king there, and if a person who has been bewitched goes to him and represents that he has been malignantly and unjustifiably laid under a spell by some unknown person, the wizard king goes through some inverted prayers and ceremonies, and utters an incantation, which forces the bewitcher to his presence. An explanation is then demanded, and if no just cause can be shown, the witch is punished and the afflicted person is freed from his ailment. Many bewitched people who have gone there to be cured have, however, never come back again, and pilgrimages thither are therefore not so common as they might be otherwise, and of course no one, not afflicted, would be reckless enough to go, as it were, into the lion's den.

But there are good witches and bad. There are the sôns, who delight in nothing so much as in killing people, afflicting them with epilepsy, fits, and divers other ailments ; and there are the wézas, who are good people, and strive to overthrow the machinations of the sôns against the welfare of mankind, while themselves learned in all the knowledge of the mystic art. Wéza simply means wisdom or knowledge, and the sorcery studied by both classes is the same. Both kinds of wise men are divided into four orders, according

to the branch of learning to which they have applied themselves more particularly.   Thus there are—

1. The Pyada wéza, the mercury wise man.
2. The Than wéza, the iron wise man.
3. The Se wéza, the medicine wise man.
4. The In wéza, the wise man learned in cabalistic signs
   and squares.

The than and in sorcerers are the most powerful and
efficacious in their workings, whether for good or evil, and
the others are looked upon more as experimenters and candidates for the higher ranks than as legitimate wizards.   To
the class of mercury wizards belong all those who make a
regular practice of the study of alchemy with a view to the
production of gold and silver, and on this subject almost
every Burman has some pet notion.   The medicine wizards
are those who set up as professional doctors on the score
of a particular knowledge of herbs and simples.   It is a
very simple matter starting as a doctor in Burma.   All you
have to do is to assert that you have acquired a special
knowledge, and set to work prescribing the most villainous-
tasted and drastic medicines you can concoct.   As long as
an undeniable result one way or the other is produced you
are sure of getting a certain amount of reputation.

The than and in practitioners have a more legitimate
title to the name of conjurers or workers in magic.   The
title of iron wizard is merely typical, and implies that the
man has a knowledge of the properties of all natural objects,
and is as capable, or more so, of acting the *rôle* of a medical
adviser as the professed doctors.   The discovery and preparation of the pieces of metal, stones, and what not, that
are let under the skin of soldiers and dacoits is carried on
by them, and this vending of charms is a regular source of
income to them.   An occasional marvel worked now and
then acts as a recommendation and advertisement of their
powers.   Thus I have seen a hmaw sayā, a kind of generic
term applied to all wonder-workers, roll up pieces of gold
and silver leaf and thin sheets of copper, and throw them
into a bowl of water.   They of course sank immediately to
the bottom, and then the sayā would make passes with his

hands and mutter an incantation, when the metal would slowly rise to the top and float there. When sceptics were present, this man would suddenly stop the charm he was uttering, and the bits of metal would either remain floating in the middle of the bowl of water or sink down again, according to the part of the spell to which he had reached. How it was done is only known to wizards of his class and sleight-of-hand people perhaps, but to the actual fact of this khôntet letpwè, as it is called, numbers of people, Europeans as well as Burmans, can testify. The conjurer is a well-known man near the village of Pantanaw, fifty miles or so west of Rangoon.

But however many miracles the than wéza may work, he is always exceeded in reputation by the constructor of cabalistic squares and symbols. These are in constant use by every Burman, or rather he gets them made and interpreted for him by a proficient. The horoscope which every one has drawn up at his birth has numbers of these mystical numbers on it, from which lucky days and dangerous combinations may be learnt. To calculate the more harmful spells the in sayā should have these data, or at any rate should know the date and hour of the victim's birth. Therefore it is a safe rule never to let a wizard or conjurer see your sadā, or to mention the hour of your birth to any one whom you may suspect of having an ill-will against you, for he might from even that one fact have a most potent charm thrown over you. These mystic squares and numbers have most extraordinary virtue. By holding up one of a particular kind for a short time you can set a house on fire. Another in engraved on a stone will make it float, and such a stone, buried in the skin of a man's body, would prevent him from drowning, unless some other magician destroyed its influence by a more potent spell. If you scratch an in on a tree or a house, you can make lightning strike it; another arrangement of the cabalistic words or numbers will preserve it from such a calamity. There is probably not a single Burman, tattooed at all, who has not several ins on different parts of his body. Some of them protect from special ailments; the most common are those which avert dangers from bullet or sword-cut.

The doings of the wizards therefore enter largely into Burmese domestic life. There is a sôn in the neighbourhood, and all the mischief which happens there is ascribed to him, while the aid of the in sayās and others is called in to frustrate his knavish tricks. The sôn is of course unknown, or the people would soon make short work of him. In remote country places, among other remnants of trial by ordeal, they still occasionally put a suspected person to the old test. A woman is suspected of being a sônma. Her hands and feet are tied, and she is placed between two boats moored out in the river. A quantity of filth is heaped upon her, and the boats are then drawn away so that she falls into the water. If she swims she is a witch, and is put to death. If, on the contrary, she sinks, it is a proof of her innocence, and the accusers are punished. To prevent her from being drowned, a rope made of green bark is tied round her waist, so that she may be pulled on shore again. The great danger from the witches is that, like the *wehrwolf*, they can assume the appearance of animals, or living people, even of one's own relations. If, however, the apparition is wounded, the same injury will be found on the person of the actual witch. Few people, however, have the courage to attack a nocturnal visitant whom they believe to be a sôn, and prefer propitiation in the shape of refections laid outside the house. In all these points the beliefs and fears coincide with those of other countries, and it is therefore unnecessary to do more than allude to them.

The rudiments of the science are contained in the volumes of the Bedin and a book on astrology and cabalistic science called the Deittôn. These are very imperfect, and individual magic-workers advance far beyond the matter to be found in them. It is said that these books were complete, but that in the time of the Lord Buddha the people, worked on by his vivid preaching, seized on all the magic volumes, together with all weapons and objects for destroying life, and heaping them together, set fire to them. But Dewadat, cousin of Shin Gautama, and always plotting harm against him, snatched several of the sections from the flames, and so a portion of the old science was preserved in the world. This tradition of course shows the attitude of the monks and the

religious towards the students of this sort of learning. Nevertheless, just as every Burman at some time in his life dabbles
a little in alchemy, so the bedin sayās and hmaw sayās, and
the magicians, good and evil, obtain believers and clients.

As the sôns are supposed to afflict people with strange
illnesses, the province of the wézas becomes very much mixed
up with that of the professional doctors. The latter cannot
complain, and the general public can see no reason why the
one should not be as good a physician as the other, for doctors in Burma take no diploma, and are not required to give
proofs of skill in the healing art to any one but themselves.
Many of them therefore are the most arrant charlatans, giving
medicines according to fancy and in unlimited quantities. On
the principle of like to like, prescriptions mainly composed of
cayenne, cloves, ginger, and the like, are made up for fever
patients, while purgatives are rigidly withheld. If a patient
says he is no better five minutes after he has swallowed a
dose, something else is tried, and so on, till the wretched
victim has a stomach loaded with drugs to the limit of the
prescriber's pharmacopœia. These quacks are too often taken
as the only representatives of Burmese medical skill, and it
is denied that any one in the country has a right to the title
of doctor at all. But it is certain that some have really useful
and efficacious remedies for ordinary ailments, such as jungle
fever, dysentery, and other frequently-met-with diseases, while
it is admitted that they are particularly successful in the
treatment of sores and ulcers. I knew of a case in Rangoon
where varicose ulcers, which had resisted the efforts of the
best English doctors in Rangoon and Calcutta, yielded to
the simples of a Burmese sethama. He used earth-oil with
an infusion of some seed or bark, and speedily effected a
cure. The Burmese *materia medica* consists of barks, leaves,
flowers, seeds, roots, and a few simple minerals, of which
they have an empirical knowledge. They especially deal in
pills and powders, which they carry about with them in little
phials of bamboo. These little cylinders are usually gilt and
painted bright red, and are always strongly perfumed. It
does not so much matter about the materials as at what time
of the moon and under what constellations the ingredients
are gathered. Whoever reaches a place within three days

of the falling of a thunderbolt and finds meteoric stones, has sufficient to set him up as a doctor at once. The scrapings of the stone, among other things, are the best possible ophthalmic medicine. Liquids are very seldom used. There are, however, two schools—the datsayās, or dietists, who trust solely to regulating the patient's food according to the derangement of the elements, which is supposed to cause his disease, and eschew drugs ; and the beindawsayās, who rely upon the exhibition of medicines. These last, the druggists, are far more numerous than the dietists. It is a great deal more easy to get a reputation with potent drugs than with a simple regulation of the diet, and accordingly an upstart doctor is always a druggist. The best advisers are those who combine the two systems, but such sensible practitioners are unfortunately few and far between.

Both assert that the human body is composed of four dat, or elements. These are—patawi daht, earth ; apaw dat, water ; tezaw dat, fire ; wayaw dat, air. Akatha, or ether, is sometimes added to these, but the doctors mostly disregard it. Earth constitutes the flesh, bones, hair, intestines, and the like members of a man. Water constitutes the fat, blood, bile, spittle, mucus, etc. Eating, drinking, chewing, and licking come from the fire element. Air produces the six kinds of winds. Any derangement of the equilibrium of these elements makes a man ill, and it is important to know the precise time of a man's birth in order to know in what proportion the dat should be present. Therefore in the case of illness an experienced doctor almost always examines a man's birth certificate before he looks at the sick man himself. Besides the derangement of the elements, diseases may be caused by kan, the influence of the sum of good and bad actions a man has done in past existences. If a man is ill of kan, nothing will cure him but the preponderance of good in his past lives. Again, a man may fall sick through derangement of his seit, or mind ; through the influence of the seasons, utu ; or, lastly, through food, ahāya. These causes, being laid down as the basis of the diagnosis, naturally do not always lead to the best results in the case of affections which are in any way out of the common run. Even in perfectly evident illnesses, however, such as low fever, two persons in the same house afflicted in the same degree with the same ailment, are treated differently, simply because they were born under the influence of different planets, which have a special control over the effects of utu and ahāya, or over the respective relations of fire and water.

The dietists are often particularly absurd in their regulation of the diet from the horoscope. Having ascertained the day on which the patient was born, they will forbid him to eat articles of food whose names commence with any of the letters assigned to that particular day, most especially those which have the same initial letter as the sick man has himself. Thus a man born on Sunday will have to eschew eggs (u), cocoanuts (ônthi), and other edibles whose name commences with a vowel. One whose birthday is Thursday must give up pumpkins (payônthi), mangosteens, and gourds (buthi), while a Monday's child must refrain from seasoning his curry with ginger (kyinsein) or garlic (kyetthônbyu), and so on through all the other days. It is worthy of note, however, that those born on a Saturday are never forbidden to eat their rice (tamin), nor those on Friday their curry (hin). An attempt to ostracise the staff of life, as curry and rice is to all Orientals, would only result in bad treatment to the too pedantic and precisely logical practitioner. Such affections are called " Monday's sickness," " Tuesday's sickness," and so on. (Taninla, Inga kan kaitthi.)

These vagaries of the dietists are, however, far from universal, and emanate mostly from the manifest quacks of the profession, just as newly-set-up druggists will imagine specially curative properties in every strange and new leaf, or seed, or mineral they come across, and manufacture such extraordinary compounds as the green powder nostrum, which was exhibited to an astonished English M.D. with the information that it contained one hundred and sixty different ingredients and was infallible in its results. No doubt it was.

There is no denying that the excitability and impatience of the people react on the proceedings of the Burmese doctors. Whenever a man falls sick he gets into a feverish state of alarm about himself, and probably sends off for several doctors at once. The first one that comes prescribes, say for the liver. If the sick man does not feel better within a quarter of an hour at the outside, the physician is paid his fee of a few annas, sixpence say, and dismissed, and another is called in. Possibly he decides that the constituent of the disturbing element is the blood—the element of water, and not that of earth—and gives a dose accordingly. Should this not be speedily effective, he too gets his sixpence and his *congé*. And so on, as long as the means of the patient or the supply of doctors holds out. One consequence of this system is, that the richer a man is, and the more doctors there are in the neighbourhood, the greater is the probability that he will die ; another equally unsatisfactory result is that the doctors, to maintain a reputation and ensure clients, are obliged to make their medicines as griping in character, as unpleasant in smell, and as nasty to taste as possible. In the larger towns many of the better-class Burmans resort now to English doctors or apothecaries. In many villages still, however, and in old-fashioned families, the patient is usually killed off by the variety of drugs given him by different doctors.

But in small towns and country villages the physicians are few, and when the se sayā cannot cure the sick man, he declares that he is possessed by an evil spirit or under a sôn's spell, and calls in the assistance of a witch doctor, a wéza of any one of the different classes, by preference, of course, an in wéza. Then there is a fresh consultation over the birth horoscope, an examination of the charms there may be on the sick man's body, a muttering of prayers and incantations, and finally the bedin sayā agrees that the man is bewitched. Thereupon he ties a rope round the patient's neck, and after chanting a formula with occasional jerks on the line, asks the demon in the victim what he has come for. If any answer is given and an object mentioned, this is taken to be the thing required, and it is placed outside the house in the road and left there all night. It will be gone by that time if it is worth taking (by men or nats). If the evil spirit does not then go out of the man, or if the tugging at the rope brings forth no answer, stronger measures are re-sorted to. He is soundly beaten with a stout bamboo, pins are stuck into him, red pepper is forced into his eyes, and the louder he shrieks and groans the better pleased are his friends and relations, for it is the witch, or the natso, that is suffering, and not the sick man at all. If this treatment does not kill or cure him, a final effort is made. A middle-aged woman, sometimes a member of the family, dresses herself up in a fantastic way, and assumes the name of " wife of the evil spirit." A shed is erected for the occasion just outside the house. Music is brought, and the woman begins to dance, slowly at first, and then gradually more and more furiously, until at length she works herself into a regular frenzy or ecstasy. Then it is supposed that the demon has passed out of the sick man into her, and that whatever answers she now gives to questions are the utterances of the demon. Consequently, whatever she directs is implicitly carried out. The instructions usually resolve themselves into offerings to be placed outside for the evil spirit at nightfall. If this fails, then the witch doctors and medicine doctors unite in declaring that the nat is too strong for them, and abandon their patient. Occasionally, if he is of a very strong constitution, he revives after that. Such performances are limited to remote jungle places nowadays. Thus, however, the provinces of the physician and the necromancer run into one another, and it is difficult to say where science ends and magic begins.

Shampooing is almost always employed in every disease, in addition to the prescriptions of the doctor ; and here, at any rate, we have real skill. The shampooers are almost always women, though most men know a little about it too. A professional has a most wonderful knowledge of all the tendons and muscles in the human body, and follows them up with a light pressure of the fingers that affords a relief in the case of rheumatism and stiffness from exhaustion, which is simply incredible to all but those who have experienced it.

In addition to their other work, the hmaw sayās are very much resorted to for love philtres and potions by both sexes. They have always an answer pat if the prescription fails : it is due to the opposition of the eingsaung nat, the guardian spirit of the house ; or the applicant has made a mistake as to the date of birth of the object of his affection

Knowledge of this latter particular is imperative, and an error of an hour or two makes all the difference in the composition of the potion.

It ought to be unsatisfactory to an intelligent Burman's feelings to think that the man who prescribes for him in a dangerous illness is possibly at the same time mixing cunning draughts for a love-sick maid, or is manufacturing an image of a girl with magical charms and drugs which shall drive the original mad and soothe the vengeful wrath of the rejected suitor. Perhaps it is on this account that a Rangoon Burman, if he falls ill out in the district anywhere, hurries back to town as fast as he can. If he cannot do that, the best thing is to call in a wéza in preference to an unknown doctor; for while the former will probably confine himself to incantations at first, the dietist will irritate all the gastric juices in your body by prescribing some new variety of food, and banning everything you have been accustomed to; while the druggist will cram you to the throat with cathartics and anthelmintics, with arsenic, fungi from bamboo roots, green vitriol, decoctions of lemon grass, borax, croton seeds, and vegetable soot.

The father of Burmese medical science was the celebrated physician Zewaka, who once cured a colic which afflicted the Lord Buddha Gautama, by simply giving him three flowers to smell. Upon the petals were strewn some potent powders which restored perfect health in a few hours. To this good medico is to be ascribed the assertion that the diseases which afflict mankind are ninety-six in number. These may vary in their symptoms according to the thirty-five tempera-ments, the forty-five accidents, the sixteen dangers, and the four elements, but there are no more than ninety-six wedana for all that. Accordingly, a very common beginning to a formal Burmese letter is to say that by his correspondent's good wishes the writer has been preserved from the ninety-six andayè; the thirty-two kan-chammā, or pieces of bad luck; the twenty-five baya, dangers from assassins, wild beasts, and the like; and finally from aneitta bala, evils of all kinds, envy, hatred, malice, and all uncharitableness : his friend's regard has kept all these things far from him, may the writer's good will be not less efficacious. Therefore it is very essential that even the most empirical doctor should know at least the names of these diseases. The mere sound of them is as good as medicine to a man with a stomach-ache.

Bewitchings, of course, do not count as diseases. Very often when a man has very strong griping pains which no amount of drugs will serve to alleviate, the doctor declares that there is an a-pin in him. Some wizard has introduced a piece of raw flesh into his stomach by means of a spell, and this goes on drawing everything to it till it kills the man. When a sick man is unable to pronounce certain letters the doctors are able to calculate in how many days or hours he will die. It is not wise to dispute this. The fulfilment of their prophecies lies very completely in their hands.

Very often images of pagodas and Buddhas may be seen outside a house in the country villages. There is some one sick within, and the pious resort to this expedient to get rid of the malady. This method is called payā tayā, and does not exclude medical advice. The figures are small, and are usually made of pasteboard or clay. A man afflicted with a headache will often hang up pictures of peacocks and hares under his eaves, along with small fans. The peacock represents the sun and the hare the moon, and the indisposition is supposed to result from sun or moonstroke. Sometimes a sayā, when he is called in, will recommend that the patient be moved a little to the eastward or the westward, if his illness arises from kan. Similar to this is the ceremony called yedaya yayi or yedaya sin. A small coffin with a tiny corpse inside it is manufactured and carried a small distance to the east or the west and there buried. When the ayôp, the effigy of the patient, has been thus disposed of, he ought to get well. These matters are decided from the sick man's horoscope, which shows from what constellations he is particularly likely to suffer harm.

The witch doctor usually has an elaborate rod called ywatan, marked all over with cabalistic figures, and often with medicines let into it. The sayā stands before the possessed person and threatens a blow. The witch or spirit in the victim then becomes anxious and pays reverence with clasped hands. It is then forced to relate exactly its name place of abode, friends and relations, and so on. The possessing demon is usually a witch, and she acknowledges that she has entered the patient from motives of hatred or revenge, The wise man could now kill the witch with his bedin if he pleased, but is usually persuaded by the relatives of the sick man not to do so. A desire not to spoil his own trade is also not without its argument. So he accepts a number of presents from the patient's family, and is then won over, contenting himself with giving the possessed person a sound thrashing as a remembrance of him and a return for the fees. Then he commands the witch to depart and not come back again. As a conclusion the victim and his relations are enjoined not to pursue the witch any farther. Sometimes, however, they are obstinate, and refuse to rest here. Then, if the affair has happened in native territory, the case is brought before the magistrate, who has the accused tied to a bamboo and thrown into the river along with the accuser, who is served in the same fashion. The one that sinks wins the case, and the loser pays all costs. In English territory the magistrate has the complainants bundled out of court.

If any one doubts the power of the hmaw sayā, he works a miracle to cure them of their scepticism, and prove that he governs all creatures. He gets an empty earthenware jar, covers it with a cloth, and repeats his spells over it. When the cloth is removed, there is smoking-hot rice and roasted fowl in the jar, and those present are allowed to eat as much as they like. If they eat with perfect belief, they will never be hungry again ; but perfect belief is practically never found. Sometimes, however, a demon gets angry at the display of power, and interferes in an officious way. He steals some of the cooked meat out of the jar, and does his best to work a counter-miracle. He never quite manages to do it, but the ceremony is disturbed by his interference and has to be gone through again. Sometimes the sayā himself indulges in a little pleasantry. The spectators see a beautiful melon so juicy and ripe that their mouths water at the very sight of it ; but when they seize a piece and already feel it between their lips, it vanishes away and they bite their own fingers. Unless they are hopelessly stupid they do not laugh at hmaw sayās after that.

The following are a few prescriptions for whitlow and bad sores from a Maulmein doctor's books :—

1. The " hand " of a tauk-tè, the big trout-spotted gekko, that haunts old trees and the thatch of houses ; or, more probably, a bit of the stem of an epiphyte called the tauk-tè's hand.

2. Sulphur.

3. The bulb of a white lily.

4. A chilli roasted.

5. Cock's dung.

Mix in equal parts, and stir while heating it, and finally add some earth oil.

Again : Take a sufficient quantity of cock's dung, add to it a small quantity of copperas, pound them well together, and then mix with earth oil and some sesamum oil.

Seven or eight dry seeds of dankwè (*Cassia fœtida*), well bruised, and then intimately mixed with a little congee (rice water), with " sufficient " earth oil added, also proves a very effective remedy.

The bedin sayā's books are partly written, partly filled, with magic figures and pictures. The squares are all formed in accordance with the ordinary Hindoo law. When the wise man is asked questions, he keeps writing down numbers and characters on his parabaik tablets and rubbing them out, chanting to himself all the time. Sometimes he shakes cowries and seeds together, and when they fall out, decides from their position which of the pictures or rhymes in his book is to be consulted. Each of these gives its own answer, but they are not always as definite in their character as is desirable. The sayā always speaks in the declamatory monotone of the linga.

The following are the names of some of the familiar spirits and their likenesses :—

Upadana Pyuda, a spirit who lives under the earth and protects the husbandman. When he comes above ground he rides on a serpent. The inquiring farmer whose cowrie refers to this picture is most fortunate.

Sadi Wazadat, a wild figure galloping on a horse. This means failure of the attempt.

Saka Bada, a monkey mounted on a goat. Denotes fertility of mind.

In another picture a crow is represented breaking a vessel full of money with its beak. Close at hand are a man and woman embracing one another. This denotes loss.

A man and his wife represented dancing together signify great gifts to the pagoda.

Another picture, which represents a husband and wife standing together in front of a house, with a horse and cow near it, denotes that the child to whom this picture may refer will be a farmer.

Near the picture of a dog, which one man holds by the tail while another hits it on the head, is written : " When the lot falls here, be not boastful, but humble ; avoid pride and assumption, for that will only raise up enemies for you."

The following are some spells :—

Take this amulet (a piece of bone carved rudely square, and with mystic figures on it), put your foot up against a thabye tree, and repeat the Ittipithaw (a form of worship in learning which one spends four or five months in the monasteries) thirty-seven times. Then you will be able to turn any given man into a ghost and make him do as you please.

Take the stalk of a betel leaf in your hand. Repeat " Ôm padan rupa wari thwa ha " seven times, and then throw the stalk at the person. He or she is sure then to listen to what you say.

The following is a charm to cause a dream about your lady-love :—Get an exact likeness of her made. Find out the hour and day on which she was born, her name and exact age. Then having begged permission from the guardian spirit of both the houses (your own and hers), chant as follows : " O Thurathadi, fairest goddess of flowers, daughter of nats most high, grant most graciously all that I desire of thee : tasa machan : without keeping back the least re-mainder ; without withdrawing a single joy : prithee do this without fail, sweet goddess of woodland love." Repeat this seven times before the figure. Then go to sleep.

CHAPTER XLV

SLAVES AND OUTCASTS

IT is a work of the greatest possible merit to build a pagoda, and the founder, prefixing Payātaga to his signature, for the rest of his life is looked upon as certain to pass into ne'ban on the completion of this his present existence. Similarly a man acquires great kutho by repairing portions of one of the old national shrines, putting up a new umbrella on the summit, setting the steps that lead up to the platform in order, or even by simply gilding afresh a few square feet on a feast day. By doing any one of these things a man sets his balance of kan on the right side and gains the good opinion of his neighbours. It is, therefore, not unnatural that all foreigners should be struck with the fact that the regular servitors of the places of worship, those who sweep the platform, carry off dead leaves, broken branches, and litter generally, and keep the place in order, are not only slaves, but are regarded as outcasts with whom the rest of the community will have no dealings and whose society is contaminating. Not only is the original parakyun a slave for life, for no one, not even a king, can liberate him or provide a substitute in his place, but his descendants, till the cycle of Shin Gautama's religion shall have come to an end and all the relics shall vanish from the earth, all his children throughout the thousands of years that have to elapse, are fixed and settled slaves of the pagoda from their birth, and any one marrying a pagoda slave, even unwittingly, becomes himself, with all the children he may have had by a previous wife, irremediably a parakyun. The reason no doubt lies in the conviction of the existence of original sin. It is desirable to have the pagoda attended to. A very small acquaintance with human nature induces the belief that this will not be done if individual effort is trusted to do the work. Therefore prisoners of war and others whom it is not convenient to put to death are dedicated to the service. So strict is the dedication that any one who attempts or connives at setting free a pagoda slave is condemned to misery in the lowest hell, awizi. The servitor of the shrine can be employed in no other duty than keeping it in order, and kings and great men are threatened with loss of power and dire destruction if they venture to employ such outcasts as servants, even in the meanest capacity.

Slavery of the familiar form known in semi-civilised countries formerly existed in Upper Burma, but the pagoda slaves are a perfectly distinct body. A person who sells himself, or is sold, by his relation for debt is in a very inferior position doubtless and cannot enjoy any very great privileges. But he can always work his release, and is not thereafter considered as lying under any particular stigma. But the parakyun are neither more nor less than outcasts. They are looked upon as unclean, and the rest of the community will have no intercourse whatever with them. So much is this the case that under British rule, which has of course freed them from their compulsory servitude, they are still looked upon with no less aversion than they were when the country was independent, and though nominally free to do as they please, have to travel into districts where they are unknown before they can find employment even of the most menial kind.

It is no explanation of the taint that the original servitors were prisoners taken in war, condemned convicts, or people expressly sentenced to this office on account of hideous crimes. The reverence for the pagoda cannot be exceeded, why then should the care of it and the surrounding buildings be considered to make its compulsory guardians vile and degraded people? In the old autocratic days it was a common thing for a pious sovereign to set apart certain villages, or a stated number of houses in those villages, for the service of the pagoda, and the victims were selected, quite regardless of personal character, by the village headman from those who were unable to buy themselves off. The cloud, therefore, which hangs over such people is all the more singular. The feeling came out very strongly in the case of a man with slave blood in him, who was appointed by the local government to be a magistrate. Subordinates declined to act under him, and resisted all he did ; the people were still more demonstrative, and petitions flowed in begging that the disgrace might be removed from their district. It was to English minds quite impossible that this should be done, and equally so that he should not receive support in the execution of his duties. The matter was far from being simplified by the natural feelings of resentment, showing itself in undue severity when occasion offered, which filled the victim of the popular clamour, and it was only by the exercise of great tact and patience that the English Deputy Commissioner was able to quiet the people, and after long persuasion gradually to set matters right. But the majority of parakyuns are far from being so fortunate. Here and there in Rangoon and Maulmein are a few men who have got into business, but it is only by carefully concealing their antecedents, and they live in constant terror that the few who know them will betray their secret and reduce them to ruin. The great bulk of the liberated, however—if they can be called liberated when they never had any direct master—find that the force of public opinion is too much for them and are driven to staying about the old source of their shame to obtain a living ; they haunt the pagoda steps and sell offerings to the pious on their way to worship, candles and prayer-flags, incense-sticks, flowers, and fruit. Few of them now resort to their old source of food, the altars, where they used to dispute the ownership of the cold rice and victuals with the crows and the pariah dogs. In Upper Burma the sellers of gold-leaf and tagônlôn are often respectable, that is to say, free men, but in the low country so great is the fear of being mistaken for a parakyun that but very few but the destitute will sell their wares on the saung-dan. At the Shwe Dagôn, in Rangoon, the vendors are almost without exception of the unclean class.

Pagoda slaves are still universal at all the greater shrines. As might have been expected, many-pagoda'd Pagān is their

greatest place.   Here there is even a king of the parakyuns,
and he enjoys a sorry mockery of state in the use of gold-
embroidered sandals, permission to wear jewellery, and the
shade of a gold umbrella when he walks abroad.   But a free
man meeting him in his grandeur would make no obeisance
and would pass him by with a grin and a gibe.   The origin
of his sovereignty is told in an old tale which proves the
antiquity of the custom and the tenacity with which the
dedication is held to.   A king of Pagān—which has not
been a capital since the fourteenth century—had suspicions
of the loyalty of a tributary sovereign, and invited him to
the great and noble city with its towers of gold and silver of
which Ser Marco Polo writes.   This monarch seems to have
had no fears, and came with but a small retinue.   Then the
Lord of the Golden Palace decreed a great feast, and when
all were assembled at the Shwezigôn pagoda, seized his unfortunate vassal by the hair, and holding aloft his sword,
dedicated the helpless man with all his followers and their
descendants for ever to the service of the great shrine, where
lies a cast of the Lord Buddha's jawbone.   Hence the petty
state of the slave-king and the great crowding of pagoda
slaves to his dominions to share his privileges.   It is
difficult to say whether the class will die out, and it seems
certain that there will be no new dedications.   It is perhaps more probable that the Pagān temple slaves are the
descendants of the Talaing King Manuha, who was brought
here a prisoner with all his people and the sacred books, by
King Anawrata from Thatôn.   As it is they marry and
increase.   Besides the parakyun, equally among the outcasts were the executioners, jailers, and lictors in Mandalay ;
lepers and incurables of all kinds, coffin-makers, and those
occupied with dead bodies and the graveyards ; all deformed
and mutilated persons and the lamaing, or government slaves,
tillers of the royal lands.   The tadaungsa are the nearest in
character to the pagoda slaves, and were probably originally
intended as a kind of reserve to draw from for a supply of
servitors to the temples.   They may not engage in any fixed
occupation for their support, and are condemned to make
their living by begging alone, but a few of them become
very rich, for they wander all over the country and occa-

sionally chance upon windfalls, but their wealth is of no use to them, for they can never retire, even in the extremest age. Like the pagoda slaves they have their headquarters in Pagān, and some of them are vehemently suspected of being runaway parakyuns from other parts of the country. But the advance in public estimation is of the slightest possible character. Among the sellers of nantagôn and other pagoda essentials, at the shrines of Rangoon, Prome, and Pegu, are here and there a few tadaungsa, tired of their wandering life; yet, notwithstanding the ill-favour with which they are regarded, they are never stinted for food.

Lepers and others afflicted with loathsome diseases, deformed and mutilated persons, are regarded more with pity than with aversion, but they are not the less outcasts, and must live in villages by themselves, or with the tadaungsa and parakyun if indeed they do not scorn to do so. They usually line the pagoda steps on a duty or feast day, and receive abundant alms, every third or fourth worshipper dropping a handful of rice or a copper coin into the basket or platter laid before them. The dislike to maimed people is very singular, and led to curious incidents in the first and second Burmese wars. The wounded men brought into the field hospitals refused to have arms or legs amputated to save their lives, and it is a matter of not unfrequent occurrence even now, in the hospitals, for a man to tear off the bandages wrapped round the stump, that he may not survive his misfortune and become a shame to his family. In some parts of the province the taint, or even the suspicion of leprosy in a family, becomes a fertile source of villainy. If the suspected person or the head of the house be at all well-to-do, heavy sums are extorted by the headman of the place in return for permission to stay on in the village, and sometimes informers make a good thing in demanding hush-money. But no amount of payments could save a man badly affected with the disease from being driven out of the town. Even in large towns the aversion is equally strong, and unless the leper is a rich man he has to live in prescribed quarters among the outcasts already mentioned. Equally despised are all those who have anything to do with funerals, either in making the coffin or digging the grave. This occupation has therefore fallen almost exclusively into the hands of the old para-kyun, and helps to keep alive the ancient feeling. It must be allowed that the ways of the sandalās do not in any way tend to conciliate the multitude.

Finally there were the pagwet, the letyataung, or thaing-gyaing, the constables, jailers, executioners, lictors, mostly confined to the neighbourhood of the native kingdom Mandalay. These merited all the obloquy that could be cast on them, but their position of quasi-authority made them more secretly hated than openly flouted. They were never allowed to enter a free man's house, even in the exercise of their office; nor could they go within the walls of the palace stockade, but many a citizen smarted under the blows of the lictor's thaing, when a great man came round a corner suddenly, and the letyataung saw a chance for a back-hander with his fasces; and it was far too easy a matter for a man to get into jail in Mandalay to make it a wise proceeding to rail at the pagwet. It was an unlovely custom in Upper Burma which made the executioner both constable and jailer, and condemned him to live on his wits. The natural result was that he lived on the prisoners, and extorted the last pice out of his victim with threats of violence, or actual torture. Pagwet means a circle on the cheek, and this ring on the face implied that its bearer had been condemned for a capital crime, and was respited to become executioner. Others had devices descriptive of their offence tattooed on the chest, as luthat (murderer), thukho (thief), damya (dacoit or highway robber). An execution in Mandalay was a horrid sight: The "spotted man" danced round his victim, made feints with his sword and burst into fits of wild laughter or yells, to shake the doomed man's nerves. It must be admitted that the spectators were very little better. A skilful blow which just slit the skin and drew blood met with an approving shout. The pagwet, like other outcasts, was buried like carrion when he died, or perhaps was simply thrown out with the town offal.

How does all this agree with the theory of Buddhism, that there is equality for all, and that the poorest man can raise himself to sublimest heights after death? The king

had and exercised the power of life and death over all his
people. He ruled in the truest sense by divine right, and
his subjects were all his slaves. The answer is—it is kan,
it is the accumulation of merits or demerits in past existences. A man is rich, powerful, and great, because aforetime
he was pious and good. Therefore now he has a right to
govern and look down with contempt on the poor. The
poor man must have been a bad man before he entered on
this existence. He deserves to be miserable ; he knows it
himself, and submits fatuously. It is true the tyrant does
not do well if he oppresses him, and perhaps may be
punished for it in a later existence, and become the slave
of him who, now a slave, may hereafter by good works attain
the rank of king. But in his present existence the great man
has the fullest right to oppress and grind down the poor
as much as he chooses. He enjoys the fruits of previous
virtues, and since he has perhaps in many existences mortified
the flesh and done grievous penance, he has now a right to
enjoy himself to the limit of his desires. Moreover, as he
has great power and riches, it is always easy for him by
much almsgiving and good works to add so much merit to
his kan as to outweigh all his sins, and in the end preserve
the balance still in his favour. This is, however, very hard
for the poor man. His station exposes him to many temptations to sin. He has but very little to give to the beikku
and to the pagodas. He has perhaps even, in order to save
himself from starvation, to shoot deer and game, and catch
fish, a mode of living which infallibly dooms him to a few
millions of years in hell, whence again he has to work up
through the upper three states of punishment before he
can enter anew upon existence on earth, there to strive to
accumulate hard-earned merit, that he may not incontinently
topple back again to nga-yè. In any case the poor man's
hope can only be directed to the future. From the seeds
sown in past worlds, tares have sprung up in the soil of his
present existence, and tares they will remain. The germ of
a higher life may be sown, but it will only grow up in a new
existence. There is happily one refuge for the man born to
poverty and misery. It is always open to him to put on the
yellow robe of the Assembly of the Perfect, but to do that

he must feel himself strong enough to beat down the fire of passions and remain steadfast to the end, for a lutwet, a man who has put his hand to the plough and turns back again, exposes himself to infinitely greater danger towards his next existence than he who has remained throughout in the world. The monastery is a house of refuge not to be lightly sought, and, sad to say, even it is not open to the outcast.

This doctrine of kan also accounts for the equanimity and callousness with which Buddhists view human misery and the taking of human life, notwithstanding the law which forbids the killing of even the smallest insect. They recognise apathetically the working out of inexorable destiny, and watch a man drowning in the river with undisturbed tranquillity, for they are not called upon or even justified in stirring a hand to prevent it. You cannot combat manifest fate.

But the outcast may not in any case enter the monastery, not even as a scholar. Even that last chance is withheld from him. He is the connecting link with the state of animals, the highest state of punishment. He is considered no better than an animal in thought; he meets with less toleration in actual life. Were he bedizened to the eyes with costly silks and priceless jewellery no girl would look at him. His wealth is of no use. He is not allowed to build a pagoda, or even to supply fresh-water pots on a wayside stand. The monk would refuse his alms; the starving free-man beggar would scorn his bounty. They will no doubt gradually disappear under British rule, but there will be those who will regret it. They may have to work hard for their living.

CHAPTER XLVI

FORMING THE NATIONAL CHARACTER

IF the nation which has no history is happy, it is difficult to
know what is to be said of the nation which has a very
voluminous history, almost all of which is, however, pure
romance. The effect on the Burmese of the fond imaginings
of the Mahā Yazawin, the great Chronicle of Kings, is most
undesirable. No defeats are recorded in those courtly pages ;
reverses are charmed into acts of clemency ; armies vast as
those that people dreamland march through its chapters ;
its heroes are of the old ballad type ; its treasures such as
might have been the produce of Aladdin's lamp. The result
has been a permanent influence on the national character.
Geoffrey of Monmouth's " Chronicle of British Kings " has
left only a faint mark on the national literature, but had the
English lived forty degrees nearer the line, they might still
be believing in Brut, great-grandson of Æneas, and the unbroken line of kings of whom King Arthur was chief. As
it is, the British Mahā Yazawin only supplied a spring for
the poets of all the after time. The Burman Chronicle, on
the other hand, has laid the foundation of the national
character. Like all hardy, strong-limbed races, the Burmans
are naturally proud ; but this innate pride has been tenfold
increased by the wonderful tales of the national annals.
What is a Burman to think when he reads in the history
of his country—there is but the one means of learning the
past—that the English have only foothold in Burma through
the clemency of a gracious king ? They might have been
crushed as effectually as the first settlers of Negraïs Island ;
they might have been driven forth as easily as their seven-

teenth-century ancestors from the factory at Bhamaw, far up
the Irrawaddy on the confines of China; but Bagyidaw, the
king, said, like the Lord Buddha, "All can take life, but who
can give it back?" The Burmese annalist relates: "The
kalabyu, the white strangers from the west, fastened a quarrel
upon the Lord of the Golden Palace. They landed at
Rangoon, took that place, and Prome, and were permitted
to advance as far as Yandabo; for the king, from motives of
piety and regard to life, made no effort whatever to oppose
them. The strangers had spent vast sums of money on
the enterprise; and by the time they reached Yandabo their
resources were exhausted; and they were in great distress.
They petitioned the king, who, of his clemency and generosity, sent them large sums of money to pay their expenses
back, and ordered them out of the country."

By the Treaty of Yandabo, extorted by the fear that the
capital would fall into the hands of Sir Archibald Campbell,
then thundering at the gates of Ava, the English acquired
the provinces of Tenasserim and Arakan, and deprived the
sovereign of two-thirds of his sea-board. The Province of
Pegu, which was annexed after the second Burmese war in
1852-53, has never been formally ceded by any treaty.
King Mindôn said, "Let them stay there; I cannot turn
them out, but I will not be written down as the king that
gave up Rangoon." Lord Dalhousie said, "A treaty with
a man like that is useless"; and he straightway fixed upon
a parallel of latitude as the northern boundary of British
Burma, and put up a line of frontier pillars along it without
reference to the Burmese Government at all. The Mahā
Yazawin said, in effect, "The foreigner was starving in his
own land, and the king bounteously granted him a resting-
place in the dismal swamps by the sea." Until the Burmese
kingdom finally disappeared the only approach to a recognition of the British possession of Pegu was an announcement
from Mindôn Min that "orders had been issued to the
governors of districts not to allow the Burmese troops to
attack the territories of Myedè and Taung-ngu, in which the
British Government had placed its garrisons." Well may it
be said that Burmese kings submitted to accomplished facts,
but did not sanction them. Shortly before the storming of

Malun, the King Mintayagyi sent a note to Sir Archibald Campbell representing that " it was contrary to his religious principles and the constitution of the Empire, to make any cession of territory, and he was bound to preserve its integrity."

Naturally, therefore, the up-country Burman thinks that his race is the bravest in all the realms of Zampudipa, the island in the south, with all its five hundred surrounding islets. The idea has been little checked by English communications and relations with the Lord of the Golden Palace. Such documents as the following are duly inserted in the Mahā Yazawin, and lose nothing in the translating. This was sent, in 1695, by Nathaniel Higginson, Governor of Madras, to the King of Ava. " To his Imperial Majesty who blesseth the noble city of Ava with his presence, Emperour of Emperours, and excelling the Kings of the East and the West in glory and honour, the clear firmament of Virtue, the fountain of Justice, the perfection of Wisdom, the lord of Charity and Protector of the Distressed, the first mover in the Sphere of Greatness, president in council, victorious in war ; who feareth none and is feared by all ; centre of the treasures of the Earth, and of the Sea ; Lord Proprietor of Gold and Silver, Rubies, Amber, and all precious Jewels ; favoured by Heaven and honoured by all men ; whose brightness shines through the World as the light of the Sun, and whose great name will be preserved in perpetual memory."

After this promising exordium the letter goes on : " The fame of so glorious an Emperour, the Lord of power and riches, being spread throughout the whole earth, all nations resort to view the splendour of your greatness, and, with your majesty's subjects, to partake of the blessings which God Almighty hath bestowed upon your kingdom above all others. Your majesty has been pleased to grant your especial favours to the Honourable English Company, whose servant I am ; and now send to present before the footstool of your throne a few toys, as an acknowledgment of your majesty's goodness, which I beg your majesty to accept, and to vouchsafe an audience to my servants and a gracious answer to my petition."

He finishes by asking leave to send a factor next mon-soon to reside at Syriam, opposite Rangoon, on the other side of the Pegu river. Edward Fleetwood was the envoy. He had to wait a long time before the gate of the palace stockade was opened; when that was done he had to bow three times to the building; half way across the esplanade he had to bow humbly three times again; then at fifteen yards' distance, and finally had to make the same obeisance to the king.

The answer to the governor, in the name of the ministers, ran as follows: "In the East, where the sun rises, and in that Oriental part of it which is called Chapudu; the Lord of water and earth, the Emperor of Emperors, against whose imperial majesty if any shall be so foolish as to imagine any-thing, it shall be happy for them to die and be consumed; the lord of great charity and help of all nations, the great Lord esteemed for happiness; the Lord of all riches, of elephants and horses and all good blessings; the Lord of high-built palaces of gold; the great and most powerful Emperor in this life, the soles of whose feet are gilt and set upon the heads of all people; we his great governor and president here, called Mahā Eggena Tibodis, do make known to the governor, Nathaniel Higginson," and so it goes on in the same strain, concluding with a notification of the presents sent—1500 viss of lac, 2500 viss of tin, 300 viss of ivory, 6 earthen dishes, and 8 lacquered boxes. This was, how-ever, more satisfactory than that which fell to the lot of Ensign Lester in 1757, when he got a concession of Negraïs Island and a commercial treaty from the conqueror, Alaungpaya. The gallant envoy received a present of eighteen oranges, two dozen heads of Indian corn, and five cucumbers. Two years later the garrison on the ceded island was massacred. The national annalist gloats over these things.

Here is another petition from the white foreigners: "Placing above our heads the golden majesty of the mighty lord, the possessor of the mines of rubies, amber, gold, silver, and all kinds of metals; of the lord under whose command are innumerable soldiers, generals, and captains; of the lord who is king of many countries and provinces, and emperor over many rulers and princes, who wait round his throne with the badges of his authority ; of the lord who is adorned with the greatest power, wisdom, knowledge, prudence, foresight, etc. ; of the lord who is rich in the possession of elephants and horses, and in particular is the lord of many white elephants ; of the lord who is the greatest of kings, the most just and the most religious ; the master of life and death ; we his slaves, the governor of Bengal, the officers and administrators of the Company, bowing and lowering our heads under the sole of his royal golden feet, do present to him, with the greatest veneration, this our humble petition."

Such documents might have flowed from the chronicler's own pen, and the Burmese historical student, in reading this unbought praise of nations, naturally takes it as honest homage due to the race, since there is now no king. So exalted an idea had the Court of the military power of the country that in 1810 a minister at Ava told Captain Canning that if proper application had been made to the king, he would have sent an army to Europe and put England in possession of France, and so ended all the troubles of the beginning of the century.

Most envoys sent to the Arbiter of Existence were treated very cavalierly in the way of interviews ; not a few in the old days waited long months without ever seeing the king at all. All, down to Sir Douglas Forsyth, in 1874, had to go in shoeless, and sit cross-legged on the floor, an unaccustomed attitude which did not tend to render the position less ridiculous. In other ways they were treated with every indignity. When King Mintayagyi heard that Colonel Symes was coming, he went away to Mingôn, to contemplate his gigantic failure at a pagoda there. Thither the colonel had to follow him, congratulating himself on the circumstance that as the king was away from the palace, there would be the less trouble in seeing him. But he found himself vastly mistaken. On arriving at Mingôn he was told to take up his quarters on an island in the middle of the river. On this barren place, shunned by all Burmese as a polluted spot, where bodies were burnt and criminals executed, he had to remain forty days, and during all that

time not the slightest notice of him was taken by the court.
Finally he was admitted on a kadaw, or " Beg-Pardon Day,"
one of those set apart for all inferiors and vassals to come
and do homage and worship at the Golden Feet.   For long
it was the invariable custom to receive representatives of
foreign states on these days.   Colonel Burney was the first
to refuse to be so treated, and he carried his point, though
the wungyis told the king the reason why he did not come
on the appointed kadaw day was because he was sick.   The
utmost protestations of Symes and Crawford failed to save
them from the humiliation.   Another favourite method of
showing contempt for foreigners and exalting the national
dignity was rather curious in its elaborate ingenuity.   Foreign
missions were provided for by a tax levied on outcasts.   The
money was only collected when an embassy was expected,
and was applied to no other purpose than providing accommodation and food for the members of the mission.   The
coin was considered too vile to be put to any other use.
Delaying the envoy at the gates was an invariable device.
Just as he came up to the entrance a band of princes, with
their followers, would turn in from a side street, and the
luckless representative of England would have to stop and
bite his nails till they had all passed in.   Colonel Burney
was delayed two hours in this way, and even Colonel Phayre,
the first Commissioner of the three coast provinces, in 1856,
had to wait on his elephant till the Eingshemin and his train
filed in before him.   Arrived at the palace, all the earlier
envoys were made to fall on their knees, and shikho to the
central spire of the royal residence.   The members of the
embassy of 1856 were nearly bullied into taking off their
hats to the pyathat.   The object was to show them as sup-
pliants at the Golden Feet, honoured by being allowed to
view his dwelling, and elevated to the summit of earthly
ambition by being admitted to an interview.   Symes and
Cox paid for their admission in this way.   Besides this
official bad treatment the plenipotentiaries were victimised
with numberless personal insults.   Even the Supreme Court
on at least one occasion refused to see Cox.   He was
knocked up long after midnight one night by a clerk who
wanted to get a nutmeg-grater to show to the king.   The

Myowun wrote to him to say that as the envoy would not take his advice he must break off all intercourse, and the English thanthaman would be good enough not to come near his house for the future.   Captain Cox had had a fence put up round his house to keep away the inquisitive rabble, at a cost of twenty rupees.   One morning when he woke up he found this had been unceremoniously carried away, and that it had been used to enclose a place near the river where the heir-apparent's head might be washed.   Finally great pressure was put upon him to take the oath of allegiance to the king ; he was to drink the water in which the muskets and lances of the guard had been dipped, and it was expressly stipulated that he should pay for his oath just as any Burman would have to do.   Scores of like details might be mentioned with regard to all the other ambassadors and residents. It will be sufficient, however, to mention that, in later years, one resident had a cane flourished over his head by a convict lictor, and that the last *chargé d'affaires* of all was chased by a howling rabble from the Mandalay bazaar to the Residency gates, which were broken in—no great exertion of strength was necessary certainly—all because he had killed a pariah dog that was snapping at his heels.

If the various Government representatives were treated in this way, non-official Englishmen could not expect great reverence to be paid to them, and it is hardly worth mentioning that in 1881 a Rangoon merchant, yelled at by convict lictors, went down on his knees while one of the leading spirits of the massacres, the Hpaung Wun, went by on his elephant.   Little wonder then that the patriotic fictions of the Mahā Yazawin were believed, and that the perusal of them was all the more greedily indulged in.   The wearing of shoes in the Palace was never settled till there had ceased to be a Lord of it.

But it is not so much the English that suffered—though occasionally a few of them did get stoned—as the smaller nations and tribes who live around and among the Burmese. It must be acknowledged that the Burman is a sad bully ; but the white strangers could reduce him to civility, if to nothing else, very speedily.   It is different with other races —some perhaps aboriginal, some invaders of Burma as much as the Burmese themselves. The Chins, the Karens, and, in some degree, even the stalwart if simple Shans, have all suffered in common with weaker nationalities from the cunning and braggadocio of the Burman. The Mahā Yazawin delights no less in recounting tales of barbaric diplomacy than in heroics about gallant generals who hold quicksilver in their mouths and advance on the quailing foe, leaping eighteen or twenty cubits in the air. For example, the chronicles of Prome relate the well-known world-story of the bullock's hide of ground. A tribe came from the East under the command of an Amazon. She obtained from the aborigines—probably now some of the hill-tribes in Arakan —a grant of as much land as could be enclosed within an ox-hide, and, following the example of Dido, cut the hide into strips. She got into difficulties, however, and would probably have been driven out had she not married a neighbouring king. A stepson of hers founded the ancient town of Tharekettara (Prome), an event said to have been prophesied by the Buddha Gautama himself, in proof whereof the Shwesandaw pagoda exists to the present day.

A story of a similar character is told with regard to the Shans. The Burmans had a quarrel with some of these big-boned highlandmen as to the ownership of a tract of fine paddy-land. The Shans were in force, and perfectly prepared to fight about the matter. The Burmese therefore resorted to craft. An old hermit was referred to on the subject. He said that the party which first finished building a pagoda of a certain fixed size should have the disputed territory. So both sides set to work. The Burmese soon found that the sturdy hillmen were distancing them. At night, therefore, the chief had recourse to stratagem. He made a framework of bamboos of the required height, had it covered with cloth, and daubed the cloth with white plaster. When daylight came, and the Shans saw the Burmese shrine complete and perfect, even to the extent of offerings of fruit and candles, their astonishment and dismay were such that they marched off straightway to the hills—ascribing the rapid erection to supernatural assistance, and never dreaming of examining the precocious payā ; whereat the Burmese chronicler chuckles with patriotic delight, and glorifies the shrewdness of his countrymen. The same story is told of the foundation of the Arakan empire by the younger of two brothers who came from India.

But it is in the relations with the milder-natured tribes, such as the Karens and Chins, or the small if warlike septs such as the Kachins, that the Burman most comes up to the truculence of the Mahā Yazawin. Out of the northern Kachins—bold robber bands, armed with queer, home-made, stockless guns—little was to be gained. They lived on the hills, and owned nothing but pigs ; but they raided on low-land villages, and the Burmans retaliated, and there were periodic seasons of mutual crucifixion. Long ago these clans had the reputation of kindly hospitality, but Burmese tyranny made most of them dangerous savages. It is different with the Karens and Chins. The former, a heavy, plethoric people, endure their wrongs with dull indifference, all but the fierce Red Karens, who kept up a perpetual guerilla warfare, after the manner of the Kachins. The Karens account for their wrongs in the following way. When Yŭwa created the world he took three handfuls of earth and threw them round about him. From one sprang the Burmans, from another the Karens, and from the third the Kalās, the foreigners. The Karens were very talkative and made more noise than all the others, and so the Creator believed that there were too many of them, and he threw another half handful to the Burmans, who thus gained such a supremacy that they soon overcame the Karens, and have oppressed them ever since.

The Chins were subjected to such long-continued and systematic ill-treatment on the part of the Burmese, that traditions accounting for this oppression actually form a part of the national religion. All mankind, they say, is descended from a woman called Hlinyu, who laid 101 eggs, from the last laid of which sprang the Chins. Hlinyu loved the youngest best ; but he had gone away, and before she found him again the whole world except bleak mountain-ranges had been partitioned out among her other children. So the Chin first man got the hills, and as compensation was given elephants, horses, cattle, goats, pigs, and fowls. Unfortunately, Hlinyu appointed the Burman brother to look after him. The Burman turned out a most wicked and unscrupulous guardian. He pretended to teach him, but only showed the blank side of the slate, so that the poor Chin never learned a single letter. He rubbed the elephant's back with cowhage, so that the Chin's bare legs were so tickled that he refused to have such an unpleasant animal, and gave all the elephants to the Burman. By similar tricks the buffaloes, the horses, and the cattle were obtained. When the Chin mounted to ride on the horse, the Burman's wife got in the way, and was knocked down ; and as compensation for the injuries she sustained, and to quiet her clamour, the horse had to be handed over. Then at the Burman's instigation the Chin went to view his buffaloes, clad in fiery-red garments. The buffalo naturally chased him up a tree, and before he could gain the earth again the buffaloes had gone the way of the elephants and horses. Ultimately nothing remained but goats, pigs, and fowls. Even the barren mountains were not left in his undisturbed possession. When the boundaries of the different countries were marked out, the Burman took very good care to mark his with stones and pillars, but he persuaded the Chin that tufts of grass were good enough for him. These were all burned away by the jungle-fires, and then the despoiled Chin had to live wherever the Burman told him. Thus the race has never had a country or town of its own, but wanders about in a nomadic way over the hills on the fringe of Burma. The well-known custom some of the frontier Chin women have of tattooing their faces is an existing proof of this tyranny. They are naturally pretty ; and this disfigurement—for they themselves acknowledge it to be such, and never adopted it in the heart of the Chin hills—was adopted to prevent the Burmese from carrying them off, as they once did constantly.

The stories of the Mahā Yazawin fully account for and justify these queer traditions of the national religion of the Chins. But it is not in such minor points that the annalist is seen at his best. It is when he vapours about Chinese and Siamese and Munipuris, who come in armies numbered by hundreds of thousands, with elephants in tens of thousands, and the guardian nats of the nations fight on their respective

sides and serve to account for Burmese retreats—then it is
that the spirit of the Mahā Yazawin comes out and streams
along in true 'Ercles vein.   And except the plays the Burman has no other literature to read.   It is not wonderful,
therefore, that he has as good an opinion of himself as the
" centennial Yankees."

> Breathes there a Yank, so mean, so small,
> Who never says, " Wal now, by Gaul,
> I reckon since old Adam's fall
> There's never growed on this 'ere ball
> A nation so all-fired tall
> > As we centennial Yankees.'

The writer might well have been a worker on the Great
Chronicle of Kings.

CHAPTER XLVII

THE LORD OF THE CELESTIAL ELEPHANT AND OF
MANY WHITE ELEPHANTS

THE *Royal History of Kings* enumerates altogether 587,000
kings, following one another in regular succession. From
Mahā Thamada, the great first ruler of land and of sea, there
were 334,569 sovereigns till the time of the most excellent
Buddha Gautama. From thence onward, the Mahā Yazawin
carefully records the sequence of the predecessors of the last
ruler of the Eastern Land, Thibaw Min. Western chroniclers
point out incredulously that the hunter Aung Zaya, who died
in 1760, founded the present dynasty under the title of
Alaungpaya (commonly written Alompra), and till his
rescue of the country from the victorious Peguans, held
no more exalted rank than that of headman of his native
village. But this scepticism ignores the doctrine of Kan,
which provides that none can succeed to the throne of the
Arbiter of Existence and Great Lord of Righteousness but
those whose merit in previous existences entitles them to it.
The king emphatically rules by what is called in the Western
kingdoms the right divine. The eldest daughter of the
reigning king was always declared tabindaing, she was forbidden to marry till the death of the sovereign. When that
occurred, if there were no sons to succeed, there was an
interregnum till the tabindaing could find a husband to
ascend the throne. This selection was not made by the
laws of passion or personal inclination, but was solely decided according to the principles of kan. A royal chariot
was harnessed to a fiery steed and driven away from the
palace with no one to guide it. The horse roamed about,

suffering no one to enter till he came to the person decided by fate to rule the country, usually some one of the royal lineage, or of some other princely line, who had wandered or been carried off from court. Then the horse waited patiently till the sleeper should wake up; the tales always represent the prince as asleep when the chariot arrives. When he rouses himself he steps into the chariot, and without guidance, the horse forthwith gallops back to the palace and the tabindaing finds a husband and the country a king. Alompra became sovereign, only in a slightly different way, but his descent from Mahā Thamada must be unimpeachable.

Long before he took up arms and won for himself the throne, the soothsayers saw about him signs that betokened his coming dignity. When he slept his arms shone like fire; vultures perched on the houses of his enemies; gorgeous butterflies and gay-plumaged birds and strange animals entered his dwelling; he dug up an ancient image of the Buddha not far from his doorstep; when he came to fight it was manifest that he was favoured even beyond the great men of old. He possessed a sword that flew through the air and cut off heads; his shoes enabled him to clear miles at a stride; his fairy spear could spit a whole line of soldiers at once; his javelin could be hurled to any distance; finally, as a fifth weapon, he had a gun which never missed its mark, and was brought down to him by a thagyā. The possession of these five weapons at once proved his right to the throne and secured his holding it. It is true that some of the omens which signalised his right have appeared in others with very different result. A Karen minlaung, or embryo king, displayed the same fire-streaming arms, and raised a rebellion since the British occupation of Pegu. He gained a considerable following, and seemed formidable for a time, till the English wise men pointed out that the fiery glow was produced by rubbing phosphorus on his skin. Then all went against him as an impostor, and he very soon vanished into the hill-country. Similarly, in 1858, a poor fisherman at Twante, a large village not far from Rangoon, dragged up in his net a small image of the Buddha. Such discoveries are always looked upon as an omen of high

destiny, and according to the common superstition, the
fisherman believed that he would rise in dignity, restore the
Talaing kingdom, and revive religion.   He announced the
supernatural call in the village bazaar.   A few desperate
characters joined him, took possession of the town, and
issued a proclamation calling upon all the faithful to rally
to his standard.   But the British civil authorities stepped in
and broke up the procession which was going in solemn
state to the pagoda to inaugurate and consecrate the fisherman in his new profession.   The claimant of royal honours
escaped at the time, but was afterwards given up by the
villagers.   In each of these cases there was deception or
misapprehension of the meaning of the omens, but the
abundance of the signs in the case of Alompra disposes of
the assertion that he was a mere adventurer.   He himself
thoroughly believed in his high destiny, and talked of it in
right royal fashion to Captain Baker, an ambassador sent to
him in 1755 by the Honourable East India Company.   This
gentleman, the commander of an East Indiaman, who, under
the instructions of his employers, evidently regarded the
great conqueror as little better than a savage, brought him a
present of a chest or two of gunpowder, a couple of muskets
and carbines, a gilt looking-glass, some red earth in bags,
and half a dozen bottles of lavender water (there is no
mention of glass beads), and offered Alompra the assistance
of the great company.   Whereupon his majesty burst into a
defiant laugh and replied in the following fashion : " Have I
asked, or do I want any assistance to reduce my enemies to
subjection ?   Let none conceive such an opinion !   Have I
not in three years' time extended my conquests three months'
journey in every quarter without the help of cannon or
muskets ?   Nay, I have with bludgeons only, opposed and
defeated these Peguans who destroyed the capital of this
kingdom, and took the prince prisoner ; and a month hence
I intend to go with a great force to Dagôn (Rangoon),
where I have an army now lying, when I will advance to
the walls of Pegu, blockade and starve them out of it, which
is the last town I have now to take to complete my conquest, and then I will go in quest of Bourno (the French
governor of Syriam, whom he afterwards actually did put to

death).   Captain, see this sword ; it is now three years since it has been constantly exercised in chastising my enemies ; it is indeed almost blunt with use ; but it shall be continued to the same till they are utterly dispersed.   Do not talk of assistance.   I require none.   The Peguans I can wipe away as thus (drawing the palm of one hand over the other).   See these arms and this thigh (drawing his loose coat-sleeve up to the armpit, and lifting his pasoh, so as to display a bare tattooed leg) ; amongst a thousand you cannot see my match.   I can crush a hundred such as the King of Pegu." (Quoted from Crawford.)

Two years later he talked to Ensign Lester in the same bombastic strain, telling him that he would go to Madras, and that if a nine-pounder shot was to hit him it could do him no harm, with a good deal more to the same effect.   He is described at this time, when he was about forty-five years of age, as five feet eleven in height, and of a powerful build, with a long, but not a thin face, the expression not being improved by a number of smallpox pitmarks.   He had a broad but very retreating forehead, a characteristic shared by all his descendants, and prominent in the case of King Mindôn.

Alaungpaya, then, was no feeble founder of the present line of successors to the great Mahā Thamada.   He certainly had the power to command, and his military successes carried the peacock flag from far away towards Dacca, down to the Siamese capital.   Assuredly he was a worthy follower of the great first king, and the Burmese believed firmly in the unbroken character of the succession.   Accordingly all the old Indian and Sakyan customs were carefully observed by the Burmese royal family.   Such were the marriage with half-sisters, and the consequent preserving unmarried of the king's eldest daughter ; the reverence of the three most excellent animals, the peacock of the sun, the hare of the moon, and the kalawaik, the carrying bird of Vishnu, whose eyes like jewels look friendly on the stranger ; and the beittheit, the consecration by pouring out of water at the accession.   Marriage with half-sisters was only allowed to the king, not to the people at large, or even to the princes of the blood-royal.   The throne was painted over with representations of the peacock and the hare, typifying the descent of the king from the solar and lunar races, which was also directly laid claim to in the title, netwetbuyin, sovereign of the rising sun. Similarly with the titles khattia, implying that he had dominion over the crops, and yaza, because he could instruct men in the laws, a somewhat doubtful ability in regard to all except perhaps King Mindôn. The consecration by beittheit was completed in three special ceremonies, as was the case with the Payālaung chosen to be the first ruler.

1. Yaza-beit, the consecrating of him as king.

2. Manda beittheit, the solemn marrying him to a queen of royal lineage.

3. Thenga beittheit, the confirmation or renewal of his engagement to abide by the laws, whereupon full powers for the government and administration of the country are conferred.

The actual coronation ceremony was latterly a mere form, but was intended to mark the claim of the Lord of the Golden Palace to be the representative of the universal monarch, the Sekyawadé king, who never makes his appearance during the time allotted to the publication and duration of the religious institutions of a Buddha. It consisted principally in incantations and sprinkling with holy water from the Ganges, performed by the pônnas, the Brahmin astrologers; the Burman yahans had nothing whatever to do with it. Besides the pônnas, only a few of the chief ministers were present. The really national part of the ceremony was the royal progress round the city moat, made seven days after the beittheit. The king left the city by the Eastern Gate, the precise moment being notified by a discharge of cannon. He then entered the state barge, a most gorgeously gilt and carved construction, surpassing even the traditional coach of the Lord Mayor of London. This boat was then slowly rowed round the moat, with music clashing all around, and bands of dancers supplying the place of a rejoicing populace. Then when the circuit had been completed, the newly crowned monarch entered again between the guardian ogres of the Eastern Gate, a fresh salvo of artillery announcing the arrival at the palace. The ceremony was simple enough, but King

Thibaw never went through it. In the first days of his reign he was afraid to leave the nandaw, lest conspirators might find the chance too good a one to lose, and later on, a fear that the delayed festival might suggest ideas of previous faint-heartedness came in the way. Consequently, though he was crowned successor to Mahā Thamada as far as the beittheit was concerned, and therefore became the source of the law, the guardian of the welfare of the country, the recipient of the revenues, and the chief administrator of justice, he was no proper successor to the warlike Alaungpaya. Possibly the failure to assume the sturdy spirit of the first of the family may account for the deficiency in some of the attributes derived from the first king, a deficiency which even the most loyal of his subjects did not hesitate to admit.

The first ruler was chosen for his strict adherence to the five fundamental precepts now incumbent on all men, and for his general sanctity. These qualities are inherent in all successors, though sometimes it is difficult to distinguish them. From them sprang four other laws incumbent on all kings and rulers. These thengaha, kingly laws, or byammazoya are as follows :—

1. Thathameda, ordaining that he shall not receive more than a tithe of the produce of the country.

2. Purithameda, ordaining that the king shall engage to pay his servants and army once every six months.

3. Thamapatha, by which the king binds himself to assist his subjects with money, and to receive payment of it within three years, without charging interest.

4. Wāsapaya, the use of courteous and fitting language, according to the age and position in life of the persons addressed.

It is to be feared that these kindly kingly laws were not found suitable to the conditions of modern society. At any rate they were not very strictly observed by Thibaw Min.

Nevertheless that monarch was very far from being such an unlovely character as most Europeans have been led to believe. It was explicitly denied by many that he drank at all ; it is certain that whatever excesses he may have plunged into in the remorse caused by the massacres of February 1879, he was assuredly not a confirmed drunkard. His worst fault was that he was easy, or call it weak-spirited if you like. It is an open secret that he was not intended to be king. His father, Mindôn Min, had a strong liking for the young yahan, but his intention, if he had any, was that the pious and well-read Nyaungyan prince, who died a refugee at Barrackpore, near Calcutta, was to be his successor, and if the court or the town had been polled, the choice would have fallen on the same burly, good-natured individual.

It must be understood that, notwithstanding the precautions for the preservation of the pure blood-royal, the system of keeping a princess tabindaing, to be married to the new ruler, it by no means followed that the eldest son of this union, or, indeed, any son by this queen at all, necessarily succeeded to the throne. It was not often that there was a recognised Eingshemin, an heir-apparent to the throne, but when there was such a dignitary, he might be the fifth, or the tenth, or the thirtieth son, the only stipulation being that he should be the child of one of the four chief queens. The nomination rested with the king. A consideration of the gruesome history of the parricide kings, who reigned in one of the countries of the Myissi Madetha, the middle country, as India is called, each of whom ascended a throne stained with a father's blood, until the horrified populace of Pataliputra revolted and exterminated the whole house; the reading of this bloody chapter in the royal annals may have prompted the custom, but it is certain that it is not often that the heir to the throne was recognised. Mindôn made no sign till his last illness came upon him. Then when it was evident that he could not survive, he named the Nyaungyan mintha and after him the yellow-robed Thibaw prince. Then palace intrigue began. The Thibaw prince, it was well known, had a passion for the tabindaing, Selin Supaya (Selina Sophia as she was called by some of the English residents in Mandalay), and the second of the Supayās, for there were three of them, was equally enamoured of the young Patama Byan. Therefore the queen-mother resolved to gratify all parties, and become herself queen dowager. She opened up communications with the then all-powerful Kin Wunmingyi, the Premier as he was usually called. That able minister saw continued power in store for himself if he could get the unsophisticated pyin-sin placed on the throne. Therefore he threw himself into the plot. The princes were summoned by a forged royal order to come before his majesty, bid him farewell, and hear his nomination of a successor. As they came up to the hmawgaw, the mirror throne room, where the kings body afterwards lay in state, they were seized separately and forthwith hurried off to prison. The Nyaungyan and his brother, the Nyaungôk prince, received timely warning, and instead of coming to the palace went straight off for sanctuary to the English Church, whence they afterwards escaped, disguised, to the protection of the British flag in the compound of the British Residency. But though they thus saved their lives, as appeared five months afterwards, when the other princes were done to death, the throne was lost, for Thibaw was left master of the situation, and soon completed his arrangements for securing his position. At first everything went well. It was necessary to retain the support of the Kin Wungyi, and that astute minister, acting on the idea that he could easily manage the raw young ex-neophyte, proceeded to draw up a scheme for a constitutional government, the greater part of which was written for him by the late Dr. Clement Williams, the first English Resident in Mandalay, and afterwards an independent trader. This constitution was published with a great flare of trumpets and much talk about the establishment of Western methods, and the raising of Burma to the rank of a first-class Eastern power. The people at large did not perceive any very radical difference, as far as the payment of moneys was concerned, under the new system. Perhaps it would have turned out well if it had lasted. But it was not destined to last.

As soon as the funeral rites of the dead king were over, and Thibaw Min had been sprinkled with the consecrated water by the pônnas, he proposed to marry " Selina Sophia," and take the younger sister, the Supayalat, along with her according to agreement. But the tabindaing was not willing. On the contrary, she took the altogether unprecedented step of cutting off her hair and entering a nunnery. The slighted golden monarch was furious. The two luckless maids of honour of the scornful beauty had their hands chopped off by the " spotted man." What became of the nun herself no one seems to know. Whether she went to her grave or to a jungle convent is a matter which neither her friends nor her enemies ever revealed. Thibaw Min at any rate had to be satisfied with the Supayalat. He very soon found that he had quite enough to do with her. The mother had always been known as strong-minded ; the daughter developed an even greater amount of determination, and between them they soon reduced the ruler of the umbrella-bearing chiefs to submission. It had never been their intention that the Kin Wungyi should derive the greatest part of advantage from the scheme for enthroning the Thibaw prince, and they gradually worked his majesty into a state of desperation. However meek he might be towards them, he soon became embarrassingly testy with his courtiers, and after a time took to using what was called Tharrawaddy's spear. Kônbaung Min, that fiery descendant of Alaungpaya, in his latter years amused himself with spearing his courtiers with a javelin he always kept by him. This trait, which soon grew into a regular homicidal mania, and led to his being smothered in the end, seemed to have broken out afresh in the young king, and the Rangoon papers began to talk of hereditary insanity. Soon, however, the whole civilised world was to be shocked. The queen mother and the Supayalat persuaded the king that he would never be safe till the princes were put out of the way. It is said that Thibaw Min at first flatly refused, and then, broken down by daily taunts, pleaded the danger from the British Government. Here also, however, he was overruled. The queen dowager called in a European (not an Englishman), and asked what would be done if all the imprisoned princes were massacred ? He answered there would be a great deal of talk and nothing more. So Thibaw gave in, and said, " Shin-ba se, let them be cleared away " ; and seventy of the royal blood, men, women, and children, were murdered in the next three days, and buried within the palace, in a long trench dug for the purpose. The eldest prince, the Mekhaya, a man nearly three times Thibaw's age, and hated for his fierce, proud demeanour, died shrieking for mercy at the hands of his own slaves, whom he had often tortured. The Thonsè mintha, equally over-bearing in his manner, and a fanatical hater of the English, whom he lost no opportunity of insulting, gained in his death an esteem he had never known while living. With his last breath he hurled defiance and imprecations at the brother whom he had always despised, and prophesied a speedy and bloody end for the "runaway monk." The weakly and gentle-mannered Maingtun murmured a prayer that the hideous sin of murder might be pardoned to its instigator and perpetrators, and then resigned his neck to the club which sent him to the blissful seats of nat-dewas. The princesses were subjected to nameless horrors, and the treat-ment of the children recalled the days when ravaging hordes marched through the land with babes spitted on their pike staffs for standards. The poor old regent of Pegu, governor at Rangoon when the British came in 1852, had his nostrils and gullet crammed with gunpowder, and was thus blown up. But the tale of horrors is not one to enlarge upon. They were conducted by those who became the king's most trusted advisers. All the three days bands of music were playing throughout the palace, and dancers posturing to divert attention from what was going on, and to drown the cries of the victims.

The custom of putting to death all dangerous rivals on the accession of a new king was without doubt almost a re-cognised thing in Burma whenever there was a new sovereign. Many Burmans defend it warmly, on the plea that it secured the peace of the country. Where there were so many of the royal blood, the appointment of one, possibly among the youngest, to the supreme power, could not but lead to discon-tent, breaking out into open rebellion when the slighted found themselves strong enough to feel hope of success for a rising. The accession of Mindôn was marked by no such atrocities, but he came to the throne under exceptional circumstances. His brother, the Pagān Min, was deposed because he would do nothing to make peace with the English, then threatening to occupy the capital, which they were so near effecting in the first war of 1826. The deposed king was allowed to live happy with his game-cocks. The people's idol, the fiery "War Prince," was passed over because he was pledged to fight to the death, and there was an explicit understanding that he, or failing him, his issue, should succeed to the royal honours on the death of King Mindôn. That pious and enlightened monarch was forced on the country by a happy necessity. But it was very different when he died. There was no war to distract the people, and further, there was a multiplicity of candidates. The Convener of the Fifth Great Synod had, during his lifetime, fifty-three recognised wives, besides an indefinite number of handmaidens. By the wives he had altogether one hundred and ten children, forty-eight sons and sixty-two daughters. Of the forty-eight sons only twenty-four were alive at the time of his death, and two of these were detained as political prisoners in India, the Myingun and Myingundaing princes, the originators of the rebellion of 1866, when the "War Prince" was killed, and the king himself had a narrow escape. The Myingundaing died many years ago in India ; the Myingun still lives on an allowance from the French Government in Saigon.

There were thus twenty-two possible successors to the Golden Throne. One was a lunatic—the Kyabin Mintha ; four were little boys under ten years of age, others were disqualified for a variety of reasons, but there remained the Thonsè, the Mekhaya, the Nyaungyan, and the Nyaungôk, all of whom were considered as having certainly greater claims than the actual successor. Thibaw Min wanted to keep them all in prison, and a range of barracks was actually being constructed for their occupation when the massacres occurred. Whatever foreigners may think, all Burmans lay the guilt of the executions at the door of the queen and the queen dowager. When some were killed, prudential motives, as well as a ghoul-like thirst for blood, prompted the murder of all, and this accordingly was carried out. Of all the twenty-four princes, excluding the king, there were left alive but four little boys in sanctuary in Mandalay monasteries, one of them barely five years old, and three refugees in India, one of the four, the Mingundaing prince, having died soon after. Of the princesses, thirty-five of whom survived their father, four were killed in the February massacres, and twenty-one kept in confinement in the palace, some of whom almost certainly died of want or external violence. The remainder were of too little account to be taken notice of. Thirty-seven queens were alive when the late king died. Thirteen fled when his illness became dangerous, and so extinguished themselves. Twenty-three were kept in underground dungeons, or under close surveillance in the palace ; one only, the mother of the Mekhaya, with fourteen of her children and grandchildren, were killed in 1879. This is rather a dismal list, and the shadow of it rested over the royal throne. Whether Thibaw Min was the direct author of the tragedy or not, the stain of the crime and the recollection of it clung to him. After its accomplishment, the king fell more and more under the malign influence of the termagant queen. The Kin Wungyi and his constitution were ignominiously bundled out of the palace. The former all-powerful minister became little more than a private citizen, and the vile conductors of the massacres were the chief in authority. With their lotteries and monopolies they had very soon brought the country to ruin, had it not been for the blessing of English rule.

Personally, Thibaw Min could not be otherwise than miserable. The harridan queen kept him in most humble subjection. Hitherto every king of Burma had had at least four chief queens, those of the east, west, north, and south palaces, of whom the southern queen was supreme. But Supayalat persisted in remaining sole controller of the royal heart. Terrible stories are told of the death by lingering torture which proved the portion of maids of honour on whose charms the unhappy king is said to have looked with favour. Such an unusual state of things, such a disgrace as a woman's slave for a king, had never befallen any country before. A son was born in the end of 1879, but he died of smallpox in the epidemic of March 1880, and a daughter in the end of the same year compared but badly with King Mindôn's three or four a year.

The king was practically a prisoner within his golden walls. No king of Burma had ever been much in the habit of leaving the palace.   Possession of it, with the vast arsenal which it contained, implied the subduing of the entire country. When a monarch went forth to worship at a pagoda or preside at some function, he left the nandaw in charge of the prince or minister whom he could best trust.   But poor Thibaw Min could trust no one, or at any rate believed that this was his state.   From the time he succeeded to the throne till he left it a prisoner, he never went outside the palace walls.

CHAPTER XLVIII

KING THIBAW

[The following three chapters remain as they were written in 1880.]

I.—A PRIVATE INTERVIEW

TIME was, when to get an interview with the Arbiter of Existence was as difficult a matter as to see the Grand Lama, or the Sherif ul Islam of Mecca. When the servants of "the Foreign Woman," Her Most Gracious Majesty Queen Victoria, protested in 1879 against the new sovereign's summary settlement of domestic matters, Thibaw swore a royal oath by the sacred hairs of Gautama, by the Lord, the Law and the Assembly, the three precious things, that he would never look on a white man again. For a year the vow was religiously kept, and ambitious "globe-trotters" and prying special correspondents were kept at a distance, and had not even the satisfaction of being admitted within the outer gate of the nandaw. In time, however, the royal coffers got low, and it was thought foolish not to make use of the barbarian merchants, seeking for monopolies and grants of forest land, and able and willing to pay enormous sums for such concessions. His majesty's ministers therefore speedily found means of relieving the great King of Righteousness from his solemn oath. The first principle of the Buddhist faith is charity. How, then, could the Lord of the Rising Sun gain more merit and advance some miles on the noble Eightfold Path better than by conquering his just personal antipathies and allowing awe-stricken foreigners to grovel before the splendour of his effulgence and worship at

459

his Golden Feet! When once they had experienced that supreme delight, his majesty's ministers might be trusted to see that the wealth of the merchants was made to subserve the royal interests. And so it came to pass that Thibaw first received a few speculators and their friends, and has ended by granting an audience to any European that can get a minister to speak for him. And so the Golden Hairs are forgotten, and the three precious things calmly flouted. Still the royal barbarian is not comfortable at these interviews. He was too curious to be dignified. He had not the fund of conversation that his father had, and he was impatient apparently of being looked at, as strangers in remote parts of China and wild beasts in zoological gardens may be supposed to be.

Securing an interview is not always an easy matter, unless you are a great capitalist, desirous of a grant somewhere. If you merely wish to see his majesty, the process is somewhat difficult. You probably apply first of all to the Chevalier Andreino, Italian Consul in Mandalay, and master of ceremonies and mysterious "doing duty" man at the Burmese Court. He may get you the desired audience, but more probably refers you to one of the higher ministers. Almost certainly these officials will say that it is impossible for you to see the king. His majesty is too busy, "working hard all day at affairs of state"; and they gaze stolidly upon you. You regret the circumstance extremely, make the minister a present of a few hundred rupees, and continue to deplore your bad luck. Then he brightens up suddenly, recollects that on such and such a day his majesty is possibly free. He will find out and do his best for you.

Next day you are told that an interview will be granted, that the king of kings graciously permits you to come and place your head under his gilded feet. If you are a wise man and have been warned by considerate friends, you will now commence to practise sitting on your feet. It is as well to rehearse the process frequently beforehand, for they must be tucked away so that his majesty cannot see them; and if you do not find the most agreeable way of effecting the concealment, your audience will be chiefly memorable to you for frightful agony, a vast amount of internal "popular language," and vows of vengeance against the ministers, who seem to have an irritating faculty of grinning all down their backs.

The journey to the palace is not a pleasant preparation. It is too hot to ride, and accordingly you decide to go in the apotheosis of a dog-kennel on wheels, which does duty for a carriage in Mandalay. There is not room for much more than one Englishman in the vehicle, and the only way you can get in is by scrambling over the backs of the bullocks. I shall never forget my first experience of a Mandalay carriage. After an exciting ten minutes spent in trying to circumvent a kicking bullock, I at length got in and sat down on the floor——there are no seats——to gaze out at the round hole by which I had got in. The rest of the party followed, each man in a kennel of his own. The beasts set off at a swinging trot over roads of the early depraved order, and in a couple of minutes we were all regretting that we did not brave the sun and ride, or even walk. However, the drivers disregard our entreaties, and hustle up the cattle all the more energetically. We pass over the moat, and through the enormous wooden gateway into the walled town. We enter by the a-mingala gate, the south-western, the only one through which corpses are allowed to be taken from the city. It is almost invariably used by Englishmen as being nearest to the Residency and the river, but no upper-class Burman will pass through it if he possibly can avoid doing so. After five minutes' more jolting we arrive at the outer stockade of the palace, and get out of our conveyances with some alacrity and a lot of bruises. Immediately inside the gate is a guard-house, with a cluster of the royal soldiery, who, as we come up, squat down on the ground and hold their Enfields in front of them at the third motion of the present, looking like frogs on a Christmas card.

We cross a wide open space, pass through the " Red Postern," and turn to the left, for it is to be a private reception, and we do not ascend the steps to the Hall of Audience. We pass a gallop which Thibaw has laid down for his ponies, and enter the Royal Gardens. They are not much to speak of. Laid out in squares, with raised paths, deep brickwork canals running in every direction, grottoes and "fads" of all sorts in every available place, they are rather tiresome, and we prefer to talk to a remarkable gentleman who meets us here. This is the Pangyet Wun, or governor of the glass manufactories—rather a mysterious title, seeing that there are no such works in the royal city. But names mean anything or nothing in Mandalay. The Pangyet Wun is the familiar example of Western flippancy triumphing over Eastern conceit and forgotten good manners. He speaks the English of the primer overlaid with the language of the young subaltern and the seafaring man on Atlantic steamers of the inferior class.

As we shake hands with him he smiles demurely, and says he regrets he cannot offer us "a liquor." "Wine or spirits, you know, are not drunk in the palace," and an apparition suggestive of a barbarian wink flits across his face. We have not long to talk with him, however. Everything, he says, is ready, and we make for a side-door into the palace, or rather into one of the numerous audience chambers connected with the nandaw, each having a name of its own, and being used according to his majesty's whim. We are to be received in the Hmaw-gaw, "the Crystal Palace," so called from the decoration of its walls, resplendent with bits of mirror and coloured glass. We have to put off our shoes before stepping into the palace, and do so not without dire misgivings, for in times gone by we had been to see King Mindôn, and have lively recollections of the nails in the floor. A Burman, they say, never likes to finish anything, and therefore does not drive home the nails in the planking of his house. People more versed in the ways of the nandaw assert that this is not the true reason, and declare that it is an ingenious method of making the presumptuous Kalā approach the neighbourhood of the Lord of Land and Sea in respectful fashion, with his eyes humbly lowered. It certainly is very effective in that way. You cannot gaze about you with any degree of freedom when you have a lurking suspicion that the next step will drive a nail into the ball of your big toe. Consequently every one used to go in with meekly downcast face, and respect to the sovereign was thus triumphantly enforced. But Thibaw disdains such petty ways of compelling outward respect. Has he not made the English Resident run away? Or perhaps it is the European experience of the Pangyet Wun that we have to thank. At any rate, the corridors and passages are covered with thick soft carpets, three or four deep, and we walk along in comfort, if with a somewhat undressed feeling.

It is not far to the Hmaw-gaw. We find the chamber almost empty. A thick carpet, woven in one piece, covers the floor, and the far side is raised a couple of feet above the rest of the room. On this dais stands a couch. The Pangyet Wun tells us to sit down and not to speak. We obey, and stare at the couch and a door behind it. Again we have misgivings. Mindôn Min used to keep visitors waiting a trifle of an hour or so, till they got so cramped that they had to be hoisted on to their legs. But it is not so with his son. He comes almost immediately, jerking himself suddenly in at the door, as if somebody had stuck a pin into him behind, walks hurriedly to the couch, kicking off his slippers on the way, and throws himself upon it, with his elbows sunk in the crimson and gold cushions. He looks straight at us for about thirty seconds, and then falls to examining his finger-nails and the carpet. He is embarrassed; his father was embarrassing. The pious potentate used to scrutinise his visitors (at a distance of twenty feet or so) through a field-glass, and people who were not overawed used to grin, which required explanation. King Thibaw comes alone, except that there is a page with cheroots. The gigantic gold spittoon and betel-nut box and other salivating and chewing paraphernalia, which were deposited before his late lamented father, are wanting. He knocks off the ash of his green cheroot on the carpet and presently lets it go out. Meanwhile the thandawsin, the royal herald, has commenced chanting our names, business, and the list of our presents. This is done in a high-pitched recitative, and takes a long time, for all the names, styles, and titles of his majesty are declaimed for a matter of quarter of an hour, each sentence ending with a long-drawn payā-a-ah.

At last it is over, and Thibaw asks if we are well. We announce that we are, and the interpreter, who throughout sees fit to translate bald monosyllables into obsequious, not to say grovelling periods, says that by his majesty's merciful permission we are in the enjoyment of perfect health. Thibaw then demands our business. The interpreter replies that we have come to view the glories of his majesty's mighty kingdom, and to lay our heads under his golden feet. This is a lengthy formality, for an epitome of the titles comes in with every answer. Thibaw looks very ill at ease, and has an occasional glance at us out of the tail of his eye. Having inquired after the well-being of the Queen, the Viceroy, the Chief Commissioner of British Burma, and his dear brothers in Calcutta, who, he hopes, are being well treated, as befits their rank, it seems as if there was going to be a sudden end to the audience, to avert which we wildly grasp at the idea of saying that we had taken tickets in the royal lotteries, but had not been successful in the drawing. His majesty twirls his cheroot over his shoulder, which is a sign that he wants a light, and says he is very sorry, but hopes we will try again. We announce that we are going to make another attempt, and add, in the desperate hope of getting his majesty into a controversy, that lotteries are considered a very bad thing for the people in Europe. The interpreter gazes for three-quarters of a second reproachfully at us and says, that by reason of his majesty's great might, glory, and clemency, we are encouraged to make a fresh venture, and that we are lost in wonder at the wisdom which has fallen upon such a method of increasing the revenue, a system which had never occurred to the unilluminated minds of barbarian financiers. Burmese is a language with which some of us are acquainted, and which affords unusual facilities for the relief of the irritated mind, but while we are hesitating as to whether we shall break through Court etiquette and address the great Lord of Righteousness mouth to mouth, Thibaw graciously remarks that he is glad to hear that the wisdom of his ministers has increased the knowledge of political economy in the world, and adds that he is unacquainted with any trade which for an outlay of two rupees will bring in a return of ten thousand. Having announced that he will give orders to his ministers and officials to show us every respect while we remain under the shadow of his throne, he suddenly gets up and vanishes as rapidly as he appeared. The Pangyet Wun calls out, " Get on your legs, gentlemen, ' long chairs ' are better than this sort of thing," and we obey with great alacrity, and are regaled outside with brandy and water of considerable potency, poured out of a teapot into teacups.

CHAPTER XLIX

KING THIBAW

II.—THE MANY-TITLED

His most glorious, excellent majesty, the present ruler of the city of Mandalay, or Yatanabông Nepyidaw, ruler of the sea and land, lord of the rising sun, sovereign of the empires of Thumaparanta and Zampudipa, and of other great empires and countries, and king of all the umbrella-bearing chiefs, lord of the mines of gold, silver, rubies, amber, and the noble serpentine, chief of the Saddan, or celestial elephant, and master of many white elephants, the supporter of religion, owner of the sekya, or Indra's weapon, the sun-descended monarch, sovereign of the power of life and death, great chief of righteousness, king of kings, and possessor of boundless dominions and supreme wisdom, the arbiter of existence, has a very bad character. He killed his brothers and sisters and he drinks gin.

He is very far from being a fool for all that. All his predecessors killed certain of their relatives too when they came to the throne ; only they had not so many as Thibaw, and there were no electric telegraphs in those days. Besides, they had not such pressing need to clear the field. Thibaw was put on the throne by a palace intrigue, and if he had not disposed of his brothers they would probably have killed him. So say all his majesty's subjects, and they ought to know. The drinking of plebeian gin is another matter, and is likely to be the ruin of the many-titled monarch. It is telling on him fast. When he came to the throne he was a very good-looking young man, the handsomest Burman in the country, people used to say. Two years and a half have, however, made a very great difference. His majesty's flat nose has become flatter than ever ; his forehead seems to have more of the snake's slope back than even the most typical of his family ; and his round face is all bloated and blotched. When we had an interview with him, he had a scratch across his face from the eye over the left cheek, and it was a question whether the queen had done it or not. It did not add dignity to a manner which was not by any means ideally kingly. It was a private interview certainly, and we did not therefore expect to see him gorgeous in a silk surcoat and spire-like tharapu or crown. But it seemed somewhat negligent to appear in a soiled white short coat and a plain check pattern, yellow silk pasoh, such as any ordinary townsman might wear. In his ears certainly were splendid gold cylinders, with magnificent clusters of diamonds and emeralds at the ends, and on his finger glistened a sapphire ring worth a monarch's ransom. There was a spray of diamonds in his hair too, but it only sufficed to draw attention to the fact that he had neglected his toilet, which is a bad sign in a young man ! All Burmans wear their long hair tied up in a knot on the top of their head. Thibaw, however, stepped out of a monastery on to the throne, and in the monasteries every one has his head shaved. The royal hair has therefore not had time to grow very long yet, and his majesty makes up his yaung, or top knot, with false tresses, as many humbler Burmans do, only they take care over it, which he does not. This is the worst sign of all ; for when a Burman ceases to take pride in his hair he must be very far gone.

There are very considerable doubts as to his majesty's legitimacy. In any case he is not a pure Burman. His mother had a good deal of wild Shan blood in her veins. Just before Thibaw's birth it was discovered that his mother was unpardonably intimate with a pôngyi, one of the mendicants of the royal monastery. The monk was thrown into prison, and died there very suddenly of official colic. The queen was sent to a nunnery, where she remained till Thibaw came to the throne. She had better have stayed there for good. A year ago there was a fearful scandal.

Some thirty people about the Court were beheaded, and the queen dowager was relegated to the convent.

Thibaw himself was brought up in an uncle's house and used to be unmercifully bullied by his cousins. When Dr. Marks, the eminent S.P.G. missionary, came to Mandalay and established a school, the late king asked what was the best age for a Burman to commence learning English. The reverend gentleman said, "About twelve years old." King Mindôn called for "all his sons that were twelve years old or thereabouts." Eleven were produced, and among them was Thibaw. The future king went to the royal school, but he sat apart from his late victims, and never came to school on the same elephant with them. He was a surly, morose boy, not very good at his lessons, and once or twice narrowly escaped the usual result of such conduct. I believe he was never actually birched, but he had several times to stand in the corner. When he left he was able to read a little, but he has forgotten all his English now. He used to be fond of cricket, and slogged away in fairly good pendulum form ; but he never would field out, and used unprincely language to any one who bowled him. He was the youngest of the batch by a month or two, and was always quarrelling with his brothers and bullying the wretched slave who attended him and carried his cheroots and betel-nut. But nobody paid much attention to his vagaries then, for he was twentieth or thirtieth son, and the Mekhaya prince, the eldest, might very easily have been his father, or even grandfather.

After he left the S.P.G. Royal School, King Mindôn made him a koyin, a neophant, in the royal monastery. There he seemed to get on better. At any rate when his novitiate was over, he passed with honours as Patama Kyaw, an examination in the Bitaghat thônbông, the three " baskets " of the Buddhist law, and sundry other volumes of ritual and controversy. This was what first drew the old king's attention to him. Mindôn Min was a very pious old gentleman, and had a particular delight in his title of Convener of the Fifth Great Synod. When therefore young Thibaw made a score in the Turanian Theological Tripos, his father bored everybody with his talk about the juvenile

divine, and was not far off imagining that he was an embryo
Budh.   Thibaw an avatar of Arimadeya!   Bradlaugh
in the Salvation Army!   Other people knew better even
then.   Even in those days Thibaw was a disgraceful little
rip.   The present Queen of the South and sundry other
little petticoats came to flirt with him and his companions
in the monastery.   An ascetic should not even look at a
woman, and the old kyaungpogo, the abbot of the royal
mendicants, was terribly scandalised, and it is whispered
about that he tied the raffish young princeling's hands up
to a tree and swished him soundly.   Some colour is
lent to the report by the fact that Thibaw dismissed the
venerable recluse as soon as he ascended the throne.   However that may be, the old king heard nothing about it, and
went on believing the " Senior Theolog " to be a miracle
of piety and learning, and the sacred cocks and hens on
Mandalay Hill had double rations for a month in honour of
the event.   Nevertheless, he did not by any means intend
Thibaw to succeed him on the throne.   The Nyaungyan
was the man he named.   But the mother of the Supayalat,
now Thibaw's queen, took the matter in hand.   She knew
that Thibaw was deeply in love with her daughter, and
thought she could easily manage the moon-struck, Pali-
spouting novice.   She communicated her views to the Kin
Wunmingyi, the head of the ministry.   That diplomatic
old gentleman was equally deceived, and thought he would
have no trouble in leading the verdant recluse as he pleased.
The matter was arranged ; the elder princes were all seized
and thrown into prison before Mindôn Min died.   Thibaw
tolerated the Kin Wunmingyi for a short time, and let
him formulate a wonderful production which the Turanian
Foreign Secretary called a constitution.   When the simple
quondam mendicant found himself firm on the throne, and
when the Nyaungyan, his great fear, had got away from
the British Residency in Mandalay, and was safe in Calcutta,
Thibaw threw off the mask.   Eighty-six of his blood
relations were battered and choked to death, or buried alive.
The Kin Wungyi's hapless constitution was crumpled up
and chucked over the frontier, and Thibaw stood forth as
the most inhuman of a long line of savage despots.   The

Kin Wunmingyi, who, after all, had been to Europe and was versed in public affairs, lost all influence, and was succeeded as adviser by the Taingda Mingyi, a statesman of the typical oriental kind, supple, unscrupulous and grasping. Thibaw even achieved a certain kind of popularity with his subjects. He insulted our representative and blustered at all foreigners, and finally frightened the Indian Government by covert threats into suddenly withdrawing the whole *personnel* of the Residency. Then it was announced by sound of gong all over Burma that the Sovereign of Land and Water, by reason of his great might and glory, had caused the hated English to flee from his sight, and would, in his own good time, carry the great peacock flag to the south, and plant it once more on the shores of the Gulf of Martaban.

It is a great triumph for the pôngyi's son, as he was nicknamed when it was safe to do so, and it will be remembered about him quite as long as the fiendish cruelty of his massacres. We have certainly not done with Thibaw yet. We cannot go on for ever keeping strong garrisons at Thayet-myo and Toungoo, our frontier stations, where the soldiers have little else to do but die of fever and cholera and heat-apoplexy. Constant scares ruin the trade in Rangoon, and, as Lord Ripon says, when we are attacked in our mercantile interests we are wounded in our most irritable point. The abrogation of the monopolies is little better than a sham, and the negotiations for a new treaty are little more sincere. Thibaw will not receive a new Resident in the Royal City, except shoeless and practically lying on his stomach. We can hardly agree to that again.

The rupture came six years later, brought about by secret treatings with France and autocratic dealings with the Bombay Burma Trading Corporation. The Burmese kingdom fell with the suddenness of a paralytic stroke, and King Thibaw was a prisoner within a month of his rejection of the British ultimatum. He now lives forgotten at Ratnagiri.

CHAPTER L

KING THIBAW

III.—A KADAW DAY

" THE princes, the governors, and the captains, the judges, the treasurers, the counsellors, the sheriffs, and all the rulers of the provinces were gathered together and fell down and worshipped at what time they heard the sound of the cornet, flute, harp, sackbut, psaltery, dulcimer, and all kinds of music."

That is an exact description of the course of proceedings in Mandalay on a kadaw day. The gentlemen of the court and band as aforesaid, in the plain of Dura, must have greatly resembled Thibaw's worshippers, though it would be unfair to compare Nebuchadnezzar with the feckless last king of the Burmans. A kadaw-né means, literally translated, " a beg-pardon day." On such occasions all the officials, the tributary chiefs, and most eminent men in the country have to come to the palace and do homage and worship at the Golden Feet. There may be as many " Beg-pardon Days " during the year as his majesty pleases, but the most regular and best-attended, as well as the most brilliant, are always at the beginning and end of Lent, which extends, roughly speaking, from June to October. The end of Lent is probably the greatest occasion of all, and the audience sometimes, as was the case in 1880, extends over three days.

During Lent, every one is supposed to fast and be pious and improve his mind generally. On the conclusion of such a period, therefore, it is fitting that all loyal subjects should renew their allegiance to the Great Lord of Righteousness, and prostrate themselves with humble regard at his magnificent feet.   The giving of presents or kadaw——no one can go near the king without a present——is represented as a deprecatory offering to avert deserved punishment for offences.

The whole town is *en fête* on such occasions.   The Lord Mayor's show, or the transformation scene in a pantomime, which are the stay-at-home Englishman's idea of supreme magnificence, are as nothing compared to the procession round the moat which encircles the city walls.   Mingyis, Atwinwuns, Sawbwas, Myosas ; officials and vassals in formidable numbers and with terrible names ; each man accompanied and adorned with his utmost possessions in the way of man, beast, gauds, and raiment, file proudly round preparatory to entering the palace.   The description of a prince's order of going may suffice to give an idea of the whole.   First come the lictors, prancing along with their fasces and hoarse shoutings, yelling to everybody to clear the way, regardless of the fact that the populace is all down on its knees by the side of the road, shikhoing reverentially. They are about half a dozen in number, and to a short-sighted man appear to be stark naked.   A closer inspection with a glass, however, reveals the fact that they have some regard for decency, if they have little for anything else.   Behind them comes the family band, braying, and clashing, and skirling its loudest.   Undisturbed by the din, stalk composedly in the rear half a dozen elephants, the first couple splendid tuskers, in complete war-array, with fighting howdahs on their backs, and brilliant housings trailing to the ground ; the second pair with ordinary furnishings, and the others with no further encumbrance than the mahaut on their backs.   As near to these as their syces can persuade them to go, caper a number of led horses, harnessed with gay scarlet saddles, and saddle flaps, with tassels of the same colour sweeping the earth.   Immediately in their rear is a bright-hued cloud of retainers, armed with guns, spears, and swords, and many carrying fans of all sorts and sizes. Floating over their head like a great red cloud, is the prince's wide satin-fringed umbrella, or perhaps it may be a gold one, if he enjoys his master's favour.   Then there is a rabble of body-servants, carrying a gold-sheathed sword, a velvet pillow, spittoons, betel-nut boxes, and a variety of other things of uses more or less obvious. Last of all, surrounded by his page body-guard, comes the mintha himself, reclining in a wan, a finely-carved litter, borne by many shoulders. Many of the officials are, of course, unable to make such a grand display as this, but every one does his utmost to surpass his fellows in some point or other, and the result is a spectacle which would furnish abundance of valuable notions to a pantomime scenic artist racking his brains for novelties.

All the retinue is left outside when they come to the palace and ascend the broad flight of steps flanked by the two great gilded cannon, and approach the nandaw, the magnificent Hall of Audience. At stated points they pay lowly reverence to the graceful spire which rises over the throne and marks the centre of the palace, of the town, of Burma, and therefore of the universe. Inside the nandaw each man has his special place, according to his rank, Englishmen being ordinarily told off with ministers of the third grade. They sit there and smoke, placidly awaiting events.

The Hall of Audience is a fine building of its kind ; a long columned chamber, open on three sides, with gilt and red pillars, and a profusion of ornaments. The walls are made gorgeous with bits of looking-glass, porcelain, fragments of coloured glass, a mosaic of queer odds and ends fastened on with a resinous gum. This style of ornamentation is peculiarly Burmese, and is really very striking, though the materials may not seem promising. The effect of the whole is unique, if a little bewildering. It is like a compound chromotrope out of order. But close inspection gives an impression of tawdriness, and the national Burmese carelessness appears through all. Round the tops of the wooden walls runs beautifully carved lattice-work, but some of it has got broken in one place, and at another all the gilding has come off. There are some richly ornamented doors, but hinges have not been available when they were put up, and they swing on a sort of ball and socket contrivance which serves the purpose, but makes close-fitting and easy movement impossible.

The throne stands at the far end of the hall on a high raised dais. It diminishes by a gradation of little ledges to mid-height, and then similarly expands, like one notched pyramid thrust down on another. Those of the royal blood sit ordinarily in front on either side of the dais, but there are lamentably few of the royal blood nowadays.

Every one is collected now. The scene is such as can be seen nowhere in the world but in Burma, and in Burma only in perfection in the Hall of Audience. A Burmese crowd is always a gay sight, but when all the highest in the land have assembled in the yôndaw, it is magnificent. The Tennysonian " wind-stirred tulip beds " is a tempting phrase, but it hardly seems sufficient. A stirabout of rainbows has an oriental sound about it, and perhaps more fitly suggests the brilliant contrasts of colour. What a magnificent sight it must be from the throne ; the eye passing over the gaily dressed figures, every face bent low to the ground, down the broad steps, and through the towering eastern gate, over spires and pagodas away to the shaggy dark Shan hills beyond, like the entries to King Arthur's palace that

> Open'd from the hall
> At one end one, that gave upon a range
> Of level pavement where the king would pace
> At sunrise, gazing over plain and wood ;
> And down from this a lordly stairway sloped
> Till lost in blowing trees and tops of towers.

Little wonder the king of Burma thinks himself a deity.

Meanwhile the collected worshippers smoke cheroots and chew betel, and talk freely. Suddenly a little bell tinkles, and every one is grovelling on his stomach in a second. A purple curtain is drawn aside, and down a long corridor, laid with crimson and gold carpet, the Sovereign of Life and Death comes with a hurried, uneven step. He is in full regal dress, and the broad gold shoulder-belt of the salwè and the towering jewelled crown on his head, seem to weigh heavily on him as he ascends wearily to the throne. Now comes the presentation of the kadaw. The actual presents are all lying tumbled in a heap somewhere, and his majesty probably never sees them at all. Lists are made out on palm-leaf, scratched on with a sharp-pointed style, and these are

brought up by a thandawgan.   The sight is in every way a
remarkable one, and quite in keeping with the semi-barbaric
character of the surroundings.   The herald starts from the
eastern gate, about three hundred yards off, and in full view
from the hall the whole way.   Across the wide open space
between the outer and inner stockades, and up between the
gilded cannon he comes, with a fantastic, prancing gait,
waving the palm-leaves at arm's length, and bowing lowly
to the ground at every ten paces.   Up the steps and between
a long double line of the gorgeously uniformed ahmudan,
and the blue-jacketed marines with the anchor on their
spiked helmets, all presenting arms.   Throughout the whole
ceremony, the courtiers within the hall, at intervals of a
minute or less, raise a long-drawn shout of payā——a word
expressive of deity.   When at last the thandawgan reaches
the throne he bows thrice, deposits the palm-leaves
reverentially, and lies prone.   They are read out in part, or
altogether, or not at all, according to his majesty's pleasure.
Then he commences to talk.   He is much more fluent in a
grand audience than he is at a private interview.   He asks
one minister how the lottery under his charge is filling up ;
another what news there is from the army now fighting
against the Shans : a French engineer is questioned with
regard to some works going on in the royal gardens ; a
governor of a remote province enjoined to be regular in
collecting the ngwedaw, the royal tax.   His monastic studies
have given him command of a copious fund of lofty moral
sayings, and these he scatters about freely, and sends away
aspirants to the royal favour exultant in the feeling that
some golden words have been addressed, if not to them
directly, at any rate to some one near them in the row.
An audience occasionally lasts a couple of hours, so that
Europeans, if they are at all stiff in the joints, are apt to get
frightfully cramped, and afford unrighteous amusement to
malicious old wuns by their uneasy attempts to find a more
comfortable arrangement of their legs.   Such receptions are,
therefore, not in favour with Englishmen, except those who
may be in the royal service, or who are negotiating for a
grant of some kind, and therefore wish to be well with his
majesty.   The king smokes a gigantic white cheroot all the

time, and chews betel simultaneously, making up the morsel
himself very often.   Many of those in the hall smoke also,
but the operation cannot be conducted with any great
degree of comfort when your nose is close to the nether
extremity of the spine of the man in front of you.   In
former days pipes were often smoked, but the bowls were
always thrust through holes in the floor made for the
purpose.

Thibaw's apparent affability at these public audiences
counteracts the effect of any other habits he may have, not
so favourably viewed by Buddhists, and there are, perhaps,
not a few of his subjects with whom he is possibly more
popular than any king of Burma has been since the days of
Alaungpaya the founder of the dynasty.   His faults are
thought to be those of his ministers and advisers.   His easy-
going indolence is the end of the desire of all his race.   But
it is not likely that his reign will be long.   There is too much
scheming and plotting going on in Mandalay just now for
that.   If Thibaw dies a sovereign he will be lucky.   In
the meantime the king rises and disappears behind the
purple curtain.   The durbar disperses immediately.   The
worshippers return home rejoicing and damn the king's
enemies.

CHAPTER LI

THE PALACE

THE palace of Mandalay lies in the centre of the four-square city, like the innermost of a series of Chinese carved boxes. The capital is a city within a city. The greater part of the wide plain from the Irrawaddy to the Shan hills, a space of about five miles broad and as many long, down to the Dôtta wadi, the Amarapura river, is laid out in wide roads running at right angles to one another, with abundance of houses of all kinds, from the brick house of the Chinaman, with its cumbrous tiles that bend in the rafters, and the white-plastered, flat-roofed habitation of the Mogul or Surati merchant, to the wood or bamboo dwelling of the Burman. They are not very close together, but there is plenty of space, and every house has its patch of garden, or clump of plantain trees, and its wide court where the buffaloes and the ox-cart can be disposed comfortably. But these only form the suburbs. The Myo, the city proper of Mandalay, is a huge walled square, each face a mile and an eighth long. The mud brick built walls are nearly thirty feet high and about three thick, backed with a heavy mass of earth, but though they would be hard to batter down, there are no guns mounted for their defence on the bastions which rise at intervals of about two hundred yards, each surmounted by an open-sided teak pavilion, carved in the usual gabled, joss-house, spire-like fashion. The crest of the parapet is deeply denticulated, with no other apparent advantage than that of ornament. There are twelve gates to the city, three on each side, but only one bridge to each three over the moat, except on the west, where there are two, one opposite the

amingala or south-west gate, specially reserved for the
passage of funerals. Outside every gate is a post bearing
the name and emblem of the gate, the latter being the signs
of the zodiac. Sixty feet, or thereabouts, from the walls,
runs all round a deep moat, about fifty yards broad, covered
in many places with the lotus plant that the Buddhist loves.
Here and there upon it float a number of royal craft, state
barges, and despatch boats, some of them richly gilded, with
the kalawaik, the crane, carved on the stern, others foundered
and lying rotting, with their lofty sterns rising high in the
air. Covering each gate is a traverse, or crenelated barbican,
of the same construction as the walls. Inside, the streets of
the city run parallel to the walls. They are wide and fairly
well kept wherever the king is likely to pass, but there is
no attempt at metalling. Young trees line the sides, and
down most of them run little streams of water. There is no
attempt at a drainage system, but the town is essentially
clean and airy, the pigs and pariah dogs acting as scavengers,
and the constant open spaces ensuring ventilation. Right
in the centre is the palace, which has two successive en-
closures. The outer is a quarter of a mile square, and
consists of a high teak palisade, very massive and compact.
Within this is a wide open space laid out as an esplanade,
inside of which is a brick wall, edged round a great part of
the way by the houses of high ministers and court officials.
The outer court has four gates, each presided over by a
special commander; the north, or water gate, being only
available for the royal barges. Except for members of the
palace household, there is only admittance to the inner
enclosure by the gate on the eastern face. There is a special
portal in the centre here, opened only for the king, and none
but the Lord of the Golden Throne may use it. All else
must enter by the taga-ni, the red postern, a cramped little
gateway, which makes the smallest man involuntarily bend
his head as he approaches the golden palace. The front of
the building is decorated with gilding and tinsel work, which
looks well when it is new, but after the rainy seasons would
be better not there at all. To the left is the Hlutdaw,
the Hall off the Supreme Council, a detached structure, raised
some feet off the ground, and perfectly open; the roof, richly

carved with flowers and figures, and adorned with the usual flamboyant pinnacles, supported on massive teak pillars, painted vermilion colour at the base, and gilt higher up. Straight ahead is the great Hall of Audience, a colonnade, or columned arcade, extending along the entire eastern front, and opening directly upon it. At the end of a pillared vista stands the throne, on a dais, reached by five steps from the level of the hall. The top is a cushioned ledge, like the box in a theatre. Just over the throne, and in the centre of the palace, which is the centre of the city, which is the centre of Burma, which is the Turanian "hub" of the world, rises the seven-roofed spire, emblematic of royalty and religion. The princes of the highest rank sit in front to the right of the throne; those of the blood-royal, but not so closely connected, to the left. Then in regular gradation, opposite one another, the wungyi, atwinwuns, wundauks, and the minor officials. On either side of the hall of audience and behind are a number of minor throne-rooms, not rooms in the English sense of the word, but simply open roofed spaces, separated from each other by skirtings of planking, covered with gold-leaf, and supported by a multitude of teak pillars, dyed for the greater part of their height a deep red. Some rooms are almost entirely gilt, others are adorned with wall-paintings, others, again, with the favourite mosaic of bits of mirror and coloured glass, framed in a gilt network. Every room is furnished with one or more stands of arms; there is a rack of sadly ill-cared-for muskets round the throne itself. The palace is, in fact, a gigantic armoury. All the cannon and guns in the country are kept there. Hence it is that when the palace is taken by a usurper, the country is conquered. The abundance of gold-leaf ought to make the effect splendid, but the quantity of alloy there is in the gilding makes it speedily lose its glitter, and the general impression is that of dinginess, if not indeed of actual slip-shod tawdriness. But to be seen at its best the palace should be visited on a great beg-pardon day, when the rough plank floors are covered with gorgeous rugs and carpets, and the halls are filled with officials dressed in all the hues of the rainbow.

There are a variety of matters to be carefully observed by all who enter, or have anything to do with the palace.

Best known is the regulation with regard to the wearing of shoes. Burmans must remove them as soon as they enter the palace enclosure, just as they would on going inside of the parawun of a pagoda or a monastery. Englishmen and white foreigners generally are required to take off their boots whenever they begin to ascend a step—the whole palace and all the buildings near it being on a brick platform some ten feet or more above the level of the ground. There are always a number of dancers and jugglers and loiterers about the royal buildings, and the necessity of being separated from your shoes sometimes leads to the loss of them altogether. It is on record that a British Resident incurred this misfortune, and had to make the best of his way, partly in a pair of Burman sandals, and partly on his stocking soles —as being preferable—to the outside of the teak stockade where his pony was waiting for him.

Another ceremony is that of shekhoing to the spire, the external emblem of the throne. All Burmans must do this at each of the gates, at the foot of the steps, and at intervals in between, according to loyalty, or the supposed friendly or hostile attitude of lookers-on. All the early English ambassadors had to conform to this regulation, notably Cox and Baker, the latter dropping on his knees. After an intermediate stage of taking off their hats, permission was gained to dispense with everything but the removal of shoes and sword. But the court rejoices in the fact that no one can pass through the red postern without bending his head, regulations or no regulations.

No arms whatever can be taken into the palace, not even —perhaps I should say, least even, in view of conspiracies— by the royal princes. Similarly, all umbrellas must be left at the outer gate of the palace, except by members of the royal household, who may carry them to the foot of the steps of the audience hall. Common people must lower them when they pass any of the gates outside. Arrest, or rough handling by the guards, would be the infallible result of non-compliance. Another rule is that you must take no money out of the palace. You may take in as much as you please.

No one in the palace, or indeed in the whole town, must sleep otherwise than with his feet turned outwards from the spire. To show the soles of the feet to the throne is high treason. This is awkward for the inhabitants of some quarters, for there is a rule applying to all Buddhists, that they must not place their feet towards the east, where the sun rises and whence the next Buddha, Arimadeya, will come, nor to the west, where the bawdi bin stands, or stood, the tree under which Shin Gautama attained the supreme wisdom. The superstition is probably derived from the Brahmins, who threaten grievous dangers to the man who places his feet on the shadow of a dewa, a king, a teacher, a saint, or another man's wife.

The frequent change of locality of the palace, and therefore of the capital, is a peculiarity of Burma. There are about a score of towns in the country which have been at one time or other the metropolis. Such are Tagaung, Old Pagān, and Shwebo, above Mandalay; Prome (under the title Tharekettara), Pagān, Sagaing, Ava, and Amarapura, below it. The last two are the best known; indeed some people to the present day persist in talking of the "Kingdom of Ava," though that once brilliant capital has been little better than a jungle for a great many years, and the lines of the old walls can only be traced with difficulty.

It is hardly correct to say, as most writers on Burma have hitherto done, that with a new king there should be a new capital. This has very frequently been the case, but the matter does not altogether depend upon the accession of a new sovereign. It is brought about by a very much more gruesome (the word is used advisedly) circumstance. On the foundation of a new capital, there are always a certain number of people buried alive. The idea is that they become nat-thein, that their spirits haunt the place where they were put to death, and attack all persons approaching with malevolent intentions. The notion is entirely due to the royal astrologers, the Brahmin pônnas, and as being repugnant to the tenets of Buddhism, is strenuously denounced by the true brethren of the yellow robe. But it fits in very well with the popular superstition regarding the existence of spirits, and has hence always firmly maintained its ground. It is a matter of common knowledge that this idea of sanctifying a building with human sacrifices is a notion which has prevailed in all parts of the world at different times, and instances of horrors of the kind are not unknown in Europe.

The virtue of the sacrifices only lasts a certain time, and when it is gone a new city should be built. There are certain signs, added to public disasters, which point out to the initiated when this alteration of site should take place. Mandalay was commenced in 1858, and two years later the seat of government was transferred from Amarapura, some five or six miles down the river. When the foundations of the city wall were laid, fifty-two persons of both sexes, and of various age and rank, were consigned to a living tomb. Three were buried under each of the twelve city gates, one at each of the four corners, one under each of the palace gates, and at the corners of the timber stockade, and four under the throne itself. The selection had to be made with care, for the victims were required to be representative people, born on special days of the week, and the boys buried were not to have any tattoo marks on them, the girls not to have their ears bored. When it was known that the troops were making the collection, no one was to be seen about the streets, except in great bands in the middle of the day. The government gave a series of magnificent dramatic performances, but no one went to see them. Eventually, however, the tale was made up, and the building went on apace. Along with the four human beings buried at the corners of the city were placed four jars full of oil, carefully covered over and protected from any damage that might come from the weight of earth pressing down upon them. These were examined every seven years by the royal astrologers, and as long as they remained intact the town was considered safe.

At the third examination in 1880, however, it was found that the oil in two of the jars was either completely dried up or had leaked out. One was pretty far gone, and the fourth alone remained in a tolerably satisfactory state. At this very time, the January and February of 1880, a terrible scourge of smallpox was decimating the town, and two of the royal house, King Thibaw's infant son, his only child, and the ex-Pagān Min, the cock-fighting king, had fallen victims. This was bad enough, but other signs portending evil had happened. One of the most valued of the crown jewels, the Nansin Baddamya, had disappeared, a huge ruby, cherished as emblematic of the fortune of the dynasty since the days of Alaungpaya. A tiger in the royal gardens escaped from his cage, a most ominous circumstance, not for the poor wretch whom he killed and half ate before he could be recaptured, but for the city and the entire kingdom. The appearance of wild animals in a town is a sign that it will speedily turn to a wilderness. It was the discovery of a tiger and some deer in the environs of Amarapura which decided the fate of that "City of the Immortals." All these circumstances, coupled with the outward and visible sign of the wrath of the spirits in the shape of the plague of small-pox, decided the pônnas at once. It was no use filling the jars with oil again, or putting in fresh ones. Such parsimonious measures would be considerably worse than useless. A full conclave of the astrologers voted by a large majority for the change of the capital. This, however, neither the ministers nor Thibaw Min would hear of. Mandalay is very different from Amarapura and Ava. There are too many solid brick houses and mills and public manufactories —none of them working, it is true, but too costly to be abandoned—in the present capital to admit of its being thrown over in the old casual way, when a royal order forced everybody to migrate, on pain of imprisonment or death. The pônnas therefore held another meeting, and it was decided that the only other alternative was the offering of propitiatory sacrifices. At the instance of the Pônna Wun, a truculent old villain, it was resolved that the number should be the highest possible : a hundred men, a hundred women, a hundred boys, a hundred girls, a hundred soldiers, and a hundred foreigners. This the king agreed to, and a royal mandate was signed, and arrests forthwith commenced. A frightful panic spread in Mandalay after the first day. Every steamer leaving the capital was crowded to suffocation, boats went down the river in dozens, and there seemed every possibility that Mandalay would be deserted. Then the ministers took fright at the indignation which the announced massacres caused in England, and the whole thing was countermanded and denied.   But upwards of a hundred people had been arrested, and some of these, when liberated months afterwards, declared that in the dark nights of terror, when no one ventured about Mandalay streets, people were buried under each of the posts at the twelve gates, as a compromise between the fear of the spirits and the fear that the English troops would cross the frontier. Each of these posts bears an image of an animal from one of the seals of the king, and before the post sits a figure of a bilu, with a thick club, to act as watchman, in case the human guard should go to sleep.   As Burman sentries generally sleep sounder than other people, the propitiation of these spirits at any rate was a very imperative precaution.   Whether the oil-jars were filled and reburied *alone* is a dark mystery.   But the smallpox left Mandalay, and the place is as happy as ever it was, which, however, is not saying much.

The British town of Mandalay is very different from that described.   The Palace stockade has gone, and with it very many of the suites of apartments, notably in the women's quarter.   The Hall of Audience for a time was converted into a Tamil Mission chapel ; the Hlutdaw into a hideous collection of clerks' offices.   This has been changed owing to the indignant protests of English visitors.   Most of the Palace Halls are now empty : even the Upper Burma Club has been turned out.

The old City has now become cantonments with a few scattered barracks, officers' quarters, and wide stretches of grass. What formerly constituted the suburbs is now Mandalay town.   The former execrable roads are now among the best in Burma.   But many of the notable buildings, the elaborate monasteries, and gilt shrines have been burnt.   Mandalay is certainly a dwindling town ; the only question is how long it will remain the second town in Burma.

CHAPTER LII

THE LORD WHITE ELEPHANT

THE importance attached to the possession of a white elephant is traceable to the Buddhist system. The form in which Gautama Buddha entered the womb of Queen Maya to be born upon earth for the last time to "teach the Law and give the millions peace" was that of a white elephant. The Saddan, or celestial elephant, was an avatar of his many existences previously. The Saddan is gifted with special endowments, and is one of the seven precious things the possession of which marks the Sekyawadé, the Mahā Chakra Vartti Raja, "the great wheel-turning king," the holy and universal sovereign—a ruler who appears in once a cycle, at the time when the waxing and waning term of human life has reached its maximum of an athinkaya (a huge period represented by a unit and 164 cyphers) in duration. Thus the possession of an undoubted white elephant stands as a sign and symbol of universal sovereignty ; and every Burmese king longed for the capture of such a treasure during his reign as a token that his legitimate royalty is recognised by the unseen powers. The great river of Burma, the Iriawaddy, is named from Airawata, the elephant of Indra, a sufficient assertion of the proper dwelling-place of all his successors. Hence the reverence of the Hindoos for the animal, and their not infrequent pilgrimages to Mandalay to see the royal creature and have a dursun, or interview of worship, with him.

All the elephants in the country, whether wild or tame, belonged to the king : whoever captured one had to give him up to the king, and he granted permission to the princes and to a few of the higher dignitaries to use them. The lucky discoverer of a white elephant was made a mingyi, and was exempted from taxes and burdens of every kind for the rest of his life. Red and spotted elephants were also held in great esteem.

White crows, rats, mice, and hares are common and easily distinguished ; but it is different with a white elephant. He is not to be considered as snow-white : very far from it. All the white elephants now existing in Siam and Burma are of a light mouse colour, somewhat of the same tint as the pale freckles to be found on the trunk of almost every ordinary elephant. This light grey is uniform all over, the spots on the trunk being white. The depth of the colour, however, varies greatly ; and there are often blemishes in the shape of darker patches which would seem to ruin an otherwise eligible candidate's claims. It has been therefore found necessary to determine some infallible test points, which will demonstrate the right of the animal to his title. Determining white elephants is quite a science, and there is a very considerable literature on the subject. The Burmese skilled men fix upon two of these tests as superior to all others. One is that the elephant shall have five toe-nails on his hind feet instead of four. This is a good way of making certain, but occasionally there are indubitably black elephants which have the sacred number of toes. These are white elephants debased by sin, labouring under the evil kan of previous existences, and therefore ineligible for the honours accorded to the real animal. The other test is considered perfectly decisive, no matter what the precise tint of the skin may be. It is this : if you pour water upon a "white" elephant he turns red, while a black elephant only becomes blacker than ever. This is the final test always resorted to in Mandalay. A swarthy specimen who had twenty toe-nails and turned red when he was washed would be forthwith installed in all the honours and emoluments of the Sinbyudaw, no matter what scoffers might say about his colour. Such a creature was the last Lord White Elephant in Mandalay. He would not have been recognised as an albino by any except those who are learned in the science and well versed in the voluminous and puzzling minutiæ of the question. To most people he seemed an impostor, for his colour was a mixture of light-brown and dingy, smoke-smirched cream colour. The eye, when you know it, is perhaps the best rough test for an amateur. The iris ought to be yellow, with a reddish outer annulus. The effect of this is decisive to the connoisseur, if only sinister to the outsider. But the red ring represents the circle of the nine precious gems. In other respects the Sinbyudaw was not attractive in appearance ; he was very big, but, notwithstanding the care taken of him, was remarkably lean and hollow-sided. His tusks, however, were magnificent—white, smooth, and curving forward in front of his trunk so that they almost met. In his young days he was suckled by women, who stood in a long row outside his palace, and the honour was eagerly sought after, for the creature was a national pride and not merely a royal monopoly. A hundred soldiers guarded his palace, and the Sovereign of the Golden Throne himself made offerings and paid him reverence. An establishment of thirty men waited on him, and among them was a Minister of State, who managed his affairs and looked after the revenues of the province that was assigned to him to "eat." His palace stood within the inner stockade and was decorated with the royal pya-that. Every day he was bathed with scented sandal water, and all his vessels and utensils were made of gold. Troupes of the palace *coryphées* danced for his pleasure, and there were choruses of sweet-voiced singers to lull him to sleep.

Nevertheless his lordship was very bad-tempered, and his attendants were much afraid of him. Such things are, however, not unknown with human kings. On one occasion the Sinbyudaw killed a man who had ventured too near, and there was a good deal of trouble and noise before the body could be got away from him. The king—Thibaw's father—heard the commotion, and inquired what was the matter. When he was told, he expressed great concern and not a little alarm for the future state of the Lord White Elephant, with the red stain of murder on him, blotting out hosts of previous good deeds. But the elephant's minister calmed his mind and restored him to equanimity by saying, " Pray do not be disturbed, payā ; lu ma hôk bu kalā—it was not a man only a foreigner."

Probably because he was so vicious, the last Lord White Elephant was never ridden, as previous incumbents were. No one but the king himself could have ridden him ; and latterly King Mindôn became very fat and feeble, while King Thibaw's nerves were not strong enough. The Sinbyudaw is king of elephants, and therefore none but a king might mount him. His royal trappings were kept in his palace, and were very magnificent. Draperies of silk and bands of rich red cloth ran from the head-stall to the back and thence to the tail, hanging in curves over the body. They were richly embroidered in gold and studded with rubies and emeralds. On the forehead was a plate of gold, recording his majesty's titles, such as was worn by every man of rank in the country up to the Arbiter of Existence himself. Bosses of pure gold and clusters of precious stones covered the head-stall, and golden tassels hung down over the ears. When he went forth to take the air, he was shaded by golden and white umbrellas. He and the king shared all the white umbrellas in the country between them. The king of men had nine ; the king of elephants two, but he had also four golden ones. Not even the heir-apparent, if there were one, had a right to use the white umbrella. He had to be contented with his eight golden shades ; the display of a white one would have been regarded as a declaration of rebellion, and would have resulted in his immediate execution. No wonder, then, that the attendants and visitors took off their shoes when they entered Sinbyudaw's palace, and that the people bowed down low and did humble obeisance when he passed through the streets. These were swept and sprinkled with water for him as for the King of the Golden Throne himself.

The Lord White Elephant's suite accounted for his irritable temper by the bad treatment which he met with in his early days. The royal coffers were low, and the English were clamouring for the last instalments of the Yandabo indemnity money. So the rents of the elephant were appropriated to pay off the troublesome foreigners. Every care was taken to soften the indignity. The king himself wrote a long address on a palm-leaf, requesting the Lord White Elephant not to take it amiss that his revenues were devoted to the payment of the barbarians.   In any case he should not suffer, for the whole sum would be refunded in two months' time.   The circumstance, however, seems to have preyed on his mind, for the bodyguard said that his majesty (the elephant) had never been the same since.

There are frequent reports of the capture of white elephants, and special questing parties are sent out every now and then.   But the candidates almost invariably fail to satisfy the water test, or the tail is not long enough, or the position of the eye is wrong, and the red ring is wanting. At any rate, genuine " white " elephants are very seldom found.   As with the king, when the Sinbyudaw died it was not permissible to say so in as many rude words.   It had to be whispered that his majesty had " departed " or " disappeared."   He used to get a royal funeral.

When Mandalay was taken in 1886 the Royal White Elephant was sent down to Rangoon, where he was to have been kept in the Zoological Gardens.   But he died immediately after he arrived.   There has been no suggestion of the discovery of a White Elephant since.

CHAPTER LIII

MINISTERS OF STATE

WHEN Mindôn Min heard in 1874 that the elections had gone against the ministry, and that Disraeli was to be Premier, he sighed, and said: "Then poor Ga-la-sa-tong (Gladstone) is in prison, I suppose. I am sorry for him. I don't think he was a bad fellow, and I gave him the Fifteenstring Salwè (the Burmese Order of Knighthood) a year or two ago." That is the Burmese notion of how to settle the Opposition. The lines of statesmen in the Royal City of Gems were not cast in pleasant places. If they rose rapidly, they came down with as much precipitation; and their fall was as crushing as ordinarily it was inevitable. The coolie of to-day might be the minister of to-morrow; and a month hence he might be spread-eagled in the court of the palace, with a vertical sun beating down upon him and huge stones piled on his chest and stomach. Or he might be treated even more summarily than this. When King Tharrawaddy succeeded he made Bagyidaw's ministers work as slaves on the roads for a time, and when this exercise had quite worn them out, charitably put them to death, without the frightful barbarities which characterised his treatment of the upstart queen dowager and her quondam all-powerful brother Minthagyi. A more recent example was that of the Naingan-gya Wundauk. This unfortunate statesman was sent in 1880 as an ambassador to the English Raj, and after eight months' stay on board of a steamer at Thayetmyo, a few miles inside the British frontier, came back to say that his mission had failed, and that in fact he had been told to go away. He did not survive long. It was a week or two

before he was admitted to see the king ; and when he did
see him the meeting was unpleasant.   Next day the portly
wundauk " died of apoplexy."

Sudden deaths were not at all uncommon.   An official
displeased him in some way, and Mindôn Min said emphatically, " I don't want to see that man any more."   The poor
wretch left the royal presence to be seized by lictors outside
and killed more or less rapidly.   A day or two afterwards
his majesty would ask where so-and-so was.   " Alas ! sire,"
was the answer, " he died of chagrin shortly after the lord of
the earth and ocean cast eyes of displeasure on him."   Then
the Convener of the Fifth Great Synod quoted a pious saw
from the Lawkanidi, and turned his mind to other matters.
He made it a special boast that never in all his reign had he
ordered an execution.   Yet many people died of " official
colic " during the time he was on the throne, and Colonel
Sladen arrived sixty seconds too late with a respite for one
of the pious monarch's own sons.   The sound of the hoofs
of the English Resident's horse as he galloped past the
astrologers' monastery to the execution ground only quickened
the headsman's sword.   The hapless Padein Mintha should
have perished with the setting sun.   There were still long
shadows slanting up from the trees by the royal foundry
when the colonel reined in and upbraided the presiding
Minister for his bloodthirsty haste.   The Lingayāma Sadaw,
when he heard the story, said the ayebaing should have been
a Buddhist and might probably become a yahanda in no
very distant existence.

Yet King Mindôn was undoubtedly a kindly man.   The
stories which occasionally appeared about him in the English
papers of twenty years or so back were not true.   He never
got a pea-rifle and " potted " his subjects from the palace
verandahs when he was bored.   They libelled him who said
he did.   He was a good Buddhist , and never took life of
man or animal.   King Thibaw was, perhaps, not quite so
strict in his notions.   When he first came to the throne he
unearthed the spear with which his grandfather Tharrawaddy
used occasionally to spit his counsellors.   The young king's
aim was not quite so good, or his purposes not quite so
deadly.   He prodded a few heralds and interpreters, and

flung the spear at one or two of his father's trusted advisers ; but it is not recorded that he ever actually killed anybody with his own hands.   In fact, he got on fairly well with his ministers, having drilled the seniors into complete submission to his wishes, and appointed among the younger members those who were most of his own way of thinking.   The most characteristic man in the Cabinet was the Hlethin Atwin-wun, better known as the Hpaungwun.   He was only of the second official grade, but none of the four wunmingyis had any real power.   They dated from the last reign, and were practically over-ridden by the younger party.   The king did, it is true, marry the daughter of the Kampat Min-gyi, but that stolid old gentleman was always remarkable for his disinclination to do anything at all, and was not at all likely to exert himself unduly for the sake of precarious pre-eminence.   Therefore the ex-Mayor of Mandalay, in con-junction with the Yanaung prince, a favourite of the Queen Supayalat's, and one or two others of the young Burman party, became the most representative ministers.

The Atwinwun wore the dragon tattooed on the nape of his neck.   Fourteen years before he was a slave, and in position little better than a coolie.   His rise from this rank might have been a credit to him if it had been effected by his own powers.   But he rose by a mere accident, and carried all the tendencies of his original position with him. In 1866, when two of King Thibaw's half-brothers, the Myingun and Myingundaing princes, rose in rebellion against their father, the late king, the Hpaungwun — he seems more familiar under his old title—was one of the guards in the palace.   After the rebels had killed their uncle, " the War Prince," they made for the Summer Palace, where the king was at the time along with Colonel Sladen, the British Resident.   The Summer Palace is a small building outside the stockade of the actual nandaw, and it was foreseen that his majesty would make immediately for the eastern gate, which is quite close at hand.   A man was therefore stationed there with orders to kill King Mindôn whenever he made his appearance.   All happened as had been surmised with one slight exception.   Royal blood in Mandalay never went outside the palace on its own legs, and when his majesty reached the gate he promptly jumped on the intending regicide's back and bade him carry him over the esplanade. The man was so overcome by the royal presence, or so slavishly accustomed to do what he was ordered, that he obeyed. When they were safe within the inner stockade he stooped down to let the king dismount, and his sword fell from the folds of his waistcloth. None but the king may carry arms within the nandaw, and the Hpaungwun, grasping the situation, snatched up the sword and cut the man's head off. Mindôn Min, with a curious regard for this mixture of barbarity and rapidity of action, made the coolie a subordinate official on the spot, and since then the Hpaungwun has gone on distinguishing himself as on this occasion. He was promoted successively through the grades of slipper-bearer, tea-server, and betel-box holder to that of the Governor of the Royal Rafts or Barges (Hpaung-wun), and Mayor of Mandalay (Myowun), which latter steps he gained through his activity in the palace massacres —loyalty and energy his patent called it. King Thibaw found in the prompt and ruthless wun a willing and enthusiastic helper in the murder of the princes and princesses. Naturally he was one of the king's firmest supporters, for Thibaw's fall meant his own certain death. His squat figure and vulturine face made him the most easily recognised of the court circle, and he repaid the aversion of English-men with a most demonstrative hatred. Perhaps this was because his features, and especially his nose, suggested a European among his forebears. As Hlethin Atwinwun, or Minister of the Interior, he had supreme command over all the lower fluviatile provinces, and had a large military force at his command. He escaped punishment and became a trader after the annexation.

Equally high in the king's favour, and not less fierce in their denunciation of the English, were the Taingda Atwin-wun and the Yenangyaung, also of the same second grade. They, too, were prominent in the massacres, and were reputed to drink curaçoa in tumblers. If they really did, it would account for a great deal. Both were slaves of the young Thibaw prince when he was a boy in the English Missionary school, and followed his fortunes into the Royal

Monastery. As chiefs of the Letthôndaw, the Royal Page Bodyguard, they had the opportunity which won their rank. A daughter of the Taingda married the Hpaungwun, and the Atwinwun in consequence gave occasional dinners to the European and quasi-European dwellers in Mandalay. The guests were, as a rule, not in a position to brave his anger by a refusal, and had to endure most elaborate indignities at his hands. All the most humiliating formalities of the palace had to be observed towards the young minister, and the *menu* was said, by the victims, to be the worst of them all. In regard to this, it must be remembered that it took a very great deal to hurt the dignity of some Mandalay Europeans, and also that they were as fickle as any mob.

These three atwinwuns were the most powerful ministers, and had greater influence with the king than any of their technical superiors. The four wungyis were, with the exception of the Upathi, of very little account with any one. The Laungshwe Mingyi had been for long nearly bed-ridden, and was not able to appear even at Mindôn's funeral. The other three had all been in Europe, but the most that can be said of the Kampat Mingyi is that he became the king's father-in-law, while the Yaw was absent for nearly two years on an expedition against the Shan mountaineers. He effected nothing warlike, and rumour said that he was so fully occupied in keeping the troops from dispersing to their homes that he had no time to fight. The fourth, however, was a remarkable man. The Upathi, better known as the Kinwunmingyi, had been very prominent for years, and he lived for twenty years after the annexation as a pensioner of the British Government. He used to be commonly spoken of as the premier on English analogy, but there was really no such dignitary known in Burma, and the Kinwungyi's substantive appointment was simply that of foreign secretary. He was twice to Europe on embassies, and his naturally acute mind was thus enlarged in its views. Had it not been for his great command over the public feeling, and his influence even over King Thibaw, there would certainly have been war between Burma and Great Britain in 1879. The foreign secretary was the representative of order ; and it was a bad thing for the country when he was almost entirely driven from power, if not from office. He was a master of oriental craft, and tided through all the intrigues against him. He held a document from the late king, granting him immunity from all kinds of death. The list is a very frightful one, and ranges from vulgar, obvious beheading to the refined cruelty of throwing on a spread-eagled victim a nest of the fierce red ants known as kāgyin, whose mandibles drive a man raving mad in little over a quarter of an hour. But the palm-leaf patent would have been of little avail without a head that was well able to take care of itself. Like many of the older and better ministers, the Upathi Mingyi came from the cloister to office. On Mindôn's accession to the throne, he at once appointed the Pakhan Mingyi from a monastery to be an atwinwun, and in no very great time to the supreme rank of mingyi, a skipping of the lower grades which was very unusual, as was also the circumstance that the new minister married one of King Tharrawaddy's widows. The Kin Wungyi was in the Pakhan's monastery, shared his rise, and when the patron, who never lost the bilious, monkish look, and the cold, stiff pôngyi's manner, obtained the deliverance, succeeded him as mingyi. Had he been permitted, the foreign secretary would have made Burma a very different country from what it was.

The Upathi was certainly a superior man, and compiled some valuable digests of Burmese law after his retirement in Rangoon, but undoubtedly the most singular of the Mandalay court officials was the Pangyet Wun. He was a polished gentleman, spoke English fairly and French and Italian fluently, and had considerably more than a veneer of civilisation. As a boy he was at school in Calcutta, and having been well grounded there, proceeded to France. There he took his degree at the Panthéon, obtained a diploma in the Central Imperial School of Arts and Manufactures in Paris, and was altogether nearly twelve years in Europe. Notwithstanding his reminiscences of Mabille and the Champs Elysées, however, he accommodated himself very well to circumstances. When the young wun returned to Mandalay, King Mindôn had a long talk with him, and finally said : " And these foreigners, then, have they in any of their cities buildings such as adorn our Royal City of Gems?" Alas! your majesty," he replied, "the luckless people have not the magnificent teak ; how, then, can they hope to raise anything comparable to the meanest of your palaces?" This courtier-like caution never deserted the Pangyet Wun. He never meddled with politics, and was content with his governorship of the glass manufactories, which meant anything or nothing, and commanded a nominal salary. But none of the ministers had any salary from King Thibaw, so that the cultured sinecurist was not worse off than his fellows. He consorted a good deal with foreigners, but averted suspicion by saying that it was merely to keep up his knowledge of their languages. No doubt he might have had a much higher post, but he had enough money, and did not care to run the risk of trying for more. That was also his view during the crisis and after the annexation.

CHAPTER LIV

THE BURMESE ARMY

THE Burmese army was not thought very much of even by the most patriotic Burman who had seen soldiers in other parts of the world. Malignant people called it a rabble ; more smooth-tongued and favourably-disposed critics were fain to acknowledge that it was deficient in discipline. In physique and courage the men were formidable enough, but flintlocks and long Enfields do not avail much against the breechloader, and when complete inability to manœuvre was added to this, it was evident that even in jungle warfare, except against an equally ill-armed foe, King Thibaw's forces would make but a sorry show. Military instruction of a certain kind they had, but it never extended beyond squad drill, and even this was but very perfunctorily learned, while movements of large bodies of men were never attempted, except the so-called reviews, which took place every now and again, and in 1879 were held within a day or two either way at the full moon of every month. These " reviews " were, however, nothing more than marches-out on a big scale, and were only useful as a means of displaying the soldier in the glory of his uniform, and giving him a little exercise. Except on these occasions, indeed, it was seldom that the soldiery appeared in military dress. Even when on guard they dispensed with every article of warlike attire, except the gun, and even that was more frequently to be found in the rack than in the sentry's hands. These military promenades, therefore, offered the most favourable opportunity of observing the royal levies.

The troops mustered at an early hour in the wide glacis

between the inner and outer stockades of the palace. There they fell in, in a theoretical formation of fours, and remained placidly waiting ; conversation went on freely, and smoking and chewing betel were not interfered with. The bogyi and other officers of rank meanwhile assembled within the inner court. After, perhaps, three or four hours' waiting, the king came out and inspected the forces through a field-glass from the head of the broad flight of steps in front of the Hall of Audience, or, perhaps, a notice was sent out that his majesty would not even view his troops in this easy fashion, and the army was saved from the—to English notions— exceedingly unmilitary attitude of grovelling on its stomach for a matter of two minutes while the king looked through his binocular.

This over, the non-commissioned officers said *hé !* and the men sloped arms and started off anyhow. Outside the eastern gate a halt was made while the bogyis, colonels of regiments, mounted their elephants, got into position, and marshalled their bodyguards round about them. The lesser bos and thwethaukgyis, "great blood drinkers," were mounted on ponies and had their personal retainers about them too. The commanding officer came at the head of his regiment, preceded by twenty pages carrying double-barrelled smooth-bores in red cloth covers. These pages were all dressed alike, according to the individual taste of the commander, in uniform turbans, tunic, and pason. The livery of the young Kachin colonel of the Fourth Regiment was the most effective—red-flowered turbans, French grey jackets, and red pasos of the wavy " dog's tooth " pattern. The colonel of the Third Regiment, on the other hand, revelled in bilious contrasts—pea-green gaungbaungs, flowing red tunics, and yellow waistcloths of what a 'Varsity tradesman would call a neat quiet plaid pattern. This bodyguard walked at either side of the road in loose Indian file to see that the way was clear. The bo himself rode an elephant, gorgeously caparisoned, with tassels and streamers trailing to the ground from the velvet-covered howdah. He was dressed in the national turban and paso, but wore a tight-fitting tunic, covered with gold lace. All of them were either smoking or chewing betel. Behind the elephant came the umbrella-bearer, or, perhaps, two or three of them if the officer had attained such distinction.

The actual civilian commander of the regiment seldom came out to the review, so that there were comparatively few gold umbrellas, but the red and green military sun-shades, with deep fringes, added perhaps more to the brilliance of the array, considered simply as a spectacle. Behind the hti-bearers came the minor officers, mounted on ponies, with the ordinary Burmese scarlet cloth saddle and tassels sweeping over the animal's flanks. Each of these minor chiefs also had his umbrella borne over his head, and a score or two of spear-men guarded the flanks of the cavalcade. Mingled up among them was a confused crowd of cheroot-bearers, spittoon-holders, betel-box carriers, and similar functionaries such as accompany a Burmese grandee wherever he goes. Behind this motley assemblage came the regimental colours. These were bifurcated red pennants, burgees bearing the number of the battalion, and leogryphs, lions, dogs, dragons, and similar distinguishing emblems for the different regiments. The standard was not very ponderous, but occasionally the bearer—he was not an officer—got tired of carrying it over his shoulder and lowered it to the trail without seeming to injure any one's sense of congruity. He was followed by the band, or a portion of it, for the musicians were scattered in twos and threes all over the regiment, usually at the head of a company, but not by any means necessarily so. Burmese music is ordinarily far from soft and gentle. At a play the trumpets blare, and the gongs, cymbals, and clappers clash and jingle and rattle in truly inspiriting fashion. But no such spirit-stirring strains are considered necessary to rouse martial ardour. A military bandsman required no preliminary education. All he had to do was to tap, tap away in the most stolid and monotonous fashion on a kyinaung. This is a brass or bell-metal gong, about the size of a dessert plate with a small round boss in the centre. The sound is sweet, and they are pitched in different keys, but a low-country Burman is at a loss to divine their precise use. The sound does not travel far, and they are not beaten in any fixed time, besides that the ahmudan would not step to it if they were ; so that if it were not for the dignity of the thing, there might just as well have been no band at all. But there they were, and they jingled away and stopped and began again in the most casual and independent possible way.

After all this came at last the ahmudan, King Thibaw's army of " immortals " in full array. They most assuredly had not a martial appearance, and there was not a semblance of discipline among them. It was just possible to make out that they were marching in column. Here and there was a ragged resemblance to an alignment of fours, achieved for a few minutes apparently more by chance than anything else. The soldiers were very gorgeous. Peony roses and sunflowers were as nothing to them. All had red tunics, but the facings, which were broad, were different in each regiment. Some were yellow, some green, some blue, some nondescript, and the effect on the red ground was not always pleasing. The trousers were very various. Blue, with a broad yellow stripe down the side, or occasionally for the sake of variety down the front or the back, green and red, yellow and maroon, scarlet and brown, were a few of the combinations. On their heads were worn helmets with burnished spikes, and a small metal dragon in front. These helmets do not suit at all with long hair. The topknot of a good many is so large that the *pickelhaube* balances on it, and wobbles about in undignified fashion.

The majority, however, found that the most satisfactory way of avoiding this was to put the helmet on the back of the head, which imparted to them a dissipated appearance, which was far from martial-looking. Not a few found the difference in weight between their ordinary silk turban and a papier-mâché or plaited wicker helmet more than they could bear, and solved the difficulty by carrying their headpiece on the end of their carbines. This met with no remonstrance or opposition on the part of the non-commissioned officers, who, armed with spears, marched at irregular intervals along the flanks of the column. The soldiers had no belts, and therefore no scabbards, and proceeded with bayonets fixed. The Fourth Regiment, commanded by the young Kachin before alluded to, had a habit, whether for the sake of distinction, or as signifying that they were prepared at any moment to give cold steel, of sloping arms in an eccentric way. Grasping the rifle at the upper band, they threw the butt over the shoulder and proceeded with bayonets sticking out in front. As a necessary consequence they did not straggle so much as the others, for if a man lagged he was wakened up by a prod from the point of the bayonet in the nape of the neck, or between the shoulders. The chief objection to this method of keeping the men at fairly regular intervals, was that a prick in the rear was as likely as not to pass right on to the head of the column, with the result of a volley of abuse and very considerable disorganisation.

The marines were the strongest in point of numbers, and far and away the best in drill. They kept their alignment very fairly, and frequently as many as three men in a section kept step. Their uniform was a blue-frogged red tunic and blue trousers with a scarlet stripe. On the helmet they wore an anchor instead of the ordinary dragon of the line. Their colonel was the Hpaungwun, Myowun, now Hlethin atwin-wun, the minister who was so energetic in the palace mas-sacres in 1879. The credit of their discipline was, however, entirely due to Commotto, a young Italian naval officer in the king's service, and engineer of all the river forts. The marines were quite a thousand strong, and their officers were mounted just like the rest. When there was practice in the war-boats, the mayor-colonel viewed the performance from the back of an elephant on the river-bank. Like all the great men, however, he did not trouble himself to go out to the reviews.

The men smoked in the ranks and hailed their friends along the route in the freest possible fashion. When a man wanted a light or a drink of water he simply fell out and went in search of it among the spectators, rightly enough assured that none of the officers would bother their heads as to the reason of his departure. All along the line of march men who had been delayed in this way might be seen scuttling along to get somewhere near their proper places. Here and there one was left far away from his regiment, having been seduced into conversation with a friend. Now and then the non-commissioned officers caught sight of an Englishman looking on, and woke up to the sudden sense of their responsi-bilities, delivering sound thwacks with the butt end of their spears on the shoulders of any stragglers within reach in most energetic and official fashion.   As a rule, however, they contented themselves with getting over the ground.   Many of the recruits viewed their trousers with very grave suspicions. They evidently thought that unless precautionary measures were adopted, the article would slip off, and therefore, with a vigilance which did credit to their sense of modesty, held on tight with one hand to their continuations.   Perhaps the tailors were to blame.   But in any case the attitude was undignified, and certainly not military.   The garment was not regarded with any favour even by the veterans.   When the ahmudan were on guard they generally wore the ordinary waistcloth and carried the trousers in one hand to show their status.   The tunics were almost never worn except at the reviews.

Between regiments came four cannon, pulled by men, and with little pennons stuck in the touch-holes.   Two gunners accompanied each two-pounder, one carrying a galvanised tin bucket and the other a big canister, intended for shot and powder, but singularly unfitted for such material on a campaign.   Sponges and rammers were wanting, and were said to be intentionally so in the hope that the guns might be mistaken for breech-loaders, and the men who drew the pieces were the bombardiers.

After the infantry, at an interval of two hundred yards, came two regiments of cavalry, numbering about five hundred lances in all.   They wore helmets of Grecian pattern, like cuirassiers, but otherwise were in the national dress.   The second of the two was the celebrated "Kathé Horse," who have won in English books on Burma a fame unknown in their own country.   They were dressed in French grey jackets and red pasos, and looked very well; but their mounts were very poor for a country where ponies are so plentiful and where it was so easy for the commander to demand their excellence.   The saddles had long flaps or wings hanging down in front to protect the riders' bare legs when riding through underwood, but it was so long since they had been in the jungle that the flaps were more of a decoration than a necessity.   Cavalry is an arm of the service of little use in a country like Burma, but with their long slender lances and splendid trappings they made a fine show, and not very much more could be said for the infantry—not so much in some cases.

The lancers were followed by the commissariat and control departments, a rabble of men carrying pots and pans and rolls of bamboo matting and boxes intended for ammunition, but containing none, and huge wicker baskets, besides a lot of other baggage which might be useful, but did not look like it. There were five or six hundred of these men, guarded by a handful of dah and spearmen.

In their wake followed the artillery corps ; first, thirty or forty two-pounders, similar to those between the different regiments, and with the same complement of men to each gun, and the same appliances. Then the elephant battery, each elephant with two jingals mounted on the howdah. These jingals, throwing a half or three-quarter pound ball, with their long pointed tails and muzzles pointed up to the skies, look very much like telescopes from a distance. In actual warfare they would probably do nothing beyond scaring the elephant. Besides the mahaut, each elephant carried a man to manage the guns. Fifty of them were loaded with this mosquito artillery, and behind them came fifty more with nothing on them but the mahaut. Many were most magnificent tuskers, and they constituted the most valuable part of his majesty's army.

Behind the elephants came the heavier guns, drawn by buffaloes, but they were apt to stick in the heavy, unmade roads, and the buffaloes themselves were not easy brutes to manage, especially on a warm day when their skin begins to crack. This battery, therefore, usually went but a short distance. These heavy guns were mostly very ancient ship guns of Portuguese, Dutch, French, and Arakanese make, and would be considered valuable in an English parish museum. They were formidable to none except primitive mountaineers, and to them chiefly from the noise they made.

As this account shows, Thibaw's army was neither threatening nor efficient, and the events of 1885 bore out the estimate. When the time came for adding Upper Burma to the British dominions it was effected with the least possible amount of bloodshed on either side. It might be supposed from what has been said that the ahmudan had no drill, but this was very far from being the case. On the contrary, drill was going on constantly inside the palace and at the various guard stations. The French and Italian officers were always instructing them, but a want of belief in the utility of mass movements rendered all their efforts useless. The recruits went through the balance-step with the utmost enthusiasm ; when it came to forming fours they were a little less ardent, but by the time they ought to have been counter-marching and right-forming company they were tired of the whole business and poked fun at the instructor. European officers called themselves, and were called, generals and colonels and what not, but they were simply drill sergeants with very unpromising material. They were allowed no uniform ; they never took command on a review day. Occasionally they complained of being insulted by their squads, and were told by a sententious mingyi that patience is one of the ten virtues which go to the making up of a true gentleman. To recompense them for their trials they made a great deal of money in a variety of ways, their salaries being the least part, and paid at long and uncertain intervals in a lump sum. The real "generals" were men who hardly ever came out at all, least of all when there was a chance of fighting. The commander-in-chief was for many months in jail, but still retained his title, and two of his sons remained in command of regiments. The men who managed the reviews and any work that was to be done were all let-thôndaw, the king's pages of honour. Few of them were over twenty, but their duties did not require much experience.

Besides the legitimate drill, conducted by the European instructors, there were other performances, the object of which would hardly be apparent to the compilers of the *Manual of Field Exercise*. The instructor, one of the junior officers, assembled the men in a big circle round about him, and proceeded in a fashion dictated to him apparently by nothing but his own fancy. He threw his gun into the air, caught it and cried *hé !* and the men followed his example to the best of their ability. He went through the same manœuvre behind his back, cried *hé !* again, and the men probably got some hard knocks in dutifully trying to imitate him. He cried *hé* and hunched up his shoulders ; cried *hé* and brought

them down again ; slapped one thigh and then the other with
a *hé;* pirouetted on one leg and brandished a jointless limb
in the air, crying *hé* vigorously, all which performances his
squad copied as best they could. The men dropped off as
they got tired, and by and by the instructor sat down himself, and the party dissolved or not as it pleased. Laughter,
criticism, and applause were constant throughout. This sort
of exercise was almost constant in the capital in 1879, and
it was pretty nearly the only drill the rural levies ever got.
These latter were dressed in the uniform of Mindôn's reign,
mostly cast-off tunics and trousers of the Madras native
infantry. They wore round soup-tureen-like helmets, with a
piece of looking-glass in front. Of these they were very
proud, but did not disdain to drink water and eat their
dinner out of them. There was only a limited supply of
these adornments for the provinces, and as a consequence it
was frequent for the man on guard to strip and hand over
his uniform to the relief, and then go home happy.

There was no musketry practice. Occasionally on feast-
days, or when his majesty went out, there was a lot of powder
burnt, but it would have been a very risky matter discharging
some of the more ancient firelocks, and so it was perhaps as
well that class-firing was not introduced. The artillery never
had any exercise. Burmans have not the same respect for
big guns that the natives of India have. They imagine that
such a big thing as a field-piece is sure to hit something, if
it is only pointed in a general way in the right direction, and
conclude therefore that any fool can manage a big gun without preliminary practice. King Mindôn appointed a French
officer to look after the gunners. This gentleman thought
he must do something for his salary——rather an unusual thing
with the king's servants——and accordingly as the men could
not be induced to drill, took a battery out to the paddy-fields
towards Yankintaung for ball practice. There he got
the guns into position and commenced firing. Loud sounds
should never assail the royal ears, and when his majesty
heard the din, he was fiercely enraged. The Kathé Horse
were sent out in a body to stop it. The over-energetic
Gaul was told that if he had not been an ignorant foreigner,
who did not know any better, he would have been made a

target for his own battery, but the Burman officer was flogged round the town. The guns were stowed away in the palace lest such an enormity might by misadventure be again perpetrated. There they remained till Thibaw Min got them dragged out for his reviews. They had never been cleaned all this time, any more than the infantry arms ever were. He was perhaps less sensitive on the score of noise, but he did not send his gunners out to practise, and they, as a rule, kept their spare clothes and cheroots and betel stowed away in the muzzles of their pieces.

The strength of the army at the disposal of King Thibaw was only limited by the number of men in the country. Every male was liable to serve as a soldier whenever he was called upon, and in 1879, when war with England was momentarily expected, levies of one man from every twenty houses, every twelve, every six, were called out, and finally an ameindaw, or royal mandate, was issued, summoning every able-bodied man in the country to hold himself in readiness for taking the field. But in ordinary times the amount of a Burmese force depended not upon the number of the population, but on the body of men the neighbourhood could feed in a collective state, for it was the district and not the Government that supported them. At the best Thibaw Min could supply not more than 25,000 and 30,000 men with muskets, more or less useless, from long Enfields to ancient flintlocks, which would be most readily induced to go off by putting them on a fire. The method of raising forces was somewhat as follows. The king, with or without the advice of his ministers, decided how many men were wanted, and informed the Hlutdaw, which thereupon issued orders to all the governors of provinces, calling upon them to muster the quota which custom had decided their districts must provide. The provincial rulers then sent their instructions to the myothugyis and taikthugyis, heads of townships and village circles, who in their turn communicated with the subordinate headman of each separate village. This last official, with the assistance of the house-reeves, singled out the men. Substitutes were allowed, and as every thugyi was absolute in his own place, he usually made a very pretty thing out of such a levy, through fines

and sums given to him to procure another man.   The whole
district was called upon to pay for the support and equipment
of its contingent, and the men who were recruited were
usually those who were unable to furnish their share of this
tax.   But the men who eventually went off as soldiers were
not by any means commonly those whom the headman first
nominated.   He expected to have money extorted from him
by his superiors, and made his arrangements accordingly,
naming all the wealthiest men in the place in his first list.
This method of raising troops is not expeditious, but nothing
under Thibaw's rule was expeditious, and it gave abundant
scope for palavering and extortion, the two chief accomplishments of the rural officials.

The inhabitants of certain districts, however, were considered the hereditary soldiers of the Alaungpaya dynasty,
and these levies were looked upon as forming the standing
army.   They held their lands by military service and were
exempt from all taxation.   They considered themselves to be
the flower of the service and adopted *Junker* manners.   A
dragon was tattooed on the back of their necks, just over the
shoulders, to signify that they specially belonged to the king,
and, strictly speaking, they alone were entitled to the name
ahmudan.   They mounted guard in the palace, and were
almost never required to leave the capital.   The chief Alaungpaya districts are in the north, round about Môtshobo, now
called Shwebo, whence the founder of the present dynasty
came.   The rural levies got all the work there was to be
done against marauding Shans and Kachins, and garrisoned
the various fortified towns along the frontier.   Many of
these contingents were armed with nothing but spears and
dahs.   At Minhla, near the old British frontier, where there
was a well-constructed fort, was posted the strongest and
best-armed detachment out of Mandalay.   Near Ava there
were three forts : one, the face of the old city wall, an earthen
rampart thirty feet thick and twenty feet high, faced on the
outside with masonry ; a second on the other side of the
river at Sagaing, and the third farther up at the bend of the
river, at Shwegyetyet.   These commanded the river at a
point where vessels proceeding up the river had to round
a dangerous reef of rocks.   But with regard to these

forts Captain Barker of H.M.'s 89th P.V., the best English
authority on Upper Burma military matters, said, " without
ditch, without flank defence, without expense magazines,
without traverses to protect the gunners, they are mere shell-
traps for the destruction of the garrison." He might have
added that they were without armament, and in 1885 they
surrendered without firing a shot. Mandalay itself has
naturally a strong position because of its inaccessibility.
To the east it is guarded by the Shan mountains and the
marshy plains below. Rivers and creeks make the approach
from the south difficult. On the north is an impassable
morass. On the west of the city are wide-spreading, thickly
populated suburbs, and the river-side is defended by a high
embankment. But the weakness of Mandalay lay in the
worthlessness of the army and the feebleness of its armament.
The kingdom of Burma was, in fact, nothing like so powerful
as it was a quarter of a century before, when the second
Burmese war was ended. When the end came Mandalay
fell to a force twenty miles away.

Note.—It has been brought to the writer's notice that several
worthy Frenchmen have been hurt by the references to foreigners in
this and in preceding and following chapters. It may therefore be
noted here that the count who sold syrups was not the Comte de
Trevelec, who was a contemporary of the Marquis de Gallifet at St.
Cyr, and that there is no reference to General de Facieu, a popular,
picturesque, and notable French gentleman. Neither were Louis
Vossion nor Monsieur Fernand d'Avéra thought of when this book was
written. Vossion was a stubborn patriot. Monsieur d'Avéra is a genial
patriot with a doubt whether France or Upper Burma has the greater
claims on him. In any case for fifty years Fernand d'Avéra has been
one of the best known and best liked men in Burma.

CHAPTER LV

JUDICIAL ADMINISTRATION

BUDDHIST law as it was administered in Upper Burma
dates from the beginning of the now existing world. The
first crime was theft ; the first punishment was a scolding,
speedily followed by a thrashing ; and the first judge was
Mahā Thamada, elected by vote of the people to be ruler
over them. No doubt there were written laws then, but
they have not come down to us. The written code in use
was given to the world by Manu, originally a cow-herd,
but afterwards a minister. He found them written in large
characters on the walls of another world, to which he was
transported when in an ecstasy. These laws formed the first
code. There have been since compiled from them eight
other codes in the kingdom of Prome and other ancient
states in Burmah. The last, called Mahā Manu Thaya
Shwe Myin, was drawn up on the foundation of the sixth
kingdom of Ava, in the year 1137 B.E. (1775 A.D.), by
Minhkaung Gyi, who, with the aid of a learned monk,
went through and carefully revised all the codes. These
laws in their integrity are those which governed Upper
Burma and now govern the whole of Burma in so far as they
regulate social relations. The codes were written in Sanskrit and Magadha, a language usually called Pali through
an error. The name Pali signifies really not a *language*,
but " The Canon," handed down to Buddhists, as composed by pious disciples from the teachings of Shin
Gautama. The Magadha or Pali code accepted is called
Manu Wunnana, from its writer and compiler, a minister of
state in Ava. It is looked upon as a commentary on, or
a key to, the codes, and contains the whole of the laws.

Besides the codes there exist also twenty standard collections of decisions, leading cases in which judgment was delivered by kings, queens, princesses, and ministers. These are by some regarded as obsolete, by many lugyis, however, considered to have still the force of law. The best known of these are :—

The decisions of Mahawthata, the embryo Budh.

„　　　　Widuya, one of the ten great avatars.

„　　　　Thudhammasari.

„　　　　Kutha.

„　　　　Dwuttabaung, first king of Prome.

„　　　　Sinbyushin.

The laws given by Manu to the ruler Mahā Thamada numbered altogether eighteen. From these all others have been framed. The eighteen original laws had regard to :—
1. Borrowing money. 2. Deposits of money. 3. Stealing and altering the appearance of property and selling it. 4. When a gift may be had back on demanding it, and when not, there being six kinds of gifts. 5. Deciding the wages of carpenters. 6. Deciding the wages of labourers. 7. Breach of promise. 8. Deciding disputes between the owners of cattle and neat-herds. 9. Settling disputed boundaries. 10. Deciding whether property purchased may be returned. 11. Accusations. 12. Theft or concealment. 13. Assault. 14. Murder. 15. Deciding the proper conduct of husband and wife. 16. The question of slavery. 17. Deciding if cock-fighting, betting, or gambling debts shall be paid. 18. Partition of inherited property.

Manu also laid down that persons appointed to administer the laws should not only have a competent knowledge of the code, but should also possess fourteen qualifications, as follows :—1. To decide in strict accordance with the law. 2. To be respectable. 3. To be of moral character. 4. To inspire awe. 5. To command love. 6. To be of good birth. 7. To be religious. 8. To be virtuous. 9. To be truthful. 10. To be talented. 11. To be devoted to the study of the law. 12. To possess honesty of purpose and intention. 13. Knowledge of the principal parties and pleaders in a suit.   14. Fearlessness in deciding cases, or being lion-hearted.

The supreme court in Burma was the Hlutdaw constituted of four wungyis, the chief ministers of state, who held their meetings in a hall within the palace, which took its name from the court.   Each wungyi (great burden) had its wundauk (prop of the burden) as an assistant to sit with him in court.   These wundauks formed the third rank of ministers, under the four atwinwuns (inner burdens), who were a kind of household ministers, or privy councillors, and sat in a special court, called the Byadeit, also in the palace.   The latter had nominally as their chief duty to deal with the monopolies which Thibaw Min set himself to establish in such abundance.   But as any man, no matter what special education or preparation he might have had, was considered eligible for any post, political, military, civil, or judicial, so both the Hlut and the Byadeit conducted all manner of business, from the external relations of the country to ordinary criminal or civil appeal cases sent up from the yôndaw, the criminal court, where the myowuns (city burdens), usually two in number, sat daily ; or from the tayayôn, the civil court, where two tayathugyis (great men of the law) presided.   In either of these inferior courts it was not at all uncommon for a wundauk, or even a wungyi, to attend and investigate important cases.   But original suits were also frequently heard before the Hlut, and many cases were decided by the wungyis or any of the subordinate officials in their private houses.   Formerly indeed this was the chief source of their salaries, for costs to the amount of ten per cent on the property under dispute went of right to the judge.   The late king instituted the custom of fixed salaries, and Thibaw Min retained it, but neglected to pay the money.   It will thus be seen that law matters, even in the capital, were carried on in a very casual, haphazard sort of a way.   There was no attempt at a distribution of public business into departments, and each individual wungyi took his part in deliberations on all kinds of subjects with as much confidence as if he were an expert.

If the capital displayed a lack of system, there was

certainly little to be expected from the provinces. The same general system prevailed in the separate districts. Each one was ruled by a governor, or myowun, appointed by the Hlutdaw or by the king, and armed with full powers, military, judicial, civil, and fiscal. Appeals might be sent from his decisions to the Hlut, but otherwise he was entirely irresponsible, as long as he was regular in forwarding the prescribed revenue to the myosa, the prince or princess, or other great personage who "ate" the province. The "town-eater" almost never went to his district, so that it was entirely at the mercy of the myowun, and might be squeezed by him as much as he thought proper and judicious. The subordinate officials varied in different provinces according to their requirements. All, however, had myosayes, secretaries, or town-clerks, nahkandaws, "receivers of the royal orders," and sikkès, chiefs in war, military officers, who formed a provincial council or court holding daily sittings and making reports to the myowun. In some districts, according to the duties, there were in addition to these an akunwun, or revenue superintendent, an akaukwun, or collector of customs, as also in riparian districts a yewun, or myitsinwun, who had a jurisdiction over the entire river. This authority, however, very often vested in one of the governors. Thus the last Wun of Minhla had power of life and death, as high sheriff of the Irrawaddy, from his own town, close on the British frontier, right up to Sagaing, not far below Mandalay. Other officials were the htaunghmu, or jailer, the tagāhmu, governors of the gates, called windawhmu in the capital, where they were very important officers, and the ayatgaung, heads of quarters, in all the larger towns. Under each governor of a province were a number of governors of the separate towns under his jurisdiction. These were called myoôk when the appointment was temporary, or only for life, and myothugyi when it was hereditary, as was most frequently the case. Besides these, in some of the provinces there were taikthugyi, governors of circles or groups of villages, each of which had its own ywathugyi, who in turn had under him sundry gaungs to look after each his specially allotted number of houses. As each of these subordinates had to send in regularly to his immediate superior a certain fixed sum, determined without regard to favourable seasons, health of the population, or anything of that kind, and as each man was judge over the people in his charge, it may naturally be supposed that the general population did not lead a very happy life. Complaints might be made against extortion and illegal decisions, but the heads· of tracts, if they had the money, could always stifle inquiry.

Some of the laws deduced from Manu's eighteen original enactments strike one as being rather singular. For example, if two men quarrel and fight and one of them is killed, there is no penalty ; but if a third party interferes and kills or injures one of the original combatants, he must pay the ordinary fine for murder, or causing hurt. Should he himself be killed, the other two are subject to no penalty. When a man is guilty of adultery with another man's wife, if it be proved to be the first time, he must pay the fine for adultery, usually the price of the woman, assessed according to the judge's opinion ; if it is her second offence, he only pays half the fine ; but if she has been guilty for a third time, he pays no penalty at all.

If one man curses another and some evil happens, he must pay twice the price of the damage incurred ; thus, if the man dies he must pay twice the value of a man ; two cows if a cow dies, and so on.

When the king dies there is a general pardon of all offences, and a remission of fines, except in the case of debt. There are also seven things which cannot be reclaimed after the death of the king under whom they were promised or given. These are :— 1. Deposits. 2. Pledges. 3. Money paid wrongly by the parties in a law-suit. 4. Things carried off by violence, or seized upon without sufficient title. 5. Promises. 6. Things secretly stolen. 7. Things that have been voluntarily given up by one man and taken possession of by another.

The decisions of Mahawthata, Princess Thudhammasari, and others are of little value from a strictly legal point of view. They are chiefly of a religious character. The princess begins by saying that her cases are to be considered as guides to nobles and judges as to the line they should follow. To an English barrister they would seem to be excerpts from the *Arabian Nights*, and as far from precedents as it is possible to imagine anything. The play of Mahawthata tells of the Lord Buddha in the birth in which he exhibited the most consummate wisdom and acumen, as in Wethandaya he embodies the spirit of liberality. In both these births, as in his last, Shin Gautama spoke from the moment he was brought forth. As Wethandaya he immediately entreated his mother for something to give in charity to the poor, and distributed forthwith the four hundred pieces of silver she gave him. As Mahawthata he appeared in the world with a plant in his hand, and, holding it up, said, "This is medicinal herb." Throughout all this life he was constantly displaying extraordinary wisdom, jealous ministers being in the habit of propounding difficult cases to him. Thus he was shown a log of sha (*Acacia Catechu*), from which cutch, stupidly called *Terra Japonica*, is obtained, and asked which was the upper end and which the lower end. He solved the problem by putting it in the water, when the lower end, as being the heavier, sank deeper in the water. Another case is exactly similar to the famous Biblical decisions of Solomon. These decisions, though they may be interesting, are hardly valuable as standard leading cases.

Some of the definitions of crimes in the Dhammathat are a little singular. Thus among the ten descriptions of assault are mentioned : "saying in regard to a lunatic, a drunkard, or a half-witted person who is ill, that he will die, and he dies"; "refusing restitution for cattle killed"; "standing near an assailant." To avoid being summoned for one of the twenty-seven kinds of abuse one must be very circumspect, for there is ground for action if one says Hé to a man, as the Mandalay people were fond of shouting Hé Kalā after Europeans. It is equally risky to address a man as nin, *i.e.* in the third person ; to say that he is "deficient in strength"; that he is a stutterer, bow-legged, broken-down, squinting, or afflicted with white spots on his body ; that he is heretical, or, finally, that he is given to using bad language.

The niceties of the law may be illustrated by the following case from the Talaing Dhammathat. A man in search

of honey climbed up a high tree to get at a hive.   His foot
slipped and he fell off a large branch on to a small one below.
He was afraid that this would not be able to support his
weight, and called out for assistance to a mahaut, who was
passing by on his elephant.   The elephant-driver held up
the hook with which he guided his animal and told him to
come down by it.   The bee-hunter seized the hook, and
while he was holding it the elephant took fright and ran
away.   There were then the mahaut hanging on to his hook
and the bee-hunter clinging to the slender branch which
momentarily threatened to give way.   Fortunately, just at
this moment four persons passed by and were called to by
both the bee-hunter and the elephant-driver to come and
save them.   They could think of no other expedient than to
hold out their clothes, which accordingly they did, spreading
them out as high above their heads as possible, so as to
break the fall.   The two men dropped from the tree on
their four preservers, but what between their own weight and
the awkwardness of the iron driving-hook, the whole six
were knocked senseless and fell on the ground.   Whilst they
lay in a swoon a doctor came up and gave them medicines
which brought them round.   When all had recovered, he
demanded his fee.   But the question was who was to pay
him.   The elephant-driver said he should not be asked to
pay because he tried to save the bee-hunter's life and was
an innocent cause of the injuries sustained by his rescuers.
The bee-hunter on his part maintained that he should not
be called on for payment, seeing that if he had not held
on so tight, the mahaut would have fallen and been killed.
Finally, the four rescuers said that it was utterly unreasonable to ask them to pay, seeing that it was through pure
generosity that they had held out their clothes to save the
lives of the mahaut and the bee-hunter and through this
act of kindliness they themselves had been hurt.   The
elephant-driver and the bee-hunter somewhat thanklessly
retorted that if a ladder had been brought, or had been
constructed, they could have come down in perfect safety
and without hurt to any one, and that therefore the four
rescuers should pay.

The question as to who is liable in this case is a nice

one, as also is the point as to who should be made defendants, and who should be the witnesses. The Talaing Dhammathat says that the incident occurred in the province of Kawdônpayit, in Hindustan, and that the case gave rise to the recognition of the root, trunk, and branches of the law, which till then had not been defined. From whom, or whether the doctor got his fee at all, we are not told.

Advocates, pleaders, or barristers were, it is stated, unknown until a case occurred when certain suitors from the jungle came before the king and were not able to understand the court language. A court official was therefore allowed to assist them and turn their rustic jargon into comprehensible speech. These as "standing before" the king were called Shéné, as it were mouthpieces for the parties to the suit, and the king, who acted as judge. The convenience derived from their superior knowledge and experience afterwards led to the establishment of a regular body of barristers.

If the laws are, some of them, somewhat singular to those who are accustomed to the scientific Indian penal and civil codes, as well as to the growth of centuries of Western practice, the method of binding over witnesses to tell the truth, or at least the book on which they are required to pledge themselves, is sufficiently startling. The Book of the Oath, Kyeinsa, is still used in British courts of justice, and it is to be hoped that all the younger members of the population know what terrible punishments they are drawing down on themselves when they hold it over their heads and promise to tell the truth ; what frightful penalties will befall them if they swerve in the least degree from the exact facts of the case. In the old times a man used always to be sworn on this book in a place where there was no shadow, or in a pagoda, and this custom was maintained to the end in native Burma. There was a special shrine for the purpose in Mandalay, and at the Shwe Mingôn Payā, near the oilwells of Yenangyaung, there is a stone, ordinarily deposited between two images of the Hentha, the Brahminy goose, which the swearer takes in his hand, lamps being lighted at the same time. The book itself might not be kept in ordinary places. Some copies were kept in the court in a specially consecrated box, some in a zayat, and some, more terrific in their denunciations, in little receptacles fixed high up in trees.

With the view of guarding thoughtless or reckless people against themselves there were certain classes enumerated who should not under any circumstances be allowed to take the oath, or to appear as witnesses. These were :— 1. Those who do not believe in the merit of good works. 2. Such people as trade with the goods of others. 3. Parties interested in the case, as well as their relations, friends, and enemies. 4. Great talkers. 5. Sick persons. 6. Old men. 7. Children. 8. Overbearing men. 9. Public singers. 10. Actresses. 11. Women of ill fame. 12. Goldsmiths. 13. Painters. 14. Blacksmiths. 15. Cobblers. 16. Asthmatic persons. 17. Low people. 18. Gluttons. 19. Gamblers. 20. Hot-tempered people. 21. Doctors. 22. Thieves. 23. Pregnant women. 24. Hermaphrodites, a by no means uncommon class in Burma. If, however, both parties to the suit gave their consent, some of these classes might be allowed to give testimony. Another curious old provision was that when one of the litigants produced a witness, he himself was not required to take the oath, while contrariwise, if he swore on the book, it was not imperative that he should call witnesses.

The Book of the Oath is not quite fixed in its length, nor in the number of the imprecations which it threatens against false witnesses. Some copies are much more diffuse than others. It is always written on palm-leaf, in the ordinary character, and these in English courts are kept wrapped up in the ecclesiastical kabbalwè, usually sewn for greater convenience. The commonest version is as follows:—

I will speak the truth. If I should be influenced by the laws of demerits, namely, passion, folly, anger, false opinion, immodesty, pride, scepticism, hard-heartedness, then may all these calamities attend me and my relations, wherever we may be, by land or by water, travelling or remaining quietly at home. May the nats who guard the sacred heavens, the athura nats and all other giants, the nats who guard the three Baskets of the Sacred Law, delivered by the most excellent Buddha, and all the other holy writings and sermons ; may the nats, the guardians of the sacred relics the holy hairs, the teeth, the jawbone, the frontal bone, and all the other relics ; the keepers and warders of countless shrines, all golden and made famous by sacred memories ; the protectors of the images and figures of the supreme Buddha ; may the nats who guard the sacred mount and all the hills of the Southern Island ; the nats who watch and ward the mighty rivers, the lesser streams, the lakes, the torrents, cataracts, and whirlpools ; the nats who preside over the vast forests and the single trees ; the nats of the sun, the moon, the stars, and meteors, the clouds, winds, mists, and exhalations ; may the nagā and the galôn, hideous dragons, and cruel birds, all bilus, ogres, demons, warlocks, all the evils that come from without the body ; may all these spirits and ill things unite to slay me and mine, to the utmost limits of kinship, if I speak not the truth.

When I and my relations are on land, let all the hideous land creatures, tigers, bilus, elephants, male and female, demons and giants, buffaloes, poisonous serpents, the cobra, and the hamadryad, the scorpion, and the centipede ; may they all seize, bite, crush, strangle, and devour us ; may the earth open and swallow us up ; a thunderbolt from heaven descend and annihilate us, if I speak not the truth.

When we travel by water may our boats sink and be shattered by storms ; may crocodiles, writhing snakes, and ravenous fishes kill and devour us, that we suddenly die, perish, and come to utter destruction, if I speak not the truth.

May the five calamities occasioned by fire, water, thieves, governors and enemies oppress us ; may we be subject to all the maladies of the body ; may we be as fools and idiots, afflicted with madness and leprosy, with all kinds of loathsome disease and evils that deform the body, with itch, scurvy, ulcers, deafness, blindness, dysentery, the plague, and all manner of mental and corporal miseries ; may we incur the hatred and punishments of judges and rulers ; may we be for ever separated from our forefathers, children, and relations, throughout all succeeding worlds ; may fire destroy our goods ; lances, swords, arrows, and knives, and all sorts of weapons cut and pierce and maim our bodies ; may I die instantly, vomiting up clotted, black blood before the assembled people, if I speak not the truth.

Moreover, if I speak not the truth, may I and all my family after death be instantly cast into the abyss of hell, there to wander for a cycle of worlds through the eight great hells, and all the smaller ones, suffering from all the torments of these places ; and when at length I shall emerge thence, may I become a pyeitta, or a thurakè, and thereafter some hideous animal, passing through all the wretchedness of the four states of punishment. Finally, when after innumerable worlds I shall at length once more become man, may I be the slave of other men a hundred and a thousand times, if I speak not now the truth.

But if I speak truth, may I and all my relations escape the three calamities, the four states of punishment, and the five enemies ; may all the ills in the body and all that are without the body keep far away ; may our wealth, honour, and estimation ever increase, and when we die may we attain the happiness of men and dewas, and speedily entering on the noble path, reach the cloudless peace of Ne'ban.

A desire to avoid denouncing on themselves all these fearsome penalties led in the old times to a good deal of trying by ordeal, a form of decision which still prevails extensively in country districts, and occasionally was made use of even in Mandalay. The forms used are those familiar in old times in other parts of the world, such as eating consecrated rice, like the first English *corsnaed*, plunging the finger wrapped in a thin palm-leaf into melted tin ; immersing accuser and accused in water to see who would remain longest below and prove his innocence or guilt. The yahans are usually present on these occasions, and recite certain formulæ beforehand, a great concourse of people assembling to see the test. The opposing parties wade into the river, or into a tank, up to the chest and then duck under, a couple of men holding a board over their heads to keep them down. The one that comes up first is cast in the case. Another form common at the pagodas is for both parties to resort thither, when the monks again recite the precepts and sundry other phrases. Then equal parts of wax are carefully weighed out, and from these candles are made for plaintiff and defendant. They are lighted simultaneously, and the holder of the candle which first burns out is adjudged to have lost the case, and judgment is delivered forthwith. The winning party, for all the friends are always present, immediately cause their band to strike up, dancers perform and songs are sung, and every token of triumph is exhibited. Unfortunately, however, for any supposed efficacy of the system, substitutes are allowed, and in addition to this bribery plays as important a part almost as it did in the law-courts themselves. The man whose money went farthest won his case, whether decided according to the principles of the Dhammathat or the lottery of the ordeal.

The punishments inflicted were sometimes very cruel, and the treatment of the prisoners occasionally savage in the extreme. In criminal cases torture was frequently applied to extort confession from the accused or evidence from the witnesses. Rich men usually suffered nothing worse than a fine. For the impecunious, sentences varied from sundry stripes with a rattan, with or without imprison-ment, to mutilation, perpetual slavery, and death. Except for debt, a man sentenced by the court to slavery became so with all his descendants for ever, and they were usually allotted to some pagoda, doomed to support life by begging as tadaungsa, or relegated to some other of the outcast classes. Death in Mandalay was almost invariably by decapitation, the agony of the condemned being occasionally prolonged by a fiendish executioner ; the custom of throwing victims to be devoured by wild beasts, or trodden to death by wild elephants in the elephant-trap, was latterly wholly given up. In the provinces, however, other methods were very frequently adopted. North of the capital " crucifixion " was particularly common. The letwakat, or wakattaing, does not at all resemble the ordinary pictorial representation of the cross. It is more like a double ladder, consisting of three stout bamboos fixed upright in the ground, three bars lashed to them horizontally with canes, and over these again two cross-bars in the shape of a St. Andrew's cross. These punishment stakes were most frequently put up on the river-bank or on sandbanks in the stream, and were particularly common where the Shan and Kachin hills come down any-where near the Irrawaddy. Sometimes the criminal was killed before he was lashed up, sometimes he was tied up first and then disembowelled with a sword-gash across the stomach, or rendered helpless by a few spear-thrusts. In either case the body was left hanging, to be picked clean by the vultures, and the bones gradually fell off. Formerly, when the mouth of the Irrawaddy was Burmese territory, a favourite method used to be to tie the convict down at the edge of the stream at low water and leave him to be drowned by the incoming tide. The fishes were often more expeditious than the vultures in devouring their prey. The favourite kind of stake for this purpose was the " stump of hell," the irregular short stem of the undeveloped trees in a mangrove swamp, looking like pinnacles or knobs rising out of the confused network of exposed roots.

But imprisonment was often worse than death. The prisons had never been cleaned out since they were made, some of them noisome underground cells, some flimsy wooden or bamboo structures open all round. The prisoners sat with their feet in the stocks perpetually, and the long bamboo which united them was occasionally triced up so far that the poor wretches only touched the ground with their shoulders. A favourite time for thus inverting them was at night. But a man who had not had enough money to satisfy the judge might often manage satisfactorily to square the jailer. If he effected that he was on the whole comfortable ; he was allowed to go away in the morning, have his meals at home, and go back and deliver himself into custody at night again. But if he had no money, or no friends to pay it for him, his best course was to die at once, indeed he certainly would before long, for the only food to be had in prison was that supplied by relatives of the convicts. If no friend brought it, the jailer certainly would not supply any. It was better to be " proclaimed," to suffer maungkyaw, than to go to jail. This was a punishment almost confined to the capital, and greatly resembling the old English naval practice of flogging an offender " round the fleet." The criminal was taken to each gate of the city, to the corners of all the chief streets, and to sundry other frequented places. At each of these points his crime and sentence were read out and he was flogged. None but the strong-constitutioned could stand it, but those who survived were free men.

Notwithstanding the severity of the treatment in the jails, the laws were really very mildly administered, and there were few whose relations could not muster up enough to secure them immunity from torture.   Capital sentences were on the whole rare, except when political considerations came in. Then there was no mercy.   Cattle-stealing was very severely punished, but murder could almost always be purged by a blood-bote.

CHAPTER LVI

REVENUE SYSTEM

THE first people, when they took counsel together and appointed a ruler to repress crime and manage the affairs of the country, agreed that each man should pay a tenth of his thale rice, and this tithe system remained in force in Burma till practically the end, not merely for supplying the royal coffers, but also for paying all public servants. King Mindôn abolished the tithe system as far as the payment of local officials was concerned, and arranged to give them fixed salaries ; but even in his time this law was somewhat of a dead letter, and under his son the last king, if governors and secretaries did not resort to old methods they got nothing. Unfortunately for the people the ancient system was by far the most profitable, and the collectors were not at all inclined to agitate for their payment at stated times from the treasury. The actual exactions of these worthies far exceeded what appeared in their black parabaik notebooks, and were in fact only limited by the possessions of their victims, and occasionally by a slight fear of consequences, if a desperate man should complain to some powerful minister in Mandalay. Then the delinquent might be turned out to make way for a friend of the wungyi's. But, alas for the people, the change, if not exactly from King Log to King Stork, was only too likely to be from a well-filled stork to a lean and hungry one.

The division of the country for the collection of revenue was identical with that for administrative purposes, and the several duties were carried out by the same persons with the same assistants. The one man was civil administrator, judge, colonel of the local militia, and revenue collector for his locality, whether province, circle, or simple village. The fixed revenue demanded by the myosa, whether prince of the blood-royal, minister of state, maid of honour, royal spittoon-bearer, or white elephant, was remitted to Mandalay by the resident lord-lieutenant of the province, together with a certain over-plus for the " province-eater's " secretary, clerk, and treasurer. The whole amounted to from sixty to eighty per cent of the money nominally raised from the people, and the money kept back was supposed to pay for the services of the myowun and his subordinates. But they would have been very much less great people if they got no more than this. It is impossible to say how much money was collected in any one district, or even in any single town. The steatite pencil records were easily effaced and altered, even if they were ever accurate, and no one knew anything of the details of taxation. A certain circle of villages was called upon to produce a certain amount of revenue to go to the capital, and as long as this was regularly paid no questions were asked. The governor divided out amongst the circles the quota each was expected to pay, and the taikthugyi in his turn made the allotment for the villages under his control; finally the village headman gave his instructions to the tithing-men, and they extorted all they could from the householders under their control. The system was admirably planned, but the working of it was execrable in its cruelty. Every Burman was the king's slave, and could not leave the district, far less the country, without the royal permission granted through the local authorities. The men who came down to reap British Burma paddy-fields in November and December had all of them to leave hostages behind, their wives and families or some near relation, to guarantee that they would return when the season was over to pay their ngwedaw.

This ngwedaw, or "royal silver," was the main source of the revenue. It was a house-tax or family-tax, not a capita-tion-tax, though its incidence was generally so arranged that it practically came to be a poll assessment, or at any rate a kind of rude property-tax. The amount of land cultivated, which naturally varied according to the number of hands

available for the purpose, served as a guide, though it seemed
to be a very misleading one, for the amount demanded in
successive years and in adjoining districts differed in the most
capricious way. Sè-einggaungs never failed to scent out
where money was, and to get the lion's share of it ; for
where the tax-collector might also be the judge, there was
small room for hesitation and attempts to shirk payment.
The myosa had a very summary way of deciding the
matter. He announced to the governor that there were so
many houses in the province, and that he was to collect three,
or five, or seven rupees a head from them. If the estimate
of the number of houses was too high, the myowun shifted
the trouble on to his subordinates ; if it was too low—but
there is no use considering that case, for it was unheard
of for a town-eater to underestimate what was due to him.

Next in importance were the imposts on produce. These
were estimated in a still more arbitrary way. A pè, a land
measure not very much different from an English acre, is
assumed to produce a hundred baskets of paddy. Of this
any amount from ten up to forty per cent was taken,
occasionally in money value, but more frequently in kind.
Such dues would be heavy enough in any case, but they
were particularly burdensome when the land did not produce
the hundred baskets, assumed to be stored in the public
granaries, where all the farmers must lodge their grain.
The amount assessed would be a good crop for an actual pè,
but when the land-measurer started with a cubit settled by
the standard of the breadth of his own hand, the result was
rarely favourable to the cultivator. Sometimes the process
was varied by imposing a tax in kind or money on every
plough, or, more often, on every yoke of oxen or buffaloes.
In a similar way, tobacco, cotton, wheat, sesamum, pepper,
onions, and all kinds of vegetables were put under
contribution. A small sum was also levied on cocoanut,
areca, and palmyra palms. Fishermen had to pay in coin
or fish-paste for each of their nets or fish-traps ; sometimes
the fisheries were farmed out. Then there were dues on
timber, and on the gums, resins, oils, and other forest produce,
and a multitude of other minor imposts ; dues on the sale of
cattle, licenses to sell various articles, a tax on brokerage,

transit dues, and so on, all imposed whenever the district offered an opportunity for them.

A fertile source of profit to the officials were the fees on law-suits and criminal cases, as well as on minor matters, such as the settlement of petty quarrels, divorce suits, and the like, which did not require to be formally tried, but could be settled in the verandah of the thugyi's house over a cheroot or a fid of betel. At the beginning of the year, and on other great kadaw days, special sums had always to be wrung out of the people to furnish the presents required to be offered to the king by all the officials, from the myosa downwards. *Corvées* and enforced duties of all kinds were frequent, and the men selected for such service could only get off by furnishing a substitute, or bribing the tithing man. The king or some great man wanted to build a pagoda, and orders were sent round to the various circles that they must furnish a regular supply of workers daily. The taik or myothugyi drew up a roster, and each man had to go and work for a certain number of days. If he failed to go he was triced up to a post or a tree and got a sound flogging. Similar forced duties were the protection of the frontier and the pursuit of dacoits. Such work was particularly detested, for the men had to keep themselves supplied with food, or get their friends to bring it to them, and this was not always an easy matter. Besides such service might last an indefinite time.

Added to all the ordinary imposts were occasional extraordinary contributions to the Crown on the occasion of entering upon war, or upon other public emergencies. The Hlutdaw in Mandalay fixed the amount, and it was divided among the governors of districts. In 1798 a call of thirty-three rupees was made from every house in the country. It was two years before the collection was finished, and the result was six million rupees. But how much more the people paid is quite another thing. Very heavy calls were also made in 1827 to meet the first instalment of the indemnity due to the British after the treaty of Yandabo. The money was sent down at dead of night to the British Commissioners, and all the people were ordered to close their doors and remain inside that they might not see the national humiliation.   As an instance of Burman carelessness in money matters it may be mentioned that when the final instalment was paid, considerably over the sum due was sent to Calcutta. When the overplus was returned, there was great discussion among the Ministers as to what could be the motive of the Indian Government in being so singularly scrupulous.

A good many districts were almost entirely exempted from taxes in recognition of special services required of them. The inhabitants of the capital were particularly well off in this respect.   They furnished the troops to guard the palace and city.   Moreover, it would have been much more difficult to oppress them with impunity, apart from the fact that if they were disaffected it would have offered a premium to rebels.   For similar reasons some of the townships about Môtshobo were free from the ngwedaw.   It was from this district that Alaungpaya, the founder of the dynasty, came, and insurrectionist princes always made for Môtshobo when they levied war.   Several villages on the Irrawaddy, in consideration of supplying the royal gilded boats, manning the royal barges, and passing on Court despatches, were relieved from the family tax.   But the petty officials took very good care that they did not grow rich on their immunities.

All these methods were more or less sanctioned by ancient custom.   Modern ingenuity and requirements, however, found out new ways of raising money.   The pious ardour of Mindôn led him to spend vast sums on the erection of pagodas and religious buildings of all kinds, as well as on the manufactories, cotton mills, foundries, and powder mills with which he crowded the suburbs of Mandalay, and closed when he got tired of them.   All this cost a very great deal of money, which even the exaction of benevolences from wealthy courtiers failed to supply.   Consequently Mindôn Min turned merchant and established a great number of royal monopolies.   The producers were allowed to sell to none but to him, and he fixed the price which he was prepared to pay.   For long, cotton, jaggery, timber, wheat, precious stones, and earth oil could only be had from the royal merchant, and the trade with British Burma was in anything but a satisfactory state.   Then in 1867, Colonel

Fytche, holding out the inducement of increased customs dues from the newly started Irrawaddy Flotilla Company's steamers, persuaded his majesty to give up all the monopolies, except those of earth oil, timber, and precious stones ; and to agree to a uniform import and export duty on all other goods and merchandise, passing between British and Burmese territory, of five per cent *ad valorem.* This treaty lapsed in 1877 and was not renewed. Nevertheless, King Mindôn did not renew the monopolies.

When his son came to the throne, he issued, or there was issued for him, a proclamation, stating that he was going to adopt Western forms of government, and expressly announcing that he had no intention of reviving the monopoly system. He was, however, with his wild, extravagant habits, very soon in as great monetary difficulties as his father, and from 1880 began steadily to sell monopolies and give grants of forest land for hard cash payments. The new monopoly buyers, haunted by a fear of British interference, and not by any means assured in their minds as to the stability of Thibaw Min's rule, were anxious to get as much money as they could, and therefore paid only the most absurdly low prices for produce. The cultivators, find-ing all their labour in vain, began consequently in large numbers to give up farming or working in the forests, the consequence of which was a still further shock to the trade with British Burma and an entire inability on the part of the population the following year to pay the house-tax. Besides the monopoly system derived from his predecessors, Thibaw Min also hit on the notion of lotteries for the replenishment of his treasury. The system worked very well for a time, and brought in great quantities of money, but latterly the loose coin of the populace had all been netted, and the lottery source of revenue was pretty nearly worked out. In 1879 and 1880 Mandalay was simply flooded with lottery-offices, each under the superintendence of a minister of high rank. Those who were able to show the king the most money were highest in the royal favour, and consequently the rivalry between these worthies ran very strong. All manner of dodges were tried to entice speculators away from all other offices to the minister's own. The Hpaung-wun,

Myowun, the lord high admiral, and lord mayor's establishment was generally admitted to be the largest and best, and it was certainly he who first began to try and allure the people. He secured the old custom-house buildings for his office, and enclosed a wide expanse round about it with a strong bamboo fence. Porous pots of deliciously cool drinking water, each pot supplied with a number of tin mugs, were arranged on stands all round the sides. The antisoporific letpet, the gigantic, but soothing, green cheroot, and the good betel lay in great heaps on the tables everywhere, and vanished with extraordinary rapidity. A dozen or more punkahs were hung up and worked by coolies, so as to calm the brains and cool the heated faces of excited clients. Later on, when other wuns and letthondaw copied his methods, the resourceful Hpaungwun added bands of music, dancing girls, and even regular dramatic performances, kept up perpetually, to the other attractions of his place of business. Some managers strove to get the better of their neighbours by giving the people unlimited supplies of palm-toddy, in the hope that the heady liquor might induce them to risk their last coins. Others hit upon the device of returning one pice—about one farthing—on each ticket taken. Others again, desperate at the thought of being unable to render a good account to their royal master, engaged gangs of bullies, who went about threatening people with violence or false accusations in the law-courts if any but their master were patronised, while the Zegyodaw Myowun, U Tha O, in virtue of his official position as keeper of the markets, sent his subordinates to the Chinese gambling-house keepers, and forced them to subscribe periodically for fifty tickets at a couple of rupees each, if they hoped to retain their gambling licenses. Fired by his example, the Yaw Shwedaik and Taingda atwinwuns also made use of their court influence to draw subscribers. Brokers and traders of all nationalities who had business with the palace were put down for a couple of hundred tickets or so, on pain of losing their contracts. One of the wundouks was advanced and heedless enough to select the Dhammayôn, a place of worship and prayer, for his lottery-office. All the old lines were upset. Drawings were held whenever the lists were filled up, no matter whether it was an uboné, or a more sacred feast, and, as a consequence, the minds of the people were kept in a state of perpetual unhealthy excitement.

Neither buyers nor sellers were to be seen in the bazaar. Cultivators sold off their farming stock and implements, and launched all their money into the state lotteries. Fathers sold their daughters, and husbands their wives, to have a final try for fortune, until the lottery managers issued a notice that they would give no more tickets in exchange for women. To fill up the totals faster, and draw in every available coin, twenty, or even more, people were allowed to club together to buy a single ticket. Business was entirely suspended, and all the people hovered about the lottery-offices, longing for the drawing, while cleaned-out speculators prowled about day and night, watching for an opportunity to thieve and rob. How it was that the plundered people did not rise against the government, or at least against the lottery managers, is a mystery, but they did not. The suburbs of Mandalay were filled for a time with ruined gamblers, until the soldiery were employed to drive them farther afield, when many made their way to the frontier, and recouped themselves by raids on British Burma villages. Eventually money failed, or the people were disillusionised, and the lottery-offices, though several remained open, drove but a very slight trade. Then Thibaw Min had to resort to other measures to meet his expenditure, and from July 1881 began disposing of monopolies right and left. Having finished the export monopolies, he commenced with those on imports. The British trade with Upper Burma was being steadily ruined, and the war which ended in the extinction of the kingdom of Burma was made inevitable.

CHAPTER LVII

LAND TENURE

In India the Raja has always been considered the chief proprietor of the soil and the lord paramount over all those who own it or dwell upon it. In Burma precisely the reverse of this system obtained. The king was indeed considered entitled to a share of the produce, and, as a matter of fact, undoubtedly got pretty nearly all of it; but the origin of the land tenure rested on an entirely different foundation. The Burmans go back to the first peopling of the earth and the appointment of the saintly Payālaung to be ruler over them. Mahā Thamada came after the lands had been pretty generally taken up by the people, and therefore the cultivators of the original thalé san had no intention of appointing him supreme landlord, when they chose him to be the source of the Law and of the administration of justice. He acquired a share of the produce of the country only by the free gift of the people, who, to provide revenues for him, of their own accord surrendered a tenth part of all their crops that he might be free to devote himself entirely to the management of the public affairs and the execution of the laws. This right to a tenth of the produce of the soil, and no more, is explicitly laid down in the Indian Buddhist code, the Dhammathat, or laws of Manu. This ancient book, which, by the way, is entirely distinct from the Indian *Institutes of Manu*, enunciates as follows in the sixth chapter: "The king, who is our ruler, must abide by the ten kingly laws. All land which is unclaimed shall be his, but he shall have no right to take all. Such lands as are cultivated by man, or have been previously reclaimed, shall

remain to the cultivator and his heirs.   But he shall have a
tenth of the produce of all rice-lands, orchards, and gardens ;
and all excise and ferry duties, as well as canals and public
works, shall belong to him.   Through a succession of worlds
the first king, the great Mahā Thamada, has established
one-tenth to be his portion for ever, and let this be regarded
as an everlasting precedent."

According to the Dhammathat there are seven methods
by which landed property may be acquired.   These are as
follows :— 1. By gift from the king.   This is made only to
soldiers and officials.   2. By inheritance.   3. By purchase.
4. By allotment from civil officers.   5. By personal reclaim-
ing from the jungle.   6. By gift.   7. By unchallenged
occupation for a period of ten years.

The first two titles are called perfect.   The remainder
are open to question, and may be disputed by any one who
can show a prior claim.   In actual fact, however, it may be
said that the man who reclaims for himself a piece of land
out of the jungle becomes by his industry proprietor of the
clearing, without reference to local authorities, village elders,
or any one at all, and has thereafter an inalienable right to
his tenure, with no dues to pay whatever, except the sum
the taikthugyi may see fit to assess him at.   That worthy's
valuation, however, always displayed an enthusiastic belief
in the fertility of the soil.   The landed proprietor could
dispose of it by gift, or he might sell it ; otherwise it descended
to his heirs and assigns in the order of succession ; the whole
right and title was essentially vested in the owner and the
heirs of his body.   The tenure was, therefore, by what lawyers
call fee-simple, udal, or allodial right.   The estate left by the
original occupier was seldom broken up.   The heirs tilled parts
of it, or gathered the whole crop in successive years ; so that
the land did not require to be split up into infinitesimal
parts.   This practice was rendered all the easier by the thinness of the population.   It was open to any one at any time
to carve for himself out of the forest a holding of his own,
and thus there was no temptation to break up the original
family acres.   It is singular that under a rule so completely
despotic as that of Burma, where every man was the king's
slave, and could not cross the borders without his permission,

the right of land tenure should always have been so fixed
and certain.   The fondness with which the people cling to
their ancestral lands has something of almost religious fervour
in its tenacity.   As long as a family remains in the neighbourhood of their inheritance nothing will persuade them to give
up their connection with it.   In Upper Burma, to the present
day, land is never sold as the term would be understood in
Europe.   The transaction which goes by the name of a sale
is, in reality, a kind of mortgaging, or, more exactly, pawning,
if such a term can be used with regard to land.

The estate passes from one occupant to another for a
certain sum of money, and it is clearly understood that if at
any time the original owner is in a position to reclaim his
property he may do so whether the purchaser likes it or not.
Farther than this even, the buyer cannot sell the land to a
third party without first obtaining the consent of its former
owner.   Notwithstanding this feeling, however, it is seldom
that a property can be found which has remained for any
considerable length of time in the same family.   This is
owing to the constant rebellions and wars between Peguans
and Burmese and Shans, which afflicted the country for five
hundred years.   All those who were not killed were driven
away from their former homes by ruthless invaders or were
drafted off to fight for the king.   In the short intervals of
peace rival governors, in desperation for means to raise the
revenues expected from their provinces, would tempt people
away from their former homes by the offer of rewards or a
reduction of body service.   Thus in some cases the proprietors
were killed out, in others they left for districts so remote that
it was impossible to retain a hold on the ancestral property,
however great their attachment to it.   As an illustration of
the sanctity attaching to ownership of land, the law concerning
church lands may be quoted from Buddhaghosha's Parables :
" Whoso shall take for himself or for another wutmye, consecrated or glebe-land, shall become a mite, or a white ant
upon that sacred ground for the whole of 100,000 cycles."

The eighteenth of the original eighteen laws given by
Manu to the king refers to the partition of property, and an
elaboration of this points out sixteen descriptions of children
who cannot claim a portion of their parents' property.   The

distinctions are more minute than is at all necessary or indeed comprehensible. They include all children born out of wedlock, among whom are reckoned such as are born before the parents have been married ten months ; all children that are purchased, or adopted by any other ceremony than that of abadita or keiktima ; and such as " from respect or affection style their guardians father or mother." The settlement of boundary marks was one of the earliest duties of the first ruler. The thale rice became constantly scarcer and scarcer, and it was determined that it would be well to give every person his share and mark it off distinctly. The appointment of persons to execute this duty was the first occasion on which executive officials were found necessary. Manu enumerated twenty-five objects suitable for legal landmarks. These included all natural objects, such as lakes, rivers, ridges, and hills, remarkable large trees and clumps of bamboos ; artificial boundaries of an equally permanent character, such as pagodas, shrines for demon-worship, zayats, or rest-houses, stone pillars and sacred posts, wells and cairns ; finally such singular distinguishing marks as heads of cattle, chaff, ashes, charcoal, sand, broken earthenware vessels, and men's bones. " Beating the bounds," one would think, must have been very necessary with the younger members of the household in the case of such perishable boundary lines as could be constituted by chaff, or even sand. In Upper Burma the cultivating population was so sparse that no difficulty was found in the matter of boundaries. In Lower Burma farms are as distinctly marked off as land-surveyors' chains can effect the operation in pointing out the little raised ridges which separate the plots of paddy land from one another. Nevertheless they are hardly such as the South of England farmers would approve.

These allodial tenures are the only ones which exist in Burma now. In independent territory there were two other kinds of holding, which were not, however, very numerous or extensive. The first of these were called thugyisa fields, and consisted of certain tracts of land near the town or village set apart for the maintenance of the headman. As that official was anything but a permanency, the tenant for the time being very seldom cultivated them himself, but let them out to farmers, who were required not only to pay him his rent, but as a rule had also to supply the revenue demanded from the owner by the State.   There was therefore no very enthusiastic bidding for his lands, but he always got a tenant somehow or other.   It would have been a bad day for the village if no one came forward.   Every man in the place would have been called upon to work for a certain period on the thugyi's paddy-fields.   These have now been merged in the State lands.

The third class of arable estates consisted of the lands known as bhanda, treasury, or royal fields.   These were the private property of the king, and were cultivated ordinarily by the outcast lamaing, crown predial slaves.   Sometimes, however, the whole of the farmers in the neighbourhood were summoned by roster to do their one, or three, or five days' work, for which they received no payment ; on the contrary, if they tried to escape they were tied up and received a dozen or two according to the humanity of the district governor. Near the capital, where oppression never was so gross as in the outlying provinces, the cultivators of the Lèdawgyi were frequently freed from all taxation but the payment of the family tax, and some even, as in the neighbourhood of Aungbinle, whose revenues were assigned by the king to the great Arakan pagoda, were let off even the ngwedaw. But these *corvées* were very irksome, for the payment of a little money would always ensure the omission of a name from the taikthugyi's list, and the work fell all the harder on the luckless remainder.   The whole of the produce of the bhanda lands belonged of course to the king, unless where he had otherwise assigned it.   What with revenue paid in kind and the crops of the Lèdawgyi, the king had granaries as vast as those which Joseph built for the king of Egypt. Mindôn Min drew from them to pay his soldiery, varying the monotony from time to time with pieces of rotten Manchester grey shirting.   Offerings to the Sacred Order, of whom he daily fed several thousands, also served to keep the storehouses within reasonable bounds.   Thibaw Min turned his grain into money with all possible expedition, and the money vanished with equal rapidity.   The Lèdaw of course became State land on the Annexation.

The only analogy to the crown lands in Lower Burma was found in the reservation of forests by the government for the preservation of teak and other valuable trees such as the thit-ka (*Cedreela toona*), thit-kado (*Pentace Burmanica*), and padauk (*Pterocarpus Indicus*), which are absolutely reserved, that is to say, no tree may be felled which has not been girdled by government forest officers, even by those who have bought the right to remove the timber. It is expressly stated that the lessee is in no case allowed to girdle trees on his own account, and the rules are in other respects of the most stringent and Oriental description. No taung-ya, or hill-gardens may be made in the demarcated tracts. A selection of rivers and streams is made which must be kept free from all artificial obstructions, whether for fisheries, irrigation, or other purposes. Unauthorised felling, cutting, marking, killing, or injuring trees of all kinds, shrubs or bamboos, the collection of wood oil, resin, and even leaves, and any interference with the soil or its produce without permission, is made penal. Even the use of existing roads and bridle-paths may, if the forest officer sees fit, be prohibited. In 1882, out of a total area of about 80,000 square miles of teak-producing forests, some 13,000 square miles were thus reserved, but this area has now been ten times exceeded. The Burman, who knows nothing whatever of game laws or edicts against trespassers, is inclined to look upon this stringent reservation of land which the ancient code declares free for all, as something far more despotic than the enforced labour and extortionate demands of national rule. Doubtless time will prove to him that it is a wise precaution to guard from destruction a slow-growing tree like the teak, and when the wandering hunter gets to understand that forest fires are a calamity and not simply an easy method of making a clearing, the State forests will come to be something less like pheasant coverts than they now are.

Otherwise, waste lands, as in old Upper Burma, are by the law of the Dhammathat open to all-comers. Any one can select for himself a tract of such land at his pleasure, and may clear and cultivate in any way he chooses, paying his tax upon it when the time for the annual assessment of land revenue comes round. In many cases, however, he is allowed to hold his land free from taxes for such a period as may be necessary to bring it into a thorough state of cultivation. In such a case as this he has to apply to the thugyi—the old hereditary officers being retained throughout British Burma —of his circle, if the land does not exceed five acres in extent. If it is above that area, application has to be made to the English Assistant-commissioner, or to the Deputy-commissioner in charge of the district, if the average of the new claim exceeds fifty. The land is then surveyed and a grant is drawn up specifying the term of years during which he shall be free from imposts. This varies according to the kind of jungle which is to be cleared away, and the kind of crops intended to be grown. The exemption is in no case for less than a year. If rice is to be grown, seven years is the longest term of rent-free tenure, but for orchard cultivation it extends to twelve years. In a few cases, where the nature of the ground necessitates, in addition to clearing away the forest growth, the digging of channels for irrigation, and the erection of dams, extension even of this long period is granted. As in France, Norway, Japan, and Switzerland, the farms are all very small, in some cases almost absurdly so. Along the old frontier the holdings averaged only about five acres, in the Rangoon district from sixteen to twenty acres is the ordinary size, but here and there are a few considerably larger. It would, however, be a great mistake to endeavour to introduce larger tenancies. It is entirely against the genius of the people, and the appearance of foreign capitalists could not be otherwise than disastrous. The present mode of cultivation is slovenly enough, and larger farms would most certainly not tend to remedy the defect, which is due in great part to the superabundance of available arable land lying waste. Burma is progressing fast enough as it is. The abundance of rich land, the facility with which rights over it can be acquired, the great demand for rice, and the ever-increasing counter demand for European goods, the fixed, though heavy taxation, the cessation of all irregular and unexpected collections, the absolute personal security enjoyed by all under the English administration : all these benefits have resulted in the trebling of the population of Lower Burma during twenty-six years since the annexation of Pegu ;

in the more than trebling of the trade—the value of the sea-borne merchandise alone having doubled and reached twelve and a half millions sterling during the ten years previous to 1881—and in the wonderful increase in revenue, which makes Burma the most valuable of all the provinces under the Indian Government.   Now that all Burma is one province the increase of revenue and the contribution paid to the Imperial Government have gone on increasing with a regularity which is almost automatic.

CHAPTER LVIII

MANDALAY AND RANGOON

[This chapter describes these towns as they were in 1881.]

AMERICANS talk, and with good reason, of the magic growth of their cities. But for mere mushroom growth, Mandalay might compare even with Chicago itself, and if we are to judge of the progress of a commercial place by the fair criterion of business results, Rangoon may hold up its head in confident rivalry with any of the typical American cities. In the middle of last century the site of Mandalay was swampy paddy land and rank jungle. Now an area of five square miles is covered with houses, many of them squalid enough certainly, and with large patches of unused land round about them, but none the less contained within the city limits. Rangoon came into British hands in 1852, and at that time possessed no commerce worthy of the name, indeed it was only known as the place for pilgrims to the Shwe Dagôn pagoda to stay at, and the residence of the Regent of Pegu, as being the guard station on the most accessible mouth of the Irrawaddy. Ten years later, ships entered or cleared from the port having a tonnage of 295,000 tons, and the imports were worth £1,200,000, the exports £1,400,000, and since that date—a year or two after Mandalay had been founded—the tonnage has increased to 1,000,000, the value of the imports to £5,000,000 sterling, and the exports to £4,000,000. In a quarter of a century the commerce of British Burma rose to nearly £20,000,000 sterling. The population has quadrupled ; public works are carried on ; education is widely disseminated ; the administration is carefully managed by British officials ; a railway,

163 miles long, has been made; there are 1300 miles of
telegraph lines; stately law courts and other public buildings
have sprung up, and so far from the work being a tax on
the Indian Imperial Treasury, British Burma has been, after
its first few years, more than self-supporting. For a considerable time it has contributed to the Imperial Treasury a clear
surplus of a million sterling. The mere figures are in themselves surprising, but they cannot be truly appreciated unless
they are read alongside the obvious, undeniable, and acknowledged prosperity and contentment of the native population.
Since the annexation of Upper Burma these figures have
been roughly multiplied by ten, and there is a steady yearly
increase which would be greater if Burma were allowed to
make use of her yearly surpluses.

As long as there was a king of Burma, Mandalay was a
larger town than Rangoon and an infinitely more picturesque
one. It still remains by a long way the second town in
Burma, but Rangoon has over-passed it in population.
While Rangoon has gained, Mandalay has lost, but there
seems no reason why it should go on declining.

The mushroom growth of Mandalay was entirely due to
an autocratic order, but the number of ancient capitals in
the neighbourhood shows that the position is an advantageous
one. The astrologers and the king settled the new site
between them, and when this was arranged a royal order
came out bidding all remove themselves from Amarapura to
Mandalay on pain of death in case of refusal. The trans-
ference of a bamboo hut is certainly no very great undertaking, and occupies less than a week in the pulling down
and setting up. But the hardship was none the less where
the people had gardens, or fruit-trees growing in their yards.
The Chinese alone remained firm. Their houses were of
the usual substantial, heavy, Celestial architecture, and, moreover, they had built for themselves an elaborate joss-house,
in splendour quite equal to the best in Rangoon. Consequently, they flatly refused to migrate the two or three miles
distance to the new capital. The astrologers were as usual
for using force, but Mindôn Min had more sense. The
Chinamen were almost all British subjects, and moreover their
dealings contributed substantially to the revenue. Their

village therefore remained, and has served to drag out a long suburb beyond the Arakan pagoda as a kind of connecting link.   Numbers of later arrivals, however, settled in the royal City of Gems, and the wealthier merchants all eventually mòved their headquarters thither, so that his majesty triumphed in the end.   The best houses in Mandalay, the only brick ones, in fact, till the British came, are all in the possession of the Chinese and Indian merchants.   Burmans had neither the right nor the money to build anything but wooden erections.   These latter have, however, the compensating advantage that they stand all but the most violent earthquakes, while the brick houses, even when they are strengthened by an elaborate wooden framework, usually collapse when there is anything like a heavy shock.

But the great majority of the houses are simply wattled huts, with large open spaces in their rear which serve to keep the town airy and well ventilated.   According to Burman custom each house has its little shop with the entire stock in trade displayed to the view of the passer-by.   As in all Eastern towns, those who occupy themselves with a regular handicraft all flock together.   Thus the umbrella-makers and sellers of saddlery live to the south of the palace, vendors of bamboo-work and lacquered boxes to the west, while the potters and miscellaneous goods shops are mostly along the street that leads to Payā Gyi, the Arakan pagoda.

There was no attempt at metalling any of the roads, except in independent times the broad thoroughfare which led up from the steamer ghaut, past the ministers' residences, up to the outskirts of the town, for Mandalay lies two miles away from the river-bank, the idea being that at Amarapura the noise of the foreigners' steamers disturbed the royal repose.   The big stones which represented the metalling on this one road were rather a trouble than otherwise, except to the vultures and egrets in the wet weather, when all around was a sea of mud, and the boulders formed an eligible coign of vantage.   Elsewhere the streets were cut into huge ruts, and the bullock-carts went along in the hot weather in a pyramid of dust, and in the rains a ploughed field would be smooth going in comparison.   But the gaily-painted carriages which always suggest a dog-kennel on

wheels to a European, were strongly built, and the fair dames
inside were used to the jolting.   It was only when the king or
one of the queens went forth that any attempt at road-mending
was carried on.   Then an ameindaw was issued, Shinbuyin
Twet daw mumi, the Golden Majesty, will make a royal
progress, and all along the route the house-reeves saw that
the rough places were made smooth, and the crooked places
straight.   Thus the main thoroughfares were kept in a state
of fair repair.   In other respects, however, Mandalay was vastly
superior to all Indian towns.   In all the city there is not a
drain, but it is equally certain that neither is there a smell.
There were no such slums as constantly offend every sense
a man has in the Black Town of Madras or the native
quarters of Calcutta.   This cleanliness was due to the exertions
of the great multitudes of swine and dogs.   The pigs formed
most efficient scavengers during the day-time, and wandered
all about in the most independent and ownerless fashion.
Charitable people, in search of merit, set out daily meals for
them, while all in common threw out their scraps and leavings
in the confidence justified by experience that nothing would
be left to decay.   The great majority of the dogs, equally
with the porkers, belonged to nobody in particular, and made
themselves comfortable under any house they chose, sleeping
nearly all day and howling and fighting all night.   These
animals were all strenuous adherents of the Old Burman party,
and cherished a most fanatic hatred for Europeans.   The old
boar ran between the legs of the white man or of his pony,
in a simulated state of alarm at his faded, ghost-like face,
and the pariah dogs let all the town know the progress of
a foreigner by their fierce barking and snapping of teeth
a yard or so off his calves.   The dogs of one street passed him
on to the next, so that it was impossible for a wandering
Briton to go about the town unobserved.   It will not soon
be forgotten how the English Assistant Resident had to run
for his life from the Mandalay bazaar.   He had killed a
snarling brute with a quick backward swing of his stick, and
the pious life-regarding populace came out upon him armed
with billets of firewood and formidable dahs.   He managed
to keep away from them, but he had a half-mile race of it,
and the Residency gates were smashed in by the mob.   Then

the guard dispersed the people.   Next day, an old lady, who claimed to be the owner of the dog, visited the big Englishman and told him she forgave him.   He was barely polite.

Burmans had no trouble with the pigs and dogs.   They found their own countrymen much more awkward to meet. There was constantly some prince or mingyi passing along the streets, and then the road had to be immediately cleared, and every one knelt humbly till the great man passed. Any delay in clearing the path, or an imagined want of reverence in the shikhoing, met with very summary punishment.   Before every dignitary rushed along a posse of half-naked lictors, yelling out to the people to bow down, and hitting round about them with their fasces and dahs. These masterful ruffians particularly loved to insult Englishmen.   During Mindôn's reign an edict was published exempting Englishmen from the necessity of getting down on their knees in the mud and dust, but ordaining that they should lift their hats.   The letyataung dearly loved to launch torrents of abuse at their victim, and make him dismount from his pony and remove his hat when the prince was half a block distant.   In the spring of 1880 an English mercantile man was actually bullied into going down on his knees.   But, as a rule, where it was possible, foreigners turned down a by-street, or into one of the waste plots of ground. This method of avoiding the annoyance was not open to a Burman.   If he tried to avoid paying due obeisance, he was denounced as a disaffected man and thrown into jail.

But there were plenty of other obstructions to be met with in the streets of the royal city.   Each householder was considered, or considered himself, perfectly at liberty to do what he pleased with the section of the road in front of his house.   Accordingly, when the spirit moved him, he calmly blocked the thoroughfare by erecting a temporary theatre for the performance of a pwè.   The construction of such a mandut did not take very long.   A framework of bamboo was run up and covered in on the roof, and one side with bamboo matting, and all was ready ; the stage was the street, and the spectators deposited themselves where they found room.   After the three or four days' performance, the stage was pulled down, and the thoroughfare was clear again.

During the season a dozen or more of these plays went on in Mandalay on the same night, and the entire population turned out to see them, thus effectually blocking as many streets as there were performances.   This might have been awkward for the ordinary wayfarer were it not that he would probably infinitely prefer staying to see the drama to continuing his journey.   Great men were not so complaisant. Two of the massacred princes, the Mekkhaya and the Thonsè, seemed to take a special delight, when they were belated on some roistering expedition, in breaking up such plebeian gatherings.   They would come sweeping down the street with all their retinue, and the spectators, deafened by the music and engrossed with the action on the stage, would get their first hint of the torrent coming from the vigorous blows dealt all round about them by the howling lictors. Everything would be disorder and alarm for a time, men and women down in the ditch, the stage deserted, and the spectators scattered far and wide.   Then, ten minutes later, they would all come back again ; there would be a few remarks concerning his Royal Highness—" very often out at unexpected times, and always making his appearance so suddenly," etc. etc. ; the bamboo erection would be propped up again, and the actors continued with the scene as if nothing whatever had happened, though the clown, no doubt, made as much fun out of the incident as he dared.

Going about at night in Mandalay was not much practised. Theatre-goers usually returned home with the rising sun. There were no lamps in the streets, and so every one who had business after dark was required to go about carrying a lantern or beating a drum or gong.   If any one ventured abroad without thus marking his movements, he was promptly arrested by the night watch, and once a man was arrested in Mandalay it cost a good deal of money to get free again, no matter how good an account he might be able to give of himself.   To save themselves the trouble of being constantly on the look-out as well as to trip up any one who tried to run away, the guardians of the peace had an unpleasant custom of tying ropes across the road an inch or two above the ground, and these were quite as effectual man-traps as have ever been invented.

When a fire occurred in the Golden City, it was usually a very big one and burned until it could find no more fuel. There were two reasons for this. The most obvious was, of course, that wood huts, with an inflammable roof like thin grass thatch, caught fire with the slightest spark ; and there was nothing in the shape of a fire-engine, even in the palace. The second was very characteristic of a despotism, and vastly more disastrous. Immemorial tradition associated a conflagration with a revolution. When an attempt was to be made to seize the throne, the attention of the people and the soldiery was always diverted by incendiary fires. Therefore when a house took fire the people found nearest to it by the night watchmen were always arrested and made responsible for the catastrophe. As a natural consequence, the moment flames burst out, not only the inmates of the house, but all the neighbours took to their heels and ran, without incommoding themselves with even the smallest portion of their property. A few of the royal troops came down after a time and unroofed a house here and there, and perhaps even pulled down some altogether, but their efforts as amateur firemen were usually of the most feeble and futile description, and the flames went on till there was nothing more to burn. Next day the unhappy burnt-out people came back and made for themselves little hovels of bamboo matting among the charred posts till something better could be run up again. The neighbouring quarters contributed something to support them, or they got their meals at the monasteries, and in a few months all traces of the fire had disappeared, the same rickety huts with the old scanty store of wares rose up again, and the scorched leaves fell off the trees and were replaced by fresh green foliage.

The population of Mandalay was a very queer one. Of the Burmans the great majority were soldiers or hangers-on of the various great men about the court. The residuum was composed of a few honest tradesmen and a vast quantity of bad characters, broken agriculturists, gamblers, thieves from Lower Burma, and outlaws from all parts. The number of yellow-robed yahans was extraordinary. King Mindôn used to give alms to five thousand of them daily. The jars of rice were arranged in long rows on a platform erected specially for the purpose, with mountains of bananas, and trays heaped up with ngapi, curries, and condiments of all kinds. Thibaw Min was not so eager for merit, and actually went the length of driving a couple of thousand of the holy men out of the capital. Still even he gave them periodical feasts, and there were at least ten thousand of the religious in the Golden City and its immediate neighbourhood. Besides these there were numerous other nationalities ; the Chinaman, smooth-shaven and prosperous as always, whether gaunt and big-boned from Yün-nan and Szuch'uan, or sleek and sturdy from Rangoon and the Straits, defying the most greedy official to rob him of his profits, and drinking his tea and smoking his opium-pipe with supreme composure and good-humour ; the bearded Surati with solemn face and Jewish tricks of trade ; the Palaung come down from the north with his bamboo rafts laden with pickled tea ; the stalwart Shan with baggy blue or white trousers and tattoo marks down to his ankles, journeying in a long caravan with sword-blades and iron-work, and a cavalcade of mountain ponies ; the heavy, easy-going Karen ; the lithe, treacherous Kachin, bringing presents perhaps from his village, and on his way down spying out villages easy to raid in a night attack ; all these, and a host of others, might be seen any day in the Royal City of Gems. There were not a few white men too, even latterly, when evil times fell upon them, and there were not the pickings that were to be had when Mindôn Min was king. But many of them were there sorely against their inclination. Mandalay had become an asylum for insolvent debtors, runaway soldiers and sailors, and unlucky adventurers from British territory, just as Rangoon used to be for India in the old Burman days. There were numbers of French and Italians in government service, as military instructors and superintendents of the various factories ; officers who had been cashiered, or disowned by their families, or were in other ways under a cloud. One Count there was, who constituted the scientific branch of the service in himself, manufactured and sold fruit syrups to the captains of steamers, preserved a pocket-handkerchief with a coronet in the corner, and carried his lands in his finger-nails. The old king was shamefully cheated by a variety of speculators, not a few of them Englishmen.

Perhaps it was his own fault. He had a perfect mono-
mania for making cannon, and thought that every white
man must have some notion of how they were to be manufactured.   Consequently, whenever some fresh wanderer
came to the royal city and requested employment, he was
brought before the king, and some such dialogue as the
following ensued : "What is your name ? " "John Smith."
" What can you do ? " " May it please your majesty, I am
a sea-cook." " Can you make a cannon ? " Whereupon John
Smith, if he was a wise man, would profess his ability to
make the attempt at any rate. A lump of metal would
be made over to him, and he would chisel and hammer
away at it and draw his monthly pay as regularly as he
could get it. When results were demanded he would either
run away, or boldly ask for a grant of money to enable him
to go to Europe to get the requisite tools. If he got it
neither tools nor man were ever seen again. Such lack
of moral principle was believed by the king to arise from
the want of a Buddhist training, and he continued to be
imposed upon to the very end. Thibaw still retained some
foreigners in his service, but they found it harder to get
their pay, and much more of a task to swindle the
Government.

Thus Mandalay presented a series of violent contrasts :
jewel-studded temples and gilded monasteries standing side
by side with wattled hovels penetrated by every wind that
blew ; the haughty prince preceded by the respited murderer, his lictor ; the busy Chinaman next door to the
gambling scum of the low country ; the astrologer, learned
in his mantras, overpersuaded by the glib talk of the Western
adventurer ; and over all hanging the fear of prison with its
nameless horrors, and the knife of the assassin.

In the beginning of the century Rangoon was in much
the same condition, except that it was very much smaller,
no better in fact than a village with the Governor's house
and stockade in the middle of it. Now it has broad smooth
roads, beautifully laid out public gardens, abundant street
lamps, spacious mercantile offices, mills, schools, jails,
hospitals, clubs, and halls. The population forms an even
more motley assemblage than is to be found in Mandalay.

There are Chinese, Japanese, Malays, Siamese, natives of India of all parts, Bengalis, Madrassis, Panjabis, Parsis, Persians, Suratis, together with Armenians, Jews, English, French, Germans, Italians, Greeks, and all the European nationalities, mixed up with the native races, Burmese, Talaings, Shans, Karens, but they are all kept in order by the strong arm of the law, which is the same for the rich man and the poor.

The same benefits are now extended to Mandalay, but it is a vastly less interesting place than it used to be. A siding from the railway cuts its way through the city wall; one of the pyathats on the battlements has thrown out corridors to make a somewhat barrack-like Government house; a carriage drive goes round Mandalay hill; the pigs have all been eaten up, and the pariah dogs are poisoned periodically by municipal order. There never were any sludgy sqwudgy creeks, but the roads, which were a passable imitation of them in the rains, are now eminently fitted for exceeding the speed limit. A, B, and C roads testify to the unromantic stolidity of the Military Intelligence Department; electric trams make it easier for the Burman to move to the suburbs and leave the town to the hustling foreigner. There are no agreeable scallywags. There are Cook's tourists instead during the three cool months of the year. The palace, instead of being tawdrily magnificent, smells horribly of bats. It has been declared to be an archæological treasure, though it is only about sixty years old, and has been horribly mishandled by unimaginative secretaries and a Public Works Department oppressed with sealed patterns.

CHAPTER LIX

ERAS, COMPUTATION OF TIME, WEIGHT, ETC.

BURMESE chronology recognises five different eras, only the last of which, however, is ever practically used. These are:—

1. The Kawza era, which was abolished by Shin Gautama's grandfather. It had extended over 8650 years, and came to an end in the year 691 before the Christian era.

2. Bodaw Insana, the Buddha's grandfather, then established an era of his own. It lasted only 148 years, or till 543 B.C., in which year Shin Gautama died.

3. The Religious era. Fixed by Ayatathat, King of Magadha in India, dating from the death of the most excellent payā, and current till A.D. 82.

4. King Thamôddayit's era, established by that monarch in A.D. 82 at Prome, and lasting till A.D. 639, or for a period of 562 years.

5. The current era, established by the Yahan Pôppasaw, when he usurped the throne of Pagān in A.D. 639. The year 1244 of this era begins in April 1882.

The changing of the eras was in most cases to avoid calamities, threatened for certain years by old prophecies, and in a few instances of eras which gained no permanent place, merely for the sake of gratifying royal vanity.

The ordinary year consists of twelve lunar months, of twenty-nine and thirty days alternately. Every third year a thirteenth month is intercalated between the fourth and fifth. The date on which the year begins in the month of April was determined by the calculations of the royal astrologers in Mandalay, and published throughout the country by the pôngyis and district officials. The Chief Secretary

to the Burma Government now fixes the day.   He consults
the astrologers theoretically and sees that it is suitable for
the polo tournament at Maymyo, the hot weather headquarters of the local government.

The months, with their corresponding English equiva-
lents, are as follows :—

Tagu	about	April.
Kasôn	„	May.
Nayôn	„	June.
Waso	„	July.

(A second, a Dutiya Waso, intercalated every third year.)

Wagaung	about	August.
Tawthalin	„	September.
Thadingyut	„	October.
Tasaungmôn	„	November.
Na'daw	„	December.
Pyatho	„	January.
Tabodwè	„	February.
Tabaung	„	March.

The days are not counted right through the month as in
the European system, but as with a watch, or as with the
" day " itself, the month is divided into two parts : the la-
san, or waxing moon, which lasts from the first to the la-byi,
the full moon ; and from the following day, the 16th, to the
end of the month (the la-gwè) comes the waning, la-sôk or
la-byigyaw.

Besides this there is a division corresponding to that
into weeks in the European system.   The seven days are
named after the eight planets, or astrological houses.   Sunday is Taninganwe (the day of the Ne Yawi or Sun) ;
Monday, Taninla (from La, or Sanda, the Moon) ; Tuesday,
Inga (from Inga, Mars) ; Wednesday, from one in the morning till noon, Bôddahu (Bôdda, Mercury) ; the rest of
Wednesday, from mid-day till midnight, Yahu (from the
dark planet of the same name, a monstrous foul nat, who
strives to swallow the sun and moon, and causes partial
eclipses by licking and pawing them ; once every three years
he attacks the sun, and once in six months the moon) ;
Thursday, Kyathabadé (from Prispati, or Pyèpati, Jupiter) ;

Friday, Thaukkya (from Thaukkya, Venus) ; Saturday, Sané (from Thawri, Saturn).   The selection of the planets to denote the days of the week by races so different now, whatever they may originally have been, as the Chinese, Scandinavians, Greeks, and all the Mohammedan tribes, is singular.

For ordinary purposes the day and the night are divided into four periods of three hours each : from six to nine, which is called ta-chetti, the first watch, one blow ; twelve o'clock, the next quarter, is announced by hni'-chetti, the second watch, two blows ; three o'clock, thôn-chetti, the third watch, three blows ; and six, le-chetti, the fourth watch, four blows.   These hours were sounded in Mandalay by alternate beating on a huge gong and drum placed in the clock-tower by the eastern gate ; and at le-chetti, sundown or sunrise, the palace gates were closed, or opened, as the case might be.   Noon is styled môn, and midnight tha'gaung ; and the word byan is added in the sense of the English P.M. Thus nayi byan thôn-chetti would be 3 P.M.

In English territory of course the English system has been adopted, and now prevails over the whole country, Upper and Lower.   For astronomical purposes, such as the casting of the horoscope and the calculations for fortunate days and the like, an exceedingly elaborate scale exists, but it is never made use of in ordinary life, though references to it in religious books are not uncommon.   The unit is a naya.   This is the period of time in which ten flashes of lightning may take place, or the time it takes to wink the eye ten times, or to throw out the arm as often.

4 Naya are equivalent to			one Kanā, an " instant."
12 Kanā	„	„	Kayā.
10 Kayā	„	„	Pyan.
6 Pyan	„	„	Bizana.
15 Bizana	„	„	Pad.
4 Pad	„	„	Nayi, an " hour."
60 Nayi	„	„	Yet, a day and night.
15 Yet	„	„	Bekkha, or side (of the moon) a half month.
2 Bekkha	„	„	La, a month.
12 La	„	„	Hnit, a year.

Besides the ordinary names given above for the twelve months, the soothsayers, for the sake of the increased learning it seems to give them, are accustomed to refer to the months by the names of the twelve signs of the zodiac called Yathi.

Thus Tagu is known as Meittha, the ram.

„	Kasôn	„	Pyeittha, the bull.
„	Nayôn	„	Medôn, the union of the procreating powers of the male and female.
„	Waso	„	Karakat, the crab.
„	Wagaung	„	Thein, the lion.
„	Tawthalin	„	Kan, the virgin.
„	Thadingyut	„	Tu, the scales.
„	Tasaungmôn	„	Pyeitsa, the scorpion.
„	Na'daw	„	Nu, the bow.
„	Pyatho	„	Makāya, the sea monster.
„	Tabodwè	„	Kôn, the water-pot.
„	Tabaung	„	Mein, the fish.

There are reckoned to be three seasons, the cold, the hot, and the wet.

The cold season, saung-dwin, heman, or hemanta utu, lasts from the first of the waning of Tasaungmôn to the first of the waning of Tabaung, from the end of November to the beginning of March.

The hot season, nwe, geman, or gemanta utu, lasts from the first of the waning of Tabaung to the first of the waning of Waso, from the beginning of March to the beginning of July.

The wet season, mo, wathan, or wathanta utu, lasts from the first of the waning of Waso to the first of the waning of Tasaungmôn, from the beginning of July to the end of November.

This is a very hard and fast division, but it is fairly accurate. The cold weather is, however, only perceptible in the early morning. Fifty degrees is about the lowest known in Rangoon, but it is colder in other stations. Still you have to journey beyond Bhamaw in the north before you come to the region of duck frosts. There is no mistake

about the rains. In Rangoon the annual average rainfall
is a hundred inches, but in Maulmein, Ākyab, and other
towns considerably over twice that amount is registered. In
Rangoon, on 3rd November 1879, between one o'clock in
the morning and two in the afternoon eleven inches fell.
Happily this sort of thing is not usual.

In Mandalay, time was calculated by means of a water-
clock, which stood in the bo-ho, the clock-tower by the
eastern gate, where were also the gong and drum on which
the watches were sounded by one, two, three, or four alternate
blows. The water-clock is a simple enough affair. It consists of nothing more than a large vessel filled with water,
in which cups are placed, perforated so that an hour—a
Burmese nayi—elapses before they sink to the bottom. It
is only at the vernal and autumnal equinoxes that the hours
of the day and night are equal. At other times they vary,
and the Burmans make a great fuss over their complicated
calculations. In July the days are longest with thirty-six
hours, the night only lasting twenty-four, while these figures
are exactly reversed in January. Any inaccuracy in Burmese computations arises from the loss of the fourth book
of Bedin (the Indian Vedas), which was destroyed in the
bonfire made by the religious of all fishing-nets, snares,
weapons of war, and such writings as are denounced in the
sacred books. It was by pecking at the ashes of this volume
that the domestic fowls of Burma acquired that astronomical
lore which induces them to crow all together at midnight
(tha'gaung kyet).

It is only, however, in the capital that the water-clock is
found, and in the rest of the country, and especially in all
the smaller villages and towns, time is only roughly indicated by a reference to the position of the sun or the moon,
or to certain daily occurrences taking place at fixed times,
as "in the morning when the sun was a span above the
horizon"; or "when the sun was as high as a toddy-palm";
"before the sky was light"; "when the light gets strength"
about half-past five; "the earliest cock-crowing time"; "when
the monks go a-begging," that is to say, six or seven in the
morning, according to the custom of the local monastery;
"monks' returning time," usually about eight, but varying,

of course, with the charity of the neighbourhood ; " breakfast time," usually eight o'clock ; " dinner time," about five ; " after mid-day " ; " sky-closing time " about 6 P.M. ; " brothers don't know each other time," that is, just after dark ; " when the lamps are lighted " ; " children's go-to-bed time," about eight o'clock ; " lads go courting time," about the same period ; " when grown-up people lay their heads down," ten o'clock in the country, twelve with the kālathas of the towns ; " all the world quiet time " ; tha'gaung gyaw, " the wee short hour ayont the twal' " ; when " the iron tongue of midnight hath told twelve," as Shakespeare has it ; a-yôn kyè-ni paw, " when the red star rises,"—all these and a multitude of others are in common everyday use, and from the simple habits of the people, and their own graphic force, are quite sufficient to mark the desired time and ensure punctuality. Many can tell the time simply by looking at their own shadow. Burmans not being yet affected by this " age of machinery," as Carlyle calls it, are quite satisfied with equally simple methods of indicating duration of time. Athet ta-daung, " a breath's space," serves to denote a moment ; " the chewing of a fid of betel " occupies ten minutes ; " the time it would take to boil one pot of rice," twenty minutes, is well known to everybody where the cooking goes on in the front of the house. These being recognised, the chewing of two betel nuts, the boiling of three pots of rice, do not imply too great an effort of mental arithmetic. The simple rural Burmans understand as little of the English system of horology as they do of the nayas, and bizanas, and pads of the royal astronomers—measures of time which nevertheless appear in all their horoscopes.

Measures of distance are described in equally picturesque language. Thus we have " a stone's throw," from fifty to sixty yards, bests on record with throwing the cricket ball being unknown ; " a call," about a couple of hundred yards ; " a musket's sound," half an English mile ; " morning meal's distance," that is to say, as far as a man could walk between sunrise and breakfast time, say six miles English ; a mu, the eighth of a taing, quarter of a mile ; a mat, twice as far ; " nga mu," literally five mus or half a taing, an English mile.

The book measures of length are, however, very elaborate.
A san-kyi, or hair's breadth, is taken as the unit.

10 San-kyi	=	one hnan, a grain of sesamum seed.
6 Hnan	=	one mu-yaw, a barley-corn.
4 Mu-yaw	=	one let-thit, a finger's breadth.
8 Let-thit	=	one meik, the width of the fist with the thumb extended.
3 Meik	=	one taung, a cubit ($19\frac{1}{2}$ inches).
4 Taung	=	one lan, a fathom.
7 Taung	=	one ta, a measuring rod.
20 Ta	=	one ôkthapa.
1000 Ta	=	one daing, one Burmese, nearly two English miles.
20 Okthapa	=	one kawtha.
4 Kawtha	=	one gawut.
4 Gawut	=	one yuzana.

A yuzana is reckoned to measure 6400 ta, that is, six
daing and 400 ta.   The daing, or post, is the standard in
common use with the Burmese for the measurement of long
distances.   It is also used as a generic term for any measure
approaching it in length, such as a league, a kos, an English
mile, and so on, as engaleik daing, an English mile.

Twelve fingers' breadths are reckoned equal to one htwa,
a span.   Ta implies measure in general, and is used as an
auxiliary to the other measures of length, as taung ta, a
cubit.

The hill tribes have a peculiar way of speaking of a
place as being "one hill" or "three hills" distant.   The
expression may be very vague, but it gives the wayfarer an
idea of what is before him which could not be expressed in
the simple statement that he had ten miles to go.   The
road might be all down hill, or all up, for all this would
convey to his mind.   Similarly river boatmen talk of "two
reaches" or "four reaches."

The measures of capacity start from the ear of corn.
One ear, ta-hnan, ought to contain 200 grains.

200 A-se, or grains	=	one let-sôn, as much as can be placed on the ends of the fingers joined together.

2 Let-sôn	=	one let-sôt, the quantity of grain which may be grasped in the fist.
3 Let-sôt	=	one let-hpet, as much grain as can be heaped on the palm of the hand.
2 Let-hpet	=	one let-kut, the quantity which may be heaped on the surface of both hands joined together.
2 Let-kut	=	one kônsa, what is sufficient for the meal of one person.
5 Kônsa	=	one pyi, a small measure.
2 Pyi	=	one sa-ywet.
2 Sa-ywet	=	one seit, quarter of a basket.
2 Seit	=	one hkwè, half a basket.
2 Hkwè	=	one tin, a basket.
4 Tin	=	one to.
20 To	=	one ta-pôn, or ta-su, a heap or two cart-loads—hlè hni' si.

The pyi is also subdivided into four salè. Practically, the only measures used are the tin, the seit, the pyi, and the salè. All depend upon the size of the tin, but as this varies not only in almost every district, but also in many parts of the same district, the results are somewhat embarrassing to merchants making purchases from the cultivators. The English have made an attempt to introduce a standard "basket," containing 2218.19 cubic inches, but without any very great success. Application for legal establishment of the standard would cause disturbance to trade and irritation of the old-fashioned people, but it is evident that it must come some day. If Burmans had the money-grubbing instincts of the natives of India it would have been done long ago, but as long as everybody gets enough to eat and there is overplus, after offerings to the monks and the pagoda, wherewith to get money for new clothes, the Burman farmer cares very little what entangled sums in arithmetic have to be worked out by the unlucky purchaser.

The standard of weight begins exceedingly low in the scale. Parama nu-myu are atoms of a subtle fluid, invisible to men, but visible to nat-dewas and the highly advanced in religion.

36 Parama nu-myu	=	one a-nu-myu, visible particles of dust, such as the motes dancing in the sunbeam.
36 Anu-myu	=	one ka-nyit-che, a gross particle, such as the dust which falls from the style, when a scribe writes on a palm-leaf.
7 Ka-nyit-che	=	one than ôk-kaung, a louse's head.
7 Than ôk-kaung	=	one môn-nyin se, a mustard seed.
3 Môn-nyin se	=	one hnan se, a grain of sesamum.
4 Hnan se	=	one san se, a grain of rice.
4 San se	=	one hkyin ywe, a seed of the *Abrus precatorius*.
2 Hkyin ywe	=	one ywegyi, a seed of the *Aden- anthera pavorina*.
4 Ywegyi	=	one pè.
2 Pè	=	one mu.
2 Mu	=	one mat.
4 Mat	=	one kyat.
5 Kyat	=	one bo.
20 Bo	=	beittha, a viss, 3.652 lbs. avoirdu- pois.
4 Beittha	=	one tula.
4000 Tula	=	one tapông, or tasu.

The only weights in ordinary use are the mu, mat, nga-mu (or hkwè), half a kyat, and the kyat. The standard weights are usually formed with a figure of the sacred hantha on them, or sometimes with the animal representing the royal birthday.

Formerly the Burmese had no stamped coinage, and the silver and gold used, mixed in greater or less amount with alloy, which necessitated the calling in of an assayer for every transaction, was always dealt out by weight. King Mindôn struck gold coins stamped with the lion and the pea-cock, silver and copper with the royal peacock, and lead with the hare. The lead coins were simply blobs of metal like a spherical bullet squeezed out of shape. One might examine thousands of them and never see a hare. Mandalay rupees, though the same size as those of the Indian Government, were not in favour in Rangoon. They usually ran to fourteen annas, so that there was a loss of two annas on each. The gold coins were practically not in circulation at all. Englishmen bought them as curiosities in the bazaar and got cheated if they did not carefully ring every one. The smaller ones, struck from the same die as the silver two-anna bit, were principally used by the king to fill silver cups presented to distinguished visitors.

Being derived from the measures of weight, the coins have received the same names. The rupee is kyat, some-times also called ding-ga, that is, a circular piece of metal, whether a coin or a medal, and the sub-multiples go by the names of the smaller weights : pè is one anna ; mu, two annas ; mat, four annas ; nga-mu, eight annas ; thôn-mat, twelve annas ; kyat-mu-din, fourteen annas, literally a rupee less two annas ; one piece is ti'-bya.

The Burmans have no bankers. In native times there were exceedingly few who would have anything to lodge with such a personage. Those who have superabundant coin almost always disperse it in giving a kyi-gyin pwè, or in building a pagoda, a monastery, digging a tank, or some such work of merit. Whatever money there may remain over is turned into use or display in the shape of fat oxen, and silver and gold cups and jewellery. These are pleasant things to look at and easily convertible into money when necessary. Burmans detest hoarding. A miser is threatened with as terrible a hereafter as a parricide. The portion of both is in awidzi, the lowest hell.

All this sort of thing shows a very unbusiness-like, certainly a very uncommercial spirit, but it is at least open to argument that the Burman is philosophically right. He cares little for the troubles of the world and the manifold questions of the day which distract the more highly cultured nations. His eyes are fixed uninterruptedly on the dark mysteries which surround our beginning, our end, and every moment of our life. The earth is only a camping-ground, in which it does not repay the trouble to establish one's self firmly and comfortably. The rich man carries his gold and silver, the poor his last handful of rice, to the pagoda, and deposits it there at usurer's interest for his future home beyond.   Let the black coolie of India talk all day and dream all night of his filthy pice ; let the greasy Chetty money-lender gloat over his bloated money-bags ; let the English merchant delight in all the refined luxuries wealth can bring him : the Burman is content if he has enough to eat and remain a free man, happy if he accumulates sufficient to build a work of merit, or give a free festival to his less fortunate brethren.   Who shall say he is not wise ?

CHAPTER LX

THE LANGUAGE

THE Burmese language is monosyllabic, and is therefore, like all the other monosyllabic languages, forced into the tonic system on account of the limited number of combinations of which the consonants admit. The multitude of meanings which a slight difference of accentuation gives to an otherwise identical sound is the greatest difficulty which a stranger has to contend with in studying the language, and never fails to land the beginner in a most embarrassing maze of complications. The modulations of the voice which European nations employ only to express astonishment, disbelief, interrogation, and alarm, become in Burmese and other Indo-Chinese tongues a means for distinguishing between words of different meaning; and this peculiarity offers particular difficulties to the phlegmatic, monotonous-voiced Englishman. It does not simplify matters that Burmese is, of all these languages, the softest and most pliable, and has therefore received the title of the Italian of the Far East. The varying cadence of the sounds produces to the ear the semblance of a chant, and all the people seem to speak in a kind of rhythm, so that as long as a man has ideas, it is not a very difficult matter to compose linga. But this only renders it more puzzling to the Occidental, and accounts for the fact that very few Englishmen learn Burmese, and still fewer speak it well. Of the mercantile community not one in fifty has any knowledge of Burmese at all; and the civil officers, who have to pass examinations before they get promotion, are but poor hands in conversation. The chief reason of this is, of course, that the European is accustomed to learn by the eye, while the Burman learns almost entirely by ear, and the language is correspondingly affected. The semi-civilised man has a gift for catching faint distinctions of sound ; and a modulation hardly perceptible to the European is enough to give to the Burman an entirely new meaning to the word. Fortunately the grammar is of the easiest possible character, and there is an extensive written literature, so that recourse may be had to the system of learning by the eye ; but this only produces book scholars, and without a knowledge of the pronunciation it is impossible to appreciate the smooth flow of the dramatic metres. Individual sentences, too, may be clear enough, and the immediate connection of subordinate ideas with the leading thought is a great help, but longer compositions can often only be understood by a careful collating of the whole meaning, when once reading aloud would make the whole idea perfectly evident to a Burman.

One of the principal features in the language is the arrangement of words in a sentence, which, as is the case also in Thibetan, is the exact reverse of the order followed in English. This is the more singular and significant to the philologist, because the surrounding Shans, Talaings, and Karens observe practically the same sequence as in English. Another peculiarity is in the nouns, adjectives, and tenses of verbs, which are all formed by the addition of suffixes or affixes to the verbal root. Passive verbs are in very many cases transformed into the active form by the aspiration of the initial consonant, and transitives from intransitives in the same way ; as kya-thi, to fall ; hkya-thi, to throw down, or cause to fall ; pyet-thi, to be ruined ; hpyet-thi, to bring to ruin ; lut-thi, to be free ; hlut-gyi, to set free. The language is written from left to right, and there are no spaces between the words, and but very few paik, or stops, to mark separate sentences, except the paik-gyi which divides paragraphs, and consists of four short perpendicular lines arranged in couples. The written characters are, all but one or two, composed of circles, or segments of circles, having acquired that shape from the original Nagari, by the custom of writing with a pointed style on palm leaves. The alphabet is derived from the Magadhi or Pali (the latter word properly meaning a text and not a language), and was doubtless imported into Burma with the teachings of Buddhism. The monosyllabic character of the language has, however, considerably changed the sound of many of the letters. There are ten vowels and thirty-two consonants, every alternate vowel having the sound of that preceding it, but considerably longer and broader in tone. The consonants are divided into groups of gutturals, palatals, cerebrals, dentals, and labials, with five liquids, a sibilant pronounced *th*, and an aspirate. In each class there are five letters; the first the simple sound, the second its aspirate, the third the sound rough and hard, the fourth its aspirate, and the fifth the corresponding nasal. The letters of the alphabet have all names descriptive of their shapes, beginning with ka-gyi and ka-gwe, "great ka" and "curved ka." Some of the names are singular; "big-bellied ta," "elephant shackles hta," "bottom indented da," "steep pa," "hump-backed ba," "bridle za," and "supine ya." The vowel *a* is inherent in every consonant, and is pronounced in every case, except when it is "killed" by the "that" mark, when the consonant itself is also killed, and the effect produced is a short, sharp, abrupt termination to the word, as if the letter were strangled in the attempt to pronounce it.

A peculiarity which Burmese shares with all the other cognate tongues is the use of help words in counting—"nouns generic" as they have been called. One cannot say in Burmese, as in English, "two dogs," "four spears," "three trees," and so forth. It is requisite to mention first the thing spoken of; second, the number or quantity of objects; and finally, the genus, or class to which they belong. Thus kwe hni'-gaung, dogs, two animals, or two dogs; hlan le-sin, spears, four long, straight things; ôn-bin thôn-bin, cocoanut palms, three trees, and so forth. The cardinal is not placed in immediate juxtaposition with the noun, but has the guiding word in between. There are a vast number of these generic nouns, and they come quite naturally to a Burman. He speaks of boxes and pots as so many "round things"; books and letters as "writings"; mats as "flat things"; horses and carts as "things to be ridden on";

coats and waistcloths as "things to be worn"; and so forth
in infinite variety. Even the numeral auxiliaries applied to
human beings vary. The Buddha, as well as superior beings
and pagodas, is spoken of as a ta-zu; kings, members of
the Sacred Order, and persons in power generally, are referred
to as ta-ba; respectable people to whom it is wished to be
polite are numbered as ta-u (so many "foreheads"); and
in ordinary conversation, mankind generally are denominated
ta-yauk. Foreigners—regarded as aliens and indeed not
entitled to rank as human beings at all, since they have
never worn the yellow robe—receive but scant reverence
from the tongues of the older people, and formerly from
Upper Burmans, the same auxiliary being applied to them
as would be used in speaking of a buffalo or a pig. Thus
you would say kalā hni'-gaung, foreigners, two animals,
or "two beastly foreigners." This has, however, now almost
died out, certainly in regard to Europeans, and is only
occasionally heard with reference to some of the least
civilised of the hill tribes. A hint of the same style of
enumeration occurs in the English "twenty head of cattle,"
and perhaps in the military "five hundred sabres," or "two
thousand bayonets," where the weapon is more typical and
perhaps of greater value than the man who wields it.

Chinese and Shan perhaps exceed the Burman language
in the number of almost identically sounding syllables, in
which the slightest difference of intonation makes a change
of sense, but most people are of opinion that it is quite rich
enough. Thus pe in its simple form may mean (1) the
palmyra palm or leaf, whence pe-sa, a palm-leaf book; (2)
an anvil; (3) to have the edge or point turned; (4) to lay
the ears back, as a horse; (5) to be dull of sight, or blunted
in feelings; (6) to be dirty; (7) an euphonic verbal affix.

Pe, with the heavy accent (denoting a lengthening of
the sound) means to give, and pe-sa in this form, to give
in marriage.

Hpe, with the heavy accent (practically the same sound
to an Englishman's ears) means (1) to scab over; (2) to
ward off evil; (3) to tack off shore with a boat in order to
gain an offing; (4) to be broken down in bodily strength or
ability.

Pè with the light accent (cutting the sound short) means (1) the stern of a boat ; (2) to steer ; (3) to be broken off, to crumble. Pè, with the heavy accent, means (1) a measure of weight equal to six seeds of the *Abrus precatorius* ; (2) any leguminous plant, such as bears seed in a pod, of which there are many varieties, including a pè-sa ; (3) to put aside, reject ; (4) madam, a familiar term applied by men to their intimate female friends ; (5) a square measure of ground ; (6) one of the four states of punishment. The last three usually have *a-* prefixed to them.

Hpè, with the light accent, means (1) to break off, as a small piece from a larger ; (2) to separate and take a different course.

Hpè, with the heavy accent, means (1) satin ; (2) a playing card, hpè-sa hpè-kye meaning to have shifting luck ; (3) to get out of the way ; (4) to remove. Kye hpè, derived from this, means to be splay-footed.

Thus we have nearly thirty separate meanings for a syllable which in rapid speaking seems, to an unpractised ear, to have throughout the same sound. This is philologically interesting, but practically it spoils the temper.

Myin means to see, high, and a horse ; and to translate the sentence " I saw a high horse," and read the same aloud, is a good test of the knowledge of the arrangement of words, of the accent, and of the power of appreciating delicacies of pronunciation.

There are not very many Englishmen who can properly appreciate the difference in sound between kyaung, a cat, and kyaung, a monastery. They are apt to lose their temper when the lesson is many times repeated. Hundreds of other instances might be given, but they would only tire and perhaps frighten off those who do not know the language, and would certainly irritate those who have begun the study of it.

It is a common saying that you cannot pronounce Burmese properly till you take to betel-chewing. This may be called smart, or flippant rather than true. It is, however, undeniable that the practice of chewing renders it very much more difficult to catch the sound of a word. The result appears in the grotesque names which have been given to

various places and things by old writers. Captain Hiram
Cox persisted in calling the town-clerks mew-jerrys, which
was neither a correct nor a dignified rendering of myosaye.
Still the stately old king, Upa-Raza, had greater cause of
complaint when he appeared in another book as " Upper
Roger."

It is certain that in rapid talk, and among the lower
classes, words do get softened down most remarkably.
Nyaung-u, the great lacquer manufacturing town, dwindles
away in the colloquial to Nyi-a-u, and the consequences
are lamentably evident in the transliteration of its name in
many English books. Similarly a youth named Tha Htun
Aung will respond to the call of A-o-aw, but this hardly
justifies the assertion that you do not need consonants in
Burmese at all.

CHAPTER LXI

SELECTIONS FROM THE LITERATURE

THE following is taken from the Mahā Yazawin :—

The Queen Shin-saw-bu

In Ava there lived a very learned pôngyi called Bamè-soda, and a rich man in the capital gave him his son Dhamma-sedi to bring up and instruct. This youth was possessed of very wonderful powers, due to virtues which he had exercised in previous existences. By means of these powers he brought to life one day a fowl which had been roasted and placed on the platter before his teacher. From this circumstance, to the present day, the place where the fowl scratched and sought its food is called Shwe Gyet-yet (the more popular legend assigns a different reason). On the same day it happened that a young hunter appeared in the monastery and begged the holy brother to teach him wisdom. As a present he had brought with him a roasted hare. He lifted the cover off the basket and the hare sprang up alive and healthy immediately and ran away. The pôngyi was very much struck at these two miracles, all the more because they happened on the same day, and he took the two highly gifted youths for his only scholars and taught them all he knew in the way of scholarship and mystic lore. Both were very zealous in their studies, but Dhamma-sedi learnt one letter more than his fellow-student.

Engwa-min, Thihathu, the Burman king, levied war upon the King of Rangoon, Bya-ngya-yan, and having defeated him, carried off his sister Saw Bomi. The young lady, who now got the name of Shin-saw-bu, agreed to share his throne on the condition that she should be allowed to institute religious ceremonies to remind her of the holy pagoda of her own Talaing town. Captivated by her charms, the king consented, and recommended to her notice, as being the most likely to give her aid, the two most highly honoured pôngyis of the capital, Dhamma - sedi and Dhamma-bāla, the ex-hunter. The wily princess managed to arrange a love intrigue with the two yahans, and by their aid succeeded in escaping to Rangoon, where in no very great time she was placed on the throne, and built a golden monastery for the two holy men to live in. Out of gratitude she wished to raise one of her two friends to share the throne with her, but the choice was a hard matter, for they were both equally well favoured, and no man could say which was the more learned. She resolved therefore to put their wit to the test and to abide by the issue.

The two holy men were summoned to her audience-chamber, where before her throne were placed two alms-bowls : one perfectly empty and plain, but decorated with the royal insignia ; the other more elaborately worked and full of the choicest delicacies. The rivals were bidden to place themselves, according to their liking, by the one or the other. Dhamma-bāla chose the juncates, but the wiser Dhamma-sedi walked straight to the royal thabeit. The latter therefore received the hand of the queen after he had left the order.

Dhamma-bāla was full of wrath and envy, and forthwith created countless armies by reciting powerful bedin linga over a bowl full of rice, every grain of which grew into a soldier. But Dhamma-sedi was skilful in the same arts, and by virtue of the additional letter which he had learned was able always to overcome the machinations of his opponent, so that at last Dhamma-balā saw himself overcome at all points, and took to flight to save his life. But he had not thrown off his long monkish robes, and his feet got entangled in them, and he fell and was overtaken by his pursuers, who killed him at a place where now the village Thengan Nyôn stands, " the spot where the yellow robe betrayed." The queen only reigned three years, but in that time she greatly enlarged and beautified the pagodas of Shwe Dagôn at Rangoon and Shwe Hmaw Daw at

Pegu. Dhamma - sedi reigned after her gloriously and highly honoured for thirty-one years.

The main points of this bit of Mahā Yaza-win history are correct. Shin-saw-bu was carried off in A.D. 1439 and did escape from Ava to be placed on the Peguan throne. Rangoon cantonments are to this day known among the Burmese as Shin-saw-bu Myo. King Dhamma-sedi was celebrated for his wisdom and for his intercourse with foreign powers. He received embassies from China, Siam, and Ceylon. He was also certainly originally a monk; his magic arts are another thing. His death is placed in A.D. 1491. The slight suggestion of the casket scene in the *Merchant of Venice* will be noticed.

The following is a favourite fable :—

Why Ants are found everywhere

All the animals of the forest came to the lion-king to pay him homage. The little ant came with the rest to bow down before the king of beasts, but the noblemen drove it away with scorn. When the king of the ants heard of it he was very angry, and sent a worm to creep into the ear of the lion and torment him. The lion roared aloud with pain, and all the animals came running from every side to offer their services and fight the enemy, wherever or whoever he might be. But none of them could do any real good. They could not get at the worm. At last, after many humble embassies, the king of the ants was prevailed upon to send one of his subjects, who crept into the lion's ear and pulled out the worm. Since that time the ants have enjoyed the privilege of living everywhere and in any country, while the other animals had all of them their special places assigned at the division of the earth.

The following, the fourteenth decision of the Princess Thudhammasari, is considered a legal precedent as well as the inculcation of a moral principle :—

The Dog, the Cat, and the Ichneumon

In the time of the Buddha Gawnagông, four pupils, a prince, a young noble, a rich man's son, and a poor man's son, received their education together in the country of Tekkatho. When they had finished their course they asked their teacher what was the value of learning. The sayā replied as follows :—Long ago there dwelt in the land of Gahapatiwetha four wealthy men who were great friends, and each sought to further his friends' plans as much as possible. At last one of them died and left an only son. The widow said to him, " My dear son, my husband, your father, Maung Ba is dead, and you take his place and succeed to all the property ; but you are still very young. It would be well, therefore, if you went to your father's three friends to acquire learning and prudence from them." With that she gave him three hundred rupees and sent him off with a company of servants.

On the way they met a man leading a dog. " Hallo ! you there," said the boy, " will you sell that dog ? " " If you want to buy him," replied the stranger, " you must give me a hundred rupees." The youth paid the money and sent the dog back to his mother. She took it for granted that her late husband's three friends had approved of the purchase, and fed the dog and took great care of it.

Another day, after he had eaten his noontide meal, he met a man carrying a cat, and called out, " I say, you sir, will you sell that cat ? " " Yes," said the man, " for a hundred rupees." The money was paid, and the cat sent back to his mother as before. She thought that this cat must have been recommended by the three merchants as a purchase, and took as great care of the cat as of the dog.

Another day, after his dinner, he came upon a man with an ichneumon in his arms, and wanted to buy it also. The man agreed to part with it like the others for a hundred rupees. The rich man's son paid the money and sent it back home. The mother, still under the same impression, looked after it as carefully as the dog and the cat.

Now the dog and the cat were domestic animals, and she kept them about the house without any concern, but the ichneumon was a wild creature, and she was in such a state about it that she wasted away. One day when the monk from the monastery came round on his usual alms'-begging tour, to receive his dole of rice, he noticed her appearance and said, " Dear me, my good supportress, how thin you have grown." The rich man's widow replied, " Yes, the reason is this : I gave my son three hundred rupees, and sent him off to his father's three old friends to learn business habits, and one day he sends me a dog, the next a cat, and then again an ichneumon ; and he gave a hundred rupees apiece for them. Now I don't mind about the dog and the cat, for they are house animals, and I get on very well with them ; but the ichneumon is a jungle-beast, and the mere sight of it frightens me so that my body and limbs and eyes are all pining away." The yahan advised her to turn the creature loose in the jungle. It is wrong to disregard the counsel of one's teachers or one's parents, and so she set the ichneumon free, not, however, without giving it some food well soused in oil to keep it alive till it was able to look out for itself.

When the ichneumon got into the forest he fell a-thinking : the rich man's son gave a hundred rupees for me, and since I came into his possession I have been well looked after and fed, and better than all, I have now got my liberty again. I must repay him the debt of gratitude I owe. Then he found in a pool in the forest a ruby ring, and carried it off to the rich man's son, and said : " This is no common ring, it possesses the power of gratifying every wish of its owner. Put it on your finger, therefore, and be sure you do not allow any one else to wear it." Thereupon he went off to the jungle again.

The rich man's son wished, and during the night a great palace with a pya-that rose up before his house. The king of the country, with all his subjects, came to see the sight, and the king gave him his daughter in marriage. Soon after this the princess's spiritual teacher came to see if he could spy out her husband's charm. He looked everywhere, but he could see nothing but the ring. He therefore came to see the princess by herself, when the prince had gone out, and after making a great number of pretty speeches to her, asked if she was sure of her husband's love. " What a stupid question," said she ; " he is only a rich man's son, and I am the daughter of a king." " Oh ! if he is so very fond of you then, you have probably been allowed to wear his ring,"

insinuated the pônna sadaw. " If I have not," returned she,
" I would like to know who should ? "   Then the reverend
gentleman went away.

A day or two afterwards, the princess asked her husband
to let her put on his ring. He was very fond of her, and so
he took it off and let her have it, but told her on no account
to show it to any one, but to wear it constantly on her
finger. The pônna came again another day when the rich
man's son was out, and began talking in his usual smooth-
tongued way. The princess said : " I have got that ring
you were speaking about the other day."   " Have you ? " said
he ; " where is it ? "   " On my finger," she said, and showed
it. He begged her to take it off and let him examine it,
and her nurse, who was also present, at last prevailed on her
to gratify the sadaw's wishes, and so at last she drew it off
and handed it to him. As soon as he got it, he slipped it
on his finger, changed himself into a crow, and flew away
to the middle of the Thamôddaya ocean, whither no one
could follow him, and there he stayed under a seven-roofed
spire.

When her husband came back and heard what the
pônna had done, he said to the princess : " You showed
the ring, though I expressly told you not to do so, and now
it is in the middle of the great Thamôddaya sea, and we shall
never be able to get it back again." He then remained
sunk in a deep melancholy.

One day a bevy of the daughters of the nat-dewas
came to bathe in a pond grown over with water-lilies, not
far from the house where the rich man's son was born.
They took off their necklaces and jewellery and laid them
down on the bank. The cat found them there, caught them
up, and ran off and hid them. The houri maidens came to
the cat and begged her to return their necklaces, saying
they were only fit for nat-dewas and not for mortal men.
The cat replied, "If I do, will you promise to make me
a road to the place where the pônna sadaw is living under
his pya-that in the middle of the Thamôddaya sea ? That
is the only condition on which I will give them back." So
the daughters of nats made the road, and the cat crept
stealthily along till she reached the spire, where she found

the pônna asleep, with the ring on his finger. She pulled it off and brought it back to her master as a return for his kindness, saying, " You paid a very large sum for me, and have fed and treated me well ever since." The sadaw, for his part, fell into the sea and was drowned, while the rich man's son, having now regained his talisman, had every wish of his heart gratified.

Some time afterwards a band of five hundred robbers came to kill the rich man's son and carry off his ring. The dog saw what their purpose was, and flew straight at the leader of the band, and bit him to death and dropped his body down a well. The other robbers were so frightened that they ran away. Next day the dog said to his master, " I did not get any sleep last night ; I had hard work to do," and then he told how the robbers had come to slay his master and pillage the place, and how he had killed their leader, and so frightened the rest away. He finished by saying, " Now I have made some return for your kindness to me. I have been enabled to save your life and property." " Aha ! " answered the rich man's son, " everybody called me a fool for giving a hundred rupees for you who are only an animal, but I owe all my fortune to three animals, each of which I purchased for that sum." Then he went away into the jungle and brought back the ichneumon and kept him in his house.

Now the ichneumon, the dog, and the cat, each of them asserted that he had a right to eat before the others. The ichneumon, because he first gave the ring to his master ; the cat, because when the gift was lost she had taken the necklaces of the dewa daughters, and so by getting a road made for her, had recovered the ring and thus restored her master's fortunes ; the dog, because, when five hundred robbers came to strip the rich man's son of what the others had given him, and to take his life, he killed their leader and dropped him into the well, whereupon the rest of the band ran away ; " and thus," said the dog, " I am the preserver, not only of our master's property, but also of his life."

At length they agreed to leave the arbitration of their dispute to the decision of Princess Thudhammasari, the daughter of King Dhammarit, who reigned at Maadarit in the kingdom of Kambawsa. She dwelt in the palace of a Tabindaing (the princess who remains single to be married to the next king), and was well versed in the Ten Laws (1. To make religious offerings. 2. To keep the commandments. 3. To be charitable. 4. To be upright. 5. To be mild and gentle. 6. Not to give way to anger. 7. To be strict in observing all the religious ceremonies. 8. Not to oppress any one. 9. To exercise self-restraint. 10. Not to be familiar with inferiors); and learned in the civil as well as the criminal code. The fame of her wisdom had spread to the eight quarters of the world, so that the most eminent men from every country came to her for judgment.

The three animals therefore came before the princess, and the ichneumon opened the case as follows : " A certain rich man's son paid a hundred rupees for me, fed me and housed me well, and set me free in the forest. Having regard for his kindnesses, I gave him a ruby ring, by means of which he obtained a palace with a royal spire, which sprang out of the earth ; therefore I am entitled to take precedence and to eat before the dog and the cat." The cat then followed, and recounted how the pônna had carried off the ring which the ichneumon had given her master, and how she had got it back again, and so had renewed all his fortunes. Then the dog stated his case, saying, " When robbers came to take from our master the ring which the ichneumon had given him, and which, when it was lost, was restored to him by the cat, I killed the leader of the band and then they all fled. Therefore I preserved not only my master's property, but also his life, and therefore I ought to have precedence over the other two. "

When they had finished their arguments, Princess Thudhammasari pronounced her decision as follows : " The dog, in addition to saving his master's treasures, prolonged his life also ; therefore he is entitled to the first place amongst you ; but, of a truth, there are none among animals who so well understand how to repay a debt of gratitude as you three do."

Thus ends the story of the dog, the cat, and the

ichneumon, from which you may learn, that although man is superior to all animals, yet kindness shown to them will always meet with its reward.

The following sermon of the Lord Buddha is the chief favourite with the Burmese. In its present form it is said to have been handed down by the favourite disciple, Ananda, who heard it from the lips of Shin Gautama himself. The Mingala-thut is one of the first books the young scholar gets into his hands after he has learnt the ordinary formulæ of worship. There are few Burmans, even in these later days, who cannot repeat the Pali text from end to end.

Mingala-thut, the Buddhist Beatitudes, or Chapter of Blessings

Praise be to Buddha the holy, the all-wise.

When the adorable and most excellent Buddha dwelt in the great monastery of Zetawun, built by the rich man Anātabein, in the country of Thawatti, there came to him a déwa at the hour of midnight, when the whole building was illuminated by the effulgence which streamed from his body. The déwa placed himself neither too far nor too near, neither to the right nor to the left, but in the proper spot, and after bowing low in humble obeisance, thus addressed the Buddha :

" Most adorable and excellent Buddha, during twelve long years, many déwas and men, desirous of reaching to the holiness of Ne'ban, have striven to discover what things are blessed, but they still remain in ignorance. Do thou therefore instruct us in those matters which are most blessed."

The Adorable replied :—

" Thou son of déwas, to shun the company of the foolish ; to pay homage to the learned ; to worship what ought to be worshipped ; these are blessed things. Déwa, mark them well.

" Thou son of déwas, to dwell among good men ; to have with one's self the conciousness of good deeds done in a former state of existence ; to guard well all one's actions; these are blessed things. Déwa, mark them well.

"Thou son of déwas, to hear and see much in order to acquire knowledge; to study all science that leads not to sin; to make use of proper language; to acquire a knowledge of propriety of behaviour (from the Wini); these are blessed things. Déwa, mark them well.

"Thou son of déwas, to treat parents with tenderness and affection; to nourish well one's wife and children; to perform no action under the influence of sinful temptation; these are blessed things. Déwa, mark them well.

"Thou son of déwas, to make offerings and give abundant alms; to act in accordance with the precepts of the law and of virtue; to assist relatives and friends; to perform virtuous actions; these are blessed things. Déwa, mark them well.

"Thou son of déwas, to avoid sin, to be most instant and strenuous in such avoiding; to abstain from spirituous liquor; to remember always the principle of accumulation of merit; these are blessed things. Déwa, mark them well.

"Thou son of déwas, to pay respect to all those who are worthy of regard; to be ever humble; to be ever contented; to be grateful for favours received; to listen to the preaching of the sacred law at the proper times; these are blessed things. Déwa, mark them well.

"Thou son of déwas, to be patient and endure suffering; to rejoice in edifying discourse; to visit the holy men when occasion serves; to converse on religious subjects; these are blessed things. Déwa, mark them well.

"Thou son of déwas, to practise religious austerities; to continue firm in the sublime truth; to study always to act in the most virtuous way; to keep the eyes firmly fixed on the attainment of Ne'ban; these are blessed things. Déwa, mark them well.

"Thou son of déwas, to be unmoved; to be of tranquil mind; to be exempt from passion; to be perfectly composed and fearless amid all earthly dangers; these are blessed things. Déwa, mark them well.

"O déwa, whoso possesses and observes these thirty-eight blessings shall never be overcome, and shall find

happiness in all things.   Déwa, mark thou them well, so
shalt thou enjoy the peace of the Ariyas."

Thus the adorable Buddha replied.

Of this sermon the venerable Bishop Bigandet writes :—
" Within a narrow compass, the Buddha has condensed an
abridgment of almost all moral virtues.   The first portion
of these precepts contains injunctions to shun all that may
prove an impediment to the practice of good works.   The
second part inculcates the necessity of regulating one's mind
and intention for a regular discharge of the duties incumbent
on each man in his separate station.   Then follows a
recommendation to bestow assistance on parents, relatives,
and all men in general.   Next to that we find recommended
the virtues of humility, resignation, gratitude, and patience.
After this, the preacher insists on the necessity of studying
the law, visiting the religious, conversing on religious subjects.
When this is done the hearer is commanded to study with
great attention the four great truths, and keep his mind's eye
ever fixed on the happy state of Ne'ban, which, though as
yet distant, ought never to be lost sight of.   Thus prepared,
the hearer must be bent upon acquiring the qualifications
befitting the true sage.   Like the one mentioned by the
Latin poet, who would remain firm, fearless, and unmoved,
even in the midst of the ruins of the crumbling universe, the
Buddhist sage must ever remain calm, composed, and
unshaken among all the vicissitudes of life.   There is again
clearly pointed out the final end to be arrived at, viz. that
of perfect mental stability.   This state is the foreshadowing
of that of Ne'ban."

Prefixed to every Burmese work is the phrase " Na-maw-
tatha bagawa-daw araha-daw thamma thamôddatha," which
has the same significance as the A.M.D.G. of the Jesuits
—" Praise be to Bagawa (the Buddha as the displayer of
the six glories), the holy, the all-wise."

CHAPTER LXII

STRAY NOTES

THERE are some curious national superstitions about the sabba-gyi or boa-constrictor. Although he is now innocuous as far as biting is concerned, he was originally the only poisonous snake. The way in which he lost his dangerous qualities is rather curious. The crow, that great benefactor to the entire race of fable writers, one day set himself to annoy the python, and declared that though he might think himself very big and very dangerous, he never killed anybody for all his biting. The sabba-gyi got very angry, and eventually spat up all his poison in a pet. It was swallowed by a great variety of other creeping things, and so the race of thanatophidians was vastly increased in numbers, if not in size, while the python would be harmless were it not for his vast strength.

Nevertheless the Tavoy fishermen make a domestic pet of him, and declare he is invaluable as a weather prophet. When they put out to sea they carry their boa with them, and he remains coiled up comfortably in the bows of the vessel until a storm is coming on. Then he promptly slips overboard and makes for the shore, and the sailors hoist sail and follow him with all possible expedition. The sabba-gyi is a much surer guide than the Meteorological Office. He is kept quite quiet and tame by being well fed on nutriment that does not excite his blood. His diet is usually eggs, with vast platters of pauk-pauk, "gummy rice," which is sufficiently heavy to deprive the eater, whether man or boa, of all desire to exert himself unduly. It is somewhat curious, as a first experience, to see the cat, the dog, and the baby curled up together in a corner with the boa, making one another mutually cosy.

The gall-bladder and fat of the sabba-gyi are much prized for medicinal purposes, the fat especially being esteemed as a sovereign remedy for rheumatism and strains.

Of the poisonous snakes the most dreaded is the ngan, or u-gwet, the "spotted forehead." This creature, the hamadryad or ophiophagus, is, as his name imports, a cannibal, and lives on his neighbour snakes. Specimens as long as nine feet from nose to tail have been killed near Rangoon, and in the forests which are his proper home he sometimes grows to fourteen or fifteen feet. Unlike all other reptiles, the ngan does not get out of the way of a man approaching his haunts, but attacks him immediately. He is worse than the walrus that roused the indignation of the French poet.

Bees are kept in a good many places in the country, but it is necessary to be very careful where you put the hives. It is a most ill-omened circumstance if wild bees make a nest under the house, or if bees of any kind fly under the floor. On the other hand, a hive on the house-top is very lucky. Honey is in great request to present to the pôngyis at various feasts, and especially for the embalming of the body of a dead brother of the Robe. After the cremation the honey is sold in the bazaar. It is not eaten by Englishmen in Burma. "Tapping the governor" does not commend itself to everybody. The hill tribes in the Shan States keep bees in hives made of blocks of wood.

Rhinoceros horns are in as great favour with the Burmans as with Chinese medical men. Shavings of the horn are considered an invaluable cure for epilepsy, and also guard against poisons of all kinds. There are two distinct species found in the eastern forests—the single and the double-horned.

Near Yenangyaung, in the petroleum district, when a new oil-well is wanted, the workmen place a marble image of an elephant on a smooth, flat stone, and surround it with gifts of all kinds, and then sit down to watch. If the elephant itself moves it indicates the direction in which borings are to be made; if not, the offering on which its shadow first falls as the sun sinks down, is marked, and a bedin sayā consulted.

A woman who has seven sons or seven daughters in unbroken succession is almost certain to become a witch ; her husband had better not quarrel with her at any rate.

At Kāma, a small place between Prome and Thayetmyo, there is a spirit flame, a kind of Jack o' Lantern, in a hollow near the town. Long ago a smith was killed in a brawl and became a nat after death. He liked his old profession and set up a nat-fire, and worked away at nights on a spectral forge. The inhabitants soon found out what was going on, and after their first terror was over used to go out in the middle of the day and leave a piece of iron, saying, "Good Mr. Spirit, make me an axe, a dah, a hoe." Next day they found it all ready made. At last a Chin—just the sort of thing one of those stupid people would do—hid himself, and just when the midnight cocks had finished crowing, up rose the smith in human shape, dressed in a red paso and a flaring red turban. He began hammering away on his anvil, welding a sword. The infatuated Chin at last shouted, "Make it quick." The demon smith whipped round on the instant and flung the red-hot dah at him, burning his cheek. The indiscreet peeping Tom took to his heels and ran. After he had got a mile away he rubbed his blistered cheek, and in after-times there rose at that place Pāpôt, "the cheek-rubbing village." A mile farther on he began to shake all over with fatigue and terror, whence the name of Tôn, "the trembling village." Finally, when he reached the site of Paukpogu, the "swelling burst," he sank down on the ground, and was found there next morning with just enough life left to tell his story. The smith never worked again, but his fire may be seen to this day. Once a year all the house fires in Kāma are put out and lighted again from the nat-mi. Should any one neglect so to pay honour to the nat, his house and all his goods will be burnt before the year is out. The resemblance to the legend of Wayland Smith at Lambourn in Berkshire is obvious. The naming of the villages is also a favourite form of Horne Took etymology prevalent all over Burma.

The common notion of earthquakes is that the earth is supported on the shoulders of four creatures called nga-hlyin. These monsters are less sturdy than the classical Atlas, and

occasionally want to shift shoulders.   When they do so an
earthquake is the result.   Others declare that the quaking of
the earth is caused by gusts of wind on the under surface of
the world.   The idea is that the solid mass of the earth
is supported on a double thickness of water, and this again
by twice its thickness of air, below which is a vacuum,
occasionally, however, disturbed by storms.   The Buddha
gave a much more extensive explanation to his favourite
disciple Ananda.   " My son," he said, " eight causes make
the earth tremble.   First, the earth lies on a mass of water,
which rests on the air, and the air on space ; when the air is
set in motion, it shakes the water, which in its turn shakes the
earth ; second, any being gifted with extraordinary powers ;
third, the conception of a payā laung for his last existence ;
fourth, his birth ; fifth, his becoming a Buddha ; sixth, his
preaching the Law of the Wheel ; seventh, his mastering
and renouncing existence ; eighth, his obtaining the state
of Ne'ban.   These are the eight causes of earthquakes."

The Law of the Wheel is the doctrine of the four great
truths : pain, the production of pain, the destruction of pain,
and the way leading to that destruction.   These constantly
revolve upon themselves, and the manifestation of these
truths is the great work a Buddha has to perform.

Omens are drawn from the appearance of the sun and
moon, and especially from the particular constellation which
presides over one's birth.   The howling of dogs, the flight
and song of birds, the appearance of any strange creature,
or of a wild animal in an unexpected place, all have their
special meaning.   So have the nervous twitchings of the eye,
or of any part of the body.   If the sun or any of the planets
approaches the moon there is danger about.   In the four
months when Venus is not to be seen, in a month when
there is an earthquake or an eclipse, and on the first or last
day of a month, it is advisable not to cut one's hair, marry,
build a house, or begin any important business whatever.
These and hundreds more may be found in the Deitton,
a book very full of singular information.   Palmistry is a
science of which every educated person professes to have
more or less knowledge.   The less a man knows, the more
truculent his deductions are.

A state envelope was a very curious affair. It was nothing else but two large elephant's tusks. Half-way up they were hollow, and on the mouth there was a heavy gold cover. The tusks were mounted in different parts with gold of no mean thickness. The letter of the lord of the Golden Throne was deposited inside, and borne to its destination with the flourish of trumpets and the braying of drums. The majesty of the Burmese king would have suffered if he had forwarded a communication to the Viceroy in a cover which cost anything under a couple of hundred pounds sterling. In similar fashion the reports of subordinate officials were written with steatite pencils on coarse black paper, and this was rolled up and put in a hollow joint of bamboo. The whole was then enveloped in cloth and sealed with a peacock seal. Communications of this kind were sometimes received by English officials on the British Burma frontier.

The following are a few proverbs :—

If you want to go fast, go the old road.

Wisdom guards life ; no one can escape bad luck. The man gifted with wisdom is never left in peace.

Every bird is handsome compared with the vulture.

A mountain is climbed by degrees ; property acquired by degrees ; wisdom learnt by degrees.

Have regard for a whole family of rats, instead of for one cat.

The more you know, the more luck you have.

A short boat is hard to steer ; a dwarf is quick in the temper.

If a cock ruffles up his feathers, it is easy to pluck him. If a man gets angry he is done for.

Constant cutting dulls the knife ; constant talking dulls the wits.

A pot half full of water is hard to carry (on the head, of course ; because the water sways from side to side) ; the less a man knows, the harder he is to argue with.

A cow that can give no milk will kick. An ignorant man is to be feared for his ignorance.

If there is much paddy (unhusked rice) in the bowl, it is hard to eat. If there is much talking it is hard to understand.

Don't speak like a mountain, it is so easy to fall off.

Eat little, stomach slender ; eat much, stomach-ache.

Beware of a man's shadow (*i.e.* his relations) and a bee's sting.

A coward tiger growls ; a coward human howls.

The well-born are fair of speech ; the low-born crooked.

A slave's son is a stupid son.

If a great man flatters you, be afraid.

A great man's sword is never blunt.

There are three chances in a nagā's stare ; there is but one in a king's. (That is to say, you may escape from the dragon, but if the king is angry with you, speedy death is all you can expect.)

Kyet-go a-yo,
Lu-go a-myo.

Blood always tells ; literally, you know a game-cock from his bones, a man from his family.

CHAPTER LXIII

A PÔNGYI BYAN

THE veneration and respect which meet the yahan all through his life are extended to his remains when he dies, or rather when he leaves this world. The monk does not "die" as a common layman does, he does not even, like the king, "ascend to the nat-déwas' village." The holy man in his last existence must have been holy in order to have accumulated the sum of merits which enabled him upon earth to remain steadfast in the sacred order. When he passes away, he "returns" to the highest heavens of nats, or to the meditative states of zān, or perhaps even to the pure and immaterial realms of arupa. Therefore a mendicant's funeral is called a pôngyi byan —the return of the great glory. Even a junior member is burnt with great solemnity and state; but when a distinguished brother dies, one famous for his learning, his austerity, or the great number of Lents he has spent in the cloister, the obsequies swell into a ceremonial which attracts people from all parts of the country.

As soon as life leaves the body, the corpse is carefully washed in the usual way by the dead pôngyi's chief supporters and some of the monastic scholars. Then the intestines are taken out and buried in a quiet corner of the monastery grounds, or near the pagoda. The cavity of the stomach is then filled up with hot ashes, sawdust, a few spices, and whatever other available substances may be presumed likely to dry up the humours, and then the skin is sewed together again. A layer of wax is sometimes spread all over the body, but more often it is simply tightly swathed in white cloth from head to foot. This linen cloth is then varnished over with wood oil, so that every particle of the corpse may, if necessary, be covered with gold leaf, and this, except in very poor neighbourhoods, is always done. Where there is not money enough, the yellow sacred garments are wrapped round the corpse instead. The arms are always folded on the chest. The body is then placed in the coffin. This is not, as is the case with laymen, made of planks, but of a single log roughly hollowed out, and with a very substantial lid. This lid is not fastened down for a considerable time, and occasionally a bamboo pipe leads from the coffin into the ground to assist in drying up the embalmed body. The fastening down of the cover is sometimes rather an unpleasant spectacle. Many of the old pôngyis keep logs in their monasteries to serve for their coffins, and these, when hollowed out, are not always a satisfactory fit. Bishop Bigandet tells of a horrible sight he witnessed, when the lid had to be crushed on with wedges and the blows of a heavy mallet. The majority of aged yahans are, however, so shrivelled and shrunken before they die, that such an occurrence, which, it must not be supposed, is any less dreadful to a Burman than it is to an Englishman, could only happen very rarely, and then probably would not be carried out in the way which so justly shocked the good bishop.

The inner coffin is then, like the body, varnished with thitsi, and gilt all over. For it is prepared an outer casket called a payaung-bông, which is as magnificent as the skill of the local artificers and the liberality of the " benefactors " permit. This sarcophagus is often very large, and is richly gilt and painted in the panels, which are fringed with the usual mosaic of bits of mirror, coloured glass, and zinc. The paintings naturally represent religious subjects, usually scenes from the life of Shin Gautama ; his famous meetings with the old man, the sick, the dead, and the monk ; his departure at night from the magnificent court of King Thudawdana ; his ascent to Tawadeintha, and the like. Rearing itself over the top of the sarcophagus is usually the figure of a nagā, recalling the pious dragon chief that sheltered the Lord Buddha from a flood of rain by coiling seven times round his body and expanding its hood as a covering.

Meanwhile, money is being steadily collected for the

remainder of the rites, and as this comes in from the elders
of the surrounding villages and the kappiyadayakas of
neighbouring religious houses, the kyaungthagyi of the
deceased's monastery sets about erecting an edifice like a
thein, a " monastery of the dead." This is a building, more
or less substantial, according to the sanctity of the departed,
built of teak, and open all round, with the tapering
ecclesiastical pya-that rising over it. Hither the coffin, with
the sarcophagus, is carried and deposited on a dais in the
centre, a slight railing serving to keep off wild animals.
Over it a large white umbrella, with a deep paper-lace fringe,
is fixed, and round about hang a number of paintings, similar
to those on the payaung-bông, some of them, however,
representing the favourite subject of the different races of
men as known to the artist—the swarthy Hindoo, the
oblique-eyed Chinaman, the Kachin with his pig on his
back, and the ghastly white-faced Englishman with dog and
gun. Others are simply grotesque, and a few horrible, in
their delineations of the horrors of hell. Nevertheless, they
are all allowed to hang there, for though it is expressly
stated that paintings are among the five species of gifts
which are not meritorious (dancing is another), the ordinary
layman thinks that the painting he gives must certainly
be an exception. Here and there in this odd kind of
mortuary chapel are also keinnaya, gay tinselled pasteboard
figures of men with birds' lower extremities, manôttha
keinnaya and nat keinnaya, the latter having the wings
and gorgeous aspect of nat-déwas. Here the body lies in
state, and there is a constant stream of pilgrims—some of
them from far distant parts of the country—who come to
say their religious sentences, make offerings of flowers and
fruit as they would at the pagoda, and contribute what they
can afford towards the remainder of the ceremony.

The body remains till the required sum is collected.
During that time numbers of festivals are celebrated at the
ne'ban kyaung ; bands of music play frequently, and the
same people often make three or four different offerings.
The lying in state usually lasts several months, sometimes
considerably over a year, and it is to be noted that a pôngyi
byan never takes place during Lent.

At last all the funds are collected. An open space outside the town is cleared of jungle, and in the centre of it is erected the funeral pyre. This is constructed of bamboo matting, pasteboard brightly painted, and covered with the usual tinsel. It is, of course, in the form of the seven-roofed spire, the number of roofs, as some think, representing the number of heavens of nat-déwas. It is square up to a height of fifteen or twenty feet, where there is a platform, on which is placed a sort of cenotaph, resembling the payaung bông in construction and decoration. Above this towers up, fifty or sixty feet higher, the bamboo canopy. When this is ready, a fortunate day is selected by the elders of the town, for they have the management of the funeral rites, to the exclusion of the brethren of the yellow robe. This is announced all over the country-side by sound of gong, and when the appointed day arrives the people come flocking from every side, each quarter or village bringing its pya-thats and padetha-bins, the former similar in construction to the spire on the funeral pile, the "wishing trees" laden with a-hlu for the surviving brethren of the pôngyi who is to be cremated. The spires are arranged round about the great central one, to be burnt along with it ; the padetha-bins are delivered at the kyaung.

There is always a great gathering round the monastery of the dead, where the sramana has been lying in state. The coffin is taken down with great ceremony, and placed on a strongly built, low four-wheeled car, surmounted by the eternal bamboo spire. Now comes a part of the ceremonial which always seems strangely absurd, not to say indecorous, to foreigners. Two, or sometimes four, stout rattan or coir ropes are fastened to the car, and forthwith all the able-bodied men present commence a frantically contested and uproarious tug-of-war. No sides whatever are selected, or numbers agreed upon. Reinforcements are always ready to back up a side which seems on the point of losing, and prematurely ending the struggle ; and when a man loses his wind he leaves go his hold and sits down to have a rest. Sometimes the rope breaks, and then the progress of the funeral has to be suspended till a new one is procured and fastened on, for there is no rule as to a side abiding by its accidents. Sometimes the contest goes on for two or three hours, and there are instances recorded where it was not till the third day that a definite result was arrived at. The explanation is simple enough to a Burman, and it is surprising that it has not hitherto been given by any writer on Burma. It is a work of the greatest possible merit to drag a pôngyi's body to the funeral pyre, and this kutho falls to the share of those who win in the tug-of-war. The late Captain Forbes said that the explanation was that "the conquering village will get the better of their losing rivals in all sports, contests, or other matters during the year." But this is impossible where the winning side may be composed of men from a score of different villages in circles remote from one another. Besides, there are no championship meetings in Burma. It is to be noted also that during the lônswèthi it is usually only the payaung bông that is on the car. The actual coffin is brought down afterwards.

At last the coffin is brought to the pyre and hoisted up to its lofty platform, beneath which is stored a great quantity of combustible material : wood soaked in oil, pitch, and abundance of scented chips. Then nothing remains but to light it. When a layman is burnt, fire is set to the pile by the nearest relations with a box of Bryant and May's matches. But this is much too worldly a method for a member of the Thenga, and even the fire obtained by the friction of a plug in a hollow bamboo—an ingenious amplification of the two dry sticks of a variety of barbarous tribes, common in most monasteries—would fail to satisfy the dignity of a pôngyi. The pyre is lighted by rockets fired from a distance. Scores of these dôn have been prepared weeks beforehand, and many have been carried round triumphantly in procession by the people who have made them, a band of music preceding, and young men and girls dancing and singing of the potency of the powder and the accuracy of the aim which will gain for them the glory of setting fire to the pyre. Each rocket has a figure of some kind, a nat-déwa, a tiger, a hare, or a bilu attached to it. Some of them are of huge size, constructed of the stems of trees hollowed out and crammed full of combustibles, in which sulphur largely predominates. Many are eight or nine feet long and four or five in circumference, and secured

by iron hoops and rattan lashings.   Up in Mandalay some
are very much larger.   These are let off at the funeral pile
from a distance of forty or fifty yards, the largest being
mounted on go-carts, and many others guided by a rope
fastened to the pya-that, the rocket sliding along by means of
twisted cane loops.   The great majority fail to have any
other effect than making a great splutter and poisoning the
air.   A few refuse to budge at all ; others topple off their
carts and fizzle erratically on the grass.   A pôngyi byan
in the old days was frequently attended with loss of life.
Some one, at any rate, of the bigger rockets was sure to fly off
at a tangent and plunge into the crowd, where its weight, to
say nothing of its fiery belchings, found one or more
victims.   Even now it is only by the strictest police
regulations and a rigorous maintaining of order among the
spectators, and system in the pyrotechnists, that like catas-
trophes do not happen.   At last some lucky dôn plunges
right into the inflammable materials piled below the bier, and
in a few minutes the flames are leaping high above the
topmost pinnacle of the spire.   Roof after roof falls, setting
fire to the offerings placed round the basement.   The joints
of bamboo explode with a noise like a pistol shot ; the crowd
cheer each separate occurrence, and when finally the central
spire falls with a hiss, a shout rises from the multitude which
suggests anything but death and pious observance.   But here
in the manôtthapyi all is changeful, sad, and unreal, and
one more death brings but nearer to the final rest of Ne'ban.

When the last smouldering embers have cooled, the
monastic brethren search for any pieces of bones that may
remain, and these are carefully gathered up and buried
somewhere near the pagoda.   Sometimes, in the case of a
particularly saintly man, they are pounded down, mixed into
a paste with thitsi, and moulded into an image of the
Buddha, which is stored up in the monastery.   The custom
followed in other Buddhist countries of erecting a shrine
over the dead is, in accordance with the teachings of Shin
Gautama, an honour but rarely accorded in Burma.   In the
Shan States they are commoner, but are rarely anything
more elaborate than a stucco-covered block of bricks, about
three feet high and pointed at the top.

CHAPTER LXIV

DEATH AND BURIAL

WHEN a Burman dies, after the first interval of poignant grief on the part of those present, the body is carried to the side of the central room of the house, abutting on the front verandah, and there deposited between the house posts. Messages are then sent to the monastery, to the friends and neighbours, and a funeral band is summoned. Meanwhile the corpse is carefully washed from head to foot, and the two big toes, and usually also the thumbs, are tied together with the chema-gyo and the letma gyo, which, if practicable, should be locks of the hair of a son or daughter ; but if this is not to be got, a strip of cotton cloth is used. The whole body then, from the armpits downwards, is closely swathed in new white cotton cloth, and when this is done the best clothes the deceased possessed are put on. If the family is wealthy the paso or tamein is often very rich and costly. The face is always left uncovered, unless there are special reasons for concealing it, arising from the cause of death. Between the teeth is placed the kado-ka, a piece of gold or silver as ferry-money to pay for the passage of the mystic river, which is known to exist, but concerning which no further particulars are to be got from any Burman. It is no doubt a relic of old demon-worship, the meaning of which is forgotten, while the custom has clung on. Charon's toll of course immediately occurs to the classical reader. Probably the race on their march from their ancestral home to Burma had to cross a big river. If the family is very poor, a copper or lead coin is used, or perhaps nothing more valuable than a betel-nut. The coin, whatever it is, is usually quietly

carried off by the grave-diggers.   None but an outcast would
venture to do such a thing.

By this time, or, if the death occurred at night, in the
early morning, the band has arrived, and commences to play
dirges in front of the house.   The Sula-gandi monks greatly
disapprove of this practice, as savouring of ostentation, and
their followers therefore often dispense with the band, as do
many Burmans in the large English towns.   But otherwise
the band is always engaged, and plays on steadily till the
funeral takes place.   Almost invariably, too, one or more of
the yahans from the monastery come along and stay in the
house, their presence being invaluable in keeping away evil
spirits, who might otherwise loiter about the place.   The
monk may or may not deliver a discourse, just as he sees fit.
The body is then put into the coffin, which is a very flimsy
kind of affair, ordinarily made of let-pan (*Bombax mala-
baricum*), a very light and porous kind of wood not unlike
deal, or sometimes of eng tree (*Dipterocarpus tuberculatus*).
This is fastened down roughly with any kind of nails that
come to hand.   A number of the relatives and friends now
come to condole and lend their assistance in making and orna-
menting the bier and hearse, most of them bringing presents
of money or food with them.   A few years ago a very
meritorious society called Upathaka was started in Rangoon,
the object of which was to provide decent and honourable
burial for all members.   The actual society did not last very
long, but it served to show that the old feeling of mutual
help still existed.   At no time, however, have the Burmans
been backward in this meitswe a-paung a-paw, which is one
of the thirty-eight points insisted on in the Mingala-thut,
the most favourite sermon of the Lord Buddha's.   Friends
and neighbours troop in with presents of a few pice, baskets
of rice, meat, fruit, tobacco, betel, and material for decorating
the bier, so that a man who in his lifetime never had a rupee to
bless himself with, receives in Lower Burma a funeral grand
enough to bring everybody connected with it under the scope
of the sumptuary laws, if it were held in King Thibaw's
territory.

The body is kept a longer or shorter time according to
the station of the deceased.   If he was rich, the preparation

of the funeral paraphernalia takes some time, and it is now-adays almost a matter of ceremonial necessity that all children and blood relations should assemble for the burial. Technically, if the death occurred on the last day of the month the funeral ceremonies should take place before midnight, certainly before the new moon appears. This rule, however, is far from being strictly observed nowadays. A poor man is buried as quickly as possible to save expense ; a rich man's obsequies last according to the pride of his family and their inclination to spend money. The coffin, called hkaung, is usually covered with tinsel paper, or perhaps gilt. The talā, the bier, is shaded by a light canopy, or spire made of bamboo, and carried by means of four long bamboo poles. This pya-that is usually most gaily decorated with coloured pasteboard, tinsel, and paintings of different kinds, and looks strangely bright and theatrical to Europeans. It is carpentered and decorated in the street before the house, for it is from eight or ten to twenty or thirty feet in height, and often overtops all the houses in the quarter.

When the day fixed for the funeral arrives the yahans are invited to the house. They usually come in numbers proportioned to the amount of alms given. There is ordi-narily an address in the house, dwelling mainly on the vanity of human wishes and the uncertainty and misery of life on earth. Then the coffin is brought out and placed on the platform made for it in the lower part of the pya-that. Over it is then thrown a paso if the deceased was a man, or a tamein or neckerchief if a woman. This usually conceals the coffin, unless it is richly gilt, or painted, as is sometimes the case, with figures of the nobler of the animals, such as lions, tigers, monkeys, and elephants. Then the distinctive garment is looped up so that all may see. Over this cloth are usually placed short sticks wrapped round with gold and silver paper, shwe bidôn and ngwe bidôn which were forbidden in Mandalay except to the officials. Equally contrary to the Yazagaing are the sanda ya-mya, two long streamers which come down from the top of the spire and are taken in the hands of as many of the personal friends as can get hold of them. The musket shots which are fired often during the processions would have entailed especially

heavy punishment under Burman rule. Latterly some
laymen in Rangoon have even been bold enough to glorify the
funerals of their relatives with keinnaya, figures of men or
women with bird-like feet and lower extremities. These
spangled toys, which are commonly to be seen in all
monasteries, are properly only used at the last ceremonies
of a member of the sacred order. But when some men are
bold enough even to flaunt the royal white umbrella, it is
hardly to be expected that the distinctive honours of the
yahans would be respected.

The procession having been formed, a start is made.
At the head come the alms intended for the monks and for
the poor, some carried by men, some by women, the sexes
going in separate lines. After this come the pyin-sin, never
in any very great numbers, unless the a-hlu be particularly
bountiful. Following them comes the band, and often a troop
of singers. These are always hired for the purpose, and their
callousness is as little to be cast up against Burman natural
affection as the unlovable doings of the mutes at an English
funeral. Close upon the musicians comes the bier carried
by six or eight young men. Then in a general crowd follow
the relations, friends, and neighbours, all on foot. Many
passers-by, total strangers, join in the procession from motives
of piety. Here and there the men carrying the bier stop
and dance in a curious fantastic way to the measures of
the dirge of the singers. The funeral *misereres* are usually
the composition of an improvisatore in the chorus, and deal
with the life and death and good actions of the deceased.
A measure called maung pyaung is the most generally used.

Occasionally there is a tug-of-war with a rope as at a
pôngyi's funeral, one side exclaiming, " We must bury our
dead " ; the other, " You shall not take away my friend."
As a matter of necessity the former party must conquer, but
they sometimes have to get recruits from the crowd before
they can manage it.

It is a matter of regulation that a funeral should never
go to the north or to the east. The graveyard is usually to
the west of the village, and the dead should all be carried
out of a walled town by a gate reserved for this purpose.
In Mandalay this a-mingala tagā was that to the south-west,

and it was avoided by those who had business in the myo
as cursed, as indeed its name imports.   Other rules are that
a corpse must never be carried towards the centre of the
town, still less can it be taken into it.   If the man has died
in the jungle, and the funeral has to pass a village, it skirts
round the outside of it.

When the cemetery is reached, the coffin is taken out
and placed on the ground near the grave.   The immediate
mourners collect round about it ; the rest of the people go
to the zayats, of which there are always several at every
graveyard.   The music stops as soon as this place is reached.
The alms are set up in order before the pôngyis, and these
again intone the five secular commandments, and the ten
good works, besides a long string of Pali doxologies.   As
soon as they have finished they leave and file off to the
monastery, the a-hlu being carried after them.   The chief
mourner at the same time pours water slowly out of a
cocoanut shell, saying, " May the deceased and all present
share the merit of the offerings made and the ceremonies
now proceeding."   This performance, called ye-set-kya, is a
regular accompaniment of all almsgiving.   The idea is that
the earth will bear witness where men may forget.   When
Shin Gautama ascended the throne under the bawdi tree,
Mān-nat, the devil, claimed that it was his, because he had
discovered it first, and all his mighty host shouted aloud
when he called upon them as witnesses.   The Lord Buddha
had no witness but the earth, and to it he appealed, asking
whether he had not achieved the Three Great Works of
Perfection, the Ten Great Virtues, and the Five Renouncements.   The earth gave testimony to this kaung-hmu with a
terrible roaring and a violent earthquake, so that Mān-nat
and all his legions fled in terror.   Hence the pouring out of
water when alms are given.

While this is going on women are walking about the
zayats distributing cheroots and sweet drinks, betel, le'pet,
and biscuits among the visitors.   The nearest relations are
carrying out the final rites.   The coffin is swung three times
backwards and forwards over the open grave, and then
lowered in.   This ceremony, called utaikthi, is looked upon
as a kind of final farewell, and after each person has thrown

a handful of earth the grave-diggers fill up the grave. These sandalās are outcasts, the name being probably derived from the Sanskrit term for the lowest caste of the Hindoos. It is considered a mark of respect to wait till the grave is filled in, and when this is over, there is some conversation in the zayat over the refreshments, and then all make their way home. The pya-that, bamboos, and other paraphernalia are the perquisites of the sandalās, and they usually get all the alms intended for the poor, though at a great funeral there is often much competition for the pasos, turbans, and pieces of muslin given away in alms. It is to be observed that there is no tombstone put up ; nothing to mark for future years where the grave was.

Though burial is becoming common with all classes, the old method of cremation still prevails extensively in the jungle districts, and was invariable in Independent Burma when the deceased had attained considerable age. When the body is to be burned, mithingyothi, it is not necessary that the coffin lid should be fastened down, and sometimes there is no lid at all. The preparations and procession are identical with that for burial. The pyre is composed of billets of wood, laid two and two at right angles to each other, quantities of sweet-smelling woods being placed in the intervals. A few billets are placed above the coffin as well as below, and at the bottom of the funeral pile is usually an iron trough into which any un-consumed bones may fall. The pyre is kindled at various points by the nearest relations, and the sandalās stay by to see that it burns freely, and that all is consumed. When the fire has burnt out, two or three of the nearest of kin come and search about among the ashes for the bones. These are washed clean with cocoanut milk, and in the case of great people in Lower Burma of late years, often with lavender water, eau de cologne, or any of Atkinson's or Piesse and Lubin's scents. They are then wrapped up in clean white cloths, and placed in a newly made earthen-ware pot, which is not uncommonly gilt, or covered with pictures of sacred events taken from the birth stories. This is then taken back to the house temporarily.

For seven days after either kind of funeral, mourning

goes on in the house. This means in wealthy houses indiscriminate eating and drinking. Cooking goes on all night, and all day relays of condoling visitors come and eat and enjoy themselves. The yahans also come every morning and receive offerings, and recite a string of Pali sentences. Friends bring contributions towards all this expenditure, but the result of it too often is that the heir finds that not only are all his father's hoarded rupees gone, but he himself has contracted a very considerable burden of debt. Even in the case of poor people, where the feasting is limited to the seventh day, great expense is incurred. The yahans are as necessary then as at the funeral, for the house must be purified, and the evil spirits who may be hanging about, as well as the leip-bya of the deceased, have to be exorcised and driven away. Then the pot containing the bones, if the dead person was burnt, is taken to the graveyard and buried, or sometimes is put into a hole near the pagoda. Superstitious people at burials sometimes affirm that they have caught the " butterfly " of the deceased in a handkerchief, and take this home to the house, where it lies till the seventh day, when it is opened after the discourse of the yahans, and the leip-bya is driven from the house. It can then give no more trouble.

Sometimes a small pagoda is erected over the cremated ashes of a highly respected relative. These are regarded simply as monuments, even when they are over a king, to whom alone of laymen in Native Burma they could be erected. They must not be used as places to offer worship, and that this may be known, the members of the sacred order ordain that such pagodas shall have no hti, no umbrella, on the top. To obviate this it is usual with the builder to dedicate the place to Shin Gautama, and thus at once secure a monument and a hti. Pagodas erected in honour of yahandas, or particularly sainted pôngyis, receive the umbrella of right, and are places very eminently suited for the pious laymen to worship at. Such temple tombs are called ayo sedi, but are not of such frequent erection as they used to be.

In some cases the relations grind down the bones to powder, and mixing this with the wood oil called thitsi, mould the paste into a small image of the Lord Buddha, which they set up in an honoured place in their houses, and make use of as the object of their morning and evening doxologies. Such images are called tha-yo.

Nowadays money and public estimation alone determine the character of the funeral ; but formerly in Mandalay, apart from the ceremonial provided for a pôngyi byan, there were five kinds suitable for a layman—one for the sovereign ; then for members of the royal family ; thirdly, for nobles, and those who had received official rank, a rather precarious and dangerous possession ; then for thuté, rich men—so designated by special patent, which placed them under the "protection" of the court, that is to say, made them accessible for the demand of "benevolences"; and finally, a funeral for ordinary people. The burials of the poor in Mandalay were gruesome spectacles. The body was carried to the graveyard in a big, roomy box, grown rickety with much use, or, more simply still, in a mat. The san-dalās had dug a hole, little more than three feet deep. If it was not long enough the body was squeezed in without any regard for relatives feelings. Enough earth to cover it slightly was thrown on by the grave-diggers, and the howls and fights of the pariah dogs at night suggested how it was that epidemics did not arise.

In the case of the funeral, say of an Atwinwun's wife, the coffin might be gilt, with a web of white cotton cloth fastened at the head—velvet was only permissible for a person of royal blood ; the bamboos composing the bier were covered with red cloth ; the pasos, tameins, and so on, given in alms, were carried on long poles, each pole borne by two men. In the procession the insignia of the wun, his umbrellas, fans, kamauk, and the rest were carried in front ; after the alms and yahans came a dozen or more young women, carrying the court dress and decorations of the deceased, then her state carriage and that of her husband, hers being usually a palanquin. The billets of wood on the funeral pyre were gilt. These honours were so greatly valued that not a single privilege would be omitted, though the husband had to borrow money for every single item. Indeed, were he to have omitted any of them, he might be in danger of losing all, as not sufficiently appreciating the dignities conferred upon him.

As soon as Mindôn Min died, or at least as soon as it was officially made known that he was dead (for there are great doubts as to whether he died on the 12th September or on the 1st October 1878, or on some date between these two), as soon as the ministerial announcement came out on the latter date, the bo-ho, the great drum and gong suspended in a tower by the eastern gate, were stopped. The new king's drum and gong were not sounded till nine o'clock in the evening of the funeral, after which they were struck in the ordinary way every three hours. Bands of soldiers and police with gongs patrolled the streets all night long to see that everything was quiet. The princes had been seized and cast into prison some time before, but there was a chance that their adherents might raise disturbances on their behalf, and this precaution was kept up for some time. Meanwhile a pagoda, to serve as a mausoleum, was being run up with the greatest expedition close to the Mint, on the eastern side of the palace, in the outer enclosure, and this was finished in four or five days. The king had specially requested that his body should not be burnt according to ordinary royal custom, and the Sin-byumè, the senior queen and chief mourner, had resolved that this wish should be respected.

The corpse was laid out in state, and on the 3rd October the greater number of the foreigners and the officials of inferior rank were admitted to look upon it. This ceremony was conducted in the Hman-nandaw, the "Glass Palace," a room in which Thibaw Min has received most Europeans since. The body lay in the fore part of the chamber on a gilt couch, or bedstead, studded with bits of glass, and was robed from head to foot in white, a piece of white satin covering the face. The royal number of white umbrellas was canopied overhead, and at the top part of the couch were arranged the regalia in a row. On this occasion the Sinbyumè and the Anauk Nammadaw, the favourite queen of the West Palace, sat by the couch and slowly waved gorgeous peacock fans. At other times the sonless queens took it in turn to watch by the body, two at a time.

Round about were grouped all the other queens and princesses, weeping piteously. The deceased king's brother, the ex-Pagān Min, the newly elected Thibaw Min, and all the high officials, were behind at the farther end of the room. Suspended over the corpse was a small flat piece of gold shaped like a heart, called thényun, and in this the leip-bya, the butterfly spirit of the departed king, was supposed to dwell till such time as he should be buried. The public lying in state only lasted a few hours, but the body remained there unaltered till the time of the funeral. It was not certainly known whether any attempt at embalming was made, but the body was very much shrunk, and contrasted greatly with the genial presence of his majesty when last he was seen alive.

The funeral took place on the 7th, at noon. It was the first that took place that day, and no other was allowed until the royal obsequies were entirely over. The city gates were shut and strongly guarded to prevent any such going forth if any one had been bold or ignorant enough to attempt it. From the gates of the interior palace stockade to the tomb, the whole route of the procession was laid with scarlet cloth, and round the mausoleum was a wide bamboo fence covered with long cloth, inside of which were some slight sheds, run up for the accommodation of the queens and the chief ministers. It is worthy of notice also that, in a favourable position to view all that passed, was erected a similar mandut for the accommodation of the late Mr. Shaw, then British Resident in Mandalay, his assistants, and the Residency Chaplain, the late Rev. J. A. Colbeck. The Resident and Assistant Resident were admitted in full uniform, wearing their shoes and swords, and it was thought that at length a solution of the great shoe-question had been arrived at, for though in the outer court this dignity had always been allowed them, the fact that later on they saw the king not very far off roused hopes of an audience at a remote date with similar appendages. But alas, the hopes were vain.

Punctually at twelve the procession left the palace gates. At the head of the cortège came the late king's wan, a huge palanquin borne on men's shoulders. Close upon it came six elephants, in royal purple and gold housings, and after them two richly caparisoned ponies. Following these were three of the mingyis and a wundauk, the fourth chief minister, the Laungshwe being too old and feeble to appear. Then came the band, called byaing-daung, on such occasions, playing an ancient royal *miserere*, and after it a great crowd of the minor officials, wearing baungs, white official hats. Behind these came a number of men and women bearing the regalia and the utensils of the royal dead, the crown, the heavy court dress, the gold betel box, the spittoon, the hentha, and the rest. Then came an empty coffin, overlaid with scarlet velvet and plates of gold, and immediately behind it the body in a ta-nyin, or hammock of white velvet, attached to a bamboo swathed in red velvet, across which was thrown a white velvet covering spangled with gold. To the ta-nyin were attached two long cloths, sanda-ya-mya, held by a multitude of queens, princesses, and exceedingly young princes (all the older ones being in jail). Above were the eight white umbrellas, and over the Sinbyumè, the chief mourner, were held three of the same royal colour. Her three daughters, one of whom, the Supayalat, became Thibaw Min's queen, were shaded by bright yellow htis, a colour which ranks even over gold. Thus they proceeded to the bamboo enclosure. Then it was announced that the new king, Thibaw Min, was coming, having just received the beit-theit, been anointed by the Brahmin Pônnas. He appeared shortly, seated in a lofty wan, at each of the four corners of which crouched a maiden with bowed head and clasped hands, the whole being carried on the shoulders of forty men. Preceding him was his bodyguard of twelve pages all dressed alike and armed with double-barrelled breechloaders in red serge cases. The Shwe nan-yin payā, the new possessor of the golden throne, remained for half an hour, looking very ill at ease, and little inclined to inspect the splendid spectacle before him. Then he gave the order for the last rites, and in accordance with custom returned immediately to the palace. The actual ceremony of burial was now concluded with as little ceremony as previously there had been superabundance of it, and in a very short time the yahans, of whom there had been a great multitude present, were superintending the carrying off of the 108 (representing the number of divisions in the foot of the Lord Buddha, and the beads on the rosary) heaps of alms piled up in great mountains in a long shed to the east of the mausoleum. This was the last of the pious king, Maung Lun, Mindôn Min, the Convener of the Fifth Great Synod.

The following is the substance of a funeral dirge sung in Mandalay by a Rangoon man whose wife had died in the royal city :—

> Gone, gone art thou, sweet wife ; gone far away,
> Fair still and charmful, stretched on thy cold bier,
> As erst thou wert upon that joyous day
> When first I wed thee ; gladsome brought thee here,
> And joyed to think that thou wert mine.   Ah me !
> The butterfly's silk wings are shred ; no more,
> Ne'er more to rest upon thy head, Mah Meit—
> Sweet name for wife : "affectionate."   Deplore
> Her death ye nats that rule forests and streams,
> The hills and vales, and greater ye who guard
> The sacred law, the holy shrines, the beams
> Of silent moon, and sunlight baking hard
> The hot-scorched earth, not scorchèd more and seared
> Than is the parchment of my tortured heart.
> Nay, bear with me, good neighbours.   Be not feared.
> I am not mad.   The nat-so hath no part
> Of me or mine.   The spaewife sure hath said it.
>
> Ay, thou wert mine when last I trod the earth,
> Ere yet, all sinful, I was born as man,
> And yet again, in yet another birth,
> I'll claim thee ; when mayhap a happier kan,
> A fairer sum of merit, hardly won,
> Will lead us on, linked-armed, to linkèd death,
> That so progressing, joyful we may run
> Through all life's changes, and with single breath,
> Through heavens and zăn and rupa, we may bound
> To Ne'ban, blissful home of rest.   So mote it be.
>
> Alas, thou wert from Hanthawaddy's plains,
> And were we there, where thou so fain hadst stayed,
> A stately pomp had honoured thy remains,
> In silk and velvet wound, with gilded shade
> Of wide umbrella's pride, and regal spire
> Had towered to the skies, all seemly draped
> With flowing cloths and princesses' attire,
> Such as now thou dost wear, from earth escaped

To heavens of nats.   Yea, and of fretted gold
With mirror-work inlaid had been this case,
The last sad dwelling of thy earthly mould ;
But here it may not be, not in this place.

In Mamye's soil the stranger finds a tomb
As poor as doth the meanest in the land.
The trumpet's wailing note, the drum's low boom
May not be heard ; all callous as the strand
That threats the sailor on a stormy night,
The law stands fast and bids the mourner pass
With smothered moan ; and hurry from its sight
The alien clay.   Far from thy home, alas !
Thy dirge e'en waxeth faint.   Oh, Awgata,
The Lord, the Law, the Order, the Three Gems,
I bow me low.   Grant me the holy calm.

INDEX

THE NORTON LIBRARY

Meditation

Man-Perfection in God-

Sri Chinmoy

Library of Congress Catalog Card no. 80-65399

ISBN 0-88497-444-8

Printed and Published by
AUM PUBLICATIONS
86-24 Parsons Blvd.
Jamaica, N.Y. 11432

Editors' Note

The main text of this book is drawn from the hundreds of extemporaneous talks and answers to questions that Sri Chinmoy has given over the past twenty-five years. Interspersed are some of his inspirational poems and aphorisms.

In selecting and organising this material, we have tried to reflect basic concerns of all those who have embarked on the meditation journey, and in order to make it more accessible to you, we have created the chapter titles and section headings. The special "How To" sections and extensive index are intended to help you develop your own meditation practice, especially if you are a beginner.

In using this book it is best to keep in mind that the same question may be answered in many different ways, depending upon who has asked the question and the particular circumstances involved. Although we have tried to choose the most general answers, every answer may not apply in your specific case. If you are in doubt, the best authority is your own heart. The book is intended to guide and inspire you and not to lay down rules. It is our hope that this book will serve as a valuable friend to you in your spiritual search.

Table of
Contents

Meditation tells us only one thing: God is. Meditation reveals to us only one truth: ours is the vision of God.

Meditation: The Language of God

Meditation: The Language of God

❦ Why Do We Meditate?

Why do we meditate? We meditate because this world of ours has not been able to fulfil us. The so-called peace that we feel in our day-to-day life is five minutes of peace after ten hours of anxiety, worry and frustration. We are constantly at the mercy of the negative forces that are all around us: jealousy, fear, doubt, worry, anxiety and despair. These forces are like monkeys. When they get tired of biting us and take rest for a few minutes, then we say that we are enjoying peace. But this is not real peace at all, and the next moment they will attack us again.

It is only through meditation that we can get lasting peace, divine peace. If we meditate soulfully in the morning and receive peace for only one minute, that one minute of peace will permeate our whole day. And when we have a meditation of the highest order, then we get really abiding peace, light and delight. We need meditation because we want to grow in light and fulfil ourselves in light. If this is our aspiration, if this is our thirst, then meditation is the only way.

If we feel that we are satisfied with what we have and what we are, then there is no need for us to enter into the field of meditation. The reason we enter into meditation is because we have an inner hunger. We feel that within us there is something luminous, something vast, something divine. We feel that we need this thing very badly; only right now we do not have access to it. Our inner hunger comes from our spiritual need.

Meditation is not an escape

If we enter into the life of meditation in order to escape from the world and forget our sufferings, then we are doing it for the wrong reason. If we enter into the spiritual life because of outer frustration or dissatisfaction, then we may not remain in the spiritual life. Today I have failed to satisfy my desires; so I am dissatisfied with the world. But tomorrow I will say, "Let me try again. Perhaps this time I will get satisfaction." But eventually we will feel that the desire-life will never satisfy us; we will feel the need to enter into the inner life. This is aspiration.

> *What is meditation? Meditation is man's self-awakening and God's Self-offering. When man's self-awakening and God's Self-offering meet together, man becomes immortal in the inner world and God becomes fulfilled in the outer world.*

In the life of aspiration, we want only God. If we sincerely want God, then naturally He will give Himself to us. But He will do it in His own way and at His own time. If we pray and meditate with sincere aspiration for certain qualities, even if God does not grant them to us, still we will be satisfied. We will simply say, "He knows best. Right now I am not ready for these things. But He will definitely give them to me the day I am ready." In the life of aspiration it is not our achievement that gives us satisfaction; it is our aspiration. Aspiration itself is our satisfaction.

Conscious aspiration and effort

Spirituality cannot be achieved by pulling or pushing. We cannot pull down spiritual light by hook or by crook. When it comes down on its own, only on the strength of our aspiration will we be able to receive it. If we try to pull the light beyond our capacity of receptivity, our inner vessel will break. How do we receive this light from above? How do we expand our consciousness so that our receptivity will increase? The answer is meditation.

Meditation does not mean just sitting quietly for five or ten minutes. It requires conscious effort. The mind has to be made calm and quiet. At the same time, it has to be vigilant so as not to allow any distracting thoughts or desires to enter. When we can make the mind calm and quiet, we will feel that a new creation is dawning inside us. When the mind is vacant and tranquil and our whole existence becomes an empty vessel, our inner being can invoke infinite peace, light and bliss to enter into the vessel and fill it. This is meditation.

> *Meditation is the language of God. If we want to know what God's Will is in our life, if we want God to guide us, mould us and fulfil Himself in and through us, then meditation is the language that we must use.*

When we think that it is we who are trying to meditate, then meditation seems complicated. But real meditation is not done by us. It is done by our Inner Pilot, the Supreme, who is constantly meditating in and through us. We are just the vessel, and we are allowing Him to fill us with His whole Consciousness. We start with our own personal effort, but once we go deep within, we see that it is not our effort that is allowing us to enter into meditation. It is the Supreme who is meditating in and through us with our conscious awareness and consent.

Each person's soul has its own way of meditating. My way of meditating will not suit you, and your way of meditating will not suit me. There are many seekers whose meditation is not fruitful because they are not doing the meditation that is right for them. If you do not have a spiritual Master who can guide you, then you have to go deep within and get your meditation from the inmost recesses of your heart.

This is very difficult for a beginner. You have to go deep, deep within and see if you get a voice or thought or idea. Then you have to go deep into this voice or thought and see if it gives you a feeling of inner joy or peace, where there are no questions or problems or doubts. Only when you get this kind of feeling, can you know that the voice that you have heard is the real inner voice which will help you in your spiritual life.

But if you have a teacher who is a realised soul, his silent gaze will teach you how to meditate. A Master does not have to explain outwardly how to meditate, or give you a specific technique of meditation. He will simply meditate on you and inwardly teach you how to meditate. Your soul will enter into his soul and learn from his soul. All real spiritual Masters teach meditation in silence.

The ultimate aim of meditation is to establish our conscious union with God. We are all God's children, but right now we do not have conscious oneness with God. Someone may believe in God, but this belief is not a reality in his life. He just believes in God because some saint or Yogi or spiritual Master has said there is a God, or because he has read about God in spiritual books. But if we practise meditation, a day comes when we establish our conscious oneness with God. At that time, God gives us His infinite peace, infinite light and infinite bliss, and we grow into this infinite peace, light and bliss.

Q&A

Q How does one meditate?

A There are two ways to meditate. One way is to silence the mind. An ordinary man feels that if he silences the mind, he becomes a fool. He feels that if the mind does not think, the mind has lost everything. But this is not true in the spiritual life. In the spiritual life, when we silence the mind we see that a new creation, a new promise to God, dawns in the mind. Right now we have not fulfilled our promise to God; we have not totally dedicated our existence to God. When we can silence the mind, we are in a position to please and fulfil God.

Another way to meditate is to empty the heart. Right now the heart is full of emotional turmoil and problems caused by the impure vital which has enveloped it. The heart is a vessel. Right now this vessel is full of undivine things, things that limit and bind us. If we can empty the heart-vessel, there is someone who will fill it with divine peace, light and bliss, which will liberate us. When we empty our heart of ignorance, God's Wisdom-Light will come and fill it.

Q If a person does not believe in God, can he practise meditation?

A If a person does not believe in God, he can practise meditation but he may not achieve anything. Meditation is the path that leads to God. If you do not believe in God, then naturally you will not follow that path.

Q Is meditation the highest reality?

A You can say that for a beginner meditation is the highest reality. But when one becomes an advanced seeker, one knows that meditation only leads to the highest reality. If someone has been living in ignorance, if he has never prayed or meditated in his life even for a minute, for him meditation is naturally the highest reality that his consciousness can achieve. But when he has practised meditation for a few years, he knows that meditation itself is not the highest reality. The highest reality is something he achieves or grows into by walking along the path of meditation.

Q As one evolves spiritually and achieves realisation, does the focus of his meditation change?

A After one has achieved realisation, it is not necessary for him to meditate the way a seeker meditates. When someone has attained realisation, which is oneness with the Supreme, his meditation is continuous. When a seeker has realised God, he does not meditate to achieve something or to go beyond something. He meditates to bring down peace, light and bliss for humanity or to awaken the consciousness of others.

From the spiritual point of view, every seeker is a beginner. The moment you want to make constant and continual progress, at that moment you become an eternal beginner.

First Things First: How to Begin

First Things First: How to Begin

❦ How Do I Start?

From the spiritual point of view, every seeker is a beginner. A beginner is he who has the inner urge to grow into something ever more divine, ever more illumining and ever more fulfilling. The moment you want to make constant and continuous progress, the moment you want to surpass yourself and enter into the ever-transcending Beyond, at that moment you become an eternal beginner.

If you are an absolute beginner, then you can start by reading a few spiritual books or scriptures. These will give you inspiration. You should read books by spiritual Masters in whom you have implicit faith. There *are* Masters who have attained the highest consciousness, and if you read their books, you are bound to get inspiration. It is better not to read books written by professors or scholars or aspirants who are still on the path and have not yet attained illumination. Only those who have realised the Truth will have the capacity to offer the Truth. Otherwise, it is like the blind leading the blind.

It is also a good idea to associate with people who have been meditating for some time. These people may not be in a position to teach you, but they will be able to inspire you. Even if you just sit beside them while they are meditating, unconsciously your inner being will derive some meditative power from them. You are not stealing anything; only your inner being is taking help from them without your outer knowledge.

In the beginning you should not even think about meditation. Just try to set aside a certain time of day when you will try to be calm and quiet, and feel that these five minutes belong to your inner being and to nobody else. Regularity is of paramount importance. What you need is regular practice at a regular time.

 Every day there is only one thing to learn: how to be honestly happy.

Some basic techniques

For a beginner it is better to start with concentration. Otherwise, the moment you try to make your mind calm and vacant, millions of uncomely thoughts will enter into you and you will not be able to meditate even for one second. If you concentrate, at that time you challenge the wrong thoughts that are trying to enter you. So in the beginning just practise concentration for a few minutes. Then, after a few weeks or a few months, you can try meditation.

When you start meditating, always try to feel that you are a child. When one is a child, one's mind is not developed. At the age of twelve or thirteen, the mind starts functioning on an intellectual level. But before that, a child is all heart. A child feels that he does not know anything. He does not have any preconceived ideas about meditation and the spiritual life. He wants to learn everything fresh.

First feel that you are a child, and then try to feel that you are standing in a flower garden. This flower garden is your heart. A child can play in a garden for hours. He goes from this flower to that flower, but he does not leave the garden, because he gets joy from the beauty and fragrance of each flower. Feel that inside you is a garden, and you can stay in it for as long as you want. In this way you can learn to meditate in the heart.

If you can remain in the heart, you will begin to feel an inner cry. This inner cry, which is aspiration, is the secret of meditation. When an adult person cries, his cry is usually not sincere. But when a child cries, even if he is crying only for candy, he is very sincere. At that time, candy is the whole world for him. If you give him a hundred-dollar bill, he will not be satisfied; he cares only for candy. When a child cries, immediately his father or mother comes to him. If you can cry from deep within for peace, light and truth, and if this is the only thing that will satisfy you, then God your eternal Father and eternal Mother is bound to come and help you.

You should always try to feel that you are as helpless as a child. As soon as you feel that you are helpless, somebody will come to help you. If a child is lost in the street and he begins to cry, some kind-hearted person will show him where his home is. Feel that you are lost in the street and that there is a storm raging. Doubt, fear, anxiety, worry, insecurity and other undivine forces are pouring down on you. But if you cry sincerely, somebody will come to rescue you and show you how to get to your home, which is your heart. And who is that somebody? It is God, your Inner Pilot.

 Early in the morning invite God your Friend, your real Friend, your only Friend, to walk along with you during the entire day.

The Inner Pilot
God can appear with form and without form. But during your meditation, it is best to think of the Supreme as a human being. The beginner should always meditate on the personal God. Otherwise, if you try to see God

in His impersonal aspect, you will be confused by His immensity. So start with the personal God and from there you can go to the impersonal God.

Today you may be a beginner in the spiritual life, but do not feel that you will always be a beginner. At one time everybody was a beginner. If you practise concentration and meditation regularly, if you are really sincere in your spiritual search, then you are bound to make progress. The important thing is not to be discouraged. God-realisation does not come overnight. If you meditate regularly and devotedly, if you can cry for God like a child cries for his mother, then you will not have to run to the goal. No, the goal will come and stand right in front of you and claim you as its own, very own.

How To

1 **Simplicity, sincerity, purity.** There are quite a few meditation exercises a beginner can try. For the seeker wishing to enter the spiritual life, simplicity, sincerity, purity and surety are of utmost importance. It is simplicity that grants you peace of mind. It is sincerity that makes you feel that you are of God and that God is constantly for you. It is your pure heart that makes you feel at every moment that God is growing, glowing and fulfilling Himself inside you. It is surety that makes you feel that meditation is absolutely the right thing.

In silence kindly repeat the word "simplicity" inside your mind seven times and concentrate on the crown of your head. Then repeat the word "sincerity" seven times silently and soulfully inside your heart, and concentrate on your heart. Then kindly repeat the word "purity" seven times inside or around your navel centre, and concentrate on the navel centre. Please do all this silently and most soulfully. Then focus your attention on the third eye, which is between and slightly above the eyebrows, and silently repeat "surety" seven times. Next, place your hand on top of your head and say three times, "I am simple, I am simple, I am simple." Then place your hand on your heart and say three times, "I am sincere, I am sincere, I am sincere." Then place your hand on the navel centre, repeating "I am pure," and on the third eye, repeating "I am sure."

2 **A favourite quality.** If you like a particular aspect of God—love, for instance—please inwardly repeat the word "love" most soulfully several times. While uttering the word "love" most soulfully, try to feel it reverberating in the inmost recesses of your heart: "love, love, love." If you care more for divine peace, then please inwardly chant or repeat to yourself the word "peace." While doing this, try to hear the cosmic sound that the word embodies reverberating in the very depths of your heart. If you want light, then please repeat "light, light, light," most soulfully, and feel that you have actually become light. From the soles of your feet to the crown of your head, try to feel that you have become the word that you are repeating. Feel that your physical body, subtle body, all your nerves and your entire being are flooded with love or peace or light.

3 **Invite your friends.** Feel that you are standing at your heart's door and that you have invited love, peace, light, delight and all your other divine friends to visit you. But if complexity, insincerity, impurity, insecurity, doubt and other negative forces appear, please do not let them enter. Try to feel that both the divine qualities and the undivine qualities have taken the form of human beings, and that you can see them with your human eyes.

Every day try to invite one friend to enter your heart's door. This will be the beginning of a divine friendship. One day you will allow only your friend love to come in; the next day you will allow your friend joy to come in. After some time, you will have the capacity to invite more than one friend at a time. In the beginning you may not be able to pay attention to more than one friend at a time, but eventually you will be able to invite all your divine friends at once.

Q I am looking for more joy in my life, but I don't feel confident about jumping into meditation to get it.

A When life is not giving you joy but you feel that you want joy, that means you are spiritually hungry. When you are spiritually hungry, you will eat spiritual food. When you are not hungry, you will not eat. For fifteen or twenty years you did not sincerely or intensely care for the spiritual life. Since you have not meditated for so many years, if you jump all at once into the sea of spirituality, you will not be able to swim. You cannot change your nature overnight. It has to be done slowly, steadily, gradually. First move around in the water, and gradually you will learn how to swim. Eventually there will come a time when you will be able to swim well. But since you have inner hunger, that means you are ready to start swimming.

No preparation, no attempt. No attempt, no progress. No progress, no perfection. No perfection, no satisfaction.

Mastering the Essentials

Mastering the Essentials

❦ Preparing Yourself to Meditate

When you meditate at home, you should have a corner of your room which is absolutely pure and sanctified— a sacred place which you use only for meditation. There you can make a shrine where you can keep a picture of your spiritual Master, or the Christ, or some other beloved spiritual figure whom you regard as your Master.

Before beginning to meditate, it is helpful if you can take a shower or proper bath. The cleanliness of the body is very helpful for the purification of the consciousness. If you are unable to take a shower or bath before sitting down to meditate, you should at least wash your face. It is also advisable to wear clean and light clothes.

It will also help if you burn incense and keep some fresh flowers on your shrine. When you smell the scent of incense, you get perhaps only an iota of inspiration and purification, but this iota can be added to your inner treasure. There are some people who say that it is not necessary to have flowers in front of you during meditation. They say, "The flower is inside; the thousand-petalled lotus is inside." But the physical flower on your shrine will remind you of the inner flower. Its colour, its fragrance and its pure consciousness will give you inspiration. From inspiration you get aspiration.

It is the same with using candles during meditation. The flame from a candle will not in itself give you aspiration, but when you see the outer flame immediately you feel that the flame of aspiration in your inner being is also climbing high, higher, highest. If someone is on the verge of God-realisation or has actually realised God, then these outer things will have no value. But if you know that your God-realisation is still a far cry, then they will definitely increase your aspiration.

When you are doing your individual daily meditation, try to meditate alone. This does not apply to husband and wife if they have the same spiritual Master; it is all right for them to meditate together. Otherwise, it is not advisable to meditate with others during your daily individual meditation. Collective meditation is also important, but for individual daily meditation it is better to meditate privately at one's own shrine.

Meditation is a divine gift. Meditation simplifies our outer life and energises our inner life. Meditation gives us a natural and spontaneous life, a life that becomes so natural and spontaneous that we cannot breathe without being conscious of our own divinity.

Posture is important

When meditating, it is important to keep the spine straight and erect, and to keep the body relaxed. If the body is stiff, the divine and fulfilling qualities that are flowing in and through it during meditation will not be received. The body should not be uncomfortable, either. While you are meditating, your inner being will spontaneously take you to a comfortable position, and then it is up to you to maintain it. The main advantage of the lotus position is that it helps keep the spinal cord straight and erect. But it is not comfortable for most people. So the lotus position is not at all necessary for proper meditation. Many people meditate very well while seated in a chair.

Some people do physical exercises and postures. These exercises, called Hatha Yoga, relax the body and bring peace of mind for a short period. If someone is physically very restless and cannot stay still for more than a second, then these exercises will definitely help. But Hatha Yoga is not at all necessary. There are many aspirants who can just sit and make their minds calm and quiet without doing any Hatha Yoga.

It is not at all advisable to meditate while lying down, even for those who have been meditating for several years. Those who try to meditate while lying down will enter into the world of sleep or into a kind of inner drift or doze. Furthermore, while you are lying down, your breathing is not as satisfactory as it is when you are in a sitting position, since it is not conscious or controlled. Proper breathing is very important in meditation.

 A soulful heart has discovered a supreme truth: to meditate on God is a privilege and not a duty.

Eyes open vs. eyes closed
People often ask me if they should meditate with their eyes open. In ninety out of one hundred cases, those who keep their eyes closed during meditation fall asleep. For five minutes they meditate, and then for fifteen minutes they remain in the world of sleep. There is no dynamic energy, but only lethargy, complacency and a kind of restful, sweet sensation.

When you keep your eyes closed during meditation and enter into the world of sleep, you may enjoy all kinds of fantasies. Your fertile imagination may make you feel that you are entering into the higher worlds. There are many ways you can make yourself believe that you are having a wonderful meditation. So it is best to meditate with the eyes half open and half closed. In this way you are the root of the tree and at the same time the topmost bough. The part of you that has the eyes half-open is the root, symbolising Mother-Earth. The part which has the eyes half-closed is the topmost branch, the world of vision or, let us say, Heaven. Your consciousness is on the highest level and it is also here on earth, trying to transform the world.

When you meditate with your eyes half open and half closed, you are doing what is called the "lion's meditation." Even while you are going deep within, you are focusing your conscious attention both on the physical plane and on the subconscious plane. Both the physical world, with its noise and distractions, and the subconscious world, the world of sleep, are inviting you, but you are conquering both of them. You are saying, "Look, I am alert. You cannot take me into your domain." Since your eyes are partly open, you will not fall asleep. So you are challenging the world of the subconscious. At the same time you are maintaining your mastery over the physical plane, because you can see what is going on around you.

How To

Breathing Exercises

1 **Breathing into the heart centre.** Please breathe in and hold your breath for a couple of seconds, and feel that you are holding the breath, which is life-energy, in your heart centre. This will help you to develop your inner meditation capacity.

2 **Becoming aware of the breath.** When you sit down to meditate, try to breathe in as slowly and quietly as possible, so that if somebody placed a tiny thread in front of your nose it would not move at all. And when you breathe out, try to breathe out even more slowly than you breathed in. If possible, leave a short pause between the end of your exhalation and the beginning of your inhalation. If you can, hold your breath for a few seconds. But if that is difficult, do not do it. Never do anything that will make you physically uncomfortable during meditation.

3 **Breathing in peace and joy.** The first thing that you have to think of when practising breathing techniques is purity. When you breathe in, if you can feel that the breath is coming directly from God, from Purity itself, then your breath can easily be purified. Then, each time you breathe in, try to feel that you are bringing infinite peace into your body. The opposite of peace is restlessness. When you breathe out, try to feel that you are expelling the restlessness within you and also the restlessness that you see all around you. When you breathe this way, you will find restlessness leaving you. After practising this a few times, please try to feel that you are breathing in power from the universe, and when you exhale, feel that all your fear is coming out of your body. After doing this a few times, try to feel that you are breathing in infinite joy and breathing out sorrow, suffering and melancholy.

4 **Cosmic energy.** Feel that you are breathing in not air but cosmic energy. Feel that tremendous cosmic energy is entering into you with each breath, and that you are going to use it to purify your body, vital, mind and heart. Feel that there is not a single place in your being that is not being occupied by the flow of cosmic energy. It is flowing like a river inside you, washing and purifying your entire being. Then, when you breathe out, feel that you are breathing out all the rubbish inside you—all your undivine thoughts, obscure ideas and impure actions. Anything inside your system that you call undivine, anything that you do not want to claim as your own, feel that you are exhaling.

This is not the traditional yogic *pranayama*, which is more complicated and systematised, but it is a most effective spiritual method of breathing. If you practise this method of breathing, you will soon see the results. In the beginning you will have to use your imagination, but after a while you will see and feel that it is not imagination at all but reality. You are consciously breathing in the energy which is flowing all around you, purifying yourself and emptying yourself of everything undivine. If you can breathe this way for five minutes every day, you will be able to make very fast progress. But it has to be done in a very conscious way, not mechanically.

5 **Total breathing.** When you reach a more advanced stage, you can try to feel that your breath is coming in and going out through every part of your body—through your heart, through your eyes, through your nose and even through your pores. Right now you can breathe only through your nose or your mouth, but a time will come when you will be able to breathe through every part of your body. Spiritual Masters can breathe even with their nose and mouth closed. When you have perfected this spiritual breathing, all your impurity and ignorance will be replaced by God's light, peace and power.

6 **One-four-two breathing.** As you breathe in, repeat once the name of God, the Christ or whomever you adore. Or, if your Master has given you a mantra, you can repeat that. This breath does not have to be long or deep. Then hold your breath and repeat the same name four times. And when you breathe out, repeat two times the name or mantra that you have chosen. You inhale for one count, hold your breath for four counts and exhale for two counts, inwardly repeating the sacred word. If you simply count the numbers—one-four-two—you do not get any vibration or inner feeling. But when you say the name of God, immediately God's divine qualities enter into you. Then, when you hold your breath, these divine qualities rotate inside you, entering into all your impurities, obscurities, imperfections and limitations. And when you breathe out, these same divine qualities carry away all your undivine, unprogressive and destructive qualities.

In the beginning you can start with a one-four-two count. When you become experienced in this breathing exercise, you will be able to do it to a count of four-sixteen-eight: breathing in for four counts, holding the breath for sixteen, and breathing out for eight. But this has to be done very gradually. Some people do an eight-thirty-two-sixteen count, but this is for the experts.

7 **Alternate breathing.** Another technique you can try is alternate breathing. This is done by pressing the right nostril closed with the thumb and taking in a long breath through the left nostril. As you breathe in, repeat God's name once. Then hold your breath for four counts repeating God's name four times. And finally release your right nostril, press your left nostril closed with your fourth finger and release your breath to the count of two—that is, two repetitions of God's name. Then do it the opposite way, starting with the left nostril pressed closed. In this system, when you breathe in, it does not have to be done quietly. Even if you make noise, no harm. But of course, these exercises should not be done in public or where other people are trying to meditate in silence.

You should not practise one-four-two breathing for more than four or five minutes, and you should not do alternate breathing more than a few times. If you do it twenty or forty or fifty times, heat will rise from the base of your spine and enter into your head, creating tension and a headache. It is like eating too much. Eating is good, but if you eat voraciously, it will upset your stomach. This inner heat acts the same way. If you draw it up beyond your capacity, then instead of giving you a peaceful mind, it will give you an arrogant, turbulent and destructive mind. Later, when you have developed your inner capacity, you can do this alternate breathing for ten or fifteen minutes.

Q Is it necessary to meditate only at home, or can we try to meditate wherever we are?

A Right now you are only a beginner. You can meditate at your best only when you are alone in your room or in the presence of your spiritual Master. If you try to meditate while driving or walking or sitting on the subway, you will not be able to go very deep. Again, it is not enough just to be seated before your shrine. While you are seated before your shrine, you have to feel an inner shrine within your heart; otherwise, you will not have a satisfactory meditation. Wherever you meditate, you must enter into your heart, where you can see and feel the living shrine of the Supreme. At your inner shrine you are safe and pro-

Mastering the Essentials

tected. You are guarded by the divine forces there. If you can meditate at this inner shrine, you are bound to make the fastest progress, because there you will meet with no opposition.

After you have meditated very sincerely for several years and developed some inner strength, at that time you will be able to meditate anywhere. Even if you are standing in the subway or walking along the street, you will not be disturbed. Eventually you have to learn how to do the highest meditation and, at the same time, be aware of what is happening in the outer world.

Q During meditation and prayer, some people concentrate on certain objects, like photographs or some other things. Is it wise for them to cling to these objects, or is it wiser for them to meditate on something that has no form, that they cannot see?

A When they meditate on something, they are not worshipping that particular thing as God. They are only receiving inspiration from that thing. I look at a candle and I see the flame, but I am not taking the flame as God. I am taking the flame as a source of inspiration. This flame inspires me and increases my aspiration to climb upward with a burning inner cry. I may keep a flower before me when I meditate. The flower is not God, although inside the flower is God. But the flower inspires me and offers me purity. I may burn incense. Incense itself is not God for me, but incense gives me a feeling of purity, and helps me in my spiritual progress.

Anything that inspires me I shall use in order to increase my aspiration, whether it is a picture, a candle or a flower. For when my inspiration and aspiration increase, I feel that I have taken one step more toward my goal. But the candle or the picture or the flower itself is not the object of my adoration.

Q Eventually, when we realise God, will all these things drop off?

A When we become expert in our aspiration-life, then no outer form will remain. We will become one with the Formless. But in the beginning, it is necessary to approach God through form. In the beginning, a child reads aloud. He has to convince his parents, he has to convince himself, that he is reading the words. If he does not read aloud, he feels that he is not reading at all. But when the child becomes adept, he reads in silence. By then, he and his parents know that he can really read, so the outer form can drop away. But these outer forms are of paramount importance during the seeker's preliminary stages. Eventually they will go, when they are no longer necessary.

Q Is it all right to meditate after eating, or is fasting desirable?

A It is not good to meditate just after eating a large meal. The body has thousands of subtle spiritual nerves. These nerves become heavy after a big meal and will not permit you to have the highest type of meditation. The body will be heavy, the consciousness will be heavy, the nerves will be heavy, and your meditation will not be good. When you meditate properly, you feel that your whole existence, like a bird, is flying high, higher, highest. But when your consciousness is heavy, you cannot go up.

So it is always advisable to meditate on an empty stomach. At least two hours should elapse between your meal and the time that you sit down to meditate. But again, if you are really pinched with hunger when you go to meditate, your meditation will not be satisfactory. Your hunger, like a monkey, will constantly bother you. In that case, it is advisable to have just a glass of milk or juice before meditating. This will not ruin your meditation.

But to refrain from eating a large meal before meditation is not the same as fasting. Fasting is not at all necessary for meditation. By fasting you can purify yourself to some extent. Once a month, if you wish, you can fast for a day to purify your existence of outer aggressions and greed. But by fasting frequently, you approach death rather than God. Fasting is not the answer for self-purification. The answer is constant, soulful meditation, unreserved love for God and unconditional surrender to God.

Q Is it necessary to be a vegetarian in order to follow the spiritual life?

A The vegetarian diet does play a role in the spiritual life. Purity is of paramount importance for an aspirant. This purity we must establish in the body, in the vital and in the mind. When we eat meat, the aggressive animal consciousness enters into us. Our nerves become agitated and restless, and this can interfere with our meditation. If a seeker does not stop eating meat, generally he does not get subtle experiences or subtle visions.

At one time the animal consciousness was necessary for forward movement. Animals are by nature aggressive but, at the same time, there is some dynamic push forward in the animal consciousness. If we had not had animal qualities, we would have remained inert, like trees, or we would have remained in the stone consciousness where there is no growth or movement. But unfortunately the animal consciousness also contains many unillumined and destructive qualities. Now we have entered into the spiritual life, so the role of the animal consciousness is no longer necessary in our life.

From the animal consciousness we have entered into the human consciousness, and now we are trying to enter into the divine consciousness.

The mild qualities of fruits and vegetables help us to establish, in our inner life as well as in our outer life, the qualities of sweetness, softness, simplicity and purity. If we are vegetarians, this helps our inner being to strengthen its own existence. Inwardly, we are praying and meditating; outwardly, the food we are taking from Mother-Earth is helping us too, giving us not only energy but also aspiration.

Some people feel that it is meat that gives them strength. But if they go deep within, they may discover that it is their own idea about meat that is giving them strength. One can change that idea and feel that it is not meat but the spiritual energy pervading one's body that gives one strength. That energy comes from meditation as well as from proper nourishment. The strength that one can get from aspiration and meditation is infinitely more powerful than the strength one can get from meat.

Many spiritual seekers have come to the conclusion that a vegetarian is in a position to make quicker progress in the spiritual life. But along with a vegetarian diet, one must pray and meditate. If one has aspiration, the vegetarian diet will help considerably; the body's purity will help one's inner aspiration to become more intense and more soulful. But again, if one is not a vegetarian, that does not mean that one will not make spiritual progress or will not be able to realise God.

Sometimes I must be silent,
For that is the only way
To know a little better,
To think a little wiser,
To become a little more perfect,
To claim God a little sooner.

The Silent Mind

The Silent Mind

❦ Quieting the Mind

No matter which path you follow for meditation, the first and foremost task is to try to make the mind calm and quiet. If the mind is constantly roaming, if it is all the time a victim of merciless thoughts, then you will make no progress whatsoever. The mind has to be made calm and quiet so that when the light descends from above, you can be fully conscious of it. In your conscious observation and conscious acceptance of light, you will enter into a profound meditation and see the purification, transformation and illumination of your life.

How will you make the mind calm and quiet? The mind has its own power, and right now this power is stronger than your present eagerness and determination to meditate. But if you can get help from your heart, then gradually you will be able to control your mind. The heart, in turn, gets constant assistance from the soul, which is all light and all power.

Emptying the mind

You must not think that when there is nothing in your mind, you will become a fool or act like an idiot. This is not true. If you can keep your mind calm and quiet for ten or fifteen minutes, a new world will dawn within you. This is the root of all spiritual progress. Right now you can make your mind calm and quiet for only a few seconds, or for a minute, but if you can maintain your calmness, poise and tranquillity for half an hour or even for fifteen minutes, I assure you that inside your tranquillity a new world with tremendous divine light and power will grow.

When you do not have any thought in your mind, please do not feel that you are totally lost. On the contrary, feel that something divine is being prepared in your pure and aspiring nature. You cannot expect immediate results. The farmer sows the seed and then he waits; he never expects the crop to spring forth all at once. It takes a few weeks or a few months to germinate. Your mind can be like a fertile field. If you plant the seed of silence and poise and cultivate it patiently, sooner or later you are bound to reap the bumper crop of illumination.

The mind is not necessary for meditation, because thinking and meditating are absolutely different things. When we meditate, we do not think at all. The aim of meditation is to free ourselves from all thought. Thought is like a dot on a blackboard. Whether it is good or bad, it is there. Only if there is no thought whatsoever can we grow into the highest reality. Even in profound meditation thoughts can come in, but not in the highest, deepest meditation. In the highest meditation, there will be only light.

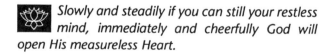 *Slowly and steadily if you can still your restless mind, immediately and cheerfully God will open His measureless Heart.*

Beyond the mind
In light, vision and reality are one. You are sitting there and I am standing here. Let us say that I am the vision and you are the reality. I have to look at you and enter into you in order to know you. But in the highest meditation reality and vision are one. Where you are, I also am there; where I am, you are. We are one. That is

34   *The Silent Mind*

why in the highest meditation we do not need thoughts. In the highest meditation the knower and the thing to be known are one.

Even reflection, which is a quiet kind of introspective thinking, is far from the disciplined vastness of meditation. The moment we start thinking, we play with limitation and bondage. Our thoughts, no matter how sweet or delicious at the moment, are painful and destructive in the long run because they limit and bind us. In the thinking mind there is no reality. Each moment we are building a world, and the following moment we are breaking it. The mind has its purpose, but in the spiritual life we have to go far above the mind to where there is eternal peace, eternal wisdom and eternal light. When we go beyond thinking with the help of our aspiration and meditation, only then can we see and enjoy God's Reality and God's Vision together.

Purifying the Mind

The mind is almost always impure, and it almost always brings in unaspiring thoughts. Even when it is not doing this, the mind is still a victim to doubt, jealousy, hypocrisy, fear and other undivine qualities. All negative things first attack the mind. The mind may reject them for a minute, but again they knock at the mind's door. This is the nature of the mind. The heart is much, much purer. Affection, love, devotion, surrender and other divine qualities are already there in the heart. That is why the heart is much purer than the mind. Even if you have fear or jealousy in the heart, the good qualities of the heart will still come forward.

But again, the heart may not be totally pure because the vital being is near the heart. The lower vital, which is situated near the navel, tends to come up and touch the heart centre. It makes the heart impure by its influence and proximity. But at least the heart is not like the mind, which deliberately opens its door to impure ideas. The heart is far better than the mind. And best is the soul. The soul is all purity, light, bliss and divinity.

1 **Becoming the soul.** In order to purify your mind, the best thing to do is to feel every day for a few minutes during your meditation that you have no mind. Say to yourself, "I have no mind, I have no mind. What I have is the heart." Then after some time feel, "I don't have a heart. What I have is the soul." When you say, "I have the soul," at that time you will be flooded with purity. But again you have to go deeper and farther by saying not only, "I have the soul," but also "I am the soul." At that time, imagine the most beautiful child you have ever seen, and feel that your soul is infinitely more beautiful than that child.

The moment you can say and feel, "I *am* the soul," and meditate on this truth, your soul's infinite purity will enter into your heart. Then, from the heart, the infinite purity will enter into your mind. When you can truly feel that you are only the soul, the soul will purify your mind.

2 **The inner flame.** Before you meditate, try to imagine a flame inside your heart. Right now the flame may be tiny and flickering; it may not be a powerful flame. But one day it will definitely become most powerful and most illumining. Try to imagine that this flame is illumining your mind. In the beginning you may not be able to concentrate according to your satisfaction because the mind is not focused. The mind is constantly thinking of many things. It has become a victim of many uncomely thoughts. The mind does not have proper illumination, so imagine a beautiful flame inside your heart, illumining you. Bring that illumining flame inside your mind. Then you will gradually see a streak of light inside your mind. When your mind starts getting illumined, it will be very, very easy to concentrate for a long time, and also to concentrate more deeply.

3 **Purifying the breath.** Before you start your meditation, repeat "Supreme" about twenty times as fast as possible in order to purify your breath. Feel that you are really growing into the very Breath of God. Unless and until the breath is purified, the mind will not remain one-pointed.

4 **God wants me, I need God.** Focus your attention on a picture. You can look at your Master's picture or you can look at yourself in the mirror. If you concentrate on your own reflection, feel that you are totally one with the physical being that you are seeing. Then try to enter into the image that you are seeing. From there you should try to grow with one thought: God wants you and you need God. Repeat: "God wants me, I need God. God wants me, I need God." Then you will see that slowly, steadily and unerringly this divine thought is entering into you and permeating your inner and outer existence, giving you purity in your mind, vital and body.

5 **Asserting control over the mind.** You can tell your mind, "I shall not allow you to go in your own way. Now I want to think of God." Repeat the name of God inwardly or aloud. Then say, "I want to have purity in my whole existence." Then repeat "purity, purity, purity." At that time you are not allowing your mind to think of impurity or of any other thing. Don't give your mind a chance to wander; simply utilise your mind for your own purpose. You have millions of things to accomplish in and through the mind. But the mind is so naughty and mischievous that if you don't utilise it, it will utilise you.

6 **Throw them out.** Each time an undivine thought enters into your mind, throw it out of your mind. It is like a foreign element, a thief, that has entered your room. Why should you consciously allow a thief to remain in your room when you have the capacity to throw him out? When an undivine thought enters into your mind, just capture the thought and throw it into the blazing fire of your inner aspiration.

7 **Strangling bad thoughts.** When a thought comes that is not pure, good or divine, immediately repeat the word "Supreme" very fast. The Supreme is my Guru, your Guru, everybody's Guru. Repeat "Supreme" very fast, and each time you use the word "Supreme," feel that you are creating a snake that will coil around the undivine thought and strangle it.

Q I am a beginner in meditation, and I find that I cannot control my thoughts. How can I have a successful meditation?

A If you are a beginner, try to allow only divine thoughts to enter into you, and not undivine thoughts. It is better not to have any thoughts at all during meditation, but it is next to impossible for the beginner to have a mind without thoughts. So you can begin by having good thoughts: "I want to be good, I want to be more spiritual, I want to love God more, I want to exist only for Him." Let these ideas grow within you. Start with one or two divine ideas: "Today I will be absolutely pure. I will not allow any bad thought, but only peace, to enter into me." When you allow one divine thought to grow inside you, you will see that immediately your consciousness changes for the better.

Start with divine ideas: "Today I want to feel that I am really a child of God." This will not be a mere feeling but an actual reality. Feel that the Virgin Mary is holding the child Christ. Feel that the Divine Mother is holding you in her arms like a baby. Then feel: "I really want to have wisdom-light. I want to walk with my Father. Wherever He goes I will go with Him. I will get light from Him."

Some people don't have ideas like this. Creative thoughts and ideas don't come. There is just a vacuum. You may ask which is better—to have many silly messages in the mind or no messages at all. But there is a negative, inconscient way of meditating which has no life in it. This is not the silent mind. It is not productive. In real meditation, the mind is silent but at the same time it is conscious.

Q Ideally, should one reject all thoughts during meditation?

A The best thing is to try not to allow any thought to enter into your mind, whether it is a good thought or a bad thought. It is as though you are in your room, and somebody is knocking at your door. You have no idea whether it is an enemy or a friend. Divine thoughts are your true friends, and undivine thoughts are your enemies. You would like to allow your friends to enter, but you do not know who your friends are. And even if you *do* know who your friends are, when you open the door for them you may find that your enemies are also there.

Then, before your friends can cross the threshold, your enemies will also enter. You may not even notice any undivine thoughts, but while the divine thoughts are entering, the undivine thoughts, like thieves, will also secretly enter and create tremendous confusion. Once they have entered, it is very difficult to chase them out. For that you need the strength of solid spiritual discipline. For fifteen minutes you may cherish spiritual thoughts and then, in just a fleeting second, an undivine thought will come. So the best thing is not to allow any thoughts at all during your meditation. Just keep the door bolted from inside.

> *There was a time when I loved you, O my thought-world. But now I love the beauty of a silence-mind and the purity of a gratitude-heart.*

Your real friends will not go away. They will think, "Something is wrong with him. Usually he is so kind to us. So there must be some special reason why he is not opening the door." They have sympathetic oneness, so they will wait indefinitely. But your enemies will wait just for a few minutes. Then they will lose all patience and say, "It is beneath our dignity to waste our time here." These enemies have their pride. They will say, "Who cares? Who needs him? Let us go and attack somebody else." If you pay no attention to a monkey, the monkey will eventually go away and bite somebody else. But your friends will say, "No, we need him and he needs us. We will wait indefinitely for him." So after a few minutes your enemies will go away. Then you can open the door and your dearest friends will be there waiting for you.

If you meditate regularly and devotedly, after some time you will become inwardly strong. Then you will be able to welcome the divine thoughts and chase away the undivine thoughts. If you are getting a thought of divine love, divine peace or divine power, then you will allow that thought to enter into you and expand. You will let it play and grow in the garden of your mind. While the thought is playing and you are playing with it, you will see that you are growing into it. Each divine thought that you let in will create a new and fulfilling world for you, and will surcharge your entire being with divinity.

After a few years of meditation you will have enough inner strength to let in even the undivine thoughts. When an undivine thought comes into your mind, you will not reject it; you will transform it. When somebody undivine knocks at your door, if you have enough strength to compel him to behave properly once he enters, then you can open the door for him. Eventually you have to accept the challenge and conquer these wrong thoughts; otherwise, they will come back to bother you again and again.

> *I am so proud of my mind. Why? Because it has started enjoying little things: a simple thought, a pure heart, a humble life.*

You have to be a divine potter. If the potter is afraid to touch the clay, then the clay will remain always clay and the potter will not be able to offer anything to the world. But if the potter is not afraid, he can transform the clay into something beautiful and useful. It is your bounden duty to transform undivine thoughts, but only when you are in a position to do so safely.

Q What is the best way to deal with undivine thoughts that come during meditation?

A The moment a negative or unaspiring thought enters your mind, you should try to use your aspiration to reject it, because during meditation everything is very intense. While you are talking or engaging in ordinary activities, you can have any kind of thought, for your thoughts are not intense at those times. But if any undivine thought comes during meditation, the power of your meditation enlarges and intensifies it. Your spiritual life grows weaker the moment you allow your mind to indulge in unaspiring thoughts during meditation. If a good thought comes, you can try to enlarge it, or you can try to lift it up to a higher level. But if you have a bad thought, try to cut it off immediately.

How will you do this? If the thought that is attacking you is coming from the outer world, try to muster your soul's will from your heart and bring it right in front of your forehead. The moment your soul's will is seen by the thought which is trying to enter into you, that thought is bound to disappear.

But if you do not have the inner capacity to do this, do not become upset. Sometimes when wrong thoughts come during meditation, the seeker feels that the strength of the wrong thought is so powerful that even if he has meditated for two or three hours, it is all useless. One ordinary thought or wrong thought comes in and he feels that he has lost everything. This is foolish. As long as you do not allow your mind to dwell on them, you should not give any importance to wrong thoughts at that particular moment.

If emotional thoughts, lower vital thoughts or sex thoughts enter into you during meditation, and you are not able to keep them out or throw them out, try to feel that these thoughts are as insignificant as ants. Just pay no attention to them. If you can feel that the spiritual power that you have received from your meditation is infinitely stronger than the power of the wrong thoughts, then these wrong thoughts cannot utilise your meditative power for their own purpose. But what often happens is that you become terribly afraid of these thoughts and dwell on them. By thinking about them and being afraid of them, you give them power.

It is true that wrong thoughts can become intense during meditation. But you can easily bring to the fore good thoughts that are infinitely more powerful. During meditation when wrong thoughts come to you, immediately try to recollect one of your sweetest or highest divine experiences. Enter into your own experience which you had a few days ago or a few years ago, and try to bring it into your mental consciousness. You will see that while you are fully immersed in your own experience, the thought from the lower vital plane is bound to leave you because the highest, deepest, purest joy is in your consciousness. Divine joy is infinitely more powerful than pleasure. The nectar-delight of your own spiritual experience is infinitely stronger than your lower vital forces. In this way you can solve the problem without leaving your meditation.

Wrong thoughts come to attack you and take away your divine feelings, divine thoughts and divine power. But when you pay all attention to divine thoughts and encourage and cherish only divine feelings, in many cases the wrong thoughts just go away. They say, "He does not care for us. We have no place here." Wrong thoughts also have their pride, and they are terribly jealous of divine thoughts. They do not care for you if you do not care for them.

So far I have been talking about thoughts that come from outside. But sometimes undivine thoughts arise from within. In the beginning it is difficult to distinguish between thoughts that are coming from outside and those that come from within. But gradually you will be able to feel the difference. The thoughts that are coming from outside can be driven back faster than the thoughts that attack you from within. But if impure and unlit thoughts arise from inside you, then you can do one of two things. You can try to feel that there is a hole right at the top of your head. Then make the thoughts flow out like a river which goes only in one direction and does not come back. They are then gone, and you are freed from them. The other method is to feel that you are the boundless ocean, all calm and quiet, and that the thoughts are like fish on the surface. The ocean pays no attention to the ripples of the fish.

Q Why is it that I am constantly bothered by thoughts?

A You are constantly bothered by thoughts because you are trying to meditate inside your mind. The very nature of the mind is to welcome thoughts—good thoughts, bad thoughts, divine thoughts, undivine thoughts. If you want to control the mind with your human will, then it will be like asking a monkey or a fly not to bother you. The very nature of a monkey is to bite and pinch; the very nature of a fly is to bother people.

The mind needs a superior power to keep it quiet. This superior power is the power of the soul. You have to bring to the fore the light of the soul from inside your heart. You are the possessor of two rooms: the heart-room and the mind-room. Right now the mind-room is obscure, unlit and impure; it is unwilling to open to the light. But the heart-room is always open to the light, for that is where the soul abides. Instead of concentrating on the mind, if you can concentrate and meditate on the reality that is inside the heart, then this reality will come forward.

If you stay in the mind-room all the time with the hope of illumining it from within, you will waste your time. If I want to light a candle, I must use a flame that is already burning, already illumined. The heart-room, fortunately, is already illumined. Once you are well-established in the heart, when you are surcharged with the soul's light, at that time you can enter into the mind-room to illumine the mind. But first you have to bring to the fore the soul's light, which is available most powerfully in the heart. The light of the soul will not torture or punish the mind. On the contrary, it will act like a most affectionate mother who feels that the imperfections of her child are her own imperfections. The heart will offer its light to the mind in order to transform the nature of the mind.

 I try to keep my mind from wandering during meditation, but I have very little success.

You are not exercising the capacity of your heart; you are only exercising the mind's power. Very often when I am concentrating on you, I see that your mind is rotating like a wheel. When the mind rotates, it is very difficult for the Supreme to act in your mind. But when your heart aspires even for a second, the Supreme opens the door and enters.

From now on, please try to feel that you do not have a mind at all. This does not mean that you will be like a brute or an animal. No! The human mind is not necessary because you have a superior instrument called the heart. If you can stay in your heart for five minutes, even if you do not pray or meditate, your consciousness will be raised.

The heart is like a fountain of peace, joy and love. You can sit at the base of the fountain and just enjoy. There is no need to pray to the Supreme to give you this or that, for you will get all the things that you want—and infinitely more—from this fountain. But you will get them in the Supreme's own way. If you can please the Supreme by staying always in the presence of your heart-fountain, your desires will be fulfilled most luminously. They may be the same desires that you have always had, but they will be touched on a very high level with luminosity. Before He fulfils these, the Supreme will transform each desire into aspiration with His light.

Q During a meditation, if there is a noise or disturbance, is it better to include it in the meditation or try to shut it out and pursue the meditation?

A Each seeker has to know his own standard of meditation. If you are a beginner, you should feel that anything that is not part of the meditation is like an intruder, and you should not allow an intruder to enter and disturb you. But if you are very advanced, and there is a disturbing sound or noise during your meditation, you can go deep into the sound itself and try to assimilate it. If you have the capacity, then in your own consciousness you can transform the attack of a powerful and challenging foreign element into an inner music, which will add to your meditation.

Q If I get creative ideas while I am meditating, should I follow them or should I just try to feel with my heart?

A As soon as you get a positive idea, you should consider it as a blessing from the Supreme. But you have to know what kind of inspiration it is. If it is an illumining inspiration, then you should follow it. If it is a creative inspiration to do something really good, then follow it. Any creative thought, anything that gives you a higher goal, should be followed. If a particular inspiration brings something new into your life and is able to transform your life, then that inspiration you should follow.

You may feel that inspiration is only in the mind whereas aspiration is only in the heart. But aspiration can be in the mind and inspiration can be in the heart. Inspiration can come to aspiration and vice versa. But inspiration must be of a very high type. Otherwise it cannot help you in your meditation at all. During meditation if you are inspired to make most delicious cookies, this kind of inspiration is a waste of time.

If it is an illumining inspiration, then please take these creative ideas as your own progress. When you get creative ideas, you have to know that they are creations from another world which want to manifest on the physical plane. When your meditation is over, you should write down the ideas. Afterwards you can elaborate on them.

Q Is it bad to expect some particular thing when we meditate?

A During your meditation just try to throw your inner and outer existence into the Supreme. You do not have to think of anything; just throw yourself into the sea of light, peace, bliss and power. But do not expect any particular divine quality or result, because then you are binding yourself and binding God. That is because human expectation is very limited. When you expect, immediately the mind acts, and then your receptivity becomes very limited. But if you do not expect, then the problem of receptivity becomes God's problem. At that time He is bound to give you everything in boundless measure, and at the same time to create the receptivity in you to receive what He has to offer.

The highest type of meditation is done in silence, with one objective: to please God in His own way. When you meditate, if you can feel that you are pleasing God in God's own way, then that is the best type of meditation. Otherwise, if you start meditating in order to get joy, you will get joy; but you will not get boundless joy, precisely because you have not pleased your Eternal Beloved, God, in His own way. What the Saviour Christ said is absolutely the highest truth: "Let Thy Will be done." Before you meditate, if you can offer the result of your meditation to the Source and say, "I wish to become Your perfect instrument so You can fulfil Yourself in and through me in Your own way," this is the highest, absolutely the highest, type of meditation.

Your mind has a flood of questions. There is but one teacher who can answer them. Who is the teacher? Your silence-loving heart.

The Silent Mind

Do you want to be happy? Then do not overestimate the power of your mind and do not under-estimate the light of your heart.

Your Spiritual Heart:
The Home of Peace

Your Spiritual Heart:
The Home of Peace

❦ Discovering Your Treasure Within

It is better to meditate in the heart than in the mind. The mind is like Times Square on New Year's Eve; the heart is like a lonely cave in the Himalayas. If you meditate in the mind, you will be able to meditate for perhaps five minutes; and out of that five minutes, for one minute you may meditate powerfully. After that you will feel your whole head getting tense. First you get joy and satisfaction; then you may feel a barren desert. But if you meditate in the heart, you acquire the capacity to identify yourself with the joy and satisfaction that you get, and then it becomes permanently yours.

If you meditate in the mind, you do not identify; you try to enter into something. When you want to enter into somebody else's house to get what that person has, either you have to break down the door or you have to plead with the owner of the house to open the door. When you plead, you feel that you are a stranger, and the owner of the house also feels that you are a stranger. Then he thinks, "Why should I allow a stranger to come into my house?" But if you use the heart, immediately the heart's qualities of softness, sweetness, love and purity come to the fore. When the owner of the house sees that you are all heart, immediately his own heart will become one with yours and he will let you in. He will feel your oneness with him and say, "What do you want from my house? If you need peace, then take it. If you need light, then take it."

One more thing: if you enter into the house with your mind, you will see some delicious fruit and immediately try to grab it. You are satisfied when you get it, even though you do not have the capacity to eat all the fruit. But if you use the heart, you will find that your capacity of receptivity is boundless. Again, if you use the mind, you will try to make a selection. You will say, "This piece of fruit is better; this one is worse." But if you enter into the house with your heart, you will feel that everything there is yours, and you will enjoy it all. The heart centre is the centre of oneness. First you identify with the truth and then, on the strength of your identification, you become the truth.

 Remain always in the sunshine of your heart until its illumining rays have also flooded your mind.

Heart and soul

If you meditate in the heart, you are meditating where the soul is. True, the light and consciousness of the soul permeate the whole body, but there is a specific place where the soul resides most of the time, and that is in the heart. If you want illumination, you have to get it from the soul, which is inside the heart. When you know what you want and where to find it, the sensible thing is to go to that place. Otherwise, it is like going to the hardware store to get groceries.

There is a vast difference between what you can get from the mind and what you can get from the heart. The mind is limited; the heart is unlimited. Deep within you are infinite peace, light and bliss. To get a limited quantity is an easy task. Meditation in the mind can give it to you. But you can get infinitely more if you meditate in the heart. Suppose you have the opportunity to work at two places. At one place you will earn two hundred dollars and at the other place five hundred dollars. If you are wise, you will not waste your time at the first place.

As long as you have tremendous faith in the mind, which complicates and confuses everything, you will be doomed to disappointment in your meditation. Ordinary people think that complication is wisdom. But spiritual people know that God is very simple. It is in simplicity, not in complexity, that the real truth abides.

I am not saying that the mind is always bad. No, it need not be. But the mind is limited. At most, what you can get from the mind is inspiration, which itself is limited. For real aspiration you have to go to the heart. Aspiration comes from the heart because the illumination of the soul is always there. When you meditate on the heart, not only do you get aspiration, but you also get the fulfilment of that aspiration: the soul's infinite peace, light and bliss.

Q I would like to know how one can reach the spiritual heart during meditation.

A The spiritual heart is located right in the centre of the chest. You can feel the spiritual heart when you are aspiring intensely, and you can also see it with the third eye. If you find it difficult to meditate on the spiritual heart, you can concentrate on the physical heart in the chest. But after you meditate there for a few months or for a year, you will feel that inside the ordinary human heart is the divine heart, and inside the divine heart is the soul. When you feel this, you will start meditating on the spiritual heart.

To reach the spiritual heart you have to feel that you do not have a mind, you do not have arms, you do not have legs, you have only the heart. Then you have to feel that you do not *have* the heart, but that you *are* the heart. When you can feel that you are the heart and nothing else, then easily you will be able to reach your spiritual heart during your meditation.

Q I find it very difficult to leave the mind and enter into the heart. What should I do?

A Just throw the mind and all its possessions into the heart. You may think, "If I throw away my mind, then how can I exist? I will become an idiot." But I tell you, the mind that you use to converse with people, the mind that you use to acquire information, the mind that you use for ordinary earthly activities, cannot take you even an inch toward God-realisation. It is lame. It is blind. It is deaf.

Try to feel that your whole existence, from the soles of your feet to the crown of your head, is the soul. Soulfully repeat, "I am the soul, I am the soul." If you can soulfully repeat this for five minutes, then the resistance of the physical mind will go away and only the soul will exist for you. Once you live in the soul and bring the soul's light forward, then this light will bring the physical mind to the higher regions or it will bring down peace from above. In either case, the physical mind as you know it will be transformed, and you will not have any more problems.

Q When I am meditating sometimes I have trouble distinguishing whether I really feel my heart or whether it is my mind that I am experiencing.

A If it is really your heart, then you will get a sense of pure satisfaction. If it is the mind, you may get satisfaction, but immediately you will also get doubt. Your experience will be attacked by other thoughts: "I am so bad, so impure, so ignorant. This morning I told a lie and yesterday I did something else that was bad, so how can I have this kind of satisfaction?" When that kind of idea comes, you will know that your experience was from the mind.

When you get an experience from the mind, you may temporarily feel very happy. But the joy will not remain, because you will not be able to establish your identification with what the mind has seen or felt or realised. But once you get an experience from the heart, immediately you will feel your oneness with it, and your joy will be lasting.

When you see a flower with your mind, you appreciate and admire it. But when you see it with your heart, immediately you feel that your heart is inside the flower or that the flower is inside your heart. So when you have an experience, if you are one with the experience itself, then you will know it is from the heart. But if you feel that the experience is something that you are achieving outside yourself, then it is from the mind.

Q What is the difference between going high and going deep in meditation?

A There is a great difference in the methods of meditation, although ultimately height and depth become one. When we want to go deep in meditation, we have to start our journey from the spiritual heart. We should feel that we are digging or travelling very deep into our heart. We are travelling inward, not backward or downward towards the feet. Below the knees the plane of inconscience starts. If we feel that we are going downward, then it is not spiritual depth we are getting but only the lower planes of consciousness. The spiritual heart is infinitely vast, so there is no limit to how deep we can go. We can never touch its boundaries, because the spiritual heart embodies the vast universe that we see, and at the same time it is larger and vaster than the universe.

When we want to go high in meditation, then we have to feel an upward direction in our meditation. Our aspiration is climbing, climbing fearlessly toward the Highest. We must pass through the thousand-petalled lotus at the top of the head. Again, the distance is infinitely vast. There is no end to our upward journey because we are travelling in Infinity. We are climbing toward the ever-transcending Beyond. In terms of distance, upward and inward are both infinite journeys toward one Goal, the Supreme.

We cannot go high by using the mind, however. We must pass through the mind, beyond the mind, and into the realm of the spiritual heart. The domain of the spiritual heart is infinitely higher and vaster than that of the highest mind. Far beyond the mind is the domain of the heart. The heart is boundless in every direction, so inside the heart is the highest height as well as the deepest depth.

The higher we can go, the deeper we can go. Again, the deeper we can go, the higher we can go. It works simultaneously. If we can meditate very powerfully, then we are bound to feel that we are going both very high and very deep. Height and depth go together, but they work in two different dimensions, so to speak. But if a person can go very high in his meditation, then he also has the capacity to go very deep.

Before we realise the Highest, we feel that there is a difference between height and depth. When we are climbing up we feel that we have reached a certain height, and when we are diving deep within, we feel that we have reached a certain depth. But height and depth are all in the mental consciousness. Once we go beyond the barrier of the mind and enter into the Universal Consciousness, we see everything as one and inseparable. At that time Reality is singing and dancing within us, and we become the Reality itself. It has no height, no depth, no length. It is all one and at the same time it is always transcending itself.

Q What will happen if I meditate on the navel centre?

A At this point in your spiritual development, it is not a good idea for you to meditate on the navel centre. This is the centre of dynamism, strength and power. If you misuse this dynamism, it becomes brutal aggression. The navel centre is also the emotional centre. With this emotion you can expand yourself and become the Infinite. But instead, if you do not have abundant purity in your nature, you will become a victim to earthly pleasure-life. You should meditate on the heart centre to get peace, love and joy. When you have these qualities, you will feel that peace itself is power, love itself is power, joy itself is power.

Q What is the relationship between the third eye and the heart centre?

A Let us say that the heart is consciousness and the third eye is light, although there is no actual difference between the two things. The third eye has infinite light and at the same time it is infinite light. The spiritual heart possesses infinite consciousness and at the same time it is infinite consciousness. But infinite light and infinite consciousness are one and the same. This moment the infinite light—which I am calling the third eye—is a building, and inside it the heart resides. But the next moment the infinite consciousness—

which I am calling the heart—can become the building, and the third eye will become the resident. They constantly change, because they are not really separate. Sometimes we see light before consciousness, while other times we see consciousness before light. The one which we see first, we feel is the source of the other. But a time comes when we see that light and consciousness are inseparable.

The heart usually embodies sweetness and love, and the third eye embodies power and illumination. But those who are very wise will feel that the third eye is also the heart, for what else is the heart except that which gives us satisfaction? And what gives us satisfaction? Only light! So if light from the third eye gives us satisfaction, then naturally we are dealing with the heart's quality. And what gives us the highest wisdom? Wisdom comes only when we go deep inside the inmost recesses of our heart, where Infinity, Eternity and Immortality play. To possess Infinity as our very own, to possess infinite light and bliss eternally as our very own, is real wisdom. So we can say that wisdom comes from the heart.

Q Is it desirable to try to open the third eye in meditation?

A The inner eye should be opened only when there is inner purity and maturity, and when neither the past nor the future will disturb you. Many times the vessel is not ready, but by means of tremendous determination a seeker does succeed in opening the third eye. Then the result is most discouraging and damaging. When you are not spiritually mature, if you see with your third eye that your mother is going to die tomorrow, then you will die today with worry and anxiety. Or if you become aware of some unfortunate incident that took place in your past, you will feel extremely miserable and you will not have the strength to continue going forward.

There are people who have opened the centre between the eyebrows before having opened their heart centre and, by the Grace of the Supreme, have not made serious mistakes in using this power. But most of the time, unless and until the heart centre is opened and the emotional part of one's nature is totally purified, the seeker will fall victim to merciless temptation if he opens the third eye. He will try to see something inwardly and immediately he will tell others, or he will try to enter into somebody out of curiosity to see what is happening in that person's nature. There are a thousand and one things which can eventually lead the seeker far, far away from the path of spirituality.

For beginners especially, it is always advisable to meditate on the heart centre. In fact, even if you are advanced, you should meditate there, because in the heart centre you get joy and become part and parcel of whatever you are meditating on. If you concentrate on the third eye, you may not have the feeling of oneness. You may see light, but you will feel that it is not yours; you will think that perhaps it was not light at all but just imagination or hallucination. Doubt may enter into your mind. But when you use the heart, the joy that you get you immediately feel is yours; the peace that you feel is yours; anything that you feel becomes yours. This is the heart's capacity for oneness.

O my heart, O heart of mine, you are my lifeboat. You sail the uncharted seas of ignorance and reach the Golden Shore of the Beyond. O sweet, sweeter, sweetest heart of mine, you are not only God's. God also is yours.

We concentrate because we want to reach the Goal. We meditate because we want to live in the heart of the Goal. We contemplate because we want to become the Goal.

Chapter 6

Concentration, Meditation & Contemplation:
Three Steps to Self-Fulfilment

Concentration, Meditation & Contemplation: Three Steps to Self-Fulfilment

❦ The Arrow and the Bow

Concentration is the arrow. Meditation is the bow.

When we concentrate, we focus all our energies upon some subject or object in order to unveil its mysteries. When we meditate, we rise from our limited consciousness into a higher consciousness where the vastness of silence reigns supreme.

Concentration wants to seize the knowledge it aims at. Meditation wants to identify itself with the knowledge it seeks.

Concentration does not allow disturbance, the thief, to enter into its armory. Meditation lets him in. Why? Just to catch the thief red-handed.

Concentration is the commander who orders the dispersed consciousness to come to attention.

Concentration and absolute firmness are not only inseparable but also interdependent divine warriors.

Concentration challenges the enemy to a duel and fights him. Meditation, with its silent smile, diminishes the challenge of the enemy.

Concentration says to God: "Father, I am coming to You." Meditation says to God: "Father, do come to me."

An aspirant has two genuine teachers: concentration and meditation. Concentration is always strict with the student; meditation is strict at times. But both of them are solemnly interested in their student's progress.

The Power of Concentration

Concentration means inner vigilance and alertness. There are thieves all around us and within us. Fear, doubt, worry and anxiety are inner thieves that are trying to steal our inner poise and peace of mind. When we learn how to concentrate, it is very difficult for these forces to enter into us. If doubt enters into our mind, the power of concentration will tear doubt to pieces. If fear enters into our mind, the power of concentration will chase away our fear. Right now we are victims to unlit, obscure, destructive thoughts, but a day will come when, on the strength of our concentration, disturbing thoughts will be afraid of us.

Concentration is the mind's dynamic will that operates in us for our acceptance of light and rejection of darkness. It is like a divine warrior in us. What concentration can do in our life of aspiration is unimaginable. It can easily separate Heaven from hell, so that we can live in the constant delight of Heaven and not in the perpetual worries, anxieties and tortures of hell while we are here on earth.

Concentration is the surest way to reach our goal, whether the goal is God-realisation or merely the fulfilment of human desires. A real aspirant sooner or later acquires the power of concentration either through the Grace of God, through constant practice or through his own aspiration.

The soul's indomitable will

When we concentrate we are like a bullet entering into something, or like a magnet pulling the object of concentration toward us. At that time we do not allow any thought to enter into our mind, whether it is divine or undivine, earthly or Heavenly, good or bad. In concentration the entire mind has to be focused on a particular object or subject. If we are concentrating on the petal of a flower, we try to feel that nothing else exists in the entire world but the petal. We look neither forward nor backward, upward nor inward; only we try to pierce the object with our one-pointed concentration. This is not an aggressive way of entering into something. This concentration comes directly from the soul's indomitable will, or will power.

When you want to practise concentration on an object, you should choose something that gives you immediate joy. If you have a Master, your Master's picture will give you immediate joy. If you do not have a Master, select something that is very beautiful, divine and pure, like a flower, for example.

We concentrate with the mind's illumining one-pointedness. We meditate with the heart's expanding vastness. We contemplate with the soul's fulfilling oneness.

Concentrating from the heart

Very often I hear aspirants say that they cannot concentrate for more than five minutes. After five minutes they get a headache or feel that their head is on fire. Why? It is because the power of their concentration is coming from the intellectual mind or, you can say, the disciplined mind. The mind knows that it must not wander; that much knowledge the mind has. But if the mind is to be utilised properly, in an illumined way, then the light of the soul has to come into it. When the light of the soul has entered into the mind, it is extremely easy to concentrate on something for hours. During this time there will be no thoughts or doubts or fears. No negative forces can enter into the mind if it is surcharged with the soul's light.

When we concentrate we have to feel that our power of concentration is coming from the heart centre and then going up to the third eye. The heart centre is where the soul is located. When we think of the soul at this time, it is better not to form any specific idea of it or try to think of what it looks like. Only we will think of it as God's representative or as boundless light and delight. When we concentrate, we try to feel that the soul's light is coming from the heart and passing through the third eye. Then, with this light, we enter into the object of concentration and identify with it. The final stage of concentration is to discover the hidden, ultimate Truth in the object of concentration.

Glimpsing the Infinite: Meditation

When we concentrate we focus our attention on one particular thing. But when we meditate we feel that we have the capacity deep within us to see many things, deal with many things and welcome many things all at the same time. When we meditate, we try to expand ourselves, like a bird spreading its wings. We try to expand our finite consciousness and enter into the Universal Consciousness where there is no fear, jealousy or doubt but only joy, peace and divine power.

Meditation means our conscious growth into the Infinite. When we meditate what we actually do is enter into a vacant, calm, silent mind and allow ourselves to be nourished and nurtured by Infinity itself. When we are in meditation we want only to commune with God. Now I am speaking in English and you are able to understand me because you know English well. Similarly, when we know how to meditate well, we will be able to commune with God, for meditation is the language we use to speak with God.

A sea of tranquillity

Meditation is like going to the bottom of the sea, where everything is calm and tranquil. On the surface there may be a multitude of waves, but the sea is not affected below. In its deepest depths, the sea is all silence. When we start meditating, first we try to reach our own inner existence, our true existence—that is to say, the bottom of the sea. Then, when the waves come from the outside world, we are not affected. Fear, doubt, worry and all the earthly turmoil will just wash away, because inside us is solid peace. Thoughts cannot trouble us, because our mind is all peace, all silence, all oneness. Like fish in the sea, they jump and swim but leave no mark. So when we are in our highest meditation we feel that we are the sea, and the animals in the sea cannot affect us. We feel that we are the sky, and all the birds flying past cannot affect us. Our mind is the sky and our heart is the infinite sea. This is meditation.

Becoming the Truth: Contemplation

Through concentration we become one-pointed. Through meditation we expand our consciousness into the Vast and enter into its consciousness. But in contemplation we grow into the Vast itself, and its consciousness becomes our very own. In contemplation we are at once in our deepest concentration and our highest meditation. The truth that we have seen and felt in meditation, we grow into and become totally one with in contemplation. When we are concentrating on God, we may feel God right in front of us or beside us. When we are meditating, we are bound to feel Infinity, Eternity and Immortality within us. But when we are contemplating, we will see that we ourselves are God, that we ourselves are Infinity, Eternity and Immortality.

Contemplation means our conscious oneness with the infinite, eternal Absolute. In contemplation the Creator and the creation, the lover and the Beloved, the knower and the known become one. One moment we are the divine lover and God is the Supreme Beloved. The next moment we change roles. In contemplation we become one with the Creator and see the whole universe inside us. At that time when we look at our own existence, we do not see a human being. We see something like a dynamo of light, peace and bliss.

> *Concentration gives the message of alertness. Meditation gives the message of vastness. Contemplation gives the message of inseparable oneness.*

Meditation vs. contemplation

If we meditate on a specific divine quality such as light or peace or bliss, or if we meditate in an abstract way on Infinity, Eternity or Immortality, then all the time we will feel an express train going forward inside us. We are meditating on peace, light or bliss while the express train is constantly moving. Our mind is calm and quiet in the vastness of Infinity, but there is a movement; a train is going endlessly toward the goal. We are envisioning a goal, and meditation is taking us there.

In contemplation it is not like that. In contemplation we feel the entire universe and farthest Goal deep inside ourselves. When we are contemplating we feel that we are holding within ourselves the entire universe with all its infinite light, peace, bliss and truth. There is no thought, no form, no idea.

In contemplation everything is merged into one stream of consciousness. In our highest contemplation we feel that we are nothing but consciousness itself; we are one with the Absolute. But in our highest meditation there is a dynamic movement going on in our consciousness. We are fully aware of what is happening in the inner and the outer world, but we are not affected. In contemplation, too, we are unaffected by what is going on in the inner and outer worlds, but our whole existence has become part and parcel of the universe, which we are holding deep inside us.

How To

Exercises in Concentration

1 **The dot.** If you want to develop the power of concentration, then here is an exercise you can try. First wash your face and eyes properly with cold water. Then make a black dot on the wall at eye level. Stand facing the dot, about ten inches away, and concentrate on it. After a few minutes, try to feel that when you are breathing in, your breath is actually coming from the dot, and that the dot is also breathing in, getting its breath from you. Try to feel that there are two persons: you and the black dot. Your breath is coming from the dot and its breath is coming from you.

In ten minutes, if your concentration is very powerful, you will feel that your soul has left you and entered into the black dot on the wall. At this time try to feel that you and your soul are conversing. Your soul is taking you into the soul's world for realisation, and you are bringing the soul into the physical world for manifestation. In this way you can develop your power of concentration very easily. But this method has to be practised. There are many things which are very easy with practice, but just because we do not practise them we do not get the result.

2 **Vision and reality.** Another exercise you can try is this. First make a very small circle on the wall at eye-level, and inside it make a black dot. It should be black; not blue or red or any other colour. Then stand facing the wall, about three and a half feet away, and focus your attention on the circle. Your eyes should be relaxed and half-open. Let the force of your concentration come from the middle of your forehead. After three or four minutes open your eyes fully and try to feel that, from head to foot, you are all eyes. Your whole physical existence has become nothing but vision, and that vision is focussed on the dot inside the circle. Then start making the object of your concentration smaller. After a few seconds try to feel that your whole body has become as tiny as the dot on the wall. Try to feel that the dot is another part of your own existence. Then enter into the dot, pierce through it and go to the other side. From the other side of the dot, look back and see your own body. Your physical body is on one side, but on the strength of your concentration you have sent your subtle body to the other side of the dot. Through your subtle body you are seeing your physical body, and through your physical body you are seeing your subtle body.

> *I concentrate for success in my life's journey.*
> *I meditate for progress in my life's journey.*
> *I contemplate for God-process in my life's journey.*

When you began to concentrate, your physical body became all vision. At that time the dot was your reality. When you entered into the dot, then vision and reality became one. You were the vision and you were also the reality. When you looked back at yourself from the dot, the process was reversed. At that time you became the vision outside yourself, and the place to which you returned—your body—was the reality. Then, the vision and the reality became one again. When you can see the vision and the reality in this way, your concentration is absolutely perfect. When your power of concentration can bring you to the other side of the point which you were calling reality, at that time your whole existence will be far beyond both vision and reality. And when you can feel that you have transcended your vision and your reality, you will have boundless power.

If you are my disciple, when you concentrate on the black dot inside the circle, you can try to see your own self there—your own face of aspiration. Feel that you exist there and nowhere else. Then try to feel that your existence, your face, your consciousness—everything—have been replaced by mine. Once you feel that your previous existence has been totally replaced by mine, you will have established your inseparable oneness with me, and my will power is bound to come into your life.

3 **My heart-friend.** Just as you can concentrate on the tip of your finger, or on a candle or any other material object, you can also concentrate on your heart. You may close your eyes or look at a wall, but all the time you are thinking of your heart as a dear friend. When this thinking becomes most intense, when it absorbs your entire attention, then you have gone beyond ordinary thinking and entered into concentration. You cannot look physically at your spiritual heart, but you can focus all your attention on it. Then gradually the power of your concentration enters into the heart and takes you completely out of the realm of the mind.

If you do not have purity in abundant measure, if countless earthly desires are in possession of the heart, then before concentrating on the heart you should invoke purity. Purity is the feeling of having a living shrine deep in the inmost recesses of your heart. When you feel the divine presence of an inner shrine, automatically you are purified. At that time your concentration on the heart will be most effective.

4. **The heartbeat of life.** Some seekers like to concentrate on their heartbeat. If you want to do this, do not be afraid that the heart will stop and you will die. If you want to be a real hero in your spiritual life, you can practise concentrating on your heartbeat. This is the golden opportunity for you to enter into the endless life. Each time you hear the sound of your heartbeat, immediately feel there your infinite, immortal life.

5. **The inner flower.** For this exercise you will need a flower. With your eyes half closed and half open, look at the entire flower for a few seconds. While you are concentrating, try to feel that you yourself are this flower. At the same time, try to feel that this flower is growing in the inmost recesses of your heart. Feel that you are the flower and you are growing inside your heart.

Then, gradually try to concentrate on one particular petal of the flower. Feel that this petal which you have selected is the seed-form of your reality-existence. After a few minutes, concentrate on the entire flower again, and feel that it is the Universal Reality. In this way go back and forth, concentrating first on the petal—the seed-form of your reality—and then on the entire flower—the Universal Reality. While you are doing this, please try not to allow any thought to enter into your mind. Try to make your mind absolutely calm, quiet and tranquil.

After some time, please close your eyes and try to see the flower that you have been concentrating on inside your heart. Then, in the same way that you concentrated on the physical flower, kindly concentrate on the flower inside your heart, with your eyes closed.

Exercises in Meditation

1 **The heart-rose.** Kindly imagine a flower inside your heart. Suppose you prefer a rose. Imagine that the rose is not fully blossomed; it is still a bud. After you have meditated for two or three minutes, please try to imagine that petal by petal the flower is blossoming. See and feel the flower blossoming petal by petal inside your heart. Then, after five minutes, try to feel that there is no heart at all; there is only a flower inside you called 'heart'. You do not have a heart, but only a flower. The flower has become your heart or your heart has become a flower.

After seven or eight minutes, please feel that this flower-heart has covered your whole body. Your body is no longer here; from your head to your feet you can feel the fragrance of the rose. If you look at your feet, immediately you experience the fragrance of a rose. If you look at your knee, you experience the fragrance of a rose. If you look at your hand, you experience the fragrance of a rose. Everywhere the beauty, fragrance and purity of the rose have permeated your entire body. When you feel from your head to your feet that you have become only the beauty, fragrance, purity and delight of the rose, then you are ready to place yourself at the Feet of your Beloved Supreme.

2 **A river of consciousness.** When you meditate, try to bring three things into your mind: purity in your entire being, humility in your entire being and gratitude in every limb, in every cell. When you breathe in and breathe out, feel that a river of divine consciousness is flowing through you without any coercion or exertion. Feel that this river of divine consciousness is flowing in and out with constant oneness with the Source, the Supreme.

3 **Offer it to God.** When you breathe in, feel that you are breathing in God's immortal qualities and when you breathe out, feel that you are offering God your ignorance.

Right now we feel that ignorance is our possession. Although we say that ignorance is very bad, we don't want to give it away. But we have to know that ignorance is not our real possession; our real possessions are peace, light and bliss. During your meditation, offer to God your false possessions and receive from God your real possessions. Ask God to take what you have and what you are and to give you what He has and what He is. What you have is aspiration, the inner cry to become divine. What you are is ignorance. Ask God to take both your aspiration and your ignorance and to give you what He has and what He is: Infinity, Eternity and Immortality.

4 **The golden being.** Try to feel that you are inside the Heart of God, the Inner Pilot. Although you have not seen the Supreme, just mentally imagine a human being who is absolutely golden. Imagine that He is right in front of you and you are inside His Heart or in His Lap or at His Feet. Do not think that you are eighteen or forty or sixty years old. Think that you are only one month old and that you are inside the very Heart of the Supreme or in His Lap.

5 **The vastness of the sky.** Keep your eyes half open and imagine the vast sky. In the beginning try to feel that the sky is in front of you; later try to feel that you are as vast as the sky, or that you are the vast sky itself.

After a few minutes please close your eyes and try to see and feel the sky inside your heart. Please feel that you are the universal heart, and that inside you is the sky that you meditated upon and identified yourself with. Your spiritual heart is infinitely vaster than the sky, so you can easily house the sky within yourself.

An Exercise in Contemplation

1 **Hide-and-seek.** Try to imagine a golden being and feel that he is infinitely more beautiful than the most beautiful child that you have ever seen on earth. This being is your Beloved Lord Supreme. You are a divine lover and the golden being is your Beloved Lord Supreme.

Now, try to imagine that your own existence and also that of your Beloved are on the top of a mountain in the Himalayas or at the very bottom of the Pacific Ocean, whichever is easier for you. Once you feel this, then inwardly smile.

After a few seconds please feel that you yourself are the Beloved Supreme and that the golden being is the divine lover. It is like a divine game of hide-and-seek. When you become the Supreme Beloved, the divine lover seeks you, and when you become the divine lover, you search for your Beloved Supreme. One moment you are the supreme lover and the next moment you are the Supreme Beloved.

In the beginning, please do this with your eyes half open. When you become expert, you can close your eyes.

Q&A

Q When I sit down to meditate, I have to concentrate so hard on keeping my mind still that I cannot contact my inner self.

A You may not know it, but you are doing the right thing. When you are trying to make your mind calm and quiet, you are concentrating. In concentration, you try to control your thoughts and emotions. Concentration has to pave the way for meditation. In order to meditate you must have already disciplined your emotional life and restless mind to some extent. When you are successful in chasing away all the thoughts that disturb your mind, sooner or later your inner self will come to the fore, like the blazing sun clearing away the veil of clouds. Right now, the inner sun is overcast with clouds: thoughts, ideas, doubts, fears and so forth. When you can chase them away, you will see that your inner self is shining, bright and radiant, right in front of you.

Q How can one know whether one is doing concentration or meditation?

A When it is concentration, there is tremendous intensity; it is like an arrow entering into a target. If you feel an intense force energising you, then this is the result of your concentration. But in meditation, there is peace and a feeling of vastness all around, especially in the mind. If you feel deep within an immense sea of peace, light and bliss, then that is due to your meditation. Meditation is all peace, poise and vastness. Intensity is there, but the intensity is flooded with luminosity. In concentration there need not be and often is not the highest luminosity.

Also, concentration wants immediate results. It is ready to do anything to achieve its goal. Meditation feels that it has infinite time at its disposal. That does not mean that meditation neglects the fleeting time. No, it appreciates fleeting time, but inside fleeting time it sees endless time. That is why meditation has infinite peace inside it.

Do not give any preference to either experience. If the Supreme wants to concentrate in you and through you, then you will allow it. Again, if He wants to meditate in and through you, that also you will allow.

Q Once we have learned how to meditate, should we no longer practise concentration?

A As a general rule, seekers who are just entering the spiritual life should start with concentration for a few months at least. Once they have learned to concentrate, then meditation becomes easy. But even when you are able to meditate, it is a good idea to concentrate for a few minutes before you start your daily meditation. If you concentrate, you are like a runner who clears the track of obstacles before he starts to run. Once the track is cleared, you can run very fast. At that time you become like an inner express train that stops only at the final destination.

Q After we have finished meditating, how do we go about contemplating?

A Contemplation comes after many years, when one is very advanced in the spiritual life. Contemplation is the highest rung of the inner ladder. Very, very few spiritual aspirants have the capacity to do even limited contemplation, and they certainly cannot do so at their sweet will.

Contemplation must be mastered before God-realisation, so it cannot be ignored or avoided. But, in your case, the necessity for contemplation has not come because your concentration and your meditation are not yet perfect. When your concentration is perfect and your meditation is perfect, at that time your contemplation will also have to be perfected. Then you will really be able to enter into the Highest.

How can you succeed in your outer life when you do not have the power of concentration? How can you proceed in your inner life when you do not have the peace of meditation?

Our prayer gives us a peaceful life. Our meditation gives us a beautiful heart.

Two Wings to Fly: Prayer & Meditation

Chapter 7
Two Wings to Fly: Prayer & Meditation

❦ I Pray, I Meditate

I pray. Why do I pray? I pray because I need God. I meditate. Why do I meditate? I meditate because God needs me.

When I pray, I think that God is high above me, above my head. When I meditate, I feel that God is deep inside me, inside my heart.

Prayer says, "I am helpless, I am impure, I am weak. I need You, O Lord Supreme, to strengthen me, to purify me, to illumine me, to perfect me, to immortalise me. I need You, O Lord Supreme."

Meditation says, "Lord Supreme, out of Your infinite bounty You have chosen me to be Your instrument to manifest You here on earth in Your own way. You could have chosen somebody else to play the role, but You have granted me the golden opportunity. To You I offer my constant gratitude, my gratitude-heart."

Prayer is purity. It purifies the mind, which is always subject to doubt, fear, worry and anxiety, and is always assailed by wrong thoughts and wrong movements. When we pray, purification takes place in our minds, and purity increases our God-receptivity. In fact, purity is nothing short of God-receptivity. Each time we pray, our inner receptacle becomes large, larger, largest. Then purity, beauty, light and delight can enter into that receptacle and sport together in the inmost recesses of our heart.

Meditation is luminosity. It illumines our heart. When illumination takes place in our heart, insecurity and the sense of want disappear. At that time we sing the song of inseparable oneness with the Universal Consciousness and Transcendental Consciousness. When our heart is illumined, the finite in us enters into the Infinite and becomes the Infinite itself. The bondage of millennia leaves us, and the freedom of infinite Truth and Light welcomes us.

Prayer says to God, "Beloved Supreme, You are mine. I claim You as my own, very own. Do grant me Your divine qualities in boundless measure so that I can be Your perfect instrument here on earth."

Meditation says to God, "O Beloved Supreme, I am Yours. You can utilise me at Your sweet Will at every moment, throughout Eternity. Through me fulfil Yourself here on earth and there in Heaven."

The best definition of prayer is to practise it daily. The best definition of meditation is to experience it soulfully. The best definition of yoga is to live it sincerely. The best definition of God is ☙ love Him, and Him only, unconditionally.

Prayer is something absolutely intense and upward-soaring. When we pray, we feel that our existence is a one-pointed flame soaring upward. From the soles of our feet to the crown of our head, our whole being is invoking and calling upwards. The very nature of prayer is to reach God by going up.

Meditation is something wide and vast that ultimately expands into the Infinite. When we meditate, we throw ourselves into a vast expanse, into an infinite sea of peace and bliss, or we welcome the infinite Vast into us. Prayer rises; meditation spreads. Meditation is constantly growing and expanding into peace, light and delight. When we meditate, we gradually see, feel and grow into the entire universe of light and delight.

Thy Will be done

When we pray, often there is a subtle desire for something, a hankering to get something or to become something. We may call it aspiration because we are praying to become good, or to have something divine which we do not have, or to be free from fear, jealousy, doubt and so forth. But there is always a subtle tendency on our part to push or pull from within.

Also, there is always the feeling of being—let us use the term 'a divine beggar'. We feel that God is high above, while we are down below. We see a yawning gulf between His existence and ours. We are looking up at Him and crying to Him, but we do not know when or to what extent God is going to fulfil our prayers. We feel that we are helpless. We just ask, and then we wait for one drop, two drops or three drops of compassion, light or peace to descend upon us. Sometimes there is a feeling of give-and-take. We say, "Lord, I am giving You my prayer, so now You please do something for me. You please help me, save me, fulfil me."

But in meditation we do not ask God for any help, boon or divine quality; we just enter into the sea of His Reality. At that time God gives us more than we could ever imagine. In prayer we feel that we have nothing and God has everything. In meditation we know that whatever God has, either we also have or we will someday have. We feel that whatever God is, we also are, only we have not yet brought our divinity forward. When we pray, we ask God for what we want. But when we meditate, God showers on us everything that we need. We see and feel that the whole universe is at our disposal. Heaven and earth do not belong to someone else; they are our own reality.

The highest prayer is, "Let Thy Will be done." This is absolutely the highest reach of prayer, and it is also the beginning of meditation. Where prayer stops its journey, meditation begins. In meditation we say nothing, we think nothing, we want nothing. In the meditation-world the Supreme is acting in and through us for His own fulfilment. The prayer-world is always asking for something. But the meditation-world says, "God is not blind or deaf. He knows what He has to do to fulfil Himself in and through me. So I shall just grow into the highest in soulful silence."

Two roads to realisation
Prayer and meditation are like two roads. Prayer is always for our own sake, for our own life, for the near and dear ones in our own small world. If we pray well, God will give us two wings to fly above. But meditation is for the entire world. When we meditate well, we feel our oneness with our own expanded reality. If we can follow the road of meditation, we are hero-warriors. At that time we can carry on our giant shoulders the entire burden of humanity. When we fulfil our meditation-life, we fulfil not only God but also ourselves and the entire world.

For those who want to realise the Highest, I always say that meditation is of paramount importance. But there have been saints in the West who have realised God through prayer only. They did not know the concept of meditation. But the intensity of their prayers and their aspiration carried them into the world of meditation and beyond. Both approaches are effective. When we pray, we go up to God; when we meditate, God comes down to us. Ultimately the result can be the same.

The necessity of prayer
If one becomes advanced in meditation, prayer is not necessary. At that time we will realise that God always knows our needs and cares for us infinitely more than we care for ourselves. Prayer is not necessary, because

we belong to God and are His property. When we renounce our personal claims and surrender ourselves completely, at that time God claims us as His very own and makes us His chosen instruments.

But until we become very advanced in the spiritual life and feel our oneness with God, prayer is necessary. If we get something through prayer, we can tell the world, "I prayed for it; that's why I got it. Look, I have this kind of closeness with my Father!" We are like children who are hungry. We ask our mother for food, and she feeds us. Yes, she would have fed us on her own, but the fact that we ask for food and our mother listens to our request gives us joy. It convinces our minds that she really cares for us. Because of our inner connection and closeness with our mother, we can ask her for whatever we want.

God could do everything for us unconditionally, but this would not give us the same kind of satisfaction. In a race, if you run the whole course, then you will be delighted if you receive a trophy. You ran very fast and finished with so much trouble, and you feel that you have earned the trophy. But if somebody who has just been a spectator gets a trophy, that person will not feel satisfied, because he has done nothing to earn it. God can give everything unconditionally, but we get more satisfaction if He gives us something after we have prayed for it or worked for it.

 What my prayer needs is a patience-tree. What my meditation needs is a gratitude-flower.

We have to know, however, that when we pray we feel that we as individuals are separated from God. We feel that He is at one place and we are somewhere else. At that time we are not in our highest consciousness where we feel that we are one with God. If we feel that we and God are one, then the question of prayer does not arise, for at that time our needs are His needs.

Prayer, we can say, intensifies our intimacy with the Supreme, whereas meditation increases our oneness with the Supreme. First we have to feel that we and God are intimate friends; then we can realise our oneness-reality with God. Before we meditate, if we can pray for a few minutes, we can develop our intimate connection with the Supreme. Then we can meditate to become one with Him.

In the highest spiritual life there is no comparison between meditation and prayer. Meditation is infinitely deeper and wider than prayer. In the West, prayer is used by seekers with considerable efficacy. But a real seeker who wants to go to the Ultimate Beyond must feel that meditation is the higher rung in the ladder to God-realisation. When we meditate, we see, feel and grow into the entire universe of light and delight.

Q I would like to know whether I should pray for something I want or whether I should just pray for God's Will to be done.

A To pray for God's Will to be done is the highest form of prayer. But a beginner finds it almost impossible to pray to God sincerely to fulfil him in God's own way. So when the seeker is just starting out, it is advisable for him to pray to God for whatever he feels he needs most, whether it is patience, purity, sincerity, humility, peace and so forth. Then God will give the seeker a little peace, light and bliss, which are the precursors of something infinite that is going to come into his inner being. Once the seeker has received some peace, light and bliss and they have become established to some extent in his inner being, at that time he will have some confidence in God's operation and also in his own life of aspiration.

When one is making very fast progress or is a little advanced, he feels that there is some reality within himself and that this reality is not going to disappoint or desert him. Then he feels that God is fully aware of what he desperately needs and is eager to supply him with those things. When a seeker feels this kind of confidence within him, that is the time for the seeker to pray, "Let Thy Will be done." At that time he can sincerely say, "God, I want to please You only in Your own way."

 Prayer is best expressed in my day-to-day life when my prayer has become a spontaneous, self-giving surrender to the Will of God.

Q How can we pray effectively?

A To pray most effectively, your prayer should be outwardly inaudible, but you may form a sentence of a few words that will convince your aspiring mind. The heart is already aspiring, but the mind needs to aspire. So it is better for the prayer to take the form of words.

You may form the sentence by writing it on the tablet of your heart. Then try to see it there. Once the words are written, you can return many times to see them. If you want to repeat the sentence, good, but it is not necessary. When you repeat your prayer you have a choice. Either write it once on the tablet of your heart and read it again and again, or continuously write the same thing—whichever gives you more joy.

How can we make our prayer most intense?

 You can make your prayer most intense by using your gratitude-heart. While you are praying, you should feel that the prayer is coming from your heart, and you have to feed the prayer with gratitude. If you do not nourish the prayer with your gratitude-heart, then your prayer will not be intense. Nothing divine will be intense unless and until you are grateful to the Supreme. At every moment your gratitude-heart must feed your inner cry. This will intensify your prayer, your aspiration, your dedication and all your spiritual qualities.

> *When I pray, I kneel down devotedly and se-cretly. When I meditate, I lift up my heart soulfully and perfectly.*

 What is the best way to pray for others?

 First, before you even start praying, you should invoke the presence of the Supreme. When you invoke His presence, He will definitely come in a subtle form. You will not see Him in a human body, but you will be able to feel His presence. Inside God's presence, try to see and feel the person for whom you are praying. If you can invoke the Supreme's presence and feel inside His presence those for whom you are praying, that will be the most effective way of helping them through your prayer.

But before asking the Supreme through your prayer to help someone, first ask Him whether you are supposed to pray for that particular person. If you get a message or inner feeling that you should pray for that particular person, only then should you do it. Suppose somebody is very sick and you want to pray to God to cure him.

You have to know that perhaps God wants him to have this experience right now for his own inner development. You have to know that God has infinitely more love for that particular person than you or any other human being could possibly have. If you ask God to cure him, you may only be opposing God's Will. But if you pray for oneness with God's Will, then God may say, "You have become one with My Will. Now I will be happy if you ask me to cure the person."

 Do you pray sometimes?

To be quite frank with you, I do not pray; nor do I have any need for meditation, although I do meditate. After one has realised the Highest and become consciously one with the Absolute Supreme, one has no need to pray or meditate. But I have a number of disciples, so I meditate for them as I used to meditate for myself many years ago. When I meditate on them, prayer is automatically there because, in trying to help them in their spiritual awakening, I am invoking God's infinite blessings, light and compassion to offer to them.

They say that prayer is the daughter of suffering. But I say that prayer is the mother of delight.

I purify my body by chanting God's name. I purify my vital by serving God. I purify my mind by emptying my mind for God. I purify my heart by meditating on God's Compassion-Love.

The Power of Mantra

Chapter 8
The Power of Mantra

❧ Chanting: Mantra and Japa

A mantra is an incantation. It can be a syllable, a word, a few words or a sentence. When you repeat a mantra many times, it is called japa. A mantra represents a particular aspect of God, and each mantra has a special significance and inner power.

If you cannot enter into your deepest meditation because your mind is restless, this is an opportunity to utilise a mantra. You can repeat "Supreme" or *Aum* or "God" for a few minutes. Also, if you get an attack on the emotional vital plane and wrong thoughts or wrong vibrations are entering into you, you can repeat *Aum* or the name of the Supreme. In this case try to do it as fast as possible. When you are trying to cleanse your mind of impurities, you must chant as if you were running to catch a moving train. During regular japa, however, just say the mantra in a normal but soulful way. But do not prolong it too much; otherwise, you will not have time to chant the five hundred or six hundred times that may be necessary.

Achieving overall purification

If you want to achieve overall purification of your nature, then japa can be most effective if you do it in a systematic way, step by step. On the first day repeat *Aum* or "Supreme" or whatever mantra your Master has given you five hundred times. The next day repeat it six hundred times; the day after that, seven hundred; and so on, until you reach twelve hundred at the end of one

93

week. Then begin descending each day until you reach five hundred again. In this way you can climb up the tree and climb down the tree.

Please continue this exercise, week by week, for a month. Whether you want to change your name or not, the world will give you a new name: purity.

While you are doing japa, if you make a mistake and lose track of the number, no harm. Just continue with some likely number. The purpose of counting is to separate your consciousness from other things. When you count, you will not be thinking of someone else or something else. While you are counting, you should try to enter into the world of silence which is deep inside the mantra. Then you will not have to count at all. Your consciousness will be focused on what you are repeating and you will begin to feel that you are meditating only on the inner significance of the mantra.

In most cases it is best to chant a mantra aloud. But after doing this for a few minutes, if you can feel that there is somebody inside—your inner being—who is repeating the mantra on your behalf, then you do not have to chant out loud. In the silence of your heart your inner being will do japa on your behalf.

Japa should be done in the morning or during the day, not just before going to bed. If japa is done when the body is tired and wants to enter into the world of sleep, the mind will just become agitated and lose its one-pointed concentration. You will only be working the mind mechanically, and you will derive no benefit. If japa is not done sincerely and soulfully, it is useless. So it should be done only one hundred, two hundred or at most three hundred times before going to bed. If you meditate before going to bed, you will invoke peace, light and bliss, but if you do japa five hundred to twelve hundred times before going to bed, you will invoke power and energy, and you will not be able to sleep.

Often when you complete your japa, you will hear the mantra being repeated inside your heart. Your mouth is not saying it, but your inner being has started repeating the mantra spontaneously.

The inner sound

During meditation sometimes seekers hear the sound of *Aum*, although they have not said it out loud and nobody in the room has chanted it out loud. This means that inwardly somebody has chanted *Aum* or is chanting it, and the meditation room has preserved the sound.

Chanting a mantra can be done while you are driving or walking along the street or standing in a public place. If you silently chant while walking along the street, you are not withdrawing; only you are trying to protect yourself from the unaspiring world. You are increasing your inner strength and inner capacity. Then, when you are inwardly strong, you will no longer have to chant; you can just move around and not be disturbed.

 Any method of spiritual discipline will have two inevitable and inseparable wings: absolute patience and firm resolution.

If you are trying to maintain a high consciousness when you are in a public place, it may be difficult for you to go deep within and bring peace to the fore. But even when you are surrounded by the noise and bustle of the outer world, you can easily bring forward a louder sound. This louder sound is not a destructive sound but one that contains indomitable power. It gives you a feeling of how potentially great and divine you are. If you can bring to the fore the divine inner sound, which comes from your heart, or if you can enter into that inner sound, then you will see that the outer noise of the world is no match for it. To your surprise, you will see that the sounds which disturbed you one minute ago will not bother you anymore. On the contrary, you will get a sense of achievement because instead of hearing noise you will hear divine music that is produced by your inner being.

The Essence of *Aum*

Aum is a single, indivisible sound; it is the vibration of the Supreme. *Aum* is the seed-sound of the universe, for with this sound God set into motion the first vibration of His creation. The most powerful of all mantras is *Aum; Aum* is the mother of all mantras. At every second God is creating Himself anew inside *Aum*. Without birth is *Aum,* without death is *Aum*. Nothing else but *Aum* existed, exists and will forever exist.

Aum is a single Sanskrit character represented in English by three letters, but pronounced as one syllable. The syllable *Aum* is indivisible, but each portion of it represents a different aspect of the Supreme. The 'A' represents and embodies the consciousness of God the Creator, the 'U' embodies the consciousness of God the Preserver and the 'M' embodies the consciousness of God the Transformer. Taken together, *Aum* is the spontaneous cosmic rhythm with which God embraces the universe.

The sound of *Aum* is unique. Generally we hear a sound when two things are struck together. But *Aum* needs no such action. It is *anahata,* or unstruck; it is the soundless sound. A Yogi or spiritual Master can hear *Aum* self-generated in the inmost recesses of his heart.

There are many ways to chant *Aum*. When you chant it loudly, you feel the omnipotence of the Supreme. When you chant it softly, you feel the delight of the Supreme. When you chant it silently, you feel the peace of the Supreme.

The universal *Aum* put forth by the Supreme is an infinite ocean. The individual *Aum* chanted by man is a drop in that ocean, but it cannot be separated from the ocean, and it can claim the infinite ocean as its very own. When man chants *Aum,* he touches and calls forth the cosmic vibration of the supreme Sound.

It is best to chant *Aum* out loud, so its sound can vibrate even in your physical ears and permeate your entire body. This will convince your outer mind and give you a greater sense of joy and achievement. When chanting out loud, the 'M' sound should last at least three times as long as the 'AU' sound.

No matter how grave a person's mistakes, if he chants *Aum* many times from the inmost depths of his heart, the omnipotent Compassion of the Supreme will forgive him. In the twinkling of an eye the power of *Aum* transforms darkness into light, ignorance into knowledge and death into Immortality.

Aum has infinite power; just by repeating *Aum* one can realise God. Everything that God has and everything that God is, within and without, *Aum* can offer, because *Aum* is at once the life, the body and the breath of God.

Q You said we can increase our purity by repeating *Aum* five hundred times a day. But for me to repeat *Aum* five hundred times a day is very difficult. Can you advise me what to do?

A If it is difficult for you to do it at one stretch, then you can do it in segments. At ten different times you can repeat it only fifty times. Say that during the day you want to drink ten glasses of water. If you try to drink all ten glasses of water at once, you will not be able to do it. So you drink one glass now and after an interval of an hour or two another glass. Then easily you can drink ten glasses of water. Instead of chanting *Aum* five hundred times all at once, early in the morning you can repeat it fifty times. Then, in an hour's time, do another fifty. Each hour if you repeat *Aum* fifty times, it won't take you more than a minute or two each time. Since you can easily offer two minutes in an hour to God, you can do your chanting in this way.

The Power of Mantra

Music has and also is the key to unlock the Heart-Door of the Supreme.

Music & Meditation: Sound & Silence

Music & Meditation: Sound & Silence

❦ A Universal Language

Music is the inner or universal language of God. I do not speak French or German or Italian, but if music is played from any of those countries, immediately the heart of the music enters into my heart, or my heart enters into the music. At that time no outer communication is needed; the inner communion of the heart is enough. My heart is communing with the heart of the music, and in our communion we become inseparably one.

Meditation and music cannot be separated. When we cry from the inmost recesses of our heart for peace, light and bliss, that is the best type of meditation. Next to meditation is music, soulful music, the music that stirs and elevates our aspiring consciousness. We cannot meditate twenty-four hours a day, but we can meditate, perhaps, for two hours a day. At other times we can play music or listen to music. When we play or hear soulful music, psychic music, immediately we are transported to a higher realm of consciousness. When we play music soulfully, we go high, higher, highest.

Each time we hear soulful music, we get inspiration and delight. In the twinkling of an eye, music can elevate our consciousness. But if we also pray and meditate, then we are undoubtedly more illumined and fulfilled than a music-lover who is not consciously leading a spiritual life. Each spiritual musician is consciously spreading God's light on earth. God is the cosmic Player, the eternal Player, and we are His instruments. But there comes a time in the process of our evolution when we feel that we have become totally one with Him. At that time, we are no longer instruments; we ourselves are musicians, divine musicians. It is the Supreme who makes the proper instrument. Then, it is He who inspires the player to play properly.

Let us not try to understand music with our mind. Let us not even try to feel it with our heart. Let us simply and spontaneously allow the music-bird to fly in our heart-sky. While flying, it will unconditionally reveal to us what it has and what it is. What it has, is Immortality's message. What it is, is Eternity's passage.

Q Can some kinds of music cause us to feel upset and change our spiritual condition?

A Yes. There is some music that is really destructive to our inner being. This music comes from the gross physical or the lower vital. Undivine music tries to awaken our lower vital consciousness and throw us into a world of excitement. The spiritual person will immediately be affected by this music.

Music has tremendous power. With fire we can burn ourselves, or we can cook and do many other good things. It is the same with music. Divine music immediately elevates our consciousness, whereas undivine music immediately lowers our consciousness and tries to destroy our sincere inner cry for a better, spiritual life. Vital music brings our consciousness down. For a few fleeting moments or hours we get a kind of pleasure; but then this pleasure takes us into a lower vital consciousness where temptation looms large. From the temptation-world we enter into the frustration-world, and from the frustration-world we enter into the destruction-world.

We all know that vital music is most appreciated all over the world. Psychic music is not very widely appreciated, and very few people appreciate the soul's music. They feel that it is like a stranger entering into their consciousness. But this is actually because spiritual music awakens the eternal tenant, the soul, that is deep within them waiting to come to the fore.

Q Can we use music to help us in our spiritual life?

A We can definitely use music to help us in our spiritual life. Music and the spiritual life are like twin brothers; we cannot separate them. How can we separate two fingers, two eyes? They live side by side. If one eye is not functioning well, then we feel that our vision is imperfect. Music and the spiritual life can easily go together; one complements the other. Music helps the spiritual seeker to go deep within to get the utmost satisfaction from life, from truth, from reality. The spiritual life, in turn, helps music to offer its capacity and its strength, which is the soul's light, to the world at large.

Q What does 'soulful' mean in relation to music?

A What do we mean by soulful music? If you say it is the music that embodies the soul, then I wish to say that you are mistaken. You have to feel that soulful music is the light that wants to express itself in a divine way. Even as darkness wants to manifest its authority on earth, light also wants to manifest its reality and divinity in a specific way. Light is the soul of everything. Light is the soul of music, the soul of love, and the soul of all art. When light divinely manifests itself in the form of music, it is the music of the soul.

Soulful music is the music that immediately elevates our consciousness to the highest. Soulful music takes us into the world of aspiration. From aspiration we enter into the world of realisation, where our inner existence is flooded with light and delight.

Soulful music is the music that wants to eventually transform our consciousness. It carries us into the Universal Consciousness and makes us feel that we are in tune with the highest, with the deepest, with the farthest.

It also makes us feel that God Himself is the Supreme Musician. When we play soulful music, we come to realise that we are not the musician; we are just an instrument. We are like a piano, violin or guitar, and it is God who is constantly playing on us. If we really play soulful music, we will feel that we are the instrument, and somebody else is singing and playing in and through us. That somebody is our Inner Pilot, the Supreme.

 God the Creator is the Supreme Musician and God the creation is the supreme music.

When we listen to soulful music, or when we ourselves play soulful music, immediately our inner existence climbs up high, higher, highest. It climbs up and enters into the Beyond, which is constantly trying to help us, guide us, mould us and shape us into our true transcendental image, our true divinity. When we hear soulful music or play a soulful piece of music, we feel a kind of inner thrill in our entire existence. From the soles of our feet to the crown of our head we feel that a river is flowing through us, a river of illumined consciousness.

Next to deep prayer or meditation, music is of paramount importance in our spiritual life. Meditation is like a direct route, or shortcut, to the goal. Music is a road that is absolutely clear: it may be a little longer, but it is quite clear of obstacles. If one can play soulful music or hear soulful music, the power of his own meditation increases. Music, soulful music, adds to our aspiration. Similarly, if a spiritual seeker wants to be a musician, even if he does not have a musical background, he will be able to be a good musician because prayer and meditation contain all capacities. You may never have studied music, but if you pray and meditate soulfully, then inside your prayer, inside your meditation, by the Grace of the Supreme, the power of music will loom large.

Q How do we know if music is spiritual and if the musician is aspiring?

A Whether or not the musician is aspiring is not your business. That is only God's business. Somebody may appear to be spiritual, but if his music brings your consciousness down, then he is not playing spiritual music. When you hear music, if it lifts your consciousness, then you will know that it is spiritual music. Sometimes the musician is aspiring and also he is playing spiritual music; at that time you are very fortunate, because you get inspiration from both the music and the musician.

Q What is the best way to become one with soulful music?

A The best way to become one with soulful music is to have the firm inner conviction while listening to it that as you are breathing in, the breath is immediately entering directly into your soul. And with the breath, you have to feel that the Universal Consciousness, divine Reality, divine Truth is also entering. Then, when you breathe out, try to feel that you are breathing out the ignorance that is covering your soul. Feel that the veils of ignorance are being lifted and discarded. If you can consciously imagine and feel this, it is the best way to become one with soulful music.

Music is God's dream. We don't have to know what it looks like or what it does. Its very existence keeps us alive.

The more you can offer gratitude to the Supreme Pilot within you, the more and the sooner you will increase your receptivity.

Receptivity: Opening to the Light

Chapter 10
Receptivity:
Opening to the Light

❦ What Is Receptivity?

Receptivity is the flow of cosmic energy and cosmic light. Receptivity is the capacity to absorb and hold the divine gifts that the Supreme showers upon you during your meditation. If you want to be receptive, when you sit down to meditate, consciously try to bring light into your being. Once you have brought light inside, direct it to the right place, the spiritual heart. Then try to grow into that light.

If you feel that you have a little receptivity, then cry for more. Do not be satisfied with the receptivity that you have. Today if it is a tiny pool, then make it into a pond, then into a lake, and finally into a vast ocean. Receptivity can be expanded gradually and endlessly. But without receptivity you will not be able to achieve anything in your spiritual life, even from countless hours of meditation.

One way to increase your receptivity is to be like a child. If the mother says to the child, "This is good," the child has no tendency to think it is bad. No matter how advanced you are in the spiritual life, you can make the fastest progress by having a childlike attitude, a sincere and genuine childlike feeling.

Gratitude
The easiest and most effective way to increase your receptivity is to offer your deepest gratitude to the

Supreme each day before you meditate. Many of your near and dear ones are not following the spiritual life, but you have accepted the spiritual life. How is it possible? It is possible because the Supreme inside you has given you the aspiration, whereas there are many, many people who are still not aspiring. You should feel that He has selected you to be spiritual. Because He has given you aspiration, you have every reason to offer Him your gratitude. He will be able to give you more receptivity if He sees that every day you are increasing your gratitude-capacity.

When you offer gratitude to God, immediately your inner vessel becomes large. Then God is able to pour more of His blessings into you or enter more fully into you with His own divine Existence. God is infinite, but only according to our receptivity can He enter into us. God is like sunlight. If I leave the curtains open, sunlight will come in. If I keep all the curtains closed, it cannot come in. The more curtains we open, the more God enters into us with infinite light. When we offer gratitude, immediately God's light comes pouring into our being.

Gratitude means self-offering to one's highest self. Your gratitude is not going to somebody else; it is going to your own highest self. Gratitude helps you identify and feel your oneness with your own highest reality.

You should always be grateful to the Inner Pilot, the Supreme. When you are grateful, your receptivity automatically increases.

 Every morning try to greet God with only one thing: an ever-increasing gratitude-gift.

How To

1 **A receptive place.** One way to get immediate receptivity is to repeat the word "Supreme" in silence over and over again, as fast as possible. First select one place in your body—let us say your third eye—and concentrate there while repeating "Supreme" as fast as possible. Then select another spot and do the same thing. It is better to go from the top downward than from the bottom upward. The place you concentrate on does not have to be a psychic centre. It can be any place you want. If you can do this in seven different places in your body, at one particular place you are bound to find yourself receptive.

2 **A child's cry.** To create receptivity when you do not have it, try to make yourself feel that you are only three years old—a mere baby. You have no mother, no father, nobody at all to protect you, and you are alone in a forest on a very dark night. All around you is darkness. Death is dancing right in front of you, and nobody is there to help you. Then what will you do? You will cry to God from the very depths of your heart, with absolute sincerity. When that kind of inner cry comes, the Supreme is bound to open your heart and make you receptive.

3 **Depend on God.** You can increase your receptivity if you feel that you are extremely helpless without the Supreme, and that with the Supreme, you are everything. This idea, this truth you can write on the tablet of your heart. Try to feel that your inner existence and your outer existence entirely depend on the Supreme. If you feel that your entire existence is meaningless and useless if He is not within you to guide you, to mould you, to shape you, and at the same time to fulfil Himself in you and through you, then your receptivity will expand. Try to feel that you are the chosen child of the Supreme just because He is utilising you, but if you are utilising yourself with your own ego and pride, then you are thousands of miles away from Him. The moment you are away from Him, you are nothing; but the moment you are one with Him with your dedication, devotion and surrender, you are everything. When you feel that you are one with Him, automatically your receptivity expands.

4 **Inner joy.** Another way to expand your receptivity during your meditation is to try to consciously feel inner joy. If you cannot feel inner joy immediately, then try to imagine for a few seconds or a few minutes that you have it. This will not be false. Your imagination will intensify your aspiration and help you to bring forward true inner joy in the course of time. The very nature of inner joy is expansion. When you expand, your receptivity will automatically increase, like a vessel that keeps getting larger.

Q I'm not as receptive in meditation as I would like to be. Why is this?

A Sometimes this happens because our consecration to the Supreme is not yet complete. Sometimes the mind resists, sometimes the vital resists and sometimes the physical or even the subtle physical resists. If there is any such resistance, negative forces can enter us, and our receptivity is lessened. Until we are really sure whether we want the life of desire or the life of aspiration, negative forces will stand between our desire and our aspiration. These forces are always on the alert. They try to separate our aspiration from our desire. Then they try to strengthen our desire and kill our aspiration, and very often they succeed. But a spiritually alert person will take aspiration and enter into desire in order to transform it. If desire enters into aspiration, then aspiration is ruined. If aspiration enters into desire, at that time desire is transformed.

At other times you may not be receptive because you have become too secure; you have become complacent. You do not feel an inner cry because you are satisfied with your material possessions or with the things that you already have in your inner life. Once you are satisfied with what you have, why should you cry for something more? When you have this kind of complacent feeling, your inner cry ceases, and your receptivity also comes to an end.

If you say no to your wrong thoughts and yes to your inspiration to become God's perfect instrument, then boundless receptivity will immediately be yours.

Aspiration-efforts always supply satisfaction-results. It may take time, at times, but the results are unmistakably sure.

Am I Meditating Well?

Am I Meditating Well?

❦ What Is a Good Meditation?

Seekers often ask how they can tell whether they are meditating properly or whether they are just deceiving themselves or having mental hallucinations. It is very easy to know. If you are meditating properly, you will get spontaneous inner joy. Nobody has given you good news, nobody has brought you any gifts, nobody has appreciated or admired you, nobody has done anything for you, but you will have an inner feeling of delight. If this happens, then you know that you are meditating properly. But if you feel a mental tension or disturbance, then you will know that the kind of meditation that you are doing is not meant for you.

If you are enjoying mental hallucination, you will feel that peace is within and restlessness is without. You are yearning for peace, light and bliss, but outwardly you are feeling a volcanic turbulence. If you are having a real meditation, a sublime meditation, then you are bound to feel peace within and without. If it is soulful meditation, you will feel your eternal existence; you will feel that you are of Eternity and for Eternity. This feeling you cannot get from a mental hallucination.

There is also another way that you can know. If you are actually entering into a higher plane, you will feel that your body is becoming very light. Although you don't have wings, you will almost feel that you can fly. In fact, when you have reached a very high world, you will actually see a bird inside you that can easily fly just as real birds do.

When it is your imagination, you will get a very sweet feeling for a few minutes; then immediately dark or frustrating thoughts will come into you. You will say, "I studied so hard, but I did not do well in my examination," or "I worked so hard in the office today, but I could not please my boss." These negative forces in the form of frustration will immediately come in. Or doubt will enter, and you may say, "How can I meditate so well when yesterday I did so many wrong things? How can God be pleased with me? How can I be having a high meditation?" But if it is really a high meditation, you will feel that your whole existence, like a divine bird, is soaring high, higher, highest. While you are having this feeling there will be no sad thoughts, no frustrating thoughts and no doubts. You will be flying in the sky of delight where all is joy, peace and bliss.

You can also know whether you had a good meditation by the way you feel afterwards. If peace, light, love and joy have come to the fore from within as a result of your meditation, then you will know that you have meditated well. If you have a good feeling for the world, if you see the world in a loving way in spite of its teeming imperfections, then you will know that your meditation was good. And if you have a dynamic feeling right after meditation, if you feel that you have come into the world to do something and become something—to grow into God's very image and become His dedicated instrument—this indicates that you have had a good meditation. But the easiest way to know if you have had a good meditation is to feel whether peace, light, love and delight have come to the fore from within.

You are now more than ready because your aspiration-bird is flying high above your mind's binding and blinding confusion-clouds.

Am I Meditating Well?

Don't be discouraged

Please do not be disturbed if you cannot meditate well in the beginning. Even in the ordinary life, God alone knows how many years one must practise in order to become very good at something. If an accomplished pianist thinks of what his standard was when he first began to play, he will laugh. It is through gradual progress that he has achieved his present musical height. In the spiritual life also, you may find it difficult to meditate in the beginning. But do not try to force yourself. Ten minutes early in the morning is enough. Gradually your capacity will increase. If you practise every day, you will make progress in your inner life.

Still, every day you cannot eat the most delicious meal. Today you may eat delicious food, and then for three or four days you may eat very simple food. But as long as you are eating, you know that you are sustaining your body. Similarly, if you have a good meditation one day, and the following day you find that you are not able to meditate well, do not become frustrated, and do not try to force yourself to meditate. When your meditation time is over, do not feel miserable even for a moment because you could not meditate. If you are displeased with yourself, then you are making a great mistake. If you cannot meditate on a particular day, try to leave the responsibility with God. If one day you cannot meditate well, feel that some other day the Supreme will again give you the blessing, inspiration and aspiration to meditate extremely well. But if you are disturbed or irritated, some of the progress that you made yesterday or the day before will be diminished or nullified. The best thing is to be calm, quiet and steady in your spiritual life. Then definitely you will continue to make progress in your meditation and in your inner life.

Q&A

Q I often find that the quality of my meditation goes up and down. I always hope that I will not fall down again, but it happens constantly.

A In the beginning everybody experiences ups and downs in the spiritual life. When a child is learning to walk, in the beginning he stumbles and falls again and again. But after a while he learns to walk properly, and finally to run. Eventually he can run as fast as his capacity will allow. But a small child cannot expect to run as fast as his father does, because his father has much more capacity.

You experience ups and downs in your meditation. When you are up, you have to feel that you are getting a glimpse of your eventual capacity. When you are down, you should simply feel that this is only a temporary incapacity. Just because you see that those who are more advanced than you in the spiritual life are running, you must not be discouraged. Once upon a time they also stumbled.

Right now the sky may be full of clouds, but a day will come when the sun will shine again with its full effulgence. When you experience low moments of fear, of doubt, of lack of aspiration, you should feel that these won't last forever. Like a child who has fallen, you must try to stand up again. Someday you will be able to walk, then run, and finally run the fastest without falling.

Q When you meditate and you cry for something, should you also make an effort to achieve it, or just let it take place naturally?

A At the beginning you have to make a personal effort; later it becomes spontaneous. Unless and until it becomes spontaneous, you have to make the personal effort. When a sprinter starts a race, his hands make such a vigorous movement. In the beginning he consciously moves his arms and hands very fast. He is making strong personal effort. But after fifty or sixty metres, when he is going at top speed, everything becomes spontaneous. At that time he is not striving to move his arms. But at the start, he did.

It is like sailing a boat. Before you start you move this thing and adjust that thing. You have to do all kinds of things at the beginning. While you are getting ready, you are very dynamic. But that is only your preparation. Still the boat is near the shore. It is only when you are actually well on your way that the boat can sail without your constant personal effort. In your meditation this spontaneous movement is an act of Grace from above.

If you are sincere, then you will say that at the very beginning of your journey God's Grace also descended. Otherwise, you would not have been inspired even to enter into the boat. But when you start out, you feel that you are making a tremendous personal effort. But there comes a time when you realise that this personal effort is nothing other than Compassion from above. Why are you getting up early to pray and meditate, whereas your friends are still wallowing in the pleasures of lethargy? It is because God's Grace has descended into you. So the deeper you go, the clearer it becomes that God's Grace enables you to make progress through your personal effort. Either God is pleased with you, or out of His infinite Compassion He is helping you.

Personal effort is of paramount importance at the beginning, because at that time we don't feel that God is our unconditional friend. As human beings, we always say that if I give you something, then you will give me something in return. But if I don't give you anything, then you are under no obligation to give me anything. But God is not like that. God gives unconditionally, whether we claim Him as our own or not. This moment I may pray to God to fulfil my desire. But the next moment, after He fulfils my desire, immediately I will say, "Oh, I don't need You. I don't want to be Your child." But God cannot do that. God always claims us as His own no matter how bad we are, because He sees that in hundreds or thousands or millions of years, He will make us perfect. A child, at his sweet will, can leave his parents; but can the parents leave the child? Impossible! Similarly, I can disown God, my eternal Father, because I am angry with Him or because He has not fulfilled my desires. But He will never disown me, because I am His child.

 Self-effort is necessary.
God's Grace is indispensable.

So personal effort is necessary because we do not feel that God is constantly loving us and blessing us unconditionally. Once we can feel that He is doing everything for us unconditionally, then personal effort is not necessary. Just because we don't have that kind of feeling, so-called personal effort is of paramount importance. But when we become sincere, when we become humble, and especially when we become pure, at that time we will feel that it is God who has inspired us to exercise our personal effort. So credit goes to God from the beginning to the end. In the beginning we give 50 percent of the credit to ourselves, because we got up to pray and meditate, and 50 percent to God, because He responded to our prayers and inspired us during our meditation. But if we are sincere, devoted and absolutely pure, then we will say that 100 percent of the credit goes to God.

Q Sometimes during my morning meditation, I fall into a doze—not a sound sleep, but just a doze. Is this a bad thing?

A Unfortunately, it is not a good thing. It is not sound sleep, but you are not fully awake either. When you meditate, you have to be absolutely dynamic. Do not allow sleepiness to enter into you. When you sit down to meditate, feel that you are entering into the battlefield where you have to fight against ignorance, imperfection and death.

Unfortunately, many seekers do not get enough inspiration to energise them for morning meditation. Some mornings you get inspiration all at once; other days you do not get any inspiration at all. If the fire is already burning inside, you do not have to do anything. But when there is no fire, what do you do? The best thing is to breathe in deeply a few times before you meditate and make your whole body energetic. This dynamic energy will help you enter into meditation. If possible, take a small quantity of hot juice or hot milk before you begin your meditation also.

Q How can I keep myself from falling asleep after about five minutes of meditation?

A First of all, before you start meditating please breathe in deeply a few times. With each breath, try to feel that a stream of energy is entering into you. Then try to feel that you are breathing in through different parts of your body: your eyes, your ears, your forehead, your shoulders, the crown of your head and so on. Feel that each of these places is a door, and when you breathe in feel that you are opening this door. At that time, energy enters into you from the Universal Consciousness.

Then try to invoke the power aspect of the Supreme. Do not invoke peace or light; only try to bring forward divine power from within or bring it down from above. This divine power will make you feel that your body is burning with fever, although you are not actually running a temperature, and immediately you will feel energised. You can also imagine a blue-green forest or field, and feel that you are walking through it. Then, no matter how tired you are, you will feel energised.

You can also pinch yourself as hard as possible, and try to feel that somebody else is pinching you. While you are pinching yourself, you have to know that it is your conscious self that is pinching your unconscious self. But you have to feel that another person is doing the pinching.

Another technique is to repeat the name of the Supreme as fast as possible. With tremendous concentration see how many times you can repeat "Supreme" with each breath. The power inside the repetition of this name will inundate your whole being and you are bound to feel a new flow of life-energy.

At meditation time always try to feel inside you a dynamic and progressive movement, but not an aggressive one. If there is a dynamic and progressive movement, then you cannot fall asleep. Inside you, feel that a train is speeding towards the destination. Feel that you yourself are an express train with only one destination. The driver of that train is constantly repeating God's name to derive energy, strength, stamina and all divine qualities. An express train stops only at the final goal, the end of its journey; on the way it does not stop at all. Your goal will be to reach or achieve a profound meditation.

Am I Meditating Well?

Q Sometimes it seems like I spend my whole time trying to keep myself awake and I don't really meditate.

A Lethargy and sleep come during meditation because sincere interest is lacking. If sincere interest is there, there will be no tendency to sleep. When a student wants to be first in school, when he has a real, sincere interest, then he studies without being forced by his parents. But some students feel that if they just pass the examination, that is more than enough. If this is their feeling, then they do not have any energetic drive or enthusiasm for their school work.

You should always try to be eager and enthusiastic about meditation. If you feel that you cannot meditate for half an hour, then plan to meditate for ten minutes. Then you will feel, "Oh, only ten minutes. Easily I can do that." If your goal is very near, then you will give it all your energy. If it is quite far, you will say, "Oh God! To keep running at top speed for such a long time is impossible." But anybody can meditate for ten minutes. If you have to run twenty miles, you will be scared to death. But if you see that the goal is within sight, then you will say, "Oh, I can easily reach it. Let me run as fast as possible."

Q If we feel tired when we sit down to meditate, how can we energise ourselves so that we don't fall asleep?

A When you feel that you are tired, exhausted, please take several deep breaths quietly and try to feel that you are breathing in from various places in your body. Try to feel that you are breathing in through the eyes, the ears, the forehead, through the crown of the head, through the shoulders and so on. When you are breathing in, if you are conscious of your breath, then you will not feel sleepy. But being conscious of your breath does not mean that you will make a sound. You will just feel that a stream of energy is entering into you with every breath.

Feel that every place you are breathing in is a door. Each time you breathe in, you open a door here, there or somewhere else. Naturally, when you open the door, light also enters, and light is another form of energy.

When you are meditating very well, you may feel that you are spontaneously doing this—drawing energy not only through your nose, but through your head and other places. Energy is available everywhere, and that universal energy wants to enter into you by various doors. Naturally, the more energy you can draw inside you, the higher will be your meditation.

How to conquer fear? With oneness within and oneness without. In oneness-light there can be no fear.

Q When I try to meditate, there is something that holds me back.

A The thing that holds you back is fear. If you want the wealth which is deep inside you, then you have to dive within bravely. Only if you have inner courage can you receive the inner wealth. Fear of the unknown and the unknowable prevents you from diving deep within. But what is unknowable today becomes merely unknown tomorrow, and the day after tomorrow it becomes known.

The vastness of truth will never harm you. It will only embrace and fulfil you. You feel afraid of something because you do not feel that that particular thing is part of you. But through meditation you establish your conscious oneness with the infinite Vast. At that time you see and feel that everything is part of you. So why should you be afraid?

Q I feel a pressure in my forehead when I meditate. What causes this and how can I stop it?

A The reason you feel pressure in your forehead is because you are meditating in the wrong place; you are meditating in the mind rather than the heart. You want to play a game, but unfortunately you have gone to the wrong playing field. When you feel pressure in your head or your forehead during meditation, it means that your mind has pulled down light and power beyond its capacity. The door to your consciousness is closed, so you are trying to break through the ceiling and pull God into your room. At that time, poor God is entering into an unprepared, unreceptive and unillumined vessel. Naturally the vessel resists, and then you get a headache.

You may also feel pressure because your mind-vessel is filled with impure thoughts and ideas. By sheer will you are trying to kill these undivine thoughts, and again the resistance of the mind causes you pain. The pressure can also mean that there is an obstruction such as fear inside you. When the mind-vessel is filled with impure thoughts and you pull down peace, light and bliss, you unconsciously become frightened. You never expected these things to be so brilliant and divine. Your mind is filled with all kinds of obscure thoughts and impurities, and suddenly divine peace, light and bliss come. At that time they seem like strangers to you, so you resist them. You are driving at top speed and suddenly you feel fear, so you try to stop.

When you feel this kind of pressure, what you should do is immediately focus your attention on your heart. Feel that you do not have a head at all; you have only the heart's soft, sweet feeling of oneness with God, your Inner Pilot. In the heart there is no fear or resistance. No matter how intensely you meditate in the heart, no matter how much peace, light and bliss you draw into the heart, you will never feel tension or pressure. There will only be joy, love and a feeling of oneness.

The safest and best way to meditate is in the heart. But if you want to use the mind, then you have to try to make the mind very calm, quiet, pure and receptive. Always feel that inside the aspiring mind there is a vessel that you can enlarge with your sincere aspiration. Try to make the vessel very large so that it can hold more purity and luminosity. But do not try to pull anything. Only let the divine Grace flow in and through you by praying and meditating most soulfully. Then you will not feel pressure or tension in your head.

Q I don't think that I am pulling, but still I get a headache when I meditate in the morning.

A In your particular case, you are meditating on the wrong thing. You are meditating on divine power, but because your inner vessel is not pure enough, instead of power, an aggressive quality comes into you. This aggression you feel as a headache. So when you meditate in the morning, you should meditate on peace. Inundate your inner and outer being with peace; then you will not get a headache. Peace itself is power; it can solve all your problems.

Q Sometimes, even though I concentrate on my heart, my head pulls down energy and I can't seem to stop it, and I just end up with a headache. Is there any way I can get back to the heart?

A The pain that you are feeling in your head is the result of resistance. What is happening is that your heart is receiving through the mind. Something is coming from above and is trying to enter into the heart, but the mind is not allowing the heart to receive fully. The mind allows the heart to receive to some extent; that is why the force is coming through the mind. But then the mind becomes jealous of the heart and it starts resisting.

At that time try to feel that inside the heart there is something which is infinitely more powerful than the mind. It is the soul, which has immense power. So bring forward your soul's inner strength and say to the mind, "You allowed me to remain quiet for a few minutes, and I am grateful. But I am still praying and meditating, I am still crying for peace, light and bliss, and now you are not allowing me to continue." Then just grab the mind and pull it into the flood of the heart.

The mind is like a naughty child. Previously it was asleep, so the mother was able to remain silent and pray to God. But now the child is awake and it wants to cause mischief. It does not want to allow the mother to aspire any longer. So what will the mother do? She will threaten the child and say, "I am still praying, I am still meditating. You must not disturb me, or I will punish you."

As long as the mind allows you to meditate, you do not have to worry. But when it starts bothering you and creating pain, that means that it does not want to allow you to receive more peace, light and bliss from above. So you have to use your soul's power and pull it into the heart.

Q When I was meditating I felt really tense. My head was hurting and I felt I was pulling. What should I do in a case like that?

If you get that kind of tense feeling, immediately breathe in and out very quickly. When the rhythm of your breathing increases, the tension goes away. Try to feel that you are climbing up a flight of stairs or a ladder that has many rungs. As you climb up you are breathing in. If you feel this ascent, then tension goes away. Tension comes when you are stuck at one place. But when you are climbing, you are like a bird flying up into the sky. When the bird is soaring, where is the tension? Similarly, if you are climbing up, there will be no tension.

Q I find your meditations very hard for me. I come in feeling beautiful. Then I feel all this pain coming into my heart and into my head. Why does this happen?

A It is not any negative force that is entering into you. Your difficulty is that when you come to our meditations, you try to pull far beyond your capacity. When I am on stage, the whole stage is flooded with light. When you sit and look at me, you try to pull this light. It is as if you are in a shop and you see all sorts of most beautiful things. Like a greedy fellow you want to buy everything, but you have in your pocket only five cents. When you try to pull beyond the capacity of your receptivity, at that time you get pain in your head or your heart.

Q Very often when I am concentrating on my heart centre during meditation, I find that my breathing is very heavy and distracting.

A In your case, you are straining your eyes while you are meditating. Your eyes are tight and stiff, and the pressure falls on your heart centre. This is very harmful to your aspiration. If you can keep your eyes normal and relaxed while you are meditating, this pressure will go away. You can keep your eyes open or closed; only don't make them unnaturally stiff.

I shall tolerate the world, I shall. Only by tolerating the world shall I be able to help my mind to ascend and my heart to transcend.

Q When I get upset with someone who does something to me, I can't meditate the way I want to. How can I overcome this?

A When you are upset, naturally you cannot meditate. You cannot welcome a friend and an enemy into your house at the same time. Your enemy is your agitation and anger, and your friend is meditation.

Suppose someone does something to you and you become angry with him. Even when several hours have elapsed and you have forgotten your anger, it can still pull you down. You have forgotten, but you have not forgiven. Unless you have forgiven, you have not illumined your anger. Sometimes you will quarrel with the members of your family and then go to sleep. The next morning you will find that you cannot meditate. You have totally forgotten the incident, but while you were sleeping the strength and velocity of your anger have increased. So it is always better to illumine the anger immediately.

When somebody does something wrong to you, try to feel that it is an extended part of your own consciousness that has made this deplorable mistake. Enlarge your heart and feel that it is you yourself who have done wrong. In that way you won't become upset. What you have to do is stop thinking of others and think only of perfecting yourself. That does not mean that you are ignoring the world's problems. No. Your own perfection will help others. When you achieve something, you will see that very thing in a small measure in others. Similarly, if you see something wrong in others, tomorrow you will see that very thing in yourself. And if you see something good in someone else but not in yourself, that particular thing will soon develop in you. If you see a person who is sincere and you are not sincere, just because you are conscious of his sincerity, your own inner sincerity will come to the fore. Your inner being will try to communicate with the sincerity of that particular person and, like a magnet, it will draw sincerity from that person or from the Supreme, who is the Source.

From now on, try to perfect your own nature instead of looking around to see whose imperfections are standing in your way. Pay all attention to your own self-discovery. When you have perfected yourself, you will see that everybody on earth will gain in perfection through you.

Q How can I tell if I am meditating too much?

A If you are meditating too much—that is to say, beyond your capacity—then you will get a kind of tension or pain in the area of the third eye. Also, you may get a haughty attitude. You may feel, "I am so divine and perfect, whereas everyone else is undivine and imperfect." If you are trying to pull down peace, light and bliss from above beyond your capacity, then you may no longer get any joy or satisfaction from your earthly activities. You may come to feel that this earthly existence of yours is useless and meaningless. If you get this kind of disgust or depression which makes you want to withdraw from the world, then you may be trying to meditate beyond your capacity.

Q When I meditate I lose energy and get tired. Is it because I meditate too much?

A No. If you are losing energy while meditating, it means that your meditation is incorrect. If you meditate well, you will gain energy. Meditation is the way to gain infinite energy, light and bliss. But if the particular method you are using is wrong, then you will lose energy instead of gaining it.

Q Is there anything I can do to always have a good meditation?

A It is through gratitude, the gratitude that is inside the heart, not inside the mind, that you can make your meditation excellent. Just for a fleeting second, remember that once upon a time you were the same as your friends and neighbours. Now look at the difference between you. It is like day and night. They may be rich on the material plane, but on the spiritual plane they are totally bankrupt. When you see the difference, automatically a spring of gratitude will well up inside you.

If you can have a drop of gratitude, inside that gratitude you will find a world of new creation. Once the seed has been sown, it starts germinating and grows into a plant. So when you are not getting a good meditation, the best thing is to think of what you were and what you are going to become. Once upon a time you could not even crawl; now you are running in the spiritual life. Once you see the difference, you are bound to have gratitude to the Supreme, for He is the Doer. It is He who has inspired you and acted in and through you. He has inspired you and He has given you the fruit of your action, so naturally your gratitude will come to the fore and you will be able to have a good meditation.

Cry within.
Meditate within. Dive within.
Your inner achievements will far
outweigh your outer imperfections.

Keeping Your Joy

Keeping Your Joy

❦ Guarding Your Inner Wealth

After you have finished meditating, you have to assimilate the result of your meditation into your inner system. Only then does it become a solid, absolutely permanent experience that is inseparably one with your existence. If you enter into a quarrel with someone or get into some unpleasant situation before the peace, light and bliss from your meditation are assimilated, then everything can be lost. Not even an iota will remain. Even by speaking with someone you can lose what you have received during meditation. Someone may come up to you and say, "How are you?" and he may take away all the peace, light and bliss that you have received. That is why you should not talk to anyone immediately after you have had a high meditation, until you have assimilated what you have received. Also, you should not eat immediately after meditation. You can move around or read if you want, but you should not eat a full meal for at least fifteen minutes or a half hour. If you are very hungry, though, it is all right to take a small quantity of milk or juice.

Normally, it takes quite a few hours to assimilate everything that you have received during meditation, and during that period you have to maintain the light that you got. How? Through your inner awareness, and by being careful of how you deal with the outside world. However, sometimes it happens that during your meditation you are receiving and at the same time assimilating. Then, when you stop meditating, it is all assimilated.

You can think of assimilation as establishing a lifelong friendship, an eternal friendship, with someone who has come into your life. If peace, light and bliss come into you during meditation and you do not make them your eternal friends, then naturally they will leave you. But if you establish an eternal friendship with them, then your friends will have an opportunity to inspire you, guide you, mould you, shape you and share with you their divine capacities and divine qualities.

Again, you have to know that assimilation is not always what the soul wants. At times the soul is eager to assimilate and keep something for quite a few days before expressing it. At other times the soul wants to reveal and manifest the qualities that it receives during meditation immediately or after only a few hours. This expression can be to others, to the atmosphere or to the Universal Consciousness. The inner wealth is like knowledge. One person may say, "Let me learn a little and teach that small amount." But someone else may say, "No, let me learn as much as I can, and then I will teach others."

Q What qualities are most important for the absorption of light?

A The absorption of light demands absolute sincerity and purity. Anybody who is one hundred percent sincere and pure in his spiritual life can immediately absorb light. The sincerity that I am speaking of is not ordinary human sincerity, but spiritual sincerity, which is infinitely more subtle. Spiritual sincerity asks whether you are ready to make all sacrifices in order to please God. If God asks you to give up everything for

His sake, if He says, "Give up everything and walk with Me, run with Me," and you are ready to do it, that is called true spiritual sincerity. Spiritual sincerity is constant inner and outer sacrifice. If there is no sacrifice in the inner life or the outer life, then sincerity cannot take birth. Constant self-sacrifice to realise the Highest is called real sincerity.

But if there is no purity, immediately you will lose the light that you have received. Purity is actually the vessel inside you which holds spiritual light, peace, bliss and power. Very often you receive things and then you lose them because impurity enters into you. Impurity does not only have to do with lower vital movements. Doubt, fear, jealousy and insecurity are all forms of impurity. One of the undivine qualities that goes hand-in-hand with impurity is self-deception, so you have to be very careful. If you want to expedite your spiritual journey, then purity must come first. Otherwise, no matter how much light you have received or are going to receive, you will not be able to keep it.

 Each conscious step of purity is a precious milestone-victory along my heart's aspiration-road.

Q At the end of meditation I feel very good. Is there anything I should do with that feeling, or any way to utilise it?

A Whatever you feel should be preserved. How can you preserve it? By offering gratitude to the Inner Pilot. Also, you can try to feel that whatever you have achieved can be transcended. If you have received or achieved a dollar's worth of peace, then next time you can try to get ten dollars' worth of peace. And if you feel that you have developed an inner muscle to receive, then you can continue strengthening that muscle. In this way you can develop a very powerful inner capacity.

Q After we stop meditating, how can we maintain the level of consciousness that we reached during our meditation?

A Here in the meditation hall we are all aspiring; that is why our consciousness is elevated. When we go home, our consciousness will go down. Some calamity may take place or we will just enter into ordinary activities, and we will lose our aspiration. Even if there is no outer disturbance, still we find it difficult to remain in our highest consciousness because we are not used to living there. We aspire for half an hour with utmost sincerity, and then relaxation starts. We feel that we have worked very hard, so now we are entitled to take rest for an hour or two. We do not value what we have achieved. We feel, "even if I lose it, I will get it back tomorrow." So we start reading a newspaper or watching television, and in this way we enter into relaxation.

If we want to maintain the height of our aspiration, then our aspiration has to flow continuously. Suppose we have meditated for an hour or so and we do not have the capacity to continue meditating. Still, we can do something which will maintain and preserve our meditation. We can read spiritual books, sing spiritual songs or listen to soulful music. We can go to visit a spiritual friend or, if that is not possible, call him on the phone and speak about spiritual matters. Another thing we can do is write about our experiences, not with the thought of publishing them but just to keep them in our consciousness. While we are writing down an experience, we are revealing our own inner light. Then, each time we read about one of our own experiences, we get new inspiration and aspiration. Even while we are eating we can remember what experiences we had during our morning meditation. Like charging a battery, we are charging our memory with spiritual energy. In this way we can remain in the spiritual flow that we had during our meditation, and keep our consciousness high until our next meditation.

If we want to maintain our height and make the utmost progress, we have to be very wise in our day-to-day lives in how we spend each second. A time will come when we will not have to have any restrictions in our life; our life itself will be a continuous flow of aspiration. But now we have to use our conscious mind in order to aspire.

 Now is the time to make good use of time. Today is the day to begin a perfect day.

Q Sometimes after meditation I lose the joy that I have received from my meditation, and I feel very bad. Why do I lose my joy?

A There are two reasons why you lose your joy. One reason is that your mind starts functioning most powerfully and vehemently. While functioning in this way, it allows obscure, impure and undivine thoughts to come in either consciously or unconsciously. When impurity enters, joy has to disappear. But if purity is well-established in the mind, the joy will last for a long time.

Another reason why you lose your joy is that your inner vessel is small, and you have taken light, which is joy itself, beyond your capacity. The quantity of light that you have received during your meditation has satisfied you, but your inner vessel is not large enough to hold it. When you lose it, you feel sad.

Q Sometimes I feel very sad when I come down from meditation.

A The sadness that you feel is quite natural, because you were in a higher world and then you had to come back to the earthly level. At that time, the worries and problems of the world enter into you. But if you meditate sincerely for a few years, these problems will not stand in your way, because when you come down from your meditation, you will have tremendous peace, poise, joy and love for humanity.

Right now you have boundless love for your child. But after you have meditated for a few years, you will have even more love for your child, because you will feel the presence of God inside him. Right now you do not feel the presence of God inside your child all the time. If he is naughty or if he breaks something, then you do not think that God is operating inside him. At that time you are exasperated and you say, "No, no, this is not God; this is the devil incarnate." But there will come a time when you will see God inside your son all the time, no matter what he does or what he says. When you progress to that point, you will not feel drained when you come down from your meditation. On the contrary, even when you enter into the activities of ordinary life you will be able to maintain the same joy, delight, peace and poise.

When you are meditating you have to feel that you are climbing a tree. You are going up high, higher, highest to collect the mangoes and bring them down for distribution. But if you feel sad when you come down, that means you want to eat them all by yourself at the top of the tree. You don't want to bring them down and share them with others. So when you go up, always go up with joy; and when you come down, also come down with joy. When you go up, feel that it is for achievement of the highest; and when you come down from meditation, feel that it is for distribution.

If you want to see the Face of God, then you must at least spend some time every day with His chosen instrument: your own heart.

Your Daily Meditation: Food for the Soul

Chapter 13
Your Daily Meditation: Food for the Soul

❧ An Appointment with God

If you are serious about your spiritual life, then you have to meditate at least once a day. If you are very enthusiastic, you can meditate three times a day—early in the morning, at noon or during your lunch hour, and in the evening. Your morning and evening meditations can be for a longer time, for fifteen minutes or half an hour, whereas your noon meditation can be as short as five or ten minutes. If it is not possible to feed your soul three times a day, then please feed it at least once. Feel that the soul is a little divine child. If you don't feed the divine child within you, it will not be able to grow and manifest your inner divine qualities and your soul's possibilities.

It is better to meditate well just once a day in the morning than to sit five or six times a day with your eyes closed and just have pleasant thoughts drifting through your head. Each time you meditate you have to feel that you are offering your life-breath to the Supreme and bringing to the fore your soul's light. Only then is your meditation worthwhile. If you feel that you can meditate soulfully only once, early in the morning, then that is enough. You have to see your real capacity, sincerity, willingness and joy. If inspiration is there, that means that you have received the sanction from the Supreme, and you will run very fast. Some people meditate during their lunch hour or when they have a coffee break in the office. That is excellent. But please meditate first thing in the morning also. If you start by doing the right thing early in the morning, then you will be inspired all day.

Morning meditation is best

If you meditate in the morning, you will find that your meditation will be most fruitful. Before the sun rises, the earth-consciousness is not yet agitated. The world has not yet entered into its daily turmoil. Nature is calm and quiet and will help you meditate. When nature is fast asleep, the animal in us or our unillumined consciousness also sleeps. At that time we are still in the world of energising and fulfilling dreams, from which reality can grow. That is why the awakened aspiring consciousness can get the most out of early morning meditation.

Once the day dawns, Mother-Earth becomes divinely energetic or undivinely restless. Especially in the West, because of its present dynamic nature, there is some feeling of irritation in the cosmos or in the outer nature. These restless qualities of the world do not have to enter into you, but usually they will. When people move around, immediately their vibration enters into you, no matter where you are. The air, the light, everything around you becomes permeated with the vibration of human activity and human anxieties. The world is standing in front of you like a roaring lion. How can you enter into your highest meditation in front of a roaring lion? But if you can meditate before the world awakens, when the cosmos is still and people around you are taking rest, then you will be able to have a deeper meditation.

Meditating during the day is very difficult. In the evening, meditation is also a little difficult, because for eight or ten hours you have been in the hustle and bustle of the world. During the day you have met with many unaspiring people, and unconsciously their undivine thoughts and impure ideas have entered into you. So unless you are inwardly very strong, you will have assimilated many unaspiring and uninspiring forces from the world. Therefore, it becomes very difficult to meditate in the evening with the same hope and freshness. If you take a shower before meditating, it will help. If you associate with spiritual people, it will also help.

In the morning all these undivine forces and experiences are out of your memory, at least for a while. During the time that you sleep, all the impurities that have come into you from others are washed away. During the hours that you are sleeping, your soul, like a divine thief, is silently observing you. An ordinary thief will steal something from you, but this divine thief will only give and give. If you need peace at one place, your soul will put peace there. The soul acts like a mother, who comes into the child's room in secrecy, early in the morning, to prepare for him the things he will need during the day. At night while you are sleeping, the soul gets the opportunity to do what is necessary for you. But during the day, when you are absorbed in the activities of the outer world, it is extremely difficult for the soul to give and for you to receive. For all these reasons morning meditation is the best.

 Beauty came to me like the morning rose.
Duty came to me like the morning sun.
Divinity came to me like the morning aspiration.

Evening meditation

If you cannot meditate in the morning, the evening is the next best time, because in the evening at least the atmosphere is becoming calm and peaceful. At noon nature is wild and restless, so your meditation may not be very deep or intense. But in the evening nature is preparing to rest and it does not disturb you. When you meditate in the evening, you can look at the setting sun and try to feel that you have become totally one with cosmic nature. You can feel that you have played your part during the day most satisfactorily and, like the sun, you are going to retire.

In the evening you are tired, and you feel that the whole world is also tired. But there is a slight difference between the world's approach to the truth and your approach. When the world is tired, it will not aspire. It wants only to rest. But you feel that your tiredness can be overcome by bringing more light and energy into your system. When you pray and meditate, at that time new life and new energy enter into you and refresh you.

A fixed time is important

Whether you meditate in the morning or the evening, it is of paramount importance to have a fixed time for your meditation. Even an infant will cry for his mother's milk at a fixed hour. If you own a store, if you always open the door at nine o'clock, then others will have confidence that they can come at nine o'clock and you will really be open. Everything has its own hour. Your inner being and your Inner Pilot, the Supreme, always observe. If you stick to a particular hour, then the Supreme has confidence in you. The Supreme says, "At this hour he is not loitering around; he is meditating. If I offer him something at this hour, he will definitely be there to receive it."

You and God should agree to a certain hour for your daily meeting. When He comes at that hour, if you are fast asleep, He will forgive you. If you are not there tomorrow, again you will be forgiven. But you will not be able to excuse yourself. Your oneness with God will not allow you to forgive yourself. Your soul will cause you such pangs that you will feel miserable. Your soul's love for the Highest is very important to you. When your Eternal Friend is coming, the host wants to be ready. The human mind is a very treacherous thing. Left to itself, the ignorant, obscure mind will try to prevent you from doing the spiritually correct thing. It will find many excuses to keep you from fulfilling your soul's wish. But if your aspiration is sincere and intense, the discipline of having a set time to meditate will help you fight against the lethargy and waywardness of the mind.

> *When you don't give countless outer things your attention, you will see that truth is looking right at you and giving you the strength to discipline your life.*

Suppose you want to meditate at six-thirty. This is your chosen hour. If you get up at seven, your own lethargy and idleness will take away all your inspiration. On the one hand, your lethargy will try to justify itself. It will enter into your conscious mind and say, "Oh, I came home very late; that is why I could not get up." Or, "For the last six days I got up at six-thirty. Since God is all kindness, today He will forgive me." There are so many ways your mind can justify getting up late. But even if you came home late, that doesn't mean that you won't do first things first. The first thing is meditation; the first thing is God.

Once you start your journey, if you do not keep moving toward your goal, then you are lost. You may think, "Today I am tired, so I will stop here and rest. Tomorrow again I will go on." But you have to know that ignorance is more alert than your own aspiration. Once you start justifying yourself, there is no end to it. Regularity will tell you that the goal is real. But if you are punctual, immediately a kind of dynamism and movement is there. Your regularity is like a motor. Because you have a motor, you know that at any time you can drive. Punctuality is when you actually turn the key and start the motor. With regularity you get only a vague idea that you will do it. But with punctuality, you actually do it.

If you are regular and punctual in your meditation, you will notice your own progress. If you can meditate sincerely and soulfully at a fixed hour every day, a time will come when you will become an expert. At that time, you will be able to meditate while doing anything, and you won't need a fixed hour. Eventually you will be able to meditate twenty-four hours a day even though you are talking to people and doing your multifarious daily activities. But for that you need many years—perhaps many lifetimes—of practice.

 No path can be too hard for you if you have one God-gift: faith in yourself.

Q How can anyone find time to meditate in the course of a busy day?

A We have twenty-four hours at our disposal, and we find time to do all kinds of things during the day. What prevents us from thinking of God for five or ten minutes a day? We have time to eat, we have time to sleep, we have time to mix with our friends, read the newspaper or watch television. We have time to do whatever we consider necessary. So when it is a matter of God, how can we say that we don't have time?

God is crying for us to think of Him. If we really care to please Him, we will find the time to think of Him and meditate on Him. But if we don't consider God important in our life, then we will always be too busy.

Q Is there a certain hour in the morning that is most conducive to meditation?

A The very best time to meditate is between three and four o'clock in the morning. This is the Brahma Muhurta, the Hour of God. No matter what your standard is, even if you are a complete beginner, you will encounter very little resistance if you meditate at this time.

The Westerner who goes to bed at twelve o'clock or one o'clock cannot expect to be able to meditate at three or four o'clock. If you want to meditate at four o'clock, you should go to bed by nine or ten the previous evening. For someone who has just entered into the spiritual life, seven or eight hours of sleep is essential. If you start sleeping only three or four hours just so that you can get up at four o'clock, it will tell upon your health. Spiritually you will derive no benefit, because you will not be able to meditate properly when you are exhausted, and the body will stand as an obstacle to your inner progress. After you make some progress in the spiritual life, then gradually you can reduce your hours of sleep. When your physical consciousness starts receiving light from above, its need for sleep diminishes.

For most people in the West, the best time to meditate is as soon as possible after you get up, before you start your daily activities. If possible you should try to meditate before seven o'clock. Before the outer world attacks you or demands anything from you, you should enter into the inner world with the idea of nourishing yourself. In this way, you are performing your inner duty before you become involved in outer activities. If you put God first in your life, then everything else will gain a more spiritual perspective. If you can please the dearest in you, who is God, before you enter into your earthly activities, then naturally you are doing the right thing.

Q Should we try to get up spontaneously to meditate or should we set an alarm?

A You should use an alarm. To get the special Grace to wake up spontaneously, you have to be a Yogi. But please, when you meditate, do not keep a clock in front of you. If you really want to meditate soulfully, just dive deep within. When you meditate, you are pleasing the Supreme. He will make you conscious of the fact that it is time to go to school or to the office. If you are really meditating, He will do this. But if you are in the sleep world, dreaming and wasting your precious time, it will not be His responsibility.

Q If you stayed up very late the previous night and are very tired when your alarm goes off, is it better to sleep longer and meditate after your accustomed time?

A You have to know how often you do it. If you are doing it every week, this is not good. But once in a blue moon it is all right. In school you study for months, and then you get a holiday. But if you want to take a holiday every day, then how will you make progress? If you have meditated for months at a particular hour and one morning you are exceptionally tired, all right. But if you go to school at a different hour every day, then how can the teacher be pleased?

Opportunities do not come every day in your life. Spirituality is like an opportunity. If you miss one meditation, you have to feel that you have really missed something, that you have travelled one step less than you could have. When you do not meditate regularly, your consciousness loses some of its capacity, and the road becomes very long. Once you relax, ignorance covers you. If you fail to get up once, then on that day ignorance has conquered you.

Suppose you go to bed at three o'clock, and when it is time for meditation you are not able to get up. But who asked you to go to bed at three o'clock? You will say it was unavoidable; you had to do something most important. But while you are up late doing that important thing, please make yourself feel that at six o'clock there also will be something unavoidable and important that you will have to do: you will have to get up to meditate. If the thing that you did late at night was so important that you could not avoid it, then I wish to say that your meditation is infinitely more important; nothing can be more important than meditation.

Sometimes our fatigue is real; sometimes it is all mental. Even if you sleep for ten hours, sometimes you feel extremely tired. Many people sleep much more than they actually need to. Often it is your mind that makes you feel you are tired and exhausted. The mind is so clever. It will make you feel that if you can sleep for only five minutes more, then you will feel much better. If you are supposed to get up at six o'clock, the mind will tell you that if your body can sleep one minute more, then you will feel better. But if you give that one minute to the body, immediately the mind will ask for five or ten minutes more, and before long it will be seven or eight o'clock. So the best thing is not to listen to the mind at all.

Q Is it bad to go back to sleep after meditating in the morning?

A If you go back to sleep and do not get up until eight or nine o'clock, then your own vital forces or the aggression of the earth, which is agitated at that hour, can enter into the result of the meditation which you did earlier, and ruin it. So it is infinitely better if you can do some other spiritual activity like reading spiritual books or singing spiritual songs.

Q If you set a time for your meditation and are able to get up earlier, should you still keep your original time?

A Yes. If your time to meditate is five-thirty in the morning, at that hour your soul will knock at your door, so you should be prepared. Choose the time that you feel is best, and stick to it. If you want, you can get up half an hour earlier in order to shower and get ready, but then you should start to meditate at your appointed time.

Q For a six o'clock meditation, will we do better if we get up at five and are up for a full hour before meditating? If we enter into activity, will we become more awake?

A It is not good if there is too much activity. If you touch a material object, immediately the consciousness of that object enters into you. If you touch a novel, immediately the consciousness of the author will enter into you. If you are drowsy and start doing housework to wake yourself up, then the housework consciousness will enter into you. If you are drowsy, it is best to take a shower. Water signifies consciousness. Once consciousness enters into you, you will not sleep. So do not enter into any activity before meditation. Just take a shower and then meditate. You can prepare yourself inwardly by reading spiritual writings for a few minutes or by singing some soulful, spiritual songs. But you should not do housework or office work.

Q If we tend to feel sleepy, is it all right to exercise before our morning meditation?

A Certainly. Doing a few exercises can make you feel more alert. It is fine to do a few minutes of hatha yoga exercises before beginning meditation.

Q What should we do if we miss our appointed hour for meditation? Should we try to make up for it at our next meditation by meditating for a longer time?

A If you have to miss your appointed hour one day due to unavoidable circumstances, do not feel miserable. As long as you have not let the hour go by out of inertia or negligence or the feeling that because you have meditated for a few days, now you deserve a rest, then you have not committed a spiritual crime. But you cannot "make up" a missed meditation by meditating longer the next time. You eat three times a day. Suppose that early in the morning you did not have breakfast, and at noon you also missed your lunch. When it is time for dinner, if you try to eat all that you have not eaten in the morning and at noon, it will only upset your stomach. If you do not eat for two or three days, and then you try to make up for the food that you missed during your fast, you will run into trouble.

With meditation it is the same. You have the inner capacity to meditate for a certain amount of time early in the morning, at noon, in the evening or at night. If you cannot follow this routine on a certain day, it is better just to meditate most soulfully at your regular hour. If you try to increase the length of time, if you try to meditate for two or three hours instead of half an hour, your physical mind will not be able to bear the pressure. Instead of creating more capacity, this will break your capacity. It will create tremendous tension in your aspiration-life. Everything has to be done systematically and gradually. Eventually you will be able to meditate for eight hours or ten hours at a stretch, but right now it is not possible.

If your aspiration is really intense, if God really comes first in your life, then you can easily adjust your outer life to make time to meditate. The inner aspiration has infinitely more power than outer obstacles. If you utilise your inner strength, then circumstances have to surrender to your aspiration. If you really want to meditate every day, then I wish to tell you that your inner aspiration will give you the power to do it. Outer obstacles can easily be overcome, because the inner life is the living expression of the infinite power. Before the infinite power, outer obstacles have to surrender.

 A spiritually established life is not an easy task. But a materially satisfied life is an impossible task.

Q How long should I meditate? Is fifteen minutes enough, or should I try to meditate longer?

A It depends on the individual. If you are able to meditate for more than fifteen minutes, do so. But it has to be absolutely sincere and soulful. To sit for an hour just to make yourself feel that you are an advanced seeker will be a mistake. The soul will not be there. You may meditate for five hours, but the meditation will not give you any joy. It will not be fruitful at all. You will only give yourself a headache. If a person can meditate for fifteen minutes most soulfully, and after that, if he feels that he has the capacity to continue, then he can continue. But if he doesn't have the capacity, then it will be a waste of time.

The best thing is to meditate for as long as you can without creating any mental tension. It depends entirely on your capacity. Increasing your spiritual capacity is like developing a muscle. Today you may exercise and become tired after five minutes. After two months you may be able to exercise for half an hour or even more, because you have developed your muscles. There is also a spiritual muscle, which is aspiration. How long and how sincerely you can cry for God depends on the strength of your inner muscle.

Q If I meditate too little, I don't have spiritual energy throughout the day. If I meditate too long, I can't maintain my aspiration.

A The problem is that you are going to extremes. Sometimes you overeat and you cannot digest what you have eaten; sometimes you don't eat at all and you feel weak. When you don't meditate enough you feel miserable, and when you meditate beyond your capacity you feel worn out. But you don't have to pull or push. You only have to discover how much capacity you have. If you meditate for only five minutes, then naturally you will not be inspired throughout the day; but if you meditate for an hour or two, you will strain your capacity, and your body will revolt. So meditate devotedly and soulfully for twenty minutes in the morning and twenty minutes in the evening, and in the afternoon if you have a chance you can meditate for five or ten minutes more. That will be ample in your particular case.

Q Why would the body revolt?

A If the physical consciousness is not powerful enough or pure enough to hold the peace, light and bliss that the psychic consciousness is receiving from above, then it will suffer. If we pull beyond our capacity, we will only break our vessel. Here capacity means receptivity. If we develop great receptivity, then no matter how much we bring down from above, we will be able to assimilate it. That is why I always advise people not to push or pull. We have to accept our life as it is and then try to transform it—not by hook or by crook, but gradually, through aspiration.

 There is a lotus deep within you, but it blooms only one petal at a time.

Q During your meditation if you feel really inspired, can you increase the length of time that you meditate?

A In the beginning it is better just to remain in a meditative mood and read spiritual writings or sing devotional songs. If you have been meditating for half an hour, then after two or three months you can increase the length of time, but do not increase it suddenly. Even if you are inspired, please increase your meditation time by degrees. Otherwise, if today you are meditating well and all of a sudden you double your meditation time, then in a subtle way pride will enter into you. You will be bloated with pride the whole day, and then the following day this pride will not allow you to meditate at all. You will think that you have received everything from your meditation, so for two weeks you will not even get up.

Meditation is like eating or taking exercise. If one day you eat too much, the next day you will have stomach problems. Or if you have the capacity to do five push-ups and one day you get inspired and do twenty, the following day you will be too sore to do even one. So always increase your capacity slowly; then you will have no difficulty. If you are inspired to meditate longer, increase your time only by two or three minutes. If your inspiration continues to increase, after a month or so your meditation will be ten or fifteen minutes longer.

Q I try to meditate for fifteen minutes a day, but I find that it takes me almost this much time to actually settle down into meditation. What would you suggest?

A If you want to meditate for fifteen minutes, try to set aside half an hour. During that half hour, you will spend some time in preparation, which is necessary if you are to have fifteen minutes of good meditation. Some people may find that they do not need fifteen minutes extra. Once they start, they can run. They do not have to take a few preliminary starts. But if it is necessary for you, then take a few practice starts. If it is not necessary, right from the beginning you can enter into your soulful meditation.

Q Today I couldn't meditate in the morning, but I was able to meditate later in the day. Why was that?

A There could be many reasons. When you tried to meditate in the morning, perhaps you needed or wanted more sleep. You did absolutely the right thing by meditating later. If you had meditated well in the morning, then the time that you spent would have left you totally satisfied. But since you felt you did not meditate properly in the morning, then the best thing was to try again later, which you did.

Q I am a housewife with small children. What advice do you have for me?

A Even a housewife with small children can easily meditate, provided you are willing to do first things first. Early in the morning before your family wakes up and you have to enter into the hustle and bustle of life, you can offer a few minutes to God. If you know that at a particular hour your children will require food or attention from you, then you can easily get up ten minutes earlier.

Then, during the day while you are taking care of your children and working in your house, you have to feel the presence of the living God inside them and all around you. Unfortunately, most people do not do that. They look upon their children and their responsibilities as their possessions and their burdens instead of seeing them as God-given opportunities to love God and to serve God. If you can feel that you love your children precisely because God is inside them, then there will be a spontaneous flow of joy and divine love. At that time your children will also feel that their mother has something special to offer.

So please try to feel that between you and your dear ones there is a bridge, and that bridge is God. You are loving your dear ones precisely because God the eternal Beloved is inside them. You are showing compassion to someone because the eternally compassionate Mother is inside you. In that way you can remain in a soulful and spiritual consciousness even while dealing with your children.

Q Sometimes when I am meditating, I feel peace and light all around me. Then someone calls me from the kitchen or some other place, and I have to stop my meditation. Then I feel frustrated.

A First of all, for your serious meditation you should choose a time when your family is not likely to require your attention. But if somebody calls you during your meditation, do not be upset. Feel that the experience that you had during your meditation was most sublime. Now you have to bring this peace, love or light to the person who has called you or distracted you. If you can do this, instead of frustration you will see the extension of the light that you have received. Then you will feel more joy, because your achievement has expanded.

What you are doing is separating your life of meditation from the world of reality. Instead, try to feel that you are bringing the divinity of your meditation into the situation which is the cause of the disturbance. By extending your meditation in this way, you will see it inside your daily activities. Meditation is not only in silence but also in the hustle and bustle of the world. You will find that you can maintain a high consciousness there also.

> *Wherever you go, go with inspiration and aspiration. Whatever you do, do with love and concern.*

Q When we've been in school all day with unaspiring people and we're in an undivine mood, how can we get rid of this mood in order to meditate well?

A Try to think that there are two rooms before you. During the day, when you were with unaspiring people, you were in the unlit room. While you were there, feel that you were caught by some hooligans who were trying to strangle you. They were trying to take away your life—your life of aspiration.

Then, when you sit down to meditate, feel that you have now escaped from that world of destruction. You could have been killed by those forces, but you have escaped into the room of peace, light and delight, which is your true home. When you have that kind of feeling, great relief and gratitude enters into you, and your existence is automatically separated from the world of unreality.

If you do not separate yourself from this world of destruction when you come to meditate, these unaspiring forces will also come. You will carry the vibration, atmosphere and thoughts from that world in your mind. It is as though somebody has thrown a heavy load onto you. You don't know who has thrown it; you are just carrying the load. So as soon as you enter into the other room, just throw the heavy bags away.

Some people take meditation as part of their schedule. They feel that one thing follows another in a continuous series: at eight o'clock they go to the office; at five o'clock they come back; at six o'clock they meditate. But it is wrong to take meditation as just another obligation. Do not unite the uninspiring incidents in your life with the fulfilling incidents. Just separate them and give importance where it is due. When you enter into the meditation room, feel that now you are entering into the real life, whereas previously you were living the unreal life. The moment you do this, you will see that the real life is welcoming you with all its inner wealth.

Q Very often I feel full of love and joy before I fall asleep, and I may remain awake without any conscious thoughts except gratitude. But I am worried about getting up in the morning. I want to be rested.

A If you cannot fall asleep but undivine thoughts are not bothering you, why not try to meditate again? If you do not feel like meditating, then you can read some spiritual books. If it is your bedtime, but you are not sleepy, then the best thing is for you to feel that God has given you an opportunity to meditate more. If you feel sleepy while you are meditating, then you can go to bed. But, if sleepiness is not bothering you, then you should feel fortunate that you can use this time for a divine purpose.

Q Could one make spiritual progress by having a week of solid meditation?

A Then more mental asylums would have to be opened. It is not possible. Only spiritual Masters can meditate for hours and days on end. Ordinary seekers have to talk and mix with people and engage in outer activities. Otherwise, the mind and nerves become very agitated. Then anger comes forward, and also a kind of subtle pride that you have been extremely spiritual for a whole week. Then the seeker becomes abnormal.

Meditating for eighteen or twenty hours a day is possible, but only when you are on the verge of realisation or after you realise God. At that time you will have acquired the capacity. But now if you try it, you will only go crazy.

Do you need happiness? Then do just three things: Meditate regularly. Smile soulfully. Love untiringly.

Keep trying! It so often happens that the last key opens the door. Likewise, it is your last prayer that may grant you salvation, and your last meditation that may grant you realisation.

Never Give Up!

Never Give Up!

❦ Cry Like a Child

Successful meditation entirely depends on our inner cry. When a child is hungry, really hungry, he cries. He may be on the first floor and his mother may be on the third floor, but when the mother hears his cry she comes down immediately to feed the child.

Let us take meditation as an inner hunger. If we are really hungry, our Father Supreme will come running no matter where we are crying. If we have intensity and sincerity in our cry, then we begin to make spiritual progress immediately. Otherwise, it can take years and years.

Again, God-realisation is not like instant coffee—something that you will get immediately. God-realisation takes time. If somebody says he will be able to make you realise God overnight, then do not take him seriously. It takes twenty years to get a Master's degree, which is based on outer knowledge. God-realisation, which is infinitely more important and more significant, naturally will take many more years. In no way do I want to discourage anyone. If your inner hunger is sincere, then God will satisfy that hunger.

If we practise concentration and meditation regularly, we are bound to succeed. If we are really sincere, we will reach the goal. But the difficulty is that we may be sincere for one day or for one week, and then we feel that meditation is not meant for us. We want to realise God overnight. We think, "Let me pray for one week,

one month, one year." After one year, if we don't realise God, we give up. We feel that the spiritual life is not
meant for us.

The road to God-realisation is long. Sometimes, while
walking along the road you will see beautiful trees with
foliage, flowers and fruits. Sometimes you will see that
there is only a road, without any beautiful scenery.
Sometimes you may feel that you are on an endless
road through a barren desert, and that the goal is im-
possibly far away. But you cannot give up walking just
because the distance seems far, or because you are
tired and have no inspiration. You have to be a divine
soldier and march on bravely and untiringly. Each day
you will travel another mile, and by taking one step at a
time eventually you will reach your goal. At that time
you will definitely feel that it was worth the struggle.

 *Love the battlefield of life, for joy is always
breathing secretly and openly in both your
victory and your defeat.*

Q&A

Q What happens if, after meditating for a few
months or a few years, you decide you want to
take a rest and then continue your journey at a later
time?

A In the ordinary life, after you have covered one
mile you can remain where you are for a while
and take rest before continuing your journey. But in the
spiritual life it is not like that. In the spiritual life, once
you take rest doubt enters into you, fear enters into you
and suspicion enters into you. All kinds of negative

forces enter into you and destroy your possibilities. Your potentiality remains the same; eventually you will realise God. But the golden possibilities that you once had are lost. You will fall back to your old ways and be lost in ignorance, and the progress that you made will be destroyed. However, the essence of the progress that you made will remain inside the soul. The essence is never lost, even though in your outer life you cannot use it. The quintessence of the progress that you made will remain inside your heart, and after five or ten years, or in your next incarnation, when you want to meditate again, this quintessence will come to the fore. At that time, if you pray to God most sincerely to enter into the spiritual life again, your previous progress will loom large in your life.

Q How can I maintain my enthusiasm to meditate every day? Some days I feel no inspiration to meditate at all.

A Some days you do not want to meditate because early in the morning you do not renew your love, devotion and surrender to the Eternal Pilot within you. Every day your Eternal Pilot is ready to feed your inner hunger, yet you may not offer Him your gratitude even for a second. If you can feel a flood of gratitude flowing inside you, then easily you can have a wonderful meditation every day.

What should you do if you feel no enthusiasm or inspiration to meditate on a particular day? For a fleeting second remember what you were before you entered into the spiritual life. When you see the difference between what you were and what you are now, automatically a spring of gratitude to the Supreme will well up inside you, for it is He who has inspired you and awakened your inner cry, and it is He who is fulfilling Himself in and through you.

Another thing you can do is to think of a time when you had a most sublime meditation, and consciously dive deep into that experience. Think of its essence—how you were thrilled, how you were jumping with delight. At first you will just be imagining the experience, because you are not actually having that meditation. But if you enter into the world of imagination and stay there for ten or fifteen minutes, power will automatically enter into your meditation and it will bear fruit. Then it will not be imagination at all; you will actually be deep in the world of meditation.

There is something else that you can also do. Try to feel that the dearest in you—either your soul, or your Master, or the Supreme—is very hungry, and that you are in a position to feed your dearest with your meditation. Your soul, your Master and the Supreme are eternally one, but take them as separate individuals. If the dearest in you is starving and you are in a position to feed him, will you not do so? If you really call someone your dearest, your heart will compel you to feed him. After you feed him, he will give you satisfaction, and in that satisfaction you become eternal, infinite and immortal. When the child is hungry, the mother comes running to feed him. After the child is fed, he gives his mother a smile. The mother sees her whole world, the entire universe, inside the smile, because the child is her universe. So, when you feed the dearest and the dearest smiles, at that time you will feel that your entire world is smiling.

Every day you cannot eat the most delicious food. In the spiritual life also, especially in the beginning, it is next to impossible to have a most successful meditation every day. Even spiritual Masters have gone through dry periods in their inner lives. But even if the food is uninspiring, still you eat in order to keep your body fit. When you meditate you are feeding your inner being, the soul. If you cannot feed the soul most delicious food each day, you must not give up trying. It is better to feed the soul something than to allow it to starve.

To maintain your inspiration, each time you sit down to meditate in the morning you have to feel that you are continuing the journey that you have already begun. You should not feel that you are beginning your journey anew. No, you should feel that you have already made considerable progress and that today you will make more progress. And each time you make progress you have to feel that you have touched a tiny portion of the goal. In this way you will feel that you are really advancing.

Even better, you should feel that your goal is not millions of miles away, but very close, right in front of your nose. If you always feel that your goal is within easy reach, but that you don't know where it is, then you will desperately cry for it and search for it. At that time, your inner being will be flooded with dynamism. If you feel that your goal is far, you become relaxed and feel that Eternity is at your disposal. But if you feel that what you want to grow into is just beside you, and that you only have to use your conscious awareness to grasp it and claim it, then you will eagerly jump into your meditation.

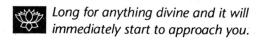 *Long for anything divine and it will immediately start to approach you.*

Only a very advanced seeker can maintain the same level of meditation each day. In the beginning you should be happy if you have a very good meditation even occasionally. When you do not have a good meditation, do not allow yourself to become a victim to frustration, for that will affect your ability to meditate the next day as well. You have to know that God wants your realisation infinitely more than you want it, so your realisation is His responsibility and His problem. If

God has not given you a good meditation today, instead of getting angry or disheartened, try to feel that He is planning to do something more important for you in some other way. If you cannot meditate one day, feel that the Supreme wanted you to have this experience, and just offer your present achievement soulfully and devotedly at His Feet. Say to Him, "These are my possessions right now—unwanted possessions—and I am offering them to You. I place them at Your Feet." If you can offer your existence to the Supreme in that way, then you will see that your daily meditations will become most fruitful.

Q Will I ever reach the point where I will always have the inspiration and aspiration to meditate?

A Right now your meditation is at the mercy of your inspiration or aspiration. When you are inspired, when you have aspiration, you are ready to meditate. Unfortunately this aspiration, this inner urge, lasts only for a day or for a few weeks and then it disappears. But when you become an expert, meditation will be at your command. How can you become an expert? If you want to become an expert singer or poet or dancer, you have to practise daily. It is the same with meditation. If you practise meditation daily, there comes a time when it becomes spontaneous; you develop an inner habit. After a while, at a certain hour you will feel compelled to meditate. You will feel that meditation is your soul's necessity, and the inner urge to meditate will never leave you. Early every morning when it is time for your meditation, your inner being will come and knock at your heart's door. Then you will have a good meditation every day.

Q Why do some people always meditate well?

A In your class at school, I am sure that you are a brilliant student. Again, there are some students in your class who do not do well at all. You are a good student because you study at home. Some of your friends do not study, so they do not do well. In the spiritual life also you have to know that some students meditate without fail every morning, noon and evening. When they meditate with all their heart and soul, God is pleased with them and intensifies their inner cry so that they are able to meditate well every day. Sincere seekers get from God additional capacity, and with that divine capacity they can always meditate well.

 My life of progress is the result of my heart's little cry and my Lord's big Smile.

Q My aspiration seems very feeble, and I'm worried it won't get any stronger in the future.

A Let us not worry about the future. Let us think of the present. As you sow, so you reap. In the past perhaps you have not sown the proper seed. Let us say your inner cry was not intense in the past, and that is why your aspiration is not strong right now. Right now you are not crying for God all the time; you do not have the feeling that without God you cannot exist. You feel that as long as there are interesting things in the world, as long as you have friends, as long as you are comfortable, you can go on. But when you feel that you can exist without water, without air, without everything, but not without God, at that time you can be certain that you will find fulfilment in the future.

If you sow a seed now, it will eventually germinate and become a plant. If we sow the proper seed—that is to say, aspiration—then the aspiration-tree will bear fruit, which we call realisation. But if we do not sow the proper seed inside ourselves, then how can we get the proper fruit? So let us not worry about the future. Let us only do the right thing today, at this moment, here and now. Try to aspire today, and let the future take care of itself.

Q How can I improve my morning meditation?

A Every morning you have to offer your gratitude to God for having awakened your consciousness while others are still sleeping, and for all His infinite blessings to you. If you offer just a fragment of your gratitude, you will feel God's Compassion. Then, when you feel God's Compassion, try to offer yourself. Say, "I will try to please You only in Your own way. So far, I have asked You to please me in my own way, to give me this and that so that I can be happy. But today I am asking for the capacity to please You in Your own way." If you can say this sincerely, automatically your morning meditation will be better.

God is ready to dawn in your mind's chaos, but being a perfect gentleman, He awaits your gracious invitation and precious dedication.

Q How do you feel about collective meditation or group meditation?

A Individual meditation should be done early in the morning at home, when you are alone. But collective meditation also has its time. When you enter into the spiritual life you try to widen your consciousness. If you claim to be a member of a larger spiritual family, then it is your duty to be of service to others. When you meditate with others you can be of real help to them, and they can be of real help to you.

Nobody meditates well every day. Let us say that today you are in a very high state of consciousness, while the person who is sitting beside you is not in his highest consciousness. If both of you are meditating together, your aspiration and even your very presence will inspire and lift up that person. Then, tomorrow it may happen that you are not inspired to go high, whereas the other person is in a high consciousness. At that time he will be able to lift you up. So collective meditation is meant for mutual help.

You have to feel that collective meditation is like a tug-of-war. Suppose that you are in a very high state of consciousness and the seeker beside you is also in a very high state of consciousness. If ten persons meditate together and they are all in a very high state of consciousness, then it is like ten persons on one side in a tug-of-war against ignorance. Since ignorance is only one person, then naturally it will lose the tug-of-war. If you are meditating at home alone and are fighting against ignorance all by yourself, then you may soon become exhausted and give up. But if you can meditate with others, it becomes much easier.

When you meditate in a group, you have to feel your oneness with others. You should not feel that you are competing with anyone else, or that you are stronger or weaker than anyone else. Each individual has to feel that he is strong only by virtue of his oneness with the others. He has to feel that he is strong because he has become one with the aspiration of his brothers and sisters.

During collective meditation try to feel that others are not separate entities. Feel that you are the only person meditating, and that you are entirely responsible for the meditation. When everyone has entered into you, when everyone is flowing in you and through you, at that time you will get the maximum benefit from your collective meditation. If twenty persons are sitting together, they have to feel that they are only one vessel. They are not individuals; they have become one vessel, and they are one in their receptivity. But each one has to feel that it is his obligation and responsibility to do his part. You cannot feel, "Oh, since we are all one, let him meditate for me."

During collective meditation you should have a good feeling for the other persons meditating with you, but do not think of them specifically. If you think of someone in particular, and that person is not aspiring, then your meditation will be on that unaspiring person and not on God. You have to feel that the highest consciousness is the goal, the target, and you are aiming your aspiration-arrow at the target. On the outer plane, if one member of the team scores a goal, that is enough. But in meditation each person has to score. If ten persons can score at the same time, only then does the group get a very high mark.

Q Is there anything wrong with seekers meditating together if they follow different Masters?

A It is not advisable for seekers following one path to meditate with seekers of another path. If you are following one path and the person sitting beside you is following a different path, in spite of your best intentions there will be an inner conflict between your aspiration and his. When you are ready to fly, the person next to you will pull you back. Unconsciously each of you will have the urge to surpass the other. He will try to go beyond you, and you will try to go beyond him. Even if you consciously say, "We are not competing," this does not help. There is an unconscious competition. You feel that your path is better than his, and he feels that his is better than yours.

It is always advisable that the disciples of one spiritual Master meditate only with those on their own path or with those who have not yet chosen a path. It is not that you are being mean; far from it. Only you feel that you live in your house and somebody else lives in his own house.

But when it is a matter of inspiration, if you want to talk with spiritual people who follow other paths, you can. You are trying to reach God, and they are trying to reach God. That means that you and they both possess inspiration. So if you speak with them, you will both get inspiration.

Q What happens if we are meditating next to someone who is thinking worldly thoughts?

A If your meditation is very high, very powerful, at that time inner fire emanates from you. If someone who is cherishing worldly thoughts sits with you, he will be compelled to give up those thoughts. Many times I have seen this when three or four people are meditating together. If one of them is in a very high meditation, then those who are cherishing worldly thoughts either have to leave the place or they are compelled from within to meditate soulfully.

When you are right, everything around you is right, for the beautiful flow that is inside your heart has the capacity to spread its fragrance of oneness-light all around you.

Q How can I maintain the peace that I feel at a group meditation when I get home?

A If you meditate at home every day, then it will be very easy for you to maintain that peace. It is very important to meditate every day without fail. Early in the morning is the best time, before the day dawns. Every day begins with new inspiration, new hope. New life is entering into us every morning, so morning meditation is indispensable for anybody who would like to follow the spiritual path.

Also, if you can mix with spiritual people, they will be able to help you. You will not ignore or hate others; far from it. Spiritual people do not hate mankind, but they have to be cautious. You have to know that your power, your capacity, is very limited. As long as your capacity is very limited, you cannot mix freely with all and sundry. So try to mix with spiritual people and meditate regularly. When you have enough inner strength, then you won't lose anything no matter what you do. Whatever you get from group meditations and whatever you get from your own meditation you will be able to preserve.

Q How can someone achieve the strength to go forward on the spiritual path?

A You have to constantly ask yourself one thing: do you want God or do you want ignorance? Both are standing right in front of you at every moment, and you must make a choice. Everybody knows that one cannot serve two masters. So when these two masters stand in front of you, you have to decide immediately which one you want. If you choose God, then you must come to Him and enter into him. And each time you find that you have come out of a divine consciousness, you have to enter into it again. If you can re-enter into God's Consciousness faithfully and quickly every time you come out of it, then eventually you will reach the point where you will not come out of it and enter into ignorance anymore. A day will come when your conscious choice of God will be permanent, and you will be totally merged in God forever.

As you begin your spiritual journey, always try to feel that you are God's child. Early in the morning you can

Never Give Up!

soulfully repeat, "I am God's child, I am God's child." Immediately you will see that whatever is dark, impure and ugly in you will go away. Later in the day, when ignorance comes to tempt you, you will feel, "I am God's child. How can I do this? I cannot enter into ignorance." By repeating, "I am God's child," you will get abundant inner strength and will power.

When you have the courage to try, you have everything, for God-revealing reality loves you and needs you.

Q How can I always maintain a strong and intense aspiration?

A The mistake that you and others make is that you have a fixed goal. If you come to a certain standard during your meditation, you feel that you have reached your goal. Or if you get a little joy in your inner life, then immediately you get a complacent feeling. You want to rest on yesterday's laurels. But I wish to say that our goal is an ever-transcending goal. Yesterday you got an iota of joy, and today you are crying to get that same iota of joy. But how do you know whether the Supreme wants you to have that iota of joy or whether He wants you go farther, higher and deeper?

In your case it happens that you always try to reach a particular goal. If you know how to run fifty metres, then after you have run fifty metres you feel that your part is over. But the Supreme does not want you to be satisfied with fifty metres. He wants you to run fifty-one, fifty-two, fifty-three, fifty-four metres. When you have a higher goal, automatically your aspiration increases. Otherwise, if you always aim at the same goal, you don't make progress, and it becomes monotonous. If you always go to the same place, after a while you don't want to go there anymore. But if you feel that your goal is constantly farther, higher, deeper, that it is ever-increasing, ever-ascending, then there is constant enthusiasm.

Joy is in progress, not in success. Success ends our journey, but progress has no end. When you have a fixed goal and you reach it, that is your success. After that, you are finished. But if you don't have a fixed goal, if your goal is going higher all the time, then you will constantly make progress, and you will get the greatest satisfaction.

So do not be satisfied with success. Aspire only for progress. Each time you make progress, that is your real success. Every day when you meditate, feel that you will go still deeper, fly still higher. Then you will be able to maintain your intensity and enthusiasm.

Q How can we maintain a good standard consistently, instead of going up and down?

A Please feel that every day is equally important. Your difficulty is that when you do something well you feel that you deserve some relaxation. Today you do a wonderful meditation, and then you feel, "Oh, since today I had a wonderful meditation, tomorrow I can relax." You feel that your meditation will maintain the same speed, but it doesn't.

Every time you meditate, you have to feel that this may be your last chance. Feel that tomorrow you may die, so if you fail today, then zero will be your mark. When the teacher gives you the examination paper today, please don't feel that tomorrow again he will give you the same examination. The past is gone. The future does not exist. There is only the present. Here in the present, either you have to become divine, or else you will remain as undivine as you were yesterday. Since you want to become divine, you should do the right thing here and now. This should be your attitude.

You should make yourself feel that today is the last day for you to achieve everything that you are supposed to achieve. If you fail today, then tomorrow again you have to feel that this is your last day. No matter how many times you fail, you should feel that each day is your last. If you feel that opportunity will come back and knock at your door tomorrow, then today you will not try. You will feel that you don't need to aspire today because you have so many tomorrows. But before those tomorrows come, the aspiration that you have today may be lost.

Do not give up. If you persist, tomorrow's peace will come and feed your mind today, and tomorrow's perfection will come and touch your life today.

As long as your heart remains an ever-mounting aspiration-flame, it makes no difference what your weaknesses are.

Meditation: The Practical Problem-Solver

Meditation: The Practical Problem-Solver

❦ Is Meditation Practical?

We say that somebody is practical when he does the right thing at the right moment in his outer life. He thinks and acts in a specific way so that others will not deceive him and his outer life will run smoothly. But no matter how clever, how sincere or how conscious we are, at times we are at a loss in the outer life. We do not know what to say. We do not know what to do. We do not know how to behave. Or, despite our saying and doing the right thing, everything goes wrong. We do not know how to cope with our outer existence; we cannot manage our lives. We sincerely want to do something or become something, but we cannot do it.

Why does this happen? It happens because our outer capacity is always limited by our limited inner awareness. But if we are practical in the inner life—that is to say, if we pray and meditate—then we will have boundless inner awareness. One who has inner awareness has free access to infinite truth and everlasting joy, and he can easily control his outer life.

The inner life constantly carries the message of truth and God. Where truth is, there is a seed. Let us allow the seed to germinate and become a tree. When the tree bears fruit, we will see the capacity of the inner world being manifested in the outer world. We always grow from within, not from without.

No matter what we do or what we say in our outer life, we are not nearing the truth-light. But if we meditate first, and afterwards act and speak, then we are doing and becoming the right thing. The inner life and inner reality must guide the outer life—not the other way around. The life-breath of the outer life has to come from the inner life. The inner reality must enter into the outer life; only then can we be really practical in the outer life.

Q&A

Q Can we answer our own questions through our daily meditations? And if so, how can we tell if the answer really comes from the heart or the soul, as opposed to the mind?

A Any question you have can be answered during your meditation or at the end of your meditation. If you go deep within, you are bound to get an answer. But when you get an answer, you have to determine whether it is coming from the soul or from the mind. If it comes from the heart or the soul, then you will feel a sense of relief and peace. At that time no contradictory thought will come to negate the answer. But if the answer does not come from the heart or the soul, then the mind will come to the fore and contradict the idea you have received.

Messages that come from the mind will have no certainty in them. This moment the mind tells you one thing; the next moment the mind tells you something else. This moment your mind will tell you that I am a very good man; the next moment your mind will say, "No, he is very bad." But the heart always offers the same message. When you sit down to meditate in the morning, it gives one message. In the evening when you meditate, you will get the same message from the heart.

If you get an inner message to see somebody—let us say your boss—you will simply go and see that person. But if the message comes from the mind, before you see him there will be many questions in your mind. Then, if you finally do see him and the result does not come out according to your satisfaction, you will curse yourself and say, "No, it was not the right thing to do. I got the wrong message."

But if the message comes from the soul, you will have tremendous conviction, and you will take both success and failure with equal satisfaction. While you are executing the message, you will not expect anything in your own way; you will not expect that your boss will be pleased with you or will do something for you. You will just do it, and whether the result comes in the form of success or failure, you will feel that you have done the right thing.

Q How can we tell if an inner message is coming from the emotional vital rather than the soul?

A You can take the vital as one runner and the soul as another runner. The vital-runner goes very fast at the beginning, with excessive excitement and enthusiasm, but he does not reach the goal. He runs about thirty metres out of a hundred, and then he cannot run anymore. The soul-runner also runs very fast at the beginning. But once the starter fires the gun, he does not stop until he reaches his goal. The soul knows its capacity and will go to the goal with utmost confidence.

When you get a message, immediately try to see which type of runner is represented. Is this the runner who will stop only when the goal is reached, or is this the runner who will run thirty metres and then lose all his energy? If the message comes from the emotional vital, you will feel that the answer you get will not take you to your goal. But if it comes from the soul, you will feel confident that it will take you to the goal.

Here is another way. When you hear a voice which is offering you a solution to a problem, imagine that a vessel is being filled. If you get the feeling of a vessel being filled slowly and steadily, drop by drop, with utmost inner security, then you will know that it is the soul's voice. Otherwise, you will feel that the vessel is being filled with a tumbler or a glass in a hurried manner. It will fill up quickly, but very soon it will begin to spill over the top. The soul will fill the vessel with utmost confidence and inner poise. If you have that kind of patient feeling, then you can know that it is the soul's voice.

A third way is to imagine a flame inside your heart. There are two types of flames. One is steady; the other is flickering. The steady flame inside your heart is not disturbed by any inner wind. But the flickering flame is disturbed by fear, doubt, anxiety and worry. If you feel that your answer is a flickering flame, then it is the voice of the emotional vital. But if it is a very steady flame rising towards the highest, then you will know that it is the soul's voice. Once you know that it is the soul's voice, you can have utmost confidence in that message.

Q Can one learn to overcome one's fears through meditation?

A Through meditation, outer fear and inner fear are bound to leave us. Now you are a victim to fear because you do not know how to expand your consciousness. But when you take refuge in your divinity, with the help of meditation, then fear has to leave you, for it feels that it is knocking at the wrong door. Now you are helpless, but fear will be helpless the moment it sees that through meditation you are in touch with something most powerful.

The very purpose of meditation is to unite, expand, enlighten and immortalise our consciousness. When we meditate, we enter into our own divinity. Divinity is not afraid of humanity, because divinity has infinite power. When we have free access to divinity, when our entire existence, inner and outer, is surcharged with divinity's boundless and infinite power, then how can we be afraid of humanity? It is impossible!

Q Can meditation protect us from all the injustice we experience in life?

A When you have to defend yourself or protect yourself, always try to use a higher weapon. If people say something and you retaliate on the same level, there will be no end to it. Again, if you simply swallow your anger, they will continue to take advantage of you. But when they see and feel tremendous inner peace in you, which you can get from your meditation, they will see something in you which can never be conquered. They will see a change in you, and this change will not only puzzle them but also threaten and frighten them. They will feel that their weapons are useless.

Peace is the most effective weapon with which to conquer injustice. When you pray and meditate, your whole being becomes flooded with peace. This is not something imaginary. You can feel peace; you can swim in the sea of peace. Then, no matter what other people do, you will feel that they are just children playing in front of you. You will say, "These are all children. What more can I expect from them?" But right now, because they are grown up in terms of years, you become angry and upset instead. If you pray and meditate regularly, you will soon feel that your peace is infinitely stronger, more fulfilling and more energising than the unfortunate situations that others create.

> *Have no fear. Nobody has any power of his own. Only God has power, and His power is another name for His sleepless Love.*

Q Is there a spiritual way to break bad habits?

A Certainly there is. Before you do anything, always meditate for a minute or at least for a few seconds. The power of that meditation will enter into the bad habit like an arrow. Meditation, the soldier, will use his divine arrows against bad habits. This is absolutely the best way.

Q Can meditation help cure physical ailments such as high blood pressure?

A Meditation means conscious awareness of our source. When we meditate, we consciously try to go to the source, which is all perfection. Our source is God, our source is truth, our source is light. Meditation takes us to our source, where there is no imperfection, no ailment. And where is the source? It is within us.

When we meditate, what result do we get in the outer life? We make our mind calm and quiet. It is almost impossible for most human beings to have peace of mind. He who does not have peace of mind is a veritable beggar; he is like a monkey in a human body. He has no satisfaction. But if we get peace of mind for one fleeting second, we feel we have accomplished a lot in life. When we have peace of mind, our vital and our body become peaceful; and where there is peace there is no disharmony. It is only in the world of anxiety, dissatisfaction, tension and confusion that there is disharmony. Otherwise, there would be no ailments.

High blood pressure, heart failure and all the diseases that we notice in God's creation are due to the presence of negative forces. These negative forces can be overcome only when we surrender to the positive force. When we meditate, we try to become a perfect channel for the positive force. The positive force is light, and the negative force is darkness. The positive force is love, not hatred. The positive force is belief, not disbelief. At each moment in our life the positive force helps us because it takes us consciously to our destination, which is perfection.

If our mind is calm and quiet, if our vital is dynamic, if our body is conscious of what it is doing, then we are inside the palace of satisfaction, where there can be no disease, no suffering, no imperfection, no obstruction to our abiding peace, abiding light, abiding satisfaction. Meditation is a means; it is a way; it is a path. If we walk along this path, then we reach our destination, which is all perfection.

Q If we are confused and nervous, how will meditation ever be able to help us?

A In the physical world, when somebody has a headache or a stomach upset, he goes to a doctor and the doctor cures him. If somebody is sick, then how can we say that he will never be well again? If he takes medicine, then there is every possibility that he will be cured. For a sick person, medicine is the answer. If somebody is assailed by anxiety, worry and confusion, meditation is the remedy. Just because he is a victim, we can't say that there will be no saviour. The saviour is there, provided the individual wants to be cured.

Suppose somebody is assailed by confusion and negative forces that deplete all his energy and take all joy out of his life. He is depressed and has surrendered to frustration owing to countless problems in his life. Let us take him as a patient: he needs a doctor, he needs treatment. When an individual is suffering from a few ailments in the mental world, he has to go to someone who has some peace of mind, some light, some inner assurance for him. This is a spiritual teacher. The spiritual teacher is like a doctor who will advise the person as to how he can free himself from fear, doubt, confusion, tension and all the negative forces that are torturing him.

Q Is it really necessary to seek help when we are suffering from mental problems? Can't we just meditate by ourselves and find the answer?

A Suppose you say, "I am suffering from certain mental difficulties, but I know the answer is inside. Now it is all night, but I feel that there is light inside my heart." This is what you feel, but you find it difficult to go deep within and discover the light. Then you have to go to someone who can bring to the fore the light that you have within you. It is as if you have misplaced the key to your own house and you don't know how to open the door. But a friend of yours comes with a light and helps you look for the key. After you find it with his help, you open the door and then he goes away. If you are ready to search in the dark for the key that you have lost, then you can try. But if you have a friend who has a light, then you can have more confidence in finding the key. So the teacher is a helper, an eternal friend who helps you in your search. When he helps you find the key, he won't keep it. He won't say it is his key. No! It is your key, your house, your light. Then you will enter into the house and get everything that you needed and wanted.

Q If we feel nervous or upset, how can we bring down peace?

A There are two ways. One way is to breathe in quietly and say "Supreme" three times very slowly. But if you find this difficult, you can invoke the Supreme as fast as possible. Fear or anxiety has a speed of its own. If you are about to be attacked by your enemy, then try to utter the name of the Supreme much faster than the speed of the attack you are getting from anger or fear. If you can do this, the Supreme will immediately conquer your anger, frustration or fear.

 Look at your heart-flower and smile. You will be able to solve your most pressing problems.

Q How can one remain calm in the mind when one has so many things to do in so little time?

A First of all, if you are not peaceful, do you think that the things you have to accomplish will be accomplished sooner? No! When you are restless and agitated, when you are full of anxiety and worries, you just add to your problems and difficulties. Suppose you have a destination which you want to reach as soon as possible. If you carry inside you undivine elements like fear, doubt, anxiety, insecurity and so forth, that means you are carrying an extra weight and diminishing your capacity. So how will you reach your goal at the earliest possible hour? Your appointed hour will be delayed.

A runner knows that if he carries extra weight, his opponents will defeat him. You have to feel the necessity of emptying your mind all the time. When doubt, fear, insecurity or any other negative forces enter into your mind, just empty them out, cast them aside so that you can run the fastest. Worries and anxieties will never help us. On the contrary, they will delay us. But if we have peace of mind, then we can run the fastest toward the goal.

Q How can we use meditation to get rid of pain?

A You should try to invoke light in order to cure pain. Pain is, after all, a kind of darkness within us. When the inner light or the light from above starts functioning in the pain itself, then the pain is removed or transformed into joy. Really advanced seekers can actually feel joy in the pain itself. But for that, one has to be very highly advanced. In your case, during your prayer or meditation you should try to bring down light from above and feel that the pain is a darkness within you. If you bring down light, then the pain will either be illumined and transformed or removed from your system.

Q One time when I was meditating I suddenly found myself thinking about some friends who needed some help. I could never describe the power I felt at this time, but I took these friends and lifted them. Two or three days later these friends were helped. Somebody needed a job and he got it, and somebody was ill and he got better. Is it related to my experience or was it mere coincidence?

A It was not a coincidence; far from it. It was your own inner being that helped them. At that time you became the instrument of the Inner Pilot, the Supreme. The Supreme wanted to help those people, and

He actually made you the instrument to help them. It was not a coincidence.

When you meditate and enter into your highest consciousness, your soul automatically tries to help your dear ones. When you enter into a very high, very deep realm of consciousness, automatically the power from within comes to the fore and you can help others. Sometimes your friends do not know who has helped them. But your soul knows and their souls know that the help has come from you. It is not your mental hallucination or ego.

> *If you can become a better listener, God's Compassion will immediately become a better adviser.*

Do not try to change the world. You will fail. Try to love the world. Lo, the world is changed, changed forever.

Meditation in Action: Serving Others

Meditation in Action: Serving Others

❦ How Do I Share My Meditation?

When we meditate in silence with utmost devotion, that is one form of meditation. When we try to dedicate our work to God or to the world, that is another form of meditation, which we may call manifestation. At that time we are serving the divinity in humanity.

In order to serve the divinity in humanity effectively, we have to consciously feel God's presence in those we are serving. While we are speaking to someone, we have to feel that we are speaking to the divinity within that person. Otherwise, if we are just helping someone in our own way without any conscious feeling of dedication to the Supreme, that work cannot be considered as a form of manifestation or as meditation in action.

If we pray and meditate, we will feel that God is inside everybody, that He is a living reality. God is everywhere and in everything, true. But if we pray and meditate, then this mental belief becomes a real, living truth to us. At that time we will consciously serve each person precisely because we know and feel that God is inside him.

If we do not see God, truth, or light in our action, then our physical mind may not be convinced of the value of the things that we are doing. Today we will serve someone and tomorrow we will say, "Oh, he is such a fool! He has no aspiration, no good qualities! Why should I serve him?" If we look at an individual without prayer and meditation, we will separate the person from the soul. But if we pray and meditate, then we will see the soul, the divinity inside each person, and we will try to bring their divinity to the fore.

If we pray and meditate, then our work will be dedicated service, and this dedicated service will help us to make spiritual progress. There are many people who work fifteen, sixteen hours a day. But their action is not dedicated service. They are only working mechanically to make money and take care of their outer responsibilities. But if we really wish to dedicate our life to God and mankind, then prayer and meditation will enable us to do so.

Q&A

Q Should a person shut himself away all alone and reject humanity in order to meditate?

A Humanity is part and parcel of God. By rejecting humanity, how are we going to embrace divinity? We have to accept the world as it is now. If we don't accept a thing, how can we transform it? If a potter does not touch the lump of clay, how is he going to shape it into a pot? He who meditates has to act like a divine hero amidst humanity.

Humanity at present is far, far from perfection. But we are also members of that humanity. How can we discard our brothers and sisters, who are like the limbs of our own body? If we do that we will only limit our own ability to act effectively in the world. We have to accept humanity as our very own. If we are in a position to inspire others, if we are one step ahead, then we have the opportunity to serve divinity in the ones who are following us.

We have to face the world and realise the Highest in the world. We do not want to lead the life of an escapist. Who escapes? He who is afraid, or he who feels that he has done something seriously wrong. We have not done anything wrong and we do not have to be afraid of the world around us. If we are afraid of the world, then we shall be afraid of everything.

Now we see a giant world of imperfection around us. We try to escape it in order to protect ourselves. But I wish to say that a far more formidable enemy than the present-day world is nothing other than our own mind. Even if we go and live in a cave, we cannot escape our mind. We carry that mind with us—a mind which is full of anxiety, jealousy, confusion, doubt, fear and other undivine qualities. This mind of ours forces us to remain in the battlefield of life. If we do not conquer our mind while living in the world, what good will it do us to merely remove our body from the everyday world?

We need not and must not enter into the Himalayan caves in order to meditate. We have to try to transform the face of the world on the strength of our dedication to the divinity in humanity. Meditation is not an escape. Meditation is the acceptance of life in its totality with a view to transforming it for the highest manifestation of the divine Truth here on earth.

Those people who only want to meditate for their own inner peace and progress, and who do not want to offer anything to the world, are selfish. Again, there are those who want to give to the world, but do not want to meditate in order to attain something worth giving. This is foolishness. If we do not possess something, then how are we going to give it? There are many people on earth who are ready to give, but what do they have? So we have to play our part. First we have to achieve, then we have to offer. In this way we can please God and fulfil mankind.

Do you want to change the world? Then change yourself first. Do you want to change yourself? Then remain completely silent inside the silence-sea.

Q Is it possible to maintain the inner peace we feel during our morning meditation throughout the day, especially when our jobs are hectic and we sometimes find ourselves in irritating situations?

A In the morning, when you pray and meditate, feel that you have gained real wealth in the form of peace, light and bliss. As you keep your money inside your wallet, so you can keep your peace, light and bliss inside your heart. With money-power, you can buy whatever you want. Similarly, the spiritual power that you get from prayer and meditation is a real power. When people are quarrelling, fighting or behaving undivinely, just bring forward the inner power which you have kept inside your heart. Peace is power, light is power, bliss is power, just as money is power. Just bring these qualities forward. The power of inner peace is infinitely more solid and concrete than any outer disturbance anybody can create on earth. Your inner peace can easily devour the irritation caused by others.

Q If we meditate well in the morning and acquire some peace, light and bliss that we can keep with us during the day, will this be noticeable to others?

A If you have achieved something in your meditation, your friends and colleagues are bound to see something pleasing, soothing, beautiful, enlightening and illumining in you. Peace, light and bliss have entered through your soul into your physical consciousness. The higher and deeper your meditation and the more you have received, the more your face and outer being will radiate and glow. After you have finished meditating, just go and look in a mirror and you will see the difference between what you are now and what you were an hour ago. This obvious physical difference is due to the fact that your physical consciousness is manifesting the light from your soul. Even as you walk along the street, you will be spreading this light. It is like a perfume that you have inside you. You are not actually using it; you are only keeping it, but it is offering its fragrance. At that time the world of aspiration and even the world of suffering, depression and despair will definitely see something in you. And it will try to follow you—sometimes with reluctance, sometimes with joy, sometimes with greed; but in some way or other it will try to follow you.

You do not have to tell others hundreds of times how meditation has changed your life. Only let them see you on one day when you have meditated well and on another day when you have not had a good meditation. The day that you have meditated well, they will see a tremendous change in you. Your very presence will inspire them.

Q How can I bridge the gap I feel between my spiritual life, which is full of joy, and my life in the office, which is totally unaspiring?

A Spiritual life does not mean that you will always be sitting in meditation with your eyes closed. When you do something in the outer world, if you can feel that you are doing it for God, then everything you do will become a part of your spiritual life. Otherwise, when you are meditating in your room, you will feel that you are doing the right thing, and the rest of the time you will feel miserable. Dedicated work is also a form of meditation.

In the morning the Supreme wants you to enter into your highest and offer your love and devotion to Him and receive His peace, light and blessings. Then He wants you to go to your office and do your dedicated service. In both cases, if you can feel that you are doing something because you have been asked to do it from within, then you will have the greatest joy. You are not the doer; you are only a dedicated instrument serving a higher reality. If you can feel this, then you will get joy no matter what you do. Even if you are doing something mechanical, something intellectual or something which is absolutely uninspiring, you will get the greatest joy because you are serving a higher cause.

You have to know that you can feel God's presence in anything you do. If you can be conscious of God while you are doing something—whether it is cleaning or cooking or working—then you will feel that God has entered into what you are doing. If you can feel God's presence within your activity, then whatever you are doing is with God and for God. If you can keep your consciousness high and maintain peace of mind while working, then your work itself is a true form of meditation.

 Each devoted moment prepares a beautiful sunrise and a fruitful sunset.

Q When people try to help humanity, isn't it partly because of ego?

A For an ordinary person who is not consciously aspiring, trying to help humanity is a positive and progressive ideal, even if it is partly inspired by ego. But those who are consciously aspiring to reach God have a different goal. Their goal is not to help, but to serve humanity—of course, in God's own way.

As spiritual aspirants, we have to know why we are doing something. Were we inspired by God? Were we commissioned by God? If our actions were not inspired by God, if we are not fulfilling God's Will, then the service that we are offering to the world will be full of darkness and imperfection. If we try to help mankind in our own way, we may think that we are serving God, but really we are just aggrandising our own ego. That kind of dedication is no dedication at all for a true spiritual aspirant.

Q What can I do if sometimes I am angry or upset and don't feel like meditating? Is it okay to do selfless service instead?

A Certainly. If your mental agitation has not affected your physical body, at that time, if you feel that you can work devotedly, you should. When you work for the Supreme, at that time you are doing meditation in the physical. You have a body, vital, mind and heart. If you cannot meditate in all parts of your being, then try to meditate in at least one part. But if all the parts of your being—physical, vital, mental and psychic—work together devotedly, then that is the best form of meditation.

Q If we give up our desires and live all the time in the inner world, how will there be any progress in the outer world?

A If you feel that we cannot live all the time in light, that we have to live in darkness for twelve hours and in light for twelve hours, that philosophy is perfectly all right, according to the standard of certain individuals. Someone meditates for one hour, and then goes out and enters into ordinary life. Someone else can meditate for several hours, while there are some people who can meditate all day and night. It is all a matter of necessity. Inner necessity compels one person to meditate for one hour and someone else to meditate for twelve hours or twenty-four hours.

When somebody meditates for an hour, he gets a kind of satisfaction. During that hour, he could have done something totally different, but he did not. He preferred to meditate. He felt that the satisfaction he would get from meditation was more worthwhile than the satisfaction he would get from working or sleeping or whatever else he would have done during that hour. After that hour, perhaps he may want to go back to the worldly life and its kind of satisfaction. It is a question of what kind of satisfaction a person wants and needs.

There are two rooms. One room is unlit and obscure right now; the other room is fully illumined. One person may say that he wants both rooms equally: "I want to remain in the unlit room for twelve hours and in the well-illumined room for twelve hours." So he is most welcome to do that. But somebody else may not feel the necessity of staying in the unlit room at all. He says, "I want to remain only in the room which is illumined."

 Yesterday I was clever. That is why I wanted to change the world. Today I am wise. That is why I am changing myself.

Then there is another person who says, "I have remained in the illumined room for twenty-four hours and I have gotten illumination. Now let me go into the other room which is still dark and illumine it with my light." This person has a big heart, so he enters into the dark room to illumine his brothers and sisters who are still in darkness. He was getting satisfaction, abiding satisfaction, in the illumined room, but this was not enough. He will be fully satisfied only when he goes into the dark room and transforms it with his light. So there are some people on earth who have come back into the world of suffering even though they have the perfect capacity to remain eternally in the world of light and delight.

If we can bring the wealth of the inner world into the outer world, then easily we can illumine this world, and this illumination is nothing other than progress. But first we must enter the inner world—the world of light—and receive something ourselves before we can offer it to the outer world. When we can do this, the inner and outer worlds will become united, and the outer world will become fully ready for the inner message. Right now the outer world is not ready, but a day will come when the outer world and the inner world will progress perfectly together.

Q Do both activity and meditation form the essence of your teaching?

A Our philosophy does not negate either the outer life or the inner life. Most human beings negate the inner life. They feel that the inner life is not important as long as their outer life is pleasant. Again, there are a few who think that the outer life is not necessary. They feel that the best thing is to enter into the Himalayan caves and lead a life of solitude, since the outer life is so painful and uninspiring.

We do not believe in living either a life of solitude or an ordinary human life—the so-called modern life that depends on machines and not on the inner reality, the soul. We try to synthesise and harmonise the outer life and the inner life. The outer life is like a beautiful flower and the inner life is its fragrance. If there is no fragrance, then we cannot appreciate the flower. Again, if there is no flower, how can there be any fragrance? So the inner life and the outer life must go together.

The most important thing a spiritual Master does for his spiritual children is to make them consciously aware of something vast and infinite within themselves, which is nothing other than God Himself.

The Guru: Your Private Tutor

The Guru:
Your Private Tutor

❦ What Is a Guru?

Guru is a Sanskrit word which means "he who illumines." The one who offers illumination is called a Guru. According to my own inner realisation I wish to say that there is only one real Guru, and that is the Supreme. No human being is the real Guru. But although the Supreme alone is the real Guru, here on earth we value time. If we find someone who can help us on our journey towards illumination, we take his help, and we may call him our Guru.

A spiritual Master or Guru is like the eldest child in the family, and the seekers are like his younger spiritual brothers and sisters. Spiritual Masters tell and show their younger brothers and sisters where their Father, the Absolute Guru, is.

The real Guru is not in the vast blue skies. He is inside the very depth of our heart. You may ask, "If He is inside our heart, then why is it necessary for us to take help from somebody else to find Him?" Although this invaluable treasure is inside our heart, we cannot see it or feel it, so we need help. A friend of ours, who we call our Guru or spiritual teacher, comes to us and teaches us how to find our own treasure.

It is not obligatory to have a living Guru, but it is certainly advisable. You know that there is a goal, and you want to reach that goal. If you are wise, you will accept help from someone who can show you the easiest, safest and most effective path to the goal. If you want to take hundreds and thousands of years to realise God, having a spiritual Master is not necessary. But if you want to reach the goal as soon as possible, then certainly it is a necessity.

If you have a Master, it facilitates your inner spiritual progress. A spiritual Master is your private tutor in the spiritual life. There is a big difference between a private tutor and an ordinary teacher. An ordinary teacher will look at a student's paper and then give him a mark. He will examine the student and then pass him or fail him. But the private tutor personally encourages and inspires the student at home so that he can pass his examination. At every moment in life's journey, ignorance tries to examine you, but your private tutor will teach you how to pass the examination easily. It is the business of the spiritual teacher to inspire the seeker and increase his aspiration so that he can realise the Highest as soon as possible.

In order to learn anything in this world you need a teacher in the beginning. To learn mathematics you need a teacher. To learn history you need a teacher. It is absurd to feel that for everything else in life you need a teacher, but not for meditation. Why do people go to the university when they can study at home? It is because they feel that they will get expert instruction from people who know the subject well. There have been a few, but very few, real men of knowledge who did not go to any university. Yes, there are exceptions; every rule admits of exceptions. God is in everybody, and if a seeker feels that he does not need human help, he is most welcome to try his capacity alone. But if someone is wise and wants to run toward his goal instead of stumbling or merely walking, then certainly the help of a Guru will be immeasurable.

Right now, perhaps, I am in London. I know that New York exists and that I have to go back there. What do I need to get me there? An airplane and a pilot. In spite of the fact that I know that the plane can take me to New York, I cannot get there without the help of the pilot. Similarly, you know that God exists. You want to reach God through meditation, but someone has to take you there. As the pilot takes me to New York, someone has to take you to the consciousness of God which is deep within you. Someone has to show you how to enter into your own divinity through meditation.

A spiritual Master comes to you with a boat. He says, "Come. If you want to go to the Golden Shore, I will take you. Moreover, once you get into my boat, you can sing on the boat, you can dance, you can even sleep; but I will bring you safely to the Shore." If you say that you do not need anybody's help, if you want to swim across the sea of ignorance alone, then it is up to you. But how many years, or how many incarnations will it take you? And again, after swimming for some time you may become totally exhausted and then you may drown.

Without a Guru, your progress will be ve'y slow and uncertain. You may get high, elevating experiences and not give them adequate significance. Or doubt may enter your mind, and you may think, "I am just an ordinary person, so how can I have that kind of experience? Perhaps I am deluding myself." Or you will tell your friends about your experiences, and they will say, "It is all a mental hallucination!" But if there is someone who knows what the inner reality is, he will be able to assure you that the experiences which you have are absolutely real. The Master encourages the seeker and inspires him. And if the seeker is doing something wrong in his meditation, the Master is in a position to correct him.

Once you complete a course, you no longer need a teacher. If you want to learn how to sing, you go to a singer and learn from him. If you want to be a dancer, you go to a dancer. Once you become a good singer or dancer, you don't have to go to the teacher anymore. In the spiritual life it is the same. You need help in the beginning, but once you become extremely advanced, you will not need anybody's help.

If someone becomes a true disciple of a Master, he does not feel that he and his Guru are two totally different beings. He does not feel that his Guru is at the top of the tree and he is at the foot of the tree. No! He feels that the Guru is his own highest part. He feels that he and the Guru are one, that the Guru is his own highest and most developed part. Therefore, a true disciple does not find any difficulty in surrendering his lowest part to his highest part. It is not beneath his dignity to be a devoted disciple, because he knows that both the highest and the lowest are his very own.

 He who inspires you is your real teacher.
He who loves you is your real teacher.
He who forces you is your real teacher.
He who perfects you is your real teacher.
He who treasures you is your real teacher.

Q Does each individual have a specific path or are all paths relatively similar?

A All the paths are not the same, although the ultimate goal is the same. There are different roads, but each road leads to the same goal. Each individual needs the guidance of a Master, and each individual has to discover his own path. Then he must follow only one path and one Master who is the leader or guide of that path.

Each individual must necessarily have a path of his own. That doesn't mean that there will not be other seekers on the path. There will be others who will want to follow the same path, but each seeker will follow it in his own way, according to his own inspiration, aspiration, and spiritual development.

Q Is it possible to follow more than one path?

A If you are practising spiritual discipline under the guidance of a Master, it is always advisable to give up your connection with other paths. If you are satisfied with one Master but are still looking for another Master, then you are making a serious mistake. You will not be able to receive what your Master wants to give you, and your spiritual progress will be very slow. Spirituality is not like a school where you have a teacher in each subject: history, geography and so on. No. God-realisation is one subject, and for that subject only one teacher is needed. So for the fastest progress, it is always advisable to find a Master in whom you have the utmost faith and then remain in his boat only. Otherwise, if you have one foot in his boat and another foot in some other boat, you will eventually fall into the water.

Q How does one know whether he is ready for a spiritual path or not?

A When you are hungry you know that you have to eat. Your hunger compels you to eat something. In the inner life also, when you are hungry for peace, light and bliss, at that time you are ready. When you have an inner cry, then you are ready for a spiritual path. When you feel the need, you are ready. If you don't have the need, then you are not ready.

Sometimes it happens that the seeker is ready and the Master is available, but attachment to the ordinary life prevents the seeker from looking sincerely enough. The other day somebody told me that she has been looking for a Master for nineteen or twenty years. I was so surprised, because I was positive that her Master is alive. If she had really been searching sincerely and crying for her Master, then she would have found him. If the aspirant is really sincerely crying for a path, then his path will present itself before him. If he really cries for a spiritual Master, either the Master will come to him or he will be able to go to the Master. No sincere effort ends in vain. If someone makes a sincere effort, then I wish to say that his inner life and outer life are bound to be crowned with success.

*What gives life its value
If not its constant cry
For self-transcendence.*

Meditating as Sri Chinmoy's Disciple

Chapter 18

Meditating as
Sri Chinmoy's Disciple

❦ Your Own Personal Guide

Each Master has his own way of teaching his students to meditate. I ask my disciples to begin their meditation by repeating the word "Supreme" a few times. The Supreme is our eternal Guru. If you chant *Aum* soulfully, it will also help you. In the spiritual life, gratitude is of paramount importance. Early in the morning when you first begin your meditation, take three very deep slow breaths, and while you are inhaling, offer your soulful gratitude to the Supreme for having awakened you and given you the inner urge to meditate. Out of millions of people on earth, He has chosen you to enter the spiritual life; so naturally you are grateful.

You may say that you do not know how to meditate. But I wish to say that once you become my disciple, once you enter into my spiritual boat, then it is the problem of the boatman to take you to the Golden Shore. After you are safely seated in the boat, you can lie down, you can sing, you can dance, you can do anything. But first you have to enter into the boat. Occasionally I give instructions outwardly to disciples who need it. But to most I do not give individual meditations. Instead, when I accept a disciple I concentrate on his or her soul and give the soul an inner form of meditation. I bring the soul forward, and the soul actually meditates in and through the seeker. The soul also convinces the heart and mind to do the right thing, so that eventually the entire being—body, vital, mind, heart and soul—will be able to properly meditate. When I concentrate on the disciple's soul, the disciple is bound to receive my inner instruction. But if the disciple can consciously create a pure vibration and keep a sincere attitude, then it is easier for his soul to remain at the fore and to receive everything from me.

Individualised meditation

In the ordinary life if ten students come to the same class in school, the teacher gives them all the same lesson. But in the case of a spiritual Master it is different. When he meditates on his disciples, the consciousness that he gives to one will not be the same as what he gives to another.

When I meditate on my disciples, I motivate and inspire each individual according to his acceptance of me and according to his capacity to receive and manifest the light that I am offering him. Out of God's infinite bounty I have the capacity to enter into each person's consciousness and soul to see what that particular individual needs most, and how he wants to manifest the divinity within himself. One individual's soul may want to realise and manifest the truth through divine power. Another individual may want to realise God through love, devotion and surrender. So first I see what the soul wants, and then I can tell the person inwardly, "You follow this method." I may not tell him outwardly, but inwardly I say, "This is the way you have to realise and manifest the truth." Then the soul may take a day, a week or a few months to convince the rest of the being how to meditate. The mind may not understand, but for meditation the mind is not at all necessary.

From time to time I may outwardly tell an individual how to meditate. But the meditation that I give is given in strictest confidence, and it is meant only for that particular individual. If he tells others and they try to use the same method, that will be a serious mistake.

Each person must go his own way during meditation because each has a particular role, a special mission on earth, to fulfil. In God's divine Play, each one has been allotted a particular part, and to perform that part one has to meditate according to one's own inner necessity.

If you feel that you are inwardly drawn to me but you have not received an individual meditation, do not worry. The best type of meditation comes when you enter into my consciousness by looking at a picture taken of me when I am in a high meditative consciousness. While meditating on my picture you do not have to think of anything. Just try to throw your outer and inner existence into my consciousness with utmost aspiration. If a thought comes to you, whether good or bad, just throw it into my picture. Each time a thought strikes your mind, feel that it is an attack, and let me have the attack. Do not encourage any thought whatsoever. In this way you can keep your inner vessel absolutely empty. If you empty yourself and give me all your thoughts and undivine qualities, then I can fill you with peace, light and bliss.

The Guru accepts

I am ready to accept from my disciples everything that you have and everything that you are. If you only want to give me the good things, that is not right. You should give me both the good and the bad. If you have fear, doubt or any negative thoughts, look at my picture and throw all your obscurity and impurity into me. Do not worry about me. I will throw these negative forces into the Universal Consciousness. But if you hold on to these things, you will only suffer. Today you will have one wrong thought, tomorrow you will have a hundred wrong thoughts and there will be no end. When these negative thoughts enter into your mind, you have to know that you actually become weak. It is as if a heavy burden has been placed on your shoulders; so naturally you become tired and exhausted.

Your Own Personal Guide   221

How do you throw negative thoughts into me? Let us say that you are jealous of someone. When you are jealous of someone, you are inwardly communicating with that person and offering him your jealous thoughts. In your mind you are formulating thoughts or ideas, and then you are consciously directing them to him. In the same way you can throw these ideas into me instead. The moment you talk to me inwardly, you have to know that you are giving me your thoughts.

When you do your morning meditation, if your sleep was not disturbed and you have not accumulated any mental garbage during the night, then there may be nothing undivine that you have to give me. At that time you can enter into me with joy, love, peace and all divine qualities. When you do this, it is like a child dealing with his own father. A child goes to his father with such joy to give him a penny that he has found in the street. The child could have used the penny to buy candy, but he felt the necessity of giving it to his father instead. And the father is so pleased that his child has given him his own possession that the father gives the child a dollar.

For my disciples, I am your spiritual father. If you give me something good or positive—a little love, a little joy, a little gratitude—then immediately I will give you boundless love, joy and gratitude in return. I will give you immeasurably more than what you have offered me. But if it is something bad that you are giving, then it will enter into my inner ocean and I will take care of it.

Meditating on Sri Chinmoy's picture
When you meditate on my picture and enter into my consciousness, you should not feel that you are entering into a foreign element or a foreign person, but that you are entering into your own highest part, your true self. You have a mother and a father, you have a husband or wife, you have children; now you can add one more person to your family. You have to feel that here

is someone who is your own—not only for this life, but forever. If you feel your oneness with me, if you feel that I am not a foreigner but a member of your own family, then automatically your consciousness, your soul, will try to associate with mine. This very association will be meditation for you.

If you look at a tree, you become one with the consciousness of the tree. If you look at a flower, you become one with the fragrance of the flower. Similarly, if you look at a picture of me in a very high consciousness, you become one with my inner divinity and reality. Sometimes when you see the ocean of light inside me, you may feel that if you enter into the ocean you will be drowned, overpowered, destroyed. At that time light is trying to enter into you and you are trying to hide. But you have to know that divine light will not expose you; it only wants to illumine you. The more light you receive, the sooner you will be illumined.

But if you feel fear, then it is better for you not to try to enter into me. Instead, you should allow me to enter into you. You can say, "Let the ocean of light come into me in a very, very small quantity, or let just a few drops of light enter into me." Your inner progress depends on your strength and receptivity, on how much of my spiritual food you can eat. If you have great inner strength, if you feel that you are strong enough to swim in the sea of light and bliss, then enter into me. Otherwise, let me enter into you. But this is only for seekers who want to follow my path.

Those who are not my disciples may think that it is the height of folly for anyone to meditate on my picture. Perhaps they feel that I am shamelessly proud. But I can assure you, a picture taken of me when I am in a very high consciousness, when I am totally one with the Supreme, does not represent my physical body or human personality. It does not represent Chinmoy Kumar Ghose. When my disciples meditate in front of my picture, they feel that they are meditating not in front of me but in front of their real Guru, who is the Supreme. The Supreme is the eternal Guru—my Guru, your Guru, everybody's Guru. But I represent Him in a personal, accessible way for those who have faith in me, just as there are other Masters who represent the Supreme for their disciples.

So when you meditate on my picture, please do not think of it as a picture of a human being. Think of the achievement and the consciousness that the picture represents. For my disciples, at least, my picture represents someone who has attained oneness with the Highest. If anyone concentrates on my picture with real devotion and aspiration, I have to help him. To serve mankind is the only reason I am here on earth.

Those who are my real disciples should not meditate on anybody's photograph but mine. Your Guru is the farmer. He is constantly cultivating the field, which is your inner life. If you do not allow him to cultivate, if you consciously or unconsciously turn to somebody else, then you are only delaying your own progress. It is not that I will mind if you put up a picture of some god or goddess in your room; I am very fond of the gods and goddesses. But if I am to carry you to the Golden Shore, then you have to be in my boat. For concentration, for meditation, for contemplation, for all inner guidance you should come to me, for you have a direct inner connection with me.

If you have a beautiful picture of a god or goddess, you can use this picture for inspiration. But if you concentrate and meditate on it, you will create tremendous confusion in yourself. One day you will look at this picture and meditate, the following day you will meditate on another goddess, the third day on somebody else and the fourth on me. Then I will be helpless. So I always tell my disciples to approach me inwardly, and I will always help them.

Love, devotion and surrender are the cornerstones of my philosophy because they make up the true sunlit path which can lead the aspirant to the Goal very fast and very safely. If you want to enter into my consciousness while looking at my picture, the best approach is that of love, devotion and surrender. If you offer your heart's love, devotion, and surrender, then you will feel my presence inside your heart. When someone becomes my disciple, he has to feel my presence in his heart and also his own presence inside my heart. When a disciple meditates on my picture, it automatically helps him in concentrating on the heart. And if he concentrates on his heart, then he will find it very easy to enter into his highest consciousness.

Meditation does not only mean sitting in front of your shrine. If you read my writings soulfully, you immediately enter into my consciousness, and entering into my consciousness is the highest form of meditation for those who consider themselves my disciples. Dedicated service is another form of meditation. When you work for me and think of me while working, my consciousness enters into you and your own consciousness is elevated. This is one of the best forms of meditation.

If you want to follow someone else's path, that person may give you different instructions. But this is what I tell my disciples. I am a spiritual teacher, but I am not the only spiritual teacher on earth; there are a few others. If you want to follow my path, I will be able to offer light to your soul. If you study my writings, if you come to our meditation meetings regularly, and if you concentrate on my picture during your own daily meditations, then I will be able to help you in your inner journey. But if you follow someone else's path, then naturally that teacher will teach you how to meditate in his own specific way.

Q&A

Q One of your pictures frightens me.

A A spiritual Master is not an X-ray machine. As soon as you stand in front of an X-ray machine you are totally exposed. When you stand in front of me I also can see everything, but I will be the last person to expose you to anybody or complain about you to the Supreme. If somebody has done something very wrong, then he may be afraid that I shall expose all his inner defects and secret misdeeds. But I am not going to expose you. On the contrary, my compassion—like a mother—will hide your imperfections. When I accept someone as my disciple, I accept all his imperfections as my very own.

So you should never be afraid of me. I am not a tiger or a lion. I am not going to devour you. Never! Even if you feel that you are darkness itself and I am the sun, no harm. The sun which shines within me is the inner sun, which only illumines. It does not expose. If it shines on darkness, it transforms it into light, and then offers this light to the world at large. So there is nothing for you to worry about.

Please, please never be afraid of me. You can be afraid of anything on earth, but do not be afraid of me. I will never harm you in any way. On the contrary, it is my business to transform your imperfections and mould and shape you into your own divinity.

Q My friend is not a disciple, but she has begun to meditate on your picture, and now she feels great fear.

A Very often people say that they are frightened by my picture. But they are not afraid of my picture. It is only a question of whether they are ready to give up certain things. Inwardly they are unwilling to give up their old habits and old life. They look at my picture and feel an ocean of uncertainty, because they are uncertain themselves about whether they really want the spiritual life, and they are afraid of what will happen if they give up their old habits. Your friend's experience may be interpreted in this way.

If one can forget the past and be ready to enter into the new, the ever-new, consciously and wholeheartedly, then one will see that the new also has its own reality— a more fulfilling reality than the past. At that time there is no fear. Fear comes only when one is unwilling to give up one's old life or is uncertain about accepting a new way of life. But usually people are unconscious of the fact that they do not want to give up their old life. Because part of them sincerely wants to be spiritual, they feel embarrassed that they are still cherishing mundane things. They do not want to admit it, even to themselves.

Anything that binds you, unlearn it. Anything that blinds you, unlearn it. Anything that limits you, unlearn it. Anything that awakens you, learn it. Anything that liberates you, learn it. Anything that fulfils you, learn it.

Q When you gaze directly at me during meditation, or when you ask us to come in front of you to meditate, I sometimes get a little nervous or frightened. I'm not sure what you are doing. Could you explain?

A When I look at you during meditation, or when I ask you to sit in front of me and meditate, at that time I am entering into you to observe what your inner and outer being want. I enter into the physical, the vital, the mind, the heart and the soul. If I see that a particular person is crying for peace, then immediately I bring down peace from above. If I see that someone else wants light, then I bring down light. According to the aspiration, necessity and receptivity of each individual seeker, I bring down different spiritual qualities from above.

Sometimes I see that a seeker does not want anything; there is no aspiration at that time. It is not that the seeker has everything; it is just that he does not have the inspiration and aspiration either to draw something from above or to receive something from me. In these seekers I just try to kindle the flame of aspiration.

In some instances you may have a better meditation when I am looking at somebody else than when I am looking at you. While I am looking at someone else, if you are in a high consciousness and you look at me, at that time like a magnet you can pull my light. Although I am looking at somebody else, more of my light can be going to you than to him. On the other hand, while I am concentrating on you, if you are thinking that all the others are now looking at you, or if your mind is counting how many seconds I am looking at you and comparing this with how long I looked at others, then you will receive very little.

Sometimes when I am blessing someone and bringing down the Supreme's infinite Compassion, that person is absolutely unreceptive. But someone who is sitting somewhere else, whose inner being is fully awake and who is most devotedly meditating on the Supreme, is receiving most powerfully. He is taking all the light that I wanted to give to the other person. At this time I am not at all displeased with the person who is receiving my light. If the person to whom I am offering it is not receptive, then naturally if someone else has the capacity, he should take it. Then, when I meditate on that person individually, if he has the capacity to receive still more, I give him more.

But sometimes it happens that when I come to that person, as soon as I look at him and meditate on him, he becomes nervous and receives nothing. Sometimes you feel that you cannot meditate properly when I gaze into your eyes or when I ask you to sit in front of me. You become frightened to death. But why should you be afraid of me? I am not a snake or a tiger. You are afraid of me because you feel that your ignorance will be exposed. Unconsciously you may think, "In the morning I told a lie or did something else wrong, and now Guru will catch me." Or wrong forces may suddenly attack you. Before you saw me, you were fine, but as soon as you stand in front of me, suddenly all the evil thoughts in the world come forward in you. But you have to know that you always had these enemies, only previously you were not aware of them. Now they are coming forward for transformation.

Do not think of me as an X-ray machine which will expose all your inner imperfections to the entire world. Instead, think of me as a mirror that will let you see what you are doing in your spiritual life. When you are in front of me, you will be able to see your own inner reflection. Whatever you have come with will be visible to you. Good thoughts as well as bad thoughts will immediately be reflected. But if you feel afraid and try to hide, or if you try to make me feel that you are this or that, then you are making a serious mistake. I know what you truly are; I know the mark you are going to get. By trying to impress me with your aspiration, you only lose whatever sincerity you have. Even if you come with only one cent of aspiration, give me that one cent with utmost sincerity. If you come with wrong thoughts, feel that these are your enemies, and separate your existence from them. Either you have to reject them and say, "They are not mine," or you have to say,

"Yes, they are mine, but I am giving them to you. These are my possessions, and I am giving you all of my possessions." Then I can take these forces from you. But if you are afraid of being exposed or of receiving what I am giving you, then you will not receive at all.

I have not come into the world to expose you and judge you. I have come only to love you and perfect you. When I look at you and concentrate on you during meditation, do not worry about what I am thinking of you. I am not thinking anything of you. I am only offering you my spiritual love, light and concern. When a child sees his mother coming to him, even if he is covered with dirt and mud, he will not be afraid. He knows that his mother will not slap him or insult him; she will only make him clean again. The moment you think that you have done something wrong—either in your mind or in your actions—feel that my concern to perfect you is infinitely greater than your concern to perfect yourself. Fear comes because you feel that you will be exposed by my light. But if you can feel that my light will only illumine and perfect you, then there will be no fear no matter how close or penetrating the light is.

Another reason you may sometimes become nervous when you meditate in front of me is because you enter into the nervousness and uncertainty of others around you. It is as if you were all students in front of an examiner. Instead of paying attention to your own inner wisdom, you look around to see what page of the textbook the other person is studying. You think that the question will come from the page that he is reading, and you also want to read that particular page. Then you start to become nervous, not because you are trying to read the same passage he is reading, but because the other person himself is nervous. He is reading a passage, but he also feels that perhaps this is not the right passage. When you start to read his passage, you enter into his consciousness and take on his uncertainty and fear.

Q Do you recommend meditating with folded hands?

A Yes, I do recommend it. If you fold your hands soulfully, it will definitely help you meditate better. If you want to increase your devotion, then always you should try to do something on the physical plane so your physical mind will be convinced. When you pray and meditate with folded hands, your reluctant, unwilling and stubborn physical mind and your entire physical being become more devoted. Everything in you becomes one-pointed.

If it is physically tiring and you are in pain, you have to know that this pain is not going to bring you satisfaction. You can pray and meditate and still go into a very high state of consciousness without folding your hands. But if you fold your hands soulfully, it definitely does help your aspiration.

Some people feel that they get ninety-nine dollars from their inner aspiration, but they need one dollar more in order to reach the destined goal. They know that folding their hands may give them that last dollar. If there is something that they can do which will immediately give them that missing dollar, then they will do it. Others feel that they do not need to fold their hands. They feel that by increasing their aspiration they will automatically get the last dollar. They are also right.

Just because so-and-so folds his hands or because you are worried what someone thinks of you, that is no reason to fold your hands. But if you feel that it increases your aspiration and receptivity, you should fold your hands. But if you do it without any spontaneous inner urge, only to impress others, then you are making a deplorable mistake. After a few days or a few months your own sincerity will come forward and make you stop. Again, just because once upon a time you were folding your hands out of deception and now you have realised your folly, that does not mean that you should necessarily stop folding your hands. It is like curiosity. Some people enter into the spiritual life out of curiosity. They do not have sincere inspiration or aspiration, but out of curiosity they come to our meetings and join our activities. Finally they see that their curiosity is getting them nowhere. At that time they stop their life of curiosity and begin to aspire sincerely. So there is no hard and fast rule.

Q Why do you sometimes ask people to look at you when they meditate?

A You are looking at your hands, but your hands will not give you realisation. I am a Master. God-realisation-consciousness is written on my face and in my eyes, not on your fingertips. You will receive much more inspiration from looking at me than from looking anywhere else.

If you can make a conscious contact with my soul, then you can rest assured that my existence on earth will act like your slave. Once anyone makes real contact with my soul and sincerely wants my help, then I am at his or her service forever. But this contact must be transformed into identification, and from identification into oneness. If a seeker can establish oneness between his soul and my soul, then I shall be always responsible for that particular human being. This is my soul's assurance.

If you want guidance, then look up with a pure heart. If you want guidance, then look within with a doubt-freed mind.

Q Sometimes even when I am meditating with you, I like to keep my eyes closed. Is this never a good thing to do?

A When I am meditating in front of my disciples, I always ask them to keep their eyes half open, because one of the ways they can receive from me is through the eyes. Sometimes I am bringing down infinite peace, light and bliss, and distributing it through my eyes. If the disciples can see these divine qualities with their own eyes in my face and in my eyes, then their physical mind will be convinced, and they will be more receptive. What I bring down you can see not only in my eyes but also in my whole face. It is like a glow that radiates around my body. If your eyes are open, then you are bound to see something.

Q When a Master brings down more light or peace than those meditating with him can absorb, what happens to it? Is it all lost?

A It is not all lost. It enters into the earth atmosphere and becomes the earth's possession. When spiritual Masters bring down divine qualities from above, Mother-Earth assimilates them as her own. Then, when someone is aspiring, he will get this peace and light from the earth-consciousness, but he will not know where it is coming from.

Q Since I started meditating with you, I have felt that my consciousness is in a different place, and I just wondered if you could comment on that.

A Since you have been coming here to meditate with us, your consciousness has begun functioning more from your heart than from your mind. Formerly, your consciousness was in the mind. When you stay in the mind, all of life seems like a dry piece of wood. But when you stay in the heart, life is turned into a sea of pure love and bliss. If you can stay there, you will gradually begin to experience a spontaneous feeling of love and oneness with God and God's creation.

 The fulness of life lies in dreaming and manifesting the impossible dreams.

Each experience is a beautiful incident inside my heart. Each experience is a powerful reality inside my soul.

Understanding Your Inner Experiences

Understanding Your Inner Experiences

❦ Fruits on the Path of Meditation

There are many roads leading to the goal. One road may have beautiful flowers on either side, another road may have only a few blossoms, and a third road may have none at all. If three seekers each follow a different road according to their soul's needs and preferences, each of them will eventually reach the goal, having had quite different experiences on their journey.

Each experience is a step towards realisation. Each experience gives you additional confidence in yourself. Each experience encourages you and energises you to march farther, and gives you enormous delight. While having the experience, you may feel the presence of an invisible guide within you, pushing you towards the goal.

Before you get the fruit that you call the goal, you may want to taste many different fruits. But only when you eat the fruit that is your goal do you get full satisfaction. Some seekers feel that they do not want any fruit but the fruit of God-realisation, so spiritual experiences, as such, are not at all necessary for them. If you have the capacity to run very fast, then you need not have thousands of experiences before realising God. Your expanding consciousness, as you grow into God, is itself a solid experience.

When you do have an inner experience, you may not be able to tell whether it is genuine or not. But only if you do not have a Master will this problem arise. If you have a Master, he will immediately be able to tell you whether you are getting fruitful inner experiences or whether you are just deceiving yourself. A spiritual Master can easily tell without the least possible doubt or hesitation.

If you do not have a Master, you can still solve this problem. Just concentrate on your spiritual heart. If the experience you are having is genuine, then you will feel a subtle tingling sensation in your heart, as though an ant were crawling there.

There are also other ways to tell whether your experience is genuine. Try to breathe as slowly and quietly as possible, and feel that you are bringing purity into your system. Feel that purity is entering into you like a thread, and revolving around your navel chakra. At that time, if you concentrate on your experience and you feel that your spiritual heart is not willing to enter into your navel chakra, you will know that your experience is a mere hallucination. But if the heart gladly enters into the navel, then rest assured that your experience is absolutely true and genuine.

Again, when you have an experience, try for a couple of minutes to feel whether you can grow into that experience or not. If you feel that sooner or later you will be able to grow into that experience, then the experience is genuine. But if you feel that reality is something else and that you can never grow into the experience, then that experience is not genuine.

When you have an experience, try to separate your outer life from your inner life. The outer life is the life of human necessity and earthly requirements. The inner life is also a life of necessity, but it is God's necessity, not your necessity—God's requirements, not your requirements. Try to feel whether it is God's necessity that is operating in and through your experience, and whether God needs and wants to fulfil Himself in and through you. If you have that kind of feeling or realisation, then your experience is genuine. Real experience comes only when you sincerely want and need the inner life, and when God needs and wants the inner life in you and through you. If you have come to that understanding, then all your experiences will be true; they have to be true.

Q Do we consciously remember all of our inner experiences?

A In the case of an ordinary seeker, when he has an inner experience, he may not consciously retain it, although the essence remains in his inner life. Even if it is a high experience, after four years or so he may totally forget it, because the ignorance in his life swallows it. He may say, "How can I have had such an experience? If I did have such an experience, how is it that afterwards I did so many wrong things? How is it that I did not meditate and pray? That means it was not such a significant experience." So his doubt devours the experience and eventually he forgets it. But in the case of a realised person, he knows that whatever he saw or felt was absolutely true. Also, he can remember the inner experiences that he had even from previous incarnations, because of his inner vision. But an ordinary seeker, even if he has had only two major experiences in his life, may not remember them at all.

Q How do we know what plane of consciousness we are in during meditation?

A A seeker can be aware of the planes of consciousness only when he is on the verge of realisation. An ordinary aspirant will not be able to know, and also it is not necessary for him to know.

There are seven higher worlds and seven lower worlds. A spiritual Master can easily be in all these fourteen worlds at the same time and see things that are happening in all the worlds. An aspirant can also be in more than one world at a time, but he will not be able to know which worlds they are. Only someone who is advanced in the spiritual life, someone who is about to step onto the highest rung of the spiritual ladder, will be able to see in which plane of consciousness he is staying during his meditation. For realised souls it is very easy.

Your spiritual Master can tell you which plane a particular experience has come from. If he tells you that a particular experience comes from the vital world or the mental world, then in the future when you get a similar experience you will be able to know that it comes from that world.

Q Is it possible to receive something in meditation and not be aware of the experience?

A Sometimes when we receive light, peace or bliss on a higher level of consciousness, the physical mind is not convinced that it has actually received anything. But it is not necessary for the physical consciousness to be aware of what has been received. Light may enter into a higher part of the emotional being and start functioning for a few minutes or a few days or even longer. There it will create a new soil, and eventually it will grow a bumper crop of inner experiences. But it may take a while for these inner experiences to enter into the gross physical consciousness.

If an experience takes place in the physical consciousness, then we can see and feel it with our senses. At that time, naturally we can rely on our own awareness. But if the experience is something very subtle, and is taking place on a higher level of consciousness, we may not be aware of it. What we are trying to do is to make the physical mind consciously aware of what is going on in the other parts of the being. If the physical and the spiritual in us are simultaneously conscious of what we are doing, then no matter in which plane of consciousness we are having an experience, we will feel it in our physical consciousness. Then we will have free access to all planes of consciousness, and the physical will not be able to doubt the reality of these subtle experiences. Otherwise, it may happen that when the Highest knocks at the door of the physical, the physical will deny it.

Q Sometimes when I meditate I feel that I am about to go through some experience, but nothing happens. What is the cause of that?

A The reason nothing happens is that you have not reached the height. You are just on the verge of it, but you do not quite reach it. It is like lighting a stove. When you turn on the gas, you have to turn the handle to a certain point before the flame comes. You come almost to that point, but you stop too soon. If you had turned the handle just a fraction of an inch farther, you would have succeeded.

It is the same with your meditation. If you had gone just a bit higher or deeper, you would have had your experience. But your attention was diverted or something made you pull back instead of going on. You failed to maintain your aspiration, and your consciousness fell. It is as if you were climbing up to the highest branch of a tree, but all of a sudden somebody called you from below and you forgot about the delicious fruit at the top of the tree and climbed down. If you can maintain your height and not respond to any call or pull from below, then you will reach your highest, and you will get your experience.

While you are praying and meditating, imagine that you are riding a bicycle. When you ride a bicycle, the wheels have to be turning all the time. You cannot balance motionless at one point. While you are meditating you have to aspire all the time; otherwise, you will fall. In the spiritual life, movement has to be constant. Either you move forward or you move backward. If you try to remain motionless, the ignorance of the world will pull you back to your starting point.

In your life of aspiration what you need is not success but progress. Progress itself is the active form of success. When you start meditating early in the morning, if you think, 'Today I have to get the highest experience, or I will feel miserable," then God may give you the experience, which you will call success. But He will not utilise You as His instrument, because you are already trying to get something from Him. You are demanding that He give you an inner experience, whereas you should be asking only for the opportunity and privilege of being His instrument to serve Him in His own way.

If you cry only to please God in His own way, if you cry only for progress, then you are bound to get all the experiences which God has in store for you, at God's own time. Right now you are trying to climb up to a great height in order to get an experience. It is extremely difficult for you to go to that height at this stage of your spiritual development. But it is very easy for God to bring the fruit down and give it to you. He is an excellent climber; He can climb up and climb down. So if you can please God, even if you remain at the foot of the tree, God will climb up on your behalf and bring the experience down, if it is His Will that you have it.

Q Oftentimes I have the feeling or sensation that I see light, but my mind doubts it very forcefully. I was wondering if the light I see is real or imaginary.

A If it is real light, if it is pure, divine light, then rest assured that your mind cannot doubt what you are seeing. The mind does not have the capacity to doubt divine light while you are seeing it. The effulgence of light is such that it will not allow any mental suspicion or doubt to enter. When the real divine light appears, at that time the mind is obliterated; it does not function at all. The entire being becomes all soul.

The mind does have the capacity to doubt divine light afterwards. When you are seeing the light, the mind is divine. After, when your consciousness descends and you are no longer physically aware of the light, the mind can gather strength and try to throw suspicion into your experience. Then you may doubt the light that you saw. If right now God stands before you, you are not going to doubt Him. But the moment God disappears from your outer vision, you can doubt God.

Because of your oneness with your body, you don't doubt your eyes or your nose. You know that they are part and parcel of your body and that your body is part and parcel of your life. Similarly, divine light is part and parcel of your real existence. How can you deny or doubt your own existence? But after the experience is over and you no longer feel the light as your own, at that time doubt may enter into you.

Q I once had an experience in which I felt the purity of God and the power and Eternity of God, but then the feeling left me.

A This was a gift of pure Grace. The Supreme, out of His infinite bounty, unconditionally offered His Grace to you. That is why this experience was possible. These things are not hallucinations. Spiritual Masters have a free access to these experiences, but seekers also can have them if they pray and meditate sincerely.

You got this experience because of God's Grace, but impurity did not allow you to keep it. Any spiritual wealth that you may have, no matter what kind it is, will be destroyed by impurity. Many people have good experiences on certain days, but the next day they indulge in lower vital life. Then all their higher experiences are destroyed. But if we refrain from enjoying vital life and emotional life, then our higher experiences grow. They grow and become very solid, like a banyan tree. So you have to be extremely careful not to indulge in the vital life if you want to retain the power of your highest experiences.

Q In meditation I have had the experience that I was totally free. But then I had to go back to my regular life, and I felt very tired and very drained.

A When you get a higher experience, it is something that will nourish you, feed you and strengthen you. If you are exhausted, if your energy is drained, it means that you have pulled beyond your capacity. Otherwise, right after meditation, you will have the strength of a lion.

Q When I am meditating well and I start to go deep within, after a few minutes I feel sleepy and my whole body goes almost numb.

A You are having the experience of silence. During your meditation your mind has totally surrendered to your heart, and the heart and the mind have both surrendered to the soul. At that time you get a feeling of static silence. Mentally you feel that you are not in this world, and that you have to come back and be very dynamic. But no! At that time the soul is operating most powerfully, and you do not have to create any movement.

This world of silence is not like ordinary sleep, where one becomes totally unconscious. On the contrary, it is a very good state. In the silence itself there is spontaneous creativity, spontaneous movement and spontaneous life—the life of spiritual awakening and spiritual revelation. Try to remain there and grow into that state with utmost sincerity, humility and devotion. You can stay there for a few days or even a month without any fear. Then you will see that the static silence will grow into dynamic silence.

If you feel sleepy when you are merely preparing to meditate, it means that inertia and lethargy are present. But if this feeling comes during a good meditation, it is not sleep at all. You are entering into the world of silence and mistaking it for sleep.

Q When I first started meditating, I had the feeling of purity and divinity flowing through each cell of my body. But now when I meditate I don't feel this, yet I think I have improved my meditation-capacity. Why is this?

A When you start to run your fastest, at the beginning you have so much alertness. Then, after thirty metres, your limbs get increased coordination. You feel totally relaxed and you may not even feel that you are running. You are not putting out any extra effort, but your speed is not slowing down. In the beginning your mind has to convince your body to move. But once you have entered into your natural stride, your mind no longer has to convince your body to run fast. You can run your fastest automatically.

Q On different occasions I have seen red, blue and white light during meditation. Could you please explain the significance of these?

A Red is the dynamic aspect of God; it represents the divine power which you are seeing inside yourself. When divinity's power enters into you, you are energised.

White is the colour of purity. It represents the consciousness of the Divine Mother. When you see white all around you, you feel that your whole physical existence is inundated with purity, from the soles of your feet to the crown of your head.

When you see a pale blue colour, it means that Infinity is entering into your aspiring consciousness. You cannot understand Infinity with your mind. The mind will imagine a great distance, expand it a little farther and then stop. But Infinity goes on expanding forever. When you see blue, try to feel that your consciousness is expanding into Infinity and that Infinity is entering into your aspiring consciousness.

Each prayer is divinely important. Each meditation is supremely significant. Each experience is soulfully fruitful.

Q I used to feel and see a golden light around my heart, but now I no longer do. How can I regain this wonderful presence?

A When this golden light, which is the light of divine manifestation, touches earth, it may not be able to remain for long. If it feels that it cannot remain in the heart because the heart is not pure enough, it will recede. But when the heart is pure, this light functions first in the heart region; then it moves into the vital and the physical.

To regain the visible presence of light is not necessary. If you want to follow a spiritual path, it is not the light that you want—it is God's constant concern for you, God's real love and blessing. When you have God's concern it can take the form of light, peace, power or any divine quality.

When a beginner sees light, he feels that he is making extraordinary progress. To some extent it is true. If God shows you light, naturally you will be inspired to dive deep into the sea of spirituality. But if God feels that what you need is peace and not light, then He will act through you in a different way.

You want to regain the wonderful presence of this light, but you will not get utmost satisfaction from seeing this light, because you will not be fulfilling God in His own way. Your highest aim is to please God in His own way. When God gives you an experience, you should be most grateful to Him. And when He does not give you one, you have to be equally grateful, because He knows what is best for you. It is your business to meditate soulfully, and it is God's business to give you light or peace or power. God will give you what He has and what He is if you give Him what you have and what you are. What you have is ignorance, and what you are is aspiration. So my request to you is to please God in His own way and not care for the things which you once had and which you now feel you are missing.

Q Would you please speak about the aura seen in meditation?

A Each individual human being has an aura. You may see your aura during your meditation, but you may also see it during concentration or even during sleep. There is no direct connection between meditation and the aura except that while you are meditating you may enter into a more peaceful consciousness, where it becomes easier for you to see an aura.

Q I have recently felt quite distinctly a force that people throw around themselves for protection, or when they don't want to speak to someone. It is like a solid object, like a wall. Is it built consciously or unconsciously?

A Usually it is built consciously. Some seekers feel that when they are around unaspiring people they need protection to maintain their high consciousness. They are afraid that the consciousness of the unaspiring people will enter into them like arrows and destroy their aspiration, so they consciously build a wall around themselves. Sometimes ordinary people who are not aspiring have a tremendous insecurity, so they also build a wall around themselves. They are afraid that others will take away whatever little wealth they have.

Spiritual Masters may build this wall to protect themselves from the attacks of the world around them. Some people who come into the presence of a spiritual Master do not want to accept anything. The moment the Master wants to give them peace or light, they attack him inwardly. Or people come to a Master without knowing what they want. Then, for example, when peace, light or bliss is offered, they feel that it is something strange, something foreign, so they reject it vehemently. Or they come to the Master with tremendous expectation and demand, saying "Give me, give me, give me!" But when the Master gives them what they need, they are not satisfied, so they attack him inwardly. For these reasons the Master creates a kind of shield for self-protection.

Each individual has a special aura of which he is not conscious. That aura goes around the person from head to foot and consciously protects him. When we meditate we may see that there is an aura constantly revolving around us. Others' auras we may also see, as people used to see them behind the Buddha or the Christ, for example. Usually these do not revolve or move. But the aura that we all have is constantly moving around us. This aura is a strong protection on the physical, vital and mental levels, but it does not protect the whole being. This aura becomes powerful only through prayer and meditation. Each day when we pray and meditate, this aura is strengthened; then it moves very, very fast. When the movement becomes extremely fast, the aura acquires tremendous strength, and at that time it is able to protect the entire being.

Q When I meditate I often feel a split in my consciousness. Part of my consciousness is in a deep meditation while another part of my consciousness is observing and carrying on a running commentary on what is being experienced. What does that mean?

A There should be no split in your consciousness. When you are properly meditating, your consciousness will become a single entity. If you feel that you are making a running commentary, then you have to know that either your mind or your vital or your physical is not totally one with your meditation. Your heart and soul are meditating most devotedly, but the mind may not be there. In our path we give more importance to the heart than to the mind. But that does not mean that we can neglect or ignore the mind. The mind has to become one with the heart so that the soul can carry both of them together. When you are meditating, sometimes your mind does not want to sit beside the heart or become one with it. That is why you are aware of this split in your consciousness. It comes from the mind. In your case very rarely does it come from the vital.

One of the Upanishads mentions that there are three kinds of meditation: gross meditation, subtle meditation and transcendental meditation. Your particular experience takes place in the first stage. In spite of having a very high meditation, you feel that your whole existence is not there. Although in your psychic consciousness you are having a very high meditation, it will not be totally fruitful, because all the members of your inner family are not participating.

In the second stage of meditation you will see that you have become totally aware of and unified in your consciousness. Now you are just using the term 'consciousness', but in that stage you will actually be able to see and feel what consciousness is. At every moment you will be able to see the divine streak of light, the all-pervading light inside you which has united you with the Highest. In this stage of meditation you become the connecting link between earth and Heaven.

The third and highest stage of meditation is transcendental meditation. In this stage you will be able to feel or see yourself as both the meditator and the meditation itself. In this stage the seer and the seen come together. This happens only in the highest Transcendental Consciousness when you go beyond nature's dance, which means temptation, frustration, anxiety, fear, jealousy, failure and so forth. But all this does not mean that in gross meditation you cannot enter into your deepest meditation. You can. But only your heart and your soul will enjoy the deepest meditation; the physical, the vital and the mind will not be able to enjoy the deepest meditation at that time. That is why it is called gross.

Q I once felt during meditation that my soul came out of the body.

A The soul can come out of the body during meditation. In some cases the soul comes to the fore so powerfully that the physical consciousness either leaves or becomes submerged or totally illumined and transformed by the soul's light.

Q While meditating I sometimes feel that my body is moving rhythmically, but when I open my eyes I see that I am not moving at all.

A The movement you feel is in the inner world, in your subtle body. That reality has not yet manifested itself in the physical, nor does it need to. If you feel that you are flying while you are meditating, you do not have to manifest this movement in the physical.

But if you feel abundant peace within you, then you should immediately try to manifest it in your eyes, in your physical consciousness. Here on earth very few people have peace. When you bring peace into the outer world and manifest it, you are solving the problems of the entire world. The world needs peace, the world needs love, the world needs all divine qualities. Your goal is to see and feel peace, light and bliss, and bring them to the fore in your outer life. By manifesting these divine qualities, you can serve mankind and fulfil God.

Q When meditating, inside I feel very strong and outside I feel very soft. But as I go deeper, I start expanding. What does that signify?

A That is excellent. You feel strong inside because you are bringing down divine peace, light and bliss into your system. The more you consciously and devotedly bring down these divine forces, the stronger you become inwardly. And these blessings from above are helping you to expand your consciousness.

Outwardly you are feeling soft, but this is not actually softness. It is inner peace and inner confidence that are growing in your outer being. When you have boundless inner strength, you do not have to display it outwardly. You do not have to clench your fists. You are relaxed because your inner strength has given you confidence. You are like a divine hero. At any moment you know you can defeat your enemy or surmount any obstruction, so you are outwardly relaxed.

 There is nothing is more powerful than peace.

Q Sometimes after meditation I touch things and find that they are not solid; they are fluid. They lose their solid state. What does this mean?

A Actually they do not lose their solid state. After a deep meditation, when you touch a wall or some other solid object, if you feel that it is soft and that you can penetrate it, you have to know that your consciousness has become identified with the consciousness of your surroundings. When you have come out of a deep meditation and touch something, you can feel your own consciousness in that thing. The solid object has accepted you and embraced you; it has opened its heart's door to become one with you.

When I touch someone from my highest consciousness, that person may not be in his highest consciousness. His mind may be roaming here and there. But if I consciously identify myself with that person, immediately I can enter into and become one with that person's consciousness.

Q When I meditate, I enter into the inner world and sometimes I see things which materialise in the outer world after a few months. Should I try to transcend this?

A What you are doing is entering into the soul's world. You do not have to try to transcend this; there is no necessity. However, you should be aware of whether or not you are crying to know these things. If you are meditating with a view to finding out what is going to happen in the future, then you do have to transcend this. If you say during your meditation, "O God, tell me what is going to happen to my husband or my son," it is a mistake. But if you are only trying to go deep within to have a profound meditation, then I can say that God wants to show you these things for a divine purpose. You should not try to transcend these experiences because, in that case, it is God's Will that you are fulfilling, and not your own desire.

Q When I meditate, I see within and without that everything is alive and has millions of patterns. I see something like a living presence in everything. Could you comment on this?

A Inside everything is God. And where God is present, life is bound to be present. Where there is life, there is God, and where there is God, there is life. Inside one thing you are seeing many varieties. The One is being expressed in many forms and many patterns. When you look at a lotus you see one flower, but it is expressed or manifested by many petals, and by leaves, the stem and other parts. In a lotus you see the manifestation of oneness through various forms. You touch one particular part of the lotus, the leaf, for example, and you say, "This is the lotus." Then you touch the stem, and again you say, "This is the lotus." God is there in all parts of the flower; that is why you feel that each part is the whole. God is present wherever life exists. God is endless in expression. He is endless in manifestation.

Q At times during meditation, I feel that my physical heart stops for a few seconds. This frightens me.

A When you feel that the physical heart stops, this is a very good experience. But you must not be afraid of it; you won't die. It means that the physical in you has totally surrendered to the spiritual in you. Many spiritual Masters, in order to enter into the higher regions during meditation, have consciously stopped their heartbeat. But only Yogis and spiritual Masters can do this at will. Out of His infinite Compassion, God has given you a glimpse of this experience. You should be very happy. When you become a Yogi, it will be up to you whether or not you want to stop your heartbeat during meditation. What it means is that the physical has totally ceased and the spiritual is reigning supreme. At that time you do not need the physical.

Q When I am meditating, I feel my head expanding, and I feel that something is pounding the top of my **A** head.

Two seemingly contradictory things are happening. On the one hand, you feel that your head is expanding. This is the purified consciousness that is expanding in your mind. On the other hand, your impure consciousness is trying to pull down light from above by force. When it does this, you feel a heavy pressure.

When the pure forces in us want to bring down something from above, there is no pressure. When our little divinity looks up and invites the highest divinity to enter, it sees its oneness with the Highest. It is like a child who sees his father. The child is not afraid because he knows this is his own father. He calls his father, and his father comes to him. But if he invites someone else's father, he may be afraid of that person. He may fear that that man will show him an angry face and say, "Why did you call me?" Because that person is unfamiliar, the child experiences a kind of uneasiness and fear.

Similarly, when the impure mind invites the highest divinity to descend, the divinity is ready to come, but the impure mind is afraid. It thinks it will be crushed. It does not get any familiar feeling. But the divine in us does get a familiar feeling when it sees the highest divinity coming down. It is the undivine in us that is always afraid of the divine, even though at times it wants to see the divine. It feels uneasy, and this gives us a severe pressure in the head.

Above the toil of life my soul is a bird of fire winging the Infinite.

Samadhi: The Height of Divine Consciousness

Chapter 20
Samadhi: The Height of Divine Consciousness

❦ What Is Samadhi?

Samadhi is a spiritual state of consciousness. There are various kinds of samadhi. Among the minor samadhis, *savikalpa* samadhi happens to be the highest. Beyond *savikalpa* comes *nirvikalpa* samadhi, but there is a great gulf between these two: they are two radically different samadhis. Again, there is something even beyond *nirvikalpa* samadhi called *sahaja* samadhi.

In *savikalpa* samadhi, for a short period of time you lose all human consciousness. In this state the conception of time and space is altogether different. For an hour or two hours you are completely in another world. You see there that almost everything is done. Here in this world there are many desires still unfulfilled in yourself and in others. Millions of desires are not fulfilled, and millions of things remain to be done. But when you are in *savikalpa* samadhi, you see that practically everything is done; you have nothing to do. You are only an instrument. If you are used, well and good; otherwise, things are all done. But from *savikalpa* samadhi everybody has to return to ordinary consciousness.

Even in *savikalpa* samadhi there are grades. Just as there are brilliant students and poor students in the same class in school, so also in *savikalpa* samadhi some aspirants reach the highest grade, while less aspiring seekers reach a lower rung of the ladder, where everything is not so clear and vivid as on the highest level.

In *savikalpa* samadhi there are thoughts and ideas coming from various places, but they do not affect you. While you are meditating, you remain undisturbed, and your inner being functions in a dynamic and confident manner. But when you are a little higher, when you have become one with the soul in *nirvikalpa* samadhi, there will be no ideas or thoughts at all. I am trying to explain it in words, but the consciousness of *nirvikalpa* samadhi can never be adequately explained or expressed. I am trying my best to tell you about this from a very high consciousness, but still my mind is expressing it. But in *nirvikalpa* samadhi there is no mind; there is only infinite peace and bliss. There nature's dance stops, and the knower and the known become one. There you enjoy a supremely divine, all-pervading, self-amorous ecstasy. You become the object of enjoyment, you become the enjoyer and you become the enjoyment itself.

When you enter into *nirvikalpa* samadhi, the first thing you feel is that your heart is larger than the universe itself. Ordinarily you see the world around you, and the universe seems infinitely larger than you are. But this is because the world and the universe are perceived by the limited mind. When you are in *nirvikalpa* samadhi, you see the universe as a tiny dot inside your vast heart.

In *nirvikalpa* samadhi there is infinite bliss. Bliss is a vague word to most people. They hear that there is something called bliss, and some people say that they have experienced it, but most individuals have no firsthand knowledge of it. When you enter into *nirvikalpa* samadhi, however, you not only feel bliss, but actually grow into that bliss.

The third thing you feel in *nirvikalpa* samadhi is power. All the power of all the occultists put together is nothing compared with the power you have in *nirvikalpa* samadhi. But the power that you can take from samadhi to utilise on earth is infinitesimal compared with the entirety.

Nirvikalpa samadhi is the highest samadhi that most realised spiritual Masters attain. It lasts for a few hours or a few days, and then one has to come down. When one comes down, what happens? Very often one forgets his own name and age; one cannot speak or think properly. But through continued practice, gradually one becomes able to come down from *nirvikalpa* samadhi and immediately function in a normal way.

Generally, when one enters into *nirvikalpa* samadhi, one does not want to come back into the world again. If one stays there for eighteen or twenty-one days, there is every possibility that the soul will leave the body for good. There were spiritual Masters in the hoary past who attained *nirvikalpa* samadhi and did not come down. They attained their highest samadhi, but found it impossible to enter into the world atmosphere again and work like human beings. One cannot operate in the world while in that state of consciousness; it is simply impossible. But there is a divine dispensation. If the Supreme wants a particular soul to work here on earth, even after twenty-one or twenty-two days, the Supreme can take that individual into another channel of dynamic, divine consciousness and have him return to the earth-plane to act.

Sahaja samadhi is by far the highest type of samadhi. In this samadhi one is in the highest consciousness but, at the same time, one is able to work in the gross physical world. One maintains the experience of *nirvikalpa* samadhi while simultaneously entering into earthly activities. One has become the soul and, at the same time, is utilising the body as a perfect instrument. In *sahaja* samadhi one does the usual things that an ordinary human being does. But in the inmost recesses of the heart one is surcharged with divine illumination. When one has this *sahaja* samadhi, one becomes the Lord and Master of Reality. One can go at his sweet will to the Highest and then come down to the earth-consciousness to manifest.

Even after achieving the highest type of realisation, on very rare occasions is anyone blessed with *sahaja* samadhi. Very few spiritual Masters have achieved this state. For *sahaja* samadhi, the Supreme's infinite Grace is required. *Sahaja* samadhi comes only when one has established inseparable oneness with the Supreme, or when one wants to show, on rare occasions, that he is the Supreme. He who has achieved *sahaja* samadhi and remains in this samadhi, consciously and perfectly manifests God at every second, and is thus the greatest pride of the Transcendental Supreme.

Q&A

Q In the highest state of samadhi, when you look at other human beings, what kind of consciousness do you feel in them?

A When one is in the highest transcendental samadhi, the physical personality of others disappears. We do not see others as human beings. We see only a flow of consciousness, like a river that is entering into the ocean. He who is in the highest trance becomes the ocean, and he who is in a lower state of consciousness is the river. The river flows into the sea and becomes one with the sea. The one who is enjoying the highest samadhi does not notice any individuality or personality in others. A human being who is not in this state of samadhi is a flowing river of consciousness, while the one who is in samadhi has become the sea itself, the sea of peace and light.

Q Do you teach your disciples any specific technique for attaining samadhi?

A No. Samadhi is a very high state of consciousness. If the beginner comes to kindergarten and asks the teacher how he can study for his Master's degree, the teacher will simply laugh. He will say, "How can I tell you?" Before we are ready to try to attain samadhi, we have to go through many, many, many inner spiritual experiences. Then there comes a time when the Master sees that the student is ready to enter into *savikalpa* samadhi. *Nirvikalpa* samadhi is out of the question for seekers right now. One has to be a most advanced seeker before he can even think of attaining *savikalpa* samadhi. *Nirvikalpa* samadhi one gets only in the highest stage of aspiration. Unfortunately, I do not have anyone among my disciples now whom I can help to enter into that state. I am very proud of my disciples. Some are very sincere and devoted, and are making very fast progress; but the time has yet to come for them to think of entering into samadhi. For all seekers I wish to say that the spiritual ladder has quite a few rungs. We have to climb up one step at a time. Samadhi, for my disciples and for the vast majority of spiritual seekers on earth, is a far cry right now.

Index

V-Z

About Sri Chinmoy

Sri Chinmoy is a fully realised spiritual Master dedicated to inspiring and serving those seeking a deeper meaning in life. Through his teaching of meditation, lectures and writings, and through his own life of dedicated service to humanity, he tries to show others how to find inner peace and fulfilment.

Born in Bengal in 1931, Sri Chinmoy entered an ashram (spiritual community) at the age of 12. His life of intense spiritual practice included meditating for up to 14 hours a day, together with writing poetry, essays and devotional songs, doing selfless service and practising athletics. While still in his early teens, he had many profound inner experiences and attained spiritual realisation. He remained in the ashram for 20 years, deepening and expanding his realisation, and in 1964 came to New York City to share his inner wealth with sincere seekers.

Today, Sri Chinmoy serves as a spiritual guide to disciples in some 80 centres around the world. He teaches the "Path of the Heart," which he feels is the simplest way to make rapid spiritual progress. By meditating on the spiritual heart, he teaches, the seeker can discover his own inner treasures of peace, joy, light and love. The role of a spiritual Master, according to Sri Chinmoy, is to help the seeker live so that these inner riches can illumine his life. He instructs his disciples in the inner life and elevates their consciousness not only beyond their expectation, but even beyond their imagination.

In return he asks his students to meditate regularly and to try to nurture the inner qualities he brings to the fore in them.

Sri Chinmoy teaches that love is the most direct way for a seeker to approach the Supreme. When a child feels love for his father, it does not matter how great the father is in the world's eye; through his love the child feels only his oneness with his father and his father's possessions. This same approach, applied to the Supreme, permits the seeker to feel that the Supreme and His own Eternity, Infinity and Immortality are the seeker's own. This philosophy of love, Sri Chinmoy feels, expresses the deepest bond between man and God, who are aspects of the same unified consciousness. In the life-game, man fulfils himself in the Supreme by realising that God is man's own highest self. The Supreme reveals Himself through man, who serves as His instrument for world transformation and perfection.

Sri Chinmoy's path does not end with realisation. Once we realise the highest, it is still necessary to manifest this reality in the world around us. In Sri Chinmoy's words, "To climb up the mango tree is great, but it is not enough. We have to climb down again to distribute the mangoes and make the world aware of their significance. Until we do this, our role is not complete and God will not be satisfied or fulfilled."

In the traditional Indian fashion, Sri Chinmoy does not charge a fee for his spiritual guidance, nor does he charge for his frequent lectures, concerts or public meditations. His only fee, he says, is the seeker's sincere inner cry. He takes a personal interest in each of his students, and when he accepts a disciple, he takes full responsibility for that seeker's inner progress. In New York, Sri Chinmoy meditates in person with his disciples several times a week and offers a regular

Wednesday evening meditation session for the general public. Students living outside New York see Sri Chinmoy during worldwide gatherings that take place three times a year, during visits to New York, or during the Master's frequent trips to their cities. They find that the inner bond between Master and disciple transcends physical separation.

As part of his selfless offering to humanity, Sri Chinmoy conducts peace meditations twice each week for ambassadors and staff at United Nations headquarters in New York. He also conducts peace meditations for government officials at the United States Congress in Washington, D.C., and recently he was invited to inaugurate a regular series of meditations at the British Parliament.

In addition, Sri Chinmoy leads an active life, demonstrating most vividly that spirituality is not an escape from the world, but a means of transforming it. He has written more than 700 books, which include plays, poems, stories, essays, commentaries and answers to questions on spirituality. He has painted thousands of widely exhibited mystical paintings and composed more than 6,000 devotional songs.

Sri Chinmoy accepts students at all levels of development, from beginners to advanced seekers, and lovingly guides them inwardly and outwardly according to their individual needs.

For further information, please write to:

AUM PUBLICATIONS
86-24 Parsons Blvd.
Jamaica, N.Y. 11432

Additional Titles by Sri Chinmoy

Beyond Within
A Philosophy for the Inner Life

"How can I carry on the responsibilities of life and still grow inwardly to find spiritual fulfilment?"

When your simple yearning to know the purpose of your life and feel the reality of God has you swimming against the tide, then the wisdom and guidance of a spiritual Master who has swum these waters is priceless. In this book, Sri Chinmoy offers profound insight into man's relationship with God, and sound advice on how to integrate the highest spiritual aspirations into your daily life.

Topics Include:
The spiritual journey • *The transformation and perfection of the body* • *The psyche* • *Meditation* • *The relationship between the mind and physical illness* • *Using the soul's will to conquer life's problems* • *How you can throw away guilt* • *Overcoming fear of failure* • *The purpose of pain and suffering* • *Becoming conscious of your own divine nature* • *The occult* • *and much more*

$10.95

Death and Reincarnation

Now in its 9th printing, this deeply moving book has brought consolation and understanding to countless people faced with the loss of a loved one or fear of their own mortality. Sri Chinmoy explains the secrets of death, the afterlife and reincarnation.

Topics Include:
▪ *Overcoming your fear of death* ▪ *Is death painful*
▪ *Postponing the hour of death* ▪ *The truth about reincarnation* ▪ *How to help those who are dying*
▪ *The soul's journey after death* ▪ *The meaning of Heaven and hell*

$4.95

Kundalini
The Mother-Power

En route to his own spiritual realisation, Sri Chinmoy attained mastery over the kundalini and occult powers. In this book he explains techniques for awakening the kundalini and the chakras. He warns of the dangers and pitfalls to be avoided, and discusses some of the occult powers that come with the opening of the chakras.

Topics Include:
▪ *Developing occult power* ▪ *The significance of the different chakras* ▪ *Concentration and will power* ▪ *Mantras to awaken the kundalini centers* ▪ *Opening the heart centre* ▪ *Sexuality and occult power*

$4.95

My Daily Heart-Blossoms
Spiritual Meditations for Every Day of the Year

In this series of 365 spiritual illuminations—one for each day of the year—Sri Chinmoy leads the reader to the inner wellspring of light from which all truth comes.

These aphorisms, poems and reflections have a familiar ring that resonates in the mind and heart long after they have been read and absorbed. They are at once simple and supremely profound . . . wisdom spilling over into poetry . . . and poetry that will carry you to new heights of realisation.

$11.95

Yoga and the Spiritual Life

Specifically tailored for Western readers, this book offers rare insight into the philosophy of Yoga and Eastern Mysticism. It offers novices as well as advanced seekers a deep understanding of the spiritual side of life. Of particular interest is the section on the soul and the inner life.

Topics Include:
- *The meaning of Yoga* - *Understanding the laws of karma* - *Self-knowledge and universal knowledge*
- *Reincarnation and spiritual evolution* - *The ego*
- *Using mantra and japa to develop purity* - *The synthesis of East and West* - *Discovering your soul's special mission* - *and more*

$4.95

Additional Titles by Sri Chinmoy

My Flute

This collection of Sri Chinmoy's poetry conveys the whole spectrum of spiritual emotions ranging from the doubts and fears of the wavering pilgrim to the ecstatic realisations of the illumined Master. Sri Chinmoy, in his role of seer-poet, writes with a power, lyricism and authenticity seldom encountered in this genre.

$3.00

The Summits of God-Life
Samadhi and Siddhi

"Essential reading for all seekers longing to fulfil their own spiritual potential."

This is Sri Chinmoy's firsthand account of states of consciousness that only a handful of Masters have ever experienced. Not a theoretical or philosophical book, but a vivid and detailed description of the farthest possibilities of human consciousness.

Topics Include:
• What is Nirvana • How to accelerate your God-realisation • The highest consciousness known to man • The Sat-Chit-Ananda consciousness • and more

$4.95

Astrology, the Supernatural and the Beyond

Sri Chinmoy describes the unseen forces that operate in and around you. You'll learn to welcome the positive forces while protecting yourself from the negative ones.

🪷 *Songs of the Soul*

🪷 *Mother India's Lighthouse*
India's Spiritual Leaders

Additional Titles by Sri Chinmoy

Inner and Outer Peace

"A powerful yet simple approach for establishing peace in your own life . . . and the world."

In this book Sri Chinmoy speaks of the higher truths that energise the quest for world peace, giving contemporary expression to the relationship between our personal search for inner peace and the world's search for outer peace. He reveals truths which lift the peace of the world above purely political and historical considerations, contributing his spiritual understanding and inspiration to the cause of world peace.

$5.95

Eastern Light for the Western Mind
Sri Chinmoy's University Talks

In the summer of 1970, in the midst of the social and political upheavals that were sweeping college campuses, Sri Chinmoy embarked on a university lecture tour offering the message of peace and hope embodied in Eastern philosophy. Speaking in a state of deep meditation, he filled the audience with a peace and serenity many had never before experienced. They found his words, as a faculty member later put it, "to be living seeds of spirituality." These moments are faithfully captured in this beautiful volume of 42 talks.

Topics Include:
▪ *The inner voice* ▪ *The quintessence of mysticism* ▪ *The secret of inner peace* ▪ *Attachment and detachment* ▪ *Self-knowledge and self-control* ▪ *The ego* ▪ *How to please God* ▪ *Fear of the inner life* ▪ *God and myself*

Meditation: Man-Perfection in God-Satisfaction

• Individuality and personality • The body's reality and the soul's reality • Intuition • Perfection • Consciousness • Inner poverty

$5.95

A Child's Heart and a Child's Dreams
Growing Up with Spiritual Wisdom — A Guide for Parents and Children

Sri Chinmoy offers practical advice on a subject that is not only an idealist's dream but every concerned parent's lifeline: fostering your child's spiritual life, watching him or her grow up with a love of God and a heart of self-giving.

Topics Include:
• Ensuring your child's spiritual growth • Education and spirituality–their meeting ground • Answers to children's questions about God • A simple guide to meditation and a special section of children's stories guaranteed to delight and inspire

$4.95

The Master and the Disciple

What is a Guru? There are running gurus, diet gurus and even stock market gurus. But to those in search of spiritual enlightenment, the Guru is not merely an 'expert'; he is the way to their self-realisation. Sri Chinmoy says in this definitive book on the Guru-

Additional Titles by Sri Chinmoy

disciple relationship: "The most important thing a Guru does for his spiritual children is to make them aware of something vast and infinite within themselves, which is nothing other than God Himself."

Topics Include:
▪ How to find a Guru ▪ Telling a real spiritual Master from a false one ▪ How to recognise your own Guru ▪ Making the most spiritual progress while under the guidance of a spiritual Master ▪ What it means when a Guru takes on your karma ▪ Plus a special section of stories and plays illustrating the more subtle aspects of the subject

$4.95

 ## *God's Hour*
Daily Meditations for Spiritual Living

The 365 aphorisms in this book should be read as meditations: tools for quieting the mind and fortifying the heart. They are meant to inspire us in our personal journey toward self-perfection, and direct our sometimes uncertain steps toward that goal.

Read the aphorisms meditatively and you'll find that they create a healing inner image. They'll show you that your potential is far greater than you ordinarily choose to believe. Each aphorism becomes a guide for the day, a source of inspiration and a signpost toward truth.

$4.95

✿ The Music of Sri Chinmoy
Flute Music for Meditation

While in a state of deep meditation Sri Chinmoy plays his haunting melodies on the electric echo-flute. Its rich and soothing tones will transport you to the highest realms of inner peace and harmony. An excellent aid to meditation and relaxation.

(Cassette) $9.95

✿ Inner and Outer Peace

A tapestry of music, poetry and aphorisms on inner and outer peace. Sri Chinmoy's profoundly inspiring messages are woven into a calm and uplifting musical composition with the Master chanting and playing the flute, harmonium, esraj, cello, harpsichord and synthesizer.

(Cassette) $9.95

✿ Ecstasy's Trance
Esraj Music for Meditation

The esraj, often described as a soothing combination of sitar and violin, is Sri Chinmoy's favourite instrument. Slowly and with haunting intensity, he seems to draw the music from another dimension. The source of these compositions is the silent realm of the deepest and most sublime meditation. Listen to the music and enter this realm, a threshold rarely crossed in the course of one's lifetime.

(Cassette) $9.95

Additional Titles by Sri Chinmoy

Silence Speaks

Sri Chinmoy plays the cello and flute. He also sings while accompanying himself on the cello and harmonium. This recording captures the intensity of Sri Chinmoy's unique style of devotional music.

(Cassette) $9.95

The Dance of Light
Sri Chinmoy Plays the Flute

Forty-seven soft and gentle flute melodies that will carry you directly to the source of joy and beauty: your own aspiring heart. Be prepared to float deep, deep within on waves of music that "come from Heaven itself." Comes with a free booklet on music-meditation.

(Cassette) $9.95

■   ■   ■

To order books or tapes, request a catalogue, or find out more about Sri Chinmoy or the Sri Chinmoy Centres worldwide, please write to:

Aum Publications
86-24 Parsons Blvd. ▪ Jamaica, NY 11432

When ordering a book or cassette, send check or money order made out to **Aum Publications.** Please add $1.50 postage for the first item and 50¢ for each additional item.

Meditation: Man-Perfection in God-Satisfaction